P9-AGL-282

WITHDRAWN

JUL 03 2024

DAVID O. McKAY LIBRARY
BYU-IDAHO

A SHIʿITE PILGRIMAGE TO MECCA
1885–1886

A SHIʿITE PILGRIMAGE TO MECCA 1885–1886

The *Safarnâmeh* of Mirzâ Moḥammad Ḥosayn Farâhâni

EDITED, TRANSLATED, AND ANNOTATED
BY
HAFEZ FARMAYAN
AND
ELTON L. DANIEL

UNIVERSITY OF TEXAS PRESS, AUSTIN

Copyright © 1990 by the University of Texas Press
All rights reserved
Printed in the United States of America

First Edition, 1990

Requests for permission to reproduce material from this work should be sent to Permissions, University of Texas Press, Box 7819, Austin, Texas 78713-7819.

♾ The paper used in this publication meets the minimum requirements of American National Standard for Information Sciences—Permanence of Paper for Printed Library Materials, ANSI Z39.48-1984.

For reasons of economy and speed, this volume has been printed from camera-ready copy furnished by the editors, who assume full responsibility for its contents.

Library of Congress Cataloging-in-Publication Data
Farāhānī, Muḥammad Ḥusayn Ḥusaynī, b. 1847 or 8.
[Safarnāmah. English]
A Shiʿite pilgrimage to Mecca, (1885–1886) : the Safarnâmeh of Mirzâ Moḥammad Ḥosayn Farâhânî / edited, translated, and annotated by Hafez F. Farmayan & Elton L. Daniel. — 1st ed.
p. cm.
Translation of: Safarnāmah.
Includes bibliographical references.
ISBN 0-292-77620-9 (alk. paper). — ISBN 0-292-77622-5 (pbk. : alk. paper)
1. Middle East—Description and travel. 2. Farāhānī, Muḥammad Ḥusayn Ḥusaynī, b. 1847 or 8—Journeys—Middle East. 3. Muslim pilgrims and pilgrimages—Saudi Arabia—Mecca. I. Farmayan, Hafez F. II. Daniel, Elton L. III. Title. IV. Title: Safarnâmeh of Mirzâ Moḥammad Ḥosayn Farahânî.
DS49.F313 1990
915.604′15—dc20 90-12174
CIP

This book is respectfully dedicated to

IRAJ AFSHAR

and

EHSAN YARSHATER

guardians of Persian culture

in the East and in the West

CONTENTS

PREFACE

The preparation of this work was expedited by the generous help of a number of colleagues whom we would like to take this opportunity to thank for their assistance. Iraj Afshar patiently responded with clarity and authority to numerous questions about technical aspects of the translation such as the identification of the many obscure places and people in Iran mentioned by Farâhâni. Mohammad Taqi Daneshpazhu helped with various textual problems, as did Mohammad Moghaddam, who also provided a copy of a rare semi-autobiographical work by Farâhâni. Farâhâni's son, Khan Malik Sasani, offered valuable information about his father's life and work. Peter Chelkowski read the manuscript and made many useful suggestions for improvements. Roger Savory gave valuable guidance in preparing the translation and graciously assisted in obtaining copies of some of the photographs reproduced in this volume from the University of Toronto library. Paul Chevedden also helped track down photographs that would illustrate Farâhâni's travels. John Williams offered advice about interpreting the Arabic proverbs cited by Farâhâni. D. W. Treadgold gave a useful critique of the sections dealing with the Caucasus. Halil Inalcik kindly shared his unparalleled knowledge about the Ottoman Empire and identified several of Farâhâni's sometimes cryptic references to Turkish places, names, and terms. David Morgan and Frederick de Jong facilitated access to various European libraries and generously provided both help and hospitality during the time spent conducting the research for the annotations to the text.

The staff of several libraries helped directly or indirectly with our work, and we wish to express our gratitude to the UCLA Special Collections Library and the libraries of the London School of Oriental and African Studies, the University of Leiden, the University of Toronto, Columbia University, the University of Texas, and the University of Hawaii. Special thanks are due to Abazar Sepehri, head librarian of the University of Texas Middle East Collection, who tracked down books and bibliographical references needed for preparing the notes, and to Colleen Hennessey, archivist at the Arthur M. Sackler Gallery in Washington, for arranging for use of photographs by Antoine Sevruguin in the Myron Bement Smith Collection of the Freer Gallery of Art/Arthur M. Sackler Gallery Archives (Smithsonian Institution).

At the University of Texas press, John H. Kyle, George Lenox, Frankie Westbrook, Barbara Spielman, Karen Crowther and David Cohen helped shepherd the book through the various stages of preparation for publication. The manuscript was carefully proofread by Jenny White, who was also able to make valuable suggestions for improved interpretation of Farâhâni's comments on Turkish history and culture. John Cotter meticulously and knowledgeably prepared the maps that accompany the text.

Finally, we thank our wives, Jody Farmayan and Ethel Daniel, for reading various drafts of the manuscript, catching uncounted errors and making useful suggestions for improvement; beyond that, we owe them a debt of gratitude that can never be fully repaid for cheerfully putting up with our many quirks during the work and caring constantly for us over the years.

A NOTE ON TRANSLITERATION

In preparing this translation, one of the most troublesome problems that had to be solved was how to transliterate from Persian into English the various personal names, place names, and technical terms found in the text. First of all, experts have not as yet reached a consensus on the most appropriate system of transliteration from Persian into Latin script. Not only do the phonetics of languages such as Italian or German dictate different systems of transliteration, there are several accepted but different ways of transliterating Persian to English. Second, this intrinsically vexing task was greatly complicated by the fact that the text is not limited to purely Persian names and terms. It also includes many from different languages sharing a common script, such as Ottoman Turkish and Arabic, as well as others which Farâhâni himself transliterated from European languages such as French or Russian. Turkish names and terms raise the additional difficulty of choosing between transliterations of the Ottoman (based on Arabic script) or using the modern Turkish forms (based on Latin script). Even for terms which occur only in Persian and Arabic, there are still substantial differences in to the way they might variously be vocalized and transliterated. To sort all this out with a minimum of confusion and some degree of consistency, it has been necessary to rely on several more or less arbitrary conventions:

1. For the purposes of this translation, a system of transliteration combining features of the systems used by the Library of Congress, the *International Journal of Middle East Studies*, and the *Great Islamic Encyclopaedia* has been followed. The main features of this transliteration scheme may be found in Table 1.

2. The same system is used for all transliterations, whether the original term is Persian, Arabic or Turkish. This primarily affects the representation of vowels and yields results which approximate in English the way the word would be pronounced in Persian. It should be noted, however, that the short vowels are rarely indicated explicitly; the vocalization and transliteration of many words is thus ambiguous or uncertain.

3. There are some exceptions to the normal transliteration conventions. For example, the Persian *eżâfeh*, or connective particle, is given as "-e" or "-ye" depending on the context. The Arabic definite article is transliterated as "ol-" without elision except after a long vowel. However, composite names including the word for God, Allah, are elided (e.g. ᶜAbdollah). The doubling in pronunciation, but not orthography, of certain "sun letters" is indicated (e.g. Amin ol-Molk, but Amin od-Dowleh.) The "dagger alif" found in Arabic words such as *raḥman* is indicated here by "a" as if it were a short vowel. It should also be remembered that there are no hyphens or capital letters in the Arabic/Persian script, and Persian is not completely consistent in the formation and orthography of compound words. No attempt has been made to regularize the representation of such features in the transliterations.

4. Almost all transliterations follow the form given by Farâhâni exactly. Thus, Arabic case endings are ignored unless indicated by Farâhâni; they are then transliterated in the form he uses even if this creates inconsistencies (for example, Abu Ayyub, Abâ Bakr, and Abi Z̲arr all use different forms of the Arabic word for "father.") However, any obvious orthographical mistakes

in the manuscript or typographical errors in the published text have been corrected; these are indicated in the footnotes.

4. Personal names are always transliterated, except in the case of certain pre-Islamic historical figures (Abraham or Alexander, for example, rather than Ebrâhim or Eskandar) or names which are recognizably derived from European languages (Napoleon, not Nâpolyun).

5. If there is a commonly recognized English equivalent of a place name or technical term, it is given in that form rather than being transliterated (for example: wakf, not *vaqf*; Trabzon, not Ṭarâbzun). Place names that cannot be positively identified are always transliterated.

Finally, it should be noted that Farâhâni naturally cites all dates according to the Islamic lunar calendar. These are retained throughout the translation, with the equivalent Christian date, as determined from the tables compiled by Faik Unat in his *Hicrî Tarihleri Milâdî Tarihe Çevirme Kılavuzu* (Ankara, 1984) given in brackets. Since the lunar year is shorter than the solar year, an Islamic date may span two Christian years. This is indicated whenever the equivalent date is ambiguous. In the notes both Muslim and Christian dates are generally given, the Muslim year preceding the Christian year and separated from it by a slash (for example, 1302/1884-85.) The Islamic solar calendar used in modern Iran is converted in the same way, but this affects only citations of recent Persian works in the notes and bibliography. It may be assumed that any date given without an equivalent is A.D.

Consonants						*Vowels, Diphthongs, & Other Conventions*			
ء	ʾ	ر	r	ف	f	ـَ	a (as in hat)	ـِ	e (berry)
ب	b	ز	z	ق	q	یٰ	â (father)	ی	i (prestige)
پ	p	ژ	zh	ک	k	ا	â (")	یَ	ay (lay)
ت	t	س	s	گ	g	آ	â (")	ِی	i (prestige)
ث	s̱	ش	sh	ل	l	ـُ	o (open)	ـیّه	eyyeh
ج	j	ص	ṣ	م	m	و	u (umlaut)	خوا	khᵛâ
چ	ch	ض	ż	ن	n	وَ	ow (bowl)	ـه	eh or at
ح	ḥ	ط	ṭ	و	v				
خ	kh	ظ	ẓ	ه	h				
د	d	ع	ʿ	ی	y				
ذ	ẕ	غ	gh						

System of Transliteration

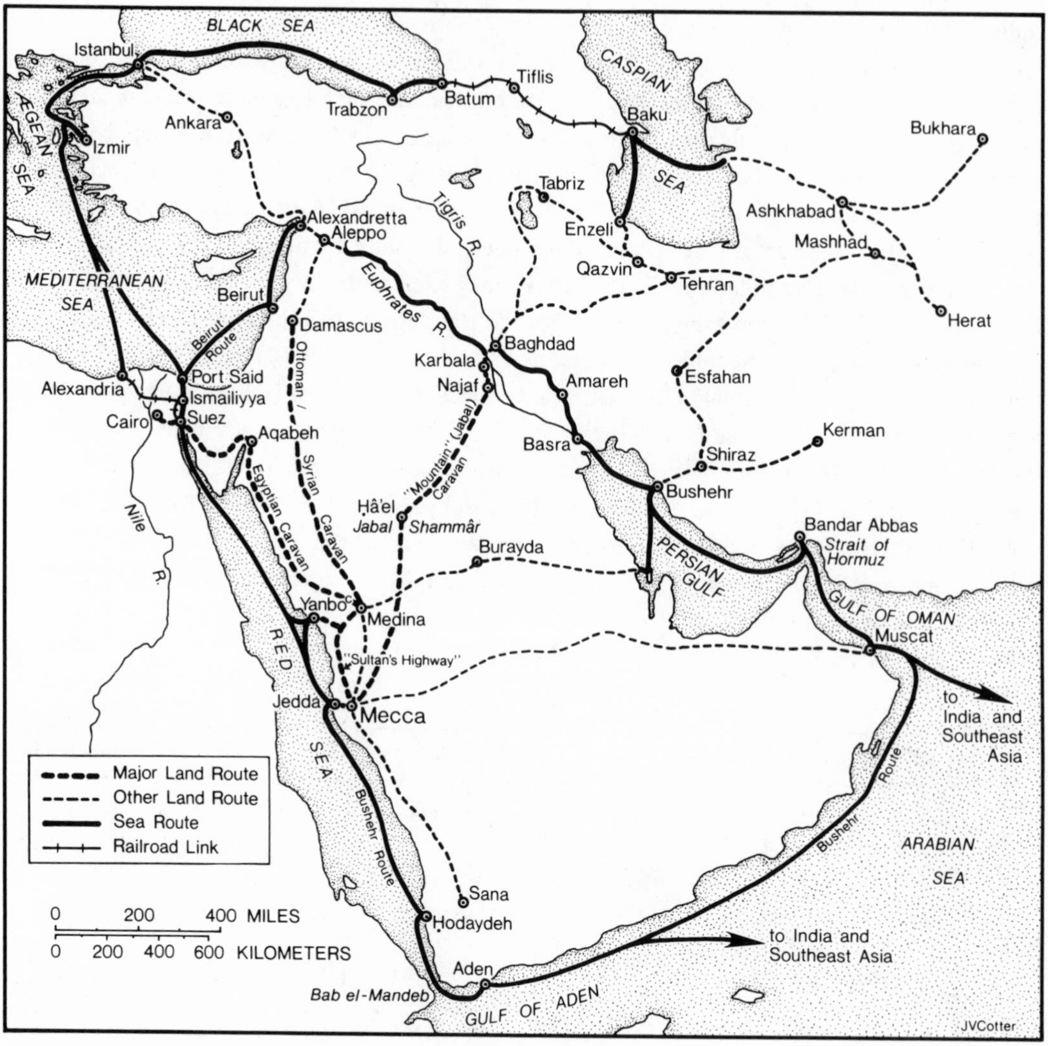

Map 1. Major pilgrimage routes in the nineteenth century.

INTRODUCTION

MEANING AND SIGNIFICANCE OF THE HAJJ FOR MUSLIMS

The most important rituals incumbent upon every Muslim are profession of the faith, prayer, fasting, almsgiving, and the hajj (*ḥajj*), the last named being the supreme pilgrimage to Mecca in Arabia, where Islam was first revealed to Moḥammad the Prophet. These five rituals are called the five pillars of Islam. Every Muslim, man or woman, who has the means and is physically capable of travel, is adjured to undertake this journey at least once in his or her lifetime. At first consideration, this fifth and last pillar of Islam may not appear to be as important to a Muslim as the first four. It can be argued that the hajj is a relatively remote religious duty since it does not directly involve the daily life of a believer. A Muslim is charged with performing it only once in his or her lifetime. Finally, the hajj becomes obligatory only when the believer can afford it. Since it is possible for pious Muslims to go through life without making the hajj, the assumption might be made that they do not bother even to think about it. Little could be further from reality than this perception, for here we are dealing with the spiritual aspects of a universal religion. Whether or not a Muslim eventually is able to accomplish the pilgrimage to Mecca is irrelevant to belief in the hajj as a pillar of Islam. True Muslims go through life in anticipation of the pilgrimage to Mecca. If the experience does not occur, it can be accepted that the fulfillment of this spiritual Islamic act is lived as he or she experiences the emotional and intellectual exaltation manifest in the concept of hajj.

The last month of the Islamic lunar calendar is called Z̲i'l-Ḥejjeh. This is the month of pilgrimage. During this month, the religious consciousness of Muslim communities throughout the world is focussed on the imminent hajj. Only a relative few are able each year to arrive in Mecca, still the annual gathering of the hajj is the world's largest religious congregation. In the year this is being written–1989–about a million and a half Muslims participated in the ritual stages of the hajj. Millions more were mentally and emotionally there. For the believers who are destined not to experience the physical reality of the pilgrimage to Mecca, it remains a life-long aspiration and inspiration.

We may ask, what is the reason for this? What sustains the concentrated interest of all races, nationalities, and classes on the hajj? What, in the end, is the purpose and meaning of the hajj? Is the hajj a ceremonial, ritualistic commemoration of the birth of Islam, a remnant of pagan Arabia which has persisted, inseparable from the fabric of a living religion? Or has it a deeper, more significant meaning? The answers to these questions are many and varied. The subject is both interesting and important, and merits a long discussion. However, for brevity's sake, we shall limit ourselves here to what are generally accepted as the primary concepts attached to the hajj.

This fifth and last pillar of Islam, the hajj, stands as a reinforcement of the *shahâdeh,* the designated first pillar of Islam. As the first is profession of the faith, the last, the hajj, is its reaffirmation. As the shahâdeh declares the oneness of God and the uniqueness of His messenger Moḥammad, the hajj maintains the vital bond that links Muslims throughout the world to each other and to God, and in this process reaffirms the unity of the Muslim community. Wherever the Muslim pilgrim's home is–the Philippines, Indonesia, Morocco, Cairo, or Detroit–when he arrives in Mecca he acknowledges the link between himself and God, between himself and the Prophet Moḥammad, between himself and fellow Muslims everywhere. The pilgrimage to Mecca for a Muslim signifies a visit to the House of God (*baytollah*), also perceived as the House of Humanity (*bayt on-nâs*). It is an attempt to approach God as closely as possible. It offers purification of the human soul and body. Here in this place God and humanity meet; races, nations, and clans disappear. Once the pilgrims perform the sacralization known as *eḥrâm*, which is the beginning of the pilgrimage, and don the garb that symbolizes this state, a sense of unity prevails. Furthermore, the concept of "I", as used in the context of "my" position, "my" clan, "my" race, and so forth, recedes from the consciousness of the believer, and the concept of "we" emerges. Here Muslims experience the true meaning of *ommat*, namely a united community with a common goal, permitting no distinctions among its constituents as to name, status, or nationality.

The hajj is based on two sources–the explicit commands of the Koran and the Traditions established by the Prophet Moḥammad. In them, believers are informed of what they must do and what they are forbidden to do at the time of pilgrimage and within the sacred precincts: There must be no shedding of blood; no hunting, nor uprooting of plants; nor wickedness; nor sexual pleasures; nor use of ornaments. Other regulations deal with such things as the gathering of pilgrims at Mount ʿArafât, offering of sacrifices of sheep and camels at the village of Menâ, and so forth. In following the Koranic commands and the sequence and patterns of actions set by Moḥammad for the formalized acts of commemoration and reaffirmation, the hajj culminates in a crescendo of spiritual bliss that the believers have come together to experience.

In the minds of the faithful, none of the pillars of Islam is so closely identified with Moḥammad as the hajj. This receives its primary importance in the conviction that Moḥammad, among all the Blessed, was revealed as the nearest approach to God, paired with the fact that the Prophet's last major act before his death was to make the pilgrimage from Medina to Mecca during February-March, 632 A.D. This event is referred to by Muslims as the Farewell Pilgrimage. The rites of the great annual hajj which are followed today by the faithful are exactly those performed by the Prophet Moḥammad in his Farewell Pilgrimage. In reenacting them, pilgrims throughout the intervening centuries attest to the profoundly moving experience of joyful emotions and a prolonged ecstasy of the spirit which are initiated as they assume the state known as eḥrâm at the beginning of the pilgrimage. The purpose of all the Islamic rituals, of course, is to bring believers closer to God. The hajj seeks to bring them closer to God, and simultaneously permits them to identify themselves with the Prophet Moḥammad, whom they consider the perfect exemplar of humanity.

RITES AND TRADITIONAL CEREMONIES OF THE HAJJ

Although the rites of the yearly hajj may appear strange to non-Muslim observers, they are supremely meaningful to the devout followers of Islam. The hajj takes place between the eighth and the thirteenth of Z̲i'l-Ḥejjeh, the last month of the year in the lunar Islamic calendar. The lunar year loses approximately eleven days annually in terms of solar calendars, returning to the same solar computation in cycles of thirty-three years. Thus, the time of the hajj comes earlier each solar year, moving gradually from spring, for instance, through winter, autumn, summer, and eventually to spring again. However, the pilgrims bound for Mecca do not concern themselves with the seasons or the weather. Hot or cold, wet or dry, at the appointed time, they make the arduous journey to offer their homage to God. It is a unique emotional experience that overshadows other realities. Years ago, one of the faithful expressed it thus: "Mecca is not a place, it is the Beginning, the Present, and Eternity."

The city of Mecca and its perimeter is called the Sacred Territory, or *Menṭaqat ol-Ḥarâm*. This is an ancient designation established, according to tradition, by Abraham, and confirmed later by the Prophet Moḥammad. Within this confine, every human, indeed every creature and every object, including vegetation, is secure. Here there is a permanent ban on fighting, hunting, and all other confrontations and violence of which man is capable. This sacred precinct is open to Muslims of all sects and forbidden to non-Muslims. It has been a sanctuary for many centuries. Within the Sacred Territory, all roads lead to the Sacred Mosque, the *Masjed ol-Ḥarâm*. This place of worship is the only significant item of architecture in Mecca. Until very recently, before the coming of the oil age, the Sacred Mosque was an unpretentious structure, the functions of which were only to protect the Kaaba and to allow the pilgrims to perform their religious observances in an orderly way. Recent expansion of the Sacred Mosque has been due to practical necessity, namely to accommodate the floods of pilgrims who every year descend into Mecca for the hajj.

The Sacred Mosque is, of course, of supreme importance in Islam, because it encloses the Kaaba, the kiblah (*qebleh*), or pivot of the world of Islam. A plain, rectangular monument, its corners roughly aligned with the points of the compass, the Kaaba is approximately fifty feet high, fifteen feet wide, and twenty feet long. It is built of large blocks of rough grey stone of dissimilar sizes, all crudely mortared with chalk. The roof is flat. It has no windows, but a single door made of brass is set about six feet above the ground. The Kaaba rests upon a base which is two feet in height that stands in the center of the vast courtyard of the Sacred Mosque. The interior of the Kaaba consists of an empty room. Outside, on the southeastern corner, there is a polished fragment of black stone set in silver and embedded in the surface of the wall. It is called simply *Ḥajar ol-Asvad*, the Black Stone. During the early period of Islam it became customary to cover the Kaaba with a cloth each year after sweeping the chamber, readying it for observance of the hajj. Initially the color of the cloths varied, according to that of the personal banner of the reigning caliph. Now, on the great occasion, it is always draped with a magnificent cloth of black brocade embroidered in gold thread with Koranic verses in beautiful calligraphy. This cloth, the *kesveh*, is newly created each year. In the past, the kesveh was made in Egypt and brought to Mecca every year in the Egyptian caravan. Now, the kesveh is always made in a factory in Mecca, specially constructed for this purpose. More than eighty weavers loom the new cloth, requiring more than 2,500 yards of fabric, and embellish it with gold. Completed, the kesveh weighs more than five thousand pounds.

For Muslims, the Kaaba marks the site of a sanctuary built by the Prophet Abraham himself, and the Black Stone, according to several traditions, is the only remaining relic of Abraham's original sanctuary. Moḥammad touched the Stone with his lips in his Farewell Pilgrimage, and since then all pilgrims have strived to do the same. The Kaaba has been rebuilt in the same form many times since the time of Abraham. The structure and its Black Stone symbolize the oneness of God and stand as the kiblah, focal point, of Islam, as all its peoples turn their faces toward it five times daily when they offer their prayers to God. In the minds of believers, the Kaaba, neither a temple nor a shrine, is truly the House of God. The Koran calls it the "first abode of mankind." The pilgrims' visit to the Kaaba during the hajj is intended to reaffirm the oneness of God and His union with humanity. Symbolic of this union is the *ṭavâf*, the act of circumambulation around the Kaaba and touching of the Black Stone.

The rituals of the hajj begin at some point of easy access to Mecca, where, by, or on, the eighth day of the month of Z̲i'l-Ḥejjeh, believers must enter, or assume, as did the Prophet Moḥammad in the year 632 A.D., the state of eḥrâm, or ritual consecration, before crossing the boundary into the Sacred Territory. Pilgrims will have cut their hair, performed ablutions, discarded their habitual clothing, and donned the garments of eḥrâm. For men, these consist of two seamless lengths of white cloth, one for covering the body from waist to ankle, and the other for draping the shoulders so that the chest and back are covered. For women, the norm is a simple, long-sleeved gown and a head covering which has no veil. Women's garments are not limited to white cloth. Several designated places outside the Sacred Territory serve as stations in which pilgrims may assume the state of eḥrâm. While putting on the eḥrâm garments, pilgrims recite the *talbeyyeh*: "I stand up for Thy Service, O God." From this moment, until they depart the Sacred Territory after performing the hajj, pilgrims are in the state of eḥrâm, in which they are required to abandon all worldly pursuits. Particularly proscribed are the use of ornaments, acts of violence, verbal strife, and sexual intercourse. The unity of mankind before God is manifest in eḥrâm: in spirit and appearance, hundreds of thousands of people from every corner of the world, with diverse cultures, races, backgrounds, statuses, and Islamic sects, become one. They look alike, talk alike, and perform alike. It is a very impressive sight. There is no annual congregation like it in the world.

After their arrival in Mecca the pilgrims begin the hajj proper (on the eighth day of the month of Z̲i'l-Ḥejjeh) by going to the village of Menâ on the eastern edge of Mecca. There they pray and meditate all day and through the night in preparation for the observances to be undertaken on the following day, the ninth of the month. When this day arrives, they go from Menâ to a plain called ᶜArafât for the rite of standing, *voquf*, which consists of praying and visiting the Mount of Mercy. It was here that Moḥammad delivered his historic Farewell Sermon, in which he established, among other precepts, two of the fundamental principles of Islam: the denunciation of the concept of racial superiority, and the identification of nobility with the degree of the believer's piety. Thus the Sermon emphasized the community and brotherhood of all believers, to which the Traditions have added the maxims that "An Arab is superior to a non-Arab in nothing but devotion," and "The noblest of you all in the sight of God is the most devout." In the evening of this day, the pilgrims proceed to Mozdalefeh, a place between Menâ and ᶜArafât, for further meditation and prayer. There they also gather pebbles for use in a rite early on the following day, after they return to Menâ. There they hurl the collected pebbles at the three masonry pillars which represent the three times that Satan tried to persuade Abraham to disobey God. This ceremony symbolizes mankind's stand against temptation and evil.

Next, on the same day as the stoning, the tenth day of Z̲i'l-Ḥejjeh, follows the Feast of the Sacrifice (ᶜId-e Qorbân). On this occasion, each pilgrim who can afford it presents a sheep for sacrifice. This is performed at Menâ also, and commemorates Abraham's sacrifice of a sheep in place of his son. It is, in addition, a thanksgiving to God, and a reminder to each believer that he should share his blessings with the less fortunate of his community. The Feast of the Sacrifice is a major holiday throughout the world of Islam. It reflects the unity of the Muslim community, and is celebrated not only by pilgrims in Menâ, but by Muslims everywhere, on the tenth of Z̲i'l-Ḥejjeh. At this point, pilgrims may end their state of consecration and resume their customary lives by removing their eḥrâm raiment, and bathe and dress in clean clothes of their preference. Afterwards, everyone, in eḥrâm or not, proceeds to the Sacred Mosque and the Kaaba in Mecca for the rite of ṭavâf, the circumambulation. This consists of circling the Kaaba seven times, beginning at the corner where the Black Stone is embedded. Two cycles of prayer follow at the Station of Abraham, which is also in the courtyard of the Masjed ol-Ḥarâm, next to the Kaaba.

With these ceremonies, the hajj is complete. However, most of the faithful also undertake a supererogatory ritual called *saᶜy*, the running, which is commonly believed to be a reenactment of the search for water by Hagar, wife of Abraham. Looking for water for her child, according to the Traditions, Hagar had run back and forth seven times between Ṣafâ and Marveh, two rocky prominences, when the angel Gabriel appeared and commanded the ground to open and water to gush forth, thus creating the well of Zamzam. Before undertaking the saᶜy, pilgrims drink from the well of Zamzam, which is located on a lower level, beneath the courtyard of the Sacred Mosque.

On the eleventh day of Z̲i'l-Ḥejjeh, pilgrims may return to Menâ and remain there for two more days. Having completed the formal rituals, and filled with a strong sense of accomplishment and spiritual satisfaction, they now have a unique opportunity to fraternize with one another. Hundreds of thousands of representatives of the worldwide community of Islam, from all quarters of the Earth, meet together for two days in a vast, austere, sun-drenched desert.

For many centuries, this is where Muslims have exchanged news, ideas, and concepts, without fear of control or suppression. These two days of exchanges and discussions have acquired special importance during recent times. Here Muslims of all origins reveal their problems, aspirations, and interests. These involve social movements, political ideas, economic strategies, and many other aspects of life and society. This varied information can be circulated from group to group throughout the entire assemblage. At present, the gathering at Menâ is no longer a primarily religious rite. It has become an impressive expression of Islamic dynamism, whereby religion, politics, social life, and the economic systems of diverse regions and nations become subjects of common interest among the peoples of Islam. They have completed the required ceremonies of the pilgrimage, the *manâsek ol-ḥajj*; they have acquired the much respected title of hajji (*ḥâjji*). Nevertheless, many may feel spiritually unfulfilled until they have visited the tomb of the Prophet Moḥammad, and prayed in the Prophet's Mosque in Medina, the city which lies about 280 miles to the north. Formerly called Yas̱reb, since the Prophet made his residence there in 622 A.D. it has been called the City of the Prophet, *madinat on-nabi*, or simply the City, al-Madina (Medina, in English). Immediately after the hajj ceremonies, those who have the desire, the time, and the means, arrange to visit Medina. Once there, they remain a week or so, making devotional visits to the tombs of the Prophet and his daughter, Fâṭemeh, one of the feminine saints most venerated by the Shi'ites. After their visit to Medina, few return to Mecca. At this juncture, the pilgrims usually turn their faces homeward and begin their return journey.

PILGRIMS' ACCESS TO MECCA THROUGH THE AGES

From medieval times onward through the nineteenth century, Meccan pilgrimages were always accomplished by means of caravans. The procedures were intelligently, and painstakingly planned, and usually safely accomplished. Initially, pilgrims in small groups left their homelands on well-established routes, using local modes of transportation. For greater security, they nearly always joined a commercial caravan, whose leaders were glad to provide protection in exchange for gold. Then, wherever they came from first, their further aim was to join one of the great hajj caravans bound for Mecca. These were sufficiently numerous, and usually departed from historical cities, or other convenient locations. The most prestigious hajj caravans in recent centuries were the Egyptian, the Syrian, and the Mesopotamian. Because of the high concentrations of Muslims with access to Cairo, Istanbul, and Damascus, and the fact that these numbers increased as these caravans proceeded to their destination, each sometimes swelled to as many as ten thousand moving persons.

The Egyptian caravan departed from Cairo and was the rendezvous for Muslims from most of northern Africa. The Egyptian hajj caravan was celebrated also as bearer each year of the new kesveh, the vast, gold-embroidered black cover for the Kaaba which, until this century, was created annually in Egypt and sent to Mecca. The Egyptian caravan set out overland, proceeded through Sinai into the Hejaz, and southward along the coast of western Arabia.

The Syrian hajj caravan, after having been joined by a subsidiary caravan from Istanbul, set out from Damascus, traversed the region later called Transjordan into Arabia, and then travelled onward to Medina and Mecca. The Syrian caravan thus served as the official Ottoman pilgrimage caravan and was thus protected by Ottoman troops and accompanied in great pomp by special Ottoman officers bearing gifts and money to be dispensed on the holy cities. Although an old treaty specified that Iranian pilgrims should join this caravan at Damascus, Shi‘ite pilgrims from Iran in fact rarely used this route.

The Mesopotamian caravan set forth from Baghdad and, travelling southward by way of the Shi‘ite holy cities of Karbala and Najaf, entered Arabia at Jomaymeh, and then, at a point west of Lineh, it turned southwestward through Ḥâ’il to meet the Hejaz road, between Medina and Mecca. This was the route preferred by many Shi‘ites, because its place of departure was much nearer Iran, and also it provided an opportunity to visit en route the Shi‘ite holy cities in Iraq. However, the political climate was seldom agreeable, the terrain was plagued by Bedouin marauders, and the climate was too harsh to make this route inviting to all pilgrims with access to it.

A second east-west route across Arabia seems to have worked well, at least for the populations of the lower Persian Gulf region. Pilgrims from southern Iran crossed the Gulf from such ports as Bushehr and Bandar ᶜAbbâs, and joined Arab pilgrims from Oman, Qatar, Bahrain, and other coastal areas, and proceeded together, via Riyadh or Boraydeh to Ṭâ’ef and thence to Mecca.

Another rather important caravan route from Yemen began at San‘a, proceeded north by way of ᶜAmrân and Saᶜdeh, and then entered the Hejaz and went thence to Ṭa’ef and Mecca. Many pilgrims from Yemen, Ethiopia, and more distant regions in Africa, joined this well-organized and quite large San‘a caravan.

The social structure of the hajj caravans was thoroughly Islamic, although each of them developed over the centuries a unique culture which was reflective of its own personality. Mainly these caravans were financed and supported by the ruler of the domain in which they originated. Each had a designated commander, the *amir ol-ḥajj*, who was responsible for the well-being of his caravan and the people in it. His power was extensive, for his decisions affected the daily lives of all members of the caravan. Having been appointed to his task by a sovereign, his authority was enforced by a military escort. He also was accompanied by an administrative staff. Since pilgrims commonly gathered to the several caravans from diverse regions, organization tended to be decentralized. Thus, various pilgrims, attracted by shared origin, marched together under their own banner. Each group spoke its own language and prepared its own food. Distinct national groups even had their own amir ol-hajj appointed by the ruler of their country of origin. These caravans were like Islamic cities on the move: some ten thousand pilgrims, men, women, and children, of all races–bound together by religion and a common goal. In eager anticipation, on foot, on horseback, on camelback, they hastened towards realization of their lives' great dream. Both the Egyptian and Syrian caravans accompanied at their van a *maḥmal* (or more correctly *maḥmel*), an elaborate construction mounted on camelback that conveyed a magnificently adorned couch, on which rested a copy of the Koran. Each maḥmal was accompanied by special attendants, who symbolized the power and authority of the ruler of the country in which the caravan originated. The pilgrims in the Egyptian and Istanbul-Damascus caravans were proud of their particular maḥmal, one representing the splendor and sovereignty of Egypt, and the other the might of the Ottoman empire.

The duration of the journeys of the hajj caravans depended on several variable factors: place of departure, the season, the weather, and the conditions of the roads. On the average, the Egyptian caravan journeyed about forty days. The Istanbul-Damascus caravan managed the distance between Damascus and Mecca in thirty days, roughly the same number of days required by the Mesopotamian caravan to reach Mecca from Baghdad. Pilgrims obliged to arrive from more distant places had to plan their journeys most carefully, often leaving home sometimes months beforehand, in order to meet the nearest hajj caravan before its appointed departure. For example, Shi'ites who journeyed from eastern Iran or Sunnites from Central Asia usually set out from their home places about one year ahead of time. Even then, there was no certainty that they would reach their caravan before its departure date. However, time was not necessarily a factor in those days. It was not always possible to follow a rigid pace or itinerary, and little anxiety was wasted on the matter. Resigned to travelling when and however they could, they simply pressed forward until their destination was reached. If they arrived late and found the hajj caravan already departed, they could remain thereabouts until the next year's hajj caravan, or proceed on their own resources to Mecca. Having chosen the latter alternative, there remained the possibility, even likelihood, that they would arrive in Mecca after the year's hajj ceremonies were over. In this event, late arrivals often remained in Mecca for a year, awaiting the next hajj season. Meanwhile, a certain amount of devotional obligation was fulfilled by performing the *ᶜomreh*, the lesser pilgrimage. Customarily, this is completed by all pilgrims upon first arrival in Mecca. The ᶜomreh is not part of the great hajj ceremony; rather, it is a brief visit to the Masjed ol-Ḥarâm, which can be undertaken at any time of year. It involves circumambulating the Kaaba and performing the saᶜy, which consists of running between the sacred hills of Ṣafâ and Marveh.

Although a pilgrimage to Mecca is not required of Muslims who do not have sufficient means, over the centuries, countless of the devout who could ill afford it have attended the hajj. This is still the case. They have worked, and still do work their way to Mecca. This often takes a very long time. For the faithful, who worked in order to earn their way to Mecca from such distances as Central Asia, Afghanistan, Central and Western Africa, or Northern India, this could take several years. It is reported, not necessarily facetiously, that one man, single when he left, arrived in Mecca with a wife and seven children. Another is said to have begun his pilgrimage in childhood and arrived as a man in his seventies. There were other hazards besides marriage and old age: Some became casualties of wars or diseases, or were enslaved, or perhaps imprisoned.

With the coming of the nineteenth century, there were changes in the ways in which Muslim travelers could approach Arabia. The Industrial Revolution in Europe led to advancements in technology which hastened the development of modern systems of travel and communications.

Although Arabia itself did not significantly change until the twentieth century, its holy places and its ports did become much more accessible to pilgrims from remote lands. Railroads and steamships were fundamental to these changes. Also of critical significance was the building of the Suez Canal, which opened Arabia to sea traffic from the Mediterranean, Europe, and the Americas beyond. Now goods could be sent and received much more expeditiously than by the old circuitous routes when an entire continent lay in the way. In effect, Mecca was suddenly closer to the inhabitants of the Ottoman Empire and North Africa. This was also quickly perceived by pilgrims coming from Central Asia, Afghanistan, India, Iran, and the Caucasus. The building of an extensive system of railways, which was one of the results of consciously enunciated British imperialism in Asia, provided fast and cheap transportation to the western ports of the subcontinent. When great numbers of hajj-bound pilgrims annually reached these ports, steamship companies were quick to make convenient and direct transportation available, through the Red Sea, with disembarkations for Mecca either at Jedda or Yanboᶜ. Comparably improved means gave access from Russia, via the Caucasus or the Caspian regions. By the time that our traveller, Farâhâni, undertook his pilgrimage, a combination of roads, steamships, and railways linked Iran and Central Asia with the Black and Red seas. Thus, Shiʿite pilgrims in this wondrous age could go to Mecca by way of the Russian empire via land routes to the Caspian; then by boat to the port of Baku; thence by rail to the Black Sea port of Batum; or they could proceed by overland caravans to the Persian Gulf, board a steamship, and travel via Aden and the Red Sea to the western coast of Arabia. Along there they could disembark at various ports, such as Jedda, Yanboᶜ, Lis̱, and Qonfoẕeh.

After the opening of the Suez Canal in 1869, European steamship companies which heretofore had frequented the Mediterranean soon established Red Sea routes to the Orient, via Alexandria and Port Said. In addition to the new uninterrupted access by sea traffic from the Mediterranean, an efficient railway system for carrying passengers was also available from Alexandria to the port of Suez. Many Iranians, particularly those of a wealthy class, took advantage of this by following a circuitous northern route to Mecca. This, in fact, is the route which Farâhâni chose. Pilgrims travelling this route left Tehran by horse carriage as far as the port of Enzeli on the Caspian. From there, they proceeded by steamboat to Baku; thence by railway through the Caucasus to Batum in Turkey; by steamer to Istanbul and onward to Alexandria. From Alexandria, they continued by rail to Suez, where steamboat accommodations were easily obtainable for passage to Yanboᶜ and Jedda, and from those ports the final stage to Mecca could be accomplished by camel caravan.

During the last three years of the nineteenth century, the most widely discussed of the Ottoman government's then current projects was that of the Hejaz railway. This plan had a devoted advocate in Sultan ᶜAbd ol-Ḥamid (1876-1909), who was greatly interested in strengthening his authority in the Arabian Peninsula, especially in the Hejaz. The project was presented to the sultan's subjects as a promotion to increase pilgrim traffic through the empire and in doing so, strengthen the ties of Islam. An "Islamic fund" was established for the railway with substantial sums contributed also by Muslims of India, China, Burma, and elsewhere.

Construction of the railway began in 1900, and was completed in 1908, stretching more than eight hundred miles from Damascus to Medina. According to statistics released by the Turkish government, the Hejaz railway carried 1,311,907 passengers between 1908 and 1913. During World War I, pilgrimage traffic was reduced to a trickle. The Ottomans used the railway chiefly for military purposes, maintaining the line of communication between the Turkish garrisons in Medina and their base in Syria. Towards the end of the War, lengthy stretches of rails and numerous bridges had been demolished by British agents, rendering the Hejaz railway useless as a pilgrimage route. It was never repaired.

Between the two World Wars, the Meccan pilgrimage was facilitated considerably by the administrative policies of the new Saudi government of Arabia. Finally, more modern means began to replace older modes of transport. The old pilgrim caravan trails were widened into fairly good motor routes. The increasing efficiency of steamships, railways, and other motorized transport made the traditional caravans swiftly decline. The conquest and subjugation of the Hejaz region by the rising House of Saᶜud increasingly insured the safety of the approaches to Mecca. The years before World War II saw a rapid rise in the numbers of pilgrims in Mecca to observe the hajj. International health records of 1933 put the number of hajj pilgrims at 55,000; at 60,000 in 1934, at 80,000 in 1935; and 100,000 in 1937. Of these, about half arrived by sea, mainly from India, Indonesia, and Malaysia.

A truly phenomenal increase came, however, after World War II. It was the age of oil and air travel which transformed the Meccan pilgrimage. First, the concept of chartered air flight was soon received as a practical extension of the travel modes of the hajj. Wherever they originated, pilgrims were long accustomed to gathering in designated places at appointed times, thus travelling onward in groups to Mecca. During the past four decades, special pilgrimage flights have brought tens of thousands of believers from the capitals of many Muslim countries directly to Jedda. Chartered pilgrimage has proved to be inexpensive, fast, and convenient. The rigors and hazards of protracted travels across many barriers now could be set aside. Pilgrims were no longer beset by the harassments of passports, visas, unfamiliar languages and dialects, and so forth. Airline companies and travel agencies now could make all arrangements in advance. Today, each pilgrim flight has its manager, who is responsible for all details. Upon arrival, representatives of each company meet their pilgrim contingents at the Jedda airport, and escort them through customs. Depending on their arrival time, pilgrims may remain in Jedda for the night, or don the eḥrâm and be driven immediately to the Sacred City, where clean hotel accommodations await them. Modern management and dependable chartering contracts have become very inexpensive and, for the most part, available to every Muslim who has the will to make the hajj. Consequently, every year during the hajj season, virtually countless pilgrims briefly invade Mecca. The hotels and guesthouses are full to bursting. The Saudi government erects vast, clean, temporary tent cities on the Plain of ᶜArafât and at the village of Menâ where nearly two million pilgrims gather for the ceremonies. Since the time of Farâhâni, the differences are staggering. When Farâhâni meticulously recorded his pilgrimage in 1885, about 40,900 pilgrims made their way to Mecca. Today, some two million of the faithful perform this religious duty. It is asserted that since ninety-eight percent of them now arrive by air, the airport at Jedda deals with some four hundred flights a day during the peak period just preceding the beginning of the hajj.

Every year at the hajj season's approach the Saudi government faces a daunting logistical effort with enviable aplomb. Although the twentieth century has brought both the air age and a pilgrim explosion to the Arabian Peninsula, this could have happened only in the new age of oil. Arabia has been transformed by oil resources development into one of the wealthiest countries in the world. The Saudi government has been able to purchase the most advanced technology thus far in existence. Some of the most modern air travel facilities yet built have recently appeared on the deserts of Arabia. Comfortable, efficient, plentiful transport whisks pilgrims over superhighways to their destinations in handsome, air-conditioned hotels in Mecca. Good and safe water, modern health facilities, abundant imported fresh produce, dairy products, and meat assure the comfort and satisfaction of the visiting pilgrims. Such is the happy destination of Meccan pilgrims in the late twentieth century, but what was it like before the present time, to survive the rigors of travel in earlier times and experience the fulfillment of participation in the traditional observances of the hajj?

MECCAN PILGRIMAGE AND TRAVEL LITERATURE

Until quite recently, a journey to Mecca from any considerable distance in the Muslim world required both courage and determination. These travellers had to face the many dangers and hardships of traversing long distances, passing through lands unknown to them, whose inhabitants often were inhospitable and sometimes predatory. Immense extremes of climate, weather, and topography relentlessly taxed their material resources and their bodily endurance. For Iranian Muslims the journey was long and arduous. They often began their travels from faraway centers such as Bokhara, Herat, Mashhad, Isfahan, Kashan, Shiraz, and others. To set out upon this lengthy and hazardous journey, which included crossing the dread, desolate Arabian desert, was a heroic act which had to be impelled and sustained by total faith. Those who undertook it were ready to die for their faith, certain of reward in the next world. However, it appears that the ultimate sacrifice was not so often exacted: Most pilgrims returned from Mecca in good health, despite the perils of the long journey. At home they told fine stories of their extraordinary adventures to welcoming relatives, friends, and wide-eyed, would-be pilgrims. Some even wrote about their experiences, not only for the sake of recording their personal adventures, but mainly for the pious purpose of providing information and instruction for their fellow Muslims. In this fashion, a distinctive genre of literature developed about the hajj–the pilgrimage–and the journeys that preceded and followed it. These works generally included information about historical geography, the routes, and various encounters with peoples and places of interest, particularly the Arabs and Arabia. The climax was an account of the hajj and the holy cities of Mecca and Medina. In Persian this genre is called *safarnâmeh*, which somehow looks inviting and mysterious, but in English it becomes literally (and prosaically), "travel book."

Such works have flourished across the Islamic world at least from medieval times to the present. A well-known example from eleventh century Persia is Nâṣer-e Khosrow's *Book of Travels*, and from the medieval Arab world we have the famous *Travels* of Ibn Battuta.†

The florescence of travel literature in Iran took place during the nineteenth century. Neither since, nor before this time, have so many fine works of this nature been produced by Persians. Their numbers are plentiful. Some have been published, but many still are in manuscript. There were several reasons for the development in Iran of this particular branch of literature during the nineteenth century. The broadly manifested Iranian literary renaissance of that time was one reason: renewed intellectual activity, energized by new ideas and changing patterns of thinking, not only transformed the structure and content of traditional Persian literature, but also endowed with new spirit some of the old literary genres which remained indispensable to Iranian culture. One of these was the travel memoir. This category was particularly encouraged under the reign and personal interest of Nâṣer od-Din Shâh (1834-96), as a means of information gathering and reporting on general conditions, both at home and abroad. Some fine examples of these are *Bostân os-Siâḥat* ("Garden of Travel"), by Ḥâjji Zayn ol-ᶜÂbedin-e Shirvâni, first published in 1310/1892-93; *Safâratnâmeh-ye Khᵛârazm* ("Journal of the Khᵛârazm Embassy"), by Reżâ Qoli Hedâyat, published in 1292/1874-75; and *Maṭlaᶜ os-Shams* ("Rising Place of the Sun"), by Eᶜtemâd os-Salṭaneh, published in three volumes between the years 1301-1303/1884-86. The shah himself wrote numerous accounts of his travels within Iran and in Europe, some of which are excellent examples of Persian prose writing.

The introduction into Iran of mechanical printing methods in the early part of the nineteenth century was a major stimulant to increased interest and change in travel literature. Making books more cheaply in less time and in vastly increased quantities helped to create a much larger reading audience as well as exciting the vanity and self-importance of traveller-authors. The many notable achievements of the Industrial Revolution proved a great boon to the production of *safarnâmeh*s; among its contributions were more efficient commercial routes and improved or new modes of transportation. The introduction of rail and steamship travel in Russia, Turkey, and India not only radically accelerated Iran's contacts with her neighboring nations, but also made for astoundingly easy access to the great world beyond. Travellers of many types, pilgrims, diplomats, heads of state, government officials, all now had more assurance of arriving at journey's end with relative ease and safety. It is true that instead of dragons, jinn, chilblains, and sunstrokes, there were newer, more fashionable perils, but on the other hand, there was promise of innumerable eye-goggling sights and events, baffling foreign cultural oddities, grand entertainments and, above all, ideas, waiting for travellers to report, and both astonish and inform the folks back home. Thus, as the nineteenth century drew nearer to the twentieth, more

† Nâṣer-e Khosrow, *Safarnâmeh*, edited and translated by C. Schefer, *Sefer Nameh; relation du voyage de Nassiri Khosrau* (Paris, 1881); English translation by Wheeler Thackston, Jr., *Nâser-e Khosraw's Book of Travels* (Albany, 1986). Ebn Baṭṭuṭeh's *Reḥleh* has been translated by H. A. R. Gibb, *The Travels of Ibn Baṭṭuta A. D. 1325-1354* (Cambridge, 1958-71); see also Ross E. Dunn, *The Adventures of Ibn Battuta, a Muslim Traveler of the 14th Century* (Berkeley and Los Angeles, 1986).

and more Iranians, many of whom were well-educated and well-informed, made extensive journeys abroad. Travel memoirs proliferated.

Travel literature written in Persian during this period included four distinct categories: accounts that dealt with general travel within Iran; memoirs concerning travels in the neighboring Russian and Ottoman empires; works written about the West, mainly Europe, and distant regions of Asia such as India and the Far East; and finally, pilgrimage literature, which consisted of accounts pertaining to the hajj, and visits to other Islamic holy places. In late nineteenth century memoirs, this time-honored genre, especially narratives of the pilgrimage to Mecca, often took its readers, en route, to some of the regions which already have been mentioned above. The content of this material depended largely on the choice of routes. Judging from the travel accounts themselves, the preferred route appears to have passed through the Russian and Ottoman empires. A person of means who lived in one of the important urban centers of Iran, away from the capital city of Tehran, and who intended to make the Meccan pilgrimage, would first travel directly to Tehran where he could virtually complete the necessary arrangements for his long journey. The traveller would depart Tehran northwestward to Qazvin, an attractive old city of historical and aesthetic interest, a former capital of Iran. From there he would turn northward and soon cross the Elburz Mountains, chiefly through relatively low river valleys, pass through the Caspian province of Gilan to the port of Enzeli on the Caspian Sea. From Enzeli, he would arrive by steamship to the Russian port of Baku; from Baku westward, through the Caucasus by railroad to the Ottoman port of Batum on the Black Sea; from there by steamship to Istanbul; from there by steamer once more, passing through the Dardenelles, the Aegean Sea, and the eastern Mediterranean, to the Egyptian port of Alexandria. From Alexandria, he would proceed by rail to Suez; there he would embark on another stretch of water to the Arabian port of Jedda. His objective now near, in a place where necessity honored tradition, he would depart Jedda by camel caravan for the last distance to Mecca.

Some of the classic memoirs of the hajj were written by Iranians who took this route, with some interesting variations. Records indicate that as many as seventeen travel accounts, safarnâmehs, of the hajj survive from the Qâjâr period (1794-1924). There may be others which as yet have not been offered to library collections, nor revealed to researchers by present owners. Of the known available works, the following have been published: *Ketâb Hedâyat os-Sabil va Kefâyat od-Dalil*, by Farhâd Mirzâ Moᶜtamad od-Dowleh, a learned uncle of Nâṣer od-Din Shâh; *Safarnâmeh-ye Tasharrof be Makkeh*, by Mahdi-Qoli Hedâyat; *Safarnâmeh-ye Makkeh*, by Amin od-Dowleh, the sharply witty vizier of Nâṣer od-Din Shâh; *Safarnâmeh-ye Ziârat-e Makkeh va Siâḥat-e Irân va Hend*, by Nâyeb oṣ-Ṣadr-e Shirâzi; *Safarnâmeh-ye Ḥâjji Mirzâ Moshtâri be Makkeh*, by Moḥammad Ebrâhim Moshtâri Khorâsâni, in verse; *Safarnâmeh-ye Makkeh*, by Sayf od-Dowleh; and finally, *Safarnâmeh-ye Farâhâni*, the subject of the present translation. When we add to the above extant works of the hajj category, other known unpublished and published religious-oriented travel accounts dating from the Qâjâr period, we have before us some twenty-nine known works. These constitute a treasure house of information on many important social and political aspects of the societies of Iran, Turkey, Iraq, Arabia, the Levant, and Egypt, offered to us by a number of literate Iranians, which present significant, interesting, and sometimes crucially important views of various social and political classes in Iran during the latter portion of the nineteenth century.

FARÂHÂNI AND HIS WORKS

The book we are presenting here is a late nineteenth century safarnâmeh of a pilgrimage to Mecca in 1885-86. The author, an Iranian notable, Mirzâ Moḥammad Ḥosayn Farâhâni, was born in 1847, and died in 1912. The manuscript of this work first came to the attention of one of the present editor-translators (Farmayan) in 1961, when he was researching an unrelated subject at Iran's National Library (Ketâbkhâneh-ye Melli) in Tehran. Earlier, this manuscript had been in the Royal Library, but later, under an act of the Parliament, it was moved to the National Library. It is a handsomely prepared manuscript and was executed by an accomplished calligrapher who was commissioned for this task by Farâhâni himself. Working from the author's first completed text, the calligrapher used a highly stylized, but readable script. Farâhâni presented this volume to Nâṣer od-Din Shâh in 1887, and it bears the monarch's signature and personal seal. Farâhâni's original copy of this work, from which the volume for the shah was copied, is in the possession of the author's son, Khân Malek Sâsâni. In some respects, it is even more handsome than the one which was presented to the shah. In his time, Farâhâni's mastery of calligraphy was widely admired. His copy of his *Safarnâmeh* is written in his personal *shekasteh* style. Although difficult to read, it is a beautiful example of the often brilliant, artfully created calligraphy of the Qâjâr period. The manuscript's original editor, Farmayan, through the courtesies of the National Library and Mr. Sâsâni, was able to obtain photocopies of both manuscripts, which he used to produce the first published edition of this work in Persian. This was published by the University of Tehran Press in 1964, under the title *Safarnâmeh-ye Mirzâ Ḥosayn-e Farâhâni*. Here, in this English translation we have named it *A Shi'ite Pilgrimage to Mecca*.‡

Farâhâni was born in the village of Âhangarân in the district of Farâhân, the present-day Arâk of northcentral Iran. His father, Mirzâ Moḥammad Mahdi, was a leading poet and bureaucrat of the early nineteenth century, who first received the title of *Malek ol-Kottâb* ("King of Calligraphers"), and later achieved the position of *Monshi ol-Mamâlek* (Chief Secretary) to the Governor-General of the province of Azerbaijan. Young Moḥammad Ḥosayn had little opportunity to receive early tutelage under his father who died at the age of eighty-eight when the child was only seven years of age. He remained in Âhangarân until, at the age of twelve, he was sent to Tehran by his mother under the guardianship of his oldest brother, Mirzâ

‡ Readers are begged to take gracious note that some 19 years later, after the revolution of a decade ago, a Mr. Masᶜud Golzâri, without permission or acknowledgement, reprinted under his own name Farmayan's work on the Farâhâni manuscript. Since at the present time there exists no copyright law in Iran, an opportunity is taken here to describe Mr. Golzâri's act as one of unmitigated piracy, and to protest it strenuously. For the sake of scholarship only do we list Mr. Golzâri's unauthorized reprint in the bibliography for this first English translation.

Moḥammad Malek. There he received the education typical of a Qâjâr bureaucrat: instruction in Persian literature, Arabic, history, accounting, and calligraphy, all of which are well-reflected in his *Safarnâmeh,* and other writings. Mirzâ Moḥammad can be said to have inherited one great talent from his father. This was calligraphy, of which eventually he became a great master. Perhaps more than any other aspect of his education, his dexterity in this art led to his employment at the age of twenty-two in the Ministry of Foreign Affairs by the well-known Foreign Minister, Mirzâ Saᶜid Khân Mo'tamen ol-Molk.

One of the goals of the shah and his chief ministers at this time was to bring about a reconciliation with the Âqâ Khân-e Maḥallâti, leader of the Ismaili sect. Earlier in the century, the Âqâ Khân had led an unsuccessful rebellion against the shah. After his defeat he escaped to India, where British authorities had given him asylum and protection. Now, the government of the shah was interested in issuing a general amnesty, and was willing thereby to welcome the Âqâ Khân and his followers back to Iran. In 1869, a special embassy was dispatched to Bombay in a negotiation effort. Although Mirzâ Moḥammad Ḥosayn Farâhâni was but a junior member of this embassy, he became its most influential one. The Âqâ Khân had been a friend and admirer of Farâhâni's deceased father, and soon accepted the son as a trusted liason between himself and the embassy's head, Mirzâ Fażlollah Khân-e Qazvini. Speedy progress was made and the Âqâ Khân accepted the shah's amnesty. It was agreed that as a gesture of good faith, first a marriage would take place between Princess Żiâ os-Salṭaneh, the shah's daughter, and Jalâl-Shâh, son of the Âqâ Khân. Afterwards, the Ismailis would be allowed to gradually return to their homeland of Maḥallât in central Iran.

The person responsible for these arrangements was Farâhâni. Consequently, in 1871, when Nâṣer od-Din Shâh was on a state visit to the holy places of Mesopotamia, Mirzâ Moḥammad Ḥosayn and Jalâl-Shâh, the Âqâ Khân's son, travelled from India to Baghdad, where they were graciously received in audience with the shah, who accorded them the honor of joining the royal entourage.

Upon the shah's return to Tehran, Farâhâni resumed work on the marriage arrangements with which he had been occupied before being swept into the royal pilgrimage. Then catastrophe struck: Jalâl-Shâh died suddenly, before his marriage day. In the resulting commotion, Farâhâni was forgotten. His promised honorarium for his endeavors in the Ismaili amnesty affair vanished in chancery. He wrote several letters of reminder, but to no avail. Then in audience with the shah, he brought up the subject. It was the wrong occasion and the shah was visibly displeased. Farâhâni found himself in disfavor. Jealousy among his colleagues made matters worse when one or more of them spread the unfounded rumor that the shah had ordered his arrest. Young and still inexperienced, Farâhâni fled in disguise, from Tehran to Kerman. This was in the year 1873.

Few details are known now of Farâhâni's life during the next seven years. The small available evidence indicates that his relationship with the shah, a man generally inclined to amiability, was soon mended. Farâhâni was given another diplomatic assignment in India, where he resided for several years (and to which he alludes in the text of his safarnâmeh). Meanwhile, his love of travel and his devotion to religious observances took him several times to the holy shrines in Khorasan and present-day Iraq, and a first pilgrimage to Mecca. Unfortunately, we have no knowledge of the particulars of his earlier Meccan journey, although there is clear evidence that he has written about some of his youthful travel experiences, which may have included his sojourn in India and his first trip to Mecca. It has been said that some of Farâhâni's possessions, household furnishings, among them some books and writings, were destroyed during several clashes with local enemies in Farâhân.

In 1882, we find Mirzâ Moḥammad Ḥosayn travelling to Khorasan as a member of the shah's entourage while the monarch was visiting that province. His assignment was to assist the shah's minister, Eᶜtemâd os-Salṭaneh in preparation of the latter's well-known book *Maṭlaᶜ os-Shams*, which dealt with the history and geography of Khorasan.

In 1885, Farâhâni set out on his great second pilgrimage to Mecca. He was inspired by Nâṣer od-Din Shâh, whom he very nearly idolized, to write a full account of his journey. This he did faithfully and in detail, when he returned to Iran in 1886. Because of its urgency, he commissioned another calligrapher to prepare the manuscript for presentation to the shah. This decision not only has deprived us of another copy of the *Safarnâmeh* in Farâhâni's own masterful calligraphy, but it also explains why there are some mistakes in the manuscript from the Royal Library. The shah was very pleased with the content of Farâhâni's work and consequently bestowed upon him the title which previously had been held by Farâhâni's father: Malek ol-Kottâb ("King of Calligraphers").

Of Farâhâni's other works, besides the *Safarnâmeh*, only two minor satirical treatises, *Ḥâlat* ("Mood") and *Âdâb os-Sorur* ("Rites of Mirth"), which were published together in 1932, have survived. Of his lost works, three can be identified: a *Divân*, or collection of poems; a *Monsha'ât*, or collection of letters; and a treatise on statecraft of the "Mirror for Princes" type, which is a time-honored genre of Persian literature. Of the last item, nothing remains, or at least nothing is known to exist now. However, we can find enough material in the *Safarnâmeh* and the *Ḥâlat* to be able to make some judgment of Farâhâni's thoughts, writings, and poetry.

Farâhâni's pen name when composing poetry was "Golbon". He apparently produced a considerable quantity of poetry, certainly enough to constitute a divân. The fragments of these, which appear in the *Safarnâmeh* and in the essay *Ḥâlat*, are in the forms of *ghazal* and *maṯnavi*. In quality they are mediocre at best and quite dull at worst. Obviously poetry was not among his talents. Farâhâni's prose writings reflect his background and his education for the Qâjâr bureaucracy. The style follows, or imitates, the style characteristics developed during the early part of the nineteenth century by such great writers of the time as Qâ'em Maqâm, Amir Neẓâm-e Garrusi, and ᶜAbd or-Razzâq-e Donboli. The single letter remaining of his lost letters, which has been quoted in the essay *Ḥâlat*, indicates clearly that his *Monsha'ât* must have been an attempt to produce a book very similar to that of Qâ'em Maqâm's *Monsha'ât*. There is no doubt that Farâhâni was well-informed in Persian literature, folktales, and folklore. He also was a man of wit and a deft and seasoned conversationalist. These qualities and accomplishments are clearly reflected in the prose of his *Safarnâmeh* and *Ḥâlat*.

From the material described above, it also is possible to perceive Farâhâni's attitudes towards religion and the religious establishment. In many ways, Farâhâni was typical of the nineteenth century Iranian bureaucratic elite class. He was extremely anti-clerical, and at the same time he was personally devout. The last portion of his little work entitled *Ḥâlat* is one of the most biting satires ever written on the Shi'ite ulama and their establishment. However, throughout the *Safarnâmeh*, the reader perceives Farâhâni's genuine piety and respect for Shi'ism. On the other hand, he criticizes sharply and speaks out boldly for abandonment of certain established Shi'i practices. For example, he finds the use of *taqeyyeh*, religious dissumulation, humiliating, and the decree concerning the ritual purity of water is to him an impracticality. He sincerely believes that Shi'ites and Sunnites should be tolerant of each other, but does not accord the same reciprocity to non-Muslims. Throughout the *Safarnâmeh*, his mistrust of non-Muslims on religious grounds is evident.

In the matter of the pilgrimage itself, the *Safarnâmeh* becomes tremendously useful as a source of information. It must not be forgotten that in writing this memoir, one of Farâhâni's chief purposes was to provide as much information as possible to the Shi'ites of Iran on the hajj, and to show them how it could be successfully undertaken. Consequently, his account covers a wide range of subjects, and presents a huge quantity of details concerning the peoples and places he comes across as he makes his way towards Mecca. The reader is informed about the quality of food and lodgings at all important stops; prices of commodities, the availability of goods, modes of transportation, fares for carriages, trains, steamships, and camels. There are ample details and warnings concerning such hazards and annoyances as bandits, dishonest guides, and corrupt officials. Every possible currency in every region he passed through is carefully discussed; the value of each is explained, and how it compares with monies in other regions. The climate in all regions and the temperaments and habits of the various peoples along his way never escape Farâhâni's scrutiny. Western readers and scholars, especially, should appreciate Farâhâni's account, because it provides something of a counterbalance to the few, but better known, nineteenth century European accounts of the pilgrimage to Mecca. In his comments, sortings of information, recordings of what impressed an Iranian Shi'ite gentleman of his day, bent on seeing for himself the supreme holy place of the Islamic world, we learn much of Arabia and the Ottoman empire as seen and interpreted by an educated, mature, intelligent Middle Easterner and Muslim. We also perceive clear reflections of Iran and its society of that time, as Farâhâni inadvertently reveals them and himself in his journal.

Regarding Farâhâni's political views, as disclosed, or implied, in the *Safarnâmeh*, like most educated Iranians of his class and day, he was conservatively progressive. He believed in need of some sort of political and religious reforms, provided they threatened neither the monarchy nor the Shi'ite religion of Iran. Like his contemporary, Ḥâjji Pirzâdeh, Farâhâni expresses his distaste for French republicanism and the movements then current in the Ottoman empire which favored republicanism. The encroachment in the Middle East of European imperialism is critically observed. The traditional enmity towards Great Britain and Russia by the Iranian bureaucratic elite is reflected in his descriptions and commentary of peoples and places in the

Caucasus and in Egypt. A representative example of this attitude from Farâhâni's *Safarnâmeh* is his description of the Egyptians' struggle against British occupation of their country. Another instance concerns the revolt of the Mahdi of the Sudan, in whom he shows considerable interest. These views can be accepted as typical of the elite class of the Iranian bureaucracy of Farâhâni's day (and later), which he represents. This is one of several areas in which the *Safarnâmeh* may be used as a valuable source in reconstructing the social history and intellectual atmosphere of Qâjâr Iran as the nineteenth century neared its close.

Assuredly, the *Safarnâmeh* can be of great value in studying the character and social behavior of the nineteenth century Iranian elite classes. In the past, many western observers, as well as contemporary social scientists, have been fascinated by Persian individualism and curious about its cultural origins. This work by Farâhâni seems to indicate that the more educated a Persian becomes, the more individualistic his attitudes become. This may be true, but the same characteristic is common among Iranians of all levels in their society, although the foundations and purposes of this individualism may change and continue to change in successively higher levels. Most Iranians proceed through life, each within his own wall of privacy and motivation. Each is sociable and gregarious to one degree or another, but each guards his aura and, commonly, each makes no effort to invade this individual territory of the personality of others. Indeed, it is quite to the contrary. Throughout this *Safarnâmeh*, the reader encounters many instances where either Farâhâni himself or other Iranians with whom he deals manifest this particular characteristic. To cite one example, the author throughout the book rarely mentions his companions. We still do not know whether he departed from Tehran alone, or if there were fellow travellers with him. A travel companion is mentioned during his stop in Rasht: "Amin-e Divân and his son, Amir Khân the Sarhang endeavored that they, too, might travel to the House of God. In the end, Amir Khân became my travelling companion." This companion is not referred to again in the context of the trip until the last day of the journey homeward when Farâhâni disembarks at the port of Enzeli in Gilan, and stands once more on his native ground. At this juncture he says in his diary: "Since the time [I] left Gilan, Ḥâjji Amir Khân the Sarhang, son of Amin-e Divan, had been [my] travelling companion. By [mutual] agreement, he was [with me] everywhere. In truth, he behaved with complete nobility, affection, and fidelity." It is regrettable that Farâhâni did not report the opinions and impressions of this companion, nor of any others throughout the lengthy journey. It would have been useful to learn how other Iranians reacted as they shared experiences in company with the author.

However, despite small complaints such as these, and a few other imperfections which readers are likely to note, we, as editors and translators, found Farâhâni's work a bounteous compendium, both accurate, relevant, and rife with voluminous detail. The book is a pleasure to read. It offers a broad window through which westerners now can view a time which is long gone. The places are still where they were, but in many ways they are greatly changed, and the same may be said of the peoples of that part of the world through which Farâhâni passed, then saved for us to see. His record is intensely interesting. It is evocative, lively, delightful, and enormously informative. It offers lavish and meticulous information on the social, political, and economic life of the Middle East of the late nineteenth century. It illuminates Russian officials as they administer the affairs of the Caucasus. It compares and contrasts western political and commercial officers in Egypt, the Levant, and India. It tells us about the Muslims of the Russian empire, the Ottomans, and the Egyptians. It speaks of places and conditions in Arabia, of the Arabs themselves, and also of the thousands of pilgrims who, then as now, come great distances in order to venerate the holy places in Arabia.

Finally, some words about our translation must be offered. This translation is based on the original Persian printed edition of the work by Hafez Farmayan (Tehran 1342/1964) and draws on his knowledge and familiarity with the manuscript to make some needed changes in the text. The page numbers cited in brackets [ ] refer to the Persian text as published in the 1964 Farmayan edition. The present English translation retains most of the editorial devices used in Farmayan's edition, such as paragraph breaks, division headings, and margin titles. For the convenience of the reader, however, the text, which was in one continuous long narrative in the original work, has been divided into seven chapters. The margin titles which in the Farmayan edition were listed as the table of contents, have been moved to where they now appear, preceding the index, under the title "Table of Subject Headings".

Exact translation between two languages inevitably is difficult; sometimes it is impossible. It is often necessary to make meanings in Persian clearer in English by adding words or phrases that are implied, but not expressly stated in the original text. Such additions have been added freely in this translation, but to distinguish them from the original text, they are always enclosed in brackets. Since Farâhâni himself notes that he was attempting to write in a clear and unembellished style, rather than the ornate and artificially complex prose preferred by many of his contemporaries, we also have tried in this translation to be faithful to the original, and as plain and literal as possible, even though this may at times produce some rather awkward English.

From the beginning of our project, we have held two purposes in mind: first, to make Farâhâni's work accessible to as broad an audience as possible; and second, to make it useful for specialists in the history and civilization of Islam and the Middle East. This is a difficult task, which always risks confusing or boring the nonspecialist with technicalities while annoying the specialist with generalities. To try to bridge the differences between the two potential audiences, we have provided extensive annotations along with the text. Different notes are intended for the use of different readers. Some are intended only to provide the general reader with some contextual information in order to further his or her appreciation of some of the allusions and nuances which would be apparent to an educated Persian reader. Other notes are intended to guide researchers and more advanced readers to accessible materials on points they may wish to pursue further. Still other notes are provided to inform specialists of technical problems involving the translation, the materials employed to resolve them, and additional sources in non Western languages dealing with matters discussed in the text. It is hoped that each reader will find the notes which serve his or her purpose and tolerate those that may seem superfluous.

We have enjoyed working on this book, and feel that our collaboration of many years, first as teacher and student and, later, as colleagues and close friends, is very successful. The responsibility in this project is equally shared by both. From beginning to end, the entire project (save for location of the manuscript and its original 1964 edition), was a joint effort. We hope that both general readers and specialists will appreciate our endeavors. For us it has been a labor of love for the Middle East and its gifts to all of us. For readers we hope it will provide useful information, as well as relaxation and enjoyment.

H.F.

E.L.D.

Fall 1989

Mirzâ Moḥammad Ḥosayn Farâhâni (1847–1912), author of the *Safarnâmeh*. (Reproduced with the permission of Professor M. Moghaddam of Tehran University)

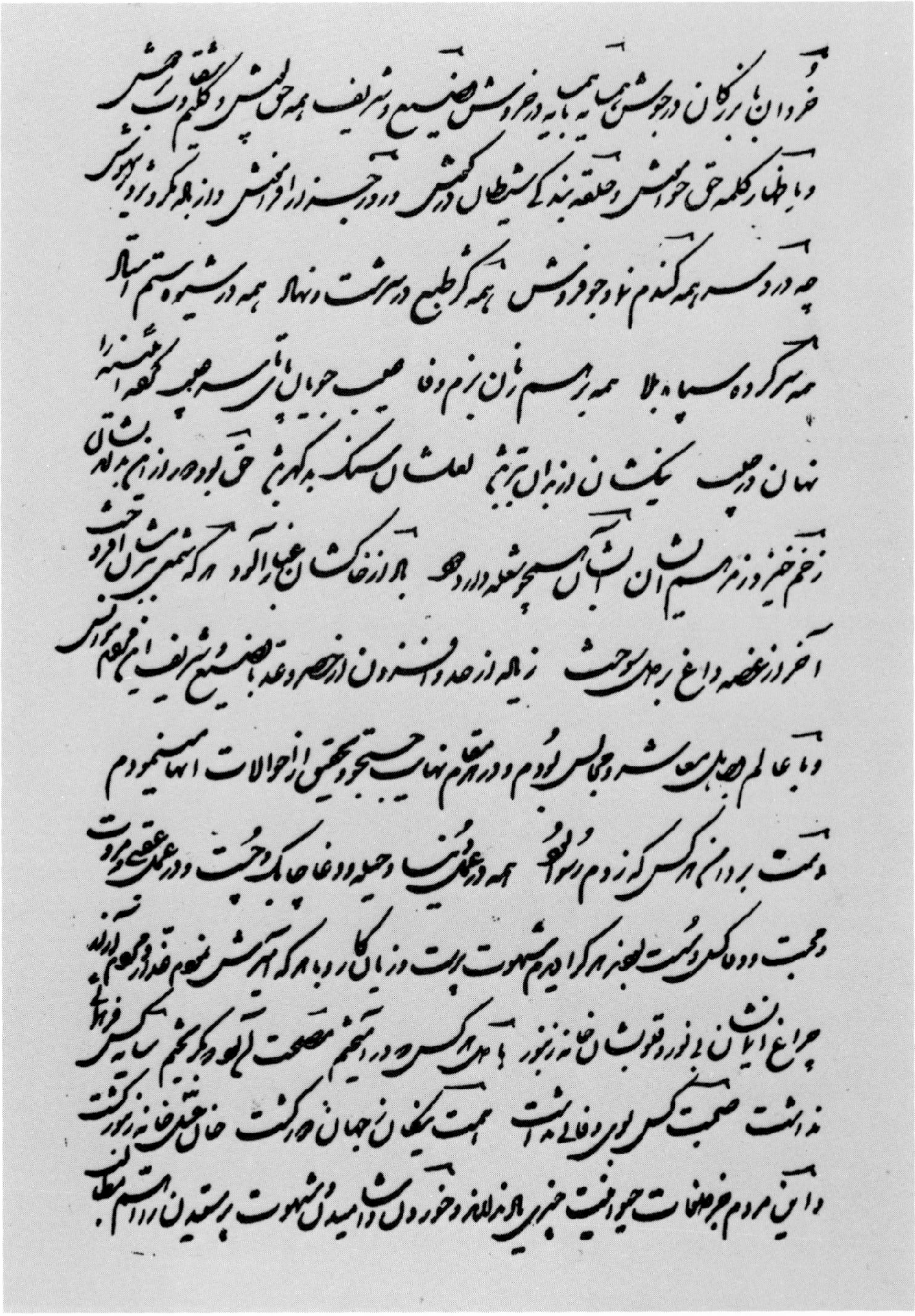

A page from the original manuscript of Farâhâni's work entitled *Ḥâlat* in the author's own handwriting. This specimen clearly shows Farâhâni's accomplished style of calligraphy. (Reproduced with the permission of Professor M. Moghaddam of Tehran University)

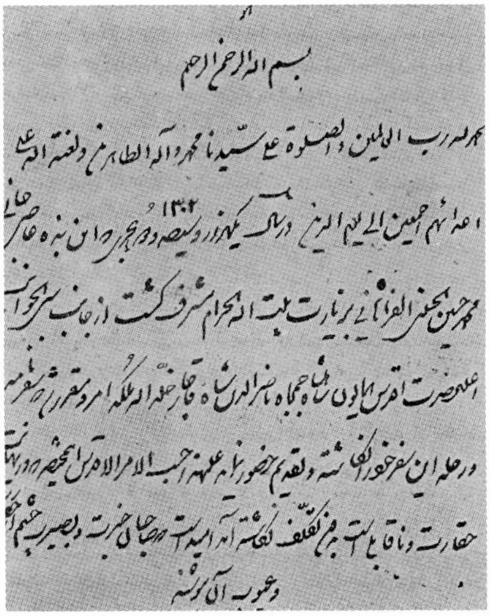

The first page of the original draft of the *Safarnâmeh* in Farâhâni's own individual *shekasteh* handwriting style. (Reproduced with the permission of Farâhâni's son Khân Malek Sâsâni)

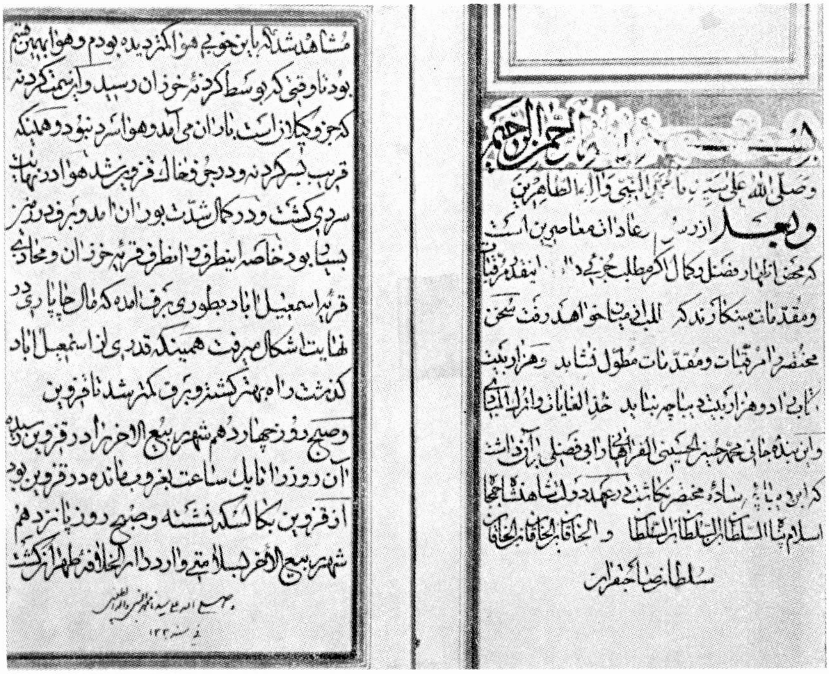

A reproduction of the first and last pages of Farâhâni's *Safarnâmeh*, the original of which is in the possession of Iran's National Library. This manuscript was presented to Nâṣer od-Din Shâh by Farâhâni in 1887 and has the Shah's seal and signature. It was loaned to the original editor (Farmayan) by the National Library in 1964 when he produced the first published edition of the work in Persian (for further information, see the introduction, page xxvi).

Nâșer od-Din Shâh Qâjâr, the reigning monarch of Iran, 1848–1896. He commissioned Farâhâni to write the account of the latter's Meccan pilgrimage. Photograph by Antoine Sevruguin, taken in the 1880s. (Courtesy of Myron Bement Smith Collection, Freer Gallery of Art / Arthur M. Sackler Gallery Archives, Smithsonian Institution, Negative number 31.1)

Tehran: Shemiran Gate. Photograph by Antoine Sevruguin, taken in the 1880s. (Courtesy of Myron Bement Smith Collection, Freer Gallery of Art / Arthur M. Sackler Gallery Archives, Smithsonian Institution, Negative number 21.2)

Tehran: Qazvin Gate. Photograph by Antoine Sevruguin, taken in the 1880s. (Courtesy of Myron Bement Smith Collection, Freer Gallery of Art / Arthur M. Sackler Gallery Archives, Smithsonian Institution, Negative number 61.5)

Tehran: Dowlat Gate. Photograph by Antoine Sevruguin, taken in the 1880s. (Courtesy of Myron Bement Smith Collection, Freer Gallery of Art / Arthur M. Sackler Gallery Archives, Smithsonian Institution, Negative number 26.4)

Doroshky: a popular mode of city transportation that was also used for long-distance travelling (see text, page 2). Photograph by Antoine Sevruguin. (Courtesy of Myron Bement Smith Collection, Freer Gallery of Art / Arthur M. Sackler Gallery Archives, Smithsonian Institution, Negative number 60.1)

A bridge on the road to Rasht (see text, page 31). Photograph by Antoine Sevruguin, taken in the 1880s. (Courtesy of Myron Bement Smith Collection, Freer Gallery of Art / Arthur M. Sackler Gallery Archives, Smithsonian Institution, Negative number 46.5)

Caspian forest near Rasht (see text, pages 43–46). Photograph by Antoine Sevruguin, taken in the 1880s. (Courtesy of Myron Bement Smith Collection, Freer Gallery of Art / Arthur M. Sackler Gallery Archives, Smithsonian Institution, Negative number 31.5)

Rice fields and farmers' houses near Rasht. Photograph by Antoine Sevruguin, taken in the 1880s. (Courtesy of Myron Bement Smith Collection, Freer Gallery of Art / Arthur M. Sackler Gallery Archives, Smithsonian Institution, Negative number 42.11)

A mosque in Rasht. Photograph by Antoine Sevruguin, taken in the 1880s. (Courtesy of Myron Bement Smith Collection, Freer Gallery of Art / Arthur M. Sackler Gallery Archives, Smithsonian Institution, Negative number 60.1)

The palace of Shams ol-Emareh at Enzeli; a fine specimen of Qâjâr secular architecture (see text, page 47 and footnote 205). Photograph by Antoine Sevruguin, taken in the 1880s. (Courtesy of Myron Bement Smith Collection, Freer Gallery of Art / Arthur M. Sackler Gallery Archives, Smithsonian Institution, Negative number 47.8)

A magnificent example of a *howz-khaneh*, a living room with fountain and pool; this was a common feature of nineteenth-century Persian mansions. Photograph by Antoine Sevruguin, taken in the 1880s; possibly the ground floor of the Shams ol-Emareh Palace at Enzeli. (Courtesy of Myron Bement Smith Collection, Freer Gallery of Art / Arthur M. Sackler Gallery Archives, Smithsonian Institution, Negative number 26.10)

Pilgrims embarking at Jedda (see text, pages 199–202); an early-twentieth-century photograph. (Reproduced from *Western Arabia and the Red Sea*, with the permission of the Controller of Her Britannic Majesty's Stationery Office)

Jedda: quarantine wharf from the boat channel; an early-twentieth-century photograph. (Reproduced from *Western Arabia and the Red Sea*, with the permission of the Controller of Her Britannic Majesty's Stationery Office)

Jedda: the main market; an early-twentieth-century photograph. (Reproduced from *Western Arabia and the Red Sea*, with the permission of the Controller of Her Britannic Majesty's Stationery Office)

Mecca: the general view at the time of Fârâhani's visit in 1885 showing the Masjed ol-Harâm in the foreground. (Reproduced from Christiaan Snouck Hurgronje, *Mekka (mit Bilder-Atlas)*, Den Haag, 1888–1889)

Mecca: view from the north; an early-twentieth-century photograph. (Reproduced from *Western Arabia and the Red Sea*, with the permission of the Controller of Her Britannic Majesty's Stationery Office)

Mecca: the interior of Masjed ol-Ḥarâm (see text, page 213). (Reproduced with the permission of the Controller of Her Britannic Majesty's Stationery Office)

Mecca: the Masjed ol-Ḥarâm, or the Sacred Mosque, as it was at the time of Farâhâni's visit in 1885. (Reproduced from Christiaan Snouck Hurgronje, *Mekka (mit Bilder-Atlas)*, Den Haag. 1888–1889)

Numbers indicate the following:

1. The gate of Bani Shaybeh
2. The Ḥejr of Ishmael
3. Building on the Zamzam Well

4–5. Portable steps for access to the Kaaba

6. Maqâm (Station) of Ebrâhim
7. Pulpit
8. Maqâm ol-Ḥanafi
9. Maqâm ol-Mâleki
10. Maqâm ol-Ḥanbali
11. Ḥamideyyeh
12. Ajyad Fort

Pilgrims' camp at Menâ in 1885. Photograph by Christiaan Snouck Hurgronje. (Reproduced from Angelo Pesce, *Makkah: A Hundred Years Ago*, London, 1986)

Pilgrims' camp at ʿArafât in 1885. Photograph by Christiaan Snouck Hurgronje. (Reproduced from Angelo Pesce, *Makkah: A Hundred Years Ago*, London, 1986)

Pilgrims' camp in the valley of ʿArafât, with the Mountain of Mercy rising in the center background. Photograph by Christiaan Snouck Hurgronje, taken in 1885. (Reproduced from Angelo Pesce, *Makkah: A Hundred Years Ago*, London, 1986)

Pilgrims' camp at Menâ in 1985. (Reproduced from Angelo Pesce, *Makkah: A Hundred Years Ago*, London, 1986)

Mecca: the aerial view, 1985. (Reproduced from Angelo Pesce, *Makkah: A Hundred Years Ago*, London, 1986)

The Kaaba, as it was at the time of Farâhâni's visit. (Reproduced from Christiaan Snouck Hurgronje, *Mekka (mit Bilder-Atlas)*, Den Haag, 1888–1889)

Mecca: the arrival of the Egyptian Maḥmal (see text, page 240). (Reproduced from *Western Arabia and the Red Sea*, with the permission of the Controller of Her Britannic Majesty's Stationery Office)

ʿOsmân Pâshâ, the Governor-General, greets the Egyptian Maḥmal. (Reproduced from Christiaan Snouck Hurgronje, *Mekka (mit Bilder-Atlas)*, Den Haag, 1888–1889)

Pilgrims in the Masjed ol-Ḥarâm during the *ṭavâf* (see text, pages 208–213); an early-twentieth-century photograph). (Reproduced from *Western Arabia and the Red Sea*, with the permission of the Controller of Her Britannic Majesty's Stationery Office)

The Ḥamideyyeh, the government's palace, built by ʿOs̱mân Pâshâ. (Reproduced from Christiaan Snouck Hurgronje, *Mekka (mit Bilder-Atlas)*, Den Haag, 1888–1889)

ᶜOs̱mân Pâshâ, Governor-General of the Hejaz at the time of Farâhâni's visit. (Reproduced from Christiaan Snouck Hurgronje, *Mekka (mit Bilder-Atlas)*, Den Haag, 1888–1889)

Sharif ʿAwn or-Rafiq, the Grand Sharif of Mecca, at the time of Farâhâni's visit. For an interesting description of Farâhâni's meeting with the Sharif, see text, pages 230–232. (Reproduced from Christiaan Snouck Hurgronje, *Mekka (mit Bilder-Atlas)*, Den Haag, 1888–1889)

Medina: the general view with Bab ol-Awali in the foreground; an early-twentieth-century photograph. (Reproduced from *Western Arabia and the Red Sea*, with the permission of the Controller of Her Britannic Majesty's Stationery Office)

Medina: the mosque and the cenotaph of the Prophet (see text, pages 260–265). (Reproduced from *Western Arabia and the Red Sea*, with the permission of the Controller of Her Britannic Majesty's Stationery Office)

Medina: the interior of the Prophet's Mosque. (Reproduced from *Western Arabia and the Red Sea*, with the permission of the Controller of Her Britannic Majesty's Stationery Office)

Yanbo[c]: the port for Medina (see text, page 284); an early-twentieth-century photograph. (Reproduced from *Arabia and the Red Sea*, with the permission of the Controller of Her Britannic Majesty's Stationery Office)

Yanbo[c]: view from the sea. (Reproduced from *Arabia and the Red Sea*, with the permission of the Controller of Her Britannic Majesty's Stationery Office)

A SHIʿITE PILGRIMAGE TO MECCA
1885–1886

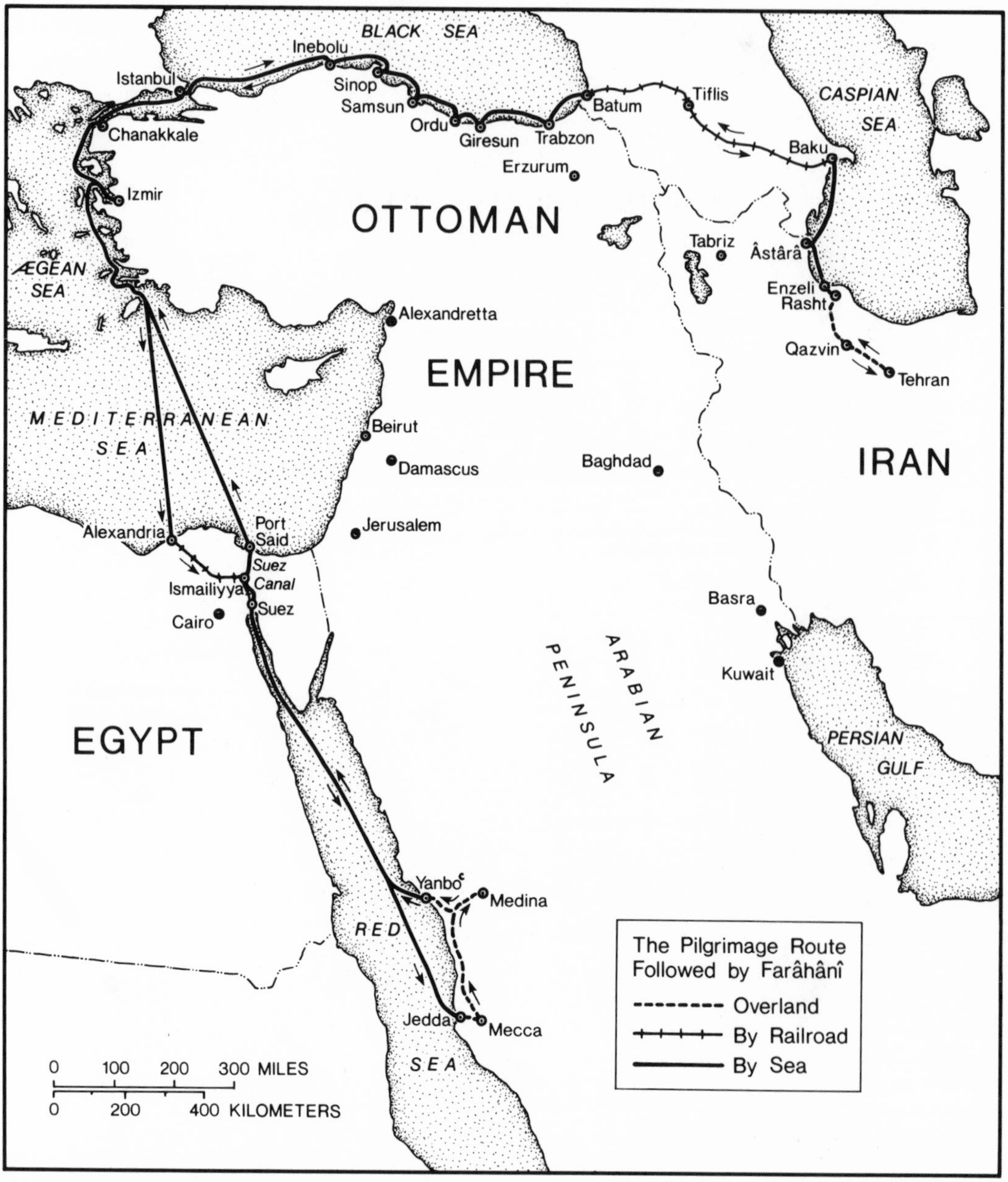

Map 2. The pilgrimage route followed by Farâhâni.

PART ONE
FROM TEHRAN TO THE CASPIAN

In the Name of God, the Compassionate, the Merciful,
May God Bless Our Master the Prophet Moḥammad
and His Immaculate Family

INTRODUCTION

One of the manners and customs of [our] contemporaries is that for the sake of full and excellent style, [even] if they only have some trifling subject, they write so much prefatory matter that the subject [itself] disappears from view. A brief speech does not justify a lengthy prologue, and it is not necessary to have two thousand lines of preface for a book of a thousand lines. "Get to the point and leave the preliminaries behind."[1] Modesty[2] has thus induced this devoted servant, Moḥammad Ḥosayn ol-Ḥosayni ol-Farâhâni, to write this short, simple preface during the reign of the august[3] Shâhânshâh, the Islam-protected Solṭân ebn-e[4] Solṭân ebn-e Solṭân, and the Khâqân,[5] ebn-e Khâqân, ebn-e Khâqân,

The Auspicious Solṭân Nâṣer od-Din Shâh Qâjâr,[6]
May God Perpetuate his Kingdom and his Rule.

The idea of visiting the House of God[7] occurred to me, so I brought up this matter with a wise mentor. He said concerning this point, "If you display any selfishness or circumspection, it will not be possible to attain such bliss."[8]

---

1 An Arabic proverb quoted by the author; see ᶜAli Akbar Dehkhodâ, *Amṯâl va ḥekâm* (fourth edition; Tehran, 1352/1973-74), pp. 10, 723.

2 Literally "ignorance" (*bi fażli*).

3 *Jamjâh*, "the equal of [the legendary Iranian king] Jam."

4 *Ebn-e* means "son of." Since this phrase uses the Arabic word for son (*ebn*), it is transliterated rather than translated. Equivalent Persian phrases will be given in translation. In some instances, the term will be represented by the conventional abbreviation "b."

5 One of the many titles used by Iranian rulers, roughly equivalent to "emperor"; in early texts it referred to the ruler of China or various Turko-Mongol princes.

6 The Shâh of Iran from 1848 until his assassination in 1896; the Qâjâr dynasty to which he belonged ruled Iran from 1786 to 1925. There is as yet no good biography of Nâṣer od-Din; for a general sketch see Mahdi Bâmdâd, *Târikh-e rejâl-e irân* (Tehran, 1966-74), 4:246-329.

7 A pious term for the Kaaba in Mecca.

8 A proverbial verse by the poet Ḥâfeẓ is quoted here but omitted from the translation; see Dehkhodâ, *Amṯâl*, p. 950.

I took to heart the saying "the lightly burdened shall be saved"[9] and recalled that "unencumbered people travel quicker."[10] [2] I entrusted myself to God and determined to travel all alone.[11]

Thus I started towards my goal with the blessing of the beloved king [Nâṣer od-Din Shâh].

DEPARTURE FROM TEHRAN

The night [before] Friday, the fourth of the noble month of Shavvâl, in the year 1302 [Thursday evening, 16 July 1885[12]], I went to the tarantass station and, three hours after nightfall, took a seat in a tarantass and departed.[13] As for the fare of the coach, the livery has several classes of transport for passengers; the fare for each varies. One is for the tarantass, which has a folding top but does not have spring-mountings or room for more than three people. The fare for the tarantass from Tehran to Qazvin, less the horse, is three tomans.[14] Another [vehicle for rent] is known as the troika, which does not have the folding top or springs and which seats three people. The fare for it, without the horse, is two tomans. Another [vehicle] is the droshky, which has a folding top, spring-mountings, and room for three people. The fare for the droshky from Tehran to Qazvin, without the horse, is five tomans. Another is the calash, which has a folding top, springs, and seats four people. The fare for it to Qazvin is six tomans. Another is the diligence, which has springs, is covered over, resembles the droshky, and seats ten people. The fare for it, without the horse, from Tehran to Qazvin is ten tomans.

---

9 The Arabic proverb "the lightly burdened shall be saved, and the heavily loaded destroyed" is attributed to Ḥasan ol-Basrî (d. 728), a famous Muslim mystic, by ᶜAli b. ᶜOs̱mân ol-Hojviri; see R. Nicholson (tr.), *Kashf al-Mahjub of Al Hujwiri* (London, 1911), p. 362; cf. Dehkhodâ, *Ams̱âl*, p. 1802.

10 A quotation from Saᶜdî; see Dehkhodâ, *Ams̱âl*, p. 941; S. Ḥayyim, *Persian-English Proverbs* (Tehran, 1956), p. 254.

11 Another verse by Ḥâfeẓ is omitted from the translation.

12 In the traditional system of reckoning dates and time followed by Farâhâni, a new day of the week begins at sunset. The period of "night" extends from after sunset to before sunrise and is divided into twelve hours; the "day" similarly consists of twelve equal hours from dawn to sunset. In converting the dates given by Farâhâni, therefore, the phrase "the night of" a given day and date will be translated as "the night [before]" that day and the corresponding Christian date, given in brackets, adjusted accordingly. In this case, for example, Friday the fourth of Shavvâl would be equivalent to 17 July 1885, but since Farâhâni was actually departing from Tehran on Thursday evening the date given is 16 July.

13 As will be apparent from Farâhâni's account, a coach service was available from Tehran to the city of Qazvin. From there, travellers had to ride horses hired from the office of the post. For comparable descriptions of the coach service and fares, see E. Orsolle, *Le Caucase et la Perse* (Paris, 1885), p. 298; George N. Curzon, *Persia and the Persian Question* (London, 1892), 1:37-38. The names used for these various vehicles made their way into Persian, as well as into English, from Russian.

14 The toman (*towmân*) was a coin, usually gold, first introduced in the Mongol period as the equivalent of 10,000 dinars; here, it is equal to 10 silver krans (cf. below, n. 16.) The value of the coinage fluctuated considerably according to the value of the metal; in general,

The horses are hitched according to the number of passengers. For example, if three people are seated in the tarantass, they charge the fee for three horses from those three passengers. [3] Moreover, a fee for one horse for the driver will also be charged. A fee for three horses may be charged, but [only] two horses will be harnessed. The fee for each horse per farsakh[15] is one silver kran.[16] From Tehran to Qazvin, which is twenty-four farsakhs, the fee for each horse will be twenty-four krans. Thus one passenger must pay twenty-four krans for the horse plus twenty-four krans for the driver's horse. This driver takes the place of an ostler.[17] If there are two or three passengers, the charge for the driver's horse is still twenty-four krans; it does not increase. Obviously, then, it is less costly for two or three people to travel together.

There is also a charge of one kran for the tarantass or calash ticket which must be presented and stamped before boarding. This ticket must be shown to the superintendent at each way-station as proof of having paid to ride the coach. It is customary that when the horses are changed at each way-station, the passengers give a one kran tip to the driver. If there are three passengers they will jointly give one kran; a kran will not be collected from each one individually.

GUARD-HOUSES ON THE WAY TO QAZVIN

It is twenty-four farsakhs from Tehran to Qazvin. Five guest-houses have been built along the way.[18] The horses are changed at each place. It

the coinage was debased during the nineteenth century. Ludwig Adamec (ed.), *Historical Gazetteer of Iran* (Graz, 1976), 1:728 gives a value of 3 shillings 4 pence for a silver toman and 7s. 4d. for a gold toman. Other sources suggest that a toman at the time of Farâhâni's journey consisted of 71 grains of gold (then worth about eighty cents.) See Charles Issawi, *The Economic History of Iran 1800-1914* (Chicago, 1971), pp. 387-88; Rabino di Borgomale, *Coins, Medals & Seals of the Shahs of Iran (1500-1941)* (Hertford, 1945); George Curzon, *Persia and the Persian Question* (London, 1892), 1:471; *The Encyclopaedia of Islam: A Dictionary of the Geography, Ethnography and Biography of the Muhammadan Peoples,* edited by M. Th. Houtsma et al., (Leiden, 1913-38 [cited herefter as EI_1]), 4:836.

15 A traditional unit for measuring distance; since it reflected a distance one could travel in a fixed period of time, the actual length varied from 2.3 to 4.2 miles (3.7 to 6.7 km.). It is more or less synonymous with the *farsang* (or parasang in common English usage). See A. H. Schindler, "Notes on the Length of the Farsakh," *Proceedings of the Royal Geographical Society*, second series, 10(1888):584-88.

16 The kran (*qerân*) was a silver coin, equal to 20 copper *shâhis* (about eight cents); see EI_1, 2:1084-85 [s.v. "Krân"].

17 The term translated here as ostler is *shâgerd châpâr*, i.e., the person (usually a boy apprentice) whose job was to accompany the travellers in order to return the horses to the place from which they had been rented. See Edward Eastwick, *Journal of a Diplomate's* [sic] *Three Years' Residence in Persia* (London, 1864), p. 212.

18 The construction of these *mehmân-khânehs* or guest-houses was a fairly recent innovation in Iran, probably inspired by Nâṣer od-Din Shâh's observations of amenities for travellers during his trips to Europe in 1873 and 1878; see Eᶜtemâd os-Salṭaneh, *ol-Ma'âṣer va'l-âṣâr* (Tehran, 1306/1889), p. 95. They are discussed in rather unflattering terms by Edward G. Browne, *A Year Amongst the Persians* (second edition; London, 1926), pp. 86-88.

is four farsakhs from each guest-house to the next. Three guard-houses have been erected between each of the guest-houses, so that there is a guard-house every farsakh. The building for the guard-house is also of necessity the home for the custodian. Some of the custodians have brought their wives and children to the guard-houses and live there. Others live alone. [4] At each guard-house which has running water near it, the custodians have planted tasteful flowerbeds, trees, and little gardens in front of the guard-house. The guard-houses which do not have [running] water nearby have had wells dug beside them. The telegraph also has lines strung along the road by the stations.

GUEST-HOUSES ALONG THE WAY

A description of the guest-houses may be presented as follows:

It is four farsakhs from Tehran to the Shâhâbâd station. By a tarantass travelling at a moderate speed, it takes an hour and a half to an hour and forty minutes. Waiting in the guest-house for the change of horses takes twenty minutes. Thus one will go four farsakhs in two hours, including the delay at the guest-house, and twenty-four farsakhs in twelve hours. It is possible to go faster or slower than this. This guest-house was built on land in Ḥosaynâbâd owned by Ḥâjji Solaymân Khân,[19] father of Moḥammad Naẓar Khân, which was appropriated by the late Grand Vizier and [re]named Shâhâbâd. Its water comes from the same [source] as that of Ḥosaynâbâd. Sometimes they take water from the Kan River and fill a cistern there, since this guest-house does not have running water. For this reason, it does not have flower-beds, a garden, or trees. The guest-house consists of four rooms, a storage area for merchandise, a kitchen, a coffee-house, and a grocery store. There is a large enclosure which is both stable and corral. Thus the barn for straw and hay, the stable, and a storage place for the coach supplies are alongside the corral. [5]

[I] did not learn exactly how many horses and workers there are at the guest-station. They said there are twenty-four horses kept here. There is an overseer who has two rooms. There is a cook, and six people are employed in the livery as grooms and drivers. The employees earn from two to five tomans a month. There are two people there, the coffee-maker and the grocer, who do not receive wages since they engage in trade for themselves. At this guest-house, it took so long for the horses to be changed that, being bored, I took up pen and paper and composed a few verses.[20] [6]

---

[19] Perhaps Solaymân Khân Afshâr (d. 1309/1891-92), who came from the Qazvin/Sâujbolâgh area? See Bamdâd, *Rejâl*, 2:116-18.

[20] The text is followed here by a *ghazal* (ode) of a dozen verses; since it contributes nothing to the text, it has been omitted from the translation. The poem, which is as

From the Shâhâbâd guest-house, one goes to Ḥeṣârak. It is four farsakhs. After two farsakhs, one comes to the Karaj bridge. The Karaj bridge has five spans and was constructed long ago. The source of the Karaj River is in the Arangeh mountains. The Solaymâniyyeh fortress, which was one of the constructions of Ḥâjji Moḥammad Ḥosayn Khân Ṣadr-e Eṣfahâni[21] and was built in the year 1226 [1811-12], is by the side of the road near the bridge. From Tehran to the bridge, the road is level and sandy; it does not get muddy during the rainy season. However, it is two [more] farsakhs past the bridge to Ḥeṣârak, and those two farsakhs are of red clay which becomes very muddy during the rainy season.

THE VILLAGE OF ḤEṢÂRAK

Ḥeṣârak is one of the villages held as crown property by the King's Council [*Divân-e Aʿlâ*].[22] It is part of the Sâujbolâgh[23] [district] of Tehran. It has nearly forty resident families. Its water [comes] from a stream that is exclusively for this village. This stream has much water in the springtime. In summer, it is half dry; there is enough [water] for the needs of the people and animals in the village but not enough for agriculture. This guest-house is situated one *maydân-e asb*[24] below the fortress. An unwalled garden, which is not unpleasant, planted with trees and flowers, has been made in front of the guest-house. It is sometimes irrigated with the scant water of the Ḥeṣârak stream. This guest-house is very attractive since it is situated on an eminence, and the Sâujbolâgh district is spread out below. The Kemâlâbâd meadow is also in front of it and is visible in the distance. The building, rooms, employees, and workers are exactly like those of the Shâhâbâd guest-house.

---

mediocre as one might expect given the circumstances of ennui which led to its composition, has as its theme the hardship of leaving someone behind when one must go on a journey; the last verse contains Farâhâni's pen name of Golbon ("Rosebush").

21 Also known as Amin od-Dowleh Mostowfi ol-Mamâlek (d. Muḥarram 1239/ September 1823). His rise from the mayorship of Isfahan to the offices of Minister of Finance and finally Prime Minister is described in Ḥasan-e Fasâ'i, *Fârsnâmeh-ye Nâṣeri*, as translated by H. Busse, *History of Persia under Qâjâr Rule* (New York, 1972), pp. 167-68; see also Bâmdâd, *Rejâl*, 3:379-81.

22 The highest ranking cabinet of ministers which would meet with the Shâh. The revenue from this property would thus be used to help cover the expenses of the Council.

23 From the Turkish name Soğuk Bulak ("Cold Spring"). It applied to the region stretching from Rayy (south of Tehran) to Qazvin. See Guy Le Strange, *Lands of the Eastern Caliphate* (third impression; London, 1966), p. 218; Adamec, *Historical Gazetteer*, 1:580; EI_1,4:186-192 [s.v. "Sâwdj-bulâḳ"].

24 Maydân (or midân) often means simply "square," but it is used here as a term for a very vague unit of measurement of distance (about one quarter of a farsakh).

THE YANGI EMÂM[25] GUEST-HOUSE

One goes from Ḥeṣârak to Yangi Emâm. It is four farsakhs. The road is level and sandy for the most part. It does not get muddy during the rainy season. [7] Yangi Emâm was a caravanserai built by the Safavids.[26] Since caravans lodged there less frequently and the founder did not [arrange for] repairs, it gradually became dirty and deteriorated and became a nest of thieves. After the guest-houses were located along this route, the caravanserai was completely renovated. The chambers along its sides were cleaned and paned doors were installed. The stables next to the caravanserai were either renovated or made into storage areas. The old ruined cistern in the middle of the caravanserai was repaired and the courtyard of the caravanserai was made into a garden with trees and flowerbeds. The high portal at the entrance to the caravanserai was rebuilt so that it comprised six clean and whitewashed rooms of various sizes, provided with carpets and furniture to be [used] as lodgings for distinguished guests. The large garden, which is nearly twelve *jarib*s [in extent] (each jarib consisting of a thousand [square] *ẕarᶜ*),[27] was laid out in front of the portal and caravanserai and planted with [various] kinds of trees, bushes, flowers, legumes, and grains. The courtyard contains three porticos with twenty-four chambers, all of which have been converted into rooms. Some of the rooms have a few mats and furnishings so that they can serve as lodgings for guests. Some of the rooms are [used as] quarters or storage areas for the employees, workers, and tradesmen staying there. Since it is the midway point and a major town and principal depot, the coach equipment or other things which have broken down along the route are brought [there] from both directions and must constantly be repaired. For this reason, the following craftsmen are always resident there, keeping shops and working: a saddler, a carpenter, a blacksmith, and a farrier. [8]

A grocer and a coffee-house keeper are there, as at most of the guest-houses. Since it is a central place, the horses and workers at this guest-house are more numerous than at most guest-houses. They say it has about forty horses and thirty workers. Next to this guest-house, a new *qalᶜeh*[28] has been constructed which houses forty families and has a public

25 The text consistently has Yangeh Emâm. This has been changed throughout to conform to standard usage; see Adamec, *Historical Gazetteer*, 1:687.

26 The ruling dynasty in Iran from 1501 to 1732.

27 The *jarib* and *ẕarᶜ* were traditional units of measurement. The ẕarᶜ was equivalent to 41 inches. The jarib was used only for measuring arable land and varied from locality to locality. It was typically 1000 to 1066 square ẕarᶜ (i.e., 0.267-0.285 acre.) See Walther Hinz, *Islamische Masse und Gewichte umgerechnet ins metrische System* (Leiden, 1955), p. 38; Fritz Rosen, *Persian Grammar* (reprinted New Delhi, 1979), p. 298; Charles Issawi, *The Economic History of the Middle East, 1800-1914* (Chicago, 1966), p. 519.

28 In this context, *qalᶜeh* does not have its usual meaning of "military fortress" or "citadel"; it is simply a large building with courtyards, stables, bath, etc. built by the landlord

bath and a *qanât*[29] that produces about one *sang*[30] of water. It is reported that Amin os-Solṭân[31] established this qalᶜeh and qanât in partnership with Amin od-Dowleh.[32] At the present time, he either has or will buy the shares of Amin od-Dowleh. Most of the drinking water for the people of the guest-house comes from this qanât. Before this, the water for Yangi Emâm came from the Kordân River.[33] Now some of the surrounding villages that used to get drinking water from the Kordân River take it from [the qanât]. Water from the river is usually used [for irrigation] in these areas, but whenever that dries up they take [water] from [the qanât].

THE YANGI EMÂM MAUSOLEUM

Near this guest-house there is a mausoleum over which a dome was built in olden times. They say two of the descendants of Ḥażrat-e[34] Musâ ebn-e Jaᶜfar[35] are buried there. At the time when these *emâmzâdeh*s[36]

---

for the residents of the village. The families selected to live in such a building were especially loyal to the landlord and looked after things on his behalf.

[29] An underground water canal used extensively in Iran to bring water from mountain sources to inhabited areas. See the article "Ḳanât" in *The Encyclopaedia of Islam : New Edition*, edited by H. A. R. Gibb et al., (Leiden, 1960- [cited hereafter as EI_2]), 4:528-33; H. Goblot, *Les Qanats: Une technique d'acquisition de l'eau* (Paris, 1979); Paul W. English, "The Origin and Spread of Kanats in the Old World," *Proceedings of the American Philosophical Society* 112(1968):170-81.

[30] A unit for measuring the flow of water; one *sang* being a current sufficient to turn a millstone. See ᶜAli Akbar Dehkhodâ, *Loghatnâmeh* (Tehran, 1946-83), 26:669.

[31] Amin os-Solṭân was a title born by two famous Iranian statesmen, Âqâ Ebrâhim Garmrudi (d. 1300/1882-83) and his son ᶜAli Aṣghar Khân (1275-1325/1858-1907). Since Farâhâni speaks of him here as being alive, he must be referring to ᶜAli Aṣghar. See Shaul Bakhash, *Iran: Monarchy, Bureaucracy & Reform under the Qajars* (London, 1978), pp. 148, 185, 377; Bâmdâd, *Rejâl*, 2:387-425; Khân Malek-e Sâsâni, *Siâsatgarân-e dowreh-ye qâjâreyyeh* (Tehran, 1338-45/1960-67), 2:140-321.

[32] Several individuals held this title, but the reference is most likely to Ḥâjj Mirzâ ᶜAli Khân, the son of Ḥâjj Mirzâ Moḥammad Khân Majd ol-Molk. He was given the title of Amin od-Dowleh in 1883 (and thus just prior to Farâhâni's journey). He became Prime Minister under Moẓaffer od-Din Shâh in 1314/1896-97. He died in 1904 at his private estate on the Caspian near Lashteneshâ. See H. F. Farmayan, "Amin od-Dowleh: Portrait of an Iranian Statesman," *International Journal of Middle East Studies* 15(1983):337-51; Bâmdâd, *Rejâl*, 2:354-66; Bakhash, *Iran*, p. 376.

[33] Ḥamdollah Qazvini, *The Geographical Part of the Nuzhat-al-Qulub* (translated by G. Le Strange, London, 1919), p. 214, has Kardận; this is corrected in Adamec, *Historical Gazetteer*, 1:400 to Kordân. On the river and village, see Eastwick, *Journal*, 1:296-98.

[34] A term of respect preceding the name of important religious or political personalities; in this case, it might be translated as "His Eminence."

[35] Musâ Kâẓem (d. 183/799), son of the sixth Imam, Jaᶜfar-e Ṣâdeq, was recognized by "Twelver" Shi'ites as their seventh infallible Imam; see EI_1, 3:741.

[36] The term *emâmzâdeh* is used in two ways. Literally it means "offspring of an Imam," and is thus a term of respect for children and descendants of one of the twelve infallible religious leaders (Imams) recognized by the "Twelver" Shi'ites. It is also used as the name for the shrine erected over the grave or tomb of one of these "saints" to which Shi'ites often make visitations to pray or make requests. See Dwight Donaldson, *The Shi'ite Religion*, (London, 1933), pp. 258-65; EI_2, 3:1169-70 [s.v. "Imâmzâdah"]. Here, the term will be transliterated when referring to a person; otherwise it is translated as "shrine."

appeared there, they were called "New Imam"[37] since they were newcomers. This same name was then given to this place. As this shrine had also fallen into ruin, the late Amin os-Solṭân had it repaired, built a little courtyard there, tiled the dome, and appointed a sayyed[38] from among the inhabitants of Sâujbolâgh as its custodian. Around this shrine and the guest-house, the traces and remains of a large [formerly] inhabited place are visible. It is known that in olden times, this had been a large place. A huge earthen tell is also here.[39] On top of the tell, traces of habitation are also visible. [9]

HASHTGARD

One farsakh from Yangi Emâm there is a place by the name of Hashtgard,[40] which is crown property. Its inhabitants are Kurds whose way of life is like that of the Naṣiris.[41] For the most part, they are highway robbers. There is a shrine in that village called the Emâmzâdeh Ja^cfar (after one of the descendants of Ḥażrat-e Musâ ebn-e Ja^cfar, peace be upon him[42]). The people of that village, the village of Yangi Emâm, the surrounding villages, and the Kurds all have great faith in him. It is popularly thought that taking an oath [in his name] produces a result very quickly; in so far as possible, no one will swear by him. Some petty thefts which have occurred in the environs have [been resolved] by having the property immediately returned and given up if the people of Hashtgard have taken the trouble to have the inhabitants of the village swear by their *emâmzâdeh*.

One goes from Yangi Emâm to Qeshlâq. It is four farsakhs. This road is clay and in rainy weather it gets very muddy. One farsakh beyond Yangi Emâm the road forks. The one which is the new road goes to Qeshlâq, and

---

37 In Turkish *Yangi Emâm* (Yeni Imam) means "New Imam."

38 A term of respect used for someone believed to be descended from the Prophet Moḥammad. See Thomas Hughes, *Dictionary of Islam* (London, 1895), p. 556.

39 This tell is still unexcavated; see Sylvia Matheson, *Persia: An Archaeological Guide* (London, 1972), p. 59.

40 Now vocalized Hashtgerd or Hashtjerd; see Adamec, *Historical Gazetteer*, 1:231.

41 Literally, "their *ṭariqeh* is the Naṣiri [or Noṣayri]." Golzâri (p. 285) suggests that the term refers to the "Noṣayri sect." The Noṣayris are an extremist Shi'ite sect found mostly in Syria, but a similar sect, better known as the Ahl-e Ḥaqq, does exist among some Kurdish tribes of northwestern Iran. See Matti Moosa, *Extremist Shiites: the Ghulat Sects* (Syracuse, 1988), pp. 185-254. However. Farâhâni consistently uses the terms *mazhab* and *ṭâyefeh* to refer to religious and ethnic groups; not *ṭariqeh*, which he generally applies to Sufi orders. Since he goes on to say that these people are brigands, perhaps the use of the appellation "protector" (*naṣir*) is simply ironic rather than a reference to a specific sect or group.

42 In Muslim texts, the names of the Prophet Moḥammad and other religious figures are often followed by various pious expressions such as the one used here. Hereafter, these will be omitted in this translation.

the other, which is the old one, goes to Gâzor Sang[43] and the shrine at Meskinâbâd.[44]

FOUR ALTERNATE ROUTES FROM TEHRAN TO QAZVIN

The old routes by which people used to go from Tehran to Qazvin varied. One went from Tehran to Kan, from Kan to the village of Kordân, from Kordân to the village of Qeshlâq, from Qeshlâq to Ḥeṣârak, and from the village of Ḥeṣârak to Qazvin. Another route went from Tehran to the village of Vâli Gard,[45] from Vâli Gard to Gâzor Sang, from Gâzor Sang to ᶜAbdollahâbâd, and from there one reached Qazvin. Another went from Tehran to Miânjub, from Miânjub to Yangi Emâm, from Yangi Emâm to ᶜAbdollahâbâd, and from there one reached Qazvin. [10] These three roads were used by muleteers. There was also a route especially for the post which went from Tehran to Miânjub, and from Miânjub to Sonqorâbâd, from which one went to Qazvin.[46]

GUEST-HOUSE AND VILLAGE OF QESHLÂQ

The Qeshlâq guest-house[47] is situated half a farsakh up from the village of Qeshlâq. It is supplied with water from the river of the village of Ziârân,[48] which is wakf property for the shrine of Ḥażrat-e Reżâ.[49] It is part of the Feshkel district in the Qazvin valley. In front of this guest-house there is an unwalled garden planted with trees, which is irrigated with water from the aforementioned river. The workers, horses, and rooms of

---

[43] Eastwick, *Journal*, 1:302 mentions "the village of Gâzir i Sang, 'the stone washerman,' so called from an impious *blanchisseur* who was metamorphosed for disobedience to the Prophet" located about twenty-seven miles from Kordân.

[44] Also written Moshkinâbâd; see Adamec, *Historical Gazetteer*, 1:464. The shrine there is described in more detail by Farhâd Mirzâ, *Ketâb hedâyat os-sabil va kefâyat od-dalil* (Shiraz, 1294/1877), p. 3.

[45] Now known as Vâlijerd or Vâligerd.

[46] On the various routes and means of conveyance between Tehran and Qazvin, cf. Solṭân Moḥammad Sayf od-Dowleh, *Safarnâmeh-ye Makkeh* (edited by ᶜAli Akbar Khodâparast; Tehran, 1363/1985), pp. 25-28, 385; Curzon, *Persia*, 1:37-39; Eastwick, *Journal*, 1:212-17. Many other travellers left descriptions of these routes and the villages along the way; Curzon, for example, mentions A. Arnold, *Through Persia by Caravan* (London, 1875); E. Orsolle, *Le Caucase et la Perse* (Paris, 1872); E. O'Donovan, *The Merv Oasis* (London, 1880); V. Baker, *Clouds in the East* (London, 1873), pp. 312-17; C. MacGregor, *Journey Through Khorasan* (London, 1878), 2:176-80.

[47] This particular station was described at some length by E. G. Browne, *A Year Amongst the Persians* (second edition; London, 1926), pp. 86-88. Contrary to Farâhâni's general observations about the new stations, Browne found that this one at least had "all the worst defects of a European hotel without its luxury."

[48] Or perhaps, more properly, Zayyârân; see Adamec, *Historical Gazetteer*, 1:708.

[49] Wakf (*vaqf*; plural *owqâf*) properties were pious endowments (usually of real property, including, as here, entire villages) for charitable purposes; as such they were tax-exempt and inalienable; see EI_1, 4:1096-1103 [s.v. "Waḳf"]. In this particular case, the revenue from the wakf had been designated to contribute to the upkeep of the shrine of the eighth Shiʿite Imam, Reżâ, in Mashhad.

this guest-house are just like those of the Ḥeṣârak and Shâhâbâd guest-houses.

The village of Qeshlâq itself contains about two hundred households. It has qanât water as well as rights to water from the Ziârân River. The village is [located between] the beginning of Qazvin [province] and the end of the Sâujbolâgh of Rayy [province] and forms part of the Bashâriât[50] district.

THE "GOLDSMITH" CLAN OF QAZVIN

From the Qeshlâq guest-house one goes to the Kavandeh guest-house. It is four farsakhs. The road is red clay and is very muddy during the rainy season. All along this road between these two guest-houses dwell the "Goldsmith clansmen" of Qazvin, who are all highway robbers. Very stealthily and vilely, they engage in theft and kill the helpless. Every chance they get, by night and day, they come to the road as if begging; if they find two or three unarmed people, they rob them of their possessions. Also along this road is an area named Ḥâjji Tappeh, which is the winter pasture for the Kurds of Qazvin. The people of Ḥâjji Tappeh are also bandits and extremely wicked. They are usually mounted and armed. [11] Every time they can, they separate ten or twelve riders from a caravan and rob them. Sometimes they also steal from the surrounding villages.

THE GUEST-HOUSE AND VILLAGE OF KAVANDEH

As for the Kavandeh guest-house, it is next to the village of Kavandeh,[51] from which it derives its water supply. A garden planted with trees has been made in front of it. Its workers, horses, and rooms are like those of the other guest-houses. The village of Kavandeh does not have a *qal^ceh*. It is a very dirty village. About forty families live there. Its water is mostly river water that comes from Zardcheh Bostân. There is also a small qanât running through the middle of the village that provides enough water for the people's drinking water. This village was one of the wakf estates of Khomârtâsh.[52] It is a wakf property for the Khiâbân mosque in Qazvin. Its inhabitants are Kurds of the Mâfi and Kubâr tribes.[53] From the Kavandeh guest-house one goes four farsakhs to Qazvin. The road is

---

50 Dehkhodâ, *Loghatnâmeh*, 9:90 has Beshâriât; for the vocalization given here, see Adamec, *Historical Gazetteer*, 1:94.

51 More commonly known as Kavandaj.

52 Khomârtâsh (d. 530/1135-36) is mentioned by Qazvini, *Gozideh*, p. 796. Because of his piety, he was called Zâhed ("the Ascetic").

53 The Mâfi (or Ma^câfi) were one of the tribes of the confederation of southern Kurdish tribes known as the Lak; see EI_2, 5:616-17; Adamec, *Historical Gazetteer*, 1:325-26, 421; Mirzâ Ebrâhim, *Safarnâmeh-ye astarâbâd va mâzandarân va gilân* (edited by Mas^cud Golzâri; Tehran, 2535/1976), p. 176. The "Kubâr" tribe is not mentioned in Adamec's list of the tribes around Qazvin or that of Mirzâ Ebrâhim; the names which comes nearest to matching it are Kalhor or perhaps Quchân.

smooth and level. It gets muddy during the rainy season, and it is extremely dry and dusty in summer. In the guest-houses along the way, nothing unusual was observed, except that food and drink were expensive for what one got.

THE QAZVIN CITY GUEST-HOUSE

The guest-house for the city of Qazvin is located in the midst of a pleasant and built-up area.[54] One of its gates fronts an avenue across from the ᶜAli Qâpu.[55] The busiest area of Qazvin is along this avenue. Another of its gates is opposite the Masjed-e Jâmeᶜ.[56] The telegraph office is also next to the guest-house. An attractive garden with trees has been created in front of the guest-house. The garden is bordered by a wooden fence. There is a pool in the middle of the garden. The building has an upstairs and a downstairs. The lower level consists of rooms, coffeehouses, and the kitchen. Some of its rooms have a little furniture and serve as lodgings [12] for ordinary travellers; some are dwellings for the employees. As for the upstairs, it contains eight rooms which are all neat, clean, painted, and have *orosi* windows.[57] Their painted doors and the furnishings are clean and nice. The rooms on the second storey are reserved for distinguished guests. Next to the yard of the guest-house is another enclosure which [serves as] the corral, stable, and tool shed. The different craftsmen stay and work there: fifty-six blacksmiths, fifteen carpenters, six saddlers, and two farriers. They make all sorts of calashes, droshkys, tarantasses, and so on, with great skill. Since the ᶜAmmârlu forest of Gilân and the coal mines are near Qazvin, most of the equipment for making calashes, etc., is kept at this Qazvin guest-house.

As for the workers and horses at this guest-house, a detailed description is appended: the overseer Mirzâ ᶜAbd ol-ᶜAli, son of Âqâ Bâqer Arbâb; secretary and accountant (two people); moneychanger (one person); servants (five people); room-keepers (five people); Iranian- and European-[style] cook (one person); chief of the stable (one person); stable workers such as drivers and so on (twenty-five people).

---

[54] Curzon, *Persia*, p. 37, judged it the finest in Iran.

[55] The "High Gate," a monumental doorway constructed during the reign of Shâh Ṭahmâsp (1524-76). See Arthur Upham Pope (ed.), *A Survey of Persian Art* (third edition; Tehran, 1977), p. 1174; Matheson, *Guide*, pp. 55-56.

[56] The usual name for the main "congregational mosque" in a city, which is suitable for use for the Friday noon prayer service and sermon.

[57] A window in a room, which may open onto a courtyard. The frame has four wooden panels inside it which can be moved up and down. The term is translated in some dictionaries as "sash-window." There is a photograph of this type of window in Manuchehr Sotudeh, *Az Âstârâ tâ astarâbâd* (Tehran, 1349-53/1970-74); volume 1, plate 123.

They say about sixty horses are kept at this guest-house. Some of them are for the exclusive use of Âqâ Bâqer. There are two hundred Qazvini troops, including the Yuzbâshi[58] and the road-guards along the way, who are under the command of Âqâ Bâqer. [13] Every time the post comes or goes, one of the road-guards accompanies the tarantass the whole way.

A BRIEF HISTORY OF THE CITY OF QAZVIN

[Qazvin] is an ancient city. Initially, Shâpur Z̲u'l-Aktâf built a citadel there and called it the Shahrestân.[59] Later, Shâpur, the son of Ardashir Bâbakân, populated the area around the Shahrestân citadel and called it Qazvin.[60] As soon as the Persian Empire fell to the Arabs, riots broke out [there.] The people left the city, and it remained devoid of inhabitants. During the caliphate of ᶜOs̲mân,[61] Valid ebn-e ᶜOtbeh the Umayyad (ᶜOs̲mân's half-brother) was appointed the governor of this region. [He] resettled people in the fort, and it became a city.

Then ol-Hâdi-bellah Musâ ebn-e Mahdi[62] built another citadel in the vicinity of that fort which was known as the "City of Musâ." One of Musâ's Turkish slaves named Mobârak built another citadel in that area and called it Mobârakâbâd. After that, authority passed to Hârun or-Rashid.[63] During the trip he made to Khorasan, he passed through Qazvin. The people complained to Hârun about being plundered by the Daylamites. Hârun ordered that a fortified wall be built around those citadels. Hârun died before the completion of the ramparts. The ramparts were completed during the reign of the Caliph Moᶜtazz,[64] through the efforts of Musâ ebn-e Buqâ in the year 254 [868]. All the citadels were occupied, and

---

58 A Turkish term which literally means "commander of a hundred men"; a rank roughly equivalent to captain.

59 Shâpur II, the "Broad-shouldered," (309-79). His building activities are well attested in the classical sources; see, for example, Abu Manṣur as̲-S̲aᶜâlebi, *Ghorar os-siar,* translated by H. Zotenberg, *Histoire des rois des perses* (Paris, 1900), p. 529. "Shahrestân" is the common term for the urban core of a city; see Arthur Christensen, *L'Iran sous les Sassanides* (Copenhagen, 1944), p. 140; W. Barthold, *Turkestan Down to the Mongol Invasion*, translated and corrected by V. Minorsky (second edition; London, 1958), p 78. Throughout this entire section, Farâhâni seems to be drawing his material from the works of the medieval historian and geographer Ḥamdollah Mostowfi Qazvini (b. 680/1281-82); cf. Qazvini/Le Strange, *Nuzhat*, pp. 62-64. For a modern history of Qazvin, see M. Sotudeh, "Târikhcheh-ye shahr-e qazvin," *Bar-rasihâ-ye târikhi* 4(1348/1969-70):95-132, 165-210.

60 Shâpur I (240-72) is usually regarded as the founder of Qazvin. Farâhâni's chronology is obviously confused in reversing the order of the two Shâpurs.

61 The third Muslim caliph (23-35/644-56).

62 An Abbasid caliph (ruled 169-70/785-86). The new quarters were founded while he was governor of the area; see Le Strange, *Eastern Caliphate*, p. 219.

63 Hârun, a famous Abbasid caliph of Baghdad (and the one most familiar to Western readers owing to his fabulous association with the *Thousand and One Arabian Nights*), ruled from 170-93/786-809. As a Shi'ite, Farâhâni uses the term *salṭanat* (meaning a secular ruler) rather than caliphate to refer to the office held by Hârun.

64 A minor Abbasid caliph who reigned from 252-55/866-69.

the city grew large. After that, in the year 373 [983-84], Ṣâḥeb ebn-e ᶜAbbâd, the minister of Fakhr od-Dowleh,[65] repaired the ramparts and erected a magnificent building which was named Ṣâḥebâbâd. [14] In the year 411 [1020-21] much damage was done to the city and the ramparts as a result of the struggle which took place between Sâlâr ebn-e Marzbân the Daylamite (the maternal uncle of Majd od-Dowleh[66]) and the people of Qazvin. The minister Ṣadr od-Din Lak[67] repaired the damage to the city and the ramparts in the year 552 [1157-58]. He [re-]built most of the ramparts and battlements with brick and mortar. Then the Mongol army destroyed the ramparts, although a few sections of them remained. At the beginning of the Safavid period, the ramparts and the city of Qazvin were both renovated. [Qazvin] eventually became the capital and seat of government. Magnificent edifices were built [there], and Qazvin remained the capital until the middle of the reign of Shâh ᶜAbbâs I.[68] When Shâh ᶜAbbâs made Isfahan the capital, [Qazvin] fell into decline and lost its luster. There are many stories and traditions concerning the noble character of Qazvin. Among them, one [handed down from] the Commander of the Faithful [ᶜAli] is, "The Prophet of God [Moḥammad] said, 'Take Alexandria and Qazvin, for they shall be conquered by my community. The two of them are two of the gates of Paradise.'"[69] A saying of Saᶜid ebn ol-Mosayyeb [handed down] from the Prophet of God is, "The chiefs of the martyrs are the martyrs of Qazvin." A saying of Jâber ebn-e ᶜAbdollah [handed down] from the Prophet of God is, "Honor Qazvin, for truly it is one of the most exalted gates of Paradise."[70] The significance of

---

65 Fakhr od-Dowleh (366-87/977-97) was one of the rulers of the Buyid dynasty of western Iran; he belonged to the senior branch which was based in northwestern Iran. Ṣaḥeb ebn-e ᶜAbbâd (326-85/938-95) was a celebrated Buyid minister; see Ebn Khallekân, *Vafayât ol-aᶜyan*, translated by Baron Mac Guckin de Slane, *Ibn Khallikan's Biographical Dictionary* (Paris, 1842-71), 1:212-17; Aḥmad Bahmanyâr, *Ṣaḥeb ebn-e ᶜAbbâd: sharḥ-e aḥvâl va âs̱âr* (edited by M. Bâstâni-Pârizi; Tehran, 1965).

66 The son of Fakhr od-Dowleh.

67 According to Ḥamdollah Qazvini, *Târikh-e gozideh* (ed. ᶜAbd ol-Ḥosayn Navâ'i; Tehran, 1339/1961), p. 776, this was Moḥammad b. ᶜAbdollah b. ᶜAbd or-Raḥim b. Mâlek, minister of [Moᶜezz od-Din] Arslân, the Seljukid sultan (556-73/1161-77.) The date given by Qazvini for the repair of the enclosure wall is 572/1176-77 rather than 552. Cf. Qazvini/Le Strange, *Nuzhat*, p. 63.

68 Ruled 1588-1629. He moved the capital from Qazvin to Isfahan around 1598.

69 Cf. Qazvini/Le Strange, *Nuzhat*, p. 63, where this tradition is attributed to the caliph ᶜOmar b. ᶜAbd ol-ᶜAziz [*sic*: read ᶜOmar b. ol-Khaṭṭâb?]

70 Jâber (d. 78/697-98) was a very famous companion of the prophet and transmitter of religious traditions; see Aḥmad b. ᶜAli ol-ᶜAsqalâni, *Tahẕib ot-tahẕib* (ed. Haydarabad, 1325/1907), 2:42-43. Saᶜid was also a well-known traditionist from Medina but not a companion of the prophet (he died around 100/718-719); see ᶜAsqalâni, *Tahẕib*, 4:84-88. This whole passage may be compared with Qazvini/Le Strange, *Nuzhat*, pp. 62-63.

this is that the slanders which are uttered about Qazvin and the Qazvinis are without foundation.[71] The land of Qazvin is very noble, and the goodness and nobleness of the people is well attested.

A DESCRIPTION OF QAZVIN IN THE YEAR 1302 A.H. [1884-5]

A description of Qazvin at the present time may be written as follows:[72] It contains seven thousand resident households, so its population is about thirty thousand. It has six hundred shops, eight caravanserais, thirty public baths, forty mosques of various sizes, nine madrasahs, and twelve ice-houses. [15]

THE QUARTERS OF QAZVIN[73]

The Darb-e Rayy quarter; the Darb-e Râh-e Chamân quarter; the Darb-e Ṣâmqân quarter (which is popularly known as the Panbeh-riseh quarter); the Qavi Maydân quarter; the Râh-e Kushk quarter; the Qumlâq quarter; the Dimaj quarter; the Ben Derakht quarter (which is popularly known as the Âkhund quarter); the Dabâghân quarter; the Khandaqbâr quarter; the Khiâbân quarter; the Sekkeh quarter; the Sharihân [quarter][74] (which is popularly known as the Sar-e Kucheh-ye Rayḥân); the Balâghi quarter; the Feshtâval quarter; the Shahrestân quarter; and the Maqlâvak[75] quarter. The enclosure wall around the city is for the most part in ruins, but its gates are still extant. Some have been renovated recently, but others remain in their old condition and are dilapidated.

GATES OF THE CITY OF QAZVIN

The names of the gates are as follows:[76]

The Râh-e Showsheh [Chaussée] gate, also known as the Râh-e Chamân, recently renovated.

The Darb-e Rayy gate, which is in its antique condition and is unrepaired.

The Panbeh-riseh gate, which has been renovated recently.

The Darb-e Kushk gate, which has been renovated recently.

---

[71] There are many popular anecdotes implying that people in Qazvin are crude, stupid or pederasts; some are recorded in Sayf od-Dowleh, *Safarnâmeh*, p. 31. It is not obvious why Farahâni should take such pains to defend the reputation of the Qazvinis; perhaps he is trying to show that he is broad-minded enough to avoid repeating such cheap jokes.

[72] Farâhâni's account is one of the best available descriptions of Qazvin in the late nineteenth century; it has been used by Anne Lambton for her excellent article on Qazvin in EI_2, s.v. "Qazvin." Cf. Sayf od-Dowleh, *Safarnâmeh*, pp. 29-31; Orsolle, *Caucase*, pp. 188-95.

[73] Cf. Adamec, *Historical Gazetteer*, 1:324.

[74] Golzâri, p. 20, has "the Sekkeh Sharihân quarter."

[75] Text: M-qâv-k. See Adamec, *Historical Gazetteer*, 1:324.

[76] Many of these gates were still in existence prior to World War II, though some were known by different names. There is a list of them in Rustam Kharegat, *A Tourist Guide to Iran* (Bombay, 1935), p. 74; cf. Adamec, *Historical Gazetteer*, 1:324.

The Qavi Maydân gate, which has been renovated recently; from this gate one goes towards Rasht.

The Khandaqbâr gate, which has been renovated recently.

The Maqlâvak gate, which has been renovated recently; from there one goes towards Tabriz.

The Sâvelân gate, from which one goes towards ᶜAmmârlu in Gilân; it has not been renovated.

The Shâhzâdeh Ḥosayn gate, which has not been renovated, and from which one goes towards Isfahan.

LARGE AND FAMOUS MOSQUES IN QAZVIN

The Masjed-e Shâh is located in the bazaar quarter. It is one of the constructions of the martyred Âqâ Moḥammad Shâh[77] which [he] did not finish but which [his successor Fatḥ-ᶜali Shâh][78] brought to completion. Its façade remained half-finished. In the reign of the pious king Moḥammad Shâh,[79] at the time Mirzâ Musâ Vazir[80] was administrator of Qazvin, [16] the façade was completed in accordance with royal command. In this period, it was also completely renovated. The fourteen or fifteen shops around the mosque are part of the wakf properties for the mosque. [The revenue from them] goes for the custodian, the muezzin, the snow-sweeper, and for the illumination of the mosque. These shops were made wakf property by the sons of the late Ḥâjji Mirzâ Rafiᶜ the Mojtahed.[81] Three shares [*dâng*[82]] of the village of Lamârd[83] are wakf property for the upkeep of the mosque. Three other shares are wakf property for the

[77] The founder and first Shâh of the Qâjâr dynasty. He ruled from 1193-1212/1779-97. He was murdered by some prisoners he had condemned to death while campaigning in the Caucasus. Although he was hardly a popular ruler, he became known as the "martyred Shâh" since he had died while engaged in fighting the infidels. See Fasâ'i/Busse, *Persia*, pp. 72-76. Contrary to what Farâhâni suggests, he only repaired this mosque; it was originally built by the Safavids Shâh Ṭahmâsb and Shâh ᶜAbbâs.

[78] The text has *khâqân-e maghfur*, "the late emperor," a conventional way of referring to the second Qâjâr ruler, Fatḥ-ᶜali Shâh (rg. 1212-50/1797-1834).

[79] The third Qâjâr Shâh, he ruled 1250-64/1834-48. He is often styled the "pious Shâh" since his reign was typified by profound suspicion of "infidel" foreigners and a reliance on the Shi'ite ulama, notably Ḥâjji Mirzâ Âqâsi (on whom, see below, n. 209).

[80] A Qâjar official (born 1198/ 1783-84); he was governor of Qazvin from 1264-69/ 1847-53. See Bâmdâd, *Rejâl*, 4:164-65 (which also reproduces an etching of him.) He is also mentioned in Reżâ Qoli Khân Hedâyat, *Rowżat oṣ-ṣafâ-ye nâṣeri* (Tehran, 1339/ 1960-61), 10: 569, 602, 630.

[81] A *mojtahed* is a Muslim jurisconsult of such recognized expertise that he is qualified to use reason and the rules of jurisprudence to reach his own independent judgment on matters of religious law: See Moojan Momen, *An Introduction to Shi'i Islam* (New Haven, 1985), pp. 203-4. On Mollâ Rafiᶜ, see below n. 134.

[82] The *dâng* was a relative measurement corresponding to one sixth of a piece of real estate.

[83] Text: Lahârd. The correct form of this name has been provided in a private communication from Professor Iraj Afshâr of Tehran, dated September, 1987.

upkeep of the Khiâbân water[-supply]. All six shares of Lamârd are administered by the children of the late Ḥâjji Mollâ ᶜAbd ol-Vahhâb the prayer-leader.

The Masjed-e Jâmeᶜ is located in the Feshtâval quarter. It is one of the constructions of ᶜEmâd od-Dowleh[84] [and] Khomârtâsh[85] ([who] was one of ᶜEmâd od-Dowleh's slaves). ᶜEmâd od-Dowleh was one of the famous governors of Qazvin. He left to attend the sultan and entrusted Khomârtâsh with the governorship of Qazvin. The latter was a devout man. He became a hermit towards the end of his life. That mosque was begun in the year 500 of the hegira [1106-7] and was finished in 509 [1115-16]. In the year 540 [1145-46] Moẓaffar od-Din Alb Arghun ebn-e Yoronqosh[86] repaired the mosque door and enlarged the existing building. There are two tablets there [which record that] Khomârtâsh made some of his property and qanâts into wakf property and then that the properties were consolidated and the names changed. There are also two tablets affixed to the gate of the mosque. The tablet on the right is Safavid, and the sense of it is that a small fee should be charged for the import of [cooking] fat and grapes at the city-gate in the year 1081 [1670-71]. On the tablet on the left side, it is inscribed that during the reign of [Fatḥ-ᶜali Shâh], in the year 1238 [1822-23], some of the supplementary excise taxes were relinquished, such as the *khâneh-nozul*,[87] the tax [17] on those travelling back and forth, the tax on workers for sentinels in the royal gardens and buildings, and the tax on snow shovelers, etc. [This mosque] used to have many wakf endowments in earlier times, but they have been lost. Now it has only a few wakf endowments. Its wakf property is managed by Mirzâ Abu Torâb.

The Balâghi mosque is located in the Panbeh-riseh quarter. It is an old building, and a very magnificent mosque, but it has been in bad shape for a number of years. Ḥâjji Mirzâ Mofid, the Shaykh ol-Eslâm[88] of

[84] ᶜEmâd od-Dowleh Buzân ebn-e Alfqosht [vocalization uncertain], who was himself the descendant of one of the *gholâms* (military slaves) of the Seljuk sultan Malek-shâh (1072-92); see Qazvini, *Gozideh*, p. 796.

[85] See above, n. 52.

[86] The text has Alb Arslân ebn-e Naqash; for the correct form of the name, see Qazvini, *Gozideh*, p. 781.

[87] That is, the duty of a private citizen or citizens to provide accommodations and hospitality for government officials when they visited the city. Though this was often regarded as an honor (and a favor which one could expect to be reciprocated), it was sometimes burdensome.

[88] Originally little more than an honorific title for a religious dignitary, the term *shaykh ol-eslâm* gradually became institutionalized as the title for the chief judge (appointed by the state) of a major town, city, or province. For an overview of the history of this office, see EI_1, 4:275-78 (especially p. 276); Richard Bulliet, "The Shaikh al-Islâm and the Evolution of Islamic Society," *Studia Islamica* 35(1972):53-67.

Qazvin, used up many of its bricks and stones to repair the Emâmzâdeh Esmâᶜil [shrine].

The Sanjideh mosque is located in the Darb-e Rayy quarter. It is not a very impressive building, but it is the oldest mosque of all. It is believed by the people of Qazvin that Ḥażrat-e Emâm Ḥasan,[89] the son of ᶜAli, prayed in this mosque, and thus they consider the mosque to be very holy. This belief has no credibility since the major historians have written nothing about Emâm Ḥasan having come to Iran. Nonetheless, it is in agreement with a story in the *Rowżat ol-aḥbâb*[90] [*Garden of the Loved Ones*] that, in the year 30 after the hegira [650-51], during the caliphate of ᶜO̱smân, Saᶜid ebn ol-ᶜÂṣ, who was governor of Kufa, set out with a great army and some of the *mohâjerin* and the *anṣâr* to conquer the province of Jorjân.[91] The two heroic Imams, Emâm Ḥasan and Emâm Ḥosayn,[92] accompanied that army, seeking the spiritual reward of performing the holy war. Thanks to their efforts, the region of Jorjân was conquered by capitulation. Despite this story, it is still doubtful that they came to Qazvin.

THE MADRASAHS OF QAZVIN

The Ḥâjji Mollâ Ṣâleḥ madrasah; the Mowlâ Verdi Khân madrasah; the Khiâbân madrasah (which is also known as the Ṣâleḥeyyeh madrasah); the Payghambareyyeh madrasah; the Ebrâhimeyyeh madrasah [18] (which is called the "New Madrasah"); the Eltefâteyyeh madrasah; the Âkhund Mollâ Ḥasan madrasah; the Ḥâjji Sayyed Taqi madrasah; and the Sardâr madrasah which Ḥosayn Khân the Sardâr built.

Each of these madrasahs has a wakf endowment. According to what has usually been written, the establishment of madrasahs and their wakf endowments began during the reign of Alb Arslân.[93] The story is told that when Alb Arslân entered the city of Nishapur and passed by the Masjed-e Jâmeᶜ, he saw a group of religious students who had gathered there and

[89] Ḥasan, Moḥammad's grandson, was the second Shi'ite Imam; d. 80/670.

[90] Text: *aḥbât*. The reference is most likely to Jamâl od-Din ol-Ḥosayni Shirâzi, *Rowżat ol-aḥbâb fi sirat on-nabi va'l-âl va'l-aṣḥâb* (ed. Lucknow, 1297/1880); see Âghâ Bozorg Ṭehrâni, *oẕ-Ẕariᶜeh elâ taṣânif osh-shiᶜeh* (Tehran, 1936-1978), 11:285-86.

[91] The *mohâjerin* or "Emigrants" were early converts to Islam in Mecca who accompanied Moḥammad to Medina after the hijra; the *anṣâr* or "Helpers" were native Medinans who converted to Islam and who co-operated with Moḥammad. Jorjân is an archaic form of the name of the area known today as Gorgân (southeast of the Caspian.)

[92] Ḥosayn, brother of Ḥasan, was the third Shi'ite Imam; he was martyred at the tragic battle of Karbalâ in 61/680.

[93] Alb Arslân was the Seljuk Turkish sultan who ruled Iraq and Iran from 455-65/1063-72. The madrasah (often translated as "college") was an institution for the teaching of religious law which spread throughout the Muslim world during the Seljuk period. The origins of the madrasah were certainly older than this, but in popular tradition the Seljuks are usually credited with inventing them as well as popularizing them. See D. Brandenburg, *Die Madrasa* (Graz, 1978) and especially George Makdisi, *The Rise of Colleges* (Edinburgh, 1981) for the most authoritative account of the historical origins of the madrasah system.

who were praising the sultan. The sultan asked Neẓâm ol-Molk,[94] "Who are they?" He answered, "They are seekers of knowledge. Their rank is more lofty than that of all people, yet of all people, their standard of subsistence is lower and more wretched. They have no fixed dwellings or residences." The sultan was moved to pity. Neẓâm ol-Molk ordered madrasahs to be built in all the regions of the sultan's empire and established endowments for them. Thus the madrasah of Neẓâm ol-Molk is still in Baghdad.[95]

MAUSOLEUMS IN THE CITY OF QAZVIN

The holy mausoleums located in the city of Qazvin are numerous. The best known of these are those several mausoleums which may be cited as follows:

One is the mausoleum of Shâhzâdeh Ḥosayn, son of the sinless ᶜAli ebn-e Musâ ebn-e Jaᶜfar,[96] which is located in the Dabâghân quarter.[97] On the plaque it is written that his martyrdom was in the year 220 [835-36]. Its dome is tiled, and the cenotaph is wooden. In the courtyard of the Shâhzâdeh Ḥosayn, there are two stones with calligraphy [by] Mir ᶜEmâd.[98] [19] The gate has exquisite inlaid work that was constructed in the year 700 and something [after 1300]. The people are utterly devoted to this shrine and consider a vow taken there to be very effective.

Another mausoleum is that of Emâmzâdeh Esmâᶜil, in which the people of Qazvin believe very strongly. They say making vows and swearing by it are extremely effective. This has been repeatedly proven by experience as miracles have been manifested. This saint's shrine is located next to the governmental buildings. Its dome is brick. Ḥâjji Naṣrollah Khân, son of Ḥasan Khân the Sardâr, renovated it. The story of the emâmzâdeh, according to what has been written in the *Baḥr ol-ansâb* [*Sea*

---

[94] A famous vizier who served under Alb Arslân and Malek Shâh for almost thirty years. He was assassinated in 485/1092, perhaps on orders from his mortal enemy, Ḥasan-e Ṣabbâḥ, chief of the "Order of Assassins" (Nezâri Esmâᶜilis). See EI_1, 3:932-36.

[95] The allusion is to the famous Neẓâmeyyeh school in Baghdad; see George Makdisi, "Muslim Institutions of Learning in Eleventh Century Baghdad," *Bulletin of the School of Oriental and African Studies* 24(1961):1-56.

[96] ᶜAli, known as Reżâ, was the eighth Shi'ite Imam. He was supposedly poisoned by the Abbasid Caliph Ma'mun in 202/817-18; the shrine of Mashhad, the most important place of pilgrimage in Shi'ite Iran, developed around his tomb.

[97] This shrine is mentioned briefly in Pope, *Survey of Persian Art*, p. 1217 (illustration 508b); see also Orsolle, *Caucase*, p. 191; Ḥ. Modarresi-Ṭabâṭabâ'i, *Bargi az târikh-e qazvin, târikhcheh-ye âstâneh-ye Shâhzâdeh Ḥosayn* (Qomm, 1361/1982-83).

[98] Mir ᶜEn âd ol-Ḥosayni (d. 1024/1615), a native of Qazvin, was one of the most famous calligraphers at the court of Shâh ᶜAbbâs. See Pope, *Survey of Persian Art*, p. 1739.

[99] There are several works, both in Arabic and Persian, with this title, and it is not certain to which Farâhâni is referring; see Storey, *Persian Literature*, pp. 183-84, 228, 230; Carl Brockelmann, *Geschichte der arabischen Literatur* (Leiden, 1934-39), SI:558, II:271. However, his comments are very close to those found in a work attributed to ᶜAlam

of Genealogies],[99] is this: After Moᶜtaṣem[100] poisoned Ḥażrat-e Jaᶜfar-e Ṣâdeq, and subsequently Manṣur the "Penny-pincher" [*Davâniqi*] came to power [*sic*],[101] Esmâᶜil, the son of Emâm Jaᶜfar-e Ṣâdeq, fled, out of fear of Manṣur, with four of his brothers towards Rayy. When they arrived at Qazvin, Sofyân-e Qazvini, who was a great friend of Manṣur, overtook them and fought them until Esmâᶜil was martyred in the city of Qazvin and was buried in the same place. His brothers fled to Rayy and Damavand.

Another one is the Payghambareyyeh mausoleum. This is also located beside the governmental buildings. They say four prophets and an emâmzadeh are buried there. Nothing is known about them or about the builder [of the tomb]. Recently, Âqâ Sayyed ᶜAli the Mojtahed had that mausoleum renovated.

Another is the mausoleum of Bibi Zobaydeh, which is located in the Panbeh-riseh quarter. According to what is written in the *Baḥr ol-ansâb*, Âmaneh Khâṭun, daughter of Musâ ebn-e Jaᶜfar, fled, after the martyrdom of Ḥażrat-e Reżâ, from Baghdad to Qazvin with Zobaydeh, Ḥalimeh, Sakineh,[102] and Âseyyeh [20] (the daughters and granddaughters of Musâ ebn-e Jaᶜfar). They all disappeared in the Panbeh-riseh quarter, and no one knows where they went.

Another is the mausoleum of Emâmzâdeh ᶜAli, which is also located in the Panbeh-riseh quarter. His genealogy is said to be as follows: ᶜAli ebn-e ᶜAwn ebn-e Amir ol-Mo'minin ᶜAli ebn-e Abi Ṭâleb. There is no doubt that this ᶜAli ebn-e ᶜAwn ebn-e Amir ol-Mo'minin was martyred in Qazvin.

Some of the children of Ḥanâneh ebn-e Zayban [ebn-e] Emâm Zayn ol-ᶜAbedin[103] were martyred in Qazvin, and some others died there, but it is not known in which mausoleum they are located.

ROYAL BUILDINGS IN QAZVIN

The old royal palaces [*ᶜemârât*] of Qazvin, which are all located adjacent to each other, are called the Dowlat-khâneh and the Arg[104] [citadel.] They are as described below.

ol-Hodâ, *Ketâb kanz ol-ansâb maᶜruf be-baḥr ol-ansâb* (Bombay, 1898), pp. 64-65. A copy of this work was apparently published in Tehran in 1280 and would have been available to Farahâni. See M. Sotudeh, "Baḥr-e naṣâb," *Râhnamâ-ye Ketâb* 11(1347/1968):298-303.

100 An Abbasid caliph (reigned 218-27/833-42).

101 Abu Jaᶜfar Manṣur, the second Abbasid caliph (136-58/754-75). His reputation for miserliness earned him the nickname "Penny-pincher." (The *dâneq* [plural *davâniq*] was one of the smallest and least valuable coins in circulation in early Islamic times.) Farâhâni's chronology is confused, since Manṣur ruled long before Moᶜtaṣem.

102 Text: Sakkeyyeh [?]; cf. *Kanz ol-ansâb*, pp. 64-65.

103 Zayn ol-ᶜAbedin was ᶜAli b. ol-Ḥosayn, also known as Sajjâd, the fourth Shi'ite Imam (died around 94/712); Zayban is probably a misreading of the name of his son Zobayd.

104 Here, and subsequently, the text reads *ark* rather than *arg*.

The ᶜAli Qâpu monumental doorway, which is one of the constructions of Shâh Solṭân Ḥosayn Ṣafavi:[105] There is a long avenue in front of it, which is also one of his creations.

The Ḥosayneyyeh palace, which is also one of the constructions of Shâh Solṭân Ḥosayn Ṣafavi: Several years ago, Sayf ol-Molk Vajihollah Mirzâ[106] renovated it according to [royal] orders.

The Khowrshid palace, which is another Safavid construction: At the present time, most of the governmental offices in Qazvin are in that building.

The Bâgh palace is also one of the constructions of Shâh Ṭahmâsb I.[107] There are some stout trees there, but the garden has been neglected and is in bad shape. The building is also ruined. [21]

The Nâderi palace, which is one of the constructions of Nâder Shâh Afshâr.[108]

The Rokneyyeh palace, which is one of the constructions of the late Rokn od-Dowleh ᶜAli-Nâqi Mirzâ:[109] This palace is now the audience hall for the governors of Qazvin.

"Arg" is usually the name for a lofty building. Originally, ᶜAmru [ebn-e] Lays̱ the Ṣaffârid built a governmental building in Ẕaranj, the capital of Sejestân.[110] Because it was lofty he called it his "Arg." After that, it gradually became common everywhere that the governmental building be called the "Arg."

---

105 This famous remnant of the old Safavid palace in Qazvin was actually built by Shâh Ṭahmâsp (940-84/1524-76); see Pope, *Survey of Persian Art*, p. 1174. It is not clear why Farâhâni should attribute it to the later Shâh Solṭân Ḥosayn (1103-35/1694-1732).

106 Vajihollah Mirzâ (1281-1322/1864-1905), a military officer, was also known at the court of Nâṣer od-Din Shâh as Sayf od-Dowleh or Amir Khân-e Sardâr. He was the son of Solṭân Aḥmad Mirzâ (the forty-sixth son of Fatḥ-ᶜali Shâh, governor of Hamadan, and author of the *Târikh-e ᶜażodi*, a collection of memoirs of the court of Fatḥ-ᶜali Shâh). He was a protégé of Moshir od-Dowleh; see Bakhash, *Iran*, p. 174; Bâmdâd, *Rejâl*, 4:396-405.

107 The Safavid Shâh from 1524-76.

108 A leader of the Afshâr tribe, Nâder eventually became shâh in the events following the Afghan invasion of Iran and subsequent collapse of the Safavid dynasty. He ruled 1148-60/1736-47. For his biography, see L. Lockhart, *Nâdir Shâh* (London, 1938).

109 A Qâjâr prince , the eighth son of Fatḥ-ᶜali Shâh, who became governor of Qazvin in 1234/1818-19 and held the post for over 25 years. See Ḥ. Nuri, *Rejâl-e dowreh-ye qâjâr* (Tehran, 1364/1985), pp. 278-80; Fasâ'i/Busse, *Persia*, p. 190; Bâmdâd, *Rejâl*, 2:496-98.

110 Farahâni uses the archaic spellings for Sistân (a province in southeast Iran) and its capital Zarang. The Ṣaffârids were one of the first independent local dynasties in the early Islamic period. Their base of power was in Sistân, where various members of the family ruled from 253/867 to as late as 900/1495. ᶜAmru b. Lays̱ was the second ruler of this dynasty (265-88/879-901). Various early Muslim geographical and historical texts allege that ᶜAmru constructed a building he called the "Arg" as a repository for the treasures acquired during his conquests. See Yâqut, *Moᶜjam ol-boldân* (Cairo, 1123-25/1906-7), 1:194; *Târikh-e sistân* (edited by M. Bahâr; Tehran, 1314/1935), 191 n. 1; Le Strange, *Lands of the Eastern Caliphate*, p. 336.

THE QANÂTS OF QAZVIN[111]

The qanât of Khomârtâsh, which was one of the wakf foundations of ᶜEmâd od-Dowleh [and] Khomârtâsh: Ḥosayn Khân Shehâb ol-Molk[112] provided funds for its restoration at the beginning of the reign [of Nâṣer od-Din Shâh]. It used to provide two sang of water, but then it was not kept in repair and now has only half a sang of water. It flows past the Masjed-e Jâmeᶜ and provides water for the Dabâghân quarter and the houses around the Shâhzâdeh Ḥosayn.

The qanât of Mollâ Khalilollah, which is known as the Mollâ Khalilâ: It is a communal wakf property. For some years, Ḥâjji Mirzâ Maḥmud Amini has provided the funds [for its upkeep.] It has about one sang of water and supplies the water for the Âkhund and Khandaqbâr quarters.

The Ṭayfuri qanât is wakf property. It now has about half a sang of water and supplies the water for some of the Râh-e Kushk quarter.

The Ḥalâl-âb qanât: This ruined qanât used to be wakf property. The people of the Râh-e Kushk quarter collaborated in renovating it and thus all the people of the quarter have obtained joint ownership of it. It has in excess of half a sang of water. [22]

The Ḥâtem Bek and Khᵛâtuni qanâts had both caved in and were in ruins. Vakil or-Raᶜâyâ[113] took an interest in restoring them and they now have half a sang of water, which supplies water for some of the Panbeh-riseh quarter.

Another is the Qanât-e Shâh, which is one of the Safavid wakf foundations. It is now in ruins and much in need of renovation. There are also three other ruined qanâts.

RIVERS FLOWING BY THE CITY OF QAZVIN

The Dizaj River: Its source is in the Rudbâr mountains and the Kuh Pâyeh[114] district.

The Aranranj River: It also springs from the Kuh Pâyeh district.

---

[111] Cf. Qazvini, *Gozideh*, pp. 779-81.

[112] Ḥosayn Khân Shâhsevân, also known as Ḥosayn Khân the Yuzbâshi, was a Qâjâr military commander who participated in the Herat campaign of 1273/1856-57 and was governor of Khorâsân until 1292/1875. In addition to the honorific of Shehâb ol-Molk, he was also given the title of Neẓâm od-Dowleh. He is mentioned in Fasâ'i/Busse, *Persia*, pp. 266, 277 and Bâmdâd, *Rejâl*, 1:393-94.

[113] This term is usually employed as the title of a provincial administrator appointed by the crown to serve as "a peasants' and artisans' ombudsman" representing ordinary citizens in conflicts with other state officials; it was also used as one of the titles of the ruler Karim Khân Zand: see John Perry, *Karim Khan Zand: A History of Iran, 1747-1779* (Chicago, 1979), pp. 215-16, 233. Here, however, Farâhâni is referring to some specific notable in Qazvin (cf. below p. 23]. Eᶜtemâd os-Salṭaneh, *Ma'âs̱er*, p. 242 indicates that the Vakil or-Raᶜâyâ of Qazvin during this period was a certain Mirzâ Esmâᶜil Khân.

[114] Here and in several subsequent places, the text has Qohpâyeh. Cf. Adamec, *Historical Gazetteer*, 1:325-26. This Kuh Pâyeh, of course, should not be confused with the better known Kuh Pâyeh district near Isfahan.

The Zuyâr River: Its source is in the Qâqazân district.

The Bisineh River: Its source is also in the mountains of Qâqazân.

Another river is the Deli Chây, which used to belong to a village named ᶜAbek. The Safavid rulers, in order to increase the city's water supply, bought that village, tore it down, and brought the water into the city. At the present time, the water still flows to the city and empties into the Bisineh River. For fifty days after Now Ruz[115] it flows to gardens, and for this the treasury collects a thousand tomans a year from the owners of the gardens. The Safavids built a water-channel from the village of ᶜAbek to the city which always provides one sang of water to the city. The royal buildings and the Khiâbân are provided with water from this river.

The city of Qazvin is situated in a valley and a flood plain. These five rivers overrun the city. In springtime, which is the season for inundations, some damage is done to the city by these rivers almost every year. If this keeps up, Qazvin will be destroyed by floods! [23] In seasons other than spring, there is very little water in Qazvin. None of the rivers is flowing, and the people suffer from lack of water. Once a dam was constructed beside the mountains so that the Shâh Rud River, in all four seasons, would produce ten to fifteen sang of water for the city. Remains of the dam are still visible in some places. The gardens of Qazvin are irrigated with water from these rivers once or twice in the spring and are never watered again until the next spring. The produce of these gardens and farms around the city is limited to grapes, pistachios, almonds, and watermelons. None of these has much need for water so they can withstand the drought. The most common thing in the gardens is the vine. In their jargon, one is said to be a "fifty-viner." Anyone who has fifty vines has income of from two thousand to fifteen thousand [dinars?[116]]. About two thousand people have vines in the gardens inside the city of Qazvin. Because they do not have a fixed water [allotment], a tax is not levied on the gardens. Rather, for purposes of taxing the gardens, they have imposed [a tax] on the weighing process: They charge a government fee on loads of raisins entering or leaving the city. This does not yield revenue to the customs; it is a separate matter and is for the [city?] administration.

ULAMA OF QAZVIN

Ḥâjji Mollâ Âqâ; Âqâ Shaykh Ṣâdeq; Ḥâjji Sayyed Abu Torâb; Âqâ Sayyed Jaᶜfar; Âqâ Sayyed Ḥosayn Zarâbâdi; Âqâ Shaykh Ṣâleḥ.[117]

[115] The Iranian New Year's Day, which falls on the Spring Equinox (March 21).

[116] The author does not specify a denomination of the currency here; in other places he usually refers to dinars after numbers of this size (there were 10,000 dinars in a toman).

[117] Several of these men are listed in Eᶜtemâd os-Salṭaneh, *Ma'âs̱er*, pp. 151, 161, 165.

PRINCES OF QAZVIN

The sons of the late Rokn od-Dowleh, of whom the most eminent is Esḥaq Mirzâ.

The sons of [Fatḥ-ᶜali Shâh], of whom the most eminent was Solṭân Salim Mirzâ. He is deceased, but his sons are still alive.

Among the sons of Ẓell os-Solṭân[118] there are Yaᶜqub Mirzâ and several others. [24]

NOTABLES AND IMPORTANT MERCHANTS OF QAZVIN

Vakil or-Raᶜâyâ and his cousins, who are all from the clan of Ḥâjji Mir Ḥasan.

Ḥâjji Mirzâ Bozorg, the Shaykh ol-Eslâm, of the clan of Ḥâjji Mir Ḥasan.

Mirzâ ᶜAbd ol-Ḥosayn, the Nâyeb oṣ-Ṣadr, of the clan of Ḥâjji Mir Ḥasan.

Ḥâjji Mirzâ Maḥmud, of the clan of Amin ot-Tojjâr.

Ḥâjji Moḥammad Ṣâdeq the merchant, of the Amini clan.

Ḥâjji Shaykh Jaᶜfar the merchant, of the Amini clan.

Âqâ ᶜAli Amin or-Raᶜâyâ, of the Amini clan.

Ḥâjji Mirzâ Mahdi the merchant, of the Amini clan.

Asadollah Khân Moᶜin or-Raᶜâyâ, one of the sons of Mowlâ Verdi Khân Mirzâ Asadollah the magistrate [*kalântar*], the son of Shahreyâr ol-Molk, of the clan of Mirzâ Moḥammad Ḥosayn ᶜAżod ol-Molk.

COMMODITIES OF QAZVIN

The commodities of Qazvin which are produced in the city and the environs and which are traded and exported [include] raisins, cotton, grains, pistachios, almonds, filberts, and cornelian cherries (which come from the river areas).

DISTRICTS OF QAZVIN

The Eqbâl district, which has twenty-four inhabited villages.

The Bashâriât district, which has thirty-five inhabited villages.

The Abharud district, which has eight inhabited villages.

The Dashtâbi district, which has forty-two inhabited villages.

The Feshkel district, which has fourteen inhabited villages.

The Kuh Pâyeh district, which has thirty-five inhabited villages. [25]

The Khar Rud district, which has thirty inhabited villages.

---

[118] Ẓell os-Solṭân, or Masᶜud Mirzâ Yamin od-Dowleh (1850-1919), was the oldest son of Nâṣer od-Din Shâh. See biographical sketch in Bakhash, *Iran*, p. 389; Guity Nashat, *The Origins of Modern Reform in Iran, 1870-80* (Urbana, 1982), *passim*; Benjamin, *Persia and the Persians*, pp. 185-88; Bâmdâd, *Rejâl*, 4:78-100; Dust ᶜAli Moᶜayyer ol-Mamâlek, "Pesarân-e Nâṣer od-Din Shâh," *Yaghmâ* 11(1337/1958-59):295-300; Ḥosayn Saᶜâdat Nuri, *Ẓell os-Solṭân* (Tehran, 1347/1968.)

The Zahrâ district, which has eighty-six inhabited villages.

The Râmand district, which has twelve inhabited villages.

The Qâqazân district, which has eighty-two inhabited villages.

The Afshâr district, which has forty-five inhabited villages.

Alamut and Rudbâr[119] are among the dependencies of Qazvin. They have eighty-five villages.

THE BOUNDARIES OF QAZVIN

The boundary of the province of Qazvin in the south is the Zahrâ district, which is adjacent to Sâvej[120] and a dependency of Hamadan. To the north, the Rudbâr and Alamut districts are adjacent to the ᶜAmmârlu district of Gilân and the summer-pastures of Râneku, Ashku, and Tonakâbon. To the east, the Bashâriât district is adjacent to the areas of Eshtehârd[121] and the Sâujbolâgh of Rayy. To the west, the Qâqazân district is adjacent to the areas of Abhar Khamseh [district] and Ṭârom.

THE MINES OF QAZVIN

The alum mine is in the Qâqazân district.

The marble quarry is in the Qâqazân district.

There are several coal mines; one of them is in the Rudbâr district and another in the Feshkel valley district.

There are several salt mines. One of them is in Rudbâr, which [also] has a spring of water that yields revenue to the state.

DEPARTURE FROM QAZVIN

Anyhow, having left Tehran on the evening [before] Friday the fourth of Shavvâl [16 July], and having arrived in Qazvin on Friday the fourth [17 July] at about noontime and waiting there until one hour before sunset, [I] mounted a post horse and set out.[122] [26]

The fare for the post horse is one kran per farsakh. Of course, it is also necessary to be accompanied by a postal service guide, and one kran per farsakh is charged as the fee for the guide's horse. The postal service guide must also be tipped one kran at each station.[123] One travels about half a farsakh through the middle of the cultivated areas of Qazvin and arrives at

119 Text: Ruddar.

120 The modern Sâveh.

121 See Adamec, *Historical Gazetteer*, 1:167.

122 This older practice of hiring horses to travel from one post-station (*châpâr-khâneh*) to the next was obviously much more arduous than the system of stagecoaches which Farâhâni had been able to use to travel from Tehran to Qazvin. Travellers who describe this postal route from Qazvin to Rasht include Eastwick, *Journal*, 1:312-30; Orsolle, *Caucase*, p. 159; Sayf od-Dowleh, *Safarnâmeh*, p. 32; Mirzâ Ebrâhim, *Safarnâmeh*, p. 171; and Eᶜtemâd os-Salṭaneh [Ṣaniᶜ od-Dowleh], *Safarnâmeh-ye Ṣaniᶜ od-Dowleh az teflis beh ṭehrân* (edited by Moḥammad Golbon; Tehran, 2536/1977), pp. 60-68.

123 These comments on the post service may be compared with those of Curzon, *Persia*, 1:30-33.

the village of Neẓâmâbâd one and a half farsakhs from the city. This village has about fifty resident households and belongs to the Amini family. One farsakh beyond Neẓâmâbâd, one reaches Ḥosaynâbâd, which has about twenty households and is jointly owned [*khowrdeh-mâlek*[124]]. Going half a farsakh past Ḥosaynâbâd, one arrives at the village of Âqâ Bâbâ. Âqâ Bâbâ is owned by Ḥosayn ᶜAli Khân, the son of ᶜAlâ' od-Dowleh the Amir-e Neẓâm.[125] It has a population of about one hundred households. It is part of the Qâqazân district. It has many trees and gardens. About two farsakhs past Âqâ Bâbâ, one arrives at the village of Mazraᶜeh. From Qazvin to Âqâ Bâbâ is three farsakhs, and from Âqâ Bâbâ to Mazraᶜeh is about two farsakhs.

MAZRAᶜEH

The village of Mazraᶜeh is situated on the slopes of the mountains and is summer-pasture land. Its water comes from springs. It has many trees. It is [both] Amini property and khowrdeh-mâlek. It has about forty resident households. The post office is in this village; that is, the post horses are kept there, so the postal courier changes horses there. First of all, this station does not have a state post office. A filthy, locally owned stable has been rented, and the government horses are kept there. Secondly, the horses at this station are extremely wretched. In all the stations along the way, the state post stations are all kept clean and have excellent horses stabled at them, except for this station. [27]

THE KHARZÂN PASS

One farsakh from Mazraᶜeh one reaches the Kharzân pass. From this direction, the ascent of the Kharzân pass is not very difficult. No point in the ascent or descent of the pass is precipitous, but the length of the pass is considerable. The descent from the other side of the Kharzân is especially long. In winter, it snows a great deal and the wind from Qâqazân blows extremely cold.

The Kharzân mountain is a broad, earthen mountain; its soil is fine with few rocks. On the slopes of this mountain, in spring and summer, the Gheyâs̱vand tribe[126] practices dry-farming. They pitch tents there and

---

124 So in the text; more often written *khordeh-mâlek*. According to Ann Lambton, *Landlord and Peasant in Persia* (Oxford, 1953), p. 432, this was landed property owned jointly by a group of peasant proprietors or other shareholders.

125 On ᶜAlâ' od-Dowleh, see Bakhash, *Iran*, pp. 148, 263; Nashat, *Reform*, p. 91; Bâmdâd, *Rejâl*, 1:89-93. On the village, cf. Eastwick, *Journal*, 1:313-14; S. G. W. Benjamin, *Persia and the Persians* (London, 1887), p. 40.

126 The name of a tribe, originally from Fârs province, which was given campgrounds near Qazvin by Âqâ Moḥammad Khân Qâjâr; cf. Nâṣer od-Din Shâh, *The Diary of H. M. the Shah of Persia during His Tour Through Europe in A. D. 1873* (translated by J. W. Redhouse; London, 1874), p. 9. Mirzâ Ebrâhim, *Safarnâmeh*, pp. 174-75, gives the name of this tribe as Qiâsvand; Dehkhodâ, *Loghatnâmeh*, 33:397 has Ghiâs̱vand.

graze their flocks and herds. In the middle of this pass and mountain, there are two populated places. The first is the village of Esmâᶜilâbâd, which has a very limited water-supply. Its agriculture is by dry-farming. Thirty households reside there. Esmâᶜil Khân Gheyâs̱vand founded it. This village is situated next to the road. About half a farsakh past there, one comes to the village of Kharzân.

THE VILLAGE OF KHARZÂN

The village of Kharzân lies in the middle of the valley along the road. It has one and a half sang of spring water. Its population is about one hundred households. It is one of the properties of Manuchehr Khân Moᶜtamad od-Dowleh[127] and is now the fief [*toyul*][128] of Jehângir Khân the Vazir-e Ṣanâyeᶜ ["Minister of Crafts and Industry"].[129] Moᶜtamad od-Dowleh built a fine brick caravanserai there, which has two [separate] caravanserais, one within the other, and many shops and stables. It is wakf property, inhabited, cultivated, and a stopping place for caravans. There is also a coffee-house and a grocery in that caravanserai. [28]

PÂCHENÂR

Past Kharzân, the road is constantly downhill in rolling country all the way to Pâchenâr. One and a half farsakhs after Kharzân, the post horses are left [behind] and one is compelled to go on foot. I sat for a while at a spring which flowed in the midst of the valley, and then, on horseback and by foot, after countless difficulties, I reached Pâchenâr. I traversed the route in seven hours. Pâchenâr village, which is by the road, consists of just one brick caravanserai and a post station. This caravanserai and post station are located on the bank of the Ṭârom River. The Ṭârom River flows from the Mollâ ᶜAli valley and enters the Shâh Rud River a little below the caravanserai.

The post station is a pleasant and attractive place with some willows and forest trees surrounding it. According to reports, Nâṣer

---

[127] Also known as Ich Âqâsi the Armenian (or the Georgian), who came to Iran from Tiflis in 1209/1794-95; he was an intimate of Fatḥ-ᶜali Shâh and Moḥammad Shâh and helped negotiate the Treaty of Turkomanchay in 1828. According to Rabino, *Provinces*, pp. 478-79, he was governor of Gilân from 1246-50/1830-35. Cf. Farhâd Mirzâ, *Hedâyat*, p.4; Bâmdâd, *Rejâl*, 4:159-63; Fasâ'i/Busse, *Persia*, p. 185 etc.

[128] The *toyul* was a type of land assignment made by a ruler to bureaucratic or military retainers in lieu of salary. The practice was abolished in 1907. See Lambton, *Landlord and Peasant*, pp. 109 ff.

[129] Jehângir Khân (1269-1309/1852-92) was the nephew of the aforementioned Manuchehr Khân and the son of Solaymân Khân Sehâm od-Dowleh (an Armenian from Tiflis who came to Iran in the early Qâjâr period). Among the circle at the court of Nâṣer od-Din Shâh he was also called Amir-e Tumâni. See Fasâ'i/Busse, *Persia*, pp. 297-99; Bâmdâd, *Rejâl*, 1:285-87. He is also mentioned as the official in charge of the state arms factory in Nashat, *Reform in Iran*, pp. 59-60.

ol-Molk,[130] during his first governorship of Gilân, had this post station constructed with sunbaked bricks, mud, and stone. Its construction is of good quality, and its horses are fine. The caravanserai is one of the constructions of Ḥâjji Moḥammad Hâdi Tâjer Miânji. Pâchenâr is the winter pasture for the Chegni[131] Kurds. At a distance of one maydân past the caravanserai, beside the road, there are about thirty small peasant houses to which the Kurds come in winter-time and in which they dwell. Pâchenâr is located low down in a valley. It is the first part of the land of Gilân. On the other side of the Kharzân pass, the weather is completely different. The soil, trees, shrubs, and steppe-land birds there are all different. There are some forest trees in the plains. About one maydân past Pâchenâr two or three rustic caravanserais of sun-baked brick and mud have been built by the road. Caravans usually stop at those caravanserais. Anyhow, I arrived in Pâchenâr three hours after sunrise [29], changed horses, and set out three hours before sunset. The road is rocky and generally passes along the left side of the mountain range. The Shâh Rud River was visible to the right of the road, sometimes far off and sometimes close by. One farsakh past Pâchenâr one arrives at the Lowshân bridge.

THE LOWSHÂN BRIDGE

The Lowshân bridge spans the Shâh Rud River, into which the Alamut and Rudbâr rivers both flow. Ḥâjji Moḥammad Hâdi Tâjer Miânji, who was a resident of Qazvin, had this bridge built in the year 1209 [1794-95] and even now, ninety-four years later, there is nothing wrong with it, and it is extremely sturdy. According to reports, it is half a farsakh from the Lowshân bridge to the village of Lowshân. Past the bridge, the Shâh Rud River lies to the left, and there are mountains on the right side near the road. Sometimes, a few small hills lie across the road. In the summer, which is the season of low water in the river, the caravans travel in the riverbed.

MANJIL

It is four farsakhs from Pâchenâr to Manjil. Two farsakhs of the way, the road is sometimes on the right bank and sometimes on the left bank of the river. For the remaining two farsakhs, the river is situated in such a way that it is not visible. These two farsakhs are rocky and often pass over hills and valleys. Close to Manjil there is a small, rocky mountain in the middle

---

130 Maḥmud Khân Qarâgozlu Nâṣer ol-Molk, the viceroy (*farmân-farmâ*) of Hamadan, was appointed to the governorship of Gilân in 1277/1860-61 and held that post for about nine years; see Rabino, *Provinces*, p. 479; Bâmdâd, *Rejâl*, 4:54-59.

131 See Adamec, *Historical Gazetteer*, 1:526, 731.

of the road; Manjil is at the top of it. It lies in a valley on a small plateau. This plateau is green and fresh and has many olive trees.

The village of Manjil has about one hundred and fifty resident households with a population of about six hundred people. There are fourteen or fifteen different shops there. Its water comes from an abundant spring. There is usually water flowing alongside the streets. [30] The brick post station has sturdy brickwork and is spacious. The upper storey has several clean white-washed rooms. This post station is one of the constructions of Moḥammad Qâsem Khân[132] the governor. It was built, in accordance with orders, during the time of his governorship of Gilân.

The wind of Manjil is famous. In all four seasons, it blows extremely hard most of the time. The wind is less in winter. It always begins to blow in the afternoon. To sum up, I arrived in Manjil one hour before sunset and left one hour after nightfall.

THE MANJIL BRIDGE

About two thousand paces past the village of Manjil is the Manjil bridge, beside which several rooms have been built to serve as a customs post. Previously, this bridge was made out of wood and was very difficult to cross. Ḥâjji Solaymân Khân-e Qâjâr Qavânlu[133] had a bridge built out of brick and mortar. In the year 1290 [1873-74], two spans of that bridge

---

132 The son of Moᶜayyer ol-Mamâlek; mentioned briefly in Hedâyat, *Rowżat oṣ-Ṣafâ-ye Nâṣeri*, 10:468, 604.

133 Solaymân Khân (1174-1220/1760-1806), the son of Âqâ Moḥammad Khân's maternal uncle, was also known as Eᶜteżâd od-Dowleh and held the governorship of Gilân for several years in the early Qâjâr period. See Fasâ'i/Busse, *Persia*, pp. 37, 83, 88-89 etc.; Bâmdâd, *Rejâl*, 2:118-24; Rabino, *Provinces*, p. 476. On the bridge and its construction see Mirzâ Ebrâhim, *Safarnâmeh*, p. 169; Sotudeh, *Âstârâ*, 1:496-97 (plate 248 is a photograph of the bridge). The Turkish Qâjâr tribe was divided into two main branches, the Qoyunlu and the Devehlu. Here, the term "Qâjâr Qavânlu" indicates that Solaymân Khan was from the Qoyunlu (=Qavânlu) branch, to which the reigning dynasty also belonged.

134 Ḥâjj Mollâ Rafiᶜ, known as Shariᶜatmadâr, was the ancestor of a long line of prominent Shi'ite religious scholars in Rasht; he died shortly before Farâhâni's visit. In addition to Farâhâni's account, Nâṣer od-Din Shâh, *Diary*, pp. 11-17, mentions him frequently and notes his work in renovating the Manjil bridge, which came to be regarded as a marvel of engineering (cf. Rabino, *Provinces*, p. 264). Eastwick, *Journal*, 1:332-33, met him and wrote of the encounter: "I went to the house of a celebrated spiritual chief, Hâji Mulá Rafi, who leads the people of Ghilán withersoever he will. I beheld an old man with a Jewish countenance, a hooked nose, and an immense white turban. We sate on the ground in a room filled with books, all manuscripts of course. We spoke of the famine, and he said he had given two túmáns, about 1*l*., to each individual of several thousand people. He did not, however, tell me that this was money collected at his instance from the rich, and that he himself gave only his influence." Kharegat, *Tourist Guide*, p. 81, records an inscription in Rasht certifying that Nâṣer od-Din Shâh had rescinded taxes on bakers at his request; see also Bakhash, *Iran*, p. 169; Bâmdâd, *Rejâl*, 5:264; Sotudeh, *Âstârâ*, 1:497; Mirzâ Ebrâhim, *Safarnâmeh*, p. 168; Eᶜtemâd os-Salṭaneh, *Ma'âs̱er*, p. 151.

were destroyed. The late Mollâ Rafiᶜ the Mojtahed,[134] in accordance with royal orders, had those two spans rebuilt and made extensive repairs to the entire bridge. This bridge has seven spans. Its central arch collapsed recently. The wooden bridge still remains by the side of this bridge. This bridge has been constructed over the Safid Rud River. One outlet of the Safid Rud is in the area of Daylam; a branch of this same river is the Shâh Rud River. It flows from the Rudbâr and Alamut area and passes below the Samirân fortress.[135] Samirân used to be a fortress among the Ṭârom mountains, but it is now in ruins. Near Manjil the Qezel Owzan River also joins it and becomes known as the Safid Rud. The mouth of these rivers is at the Caspian Sea. The district of Raḥmatâbâd is on the right side of the Manjil bridge, [31] and to its left is the district of Rudbâr Zaytun. Past the bridge is the first bad part of the Gilân road. Previously, the road was in repair and revetted with stones. Now the revetment remains in some places and is ruined in others. It gets muddy in the rainy season. Even in the places where there is revetment, the pack animals travel with difficulty because the stones are uneven. The village of Rudbâr Zaytun is one farsakh past Manjil. All along this one farsakh, the Safid Rud River is to the right of the highway, and all along the left side are huge rocky mountains. When one wants to enter Rudbâr, one descends precipitously and with extreme difficulty from these rocky mountains.

THE VILLAGE OF RUDBÂR

The village of Rudbâr has two sections: one is upper Rudbâr and the other is lower Rudbâr.[136] In all, it has nearly five hundred households, which makes about two thousand five hundred people. One hundred families are Armenian. Several caravanserais for pack animals and about sixty or seventy shops have been built along the road. Some of the shops and the coffeehouse are open at night for the purpose of trading with travellers passing through. The late Ḥâjji Mollâ Rafiᶜ was a native of this same village of Rudbâr. There are many olive trees in the mountains and around the village. All of the trees are privately owned. Each tree yields a profit of half a kran to three krans. It is one farsakh from Manjil to Rudbâr, and four farsakhs from Rudbâr to Rostamâbâd. For some distance on the way out of Rudbâr, the olive trees are alongside the road so that one must pass through the midst of them. All along these four farsakhs, [32] the Safid Rud River is situated on the right-hand side for the length of the road. On the left is the mountain and a sparse forest. The

---

[135] This was one of several famous fortresses in the environs of Qazvin held by the Esmâᶜili "Assassins" from the eleventh to the thirteenth centuries. See Yâqut, *Moᶜjam ol-boldân* , 3:135-37; Matheson, *Persia*, pp. 58-59.

[136] Cf. Rabino, *Provinces*, pp. 209-11.

road is paved with stones in some places. It is not level and goes up and down until three quarters of a farsakh before Rostamâbâd, [where] it is situated on the Rostamâbâd plateau.

ROSTAMÂBÂD

Rostamâbâd is a district of seven or eight villages.[137] Inasmuch as these villages are the property of landlords in Rasht, they do not have their own headman (*nâyeb*). The post station is located in a village named Poshteh and is built on elevated terrain so that it has a view of most of the plateau. This post station is also one of the constructions of Moḥammad Qâsem Khân the governor, who built it according to orders. It is very spacious and solid and constructed of brick and mortar. It has several clean and whitewashed rooms. There are always twelve horses stabled there. About one farsakh past the Rostamâbâd post station, one arrives at the toll station of Naql-e Bar, which is in the middle of the road in the midst of the forest. To that point, the forest trees had been sparse, but from there on the trees are very sturdy and numerous. In this forest, there are many silk trees.[138] It was the season for them to blossom, so it was very pleasant and agreeable. Everywhere, the open road winds up and down. It has stone revetment and mud [surfacing]. The forest is all around until a place where it becomes completely mountainous. That place is called Safid Kotaleh,[139] which means "White Hill."

THE EMÂMZÂDEH HÂSHEM

Coming down from Safid Kotaleh, the first level ground is at the Emâmzâdeh Hâshem. It is three quarters of a farsakh to the shrine. There again the ground is level and the road is smooth. To the right and the left, on both sides of the road, there are many pleasant forest trees. I have not yet seen the genealogy of this emâmzâdeh in any book. [33] In the yard of his mausoleum, there are several tall, old cedar trees. There is a brick caravanserai beside the road near the shrine, which they say is one of the constructions of the Safavid rulers. It is now in ruins, and no one stays there. Its restoration could be undertaken with a modest amount of revenue.[140]

---

137 Cf. Rabino, *Provinces*, pp. 212; Ḥasan Shams Gilâni, *Târikh-e ᶜolamâ va shoᶜarâ-ye gilân* (Tehran, 1327/1948), p. 28.

138 These "silk trees" or silk acacias are often mentioned by travellers in this region; see Augustus Mounsey, *A Journey Through the Caucasus and the Interior of Persia* (London, 1872), pp. 318-19; Orsolle, *Caucase*, p. 152.

139 Rabino, *Provinces*, p. 209 has "Sefid Katelè" and notes that it was located 52 km. from Manjil.

140 Text: *tankhᵛâh*, a term for income from land taxes, part of which is designated for drafts on the treasury for salaries, stipends, and so on. See V. Minorsky (tr.), *Tadhkirat al-Mulûk: A Manual of Safavid Administration* (London, 1943), p. 152. On the shrine, see Gilâni, *Târikh-e ᶜolamâ*, p. 28.

KOHDOM

The village of Kohdom[141] is one farsakh past the Emâmzâdeh Hâshem. A post station is located there. The post station is very solidly built and grand. It is one of the constructions of Moḥammad Qâsem Khân the governor, who also built several small bridges near Kohdom. A dozen horses are also kept at this post station.

Kohdom is the name of both the district and this particular village. The populated area of this village of Kohdom is scattered through the forest, not concentrated in one particular place. Two or three houses are in one spot of the forest, as is usually the case in villages in Gilân. In any event, there are about fifty households. A barrage has been built across the Safid Rud which is used for irrigation for agriculture there. From Rostamâbâd to Kohdom, there are several streams along the way, one of which is the Siâh Rud (across which the late Ḥâjji Mollâ Rafiᶜ built a bridge with a bequest[142] from Ḥâjji Abu'l-Qâsem Yazdi[143]).

It is five farsakhs from the post station of Kohdom to the city of Rasht, but the postal couriers calculate it as six farsakhs and collect the fare for six farsakhs. The road is smooth the whole way, with trees on both sides of the highway. It is three farsakhs to Bâzâr-e Sangar.[144] Bâzâr-e Sangar is a marketplace located on the road two farsakhs outside of Rasht. Ḥâjji Moḥammad Ḥasan Moᶜin ot-Tojjâr Rashti, with the assistance of Akbar Khân [34] Bayglarbayki,[145] built this bazaar. One branch of the Safid Rud flows through Sangar, so a bridge is built over it. The two farsakhs from Bâzâr-e Sangar to Rasht are smooth the whole way, with fresh and verdant forest trees arranged along the highway.

THE JOURNEY BETWEEN TEHRAN AND RASHT

Anyhow, I left Tehran on the evening [before] Friday, the fourth of the month of Shavvâl [Thursday, 16 July], and arrived in the city of Rasht on Sunday the sixth of the month of Shavvâl [19 July] two hours before sunset. Thus the journey, from the departure from the capital to [my] arrival in Rasht, including time for eating, resting, and travelling, took sixty-six hours.

---

141 Farhâd Mirzâ, *Hedâyat*, p. 6, explicitly gives this vocalization of the name. The village is described at some length by Orsolle, *Caucase*, pp. 163-64; see also Rabino, *Provinces*, p. 215. The *Ḥodud ol-ᶜâlam*, translated by V. Minorsky, *Ḥudûd al-ᶜÂlam: The Regions of the World, a Persian Geography 372 A.H.-982 A.D.* (revised by C. E. Bosworth; London, 1970), p. 390, identifies this town with the Kutom of the medieval geographers.

142 *S̱ols*; the third of a Muslim's property which may be freely disposed of in a will (the other two-thirds being distributed according to fixed regulations).

143 Cf. Nâṣer od-Din Shâh, *Diary*, p. 13; Farhâd Mirzâ, *Hedâyat*, p. 6.

144 Now more commonly known as Dowshanbeh Bâzâr; see Adamec, *Historical Gazetteer*, 1:565.

145 A prominent local dignitary who was in charge of the customs office for Gilân and Mâzandarân for six years. See Bâmdâd, *Rejâl*, 1:165.

The post station is on the outskirts of Rasht and is located next to the Kalâseh Rudbâr River. The late Ḥâjji Mollâ Rafiᶜ built a bridge across this stream with a bequest from Ḥâjji Moḥammad Bâqer Kâshi.[146] The city is just past the bridge.

THE CITY OF RASHT

The city of Rasht is not of ancient origin. It was founded in 900 A.H. [1494-95] under the name of Rasht.[147]

The length of this city: in one direction, it ends at this same Manjil bridge which is over the Kalâseh Rudbâr River (and from which one goes towards [Persian] ᶜErâq);[148] in the other direction it ends at the Chomârsarâ bridge which is over the Gowhar Rud River (and from which one goes towards Fuman).

The breadth of this city: in one direction it ends at the Nâṣereyyeh plain, from which one goes to the surrounding villages; in [the other] direction it ends at the Kalâseh Rudbâr River, from which one goes to the Kucheṣfahân[149] and Lâhijân road. [35] So the Kalâseh Rudbâr River is located along the width of the city on one side and the length of the city on another side.

THE QUARTERS OF RASHT

The Kiâb quarter; the Zâhedân quarter; the Bâzâr quarter; the Ṣayqelân quarter; the Chomârsarâ quarter; the Khomeyrân-Zâhedân quarter; [and] the Khomeyrân-Kiâb quarter.[150]

Two of its quarters are populous and esteemed. Most of the notables and great merchants are located in these two quarters.

One is the Kiâb quarter. The government building, the arsenal, the telegraph office, the British consulate (which is state property), the Sabz[eh] Maydân, the houses of the Ḥâjji Moḥammad Khâni clan

---

146 Perhaps Ḥâjji Sayyed Moḥammad Bâqer Shafti (1180-1260/1766-1845)? See Bâmdâd, *Rejâl*, 3:304-7.

147 As a district, if not as a city, Rasht was much older in origin than Farâhâni's dating suggests. It was, for example, mentioned in the anonymous tenth century geographical treatise entitled *Ḥodud ol-ᶜâlam* and described at some length by Qazvini in the thirteenth century: see Minorsky, *Ḥudûd*, pp. 137, 390; Qazvini/Le Strange, *Nuzhat*, p. 159. It was made the capital of the province of Gilân by Shâh ᶜAbbâs I. Other travel accounts describing Rasht in the nineteenth century include Sayf od-Dowleh, *Safarnâmeh*, pp. 36-38, and Mirzâ Ebrâhim, *Safarnâmeh*, pp. 167-71; see also Rabino, *Provinces*, pp. 70-81; Sotudeh, *Âstârâ*, 1:243-324; B. Nikitine, "Resht," in EI_1, 4:1142-45.

148 Here and in subsequent references Farâhâni means by ᶜErâq ("Iraq") the area south of Qazvin called "Persian Iraq" (ᶜErâq-e ᶜAjam) by early Muslim geographers; it is sometimes referred to as Arak in modern Persian.

149 Text: Kucheh Eṣfahân; see Mirzâ Ebrâhim, *Safarnâmeh*, p. 166; Adamec, *Historical Gazetteer*, 1:380; Rabino, *Provinces*, pp. 216-17; Gilâni, *Târikh-e ᶜolamâ*, p. 27.

150 Cf. Mirzâ Ebrâhim, *Safarnâmeh*, p. 167; Sotudeh, *Âstârâ*, 1:247-48 (following Gmelin). Rabino, *Provinces*, pp. 71-72 and Nikitine, "Resht," EI_1, 3:1143, give slightly different lists of the names of these quarters.

(Maḥmud Khân, Ḥâjji Ma^cṣum Khân, and Naṣrollah Khân), and the houses of the sons of Mirzâ ᶜAbd ol-Vahhâb the Mostowfi are all in this quarter.

The other is the Zâhedân quarter. The residences of officials connected with the government, the houses of Amin-e Divân,[151] the house of Bayglarbayki and his family, the houses of the late Mirzâ Musâ Nâyeb, the late Mirzâ Zaki Nâyeb, Ḥâjji Mirzâ Naṣir Ṭâyefeh, and Ḥâjji Ḥâkem, the houses of most of the clan of Ḥâjji Samiᶜ, the house of the late Ḥâjji Mollâ Rafiᶜ, the house of Ḥâjji Moḥammad Ḥasan Moᶜin ot-Tojjâr and Malek ot-Tojjâr,[152] the house of the Russian consul (which is state property), and the buildings which the Republic of France used to have in Gilân are all in this quarter.

This city has about five thousand houses, with two families living in each house. Each household has [about] four members, so the population is about 40,000 people. There are about two thousand shops in the bazaar and the [various] quarters [of the city].

MOSQUES OF RASHT

The Masjed-e Jâmeᶜ[153] is one of the constructions of Ḥâjji Jemâl, the father of Hedâyatollah Khân Rashti.[154] [36] Several of the merchants of Rasht had it repaired and added to the original building in the year 1278 [1861].

The mosque of Ḥâjji Samiᶜ: Ḥâjji Mirzâ Naṣir, known as Ḥâjji Ḥâkem, has made extensive renovations of [this,] his grandfather's mosque.

---

151 On Farâhâni's friend Amin-e Divân, see below, Part Seven, n. 101.

152 "Chief Merchant." This term, and others like it which Farâhâni has been using (Amin ot-Tojjâr, Moᶜin ot-Tojjâr, etc.), are often equivalent to names and so are generally transliterated rather than translated. However, they are titles used by important merchants in a way similar to the titulature of bureaucratic officials. See W. M. Floor, "The Merchants (*tujjâr*) in Qâjâr Iran," *Zeitschrift der Deutschen Morgenländischen Gesellschaft* 126(1976):107-12.

153 Sotudeh, *Âstârâ*, 1:254-55, citing Eᶜtemâd os-Salṭaneh's *Mer'ât ol-boldân*, 4:119-20, says that the general belief is that this mosque was founded by Ḥâjji Jemâl, father of Hedâyatollah Khân Rashti, while others believe it was built by Hedâyatollah's mother. He also mentions the repair of the mosque by various merchants in 1277-78. Cf. Rabino, *Provinces*, p. 74; Gilâni, *Târikh-e ᶜolamâ*, p. 22.

154 There have been several prominent individuals with this name in Gilân. The reference here is most likely to Hedâyatollah Khan (often known simply as Hedâyat Khân, as in subsequent passages in Farâhâni's account) who was the virtually independent ruler of the province just prior to the establishment of the Qâjâr dynasty. He was defeated by the Qâjârs in 1196/1781-82 and killed during a subsequent effort at revolt (1201/1786-87). Another Hedâyatollah Khân (also called Khânlar Khân) was appointed governor of Fuman by Fatḥ-ᶜali Shâh; he was murdered in 1848. See H. L. Rabino, "Rulers of Lahijan and Fuman," *Journal of the Royal Asiatic Society* (1918), p. 90; Rabino, *Provinces*, pp. 473-75 (citing the first-hand observations of Gmelin).

The mosque known as the mosque of Ḥâjji Moḥammad Khân, who is the grandson of Hedâyat Khân. This mosque is next to the government building.

The mosque of Ḥâjji Mollâ Ṣâdeq, who is known as Ḥâjji Mojtahed.

The mosque of Mollâ Ḥasan, known as ᶜAli Ḥosayni.

The Kiâb mosque, whose founder is unknown.

The Ṣafi mosque, which is said to be one of the constructions of Shâh Ṣafi.[155]

The mosque of Ḥâjji Moḥammad Karim the merchant.

THE MADRASAHS OF RASHT

The Jâmeᶜ madrasah, the founder of which is the same as the founder of the Masjed-e Jâmeᶜ. A group of merchants jointly had it renovated in the year 1270 [1853-54].

The Mostowfi madrasah, which is one of the constructions of Mirzâ Bâbâ, the father of Mirzâ ᶜAbd ol-Vahhâb the Mostowfi.

The Ḥâjji Moḥammad Khân madrasah (the person named being the grandson of Hedâyat Khân).

The Ḥâjji Samiᶜ madrasah, which is one of the constructions of the grandfather of Ḥâjji Ḥâkem, who had made extensive renovations to it.

The Ḥâjji ᶜAli Akbar the Merchant madrasah, which is one of the constructions of the father of Moḥammad Âqâ the Malek ot-Tojjâr.

The Ḥâjji Mollâ Ṣâdeq madrasah, which is one of his constructions. [37]

The Ḥâjji Ḥasan Kalântari madrasah.

The Ḥâjji Moḥammad Karim the Merchant madrasah.

The Ḥâjji Esmâᶜil Khân madrasah.

MAUSOLEUMS IN THE CITY OF RASHT

One is the Khᵛâhar-e Emâm ["Sister of the Emâm"] mausoleum.[156] According to popular belief, she was the sister of Ḥażrat-e Reżâ and was named Fâṭemeh. In written accounts, it is mentioned as the Lâl Showi ["Become Mute!"] shrine. They say that originally no one knew that a shrine was there. Then a drunken person passed by that place and, in a state of mirth and intoxication, uttered some impious words. A voice was heard to say "Become mute!" A few days later, he became mute. That place was excavated, the tomb was seen, and a tablet erected. A small

---

155 A Safavid monarch (1629-42). The mosque, however, would seem to be much earlier since both Nikitine, "Resht," EI_1, 4:1143 and Rabino, *Provinces*, p. 75 (citing Ḥasan Rumlu's *Aḥsan ot-tavârikh*), mention it as the oldest mosque in Rasht and one of the places where Shâh Esmâᶜil had taken refuge. See also Sotudeh, *Âstârâ*, 1:283-86, and plates 172-76.

156 On this building, see Mirzâ Ebrâhim, *Safarnâmeh*, pp. 167-68; Rabino, *Provinces*, p. 75; Gilâni, *Târikh-e ᶜolamâ*, p. 22; Sotudeh, *Âstârâ*, 1:293-96 and plates 189-93.

mausoleum was built over it. In the year 1282 [1865-66] Mollâ Ḥasan ᶜAli Ḥasani, who was one of the ulama of Gilân, sold shares and collected funds for the renovation of the mausoleum. He had the mausoleum enlarged, but he died before it was completed. The late Ḥâjji Mollâ Rafiᶜ also built a monumental portal there. According to reports, in the time of the administration of the governor ᶜAbdollah Khân,[157] funds were provided by the state treasury for the repair of this shrine, but they were not used. This shrine is highly venerated; the people believe in it completely and are devoted to it. It is a public place of refuge [*bastgâh*].[158] Vowing and swearing by it is considered to be very efficacious.

Another is the mausoleum of Âqâ Sayyed Abu Jaᶜfar, who is said to be one of the sons of Ḥażrat-e Musâ ebn-e Jaᶜfar.

Another is the mausoleum of Âqâ Fakhrâ, who is said to be the son of an emâm.

Another is the mausoleum of Chelleh-khâneh, at which they say some ascetics stayed for forty days [of self-mortification]. [38]

THE TAKYEHS OF RASHT

[Rasht] has about fifteen or sixteen *takyeh*s of various sizes.[159] The best known of these takyehs are listed below; at present, the Ḥaydari[160] and the Neᶜmati[161] orders are practiced.

---

[157] ᶜAbdollah Khân, often referred to as "the Governor" (*vâli*), was designated by Kamrân Mirzâ the Nâyeb os-Salṭaneh to replace Żiâ ol-Molk as administrator of Gilân in March, 1879. According to Rabino, *Provinces*, pp. 483-84, he held the post for seven years, during which he exploited the populace mercilessly; finally, his brother was chased out of Lahijân and he himself was replaced as governor by Moshir os-Salṭaneh in 1884, just prior to Farâhâni's visit. On the political feuding that this may have produced, see Farâhâni's account of the bazaar fire, which follows below, p. 43.

[158] Accused criminals or other individuals sought by government authorities in Iran could claim sanctuary (*bast*) within the precincts of certain mosques or shrines; as long as they remained there, they were immune to arrest by the secular authorities. See, for example, Browne, *Year Amongst the Persians*, p. 174.

[159] *Takyeh*, literally "pillow" or "resting place," originally referred to any place where a Sufi saint had stayed and thus, by extension, a retreat or lodge for members of the institutionalized Sufi (mystical) orders. (See Hughes, *Dictionary*, p. 626.) In Iran, as a Shi'ite country, the takyeh was really little more than a hall used as a place for performance of passion-plays (*taᶜzeyyeh*). In this sense, it might almost be translated as "theater." See Jean Calmard, "Le Mécénat des representations de ta'ziye. I. Les Précurseurs de Nâṣeroddin Châh," *Le Monde Iranien et l'Islam* 2(1974):73-126, and "Le Mécénat des representations de ta'ziye. II. Les Débuts de règne de Nâṣeroddin Châh," *Le Monde Iranien et l'Islam* 4(1976-77):133-62; Samuel Peterson, "The Ta'ziyeh and Related Arts," in Peter Chelkowski (ed.), *Ta'ziyeh: Ritual and Drama in Iran* (New York, 1979), pp. 64-74. On the many takyehs in Rasht, see Rabino, *Provinces*, pp. 86-88; Sotudeh, *Âstârâ*, 1:268, 277.

[160] A Sufi order founded by Quṭb od-Din Ḥaydar az-Zâvoji (d. 630/1234). It was centered in northeastern Iran but later spread to Syria, Anatolia, and India. See J. Spencer Trimingham, *The Sufi Orders in Islam* (London, 1971), p. 39.

[161] A Sufi order founded by Nur od-Din Moḥammad ebn-e ᶜAbdollah (730-834/1330-1431), who claimed to be a descendant of the fifth Shi'ite Imam, Moḥammad Bâqer.

The ᶜIsâ Khân Eᶜtemâd od-Dowleh[162] takyeh which is next to the government building; the Vâdiollah takyeh; the Âqâ Fakhrâ takyeh; the Ṣayqelân takyeh; the Ḥâjji Moḥammad Karim the Merchant takyeh; and the Khomeyrân takyeh.

THE PUBLIC BATHS OF RASHT

The public baths of Rasht are opposite the Kucheh ["paved street"?]. Because of the quantity of moisture [in the soil], they cannot be excavated very deeply. There are seventeen public baths, of which the best, largest, and cleanest are the Abu Ṭâleb baths, the Nâyeb baths, the Mashhadi Âqâ Bozorg baths, and the Moᶜin ot-Tojjâr baths.

CARAVANSERAIS OF RASHT

There are twenty-two or -three commercial caravanserais in the city. A list of the most reputable and best known of these is appended: the Golshân caravanserai; the Malek ot-Tojjâr caravanserai; the Mirzâ Baba caravanserai; the Seh Dowlat caravanserai; the Taqi Ḥâjji Mollâ Rafiᶜ caravanserai; the Gomrok-e Kohneh caravanserai; the Shisheh Bozorg caravanserai; the Shisheh Kuchek caravanserai; the Kâshi-hâ caravanserai; the Akbar Khân Bayglarbayki caravanserai; and four Armenian caravanserais.

THE CITADEL

The citadel and offices of government officials in this city are in the Hedâyat Khân palace, which originally was built by Hedâyat Khân. It comprises an inner room, an outer room, a private chamber, and a stable. Moḥammad Qâsem Khân, the governor, made extensive repairs to it. Nâṣer ol-Molk also made some repairs during his first governorship.

THE WATER AND CLIMATE IN RASHT

The houses in this city are very spacious. The roofs are made of red tiles [*sofâl*]. [39] The climate of this city is very oppressive and humid. The worst area of Gilân, in respect to climate, is the city of Rasht and the borough of Râneku.

In all of Gilân, water for drinking and other uses is well water. Every house has one or two wells that are dug down from one to three zarᶜ until they reach water. The well water has an odor; that is, it is unpleasant and causes gas. The odor is especially bad from morning until noon. There is

---

He died in the Iranian town of Mâhân, where his tomb became the spiritual center of the order. See Trimingham, *Sufi Orders*, pp. 101-2. Rabino, *Provinces*, p. 479, mentions a bloody clash between the members of this order and its Ḥaydari rivals in 1861.

[162] ᶜIsâ Khân, known as Vâli and Eᶜtemâd od-Dowleh (d. 1278/1861-62), was the son of Amir Qâsem Khân Qâjâr-e Qavânlu and held the governorship of Gilân in 1271/1854-55. He received the honorific of Eᶜtemâd od-Dowleh in 1275/1858-59. See Bakhash, *Iran*, p. 91; Bâmdâd, *Rejâl*, 2:510-12.

very little running water in the alleys in Gilân except in the districts of Kuh Pâyeh and Ṭavâlesh which do have running water in the alleys.

In the city of Rasht, Hedâyat Khân established a canal and a barrage to bring water from the Gowhar Rud River, which is located at the edge of the city, to the center of the city so that all the alleys would have running water. Later, the barrage was ruined, but the waterless canals remain in the alleys.

It rains in all four seasons in this city. Sometimes, one will not see the sun for forty or fifty days. One of the curiosities about this is that any day the jackals howl and the dogs bark back at them, the sun will shine the next day. If they don't bark back, the sun will not shine. This has been written about in old books about conditions in Gilân and has repeatedly been proven correct by experience. If it rains in Gilân in the summertime, the weather will necessarily be cold and this will be a disaster since the silkworm eggs will be destroyed and a loss sustained. If it does not rain, then first of all there will be many diseases and, second, the rice crop will be a complete loss. So whether it rains or not in the summertime, agriculture will inevitably suffer either way. [40] It is very seldom that both crops will be good in the same year, and that a disaster does not befall one of them.[163]

It both snows and sleets in this city, but it snows more than it sleets. Some years it snows a great deal in Gilân, and some years it does not snow at all. The popular belief is that every year that it snows a lot, that year will have good rice and silkworm crops and few diseases. When it snows, they prepare pits for storing ice in the highlands and hills. As soon as the snow hits the ground, they heap it up in those pits and cover it with herbage called *karaf*[164] and pile dirt up over it so that it stays cold naturally. That herbage protects the snow and ice, which they use in summertime, from the heat. Every year that it doesn't snow, the trees blossom two or three times and yield two crops. When the snow and ice are very scarce, the people suffer in summertime. For the well-to-do, ice and snow are brought to the city of Rasht from Mt. Dalfak,[165] which is near Raḥmatâbâd in ᶜAmmârlu.

[163] On the importance of sericulture in Rasht and the problems which affected it (such as the silkworm plague of 1866), see W. Barthold, *An Historical Geography of Iran* (translated by Svat Soucek; Princeton, 1984), pp.235-37; H. Rabino, *L'Industrie séricole en Perse* (Montpelier, 1910); Adamec, *Historical Gazetteer*, 1:538-39; Ahmad Seyf, "Silk Production and Trade in Iran in the 19th Century," *Iranian Studies* 16(1985):51-71.

[164] Manuchehr Sotudeh, *Farhang-e gilaki* (Tehran, 1332/1953), discusses the term *kherf* in Gilaki dialect, which may be the plant (*Ahyrium filix*) Farâhâni has in mind.

[165] Also known as Darfak Kuh; see Adamec, *Historical Gazetteer*, 1:135. Eastwick, *Journal*, p. 325, noted the perennial ice caverns on its summit.

COMMERCE IN RASHT

The goods of Gilân which can be traded are rice and silk exclusively. Woven goods and embroidery[166] are also common and are both exported and used locally. Some villages make very good silk stuffs. Ḥâjji Moḥammad Ḥasan Amin-e Dâr oż-Żarb ["the Mintmaster"][167] recently built a silk-weaving factory beside the Kalâseh Rud[bâr?] River, which is now very successful.

The common measure of weight in Gilân is the *mann-e shâh*. Oil and other things which are imported from Russia are measured by the Russian pood, which is equivalent to five and a half *mann-e tabriz*.[168] Fruits, straw, fodder, firewood, coal, etc. are measured by the load, not by weight. [41] Rice is measured by the *kayl*.[169] The kayl there varies. In some districts, the kayl is one mann-e shâh, and in other places it is half a mann more. The *quti* there is four kayls (in the new kayls). The kayl of some districts used to be one mann and a fraction, so that a quti, which is four kayls, was about three mann according to the *shâh* weights. Some districts, such as Râneku and Pashmechâh[170] of Lâhijân, have a kayl equal to half a mann and a fraction, so that one of its qutis, which is four kayls, equals two and a half mann-e shâh.

DIET OF THE PEOPLE OF GILÂN

The most common foods of the people of Gilân are rice, fowl, fish, and green vegetables. The varieties of waterfowls, poultry, and fish are

---

166 The terms used here, *shaʿrbâfi* and *golduzi*, are actually untranslatable technical terms for two local crafts in Rasht, the former a variety of weaving finely spun silk and the latter a way of embroidering cloth with pictures of flowers.

167 Also known simply as Amin oż-Żarb (1253-1316/1837-99), he was the most prominent businessman and entrepreneur during the reign of Nâṣer od-Din Shâh, called by E. G. Browne, *The Persian Revolution of 1905-1909* (Cambridge, 1910), pp. 407-8, "one of the richest men in Persia." He has attracted the attention of historians not only because of his role as the leading capitalist of his day but also because of his close association with the Muslim reformer Jamâl od-Din ol-Afghâni. An autobiographical notice may be found in *Yaghmâ* 15(1341/1962-63):29; he is also the subject of a monograph by Khosrow Moʿtażed, *Ḥâjj Amin oż-Żarb: Târikh-e tejârat va sarmâyeh goẕâri sanʿati dar irân* (Tehran 1987); see also Bâmdâd, *Rejâl,* 3:348-62; Z. Z. Abdullaev, *Promyshlennost i zarozhdenie rabochego klassa Irana v kontse XIX-nachale XX vv.* (Baku, 1963) as translated in Charles Issawi, *The Economic History of Iran 1800-1914* (Chicago, 1971), pp. 43-48. On the silk-reeling factory, see Sotudeh, *Âstârâ*, 1:302; Abdullaev/Issawi, p. 48.

168 The weight of the *mann-e tabriz* ("mann of [the city of] Tabriz") varied from time to time and place to place but was generally equivalent to 2.9-3.2 kg. The *mann-e shâh* was double the weight of the mann of Tabriz (i.e., about 6 kg.). The weight of the Russian pood was 16.38 kg., in good accord with Farâhâni's calculations. See Hinz, *Masse und Gewichte*, pp. 17-20; Issawi, *Economic History of Iran*, p. 389.

169 The kayl was a measure of volume as well as weight; Hinz, *Masse und Gewichte*, p. 40, does not give a value for Iran but mentions 22.08 liters/17 kg. for the kayl of Damascus. Rabino, *Provinces*, pp. 66-67, discusses the local Gilâni weights and gives a value of one and a quarter mann-e shâh for the kayl.

170 Dehkhodâ, *Loghatnâmeh*, 11:378 has Pashmchâh. Sotudeh, *Âstârâ*, 2:79 suggests Pâshmechâh; Farâhâni himself uses this form of the name below, Part Seven, p. 320.

excellent. Good, fragrant greens are to be found. They consume bread infrequently, unless someone has been to [Persian] ᶜErâq and grown accustomed to eating bread. The peasants have an aversion to eating bread and never consume it.[171]

FRUITS OF GILÂN

There are also many kinds of fruit in Gilân, except almonds and pistachios which are not grown. Its citrus fruits are good and plentiful, especially in the areas in which the cold and snow are less, such as Enzeli and Râneku.

As for the non-citrus produce in Gilân, only the plums, pears, and quinces are excellent. The broad-beans and lettuce of Gilân are very good and commendable.

THE ULAMA OF RASHT

Ḥâjji Mir[zâ] ᶜAbd ol-Bâqi; Mollâ Moḥammad ᶜAli the Emâm Jomᶜeh ["leader of the Friday prayers"]; and Âqâ Shaykh Javâd, [42] the son of the late Ḥâjji Mollâ Rafiᶜ.[172]

NOTABLES OF RASHT

Mirzâ Moḥammad ᶜAli Khân Amin-e Divân; Ḥâjji Mirzâ Naṣir, known as Ṭâyefeh, who is one of the clan of Ḥâjji Samiᶜ; Ḥâjji Mirzâ Naṣir, known as Ḥâjji Ḥâkem, of the clan of Ḥâjji Samiᶜ; Akbar Khân Bayglarbayki and his brothers, the sons of Mirzâ ᶜAbd ol-Vahhâb the Mostowfi; ᶜAbd ol-Ḥosayn Khân the son of Maḥmud Khân; Ḥâjji Moḥammad Ḥasan Moᶜin ot-Tojjâr; and Moḥammad Âqâ-ye Malek ot-Tojjâr.

OFFICES OF FOREIGN STATES

There are two consulates of foreign countries in the city of Rasht. One is the consulate of Russia, and the other is the consulate of England. There are about two thousand Armenians in the city and surrounding areas, some of whom are subjects of the state of Iran and some of whom are foreign nationals.

THE GILÂN DISTRICT

The city of Rasht is a provincial capital and the residence of the governor-general [*vâli*]. The representative of the central government for business matters and the like is Ḥâjji Mirzâ Naṣir, known as Ḥâjji Ḥâkem, who has held the governorship of the city for several years.

---

171 Cf. Adamec, *Historical Gazetteer*, 1:196; Rabino, *Provinces*, p. 29; Orsolle, *Caucase*, p. 171.

172 Golzâri, p. 42 has "...[and] the son of the late Ḥâjji Mollâ Rafiᶜ." On ᶜAbd ol-Bâqi see Nâṣer od-Din Shâh, *Diary*, p. 14; Eᶜtemâd os-Salṭaneh, *Ma'âs̱er*, pp. 175, 220; Gilâni, *Târikh-e ᶜolamâ*, pp. 107-8; on Mollâ Moḥammad see Eᶜtemâd os-Salṭaneh, *Mer'ât ol-boldân* (Tehran, 1294-96/1877-79), 3:vii (in the appendix or *Sâlnâmeh*); this latter source also mentions an Âqâ Shaykh Javâd among the ulama of Rasht.

THE LÂHIJÂN DISTRICT[173]

The residence of the governor [*ḥâkem*] is the borough of Lâhijân. Its governor is Mirzâ Ḥasan Khân, the son of Amin-e Divân. For more than one hundred and fifty years, the governorship there has belonged to Amin-e Divân and his ancestors, except for the five years that Fażlollah Khân, the brother of ᶜAbdollah Khân, was the governor.

THE LASHTENESHÂ DISTRICT[174]

[This] used to be considered part of Lâhijân. Most of its villages are the crown property of Khosrow Khân the Georgian.[175] These crown villages are entrusted to Amin os-Solṭân. Akbar Khân Bayglarbayki is the governor there on behalf of Amin os-Solṭân. The former has himself appointed someone else [to serve in his stead].

THE FUMAN DISTRICT[176]

[This] does not have a specific borough as the residence for a governor. [43] Its governor is ᶜAbd ol-Ḥosayn Khân ebn-e Maḥmud ebn-e Ḥâjji Qâsem Khân ebn-e Ḥâjji Moḥammad Khân.[177] [His family] has governed this district for years. ᶜAbd ol-Ḥosayn Khân always resides in the city of Rasht and sends out a deputy in his stead.

THE TULEM DISTRICT[178]

[This] is part of Fuman and is one of the crown properties of Manuchehr Khân Moᶜtamad od-Dowleh. It is beside the sea. Its government is sometimes held by the governor of Fuman, and sometimes it is part of the administration of Gilân.

THE RÂNEKU DISTRICT[179]

[This includes] three districts and is called the "Three Districts" [*Boluk-e s̱alâs̱eh*]. Its governor's residence is at the river harbor town [*forżeh*] of Langarud. There is a river there which joins the sea at the

---

[173] Cf. Sotudeh, *Âstârâ*, 2:69-214; Mirzâ Ebrâhim, *Safarnâmeh*, pp. 162-64; Rabino, *Provinces*, pp. 291-334.

[174] Text: Lashtehneshâ; this name is variously spelled in Persian as well as in English transliterations; the main town of the district is also called Jowrshar. See Sotudeh, *Âstârâ*, 1:423-60; Mirzâ Ebrâhim, *Safarnâmeh*, p. 199; Rabino, *Provinces*, pp. 248-58.

[175] He was appointed to the governorship of Gilân in 1234/1818-19 by Fatḥ-ᶜali Shâh and took advantage of his office by buying up most of the villages in the district at artificially low prices; see Bâmdâd, *Rejâl*, 1:479-80; Rabino, *Provinces*, pp. 250-52 and 477-78.

[176] See Mirzâ Ebrâhim, *Safarnâmeh*, pp. 194-196; Sotudeh, *Âstârâ*, 1:154-69; Rabino, *Provinces*, pp. 161-81. The *Farhang-e joghrâfiyâ-ye irân* (reprint; Tehran, 2535/1976), 2:202, vocalizes this name as Fowman.

[177] Also known as Modir ol-Molk; he became governor of Fuman in 1295/1878; see Bâmdâd, *Rejâl*, 5:141. On this family, see Rabino, *Provinces*, pp. 179-81.

[178] See Mirzâ Ebrâhim, *Safarnâmeh*, pp. 197-98; Sotudeh, *Âstârâ*, 1:226-29; Rabino, *Provinces*, pp. 191-96. *Farhang*, 2:65, has Tulam.

[179] On Raneku[h] and Langarud, see Mirzâ Ebrâhim, *Safarnâmeh*, pp. 158-60; Sotudeh, *Âstârâ*, 2:215-306; Rabino, *Provinces*, pp. 335 sqq.

estuary of Chomkhâleh.[180] It is a large port. Its governor is Mirzâ Musâ Khân ebn-e Mirzâ Mahdi Khân ebn-e Mirzâ ᶜAbd ol-Bâqi ebn-e Ḥâjji Mahdi, known as Ḥâjji Âqâ Bozorg. All of these have had the title of Monajjem-bâshi ["Chief Astrologer"], and they have held the governorhip there for years.[181]

THE DAYLAMÂN DISTRICT[182]

Its governor's residence is the populous village named Siâh Kal.[183] Its governor is Ḥabibollah Khân ebn-e Abu'l-Fatḥ Khân ebn-e Moḥammad Reżâ Khân.[184] The governorship of this district has belonged to [this family] for years.

THE SHAFT DISTRICT[185]

[It] has a small borough which is the governor's residence. Previously, the sons of Naṣir Khân and Neᶜmatollah Khân were governors there. Six or seven years ago that clan was deposed from the administration. Every year [the post] is given to someone else. This year the son of Mirzâ ᶜAbd ol-Vahhâb is the governor.

THE PORT OF ENZELI

[It] and the Four Ports [Chehâr Forżeh[186]]: since Akbar Khân Bayglarbayki is in charge of the border and the customs there, [44] the governorship there has also belonged for several years to Bayglarbayki, who appoints a deputy.

THE RAḤMATÂBÂD DISTRICT[187]

[It] does not have a borough for the governor's residence. Its governorship used to change every year. For some years now, it has been under Mirzâ Moḥammad ᶜAli, the son of Mirzâ Fatḥ-ᶜali of the clan of Ḥâjji Samiᶜ.

---

180 The name of a village and the eastern arm of the Langarud River; see Adamec, *Historical Gazetteer*, 1:132; Rabino, *Provinces*, p. 344. *Farhang*, 2:82, has Chamkhâleh.

181 On this family, see Bâmdâd, *Rejâl*, 4:165-68; Rabino, *Provinces*, pp. 344-45; Fasâ'i/ Busse, *Persia*, pp. 80, 85, 110; Hedâyat, *Rowżat oṣ-ṣafâ*, 9:409-10.

182 See Mirzâ Ebrâhim, *Safarnâmeh*, p. 199; Sotudeh, *Âstârâ*, 2:13-67; Rabino, *Provinces*, pp. 277-90.

183 Text: Gol. On the name, see Sotudeh, *Âstârâ*, 1:14; Adamec, *Historical Gazetteer*, 1:610; Rabino, *Provinces*, p. 277; *Farhang*, 2:161. Minorsky, *Ḥodûd*, p. 390 says that this is the name of the district southeast of Lâhijân in the environs of Barfjân.

184 On the rise of this family and its role in destroying Hedâyat Khân in early Qâjâr times, see Rabino, *Provinces*, p. 281.

185 See Mirzâ Ebrâhim, *Safarnâmeh*, pp. 191-93; Sotudeh, *Âstârâ*, 1:216-24; Rabino, *Provinces*, pp. 197-208.

186 Sotudeh, *Âstârâ*, 1:231-39 gives the name as Chehâr Fariżeh; *Farhang*, 2:87, has "Çahar farize." On these four ports (known by various names), see also Mirzâ Ebrâhim, *Safarnâmeh*, p. 202; Rabino, *Provinces*, p. 146.

187 The name Raḥmatâbâd is often linked with or used interchangeably with Rudbâr. On the two districts, see Mirzâ Ebrâhim, *Safarnâmeh*, pp. 181-90; Sotudeh, *Âstârâ*, 1:461-80; Rabino, *Provinces*, pp. 109-214, 270-76.

THE RUDBÂR ZAYTUN [OLIVE] DISTRICT

Olives are its chief crop and source of income.[188] Its borough is on the road to Qazvin. Its governorship used to vary. This year it is under Mirzâ Ṭâher, the son of Mirzâ ᶜAbd ol-Vahhâb, who has appointed a deputy.

THE ᶜAMMÂRLU[189] DISTRICT

This is [the same as] Kuh Pâyeh. It has crops of rice and silk as well as wheat, barley, other crops, and livestock. It is adjacent to the district of Qazvin and is the link [*barzakh*] between Gilân and [Persian] ᶜErâq. Its governorship varies. This year, it is under the son of Mirzâ ᶜAbd ol-Vahhâb, who has appointed a deputy.

THE GASKAR[190] DISTRICT

It does not have a borough and its governorship always used to change. This year it is under Akbar Khân Bayglarbayki, who appointed his own deputy.

THE MÂSULEH DISTRICT[191]

It does not have any cultivation of rice or silkworms, but it does have barley and wheat. Most of its men are excellent blacksmiths and iron workers. It is adjacent to the territory of Ṭârom and Zanjân. Its governorship varies; this year it was under ᶜAbd ol-Ḥosayn Khân.

THE ROSTAMÂBÂD AND KOHDOM DISTRICT

[This] does not have a specific deputy or governor since its proprietors are mostly landlords in the city of Rasht. The governor of Gilân collects the taxes for each village from its proprietor in the city of Rasht.

ṬAVÂLESH[192]

[This] is one of the dependencies of Gilân. It has winter-pasture and summer-pasture villages. The crops and produce of its winter estates are rice and silkworms, and the produce of its summer estates are wheat and barley. [Its] five districts, as determined, are: Kargân Rud,[193] [45] which has been administered for several years by Noṣratollah Khân;[194] Ṭâlesh

---

188 Cf. Adamec, *Gazetteer*, 1:547; Rabino, *Provinces*, pp. 51, 210.

189 This is a term used several times by Farâhâni to refer to the mountainous area along the Shâhrud between Qazvin and Gilân; it gets its name from the Kurdish ᶜAmmârlu tribe which Nâder Shâh established in that area. See Adamec, *Historical Gazetteer*, 1:382; Sotudeh, *Âstârâ*, 1:493-95, 501; Mirzâ Ebrâhim, *Safarnâmeh*, pp. 186-88; Rabino, *Provinces*, pp. 259-67.

190 Text: Kaskar. See Mirzâ Ebrâhim, *Safarnâmeh*, pp. 198-99; Sotudeh, *Âstârâ*, 1:187-97; Rabino, *Provinces*, pp. 153-60; Adamec, *Historical Gazetteer*, 1:185. *Farhang*, 2:281, suggests Gasgareh as the correct vocalization.

191 Cf. Sotudeh, *Âstârâ*, 1:129-40; Rabino, *Provinces*, pp. 183-90.

192 Another form of the name Ṭâlesh, i. e. the Caspian littoral from Gilân proper to the Muqân steppes. See Adamec, *Historical Gazetteer*, 1:641-42; Rabino, *Provinces*, pp. 89-100; Sotudeh, *Âstârâ*, 1:35-50; Mirzâ Ebrâhim, *Safarnâmeh*, pp. 212-17; Sayf od-Dowleh, *Safarnâmeh*, p. 42.

193 Text G-rgân Rud; see the sources cited in the preceding note. *Farhang*, 2:229 has Karkân.

194 The text in Mirzâ Ebrâhim, *Safarnâmeh*, p. 198, suggests that this name might be read Naṣrollah Khân.

Dulâb;[195] Asâlem;[196] the Shândarman[197] district; and the Mâsâ[198] district. The governorship of these four districts varies.

CONFLAGRATION IN THE BAZAAR OF RASHT

As it happens, I arrived in Rasht the evening of Sunday the sixth of the month of Shavvâl [19 July] and spent the night [before] the seventh at the house of Amin-e Divân.[199] Monday evening, Ḥâjji Mirzâ Naṣir Ṭâyefeh–we had been friends for a long time–came to visit and invited me to his home. I went to his house the night [before] Tuesday the eighth. After having dinner, sleeping, and awakening two hours before dawn, I perceived that Ḥâjji Mirzâ Naṣir and his son, Ḥâjji Moḥammad Âqâ, were awake and conversing. I inquired about the conversation and learned that the bazaar had caught on fire and there was a conflagration. They were about to gather up the household effects. I heard different accounts concerning the fire, as everyone told something according to his own suppositions. Some said that the fire was of natural causes: The night before, at six o'clock, a lightning bolt had struck the firewood at a cook's shop and kindled a fire. Others said that some cinders from the cook's shop had fallen on some brambles and firewood that were there, and as soon as it was kindled it spread to another in which there some kerosene. In that same kerosene-seller's shop, two or three mann of gunpowder had been brought so it could be sold covertly to villagers. When the fire reached the kerosene and gunpowder, it immediately flamed up fiercely and spread to a nearby forage-seller's shop. The night watchmen were informed, but they could not extinguish it.

Some said that a man named Ḥosayn, who was also known as Ḥosayn Khâldâr ["the Tattooed"] [46] and who was a famous brigand who had committed murders in the time of the governorship of ᶜAbdollah Khân, had recently been captured. Moshir os-Salṭaneh had put him to death three days previously, so some of the aforementioned's confederates set fire to the city in order to avenge his death, and specifically set fire to the firewood in the cook's shop.

It was the belief of others that rowdy partisans of ᶜAbdollah Khân, the [former] governor, were always getting together and looking for a way to

195 See Sotudeh, *Âstârâ*, 1:83-92; Rabino, *Provinces*, pp. 107-14.

196 Mirzâ Ebrâhim, *Safarnâmeh*, pp. 209-211; Sayf od-Dowleh, *Safarnâmeh*, pp. 41-42; Sotudeh, *Âstârâ*, 1:69-74; Rabino, *Provinces*, pp. 101-6.

197 Text: Shandarmin. See Mirzâ Ebrâhim, *Safarnâmeh*, p. 198; Adamec, *Gazetteer*, p. 599; Sotudeh, *Âstârâ*, 1:107-11; Rabino, *Provinces*, pp. 115-18.

198 Probably an orthographical error for Mâsâl; see Mirzâ Ebrâhim, *Safarnâmeh*, p. 198; Adamec, *Historical Gazetteer*, p. 441; Sotudeh, *Âstârâ*, 1:118-22; Rabino, *Provinces*, pp. 119-31; *Farhang*, 2:281.

199 This house was regarded as one of the finest in Gilân; although it is no longer in existence, there is a mention of it (with a good photograph) in Sotudeh, *Âstârâ*, 1:249.

ruin Moshir os-Salṭaneh, until that night when they made use of the opportunity to set fire to the firewood in the cook's shop and the fodder shop (which were next to each other); it then became a conflagration. In any case, that same night, the officials, ulama, notables, residents of the city, and people from the surrounding villages were alerted and gathered together. A large group of people, men and women, assembled in the alleys and streets. Some were sighing and groaning and crying; some were carrying off their belongings; some were upset and staring dumbfounded. Because of the degree of consternation, they were not among those who were extinguishing the fire nor did they have implements for putting it out. The fire blazed up so much that one could not approach closer than fifty paces [to it]. All [the people] were exerting themselves in carrying out the goods of the shops. The confusion reached a point where everyone was giving out money and goods to anyone without seeing or knowing [who they were], and those carrying things went anywhere they pleased. The porters carried away many of the people's possessions and did not return them. Some things fell into the hands of the destitute, and it was not known who had taken them.

The conflagration began at the sixth hour of the night and lasted until almost noon of Tuesday the eighth [21 July]; so it lasted for twelve hours. [47]

From an hour before dawn, the governor and many of the ulama, the sayyeds, and the notables were all trying to extinguish the fire. They were cutting the wood down [from buildings] with scythes and saws to isolate the blaze, but it did not help. The wailing of the men and women was loud; the city that night was like daytime. The homeowners whose houses were near the bazaar were carrying or moving their property and possessions to outlying places. Moshir os-Salṭaneh and the notables were weeping and showing remorse [in response to] the wails and complaints of the people. The women were cursing Moshir os-Salṭaneh loudly and reviling him: "You have brought this on us!" Among others, a sayyed addressed and rebuked Moshir os-Salṭaneh, "Your bad luck will burn up all Gilân!" The notables restrained the sayyed from saying such things. Finally, the fire was broken up and extinguished.

DAMAGE CAUSED BY THE FIRE

After putting out the fire, it was learned that about 1,150 shops in the bazaar, seventeen caravanserais, a mosque, a madrasah, a takyeh, and two public baths had burned. That is, the wood burned off the shops which had wooden coverings; some of the caravanserais were half burned up and some lost six or seven rooms; and the mosque, madrasah, and baths were partially burned. The loss of property, such as shops, caravanserais, and so on, was conjectured to be more than fifty thousand tomans. It was also said that the loss from smoke damage and loss of goods was seven or eight thousand tomans. Although after the fire, in order to insure that the things which had been lost could be found and not taken outside the city, the government issued a proclamation that no one could carry belongings outside the city without a permit, and even though many of the household goods that had disappeared were found and a few goods that had been lost were recovered from houses [48], nevertheless many things were still lost or had disappeared. In this fire not a single private home burned down, and no personal property or belongings at all were burned, and not a single man or woman perished. However, there was a Turkish fellow named Mashhadi Moḥammad who had some trust funds in a chest. At the time of the fire, out of great concern, he gave that chest to an unknown porter to carry to someone's house. The porter did not find so-and-so's house and carried it to someone else's house. When [the man] went after the porter and saw that the chest of funds had not arrived, he dropped dead at once in utter terror. They took up his bier. Later the money and the chest were both found. It was not known whether he also had funds other than those which had disappeared.

WEAKNESS OF MOSHIR OS-SALṬANEH'S ADMINISTRATION

Two things have caused the weakness of Moshir os-Salṭaneh's governorship and financial administration in Gilân.[200] One of these things was the fire. The other was that when Moshir os-Salṭaneh first went to Gilân for the purpose of handling financial matters, he supervised the finances with complete impartiality and unselfishness; he did not distinguish between the notables and the commoners. But greed appeared in his work during the second time he came as administrator. He and his employees collected exorbitant sums in return for reducing the taxes on people. They changed and altered completely the first tax-audit. Second, he knew that it would strengthen his administration if he colluded with the mollâs and the notables and threw their burdens on the shoulders of the commoners, so he acted in this manner. Since his actions were tainted by greed and self-interest, he did not settle matters quickly and was negligent. He did not give a correct financial statement to anyone, which everyone

[200] Rabino, *Provinces*, p. 484, confirms much of what Farâhâni suggests; he notes that Mirzâ Aḥmad Moshir os-Salṭaneh was appointed governor of Gilân in 1884 after protests over tax abuses by the former governor but was forced to leave after the fire of 1885. He was succeeded by his old rival ᶜAbdollah Khân. See also Eᶜtemâd os-Salṭaneh, *Ma'aṯer*, p. 32; Bâmdâd, *Rejâl*, 1:100-102 (with photographs).

knows is the proper thing to do. If he did give a statement to anyone, it would be confusingly erased, crossed out, or scratched up so that there was room for denial and dispute on every line of it, [49] and every phrase could be altered. Everything pertaining to his duties was ambiguous; nothing was known about how much the taxes for each district or person might be. If this was not at least suspected, when, after the previous reduction of taxes that the treasury had given Gilân, fifty thousand tomans in excess taxes were taken from Gilân, it was because it was done under circumstances such that no one would complain and everyone would be satisfied. Despite all this, Moshir os-Salṭaneh was only one person, and he did not compel anyone to give a "consideration" [*taᶜârrof*][201] to the government as well; whatever he collected as a "consideration" was for himself and not for other people. Thus the inhabitants of Gilân were satisfied and grateful for his administration.

No more than this can be written on this point.[202]

DEPARTURE FROM RASHT

I had arrived in Rasht the evening of the sixth of Shavvâl [19 July], and I stayed there for eight days. During those days [while] I was staying there, Amin-e Divân and his son Amir Khân the Sarhang[203] endeavored that they too might travel to the House of God. In the end, Amir Khân became my travelling companion. We left for Enzeli the morning of Monday the fourteenth of Shavvâl [27 July] amidst congratulations and good wishes. Amin-e Divân and some other notables escorted us to Pir Bâzâr. It is about one and a half farsakhs from Rasht to Pir Bâzâr. It has been built up all along the way, and on both sides are forest trees, silk trees, and cultivated areas. It is said that the most populous and prosperous lands of Gilân are these villages and fields between Rasht and Pir Bâzâr.

PIR BÂZÂR

Pir Bâzâr lies to the north of Rasht and is situated beside a stream. [50] It has a two storey caravansarai constructed of wood with several rooms, a portal, and stables. A fodder-store, green grocery, and coffeehouse are in front of this caravanserai. The proprietor of the caravanserai and the shops is named Ḥâjji Mir Qâsem, one of the distinguished landlords of Rasht. Pack-horses, saddles for rent, and freight wagons are always found in Pir Bâzâr for the purpose of moving or transporting goods and people.

---

[201] Any act of courtesy, respect or deference, including financial offerings, from one person to another. On the many nuances of this term, see William Beeman, *Language, Status and Power in Iran* (Bloomington, 1986).

[202] Two hemistichs from a poem by an unidentified author are quoted at this point in the text; they are omitted from this translation.

[203] "Sarhang" was a military rank roughly equivalent to colonel; see Curzon, *Persia*, 1:591.

Often several rowboats are stationed on the water at Pir Bâzâr waiting for cargo and passengers, especially on the days when the steamer is coming to or going from Enzeli. We rented one of those rowboats, which was large and had six oarsmen, for eight krans. We said farewell to those seeing us off, seated ourselves in the boat, and set out with Amir Khân, son of Amin-e Divân, and two or three servants whom we were sharing. By water, it is about five and a half farsakhs from Pir Bâzâr to Enzeli, which takes about four hours by rowboat. One farsakh of this distance is by river, which has fresh water. It is usually about ten z̲arᶜ wide. The banks of the river are forested or have attractive farms. After that, one comes to the Mordâb [lagoon]. The water is a little rough at the place where the river enters the Mordâb. Some places in the river and the Mordâb are shallow, so that the boat runs aground on the mud, but it is not dangerous. We arrived in Enzeli four hours before sunset and disembarked from the boat next to the customs house.

ENZELI

Enzeli[204] is a pleasant port and has great potential for prosperity in every respect. In all four seasons, it is green and pleasant. Tropical and cold-weather fruits [51] can be found there. In particular, its citrus fruits are excellent, inexpensive, and plentiful. The river is on one side of it, and the lagoon and the sea are on the two other sides; thus it has water on three sides and one side is dry land, which goes to Ṭavâlesh. Any place where one digs down two z̲arᶜ in the soil of Enzeli, fresh and wholesome water flows out. I have never seen another port as excellent as this in regard to the water supply and the good growth of citrus trees. Its resident households number about two thousand, so its population is approximately eight thousand people. It has 250 shops, three public baths, five or six mosques of various sizes, one church, twenty or thirty Armenian and foreign merchants, an arsenal, an armory, and three governmental buildings.

GOVERNMENTAL BUILDINGS

One is a tower called the Shams ol-ᶜEmâreh. It is a magnificent palace consisting of five storeys, to the east and north of which is the sea. All the storeys have porticos and galleries on all sides. It is built of brick and mortar, except for the galleries, which are of wood. Its ceilings are of

[204] Enzeli was founded in 1815 during the reign of Fatḥ-ᶜali Shâh. It remained a very modest settlement as late as 1859. As the Russians improved transport routes across the Caucasus and the Caspian, Enzeli gradually became Iran's most important port on the Caspian Sea. Its name was changed from Enzeli to Bandar-e Pahlavi by Reżâ Shâh in 1936; since the Iranian revolution the name has reverted to Enzeli. On the city, see Mirzâ Ebrâhim, *Safarnâmeh*, pp. 200-202; Sayf od-Dowleh, *Safarnâmeh*, pp. 39-41; Rabino, *Provinces*, pp. 133-52; Adamec, *Historical Gazetteer*, 1:165-67; Sotudeh, *Âstârâ*, 2:231-35.

painted wood. Every storey has furniture and furnishings such as beds, tables, chairs, etc.; the only thing is that they are somewhat worn out. The height of this tower is twenty-two Iraqi ẕarᶜ. This palace was begun by royal command at the time of the administration in Gilân of Mirzâ Saᶜid Khân,[205] the Minister of Foreign Affairs, but not finished. Mirzâ Moḥammad Ḥosayn Khezâneh, who served as deputy-governor on behalf of Moᶜayyer ol-Mamâlek the Neẓâm od-Dowleh,[206] finished it. The little that remained unfinished was completed during the administration of Moᶜtamad ol-Molk the Moshir od-Dowleh.[207] For the most part, Akbar Khân Bayglarbayki supervised the construction of this palace. Another of these buildings is known as the Moᶜtamad od-Dowleh palace, [52] which Manuchehr Khân Moᶜtamad od-Dowleh built according to [royal] orders during the first part of this ever-enduring [Qâjâr] dynasty. It is a very nice, two-storeyed building of brick and mortar. Another is known as the Ṣadrâ palace, which was constructed according to the instructions of Mirzâ Ḥosayn Khân Sepahsâlâr,[208] during his term as Prime Minister. This is an excellent palace. In the courtyards of all these palaces fruit-bearing citrus

[205] Mirzâ Saᶜid Khân Anṣâri (1231-1301/1816-84), known as Mo'tamen ol-Molk, was secretary to the Grand Vizier Amir Kabir and served as governor of Gilân in 1286/1869-70. See Bakhash, *Iran*, p. 386; Bâmdâd, *Rejâl*, 2:66-70. This and Farâhâni's subsequent comments on the construction of the tower are confirmed by Nâṣer od-Din Shâh, *Diary*, p. 16. There is a sketch of the building in Benjamin, *Persia and the Persians*, p. 25, and a good photograph in A. V. W. Jackson, *Constantinople to the Home of Omar Khayyam* (New York, 1911), facing p. 82; see also Orsolle, *Caucase*, p. 150; Sayf od-Dowleh, *Safarnâmeh*, p. 40.

[206] These titles were held by two Qâjâr officials, Dust ᶜAli Khân Moᶜayyer ol-Mamâlek and his son Dust Moḥammad Khân. Dust ᶜAli Khân held the governorship of Gilân in 1283/1866-67 and again in 1288/1871-72. As his title Moᶜayyer ol-Mamâlek ("Assayer of the Empire") suggests, he was primarily associated with affairs concerning the treasury and mint. On this family, see Dust ᶜAli Khân Moᶜayyer ol-Mamâlek, *Rejâl-e ᶜaṣr-e nâṣeri* (Tehran, 1361/1983), pp. 33-42 and 143-57; Bakhash, *Iran*, p. 382; Fasâ'i/Busse, *Persia*, p. 374; Bâmdâd, *Rejâl*, 1:495-500; Benjamin, *Persia and the Persians*, pp. 206-13 [Persian translation in *Yâdgâr* 4/v(1326/1947-48):61-67].

[207] Yaḥyâ Khân Moshir od-Dowleh (1247-1309/1831-92), also known as Moᶜtamed ol-Molk, in addition to an important career of his own, is noteworthy as the brother of Nâṣer od-Din Shâh's powerful Prime Minister Mirzâ Ḥosayn Khân Moshir od-Dowleh Sepahsalâr. Yaḥya Khân inherited the title Moshir od-Dowleh after his brother's death in 1881. He was very active in the Foreign Ministry and held posts in Bombay, Tiflis, and Istanbul. See Bakhash, *Iran*, p. 385, etc.; Nashat, *Reform*, passim (esp. pp. 25-42); Bâmdâd, *Rejâl*, 4:438-72; ᶜAbbâs Eqbâl, "Yaḥyâ Khân Moshir od-Dowleh," *Yâdgâr* 3/i(1325/1946-47):32-51.

[208] Prime Minister under Nâṣer od-Din Shâh from 1871-73; see the preceding note. Discussions of his career may be found in many books on Qâjâr Iran; particular reference may be made to Hafez Farmayan, "The Forces of Modernization in Nineteenth Century Iran: A Historical Survey," in William Polk & Richard Chambers (eds.), *Beginnings of Modernization in the Middle East* (Chicago, 1968), pp. 129-32; Nashat, *Reform*, passim; Bâmdâd, *Rejâl*, 1:406-26; Khân Malek-e Sâsâni, *Siâsatgarân-e dowreh-ye qâjâreyyeh* (Tehran, 1338-45/1960-67), 1:1-57; Eᶜtemâd os-Salṭaneh, *Ṣadr ot-tavârikh* (Tehran, 1349/1970), pp. 260-82.

trees have been planted in a regular pattern, and some flowers and bulbs have also been set out. [The gardens] are extremely clean and neat.

THE ARSENAL

The arsenal is also next to the sea and is unfinished. There are about twenty cannons in it which they say Ḥâjji Mirzâ Âqâsi[209] cast, with Amin-e Divân as overseer, during the reign of the late Shâh [Moḥammad Shâh]. Many armory implements which were made there at the time of Ḥâjji Mirzâ Âqâsi used to be [kept] in it, but now most of the equipment is ruined and wasted. For example, there is a chain which was made for the Ghâziân[210] bridge. About sixty artillerymen, who are relieved each year, are always garrisoned in Enzeli. There are also Anzâni[211] riflemen [posted there] who receive a salary from the treasury for this purpose. However, they do not have a commander, nor were the guards ever at their posts. There is a tall lighthouse near the arsenal that was built at the initiative of the state treasury in order to shine a lamp to guide ships at night. About fifty tomans are collected for this purpose from the treasury. Each night they light an oil lamp, the expenses for which are only six or seven tomans.

A small steamboat belonging to the state of Iran [53] is always anchored across from the government building, and several government boats are also there. The captain of the ship is someone named Âqâ who was a native of Baku. He was a Russian subject who married a woman in Enzeli and chose to live there. They say there are not more than ten or twelve employees of the ship whose salaries are no more than about three hundred tomans per year. The steamboat never leaves without authorization and permission from the government of Gilân. The steamboat goes only as far as the mouth of the Pir Bâzâr River.

---

209 Ḥajj Mirzâ ᶜAbbâs or Mollâ ᶜAbbâs of Erevan was Prime Minister under Moḥammad Shâh for 14 years. Although E. G. Browne, *Year Amongst the Persians*, p. 127, recorded some verses mocking his fondness for expenditures on cannons and irrigation projects, his reputation as a capable minister has been rehabilitated by more recent scholarship: See Eᶜtemâd os-Salṭaneh, *Ṣadr ot-tavârikh*, pp. 152-95; Ḥosayn Saᶜâdat Nuri, "Ḥâjj Mirzâ Âqâsi," *Yaghmâ* 20(1346/1867):17-25; idem, *Zendegi-ye Ḥâjj Mirzâ Âqâsi* (Tehran, 1356/1977); Bamdâd, *Rejâl*, 2:203-9; Fasâ'i/Busse, *Persia*, p. 241; Khân Malek-e Sâsâni, *Siâsatgarân*, 2:1-139.

210 Here and throughout the text the author spells the name of this place as Qâziân.

211 According to Sotudeh, *Âstârâ*, 1:235, Anzân is the name of a district near Astarâbâd; riflemen from there were conscripted for government service and posted to Enzeli beginning in 1230/1814-15. Rabino, *Provinces*, p. 140, also mentions the "Anezâni, descendant de quelques fusiliers d'Anezân dans l'Astarâbâd" sent to garrison Enzeli in 1815; he notes that they received "un traitement de 1.400 tomans."

212 According to Rabino, *Provinces*, p. 138, the customs office was usually in the hands of the Daryâbaygi family; perhaps this is another form of the name. See above, n. 145.

ADMINISTRATION

The official in Enzeli in charge of customs is Akbar Khân Bayglarbayki.[212] He is not personally involved in the administration because of his numerous other duties. His nephew Mirzâ ᶜEnâyatollah is entrusted with the business of the administration on his behalf, but the latter is young, inexperienced, and usually intoxicated or drunk. The administration of this important frontier post should be taken more seriously.

There is also an agent[213] in Enzeli who is the consular deputy on behalf of the Russian government.

THE MIÂN POSHTEH QUARTER

There is a place in Enzeli named Miân Poshteh[214] which is a small islet situated in the middle of the water. The heirs of Mirzâ ᶜAbd ol-Vahhâb the Mostowfi have a garden there named Yusofâbâd. The fields of this place formerly were very flourishing and desirable. Now it has become undesirable because of repeated water damage.

GHÂZIÂN

There are several villages situated beside the lagoon, such as Ghâziân, which is located across from Enzeli. It is crown property held by the treasury and is currently entrusted to Akbar Khân Bayglarbayki. [54] This village is also very well suited to be a prosperous place. It is possible to go via a dirt road from this village to all the districts of Rasht. [The road] runs eastward, alongside the sea, to the districts of Lashteneshâ, Lâhijân, and Langarud. One could construct a bridge between Ghâziân and Enzeli to connect them with each other. The breadth of the lagoon that enters the sea between Enzeli and Ghâziân is 360 z̲arᶜ. For 108 z̲arᶜ of these 360 z̲arᶜ, the depth of the water is from seven to eight z̲arᶜ. The depth of the rest is from half a z̲arᶜ to no more than three z̲arᶜ. The breadth of the entire lagoon is about two and a half farsakhs. Its length from Ghâziân to the Tulem district, which is in excess of three farsakhs, is crown property. There is fishing in several places along this lagoon under the auspices of the fishery concession.[215]

---

213 Both editions of the Persian text consistently read this word as *akhbat*. This is an obvious orthographical error; transposing the dots for the consonants "kh" and "b" would yield "j" and "n" respectively; i. e., the word should be *ajant* (agent.)

214 Cf. Mirzâ Ebrâhim, *Safarnâmeh*, p. 201; Rabino, *Provinces*, p. 145.

215 Text: *shilât*. In the Caspian region, particularly Gilân, there are certain areas along the banks of the the rivers flowing into the sea that are considered suitable for fishing and are thus permaı ently reserved for that purpose and leased yearly through bidding to fishermen. The leasehold includes the banks of the river and the parts of the river where fishing nets are cast as well as a number of buildings that serve as living quarters for fishermen during the fishing season and as places where fish are cleaned and stored before being sent to market. The entire location—that is, the fishing area, river bank, buildings, wharfs and wharfage—is called a *shil* (plural shilât). There may be several shils on one river;

THE FISHERY

The fishery [controls] fishing for edible and inedible[216] fish in the lagoon and the streams that belong to the state of Iran from the Atrak to Âstârâ.[217] At present it has been leased to Lianozov[218] the Armenian for 58,000 tomans. It is much more profitable than this amount. The places which are fished are as follows:

In Enzeli and Ghâziân; in the village of Mobârakâbâd; in the village of Jifehrud;[219] in Pir Bâzâr; in Kutomjân;[220] in Âbkenâr; in the crown property district of Tulem which is adjacent to the Mordâb [lagoon]; in the village of Bahamber that is part of the Gaskar district; at the mouth of the Safid Rud; in the village of Ḥasan-ᶜAli Deh and the village of Rudposht, which are both part of Lâhijân; at the mouth of the Langarud, which is two farsakhs from [the town of] Langarud and where the lagoon and stream enter the sea; in the villages of Kisom, Ebr[â]himsar, and Rashtâbâd which are all [55] part of Lâhijân and located beside the Safid Rud; in Sorkh Rud, which is part of Mâzandarân; in Farâ Konâr,[221] which is part of Mâzandarân; in Mashhadsar,[222] which is partly in Mâzandarân; in Jikrud, which is part of Mâzandarân; in Miân Kâleh,[223] which is part of Mâzandarân; in Lârim, which is part of Mâzandarân; in the village of Marz,[224] which is part of Tonakâbon;[225] in Qoltaq,[226] which is part of Astarâbâd; and in the Atrak.

---

there are thus hundreds of them throughout the Caspian region. As Farâhâni notes, they were monopolized at the time of his visit by a Russian entrepreneur (see below, n. 218). On this term, see Moḥsen Shafiᶜzâdeh, "Maᶜni-ye shilât," *Yâdgâr* 2/vi(1324/1945):33.

216 Literally, fish that are "lawful and unlawful" (for Muslims to eat according to the dietary laws of Islam). To simplify the translation, this has been translated here and in subsequent occurrences as "edible and inedible."

217 Text: Astarâ.

218 Text: Liânrof; the spelling of the name varies in different sources. A concession of fishing rights along the Persian coast of the Caspian was granted to the Lianozov brothers of Astrakhan as early as 1876 and renewed repeatedly thereafter until the abrogation of such concessions in the Pahlavi era. The most detailed account of this is Ebrâhim Taymuri, *ᶜAṣr bi khabari yâ târikh-e emteyâzât dar irân* (Tehran, 1332/1953-54), pp. 276-307, which gives the texts of the concessions and photographs of the concessionaires; see also Rouhallah Ramazani, *The Foreign Policy of Iran* (Charlottesville, 1966), pp. 225-26; Firuz Kazemzadeh, *Russia and Britain in Persia* (New Haven, 1968), p. 207; Adamec, *Historical Gazetteer*, 1:55 (s.v. Âstârâ), 1:166 (s.v. Enzeli), 1:199 (s.v. Gilân), 1:442 (s.v. Mashhad-i Sar); Rabino, *Provinces*, pp. 44, 139.

219 Usually known as Jafrud.

220 Kutomjân = Kotomjân.

221 Probably Farikanâr (Fereydun Kenâr); see Adamec, *Historical Gazetteer*, 1:170.

222 This fairly important port near the mouth of the Bâbol River became known as Bâbolsar during the Pahlavi period.

223 Perhaps Miân Kelâ? See Adamec, *Historical Gazetteer*, 1:457.

224 The same place as Marzeh today?

225 During the Pahlavi era this city was called Shâhsavâr (and is so indicated on most maps); since the Islamic Revolution, the name has reverted to Tonakâbon.

226 Golzâri, p. 55, has Q-t-l-q.

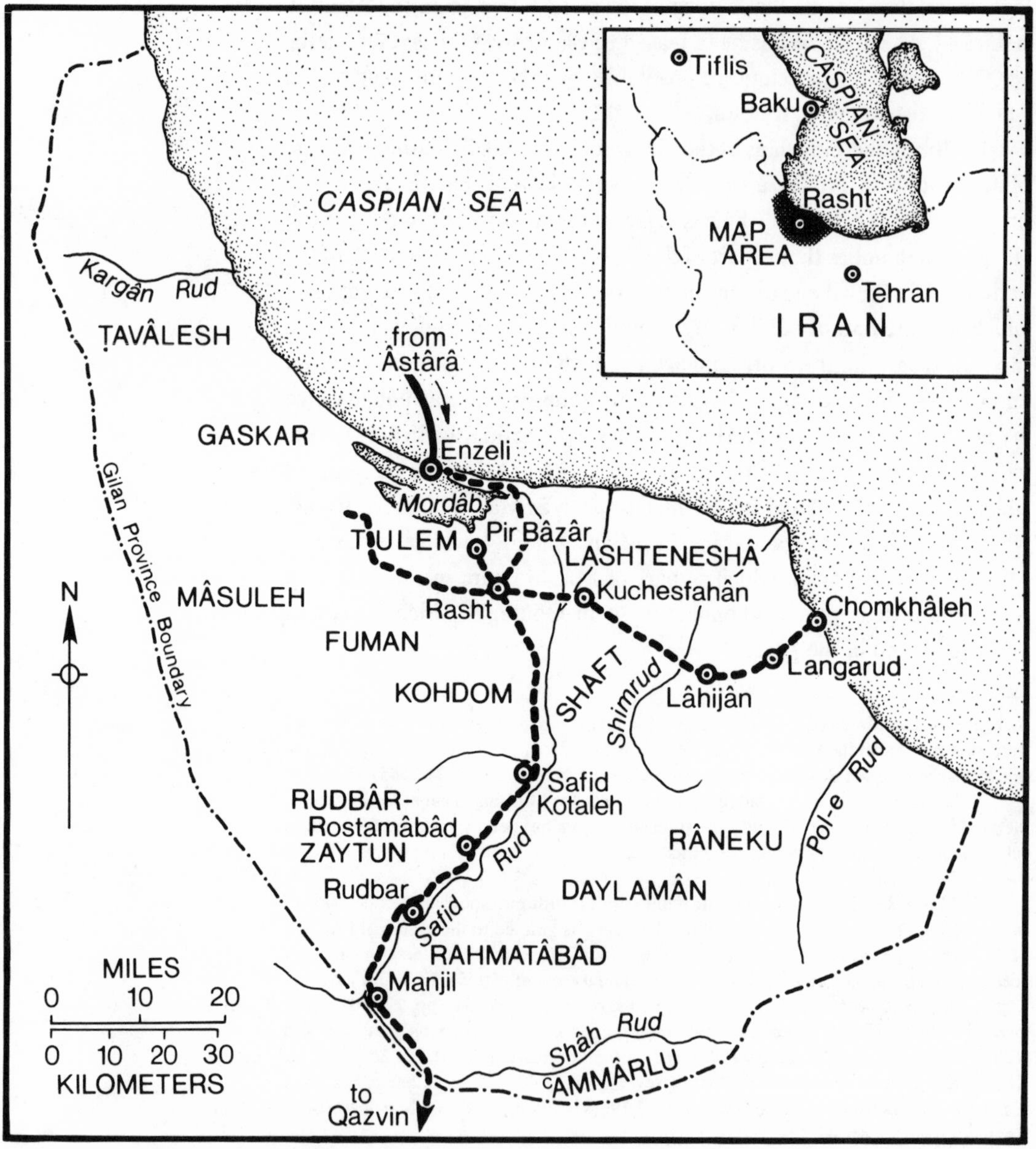

Map 3. Farâhâni's travels in the province of Gilân.

PART TWO
FROM BAKU TO BATUM

NAVIGATION ON THE CASPIAN SEA

Only ships of the Russian state and its subjects operate on the Caspian Sea.[1] There are five government steamships which transport the post and cargo as well as passengers. These government steamers call twice a week in summer and spring, once on Monday and once on Friday. At the end of fall and in winter, they call once a fortnight. As for the merchant vessels belonging to Russian subjects, there are several but they do not come and go with regularity. Because the Enzeli pier is in poor condition and the water is rough, especially in the channel between the sea and the lagoon, the boats do not approach close to Enzeli but remain anchored one or two farsakhs from Enzeli. The cargo and passengers are transported to land by launches. Although the oarsmen of Enzeli are extremely talented and skillful, nevertheless it is very frightful for the passengers in the launches because of the agitation of the waves, especially when it is windy or there are squalls and storms; one can never go by launch to the steamer [then.] Recently they brought a small steamer here from Russia. It is always stationed in Enzeli and is designed especially to carry the post for these five steamers. The cargo and passengers of each of the five steamers that go back and forth are transported from land by the small steamer; [56] no fare is collected. As for the commercial steamers, their cargo and passengers are conveyed from land as before by launches; a fare is collected for this.

STEAMSHIP FARES BETWEEN ENZELI AND BAKU

There are two offices near the Enzeli customs caravanserai– one for the agent of the government steamers, and one for the commercial steamers. Travellers must first go to these offices to

[1] The Caspian had been a virtual Russian lake since it was closed to Iranian warships by the Treaty of Golestân (1813). At the time of Farâhâni's journey, the Russian Kavkaz-Merkur ("Caucasus and Mercury") line, founded in 1861, dominated transport by this route: See Eastwick, *Journal*, 2:21; Curzon, *Persia*, 1:27; Jackson, *Constantinople*, pp. 82-83; Adamec, *Historical Gazetteer*, 1:166-67 (s.v. Enzali) and 1:535-36 (s. v. Rasht); Issawi, *Economic History of Iran*, pp. 160-65; Taymuri, ᶜ*Aṣr bi khabari*, pp. 250-73.

purchase and pick up tickets. The scale of fares for the steamers varies according to the date. Usually the fare from Enzeli to Baku by third class (which is on deck) is about five *manât*.[2] Second class (which is in the second [class] cabins) is nine manât. First class (which is in the first [class] cabins) is fourteen manât. Sometimes it may be more or less. The value of the manât fluctuates from three to three and a half Iranian krans. An account of that will be recorded in the proper place. They allow one *pood*[3] [of baggage], which is five and a half mann-e tabriz, for each passenger and do not collect a separate fare [for it]. Whenever a passenger has a load in excess of one pood, they weigh his baggage and collect a separate fare for the excess. This procedure applies only to the steamers which operate on this sea. Steamers on other seas do not restrict the load a passenger may have and do not require a separate fare.

THE SEA VOYAGE

Anyhow, we purchased tickets and, one hour before sunset, took seats on the small Russian steamer that comes to land. In a period of six minutes, we reached and boarded the government steamer named the *Constantine*.[4] [57] The steamer remained there taking on cargo until three hours of the night had passed; then it departed.

THE CASPIAN SEA

The Caspian Sea [*Baḥr-e Khazar*] has been called the Ṭabarestân Sea, the Jilân Sea, the Jorjân Sea, the Âbaskun Sea and the Khorasan Sea;[5] all of these are one and the same. According to what has been written, "Khazar" is the name of the son of Yâfes̱ ebn-e Nuḥ[6] the Prophet who, in the course of travelling, founded a city to the north of this sea near the Volga River[7] and named it after

---

[2] The term *manât* is derived from the Russian *moneta*, meaning simply coins or money, but is used in Persian as the rough equivalent of rouble. See Farâhâni's discussion of Russian currency and n. 148 below.

[3] Text: *put*. Farâhâni explains this and other Russian weights below, p. 64.

[4] This same ship is mentioned by several other travellers; mention may be made of the amusing accounts in Nâṣer od-Din Shâh, *Diary*, pp. 17, 424-26; Arnold, *Caravan*, 1:116-18.

[5] Jilân and Jorjân are Arabicized spellings of Gilân and Gorgân respectively. Âbaskun was an island port in the southeast of the Caspian Sea; it was submerged when the Oxus River temporarily changed course and emptied into the Caspian: See Le Strange, *Lands of the Eastern Caliphate*, pp. 376, 379, 456-57. Throughout this section, Farâhâni's account echoes that of Qazvini/Le Strange, *Nuzhat*, pp. 232-33. The traditional Muslim accounts of the Caspian have been summarized in Aḥmad Barimâni, *Daryâ-ye khazar* (Tehran, 1326/1947-48), pp. 10-22.

[6] The Arabic form for the name Japheth, son of Noah. The supposed descent of the Khazars from Japheth was a common idea: see D. M. Dunlop, *The History of the Jewish Khazars* (Princeton, 1954), pp. 12-14.

[7] The text has Atel, which was the old name for the Volga.

himself. The sea took the name of that city. After that, Jorjân, Jilân, Ṭabarestân, etc. flourished around that sea, and so the sea was called by the name of each [of them].

The length of this sea from east to west is about two hundred and sixty farsakhs; its breadth is about two hundred farsakhs. It is not deeper than 517 fathoms. Some have given its circumference as about 1,600 farsakhs. This sea does not have tides and does not connect with any other sea. It is very turbulent. There is mud and sediment on its bottom. There are no valuables[8] or profitable products in it except for fish, both edible and inedible.

On the eastern side of this sea are the Khᵛârazm and Bolghâr deserts[9] and some areas of Daylam, Ṭabarestân, and Jorjân.

On its western side are Kizliar,[10] Shirvân,[11] the territory of Lân,[12] and Derbent.[13] On its southern side are Gilân and Ṭavâlesh and some of Ṭabaristân, Astarâbâd, and a part of Turkistan.

On its northern side are the Qepchâq desert and the land of the Khazars and Ḥâjji Tarkhân.[14]

Many large and small rivers flow into this sea, among which are these:[15] [58]

The Gorgân[16] River, Atrak River, Terek River, Nekâ River,[17] Emba River,[18] Volga River,[19] Kuma River, Ural River, Kura River, Samur River, Shâh Rud River, Qezel Owzan River, Kalâseh Rud[bâr?] River, Gowhar Rud River, Shimrud[20] River, Lahijân

---

8 Literally, "jewels." Farâhâni has in mind such things as pearls and corals.

9 Khᵛârazm is the term for the area south of the Aral Sea; by Bolghâr desert, Farâhâni means the Russian steppes north of the Caspian.

10 Text: Qezlar. Kizliar is the name of both a gulf in the northern part of the Caspian Sea and a city near the delta of the Terek River in Daghestan; see A. M. Prokhorov (ed.), *Great Soviet Encyclopaedia* (New York, 1973-83), 12:533.

11 Muslim name for the provincial area around Baku, with its capital at Shemakha. See Barthold, *Historical Geography*, p. 228; Le Strange, *Eastern Caliphate*, pp. 179-81.

12 So in the text. The [A]Lân (Alans) were a people living near the Black Sea coast, not the Caspian. Farâhâni may have meant Arrân, the Muslim name for a province west of the confluence of the Kura and the Araxes, bordering Armenia. See Barthold, *Historical Geography*, p. 227; Le Strange, *Eastern Caliphate*, pp. 176-79.

13 Text: Bâb ol-abavât; read Bâb ol-abvâb (Derbent).

14 Ḥâjji Tarkhân is another name for Astrakhan; see EI_2, 1:721.

15 Farâhâni's list may be compared with the one given by Barimâni, *Daryâ-ye khazar*, pp. 27-46.

16 Text: Jorjân.

17 Text: Tekâ.

18 Text: Âmbâ.

19 Text: Atel (an archaic name for the Volga).

20 Text: Shemrud.

River, Harâz River,[21] Bâbol River, Châlus River, Tâlâr[22] River, Tejan[23] River, Marz River, Rudsar Stream, Langarud River, and the Pol-e Rud[24] River.

FROM ENZELI TO BAKU

From Enzeli to Baku is 350 verst[25] (an explanation of "verst" will be given in the proper place.)

Three hours after nightfall [before] Tuesday the fifteenth [Monday night, 27 July], the steamer left Enzeli. After travelling for nine hours, and first passing by the village of Kargân Rud, which is a port and is on Iranian territory and belongs to Asad Khân of Ṭavâlesh, it arrived at Âstârâ and stopped there.

ÂSTÂRÂ

Âstârâ is in the middle of a forest right on the border between Iran and Russia. There is a stream in it which is the demarcation between the territory of Iran and Russia. This side of the stream is part of Ṭavâlesh and belongs to Iran, and the other side is part of Russia. There are about two hundred households in both parts of Âstârâ.[26]

[At Âstârâ] a Russian customs officer comes from the shore to the steamer. He puts the ship's cargo into the ship's hold and seals the door of the hold. It is opened in Baku, so there can be no trickery in the ports along the way and nothing [can] be smuggled past the customs.

Also [at Âstârâ], an official in charge of passports collects and inspects the passenger's passports; the captain returns them to the owners in Baku lest there be some deception along the way. [59]

THE PORT OF LENKORAN

The steamer stayed in this port until one hour after noon taking on and unloading cargo and [then] set out. After a journey of three and a half hours, it arrived at Lenkoran and dropped anchor. Sal'yany[27] and Lenkoran are both ports and are near each other.[28]

---

21 Also spelled Harhaz; see Adamec, *Historical Gazetteer*, 1:225-26.

22 Text: Tâlâv.

23 Text: Tijan.

24 Text : Poleh-rud.

25 A Russian measurement of length equivalent to about 3,500 feet. See below, p. 68 and n. 61.

26 For more detailed descriptions of Âstârâ, see Mirzâ Ebrâhim, *Safarnâmeh*, pp. 218-19; Sotudeh, *Âstârâ*, 1:8-23.

27 Text: Sâlyân. Farâhâni must be referring to Sal'yany, although its location does not quite match his description. See Orsolle, *Caucase*, p. 147; Sayf od-Dowleh, *Safarnâmeh*, pp. 50-52.

28 Cf. Orsolle, *Caucase*, pp. 148-49; Sayf od-Dowleh, *Safarnâmeh*, pp. 46-48.

Lenkoran is the more populous. It has about fifteen hundred resident households, one hundred and fifty shops, several caravanserais, four or five mosques, and two churches. They say it has a very pleasant climate and is attractive. Varieties of fruit, such as pear, plum, apple, and quince, were brought on board the steamer for sale.

The steamer also stayed there for five hours and set out at five hours past nightfall [before] Wednesday the sixteenth [29 July].

A little past Sal'yany, the sea water is very muddy. They say the Kura[29] River flows into the sea a little further up, and that causes the water to become muddy.

According to accounts, there are two small islands between Sal'yany and Baku named Kuchuk ["Little"] Zireh and Boyuk ["Big"] Zireh.[30] Neither has any inhabited place that might be a port and a place for ships to stop. The steamer travels from Lenkoran to Baku in ten hours. Wednesday the sixteenth of the month of Shavvâl the Noble [29 July], two and a half hours before noon, the steamer arrived off shore from Baku and dropped anchor. From Enzeli to Baku by commercial steamship at a moderate [speed] and without delays takes twenty-three hours. [60] Otherwise, there are delays in ports along the way according to the ship's cargo.

THE DOCK AND HARBOR OF BAKU

The dock and harbor of Baku have been built so well by the government that it is not necessary to take a launch. The steamers come up adjacent to the dock. The dock has been constructed of wood and iron next to the sea [and] out over the water. A bridge has been constructed on it [which] connects [it] with the city. For the cost of building this dock, every steamer which anchors at the dock must pay a fee to the government agents according to the weight of the ship and the amount of [its] cargo.

At the dock, there are employees on behalf of the steamer company who open the hold of the ship and check and weigh the cargo. They allow each passenger one pood, which is five and a half mann-e tabriz, of baggage and small belongings such as ewer, samovar, hookah, and carrying-case. They charge a separate fare from the passengers for the rest of the luggage and goods.

---

[29] Text: Kord. The Kura is in fact a notoriously muddy river.

[30] There are several small islands between Lenkoran and Baku, and Farâhâni could be referring to the small pair of islands known as the Ostrov Kumani. It is perhaps somewhat more likely that he mistook the two long, narrow strips of land known as the Sara peninsula and the Kurinskaya sandbar for islands.

Customs officials are also present right on the dock. They very carefully search and inspect the goods and possessions. Without exception, they collect additional duty for every item which enters Russian territory. A description of the duties and the injustice of the customs officers will be written at the appropriate place.

Also on the dock, there are workers on behalf of the government who take care of the passports. They scrutinize the passports very carefully. They do not allow anyone without a passport to enter their territory. If there should be anyone without a passport, they do not accept any excuse and turn [him] back. Individuals who are Iranians must have a passport issued by the government, [61] and that passport must be endorsed by the Russian embassy in Tehran or one of the Russian consuls stationed in the ports must sign and endorse [it]. Passports without the endorsement and signature of the embassy or the Russian consulate at that locality will not be valid.[31]

After the individuals arrive at the dock, [the officials] take up their passports without charging a fee for the passports and send [them] for the endorsement of the Baku officials. The next day, or the day after next, they are sent to the Iranian consulate which is located in Baku. The Iranian consul endorses [them]; they charge about 2,500 dinars in Iranian money per passport for his endorsement.

THE CITY OF BAKU

In the afternoon, having finished with the passport business and the customs and so on, [we] entered the city of Baku. There are numerous caravanserais and several guest-houses in Baku which serve as lodgings for foreign travellers. There are three caravanserais in which citizens of Iran are living, and Iranian travellers lodge there. Two [of them] are the caravanserais of Ḥâjji Shaykh ᶜAli, and one is called the caravanserai of Mashhadi Ḥâjji Âqâ. Shaykh ᶜAli and Ḥâjji Âqâ are brothers, Shi'ites, and are both still living. They are respected merchants of Baku and are Russian subjects. We stayed at the large caravanserai of Ḥâjji Shaykh ᶜAli.

Baku is in the fifth clime,[32] beside the Caspian Sea. Its soil is sandy. It is adjacent to the sea on two sides; the north side is a peninsula. They say it is one of the constructions of Anushirvân

[31] Obviously, the use of the passport (*taẕkereh*) was still something of a novelty; cf. Sayf od-Dowleh, *Safarnâmeh*, p. 75.

[32] Farâhâni is following one of the systems devised by the medieval Muslim geographers to divide the world into various "climes" or regions according to their climate and distance from the equator: see EI_2, 2:1076-78 (s.v. "Iḳlîm").

Sâsâni.[33] It was named "Bâd kubeh" due to the strongly blowing wind ["bâd"] and Baku ["Bâkubeh"] is an abbreviation of that.[34] Sometimes the wind blows so strongly that it causes severe damage to buildings and living creatures. Therefore most of its buildings have been made of stone. [62]

The kings of Shirvân[35] built three very sturdy concentric fortresses with towers out of stone [there]. Between each fortress was dug a very deep moat; the sea water reached up to the wall of the old citadel.[36]

Due to the sturdiness of those fortresses, most of the Shirvânian kings used to keep their treasuries and tombs in there. They had buried their deceased notables inside those citadels. Thus Shâh Esmâᶜil, during [his] war with the Shirvânshâh, seized that fortress and confiscated the treasures of the Shirvânshâh. Out of inveterate enmity, he broke open the tombs of several of the Shirvânian kings who were buried there, exhumed their bones, and burned [them].[37] After that, the breastwork of those fortresses was taken down and the fortresses became ruined. People built houses inside the fortresses and lived there. The city was usually in the possession of the kings of the Caucasus and the Shirvânian kings. In the year 1138 [1725-26], it came into the possession of the Russians. In the year 1148 [1735-36], the government of Iran delivered it from Russian control, but in the year 1178 [1764-65] it again came into Russian possession.[38]

---

33 One of the most celebrated of the Sassanid kings (ruled 531-79).

34 Bâd kubeh means "wind-beaten." This etymology of the name may be fanciful: see EI_2, 1:966; A. Kasravi, "Bâku," *Armaghân* 10(1311/1932-33):81-87; Jackson, *Constantinople*, p. 27.

35 Shirvân refers to the district along the Caspian east of the Kura; the capital was usually at Shemakha. The title Shirvânshâh or Sharvânshâh was used by four distinct dynasties of rulers of the region from Baku to Shemakha in periods ranging from pre-Islamic times to the sixteenth century. See V. Minorsky, *A History of Sharvân and Darband* (Cambridge, 1958); B. Dorn, "Versuch einer Geschichte der Schirwanschahe" and "Geschichte Schirwans under den Statthaltern und Chanen von 1538-1820" in *Beiträge zur Geschichte der kaukasischen Länder und Völker* (reprint; Leipzig, 1967), pp. 523-602 and 317-434; Minorsky, *Ḥudûd*, pp. 404-5.

36 On the palace-complex of the Shirvânshâhs in Baku, see *Great Soviet Encyclopedia*, 29:604; L. Bretannitsky, "Baku's Historic Inner City," *Crossroads* 1(1977):37-40.

37 The Shirvânshâhs had long been the nemesis of the Safavid family. Shâh Esmâᶜil's subjugation of Shirvân took place in 1509-10: see Michel Mazzaoui, *The Origins of the Safavids* (Wiesbaden, 1972), pp. 76-82; Eskandar Beg Monshi, *History of Shah 'Abbas the Great* (trans. R. Savory; Boulder, 1978), pp. 43-44.

38 Farâhâni's history is a little imprecise but essentially correct: Taking advantage of the Afghan invasion of Iran, Peter the Great compelled Shâh Ṭahmâsp to cede Baku and other Caucasian territories in 1723. As the price for an alliance

At the present time, Baku does not have a fortress or moat. It is located on the slope of a dry, rocky mountain so that its houses of three or four storeys are situated in successive tiers on the slope of the mountain. Its streets are all wide and clean and paved with hewn stone and pebbles. Gaslights are set up in all the streets. It has about ten thousand resident households, which is a population of about forty thousand people.[39] [63] A quarter of the population is Armenian and Russian; the rest are Muslims and "Twelver" Shi'ites.[40] It has about ten mosques of various sizes, twelve churches, five public baths in the Iranian style, and three thousand shops, most of which are unroofed and two storeys high.

ANTIQUITIES IN BAKU

One of the ancient monuments in this city is an old citadel which formerly was the Muslims' bazaar. There are three mosques in that citadel, one of which is called the Masjed-e Jâme^c^. This mosque does not have a courtyard and consists merely of a large covered *shabestân*,[41] in the middle of which has been made a place without a roof like a *chahâr-tâq*.[42] A stone plaque is set up on the mosque and it is inscribed [in Arabic]: "The Solṭân, son of the Solṭân, Shaykh Khalilollah built this mosque in the year 708 [1308-9]."[43] On one side of the old citadel is a tower which is solidly built out of brick and mortar. It is forty z̲ar^c^ in height and has been restored. In order to guide ships at night, a lamp is put in it. It is called the "Maiden's Tower."[44]

against the Ottomans, Nâder Qoli (the future Nâder Shâh) forced the return of Baku and Derbent in 1735. It would be more accurate to say that Baku was an autonomous khanate by 1764; it was not retaken by the Russians until 1804 and was formally ceded to them by the Treaty of Gulistan (1813); Farâhâni may be overlooking this in order not to draw attention to the fact that it was the Qâjârs who lost this territory. For a full account of Baku's history, especially under Russian rule, see J. D. Henry, *Baku: An Eventful History* (London, 1905).

[39] Farâhâni must be referring only to the population of the inner city; official statistics showed the population of Baku in 1879 to be 112,000.

[40] Some estimates of the Persian population of Baku and other Russian cities was attempted by Hassan Hakimian, "Wage Labor and Migration: Persian Workers in Southern Russia, 1880-1914," *International Journal of Middle East Studies* 17(1985):443-62. Strangely, Hakimian did not take account of the information provided in Farâhâni's narrative.

[41] A kind of dormitory sometimes attached to large mosques; it could be used either for sleeping or the performance of supererogatory night prayers.

[42] A kind of hall composed of a courtyard flanked by four walls with arches often supporting a cupola or dome covering all or part of the courtyard.

[43] This would seem most likely to refer to Solṭân Khalil[ollah] (ruler of Baku 821-60/1418-56); see Minorsky, *Sharvân*, p. 131. Perhaps Farâhâni misread or forgot the date on the inscription.

[44] Text: Borj-e Dokhtar. On this twelfth-century monument, see *Great Soviet Encyclopedia*, 8:571; M. Useinov, L. Bretanitskii, and A. Salamzade, *Istoriia*

MAUSOLEUMS

One farsakh from the city there is the shrine of Bibi Haybat, named after one of the children of Ḥażrat-e Musâ ebn-e Jaʿfar, in whom many people have faith. They are always visiting [this shrine] and praying for things. The people's belief is that this emâmzâdeh was the younger sister of Ḥażrat-e Reżâ [whose] proper name was Fâṭemeh. She went to Ṭus for the honor of being in the presence of the Ḥażrat. Along the way she heard of the news of the death of the Ḥażrat and out of fear of the hypocrites she went to Gilân and from there to Baku. She died in this village, now known as Deh-e Shaykh. There were Shiʿites in this village; they buried [her] and protected her grave. The tomb is in a mosque of ancient construction. Around the mosque are graves of inhabitants of Baku. [64]

WATER AND CLIMATE

This city has very little water and few trees. Nonetheless, there are three springs. The government has constructed three or four cisterns in the middle of the city. Water-carriers take the water from these cisterns to the houses of the city on foot or by horse. They charge a fee for the water. The water is also not very wholesome. There are wells in most houses, but they must be very deep and their water is brackish, bitter, and can't be consumed.

The trees are also confined to these small gardens which are public places. These trees were forest trees and withered from lack of water. In some of the houses are found a few flowers such as geraniums, stork's-bill, and evening stock. The climate is humid because of the proximity to the sea. It is not possible to sleep outdoors. Nevertheless, its soil is very dry and has no moisture because of the oil in the vicinity. The curious thing about this is that the people of Baku, despite their water and climate, are very plump and fair and in good physical condition. One of the customs of the people is that they eat [only] one meal a day. Their regular meal is confined to lunch. They do not eat dinner at night. They are awake most of the night visiting with each other.

OIL WELLS

On the outskirts of the city as far as the village of Bâlâkhâneh, which is two farsakhs from the city, there are many oil wells, a few of which are state owned but most of which are privately owned. The main commerce in Baku now is the trade in oil which goes to Iran,

---

arkhitektury Azerbaidzhana (Moscow, 1963), pp. 62-65; Jackson, *Constantinople*, pp. 36-37 (with a photograph). The legend which caused it to be called the "Maiden's Tower" is recounted in J. M. Hone and Page Dickinson, *Persia in Revolution with Notes of Travel in the Caucasus* (London, 1910), pp. 167-68.

Europe, and the Ottoman Empire. There are many people who for years have dug wells on their own and labored and have not yet struck oil and have suffered severe losses in the enterprise.[45] Usually those wells are dug down about eight z̲arᶜ where they strike oil. After striking oil, they set up canals and tanks near the well so that as soon as oil is struck, it gushes up all at once, comes out of the well, empties into the canals, and flows into the tanks. [65] They take it out of those tanks, allow it to settle, and refine it in the factories. After the purification and refining, a third of it becomes kerosene[46] [suitable] for burning and is sent to the provinces. The other two thirds are burned in place of coal in the ships and factories in that immediate area. The principle oil field is in Bâlâkhâneh where many factories have been built. Every day fifteen thousand poods of oil are conveyed from there to the city. They also refine crude oil there and make kerosene.

ANCIENT FIRE TEMPLE IN THE VILLAGE OF SORÂKHÂNI

Three farsakhs to the northeast of the city there is a village named Sorâkhâni[47] where there has been a fire temple since ancient times. Some Zoroastrians and Hindus still come on pilgrimage there. Several Indians are always staying in this village. The fire temple is in the shape of an open square building in the middle of which there is a pit from which the fire comes out. There are chambers around it with a small opening between each chamber and the pit. There is a covering over the openings; whenever they want, they open the covering of the opening, touch a lighted match to the opening, and at once the gas is ignited like a lamp. It is the same

---

45 The extensive petroleum resources of the Baku area were known and exploited even in antiquity; the first modern drilling for oil there occurred in 1842. The industry had been opened up to private enterprise in 1872; this, plus the completion of the railway link in 1883, resulted in a considerable boom in prosperity for Baku. See Benjamin, *Persia and the Persians*, 18-20; Henry, *Baku, passim*; EI_2, 1:967; *Great Soviet Encyclopedia*, 2:556-57; Orsolle, *Caucase*, pp. 130-42; a very detailed account in Charles Marvin, *The Region of the Eternal Fire* (London, 1891), pp. 154-311; J. A. Martellaro, "The Acquisition and Leasing of the Baku Oil fields by the Russian Crown," *Middle Eastern Studies* 21(1985):80-88; J. P. McKay, "Entrepreneurship and the Emergence of the Russian Petroleum Industry, 1813-1883," *Research in Economic History* 8(1982):47-91; Issawi, *Economic History of Iran*, pp. 326-34.

46 Here Farâhâni uses the term *jowhar-e naft* (which he may have coined himself) to denote a refined petroleum product, presumably kerosene. Later, he uses the more common term, *naft-e safid*, to refer to kerosene.

47 Text: Sarâkhâli. See Jackson, *Constantinople*, pp. 40-57 (many photographs); Mounsey, *Journey*, p. 329; Orsolle, *Caucase*, pp. 139-42; Arnold, *Caravan*, 1:131-34; drawing in Edgar Boulangier, *Voyage à Merv* (Paris, 1888), p. 369.

everywhere in this village. Any place they want to ignite a fire, they dig down into the earth to a depth of one *chârak*[48] to half a ẕarᶜ. They put an external flame such as a match to the dug up earth and at once it is kindled and blazes like a fire. However, its heat is not very great. It has no smoke. It cannot be extinguished with water, but if a little earth is poured on it, it is extinguished. [66] Sometimes the fire is ignited spontaneously without the ground being dug up or disturbed. If [people] want to take the fire to another spot, they place a leather bag (*anbân*) opposite the excavated earth. When the bag is full of gas, they stop it up and move it. Anywhere a fire is needed, they put an iron pipe on the tip of the bag, touch an external flame to the tip of the pipe, and the end of the pipe is ignited and gives off light in the manner of a gas-lamp. As long as there is some of that gas in the bag, it is lighted; after that, it will go out. In this village of Sorâkhâni, factories have also been set up for refining oil [using] the natural [gas] fire from the earth. There is also an oil field in the midst of the sea. Coming up from below, its oil floats on the water. They go close to it by launch, light a rag or [piece of] wood and throw it on the sea in the same place where the oil is floating. Immediately that spot of the sea is inflamed until all of its oil burns up. They must skillfully beat back the flames, so the fire doesn't reach the boat.[49]

IRANIAN SUBJECTS IN SORÂKHÂNI

There are very few subjects of foreign countries in this city. There is no consul stationed there. There may be about three hundred Iranian subjects there, five or six of whom are merchants and the rest are tradesmen and workers on the boats. Most are from Gilân and Mâzandarân.

The consul of Iran posted there is someone named Mirzâ Maᶜṣum, who used to be one of the employees of the Tiflis consulate. Then he came to the capital and afterwards he was appointed as a consul. I happened to meet the aforementioned and perceived that he is very immature and inexperienced. One of the sayings of Ardashir Bâbakân is that "Many an army is defeated, much property is plundered, and many treaties are broken [by using] inexperienced and injudicious messengers and envoys." [67]

---

48 One quarter of a ẕarᶜ; i.e., approximately 28 cm.

49 The various phenomena associated with the oil and gas resources of Baku impressed many travellers who commented on them: see, for example, Qazvini/Le Strange, *Nuzhat*, pp. 198-99; "Le Feu Perpétuel de Baku," *Journal Asiatique* (second series) 11(1833):358-84; Percy Sykes, *A History of Persia* (third edition; London, 1951), 1:110; Augustus Mounsey, *A Journey Through the Caucasus and the Interior of Persia* (London, 1872), pp. 329-30.

COMMERCE

The commercial goods which are the specialties of this particular city are oil and saffron which are exported everywhere. There is also some production of opium in the villages. The goods which are brought there from the Caucasus and area of Shirvân and sold in quantity are Shirvâni shawls, furs, and squirrel pelts.

Products of Moscow and St. Petersburg[50] are also numerous there, such as: calashes, droshkys, samovars, covered dishes, clocks, weapons, excellent blankets, some haberdashery equipment, etc. Products of Iran which are sold there are mostly rice, edible and inedible fish, silk, and brown sugar.

MONEY IN BAKU

The manât and the imperial are the common currency [in] Baku. The manât is a printed paper note which is printed [in denominations] from one manât to one thousand manâts. Iranian money is also accepted. Its value varies like the worth of the imperial in Iran. Sometimes three Iranian krans equal one manât, and sometimes three krans and five shâhis to three and a half krans make one manât. The new Iranian kran is valued higher than the old kran. The new Amin os-Solṭâni kran is in more common use than the old krans. There are many moneychangers and merchants here who accept Iranian money. They take it and send it back to Iran to purchase rice, muscovado,[51] fish, and silk. It is advantageous for whoever has krans to exchange them there for manâts and to take the manât along. [68] All the pilgrims and people passing through do this. We also exchanged our money for manâts and some imperials, but as it turned out the exchange rate for the manât was better than for the imperial. A complete description of Russian money will be given in the proper place.

WEIGHTS

The customary weight [used in] Baku is the Russian *girvânkeh* which is [equal to] eighty-eight meṣqâls or five and a half of the *sir-e tabriz*. Eight girvânkeh [equal] one mann and four sir-e tabriz. Another [weight] is the pood, which [equals] about five and a half mann-e tabriz.[52]

---

[50] Text: *Peṭr*.

[51] This is based on reading *sheker-e mazândarân* instead of *sheker-e mazândân* as in the text; see F. J. Steingass, *A Comprehensive Persian-English Dictionary* (reprint; London, 1963), p. 792.

[52] The *meṣqâl* was about 4.6 grams; the *sir* was 16 miskals or 74 grams. See Fritz Rosen, *Persian Grammar* (reprint; New Delhi, 1979), p. 298; Issawi, *Economic History*, p. 389. It is not clear to which weight Farâhâni is referring as girvânkeh, but he presumably means the funt (410 grams) since 88 mesqals would be 405 grams.

ADMINISTRATION

Most of the government employees in Baku are Russians. Outwardly, they act in such a way that everything [seems] completely orderly and free and no one bothers anyone else. But in actuality it can be said that it is utterly without order, and no one is secure in life, property, or his own affairs. One cannot spend a tranquil night in one's own home. There are many criminals, and few nights go by that there are not robberies in homes and [on] the streets or two or three people are not killed. If someone wants to travel by night from one quarter to another, he must first of all be [in the company of] five or six people–one or two people would not dare to go [alone] from one quarter to another. After a theft or murder takes place, and they complain to the government, nothing is done. As it is said, "They think the uncaptured thief is a king." Proof is required; it is not possible to prove it easily, so they are compelled to tolerate the loss of life and property.

CORRUPTION AND DEBAUCHERY

One of the things which the people have implemented as a means of freedom and comfort is that whores and young male prostitutes are permitted to indulge in debauchery. If, for example, someone quarrels with his wife or young son, straightaway that woman or boy goes to the coffeehouses or the brothel [69] and says, "By my own wish, I want to engage in debauchery." It never occurs to anyone to prevent them or to force them to leave there and not permit them to engage in debauchery. In reality, this is a kind of sanctuary [*bast*]. Thus one is not in control of his honor, and the men are [thus] extremely afraid of their own wives and juvenile children. As a result of feeling jealousy and disgrace at this having happened, men who have been afflicted by this situation have often taken opium and poison and died. I don't understand the meaning of this [sort of] freedom.[53]

ETHICS AND RELIGION

Generally, the middle and lower [classes] of Russians, in so far as [I] have seen, are very impolite, wicked, devious, coarse, rude, unjust, harsh, haughty to the peasants, and careless. The institution of marriage does not have much sanctity among these people. Usually when anyone desires someone, they have intercourse without informing father, mother, or monks. They pay no attention to the priests and their own canon law. They imagine the most fanciful things about our prophet Jesus, his family, the disciples, and

[53] A verse couplet quoted here by Farâhâni is omitted from the translation.

religious law. They exceed all bounds in drinking wine; they know neither day nor night, right time nor wrong time, too much nor too little. Usually they are so drunk they are senseless. They do not know or understand anything about purity and modesty which are the norms of humanity, but which are not understood by them at any level. There are few Russians who do not drink one mann of wine in a day. Their drink is usually wine. They do not have the sense or intelligence to make or drink any other beverage.[54]

DIET OF THE PEOPLE

Their food is mostly beef and pork. [70] Their meals are extremely dirty and bad. In truth, the lot [of them] are wild, uncivilized animals who consider the things of the world all the property and possessions of their fathers, "as if they were frightened asses fleeing from a lion."[55] In particular, the members of their military, upon whom the state is utterly dependent for its security, have become perfectly brazen and have no regard for civility and are extremely unjust. In India, I saw many Englishmen and associated with high and low. Although they too are very deceitful, cunning, time-serving, hypocritical, and don't understand friendship and camaraderie at all, still in outward behavior they do act justly and humanely and have a mildness, dignity, and orderliness. Anyway, both of these two peoples have faults that this is not the place to list. The ignorant suppose that all the best examples of humanity and order are in foreign countries and among foreign peoples. It is a famous proverb: "The neighbor's chicken seems like a goose."[56]

Let us leave this matter. The Khorâsâni, Astarâbâdi, Mâzânderâni, and Shâhrudi pilgrims were travelling via Ashkhabad, Tâzeh-shahr[57] and Bandar-e Gaz. After travelling for two days and

[54] In these paragraphs, Farâhâni may seem to be rather excessive in his criticism of the Russians. On the other hand, it should be remembered that Baku during the oil boom did have a wild life. The English travellers Hone and Dickinson, *Persia in Revolution*, p. 159, also wrote that Baku "is a Mecca of adventurers" where "an enemy may be disposed of...at a cost of five roubles" and where "prosperous citizens are kidnapped in broad daylight" and "the average number of murders per day is five." They also quote the famous rebel Shâmel as saying, "Alexander the Great took a dislike to this district on account of its barrenness and he turned it into a place of exile for all the criminals of the world" (p. 166).

[55] A verse from the Koran, 74:50-51.

[56] A slightly variant form of a popular proverb; see Dehkhodâ, *Amsâl*, p. 1029; Ḥayyim, *Proverbs*, p. 373. The meaning, of course, is similar to that of "the grass is always greener on the other side of the fence." This proverb is followed by a verse, omitted from the translation, which makes much the same point.

[57] A name often given to newly founded towns (it means "New Town"); here it presumably refers to one of the new Russian port towns on the eastern littoral of the Caspian.

nights by sea, they arrived at Baku. At this time, ten or twenty of the pilgrims who had come from those provinces met up with us in Baku and became our travelling companions.

FROM BAKU TO BATUM

Having arrived in Baku on the afternoon of Wednesday the sixteenth, we left Baku at noon on Thursday the seventeenth of the month of Shavvâl [30 July], took a calash, and went to the train station.

THE RAILWAY

There is a railroad from Baku to Batum.[58] It is called the "chemin de fer." [71] "Chemin" in French means "road"; "de" is the connective preposition; and "fer" means "iron." The train[59] goes daily from Baku to Tiflis and Batum. The Baku station is half a farsakh from the city. It is a very good building, spacious, and constructed with an upper and lower storey. A guard and [some] workers are there. There are several counters. One is reserved for issuing and collecting tickets. One must first of all pay for and get a ticket at that counter. Another is reserved for carrying and taking delivery of baggage, of which each passenger may have one pood (which is five and a half mann-e tabriz). They allow baggage, samovar, water-pipe, carrying-case, and water-vessel without charging a separate fee.

---

[58] The Tsarist government, in conformity with its policies for pacifying and developing the Transcaucasian provinces, began construction of a railway from the port of Poti to Tiflis in 1867. Construction, carried out by an English company, was completed in 1872. After the Russo-Turkish War in 1878, the Black Sea terminus was transferred to the port of Batum and the line extended from Tiflis to Baku. The opening of this transportation route had a stimulating effect on the economy of northeastern Iran, but the imposition of stiff customs duties by the Russians soon made it less attractive as a link to European markets: See Charles Issawi, "The Tabriz-Trabzon Trade, 1830-1900: Rise and Decline of a Route," *International Journal of Middle East Studies* 1(1970):18-27; *idem*, *Economic History of Iran*, p. 165. Once the Transcaucasian railroad was opened to passenger traffic, however, it quickly became a popular means of connecting Iran with the Black Sea maritime routes since it alleviated the problem of making either an arduous overland trip across the rugged Caucasus or the longer detour via Tzaritzina and Taganrog. As Benjamin, *Persia and the Persians*, p. 13, reported, "...the railway between Tiflis and Batum had been opened about ten days before our arrival in Tiflis. Otherwise, instead of riding comfortably from that city to Bakû by rail in twenty-four hours, we should have been obliged to go over the route in springless troikas, over a rough, treeless road, traversing barren plains and mountains infested by brigands, and weeks would have been required to accomplish the distance."

[59] Literally, "steam calash." This is apparently a neologism, perhaps coined by Farâhâni himself. It should be remembered that there was no railroad in Iran during this period and consequently the Persian vocabulary for denoting such things was not yet fixed.

If the baggage is in excess of one pood plus these utensils, they collect a separate fare of about eighty-five krans in Iranian money for each mann-e tabriz from Baku to Batum. This baggage and the additional items may not be taken with the passenger; they are transported in a separate coach. After they pick up and take delivery of the baggage, and collect the additional fare, they give a receipt for it. This receipt [serves] as token and proof of [deposit of] that baggage. One shows that receipt at the place of destination and collects one's own items. Thus one will not see one's baggage and utensils before the place of destination. The baggage and items will not be harmed and will not suffer from loss or damage. There is also one counter for delivering baggage. There is also one counter for the tradesmen and craftsmen [working on] the coaches. Another counter is [for] public dining. Another counter is for the supervisors of the workers. [72]

STATIONS ALONG THE WAY

There are thirty-six stations from Baku to Batum. That is to say, from Baku to Ganjeh[60] there are seventeen stations; from Ganjeh to Tiflis three stations; and from Tiflis to Batum sixteen stations. The separation of each station from the next is from twenty-one verst to thirty verst. They have built a station wherever there is water and an inhabited place.

There are five hundred sagene per verst. Each sagene is three Russian zar^{c}. A sagene is [equal to] two zar^{c} and one Iraqi gereh. One verst, that is five hundred sagene, is [thus] fifteen hundred Russian zar^{c}, which equals 1,033 Iraqi zar^{c}. However in commercial transactions 1,500 Russian zar^{c} are reckoned as 1,050 Iraqi zar^{c}. The chatvar is one fourth of a verst, or 375 Russian zar^{c}. According to this method, six verst are [equal to] 6,180 Iraqi zar^{c} (six thousand of them equal one farsakh, so [that is] 180 zar^{c} in excess of a farsakh).[61]

---

[60] Ganjeh was the Muslim name for the city renamed Elizavetpol in the Tsarist period (now Kirovabad). It is described at some length by Sayf od-Dowleh, *Safarnâmeh*, pp. 64-66, who travelled this route prior to the construction of the railway.

[61] Farâhâni's account may be clarified by reference to the following table:

Russian	*Metric*
sagene	2.134 m.
verst	1.067 km.
Persian	
gereh	4.29 cm.
zar	1.04-1.12 m.
farsakh	3.7-6.7 km.

The stations are all different. Each one that is located in a principal town [*markaz*], where there are many travellers and passers-by, has more rooms, buildings, and workers. From each station to the next in terms of time takes from twenty-two or -three minutes to thirty-five minutes. In each station, [the trains] stop from two minutes to half an hour. Stops at a station which is in a principal city will be longer. They will stop at the Tiflis station for most of an hour. If a place along the way has fallen into disrepair, the motion of the coach will be greatly delayed, or it will stop. [73] The coach which carries the post goes on Mondays and Fridays and will also travel faster than this. Its halts at the stations will also be less. When [the train] stops, they ring a bell three [times] so that the passengers will be informed and [can] come out to relieve themselves. When the third bell has been struck, [the train] will start moving without hesitation.[62] They have divided up all of the railroad [into sections] and put up markers inscribed in Russian beside the railroad at every verst. There are workshops and craftsmen at every station for construction and repair of the coaches. The stations which are located in a principal city have more workshops and repair tools. In all the stations, there are troops and an officer as sentinels. Every station which is in a principal city has more troops and the rank of its officer is higher.

There are four sentry posts between each station and the next. Each [serves] as the residence for one family. All along the way, at intervals of one verst, a sentry and custodian are standing. If they raise a green flag, it signifies that that section is safe and the coach goes along quickly. If they raise a red flag, that is a sign that the railway is in some disrepair and the coach must travel slowly and with caution. If they raise a red and black flag, it is a sign that the railway is in bad shape and the coach must stop until the obstruction is removed. At night, in place of these flags as signals, they light green and red lanterns in the same manner as described. The telegraph line is strung out all along the side of the railway. One is able to telegraph from any station to another station. They give information by telegraph about every section of the railway which is in disrepair. [74]

THE FARES

The fare of the coach from one station to the next in third class (which is the place for ordinary passengers) is a paper half-manât, and at each station half a kopek in silver coinage is also collected as

[62] On this practice, cf. Jackson, *Persia*, p. 2.

"ticket-money." So the third class fare from Baku to Batum (which is thirty-six stations) consists of eighteen manâts and eighteen kopeks: eighteen manâts is the money for the coach-fare at half a manât per station, and eighteen kopeks is the money for the ticket paper. Eighteen manâts and eighteen kopeks is approximately five tomans and 8500 dinars in Iranian money. The fare for the second class coach is twice the third class fare, or thirty-six manâts and thirty-six kopeks, which is approximately eleven tomans and seven krans [in Iranian money]. The first class fare is three times the third class [fare], or fifty-four manâts and seventy-two kopeks [*sic*], which is about seventeen tomans and six krans in Iranian money. These three classes are not very different in comfort, except that the third class, by virtue of being closer to the engine, has more swaying and vibration. Because the first class [coach] is further from the steam engine, there is less vibration and swaying. The walls of the first class coach are velvet covered; its furnishings and implements and lights are new and clean and neat. The walls of the second class coach are covered with broadcloth or plaincloth, and its furnishings are not very clean. The walls of the third class coach are of wood, and it does not have any furnishings.

THE SITUATION ON THE TRAINS

The employees of the coach, such as servants, etc., are usually Russians. If anyone is careless, these employees will steal his belongings with utter nimbleness and agility. [75] If, after the theft, the individual complains to anyone, he will never get anywhere because in all the stations the passengers are continuously changing, some going and some coming, so no one can be caught. Thus the individual must be extremely watchful and protect his property.[63] In the coach, men and women, Muslims and infidels, are mixed together. There is no way to avoid it. The status of everyone is equal. Everyone in every class who has obtained a ticket sits anywhere [he wants], and there will be no preventing it. In all the stations, most foods and drinks are found. Every station which is in a principal town has more foods, but the price of everything is expensive. In some stations, foods and fruits are brought for sale from the surrounding villages and are offered cheaply.

---

[63] Cf. Benjamin, *Persia and the Persians*, p. 12: "...thieves so abound that nothing must be left in the cars unguarded."

THE PROBLEM OF WATER ALONG THE WAY

In the stations, the water to be used by Muslims and infidels is the same.[64] Everywhere, there are barrels and wooden or iron vessels that do not hold one *korr*[65] of water. The cup and little vessels are put on top of that so that Muslims and infidels dip that vessel in the barrel and take out water. If someone on the steamers, coaches, and trains is conscientious about [religious] precautions, it will be hard on him since [the water] will never be [ritually] pure. Generally speaking, there are two points which can provide ease of mind, [ritual] purity, and comfort while on the steamers and locomotive coaches.

The first point is that a small quantity of water may not be regarded as impure subsequent to contact with something [ritually] impure; that is, if the [amount of] water [available] is less than a korr, then it is not made impure by contact with things such as a water

---

[64] The problem which Farâhâni is preparing to discuss is an important one in Islamic law in general but especially in the context of Shi'ite law. In order to perform the prayers and other religious rituals, a Muslim must be in a state of ritual purity (*ṭahârat*). This ritual purity is maintained by either washing parts of the body (*vożuᶜ*) or the entire body (*ghosl*). The latter, more complex, ablutions are required by certain major pollutions (*najâsat*). According to much of traditional Muslim law, especially Shi'ite law, coming into physical contact with a non-Muslim or various things used by a non-Muslim constitutes a major pollution. Thus travelling abroad presented a number of difficulties for a Muslim like Farâhâni in terms of maintaining one's ritual purity or even finding water that could be considered "clean" for drinking. For a translation of the opinions of Ḥelli, a prominent medieval Shi'ite jurist, on this matter, see A. Querry, *Droit Musulman. Recueil de lois concernant les Musulmans schyites* (Paris, 1871), 1:1-42.

[65] The determination of whether water was ritually pure or not depended on a number of factors such as its source and its volume. The volume of the *korr* varied from one of school of law to another and was even a matter of dispute among Twelver Shi'ite authorities. In the notes to his translation of Ḥelli's legal treatise, Querry, *Droit Musulman*, p. 3 n. 1, writes: "Il existe une divergence relativement au poids qui soit de base au *korr*: les uns sont d'avis que cette base est le *rotl médîni*, et les autres se prononcent pour le *rotl érâkî*; cette dernièr opinion prévaut aujord'hui. Le rotl éràki se compose de 68 1/4 miskâls, poids du commerce en usage aujord'hui; le *korr* comprend 1200 rotl érâkî, ce qui donne en poids du commerce actuel (à 640 miskâl ou *batmen* de Tîbriz) 121 batmen et 629 miskâl, équivalant à 393 kilogrammes 12 grammes." Among modern accounts, Âyatollah Khomayni, *Resâleh towżiḥ ol-masâ'el*, translated by J. Borujerdi as *A Clarification of Questions* (Boulder, 1984), p. 4, holds that "kor water is an amount of water that fills a container measuring 3.5 spans each in length, width, and depth, weighing 128 Tabriz man less twenty mesghals which is equal to 383.906 kilograms." In any event, water in a container of this size did not become ritually impure if touched by anything unclean unless its smell, color, or odor changed. A smaller volume of water was generally held to become unclean if any unclean object came into contact with it; see Querry, *Droit Musulman*, 1:3-4; Khomayni, *Clarification*, p. 5. The point that Farâhâni is making here is that since the water containers on the trains, which can be used by non-Muslims, do not contain the minimum volume of water, both the water and the cups would be ritually "unclean" and thus improper for use by Muslims.

cistern, pitcher, cup, etc. which are polluted, unless the color, smell, or flavor has been changed by the impurity. This problem is a novel one, and it is not necessarily a [religious] offense that should cause anxiety. [76]

OPINIONS OF SHI'ITE ULAMA PERTAINING TO WATER

A number of Shi'ite ulama of early and recent [times] have held opinions about this problem. For example, among the early [authorities], the late ^{c}Omâni,[66] the late Sayyed Mortażâ,[67] and Ḥasan ebn-e Abi ^{c}Aqil[68] did not consider that a small amount of water was impure because of contact with an impurity. Among recent [authorities], the late Sayyed ^{c}Abd ol-Karim, author of the *Ketâb-e Dorr^{an}* [?],[69] the late Mollâ Moḥsen,[70] and the late Shaykh Yusof Baḥrâni[71] believed the same thing about this problem; several other contemporary ulama besides these have maintained the opinion of [its] ritual purity. Twenty-five authoritative hadiths have been transmitted maintaining the ritual purity of a small amount of water subsequent to contact with something unclean, and twenty-six

---

[66] Abu Moḥammad (or Abu ^{c}Ali) Ḥasan ebn-e Abi ^{c}Aqil, a Shi'ite narrator of religious traditions contemporary with the great Kolayni (d. 329/940); see Dehkhodâ, *Loghatnâmeh*, s.v. ^{c}Omâni; Moḥammad Solaymân Tonakâboni, *Qeṣaṣ ol-^{c}olamâ'* (Tehran, n.d.), pp. 429-30 (#126). Tonakâboni confirms that ^{c}Omâni was one of the first of the Shi'ite ulama to take the position that a small quantity of water did not become ritually unclean upon contact with an impurity.

[67] Presumably ^{c}Ali b. Ḥosayn Sharif (or Sayyed) Mortażâ, known as ^{c}Alam ol-Hodâ (355-436/966-1044), a highly respected descendant of Imam ^{c}Ali and a Shi'ite theologian in Baghdad; see Tonakâboni, *Qeṣaṣ*, pp. 406-10 (#98); Browne, *Literary History*, 4:405; Momen, *Introduction to Shi'i Islam*, p. 311; W. Madelung, "A Tradition of the Sharif al-Murtaḍa on the Legality of Working for the Government," *Bulletin of the School of Oriental and African Studies* 30(1980):18-31; H. M. Tabatabai, *An Introduction to Shii Law: A Bibliographical Study* (London, 1984), pp. 34, 41-43; Waḥid Akhṭar, "Al-Sayyid al-Murtaḍâ: His Life and Works," *Tawḥid* 4/i(1407/Sept.-Nov. 1986):125-52.

[68] This is ^{c}Omâni's proper name (see above, n. 66); perhaps Farâhâni has mistakenly identified them as two separate people.

[69] So in the text; the reference may be to ^{c}Abd ol-Karim Jazâ'eri (d. 1215/1800-1801), author of the *Ketâb od-dorar ol-mansureh fi'l-aḥkâm ol-ma'sureh*; see Moḥammad Moḥsen Âqâ Bozorg-e Ṭehrâni, *Ṭabaqât a^{c}lâm osh-shi^{c}eh* (Tehran, 1954-58), 2/ii:730 (#1404).

[70] Muḥammad b. Mortażâ b. Shâh Maḥmud of Kashan, known as Mollâ Moḥsen-e Fayż (d. 1091/1680). Although he was the author of *ol-Vâfi*, a highly regarded Shi'ite compendia of hadiths, he was an Akhbâri and unconventional enough to be described by Dwight Donaldson, *The Shi'ite Religion* (London, 1933), p. 301, as "more of a mystic and a philosopher than a theologian." See Momen, *Shi'i Islam*, pp. 113, 174; Tonakâboni, *Qeṣaṣ*, pp. 322-33 (#76); Browne, *Literary History*, 4:432-35.

[71] Yusof b. Aḥmad b. Ebrâhim Baḥrâni (d. 1186/1772-73), author of numerous books on Shi'ite religious law and tradition; see Tonakâboni, *Qeṣaṣ*, pp. 271-74 (#45); Momen, *Shi'i Islam*, pp. 118, 175.

hadiths have come down maintaining its ritual impurity. The late Shaykh Moḥammad Ḥasan in his book *Javâher ol-Kalâm* [*Jewels of Discourse*][72] collected and related all the hadiths about purity or impurity in connection with this problem. One cannot dismiss the hadiths [affirming] its ritual purity as dissimulation because the Sunnis believe in its impurity, not its purity.[73] Since numerous hadiths from the Imams are extant, and the ancient and recent Shi'ite ulama maintained the opinion of [its] purity, it is obvious that this problem in olden times and recently was and is [a matter] of recommendation, not an absolute obligation which it would be irreligious to oppose. Since the religious ulama hold opinions of [its] impurity and [its] purity, and have at hand many hadiths about both, both are equally valid and both opinions can be followed. However, those holding to [its] purity are to be preferred since those believing in [its] impurity have fallen into a quandary with regard to fixing and quantifying the amount of a korr according to the narrations of the Imams. Since this question "has become a general necessity at all times", people must pay attention to it. Thus the Imam would not leave such an important question, about which people depend on him every hour, vague and obscure. [77] In conclusion, this is a major problem which needs explication and explanation, mention and guidance, beyond that which it is possible to write in this unscholarly book. The aim is only to show that if one follows the ulama who hold that small quantities of water, upon contact with something unclean, do not become ritually impure, it will be a considerable help to his peace of mind, and his [maintenance of] ritual purity on the boats and trains will be facilitated.

VIEWS OF SHI'ITE ULAMA ON MAINTAINING PURITY

The second point which will facilitate things for a Muslim [*shakhṣ*] on the boats and trains is that of the ritual purity of

72 Shaykh Moḥammad Ḥasan Najafi (1788-1850), son of Shaykh Moḥammad Bâqer Najafi. See Tonakâboni, *Qeṣaṣ*, pp. 103-6 (#14); Tabatabai, *Introduction*, p. 93; Momen, *Shi'i Islam*, p. 318; Juan Cole, "Imami Jurisprudence and the Role of the Ulama," in N. Keddie (ed.), *Religion and Politics in Iran* (New Haven, 1983), pp. 40-41; Bâmdâd, *Rejâl*, 3:364-65. The book mentioned is one of the foremost explications of Shi'ite religious law. The various printed editions of the text are catalogued in Khân-Bâbâ Moshâr, *Fehrest-e ketâb-hâ-ye châpi-ye fârsi* (Tehran, 1337-42/1958-63), cols. 261-63.

73 Twelver Shi'ites could practice dissimulation (*taqeyyeh*) or concealment of their true religious beliefs and practices in order not to draw attention to themselves and thereby to avoid possible persecution. Thus only hadiths which *agreed* with Sunni practice could be dismissed as examples of dissimulation. For further references and Farâhân's own critique of taqeyyeh, see below, Part Five, pp. 229-30 and n. 115.

non-Muslims [*ahl-e ketâb*].[74] A number of great Shi'ite ulama have held this opinion; for example, the late Shaykh-e Mofid[75] considered that touching[76] non-Muslims was disapproved but neither forbidden nor [a cause of ritual] impurity. The late Shaykh Ṭusi[77] and the late ᶜOmâni also wrote in this manner in their treatises and creeds. Although this problem is one of discretion [rather than an absolute religious obligation], and there is no explicit verse in the Koran which might be definitive about the ritual impurity of non-Muslims, yet the immaculate Imams have insisted on the ritual impurity of the non-Muslims. Many of the ulama have also held the opinion of their ritual impurity. Some recent ulama have also held the opinion of their impurity. Thus this problem of impurity has almost become one of religious obligation [rather than discretion], and one should know the rules concerning impurity. Knowing about ritual impurity is a matter of honor for the people of Islam. Nevertheless, the problem is one of discretion. If one follows the religious scholar [*ᶜâlem*] of the Ḥayy Mosque,[78] who believes the non-Muslims may be ritually pure, one can, when obliged, associate with the non-Muslims and things will go easier on one in foreign countries. And I have heard that one of the great contemporary ulama considers the non-Muslims pure, but out of regard for the majority of religious scholars does not express this idea. [78]

DEPARTURE FROM BAKU

Anyway, I seated myself on the train and set out from Baku on Thursday the seventeenth of the month of Shavvâl [30 July] six hours

---

[74] The *ahl-e ketâb* or "people of the book" are those belonging to certain other revealed religions, such as Jews and Christians. According to most Shi'ite legal authorities, even slight physical contact with non-Muslims made a Muslim ritually impure. See, for example, Querry, *Droit Musulman*, 1:44.

[75] Abu ᶜAbdollah Moḥammad b. Moḥammad b. Nuᶜmân ol-Baghdâdi (ca. 336-413/948-1023) was one of the greatest medieval Shi'ite religious scholars, credited with writing over two hundred books. See the biographical sketch in his *Ketâb ol-ershâd,* translated by I. Howard, *Kitâb al-Irshâd: The Book of Guidance* (London, 1981), pp. xxi-xxxiv; Momen, *Shi'i Islam*, p. 317; Tabatabai, *Introduction*, pp. 40 ff.; Tonakâboni, *Qeṣaṣ*, pp. 398-406 (#97); Browne, *Literary History*, 4:405.

[76] Literally, "[physical] contact...[involving] moisture."

[77] Shaykh Abu Jaᶜfar Moḥammad b. Ḥasan b. ᶜAli Ṭusi, known as Shaykh oṭ-Ṭâ'efeh (385-460/955-1067), was a pupil of Shaykh-e Mofid and eventually succeeded him as the pre-eminent Shi'ite scholar in Baghdad. He authored a number of books, including two collections of hadith and a treatise on jurisprudence. See Donaldson, *Shi'ite Religion*, pp. 286-88; Momen, *Shi'i Islam*, p. 321; Tabatabai, *Introduction*, pp. 44-45; Tonakâboni, *Qeṣaṣ*, pp. 414-16 (#100); Browne, *Literary History*, 4:405; EI_1, 4:982.

[78] Unidentified.

before sunset. I came out from the city to the station named Khaygi. This expanse is known as the "place of cemeteries" since the earth is dry, without water or grass, full of dust and extremely hot.

THE ÂQ JAQÂBIL STATION

Past here to the station of Âq Jaqâbil,[79] which is in the Sal'yany district, is open space; on the right side are mostly dry mountains; the left side is very dusty, with little water and grass, and is hot. The road to the district seat of Sal'yany is from this station. From there to the district seat of Sal'yany by the post-horse coach takes twelve hours and is twenty-four farsakhs.

THE KYURDAMIR STATION

Past the Âq Jaqâbil station to the station of Kyurdamir,[80] which is in the Shirvân district, some villages are found on the left and the right near the railway. The climate is somewhat better and cooler. The road to the city of Shirvân[81] is from this station, so that from there to the city of Shirvân by the post-horse takes ten hours and is nearly twenty farsakhs. Past this point, the mountains were usually nearby, and villages full of streams and trees were visible. The weather was nice until [we] reached the Geokchay station.[82] The road to the district seat of Geokchay is from this station. From there to Geokchay is five verst. One goes by horse or donkey. After that one arrives at the Shamkhor[83] station, which is the beginning of the Ganjeh district. One reaches from there the station named Ganjeh. The road to the city of Ganjeh is from the station named Ganjeh. From there to the city of Ganjeh is two verst. One usually goes on foot. It is three stations from here to Tiflis. Past here, the weather changed greatly and became cold. In some places, snowy mountains were visible from near and far. Many streams, trees, and villages were apparent on the right and left. [79] There were seven or eight streams close to the railway, over which iron bridges had been erected. The coach passed over the bridges. The coach arrived at the city of Tiflis on Friday the eighteenth of Shavvâl [31 July] at five

---

[79] Referred to in various Western sources as Adji-cabul or Adzhikabul (now Kazi Magomed). There were plans to extend a branch line of the Transcaucasian Railway from this station to Tehran; see Marvin, *Eternal Fire*, p. 149.

[80] Text: Kordamir.

[81] I.e., Shemakha?

[82] Here and in subsequent places the text has "Gu-ye Chây." This is certainly a misreading of Gukchây (= Gökçay/Geokchay).

[83] Text: Shamgur. Shamkhor, however, is between Ganjeh and Tiflis, not Geokchay and Ganjeh as the passage here implies. Perhaps Farâhâni mistook the Yevlakh station for Shamkhor? Cf. Sayf od-Dowleh, *Safarnâmeh*, p. 67.

o'clock in the morning. So [the journey from] from Baku to Tiflis, including stops at the stations along the way, took seventeen hours. This coach stops one hour in Tiflis for cargo and passengers and [then] sets out for Batum.

TIFLIS

[Tiflis] is part of the fifth clime and used to be the capital of Georgia. Some have said that it is one of the constructions of Anushirvân.[84] Esḥaq ebn-e Esmâᶜil, a client of the Bani Omayyeh, built its citadel and ramparts. Its houses used to be roofed with pinewood. [80] Because Motavakkil sent Boqâ there to fight Esḥaq but Esḥaq did not want [to come out] to have battle with him, Boqâ ordered oil-throwers to be used. So they threw containers of oil onto the city until the fire spread. Most of the city burned, and many people perished there.[85] It is the belief of some that [the city] was one of those founded by Alexander the Great [*Rumi*], as alluded to by Neẓâmi in the *Eskander-nâmeh* [*Alexander Epic*].[86]

---

[84] [Marginal note]: "Some have written that the founder of Tiflis was [one of] the Georgian sultans or Khazar sultans. In the era of the caliphate of ᶜOs̱mân, this city was conquered by the army of Islam commanded by Ḥabib ebn-e Maslameh and came into Muslim possession. In the year 550 after the hegira [1155-56], the Georgians again took possession of it. Many Muslims were killed. In the year 623 A.H. [1226], Solṭân Jalâl od-Din the Khᵛârazmshâh sent an army to Georgia and took possession of the city. Many Georgians were killed. He left a governor and army there and returned. After [his] return, the inhabitants revolted against the governor's bad behavior and gave possession of the city to the Georgians. The Georgians, fearful lest the Khᵛârazmshâh send another army, burned the city and [the people] dispersed. After the death of the Khᵛârazmshâh, they populated [it] again. Thereafter, it was sometimes in the possession of Georgia, sometimes in the possession of the Shirvâni kings, and sometimes in the possession of the Ottoman sultans. Thus in the time of Solṭân Morâd Khân it came into Ottoman possession. Sometimes it was in the possession of the Pâdeshâhs of Iran." On Tiflis and its history, see Sayf od-Dowleh, *Safarnâmeh*, pp. 71-79; Gamba, *Voyage dans la Russie méridionale* (Paris, 1826), 2:154-84; Baron de Baye, *Tiflis, souvenirs d'une mission* (Paris, 1900); EI_1, 4:752-63; Moritz Wagner, *Travels in Persia, Georgia and Koordistan with Sketches of the Cossacks and the Caucasus* (London, 1856), 1:137 ff.

[85] This story is related by several early Muslim historians. Apparently this Esḥaq b. Esmâᶜil, claiming to be a client (*mawlâ*) of the Omayyad (Umayyad) family (the ruling dynasty of caliphs from 661-750), had made himself the autonomous ruler of Tiflis and its environs. The Abbasid caliph Motawakel (847-61) sent his Turkish general Boqâ on a campaign to Armenia in 238/852-53. See Aḥmad b. Yaḥyâ ol-Balâẕori, *Ketâb fotuḥ ol-boldân*, translated by P. K. Hitti, *The Origins of the Islamic State* (New York, 1916), 1:330-32; Abu'l-Ḥasan ol-Masᶜudi, *Moruj oẕ-ẕahab*, edited and translated by C. Barbier de Meynard and Pavet de Courteille, *Les Prairies d'or* (Paris, 1861-77), 2:65; Moḥammad b. Jarir Ṭabari, *Târikh or-rosol va'l-moluk*, edited by M. de Goeje (Leiden, 1879-1901), 3:1414-15; EI_1, 4:753-54.

[86] The Persian poet Neẓâmi (1140-1217) was born in Ganjeh and was thus a native of the Caucasus. His epic poem about Alexander has been described by Minoo Southgate, *Iskandarnamah: A Persian Medieval Alexander-Romance* (New York, 1978), pp. 173-79. The verse quoted by Farâhâni from the *Eskander-nâmeh* is omitted from this translation.

Georgia has always been an autonomous principality and had separate governors and rulers. The governors there have usually been vassals of the ruler of Iran. Sometimes, when they have been rebellious, the powerful rulers of Iran have invaded that principality and conquered it and taken spoils. Thus the Amir Timur Gurakân, in the year 988 [*sic*; 1580-81],[87] vanquished this city and caused much destruction and tore down the church and several places of worship of the Christians. The pious Âqâ Moḥammad Shâh the Qâjâr also conquered Tiflis in the year 1210 [1795-96], during the rule of Eregli Khân the Georgian.[88] He tied up the priests and threw them into the river Kura, killed many [people], and destroyed some of the places of worship of the Georgians.

Previously, the inhabited areas and the citadel of this city were situated on the southern slopes of the mountain. The citadel named Narikala[89] was on top of this same mountain. Many springs, some of which had hot water, flowed on the southern side of this same mountain. Over each spring various rulers have built domed structures to serve as baths.

The present city of Tiflis stretches out along the middle of the valley. It is not very wide. There are mountains north and south of it. The southern mountains are taller and more rugged. [81] At its top there are still remains of the ancient tower and ramparts which were previously the site of Narikala and the residence of the governors of Georgia. Now, most of the inhabited areas and markets are on the south side. The north side is the quarter of the Europeans,[90] in which the buildings and streets are clean and spacious. The mansion of the Vice-Regent, arsenal, armory,

---

87 Thus in both editions of the text. However, Timur (Tamerlane) captured Tiflis in 788/1386 (and subsequently sacked it in 805/1403-4). In Arabic manuscripts, the words "seven" and "nine" are easily confused, so the date 988 is probably a misreading of 788. The title "Gurkân" is a variant of Kurakân (from Turko-Mongol *güregen*, "son-in-law of the khâqân," alluding to Timur's relation by marriage to the family of Chingiz Khân.) See Percy Sykes, *History of Persia*, 2:125; EI_1, 4:757, 777.

88 The reference is to Erekle II (1720-98), king of Kakhetia (eastern Georgia). See Watson, *History of Persia*, pp. 89-94; F. Brosset, *Histoire de la Géorgie* (St. Petersburg, 1849-57); EI_1, 4:761; *Great Soviet Encyclopedia*, 10:47.

89 Text: Nârin-qalᶜeh. On this edifice, parts of which date back to the fourth century, see *Great Soviet Encyclopedia*, 25:421; Orsolle, *Caucase*, p. 43; P. Ioselian, *Opisaniye drew nostey Tiflisa* (Tiflis, 1866), pp. 238 ff. There are two fine photographs, taken not long after Farâhâni's visit, in Jackson, *Persia*, facing p. 5 and p. 14.

90 "Franks." The reference is probably to the colony of German refugees settled in Tiflis.

carpentry-shop, and hospital are on the north side. Most of the houses are located in the valley and on the slopes and top of the mountain.

THE KURA RIVER

The Kura River passes through the middle of the city of Tiflis. There are some large constructions along the bank of the river which lift up the water of the Kura by pumps and cause the water to flow off. They have built an iron bridge across the Kura. Previously, there was a wooden bridge. This bridge is one of the constructions of Prince Vorontsov,[91] the former governor of the Caucasus, a bronze statue of whom has been set up next to the bridge. Seven cannons have been placed around that statue, facing towards it.[92] There, the river has two branches. A bridge of one span has been built over one branch, and [one of] six spans over the other branch. In between these two branches of the river there are houses and shops.

As for the source and course of the Kura River, it is confirmed in the old books about this area that it rises in a place abounding in springs in the mountains of Georgia. At first, it passes through the country of Georgia;[93] then it passes through Abkhazia,[94] and reaches Tiflis. From there it goes to Hireh[95] and the districts of Shamkhor and from there flows to the district of Sal'yany. Along the way, small streams join it. Finally, it flows into the Araxes River after passing Barda[96] and empties into the Caspian Sea. [82]

---

91 Text: Doronsof. Prince Mikhail Seminovich Vorontsov was Viceroy and Governor-General of the Caucasus from 1844-54; see Wagner, *Travels*, 2:71-105; *Great Soviet Encyclopedia*, 5:603; L. H. Rhinelander, "Russia's Imperial Policy: the administration of the Caucasus in the first half of the nineteenth century," *Canadian Slavonic Papers* 17(1975):218-34; *idem*., "Viceroy Vorontsov's Administration of the Caucasus" in R. G. Suny (ed.), *Transcaucasia* (Ann Arbor, 1983), pp. 87-104. There is a view of the bridge in Jackson, *Persia*, facing p.7; cf. Orsolle, *Caucase*, pp. 42-43.

92 Text: *tup-e vâruneh* (literally, "inverted cannons").

93 Text: Khararân. Although perhaps an orthographical error for Khazarân (Khazars), it seems more likely to be an error for Jorzân (Georgia). Some early Muslim geographers (whom Farâhâni may well be paraphrasing) distinguished between eastern Georgia and the area around Tiflis since the two areas were ruled by different branches of the Baghratid dynasty. See Minorsky, *History of Sharvân*, p. 164, n. 5 (commentary on Mas^{c}udi's account).

94 Text: "Ijâz province."

95 Farâhâni may have in mind Hirak/Sirak which, according to Qazvini/Le Strange, *Nuzhat*, p. 93, "forms the summer quarters of Barda^c, it being a most pleasant and fertile place, with running streams, rich pasture-lands and excellent hunting grounds."

96 Text: Bard^{c}eh. In many texts the name is given as Barza^{c}eh. See W. Barthold, "Bardha^{c}a," EI_1, 1:656.

VIEWS OF MO^c^TAMAD OD-DOWLEH FARHÂD MIRZÂ

His Excellency Ḥâjji Mo^c^tamad od-Dowleh,[97] in his own travel book (based on the book by Orlovsky [?],[98] the governor of the province of Tiflis), has determined what may be summarized here: The [Kura River] rises in Ottoman Armenia in an area abounding in springs on the slope of a high mountain which is named Mutel-jân. The largest of those abundant springs are Marjân-su and Bunjuq-bunghâr.[99] It flows for ninety verst in Ottoman territory. Then it enters the kingdom of Russia and passes by the Oskhur[100] valley, Borzhomi,[101] and Kârtil.[102] The estate of Borzhomi is the summer-residence of the Vice-Regent. From the Ottoman frontier to Borzhomi, it flows for ninety-five verst in Russian territory; from the estate of Borzhomi it flows for two hundred verst to the frontier of Tiflis. Then it enters the territory of Ganjeh and reaches the district of Sal'yany that is part of the province of Baku. According to this [same account], the rivers that join the Kura from the beginning to Sal'yany, in proper sequence, are:

In the vicinity of Akhalkalaki,[103] the Akhâlgalâ-chây stream;[104] in the city of Akhaltsikhe,[105] the Boskhuf-chây stream;[106] between

97 Farhâd Mirzâ Mo^c^tamad od-Dowleh (1818-88) was the eleventh son of ^c^Abbâs Mirzâ and an uncle of Nâṣer od-Din Shâh; see Esmâ^c^il Ṣafâ, *Sharḥ ḥâl-e Farhâd Mirzâ Mo^c^tamad od-Dowleh* (Tehran, 1366/1987); Mo^c^ayyer ol-Mamâlek, *Rejâl*, pp. 161-66; Bakhash, *Iran*, p. 385; Bâmdâd, *Rejâl*, 3:86-92; Storey, *Persian Literature*, p. 204. He was quite accomplished as a writer and the author of several works including the *Zanbil* (a collection of poetry published in Tehran, 1329/1911); the *Jâm-e jam* (a translation of W. Pinnock's *Comprehensive System of Modern Geography and History*, published in Tehran in 1273/1856); and an account of his own pilgrimage to Mecca in 1292-3/1875-76, the *Hedâyat os-sabil va kefâyat od-dalil* (Shiraz, 1294/1877). Farâhâni has probably taken the material in this section from the *Hedâyat os-sabil*, pp. 42-43.

98 Text: Orlufâski. This is probably the same governor of Tiflis mentioned by Arthur Cunynghame, *Travels in the Eastern Caucasus* (London, 1872), p. 261 as a source of his information about the geography of the Persian frontier. Farhâd Mirzâ, *Hedâyat*, p. 42, says that this book was translated for him by Mirzâ Fatḥ-^c^ali [Âkhundzâdeh].

99 Farhâd Mirzâ, *Hedâyat*, p. 42, has Bunjuq Punghâr and, as a variant, Chunjuq Bunghâr. Bunghâr is probably a corruption of Turkish *pınar* (spring).

100 The identity of this place is uncertain; Farhâd Mirzâ, *Hedâyat*, p. 43, has Âskhur.

101 Text: Bârzhum.

102 This may be a corruption of Karthli (Iberia or Georgia). Since Farâhâni indicates below that the Araghvi enters the Kura just before "Kârtil," this would imply Mtskheta, the ancient capital of Georgia.

103 Text: Akhâlgalak; Farhâd Mirzâ, *Hedâyat*, p. 43, has Akhâlkalak.

104 The Paravani?

105 Text: Akhasegheh; Farhâd Mirzâ, *Hedâyat*, p. 43, gives the vocalization Akhseqeh.

106 Farhâd Mirzâ, *Hedâyat*, p. 43, has Paskhuf; perhaps a corruption of the name of the village Posof near the Kobliani?

Oskhur and Kârtil these four streams: the Liakhvi,[107] Lekhur [?], Ksani[108] and Araghvi; at the frontier of Tiflis, these four separate streams: Teryâlet,[109] Sumâsi,[110] Alget[i], and Khrami;[111] in the territory of Ganjeh, these four separate streams: Kurân,[112] Qâneq,[113] Terter,[114] and Qâchin;[115] and finally in the territory of Baku, near the village of Javâd-âb,[116] the Araxes River also joins the Kura and together they flow into the Caspian Sea.[117]

The ancients wrote concerning the special features of the water of the Kura River that its water is very salubrious. [83] Animals and human beings who fall into it take a long time to drown and die. Thus it is told that one time a drowning person they pulled from the Kura River was still breathing. When he came to his senses, they inquired about what had happened to him. It was learned that he had fallen into the water six days previously five stages upstream and had not died. Those present felt sorry for him and sought food for him. In the meantime, a wall under which this person was sitting collapsed all of a sudden and this person died underneath the wall. The responsibility [for this] rests with the one who told it!

Before the Kura River reaches Tiflis, they have constructed a barrage across the Kura named Qarah-yâzi so that a stream of water from the Kura flows to the villages and farms beside the city. Around the city, they have also constructed other barrages so that its water flows to the gardens and houses on the southern side of the city. By means of this, that side of the city has flourished. They have built nice houses and theaters [there]. This area is called Kucheh-ye

---

107 Text: Lekhvâ.

108 Text: Kesân.

109 The Turianchay?

110 Farhâd Mirzâ, *Hedâyat*, p. 43, has Sumâsati.

111 Text: Ḥerâm; Farhâd Mirzâ, *Hedâyat*, p. 43, has both Ḥerâm and Kherâm.

112 The Geranchay?

113 The Indzhechay?

114 Text: Ternez.

115 Farhâd Mirzâ, *Hedâyat*, p. 43, has Khâchin, certainly referring to the Khachinchay.

116 Javâd was the old Muslim name for the toll bridge across the Kura just below where it met the Araxes (near modern Sabirabad). See Minorsky, *Ḥudûd*, p. 398.

117 [Marginal note:] "The Kura River has also been called the Kay-Khosrow River. The Zoroastrians believe that after Kay-Khosrow was born, he was thrown into this river in infancy, owing to fear of Afrasiyab. The water did not drown him; thus it was named the Kay-Khosrow River." Kay-Khosrow is the hero of one of the most famous episodes in the legendary epic history of ancient Iran. His father was the prince Siâvosh, who had to take refuge with Afrâsiâb, ruler of Iran's traditional

Mojtahed; originally Âqâ Mir Fattâḥ known as Tabrizi had a great garden and house there. Then they were confiscated by the state; part [of the estate] was broken up and sold and some of its lands were made into a public park.

Also, in some places of the city, for the purpose of watering parks and vegetable gardens, they have set up wheels and attached jugs to them and pull up a lot of water with oxen, donkeys, and horses. This is also practiced alongside the Tigris and the Euphrates at Baghdad. In Kermân and Fârs also water is lifted up from wells in this manner, and the cultivated land irrigated.

WATER AND CLIMATE

In any case, the water of this city is agreeable and wholesome. [The city's] weather is variable, and tends to be cool. Thus even in this season, which is the middle of summer, there are fresh cucumbers and raspberries, [84] and the summer-quarters are quite cool. In the city and suburbs, there are many trees and flowers and vegetables; most houses have flower-beds and trees.

CROPS OF TIFLIS

The fruits [of Tiflis]–for example yellow plums, pears, grapes, hazelnuts, pistachios, quince, apples, peaches, figs, raspberries, cucumbers, and watermelons–are all abundant and cheap, but none of the fruits are of exceptional quality.

The crops from Tiflis and its environs are mostly tobacco, maize, and wheat.

DIET OF THE PEOPLE

The food of the people is mostly bread and meat. Its wheat does not have the flavor of Iranian wheat. They also bring rice from Rasht, but it is very expensive and rarely eaten. Pork and sow's milk[118] are often consumed. In the outlying villages, there are herds of domesticated swine, like herds of sheep, from which they derive considerable profits.

---

rival, Turân. His mother was Afrâsiâb's daughter, Farangis. After Afrâsiâb treacherously murdered Siâvosh, Kay-Khosrow was raised among the Turânians; eventually, he was recognized as the legitimate king of Iran and avenged his father by defeating and killing Afrâsiâb. It is interesting that Kay-Khosrow is sometimes identified with Cyrus the Great, from whom the Kura also takes its name. See Clément Huart, *Ancient Persia and Iranian Civilization* (London, 1927), p. 211; Sykes, *History of Persia*, 1:137.

[118] So in the text (*shir-e khuk*). It may be that Farâhâni, as a Muslim who considers the consumption of pork offensive, may simply be overstating things to make the point that he finds himself among infidels.

POPULATION AND RELIGION

The population of this city is about 30,000 households, which is about 120,000 people.[119] It has about 4,500 shops and seven or eight commercial caravanserais. The people there are very handsome and healthy looking. Two parts of the city [are populated by] native Georgians and Armenians, one part by Russians and foreign Christians, and one part by Muslims, half Sunnis and half Shi'ites. The Muslims there are like Christians: They never obey the dietary laws [of Islam]; they eat [Christian] food and animals slaughtered by Christians; and they use all kinds of intoxicating beverages.

CHURCHES

There are about one hundred churches in this city, three or four of those churches being especially venerated. [85] Each year, on a special day which is a Christian holiday, most of the people gather there and pitch tents and enjoy themselves. One of the churches is named for Kheżr the prophet.[120] In the belief of the local people, it was the birthplace of the Prophet Kheżr.

In the midst of the city, on the southern summit of a mountain, there is a church at which the tomb of Shaykh Ṣanᶜâ[121] is said to be. The Georgians believe strongly in Shaykh Ṣanᶜâ, and it is a place of pilgrimage. Once each year, most of the people of the city and the surrounding villages come in truly huge crowds on pilgrimage to the shaykh['s shrine], making vows and supplications.

MOSQUES

In Tiflis, there are about twenty mosques of various sizes. One large mosque is for the Sunnis, and one large mosque for the Shi'ites. It is said that Shâh ᶜAbbâs I built the large Shi'ite mosque and established its wakf endowment. The income from those endowments each year is about ten thousand manâts. The Russian government, upon the recommendation of the religous scholars of each sect, appoints a Shaykh ol-Eslâm for the Shi'ites and one for the

---

119 The population in 1897 was recorded at 160,000; see *Great Soviet Encyclopedia*, 25:427.

120 "The Green One," a popular, but obscure, Muslim saint. He is often thought to be the "servant of Moses" mentioned in the Koran (18:59-81). In popular beliefs, he was often confounded with Elijah or St. George. See A. Augustinovic, *El Khader and the Prophet Elijah* (Jerusalem, 1972).

121 The principal holy places in or near Tiflis were the Sioni Cathedral, the Metekhi Cathedral, and the Shrine of St. Abo (see Wagner, *Travels*, 2:40, 129-30). From the spelling of the name, the Sioni Cathedral would seem the most likely place to which Farâhâni might be referring. Golzâri (pp. 302-3) attempts to identify Shaykh Ṣanᶜâ with the Shaykh Samᶜân whose story is told by Farid od-Din ᶜAttâr in the *Manṭeq oṭ-ṭayr*, translated by Afkham Darbandi and Dick Davis, *The Conference of the Birds* (New York, 1984), pp. 57-75, but this seems rather implausible.

Sunnis. The authority for the courts of each of those two sects is that of its respective Shaykh ol-Eslâm.[122] The Shaykh ol-Eslâm himself deputizes trustworthy mollâs for all the towns of the Caucasus so that the courts in each town are under the mollâs sent by the Shaykh ol-Eslâm. The Shaykh ol-Eslâm has many followers and employees such as ferash, chief ferash, tax collectors, police, etc. The wakf properties of each sect are also controlled by the Shaykh ol-Eslâm. He must use the profits from them for specific [religious] purposes and needy persons. It is a requisite that the Shaykh ol-Eslâm be a Russian subject and an inhabitant of the Caucasus.

IRANIAN SUBJECTS RESIDENT IN TIFLIS

In the city of Tiflis and the surrounding villages there are about four thousand people who are Iranian subjects, such as merchants, tradesmen, or farmers. [86] One hundred are merchants, and the rest are tradesmen and farmers. No very prominent merchants reside here.

SUBJECTS OF FOREIGN STATES

The governments of Iran, the Ottoman Empire, and England have commissioners and consul-generals there. The commissioner for the state of Iran is Mirzâ Moḥammad ᶜAli Khân Moᶜin ol-Vezâreh,[123] son of the late Mirzâ Ebrâhim Khân.[124] Since he was in Bombay for some years, he knows English and Hindi very well, both spoken and written. The commissioner there receives from Iranian subjects about six thousand manâts, which is nearly two thousand tomans in Iranian money. For example, in this year, Moḥammad Khân, an Iranian subject who was the Tâjer-bâshi[125] of the Iranian merchants in Tiflis, died. Three thousand manâts from a village belonging to him were received by the commissioner. He handles all legal matters involving Iranian subjects. The officials of the province of the Caucasus never interfere with this. Transit visas are not often used there, but [the commissioner] does issue residence visas to citizens of his nationality. The commissioner's residence is located in an elevated place that is very pleasant and overlooks most of the city.

---

122 On this important religious office see above, Part One, n. 88; for another report on the Shaykh ol-Eslâm of Tiflis see Baron de Baye, *Tiflis*, pp. 23-24.

123 Perhaps the second secretary of the Iranian embassy in London mentioned by Bakhash, *Iran*, pp. 316-17?

124 Text: Ebrâhemi-Khân.

125 That is, the leader of the Iranian merchant community. See above, Part One, n. 152.

COMMERCE

The commerce of this city at present is dominated by Moscow and Russia, coming from there to here. Previously, it was an open transit route and goods came from most of the states of Europe to here, and from here were carried to the states of Iran and the Ottoman Empire. Now this commerce is blocked, and the income of the merchants has been restricted.[126] There are some other types of trade such as silk and the products of Rasht and Khorasan. The [chief] product of this city itself is mostly tobacco. Various kinds of tobacco are grown and exported. [87] In the villages here, since there are many sheep, good wool is produced. The wool trade here is very active and profitable.

There are two or three textile factories in Tiflis. It has a silk-weaver's business [*sha'rbâfi*] and a small iron-worker's shop for knives, scissors, and cutlery.

THE HOSPITAL

On the north side of the city they have built a public hospital which is very large and pleasant and orderly. It has room for three hundred patients. Muslim and Christian patients, both men and women, are there without distinction. It also has male and female employees who take care of everything.

THE MUSEUM

Near the garden and building of the prefecture, there is a building called the museum.[127]

First of all, products of all the ancient and modern kingdoms are displayed in the rooms of this building for viewing.

Second, there are some live birds there and models of animals such as various fowls, bats, dolphins, camels, crows, vultures, and so on.

Third, they have preserved some dead animals of various sizes, such as tigers, leopards, water-buffalo, wild boar, etc., in such a way that they cannot be distinguished from live ones [just] by looking [at them].

Fourth, various types of minerals, forest woods, and plants with pretty leaves and flowers are displayed there as specimens.

They collect some money from each person who comes for a visit and allow him to pass through.

---

126 Cf. Issawi, "Tabriz-Trabzon Trade."

127 The Caucasian Museum run by Gustav Radde. Volume VI of G. Radde, *Die Sammlungen des kaukasischen Museums* (Tiflis, 1901-12) has a detailed description of the museum (with many photographs) and a biography of the curator; see also Jackson, *Persia*, p. 9 (photograph facing p. 7).

THE HOT SPRINGS

There are seven hot springs on the mountain south of the city.[128] Right at the springs, a person is afflicted by the smell of sulphur. [88] They have built a bath near these springs so that the hot water for the baths is the water from the springs. It is extremely hot. They have made a kind of filtration system so that the smell of sulphur from the water is not noticeable in the bath. These natural hot waters make the hair very soft and smooth, but they are harmful to most people and cause illness.[129]

THE THEATERS

There are two theaters in this city. One is called the Georgian Theater, and one the Russian Theater. Another theater has also been opened recently which is named the Municipal Theater. Three years have been spent building this theater and acquiring its furnishings, and yet it is still unfinished. It will be very large and grand.

RECREATION SPOTS

One of the places for enjoying oneself is the "Boulevard," which is a popular place to visit and [has] a park. It is large, and the park has an iron fence. They have placed cast-iron chairs and benches around the park. In the middle of the park, there is a large pool. Water flows into it from the Kura River so that many fountains spout up. This park is in three tiers. There is a small building for providing tea, coffee, and cigarettes at the last level.

Another of the places for enjoying oneself in Tiflis is popularly known as the "Club Building" [*emârat-e qlub*], one large room [of which] is where the military personnel meet, another is where business men meet, and another where tradesmen meet. They get together at night in this building, music is played continuously, and attractive female singers sing and play. The people at each of these clubs do as they please, some occupied with listening, and some occupied with reading newspapers and books. These groups have conversations and discussions of their affairs with each other in complete comfort. [89] In each club, employees taking care of the rooms bring immediately whatever anyone wishes to eat or drink and at the end collect the price for whatever was consumed. People [belong] to these clubs on a yearly basis and keep their membership tickets at hand. The annual fee for the officer's club (military men)

---

[128] These springs were famous; the Georgian name for Tiflis comes in fact from the word for "warm" (tbili); see *Great Soviet Encyclopedia*, 25:427.

[129] It is remarkable that Farâhâni seems unaware of the therapeutic value of the springs and regards them as a bath rather than a spa.

is twenty manâts. The annual fee for the business man's club is sixteen manâts per person. The amount for the tradesman's club is eleven manâts per person. One night each week, a member may bring his wife along. The men and the ladies eat and drink together and go on walks and talk and play. It is required that these ladies who accompany the men to the club once a week not be boisterous, contentious, or dissolute in appearance. There is a specific number of annual memberships in each of these clubs. Beyond that number, additional [people] are "unofficial members" [*birun-nevis*]. These unofficial members must pay more than the required amount each year until some [member] quits or dies. If some person quits or dies, [he takes his place] and will pay a yearly amount like another member.

If a person wants to join one of these clubs temporarily, he must have one of the official, yearly members of the club give a guarantee of his suitability and good behavior. They certify in their records that so and so has stood as guarantor for so and so to enter such and such a club. Then he receives a ticket and accompanies the one vouching for him to the club. A temporary member of the officer's club must pay three manâts per night; a temporary member of the business man's club two manâts per night; and a temporary member of the tradesman's club one manât per night. If this temporary member wants to come to the club the night the ladies come, [90] he must pay double the amount mentioned.

Three nights a year they allow general admittance to all the clubs so that anyone who wishes may come to enjoy himself without anyone having to stand as guarantor. On these three nights, whatever funds are collected beyond the expenses of the clubs are given to the poor and to wayfarers. This building and the clubs are considered a kind of free-masonry,[130] and the expenses and profits are [those of] that company. That is, several individuals, with the permission of the government, enter into partnership, rent this building, and acquire this equipment. Their income and expenses are determined and registered in the account-books. Whatever the

---

[130] Farâhâni is using the term "free-masonry" in the vague sense it had in nineteenth century Iran, when it was applied to a variety of economic, political, and social associations. The term may have occurred to him in this context because two of the leading Iranian advocates of free-masonry, Malkam Khân and Âkhundzâdeh had been associated with each other in Tiflis. See Hamid Algar, "An Introduction to the History of Freemasonry in Iran," *Middle Eastern Studies* 6(1970):276-96; Esmâʿil Râ'in, *Farâmushkhâneh va frâmâsunri dar Iran* (Tehran, 1348/1969).

profit is after paying the expenses the partners divide. There are male and female servants and cooks for the building and the club who have fixed monthly salaries and collect them month by month.

NEWSPAPERS OF TIFLIS

In this city, there are three newspapers which are printed and published in the Turkish language. One is named *Light of the Caucasus* [*Żiâ'-e Qafqâz*]; one is named *The Translator* [*Terjomân*] in Bâghcheh-sarây; and one is named *The Album* [*Keshkul*]. None of these three newspapers is very distinguished or remarkable–they are Turkish.

THE COSSACKS

The inhabitants of this area [come from] various ethnic groups [*ṭâyefeh*]. One group [is that of] the Cossacks [*Qazâqs*][131] who are very healthy and tall and who are instructed from childhood in horsemanship and archery. Most of them serve in the government; occasionally, they also engage in agriculture. However, they do not pay taxes to the government. Their form of taxation is by providing cavalry. The horses and harnessings are their own, and they take implements of war such as rifles, lead, and gunpowder from the government. While they are away from home on duty, the state provides stipends for them. The dress of their men and women resembles [that] of the Turkomans. [91]

THE CHECHEN

The Chechen[132] are another group. This group is also of tall stature, with long hair and yellow complexion. They descended from Mongols who decided to settle here. They belong to the Shâfeᶜi rite [of Islam]. Their dress is like that of the Turkomans. They are never obligated to provide cavalry or soldiers for the state. The Cossack and Chechen groups are both experts at singing and dancing.

THE CIRCASSIANS[133]

This group is fair skinned with black hair. They are Sunnis. Their dress is close to the dress of the Turkomans. They have strange customs and are not very religious.

[131] By Qazâq, Farâhâni is probably not referring just to the Kazakhs but to the more diffuse groupings of Turkic and Ukrainian peoples known loosely as the "Cossacks." See Ronald Wixman, *The Peoples of the USSR: An Ethnographic Handbook* (Armonk, 1984), pp. 50-52.

[132] The text consistently reads *ḥechen*. The Chechen were a Sunni Muslim people, probably of Caucasian origin and closely related to the Ingush and Nakh. See Wixman, *Peoples of the USSR*, pp. 43-44; Shirin Akiner, *Islamic Peoples of the Soviet Union* (revised edition; London, 1986), pp. 175-81.

[133] As used by Farâhâni and many other writers, the term "Circassian" (*Cherkess*) refers to a variety of peoples in the Caucasus; most were Sunni Muslims. See Wixman, *Peoples of the USSR*, pp. 45, 49; Akiner, *Islamic Peoples*, pp. 230-36.

THE LEZG[134]

This group is also tall in stature. Many of them possess landed property, affluence, riches, and wealth. Formerly, the Georgians were held in relation to them as slaves and slavegirls. Their dress for women and men is the *kamarchin*,[135] like the dress of the ancient inhabitants of Iran.

THE GEORGIANS

This group is one of the Christian sects. Their [style of] dressing is a mixture of European ["Frankish"] and ancient Iranian clothing. They are very handsome, ruddy-complexioned, with black hair. They are very timid and cowardly and pleasure-seeking. Many lack wit and perspicacity. They while away much of their time seeking pleasure, feasting, and being neglectful [of their social responsibilities].

THE ARMENIANS

This group is also one of the Christian sects. Most [of them] are short and ugly and dirty. Some are occupied as cultivators and some are occupied as tradesmen. Previously, they used to be very pious and religious. They had numerous fast days during the year. On the fast days, they would never go to work and refrained from pleasure and mirth and music. Their chief fast-days lasted for seven weeks. Now they have become irreligious and do not observe these kinds of rites. [92] It is curious that although the Armenians and Georgians are both Christians, they do not intermarry.

THE MÂLÂGHÂN[136]

This type is mostly slender, blond, and ruddy. They are one of the Christian sects, but they do not have priests. Their custom is that three or four of the elders and wise men of their people are appointed as priests and headmen, and they refer their affairs to them. They do not put pictures of Jesus and Mary in their churches. They pray [facing] in any direction. They consider pork, araq, wine, tobacco, pipes, cigars, garlic, onions, and fish without scales to be

---

134 Text: Lagzi. The name of these people is given in English in a variety of forms: Lazg, Lezg, Lezgh, Lezghin, etc. Farâhâni, like most writers, is probably using it in a general sense to refer to many distinct peoples of Daghestan. See Wixman, *Peoples of the USSR*, pp. 125-26; Akiner, *Islamic Peoples*, pp. 138-43; and the article "Lazg" in EI_2, 5:729-30.

135 That is to say, it is pleated or has folds.

136 As Farâhâni's description makes clear, he is referring to a religious, not an ethnic, group; this must be the Molokan, who rejected the church, the church hierarchy, icons, fasting, and other aspects of Orthodoxy: See V. Druzhinin, *Molokane* (Leningrad, 1930); Stephen Graham, *A Vagabond in the Caucasus* (London, 1911), p. 235; *Great Soviet Encyclopedia*, 16:476; A. I. Klibanov, *History of Religious Sectarianism in Russia (1860's-1917)* (London, 1982), pp. 151-225. Farâhâni's information probably comes from Farhâd Mirzâ, *Hedâyat*, pp. 310-11.

forbidden. They fast three nights. They wash and shroud their dead, place them in a wooden coffin, bury them in a very deep tomb, and pray over them. Some consider circumcision lawful, and they often observe the regulations of Islam.

THE TURKS

Some of these originated from the Mongol group and some were from the province of Azerbayjan. All are fat, corpulent, ruddy or fair. Their dress resembles Iranian dress. They are of the Shi'ite religion.

THE ARMY

Because Tiflis is the capital of the Caucasus and the residence of the Governor-General [*farmân-farmâ*], ten or twelve thousand Russian troops are usually garrisoned there. The troops go from there to any place in the Caucasus they may be needed. Russian troops are levied from the nobles and commoners. They enter training at the age of twenty-one and remain in the barracks for five years occupied with training. They also travel for five years, so they remain in service to the age of thirty-two, and then they are discharged. [93] The people of the Caucasus and Qarâbâgh are exempt from this duty to the age of twenty-five. However, this will apparently be the last year of this exemption.

GOVERNMENT SPIES

One of the laudable practices frequently used in the Russian Empire is the appointment of secret spies in every city and town.

There are few quarters, streets, guest-houses, or coffeehouses where a correspondent is not concealed; indeed, there are informants in every household of any importance. In this way, they are informed about every spot of their kingdom. This procedure has always been one of the customs of great rulers. In this way, Ardashir Bâbakân was aware every morning of any event that occurred in his kingdom. He appointed secret correspondents in other domestic and foreign provinces.

Among the sayings of Buzarjmehr[137] is that twelve things are necessary to uphold the monarchy: First, abstinence from concupiscence, anger, and haughtiness. Second, honesty in speech and fidelity to promises and agreements. Third, consultations with wise men. Fourth, honoring and respecting the nobles and scholars according to the degree of their intelligence and understanding.

[137] Common name for a semi-legendary minister of Khosrow Anushirvân (sixth century A. D.), famous for his wisdom, justice, and political finesse. See Dehkhodâ, *Loghatnâmeh*, fascicle 173, p. 366; EI_2, 1:1358-59 [s.v. "Buzurgmihr"].

Fifth, investigation of the conduct of tax collectors and judges, rewarding the good and punishing the bad. Sixth, careful investigation into the condition of prisoners and criminals, duly punishing those who have done wrong and releasing the innocent. Seventh, making the roads and streets safe. Eighth, acquiring implements of warfare of good quality. Ninth, sound policy in disciplining the peasants. Tenth, respecting children, relatives, and the tribes. Eleventh, providing income for ministers, boon companions, bureaucrats, and soldiers according to their merit. Twelfth, appointing spies in every province in order to be informed confidentially and quickly about events. [94]

Whenever Bahman ebn-e Esfandiâr[138] appointed an agent to a place, he sent a secret informant along with him. If the agent's conduct was good, he was held in esteem; if not, he was deposed.

DEPARTURE FROM TIFLIS

Having arrived in Tiflis Thursday morning the eighteenth of Shavvâl [*sic*], I set out from Tiflis seated in the train coach on Friday morning the nineteenth[139] at the crack of dawn. There are sixteen stations from Tiflis to Batum.

DESCRIPTION OF SIGHTS ALONG THE WAY[140]

From the suburbs of the city through which we passed, an expansive plain was reached. The mountains receded. Many villages were visible from far and near, on the left and right, on the slopes of the mountains. Then [we] descended into valleys which were surrounded by forests. Clear streams and rivers flowed in most of these valleys. Some of the places beside the mountain consisted of dry-farms and forest trees resembling little gardens. Sometimes great mountains full of snow were visible. Beside the valleys, some stone houses in good condition had been built which were the dwellings of Armenians and Georgians. Herds of sheep, cattle, pigs, and mares were busy grazing in these meadows and fields.

---

[138] A legendary pre-Islamic hero king of Iran, sometimes identified with Artaxerxes Longimanus [Derâzdast]. The legend of Bahman is recounted by Ferdowsi in the *Shâhnâmeh*, abridged translation by R. Levy, *The Epic of the Kings* (London, 1967), pp. 218-20; S̲aᶜâlebi/Zotenberg, *Rois des Perses*, pp. 377-78 etc.

[139] Farâhâni's dating is confused here: He states above that he arrived in Tiflis on the morning of Friday the eighteenth, which was in fact a Friday. Presumably he left on Saturday the nineteenth (1 August 1885).

[140] Farâhâni's description of the route from Tiflis to Batum is much less detailed than that of Sayf od-Dowleh, *Safarnâmeh*, 80 ff., who visited Gori, Kutais, etc. The ease of Farâhâni's travel by the railway is in sharp contrast to the difficulties faced by travellers of the earlier period; cf. Mounsey, *Journey*, pp. 28-36.

Numerous rivers flow alongside the railway so that iron bridges have been erected for the train to pass over them. Every place along the way where there was a mountain, they cut a tunnel through it. For example, they have bored through the mountains in three places along the way so that the train can pass through them. One is near the Bi Ji Tuban station where the train is inside the mountain for about forty seconds,[141] and another also takes twenty-five seconds, and yet another also twenty seconds. [95]

In short, this route was very pleasant. Most of the time, hilly country, forests, streams, and greenery were [visible along the way] until, two stations before Batum, the sea came into view. Sometimes the railway was close to the sea, and sometimes it was far away. Three hours before nightfall on Saturday the twentieth of Shavvâl[142] we arrived at Batum; so from Tiflis to Batum, allowing for the delay in the stations, takes about fifteen hours. Anyone who goes directly from Baku to Batum takes altogether thirty-three hours: That is, from Baku to Tiflis is seventeen hours travel time; the train stops in Tiflis for one hour and passengers disembark and board; and it goes from Tiflis to Batum in fifteen hours. The trip may be longer or shorter than this according to difficulties caused by damage, congestion, or disrepair.

BATUM

Batum is a port located on the slopes of forested mountains along the sea. On its right side is the river Chulug, and on its left side is the Churuq,[143] but neither is near the city. Formerly, it was one of the old possessions of the Ottoman Empire, and the chief port of the Russian Empire on this sea was Poti, until in this last Russo-Ottoman war this port also came into the possession of the Russians.[144] They built the railway line, and Batum became the

---

[141] Farhâd Mirzâ, *Hedâyat*, p. 46, makes it clear that this is the tunnel between Surâm (Surami) and Bi Ji Tuban (marked on some maps, such as that in Marvin, *Eternal Fire*, as Bejeloubani); on the Surami tunnel, cf. Curzon, *Persia*, 1:64-65.

[142] The chronology is still confused; as he notes below, the twentieth of Shavvâl was a Sunday.

[143] This sentence is confusing: Both the Çolok and the Çuruk-su are north of Batum; the river to the south is the Adzharis.

[144] I.e., the Russo-Turkish war of 1877-78. The Russians, despite advances elsewhere, failed to capture Batum, which was very heavily fortified. The Ottomans, under pressure from the British, ceded it to Russia as part of the agreement reached at the Congress of Berlin. See W.E.D. Allen and Paul Muratoff, *Caucasian Battlefields* (Cambridge, 1953), pp. 123 ff.; W. N. Medlicott, *The Congress of Berlin and After* (London, 1938), pp. 101-25. A description of the city under Ottoman rule may be found in Sayf od-Dowleh, *Safarnâmeh*, p. 90.

transit port and traffic from Poti decreased.[145] The distance between Batum and Poti is about six farsakhs by sea. In olden times, this Batum was part of Georgia and [was] a fortress. It is not improbable that this place is the "Fortress of Tum" in Georgia which the Amir Timur conquered.

At present, its population is about two thousand households, which is about eight or nine thousand people. Very orderly and well kept bazaars and shops and streets have been built. [96] Most of the shops and houses from earlier times have been torn down for the sake of improving the streets. They have built a very large station for the railway trains and made a new public park beside the sea which is a promenade for the common people. They have also built five or six guest-houses and hotels for the public. The old citadel there, which used to belong to the Ottomans and was on top of an earthen hill, has been fortified. Cannons have been set up on top of all its towers. The gun-carriages are on iron tracks like a railway, so that one cannoneer can move a very large cannon wherever he wishes.[146]

The Russians are very determined to make this city flourish. For example, for the sake of cheapness and abundance of goods, they have decreed that they will not impose customs duties on anything imported into this city.[147] Generally in the Russian Empire they collect as much in customs duties as they possibly can on whatever enters the empire from abroad (a description of this will be recounted [in the account of my] return). As for whatever is exported from its territory, both goods of its country and goods from foreign countries, [they] are not subject to any customs duties. This is so goods from abroad do not enter their country, and their own country's goods can be bought and exported without customs duties.

---

[145] Among European travellers in this region, Mounsey, *Journey*, pp. 11-36, noted Batum's lack of development under Turkish rule and the great difficulties in travelling through the Caucasus during his trip in 1865, in order to point out the advantages that could be derived from rail links with Tiflis. His account makes an interesting contrast with that of Farâhâni and European travellers after the completion of the railroad, such as Marvin, *Eternal Fire*, pp. 111-24, and Edgar Boulangier, *Voyage à Merv* (Paris, 1888), pp. 32-70.

[146] Marvin, *Eternal Fire*, p. 99, and several other travellers noted that the Russians were forbidden to fortify Batum under the terms of the Treaty of Berlin but did so anyway, usually claiming that they were building "barracks."

[147] In accordance with Article 59 of the Treaty of Berlin, Batum was given the status of a free port until Russia repudiated that article of the treaty in July, 1886. This matter and others related to Russian efforts to develop Batum (and the concern this caused some policy makers in Britain) are discussed at some length in Marvin, *Eternal Fire*, pp. 99-124.

This port has a large customs house. Most of the transit of Iranian subjects, such as pilgrims and travellers to Istanbul and Egypt, is from this port. Individuals who exchanged their Iranian money in Baku for manâts and imperials change [them] to Ottoman lira here. [97] It is profitable and convenient to change [the money here].

MONEY IN CIRCULATION IN RUSSIA

At this point, the money currently used in the Russian Empire must be described.[148] They have a copper coinage called the kopeck. These are minted in several denominations: two kopecks, three kopecks, and five kopecks; five of those kopecks equal one shâhi manât. Their silver coinage, named *churk* [?], is minted [in denominations] from five kopecks (which equal one shâhi manât) up to one manât; so ten of these kopecks equal two shâhi manâts, and fifteen kopecks equal three shâhi manâts, and twenty kopecks equal one ᶜabbâsi manât. (The well known *chatvar* ["quarter"] which is brought to Iran equals one ᶜabbâsi manât; five of these chatvars equal one manât.[149]) They also have silver coinage for five shâhis, six to ten shâhis, and fifteen shâhis; silver manâts are also minted. The value of the silver manât also fluctuates at times; usually its value is 140 kopecks. The value of the paper manât is one hundred kopecks. The silver manât is very rare, even by name, but silver money smaller than the manât is plentiful although much of it is silver alloyed with copper and pewter, and its alloy is greater than its silver [content]. Most of the money which is in use and circulation is this paper manât, which is in [denominations of] one manât to one thousand manâts. The manâts have many differences in color, paper, and writing. In this area, one toman of Iranian money equals three manâts and one shâhi manât to four manâts, since the value of every manât fluctuates from three Iranian krans to three and a half krans.

---

[148] Farâhâni's discussion, here and throughout the text, may be clarified by keeping the following points in mind: As always, the value of a denomination of currency was affected by whether it was issued in paper or metal and, if metal, by variations in the relative value of silver to gold. The manât (more or less equivalent to the rouble) could be a paper note or a silver coin. It was usually issued as a paper note which would, in theory, be worth 100 kopecks. The silver shâhi manât (piatek) was 5 kopecks; the silver ᶜabbâsi manât (dvougrivenii) was 20 kopecks. See Georgii Mikhailovich, *Monnaies de l'empire de Russie, 1725-1894* (Paris, 1916) and V. I. Petrov, *Catalogue des monnaies russes* (Graz, 1964).

[149] This may reflect some local variation in the value of the currency; normally the chatvar (tchetvartak) should equal 1/4 rouble or 25 kopecks.

[150] The imperial should be equal to ten roubles.

Their gold money is the imperial, the value of which varies from eight paper manâts to eight and a half manâts,[150] which is twenty-four to twenty-five and a half Iranian krans. [98] Also, one of their coins is named the ducat, the value of which is usually three paper manâts.

The Ottoman lira there varies in its value from eight manâts and three ᶜabbâsi manâts to nine manâts and two ᶜabbâsi manâts, which may be from twenty-six to twenty-eight Iranian krans.

PRODUCTS OF THE PORT OF BATUM

This city does not have much trade in its own products, but rather the goods of Moscow and Russia. Sometimes wool, silk from Rasht, felt, and petroleum for transport to Istanbul and other Ottoman cities pass through here. It also has no great merchants.

FOREIGN SUBJECTS

There is a deputy-consul here on behalf of the Ottoman government. Some of the land-owners here were formerly Ottoman subjects and now retain that citizenship. Their legal affairs are handled by this deputy-consul.

There is also a deputy-consul here on behalf of the English government. There are about twenty English citizens.

On behalf of the Iranian government, there is sometimes a man named Tekrân, an Armenian who used to be a merchant and now is bankrupt and appears to be a dishonest and inefficient individual. Sometimes a temporary official comes here on behalf of the consul in Tiflis during the pilgrimage season. At this time, he was someone named Ḥâjji Âqâ Bayk. There are about twenty persons in this city who are Iranian subjects such as proprietors of coffeehouses, brokers,[151] bricklayers, and so on. But save us from the likes of these coffee-men and brokers![152] [99]

At first they declare with great warmth their common nationality and common religion; then they swindle the pilgrims as much as they can, with every kind of trickery. For example, they insist that the pilgrim's passport must be taken for the endorsement of the Iranian consul, the Ottoman consul, the English consul, and the administration of Batum and that this takes one or two days to get through. The pilgrims, who are also in a hurry to leave are

---

[151] The term translated here and subsequently as "broker" is *dalâl*. This was a person who attempted to serve, always with an eye to turning a profit for himself, as an intermediary for travellers in many respects—giving advice, helping with shopping, arranging housing and meals, etc.

[152] A hackneyed verse quoted here by Farâhâni is omitted from the translation.

helpless: whatever money the brokers demand the pilgrims give for the sake of not being delayed. They take the passports, put some meaningless writing on them, and give them back. Endorsement of the passport in Batum is never needed. Another example of the activities of these Iranian brokers and coffee-shop owners is that they implore the pilgrims, with every [appearance of] sincerity, "If you have any dutiable goods [with you], conceal [them] in a pocket or hat or mattress or pillow." The poor pilgrim is deceived by their words and hides his things. Meanwhile, they make a deal with the customs officers and then inform them that this pilgrim has concealed dutiable items in such and such a place. The customs officer extracts the goods, imprisons the duped pilgrim, and collects a criminal fine in addition to the customs duty. In this way way, the brokers get a share. The Armenian Tekrân collaborates with them and a portion [of the take] goes to him.

SHIPPING COMPANIES

As for the steamship companies that are here, a detailed list follows. The post of each government goes via the steamship company of its own nationals: the Austrian company known as Lloyd;[153] the Compagnie Messagèries Français; a French company named Paquet; a French company named Français [?];[154] and a Russian company. One ship from each company comes every week. Sometimes an English ship also comes, but it is not [part of] a company and is without order or regularity. [100]

THE HARBOR OF BATUM

The harbor of Batum is a very good harbor. They have done an excellent job of lining the seashore with stone and have built a wooden pier at which the large steamers can dock. One side of the pier is adjacent to land, so one boards the steamers without the trouble of taking a launch. On account of the expenses of building the harbor, they have ordered that all ships which enter this gulf pay a fee.

---

153 Text: Lut. On the shipping companies in Batum, and the success of the Austrian Lloyd Co., see P. E. Schoenberg, "The Evolution of Transport in Turkey (Eastern Thrace and Asia Minor) under Ottoman Rule, 1856-1918," *Middle Eastern Studies* 13(1977):359-72; Curzon, *Persia*, pp. 27-28; Issawi, "Tabriz-Trabzon Trade."

154 Text: *f-r-s-n-h* (vocalization uncertain).

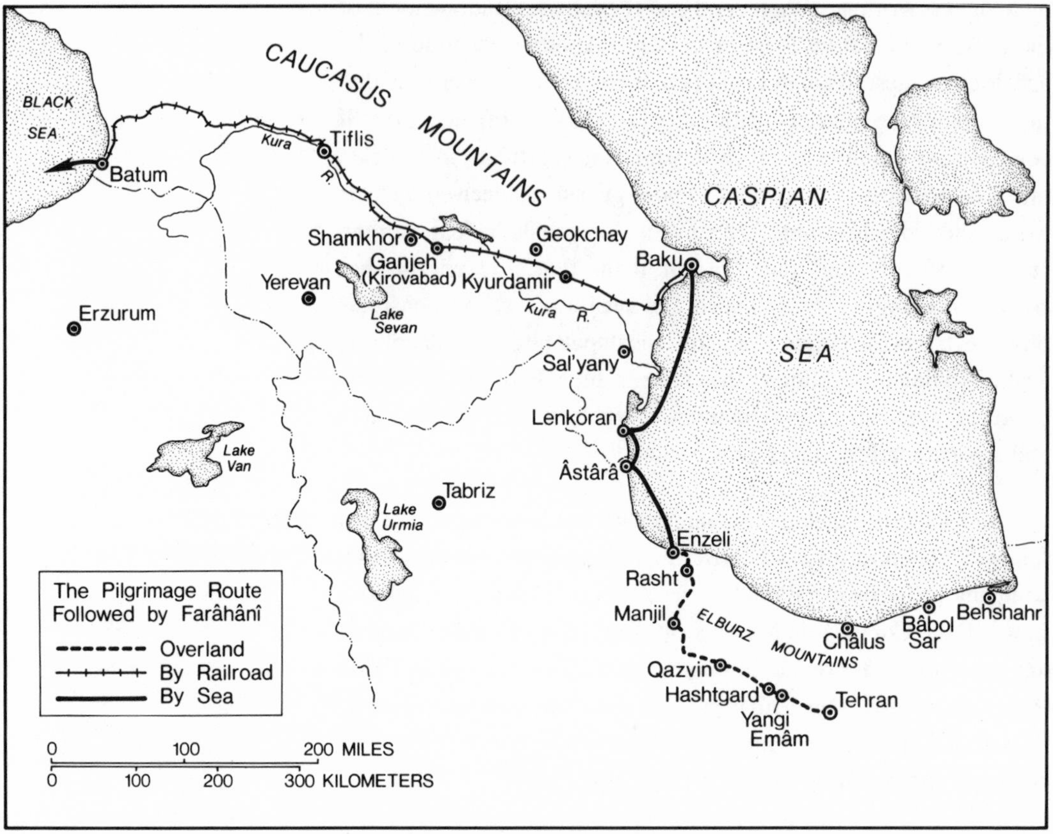

Map 4. The pilgrimage route followed by Farâhâni: Tehran to Batum.

PART THREE
THE OTTOMAN EMPIRE

DEPARTURE FROM BATUM

From Batum, some Khorâsâni, Gilâni, and Âẕerbayjâni Turkish pilgrims and I took places on the steamer named *Alexander the Second*, which belongs to the Russian company, at sunset on Sunday the twentieth of Shavvâl [2 August]. This ship and its furnishings were very clean and neat. Its fare for third class, which is the place ordinary people sit, is nine manâts; the fare for a second class cabin is twice that of third class, or eighteen manâts; and the fare for a first class cabin is three times that of third class, or twenty-seven manâts.

From Batum to Istanbul is 626 Arabic miles, which is a journey of sixty-eight hours by commercial steamer at a moderate speed. So each hour [the steamer] goes nine miles, which is three farsakhs; the rest of the time is spent waiting in the ports and harbors and the Bosphorus.

THE BLACK SEA

This Black Sea is called the "Black Sea" in every language: the Arabs call it Baḥr-e asvâd [*sic*]; the Greeks called it the Pontus; the Turks say Kara Deniz; and in French they say Mer Noire.

Europeans have delimited it in this manner: [101] In the north it is bounded by European Russia; in the northeast by the Caucasus mountains; in the south by Asia Minor, and in the west by the European part of the Ottoman Empire. The length of this sea from northwest to southeast is 140 parasangs. Its breadth varies from 93 parasangs to 53 parasangs. Its utmost depth is 1,050 fathoms. On the surface, its water appears black, but in a container a small quantity is not black. Owing to the many rivers that empty into this sea, its water is sweeter than the water of other seas. For this reason, its fish are not commendable, and it is a sea without profit. Pearls and coral and so on are never obtained in it. They say the "*Majmaᶜ ol-baḥrayn*" which the glorious Koran mentions is this very sea.[1]

---

[1] A phrase meaning "confluence of two rivers [or seas]" which occurs in the Koran, 18:60.

THE JOURNEY BY SEA

The first night we set out, the weather was very mild and the steamship travelled quite smoothly. The saying of the sage Bâselus[2] came to mind, who said "As for ships sinking, be afraid of that time when they are going well and smoothly." Two or three hours after nightfall the wind picked up, and the weather became overcast. The sea got very choppy, so that water came up to the highest point of the ship. Many men fell down and began to moan and groan. Mollâ Reżâ-ye Astarâbâdi,[3] who is considered one of the ulama of Astarâbâd, became seasick in these conditions and fell down saying, "What was Mecca that I should come to this? Now that I'm dying, I wish that I had paid someone to perform the pilgrimage for me and not have experienced these troubles myself." One of the landlords [owning] estates in Khorasan (where cotton is usually grown and is very profitable) was saying at that time, "Oh that which is carded! I wish your seeds had disappeared so we would not be obliged to make this pilgrimage!" In any case, the first thing in the morning, the weather became mild and the storm subsided. [102] The travel time from Batum to Trabzon by steamship is not more than eight or nine hours. Owing to the storm, [the ship] moved very slowly on the day of arrival at Trabzon harbor. It anchored beside the Trabzon harbor two hours after sunset.

THE PORT OF TRABZON

Trabzon is an abbreviated form of "Ṭarâbezun." In books, it is written [either] "Ṭarâbezun" or "Aṭrâbazandeh." According to a story, the army of Ardashir Bâbakân came near this place, and his troops obtained much honey in the forested area. After they had eaten it, it was learned that there was poison in it, and many of the troops perished because of that.[4]

The custom of the commercial ships upon arriving at Trabzon is this: They stop for eight or twelve hours or more in this port due to the need to unload cargo and to attend to business. After the

[2] Perhaps Basilius? See Franz Rosenthal, *The Classical Heritage in Islam* (Berkeley, 1975), pp. 36, 132. The proverb is reminiscent of St. Augustine's "Fear the sea, even when it is calm."

[3] This is apparently the same religious dignitary discussed by Eᶜtemâd os-Salṭaneh, *Ma'âs̱er*, p. 15 (Afshâr edition, p. 206); Farâhâni mentions him again in his listing of Iranian notables making the pilgrimage the year of his own journey (below, Part Four, p. 191.) It would appear that he was killed shortly after the pilgrimage, as Eᶜtemâd os-Salṭaneh calls him a martyr (*shahid*) implying that he was dead at the time of the publication of the *Ma'âs̱er* in 1306/1889.

[4] Cf. Sayf od-Dowleh, *Safarnâmeh*, pp. 90-91; Farhâd Mirzâ, *Hedâyat*, p. 51. Trabzon is famous for its honey production; stories about armies finding poisoned honey in the environs of the city go back at least far as the one recorded in Xenophon, *Anabasis*, IV, 8:20-21.

amount of time the steamer will stay in Trabzon has been determined, they inform the passengers so that anyone who wishes may enter Trabzon. Several fellow travellers and I took a rowboat and went into Trabzon. The Trabzon harbor has been somewhat improved, but it is necessary to take a rowboat. It is not like the Russian harbors.

Anyway, [my] friends and I, along with Ḥâjji Moḥammad Bâqer, a merchant from Milân who was one of [our] friends and companions, went to the house of Ḥâjji Sayyed ᶜAli Âqâ the Merchant, nephew of the late Nâẓem ot-Tojjâr Tabrizi. The aforementioned is very good-natured, cheerful, hospitable, and intelligent. He received us warmly and arranged a full lunch in the Iranian style. In order to honor [us], he also invited a number of [other] merchants. We ate lunch and then went out to sightsee in the city. There are no droshkys or coaches or horses for hire here; even the dignitaries usually go on foot in the streets. [103]

This city is located next to the sea on the side of the mountains and amidst a valley. Three sides of it are mountainous, and because of this its streets go uphill and downhill and its houses are arranged in tiers on the side of the mountains. On the top of a rocky mountain, which is in the city and next to the sea, they have erected the government citadel, bastion, and artillery post. There is always a regiment or two garrisoned in this city and its environs.

The ruins of the old citadel and towers which were built of stone and plaster still remain. There is a deep valley in the middle of town from the midst of which flows a stream. There are houses, tier by tier, on the sides of this valley. They have built a wooden bridge at the top of the valley. There is a square there called Qâbâq Maydâni.

POPULATION AND ADMINISTRATION

This city has a population of about eight thousand households, which is thirty thousand people. It has two thousand shops and eighteen baths. There are sixty districts and places in its environs: that is, there are three mutesarrifats, and each mutesarrifat has twenty *qâ'em-maqâm*s and *modir*s in its administration. Each qâ'em-maqâm and modir is the prefect of one district.[5]

[5]The Ottoman administrative system recognized two types of provinces, major provinces (*velâyat*) headed by a governor-general (*vâli*) and smaller subdivisions governed by a *motaṣarref* (the *sanjaq* or *levâ*, usually referred to in English as the mutesarrifat). The sanjak was divided into smaller administrative units known as the *każâ* and *nâḥiye*, headed by a qâ'em-maqâm (or *kaymakam* in Turkish) or modir (Turkish *müdür*). See Carter Findley, *Bureaucratic Reform in the Ottoman Empire*

RIVERS AND DRINKING WATER

There are two rivers in the midst of this city, one named the Değirmen-dereh and one named the Sürmene.[6] Water from these two rivers flows to most of the houses. The small springs in the city are numerous. Its drinking water comes from these springs. Its river water is heavy and bad-tasting.

POPULAR PROMENADES

The environs of this city are very green and pleasant. There are some forest trees in the streets. One of the attractive places of the city is the Boztepeh mountain, where there is a tomb famous as [that of] Akhi Evrân[7] of the dervishes. [104] It is said that he was one of the servants of the Prince of Martyrs.[8] The Ottomans have faith in him and make supplications and vows [there].

Also in the middle of the city, there is a garden and coffeehouse which has running water and many trees. It is a pleasure place for the populace. Its name is the "Casino." There is another mountain next to the city named Qâriq [?] which is attractive and a summer retreat for the populace.

FOREIGN SUBJECTS

There are three consuls here: the Consul of Iran, the Consul of Russia, and the English Consul. At this time, the Consul of Iran is Ḥâjji Mirzâ Ḥosayn Khân, son of Żiâ os-Salṭaneh,[9] but he himself had gone to Berlin as the companion of Moᶜin ol-Molk the ambassador. His two sons, aged eighteen and twenty, were here and came to see me and accompanied me everywhere. They knew the French and Turkish languages well and are still busy acquiring French science and writing.

There are about eight hundred Iranian subjects in Trabzon and its environs, of whom fifty are merchants and the rest are tradesmen and so on.

(Princeton, 1980), pp. 275, 286. On the velâyat of Trabzon, see *Ṭarabzun velâyateneh makhṣuṣ sâlnâmeh* (Trabzon, 1316/1898).

6 The printed texts have "r-k-r-yan dereh" and "mir-m-neh" respectively; they have been identified with the help of Professor Halil Inalcik.

7 Text: Akhi Ehervân. Akhi Evrân was a semi-legendary Turkish Sufi saint often associated with Ḥâjji Bektâsh (patron saint of the Janissary troops). His tomb is at Kırşehir, not Trabzon, so the reference here is not entirely clear. See EI_2, 1:324-25.

8 The Emâm Ḥosayn, martyred at Karbalâ.

9 This was the name of two Qâjâr princesses; one was the seventh daughter of Fatḥ-ᶜali Shâh; the other was the third daughter of Nâṣer od-Din Shâh. See Bâmdâd, *Rejâl*, 6:155 n. 3 and 1:75 n. 1. It is not clear whether either of these was the mother of this Mirzâ Ḥosayn Khân.

FAMOUS MERCHANTS

The names of the great merchants there are as follows: Ḥâjji Sayyed ᶜAli Âqâ, nephew of Nâẓem ot-Tojjâr; Ḥâjji Mollâ ᶜAli Kho'i; Ḥâjji ᶜAli Aṣghar Kho'i; Mollâ Abu Ṭâleb Kho'i;[10] Âqâ Moḥammad ᶜAli Kho'i; Âqâjân Kho'i; Karbalâ'i Kâẓem Tabrizi; and Âqâ Maḥmud Salmâsi.

TRADE

The commerce of this city is of two types. One is trade in its [own] products, which are as follows: It has beans, hazelnuts, potatoes, tobacco, linen, socks, woven goods, and a little ironworking. [105] The other is trade in goods from outside, the chief ones being sugar, lump-sugar [*qand*], and dried fruits. Trade in silk from Kashan is also quite profitable here.

Merchandise passes from Istanbul to Iran through Trabzon, reaching Tabriz by muleteers overland from Trabzon in twenty-four days.

THE TELEGRAPH

By chance, I happened to go to the telegraph office in this city. First of all, the officers of the telegraph station were all natives of the city of Trabzon. Second, they were all drinking to excess, and I found them drunk and stupefied. In this situation, a parenthetical thought crossed my mind, which is this: One group believes that the telegraph is a new invention and that it was invented by the French. [Another] group of scholars insist that some of the Greek sages invented the telegraph in the time of Alexander the Great. Thus Neẓâmi, on orders of Alb Arslân, versified the exploits of Alexander[11] according to the histories of the Muslims, Jews, Christians, and Hindus, and in the section on the inventions and great works of Alexander, he says [something that might be interpreted as referring to a kind of telegraph[12]].

There is also a reference to the telegraph in another place.[13]

It is no longer known what type of telegraph instrument it was. Logically, [A]nushirvân's "chain of justice"[14] also resembles the

---

[10] Also mentioned by Farhâd Mirzâ, *Hedâyat*, p. 267.

[11] The reference is to the *Eskandarnâmeh*; see above, Part Two, n. 86.

[12] Farâhâni quotes here a line from Neẓâmi; it seems irrelevant, however, and is omitted from the translation.

[13] Farâhâni quotes another rather pointless verse, presumably from Neẓâmi; it is also omitted from the translation.

[14] According to Neẓâm ol-Molk/Darke, *Book of Government*, p. 41, Anushirvân "commanded that a chain should be set up with bells attached to it, within the reach of even a child of seven years old, so that any plaintiffs who came to the court would not need to see a chamberlain; they would pull the chain and the bells would ring; Nushirvan would hear it and redress their grievances."

telegraph since the subjects [were able] to speak directly to the ruler without intermediary. After that period, it was neglected and lost until the beginning of the French Republic. [106]

In the year 1209 [1794-95], this invention was revived in France by means of signals, not in the present manner. In the year 1236 [1820-21], the electric telegraph was invented in France, and it came into use in the Ottoman Empire in the year 1260 [1844-45].[15] Now, I am not here [affirming] the newness or the antiquity of the telegraph; rather my purpose in this discourse has two points. The first is that the officials of the telegraph office of every district must not be appointed from the people of that same district because a telegraph operator from the people of the district is the friend or acquaintance or relative of some people and naturally he will secretly communicate anything that may relate to his friends or kindred to his companions. Or he is the enemy of others and hostile to someone and naturally will discuss something detrimental to his enemies for the sake of appearing brave and capable. Then many affairs will remain hidden owing to the spite of someone among the telegraph officials, and many matters will be divulged. Of necessity, trouble would result from these disclosures. It is the same with judges and tax-collectors from the people of a district. So it is better that every year in every district the telegraph officials be renewed in order that the telegraph officials do not become friends or acquaintances with the populace and affairs remain confidential.

The second [point] is that telegraph officials must not be drunken and intoxicated and addicted to wine.

AN ANECDOTE

There are three types [of people] whose being drunk and intoxicated and addicted to wine is not right. One is the private attendant of the sultan known as the *ᶜamaljât-e khalvat*.[16] Another

---

[15] Farâhâni is surprisingly correct about the signaling system devised in France by the Chappé brothers in 1794. The electric telegraph, of course, was invented independently in the United States and England and patented in 1837. One may guess that Farâhâni's source of information about this was a Frenchman or his anti-British sentiments are clouding his judgment. The telegraph was not introduced in the Ottoman Empire until 1855 and the time of the Crimean War; the system was developed primarily during the period 1864-76. It was introduced in Iran by Malkam Khân in 1859; after 1864, it was developed extensively there as part of the British efforts to establish telegraph communications with India. See John Reid, *The Telegraph in America* (New York, 1879); Bernard Lewis, *The Emergence of Modern Turkey* (Oxford, 1968), pp. 185-87; Farmayan, "Forces of Modernization," p. 150; Nashat, *Reform*, pp. 157-58.

[16] An office similar to that of a royal chamberlain.

is the type of scribe known as *monshi*.[17] And another is the telegraph official. The drunkenness and wine imbibing of any one of these three groups will in the end cause much trouble and mischief. [107] No matter will remain secret since all three of these groups are people [dealing with] secret and private matters. Concealment of secrets is not compatible with wine-drinking.[18]

A STORY

Thus the author of the *Târikh-e Bayhaqi* [*Bayhaqi's History*][19] writes, "ᶜAbdus, who was one of the ᶜamaljât-e khalvat of Solṭân Masᶜud, son of Solṭân Maḥmud, son of Seboktekin, revealed the sultan's secrets in the company of drunkards, and this very point was one of the causes of the extinction of his dynasty." A summary of this story[20] is that Solṭân Masᶜud, in accordance with the suspicious and despotic character he had, and owing to the backbiting of Bu Sahl-e Zowzani and some other of his intimates, had ᶜAli Qarib Dâryâq [*sic*][21] and Sepahsâlâr Ghâzi, who were among the great ministers of the Maḥmudi government,[22] imprisoned. One of the notables of the Maḥmudi government who remained in office and had a retinue and an army was the Khᵛârazmshâh Altuqâsh [*sic*].[23] [108] Solṭân Masᶜud consulted with his close advisors on capturing him and decided that the close advisors write a rescript to the tribal chief [*qâ'ed*] Monjuq to get rid of the Khᵛârazmshâh. The rescript was drawn up and sent out. ᶜAbdus told this story at a drinking bout to Abu'l-Fatḥ Ḥâtemi, and Abu'l-Fatḥ retold it at a drinking bout with Abu Moḥammad Masᶜadi, the agent of the Khᵛârazmshâh. Masᶜadi

---

17 A private secretary.

18 Farâhâni quotes five lines of verse by an unidentified poet; they are omitted from the translation.

19 A masterpiece of early Persian historiography, written by Abu'l-Fażl Bayhaqi (386-470/996-1077). It was a detailed history of the Ghaznavid dynasty (the main line of which ruled in eastern Iran and Afghanistan from 366-582/977-1186). The surviving fragments deal primarily with the reign of Masᶜud (421-32/1031-41.) There are several editions of the text, notably that of ᶜAli Fayyâż, *Târikh-e Bayhaqi* (Mashhad, 1971). For an analysis of it see Marilyn Waldman, *Toward a Theory of Historical Narrative* (Columbus, 1980).

20 This is based on a long section in the *Târikh-e Bayhaqi*, pp. 402 ff. Farâhâni's version is translated as he presents it, even though it misspells many names and is at some variance with Bayhaqi's original text.

21 The text should probably read "and Aryâroq."

22 The government [*dowlat*] of Solṭân Maḥmud of Ghazna (388-421/998-1030).

23 Read "Altontâsh"; the former slave of Seboktekin who held the governorship of the province of Khᵛârazm for many years (408-23/1017-32). On the botched plot to assassinate him, see C. E. Bosworth, *The Ghaznavids* (second edition; Beirut, 1973), pp. 60-61.

immediately wrote the details in code and sent a messenger to the Khᵛârazmshâh. Simultaneously with Qâ'ed-e Monjuq's receipt of the news, the Khᵛârazmshâh was informed of the sultan's intention and put Qâ'ed-e Monjuq to death. The news reached the sultan, who excused himself with the Khᵛârazmshâh by claiming that it was a lie. Nevertheless, the Khᵛârazmshâh never again felt secure and initiated an investigation of this point. For the rest of his life, the Khᵛârazmshâh remained in discord with and outside the domination of the sultan. After the murder of the Khᵛârazmshâh, his son Hârun, for the same reason, was not secure and manifested his opposition. The first trouble and disturbance which existed in the Masᶜudi regime was this very matter of Khᵛârazm.

My purpose in citing this story is that people who drink wine should not be entrusted with secrets. Although the requirement of sound judgment is that one not reveal personal secrets to anyone, [this applies] especially to wine-drinkers and so on: "The man who is master of the world is the man who depends on no man."[24] [109]

"Every secret which goes beyond two people becomes public" is [a maxim] attributed to His Eminence the Commander of the Faithful ᶜAli.[25] In truth, this same thing has been expressed by the proverb, "Nothing should be said in private which should not be said in public."[26]

Plato was asked, "Who is the weakest of men?" He answered, "The one who is unable to keep a secret concealed."

DEPARTURE FROM TRABZON

Anyhow, we departed from Trabzon at about sunset, accompanied to the end of the pier by the sons of Ḥâjji Mirzâ Ḥosayn Khân and a group of merchants. Ḥâjji Sayyed ᶜAli Âqâ,[our] host, came [all the way] to the steamer with a group of merchants. The steamer departed at sunset and arrived at the port of Giresun[27] at seven and a half hours after sunset [of the night before] Tuesday the twenty-second [midnight, 3-4 August]. The steamer dropped anchor there and stayed about one hour loading and unloading.

---

[24] A proverbial saying; quoted in Arabic in the text. The proverb is followed by two Persian verses by an unidentified poet; they are omitted from the translation.

[25] The proverb is quoted in Arabic; often attributed to ᶜAli, it was also used by a number of Persian poets: see Dehkhodâ, *Amsâl*, p. 1226.

[26] A proverbial saying attributed to the poet Saᶜdi; see Dehkhodâ, *Amsâl*, p. 957.

[27] [Marginal note from the original text:] "It is 68 miles from the port of Trabzon to Giresun."

THE PORT OF GIRESUN

Giresun is one of the ports which is a modirate; it is one of the dependencies of Trabzon. It has about two thousand resident households, which is a population of seven or eight thousand people. Its harbor is very bad.

THE PORT OF ORDU

After travelling from Giresun, [the steamer] entered a port named Ordu on Tuesday morning at seven o'clock and anchored there unloading and collecting the post. On the way between the port of Giresun and the port of Ordu, there is a little port named Cape Yuros.[28]

The port of Ordu is one of the dependencies of Trabzon and the seat of a qâ'em-maqâmate. It has about one thousand resident households and 150 shops. Its population is four thousand. Its harbor is very bad. The steamer stayed there two hours and departed. [110]

THE PORT OF SAMSUN

One hour before sunset, it reached the port of Samsun and anchored. Between the ports of Samsun and Ordu there are two small ports named Cape Yasun[29] and Cape Vona.[30] Because the steamer was late arriving at this port, and it had cargo and passengers, it stayed in this port the night [before] Wednesday and the day of Wednesday the twenty-third [5 August] until sunset. Because of the extended layover, most of the passengers went into Samsun.

THE CITY OF SAMSUN

Samsun is located on the slopes of the mountain. Its environs are forested. It is [part of] the province of Amasya. It is twelve farsakhs to the city of Amasya. [Samsun] is a mutesarrifat. It has six thousand resident households, so its population is twenty thousand people. It possesses one thousand shops and eleven baths. All the streets are paved with stone, and trees are planted in many places. According to reports, the water is very good and the weather very mild there. There are deputy consuls in this port on behalf of the governments of Iran, Russia, and England, who are appointed from the consulates located in Trabzon. There are about 300 Iranian

---

28 Cape Yoros is near the Bosphorus, so it is not clear to which port Farâhâni is alluding; the only town of any size between Giresun and Ordu is Bulancak.

29 Text: Pâsun. Throughout this section, Farâhâni uses the term "Kayb" for Cape rather than the Turkish *burun*.

30 The text has "Vuneh" which probably refers to Vona (a town east of Yasun Burnu); another possibility is Ünye (the first city west of Yasun Burnu).

subjects in this city who are tradesmen and merchants. The goods which are produced there are tobacco and cigarettes.[31] The cigarettes of Samsun are very well known and excellent; most of the trade in this is in export to Europe.

THE ROAD FROM SAMSUN TO DIYARBAKIR

In Samsun, there is a road which goes overland to Arab Iraq. That is, if one goes by good horses, one arrives at Diyarbakir in fourteen days; and if by caravan and muleteer, one may arrive in twenty-eight days to a month. [111] From Diyarbakir by *qoffeh kalak*[32] one will reach Samarra in seven days. The cities which may be seen along this route are: first Amasya, which used to be a large and great city, and whose buildings were renovated by Solṭân ᶜAlâ od-Din Kayqobâd the Saljuqi.[33] It is now a large city. Then one comes to Ḥâypot,[34] then to Tokat, then to Sivas, which has copper and silver mines, and then to Diyarbakir. According to reports the route is very safe and flourishing. Every hour a village beside the road comes into view.

DEPARTURE FROM SAMSUN

In short, the steamer left Samsun Wednesday the twenty-third at sunset [5 August]. Travelling until seven hours after nightfall (nearly until dawn), it arrived at a port named Sinop. This port is a dependency of Trabzon and a qâ'em-maqâmate. It has about five hundred households, fifty shops, and a population of two thousand. It is not customary that every steamer stop at this port. Our steamer stayed four hours there loading and unloading because it had cargo for there and set out again at two hours past sunset [the night before] Thursday the twenty-fourth [Wednesday evening, 5 August]. Along the way, a fortress in the middle of the sea was visible, but [I] did not learn its name. One hour before noon on Thursday, [the steamer] entered the port of Inebolu and anchored.

THE PORT OF INEBOLU

Inebolu[35] is a small borough which is part of the province of Anatolia. A river flows through the middle of it. It is a qâ'em-

---

[31] The text has the term *pâprus*, literally "papyrus," which in the dialect of Gilân means cigar or cigarette (probably derived from the Russian?); see Moḥammad Moᶜin, *Farhang-e fârsi* (Tehran, 1362-64/1983-85), s. v. "pâprus."

[32] A type of small, round boat, often made of inflated animal skins, used for navigation on the Tigris-Euphrates rivers.

[33] The Saljuq dynasty of Rum (Anatolia) had three rulers of this name during the period 616-707/1219-1307; it is not clear to which one Farâhâni is referring.

[34] Farâhâni seems confused here; the reference may be to Harput (Elaziğ) which is actually between Sivas and Diyarbakir.

[35] [Marginal note:] "It is 125 miles from Samsun to Inebolu."

maqâmate. It is located on the side of a forested mountain. Other forested mountains are numerous near it. It has approximately two thousand households, which is a population of eight thousand, with 250 shops. The city is full of streams and trees and is attractive. Its weather is very humid. [112] There is no consul or official there from foreign countries. No citizen of Iran was found there. Since this port is adjacent to the forest, its trade is limited to lumber and wood which are carried to Istanbul. The steamer loaded a lot of wood and lumber there. The steamer left Inebolu two hours before sunset.

THE JOURNEY FROM INEBOLU

Passing on from there, the mountains and seacoast were always close by. From Batum to this point, the province of Anatolia is on the port side and the shore is usually close by. Forested mountains and green, pleasant, and attractive valleys are visible; in some of the valleys, farms and inhabited areas could be seen. Sevastapol is to starboard.

THE STRAITS AT ISTANBUL

Five hours past Inebolu, the coast was no longer visible until near the Bosphorus.[36] The steamer reached the Bosphorus on Friday the twenty-fifth of Shavvâl [7 August] at noon.

THE CITY OF ISTANBUL

"Islambul" was called Istanbul by the Greeks, and the Romans [called it] Constantinople.[37] Constantinople was founded by Constantine, which is the name of one of the Caesars of Rome. Some consider it one of the regions of the fifth clime, and others part of the sixth clime. It is located on a forested peninsula, three sides of which–the eastern, western, and southern–are adjacent to the sea, and the northern [side] next to the mainland. This peninsula is six farsakhs in length. It was also a great city in antiquity and the capital of the Roman Empire. Its people were originally Romans descended from Esau, son of Isaac, son of Abraham.[38] [113]

---

[36] [Marginal note:] "It is 232 miles from Inebolu to the Bosphorus." Here and in subsequent references, Farâhâni uses the term *boghâz*, which can mean "straits" in general or the Bosphorus in particular. If the specific reference seems clear, it translated here as Bosphorus; other ambiguous usages are noted.

[37] Farâhâni consistently uses the popular term *eslâmbul* to refer to the city. The name Istanbul probably was derived from the Greek phrase *is tin polin* ("into the city"); see below, n. 48. Here and in other places, Farâhâni uses "Rome" and "Roman" to refer to the empire and people of Byzantium (as did the "Byzantines" themselves).

[38] The text has ᶜAyṣ ebn-e Esḥaq ebn-e Ebrâhim, the Arabic (Koranic) form of the name. On Muslim traditions tracing the ancestry of the Romans back to Esau, see, for example, Masᶜudi, *Prairies*, 1:88-89; 2:293-95.

THE NARRATIVE OF NÂṢER-E KHOSROW

Nâṣer-e Khosrow[39] writes that the tomb of Esau is in one of the villages of Acre.[40] Esau grew up in Acre; then he had many children, and they became dispersed. This clan at first were monotheists; then several became idolaters and one group followed the teachings of the Greek sages. Their rulers were named Caesar until the Caesar named Feyâvos or Felinunos [?] became Christian.[41] Then the Roman pagans attacked him for this and put him to death. The Christian religion was neglected again until the time that Constantine son of Qirun[42] came to power and built this Constantinople and made it the capital. According to records, this city originally had two city-walls. The elevation of the inner wall was seventy-two *gaz*,[43] and its breadth was twelve gaz. The elevation of the outer wall was forty-two gaz, and its breadth was eight gaz. The separation between these two walls was sixty gaz. There were 1,020 towers on these two ramparts, and several soldiers were stationed on every tower.

A NARRATIVE FROM THE "TOḤFEH OL-MALAKEYYEH"

The author of the *Toḥfeh ol-malakeyyeh* [?][44] writes, "This Caesar named Constantine at the end of [his] lifetime was afflicted by the disease of leprosy. One of the pagan priests told him that he must kill a group of children and sit in their blood until the disease was cured. This speech resolved Constantine to do so, but at night

---

[39] A famous Persian poet, traveller, and propagandist for the Fatimids (394-481/1004-88); author of a famous travel book recounting his own pilgrimage to Mecca in 437/1045. See C. A. Storey, *Persian Literature, A Bio-Bibliographical Survey* (London, 1953), 2:1138-1141; there is an edition and translation of this by Charles Schefer, *Sefer Nameh; relation du voyage de Nassiri Khosrau* (Paris, 1881) and a more recent English translation by Wheeler Thackston, *Nâser-e Khosraw's Book of Travels (Safarnâma)* (Albany, 1986).

[40] Cf. Schefer, *Sefer Nameh*, pp. 51-52; this detail is the only part of this passage that comes from Nâṣer-e Khosrow's account.

[41] The text is obviously corrupt here, as well as being second-hand information. The reference is probably to the Emperor Philip the Arab, who was rumored to have been a Christian (the spelling of the name might be confused with that of his associate, the Bishop Fabian, whom Decius executed upon Philip's death): see Eusebius, *The History of the Church*, translated by G. A. Williamson (New York, 1965), p. 273 [6.39:1-5].

[42] Constantine's father was named Constantine Chlorus.

[43] A unit of measurement which was used inconsistently but which was roughly equivalent to the English ell (45 inches.)

[44] Brockelmann, *Geschichte*, G II:126, mentions a work entitled *ot-Toḥfeh ol-malakeyyeh fi'l-as'eleh va'l-ajvebeh ol-falakeyyeh*. Although it is an astronomical treatise, such works often contain astrological prophecies and so could conceivably be the source of Farâhâni's anecdote. However it is in Arabic and is only known to exist in a manuscript in Cairo. It is thus not likely that Farâhâni would be familiar

he saw in a dream several of the Apostles of Jesus who said to him: If you want this disease to be removed from your body, seek a remedy from the Roman patriarch. Thus, upon awakening, he summoned the Patriarch and beseeched [him] for a cure. The Patriarch said, 'That cure is reserved for members of the Christian community.' Constantine converted, the Patriarch prayed, and the Caesar was healed.[45] At the same time, twelve thousand people of this city [114] became members of the Christian community. Gradually, the Christian religion became widespread, and great churches were built. One of the churches was thought to be on the site of the manifestation of the Apostles. Another church was supposed to take the place of the Bayt ol-Maqdes.[46] There were images there of the twelve disciples made out of gold, until in the year 858 [1454] [*sic*] Solṭân Moḥammad, called Fâteḥ ["the Conqueror"], conquered Constantinople and compelled the people to follow Islam.[47] He destroyed some of the Christian places of worship and changed some into mosques. The gold and silver statues were all broken up and minted into coins. He named the city in Turkish 'Islambul' which means 'Islam abounded.'[48] The date of the conquest is found in [the chronogram] 'a pleasant city.'[49] From then to the present day, it has been the capital of the Ottoman sultans."

---

with it, but he may have seen the work quoted in some other source. There is also a manuscript in Persian called the *Toḥfeh-ye malaki* by ᶜAli Besṭami (fl. 1626-72); however, it is described by Storey, *Persian Literature*, pp. 209-10, as a translation of a life of Emâm Reżâ and is thus probably not the work to which Farâhâni is referring.

45 This is a somewhat garbled form of the legend of St. Sylvester (the basis for the "Donation of Constantine") which somehow was picked up and repeated by Muslim authors.

46 In the case of the first church, Farâhâni (or the author he is following) is clearly alluding to the Church of the Holy Apostles; what he means by the church which was to take the place of (or to be in the place of) the Bayt ol-Maqdes, presumably the Church of the Holy Sepulcher in Jerusalem, is not clear.

47 Moḥammad II (or Mehmet II), known as the Conqueror, was Ottoman sultan briefly in 848/1444 and again from 855-86/1451-81. The conquest of Constantinople took place, of course, in 857/1453. Contrary to Farâhâni's statement, he did not force the people to become Muslims. The classic study of this ruler is Franz Babinger, *Mehmed der Eroberer und seine Zeit* (second edition; Munich, 1959) which has been translated into English by Ralph Manheim, *Mehmed the Conqueror and His Time* (Princeton, 1978).

48 On this popular etymology and the origins of the name Istanbul, see Babinger, *Mehmet the Conqueror*, p. 102; S. Runciman, "Constantinople-Istanbul," *Revue des études sud-est européennes* 7(1969):205-8; EI_2, 4:224 (s.v. "Istanbul").

49 *Baladeh ṭayyebeh.* Each letter in the Arabic alphabet also has a numerical value; adding the value of the letters in a word or phrase was a common way of expressing a date in the form of a chronogram.

A NARRATIVE FROM THE "MASÂLEK OL-MAMÂLEK"

Aḥmad ebn-e ᶜOmar, author of the *Masâlek ol-mamâlek* [*Roads of the Countries*],[50] writes, "In the palace of the Caesars of Rome one room was locked up. None of those rulers opened the lock; instead every Caesar put another lock on it until twenty-four locks were accumulated on it. The last Caesar determined to unlock those doors and locks and to learn the secret of that room. Although monks came to dissuade [him], he refused and unlocked the door. Inside, he saw several images in the form of Arabs with pikes mounted on horses and camels. All agreed that in that year the kingdom would slip from the possession of the Christian Caesars and enter into the possession of the Muslims."

HISTORICAL REMAINS

At present, some of the ruins of the ancient fortifications of this city are extant. In the middle of the inhabited part of the city there is an old stone wall with some of the towers, most of which have been demolished. Adjacent to it there is another old wall which used to consist of seven interconnecting fortresses. The Turks call it Yedi Küle. [115]

ENTRANCE INTO THE STRAITS

Anyhow, the steamer remained at the entrance to the Bosphorus for a while. The second captain went by rowboat to the telegraph station which was at the entrance to the Bosphorus and advised of the arrival of the steamer and requested permission to enter the straits. As soon as permission was received, it entered the Bosphorus.

On both sides of the Bosphorus, fortresses, bastions, and towers have been built, and on every fortress there are cannons and arsenals. On both sides of the Bosphorus, there are hills and promontories. Back of that there are mountains and forests. On these hills and promontories beside the Bosphorus, some pine, cypress, oak trees and so on are visible. These trees do not need irrigation. They are always kept verdant by the moist climate. On both sides of the Bosphorus, nice buildings have been erected, scattered in some places and close together in others. There are

---

[50] This is the title of several Arabic and Persian geographies; none is by an author named Aḥmad b. ᶜOmar. Farâhâni may be referring to the work of Aḥmad b. Sahl ol-Balkhi, preserved by Eṣtakhri under this title (and subsequently translated into Persian). However, since the anecdote assumes the fall of Byzantium, the source would seem to be a fairly late work (such as Aḥmad ol-ᶜOmari's *Masâlek ol-abṣâr fi mamâlek ol-amṣâr*) rather than one of the classical writings known by this title. Cf. Muḥammad Niẓámu'd-Din, *Introduction to the Jawámiᶜu'l-Ḥikáyát* (London, 1929), pp. 101-3, 248.

large or small gardens in most of the buildings. Fruit trees, legumes, and garden and potted flowers are grown. Because of this, the city appears very green and pleasant. The right side of the Bosphorus is called the Asiatic and the left side the European. From the beginning of this strait to its end is reckoned to be six parasangs. For the most part, the city of Istanbul is beside the Bosphorus. Along this same strait, in front of the royal buildings, three or four government warships are always anchored.

CUSTOMS

After the steamer entered the Bosphorus, it travelled extremely slowly. One farsakh before the harbor, since this was a large ship, a small escort steamer from the same company came and guided it to the harbor, until it arrived near the customs house and anchored. There were many large and small steamers and sailing vessels and rowboats. After permission from the naval commissioners, the passengers boarded rowboats and crossed the water to the gate of the customs house. [116]

At the edge of the quay, there are several people on behalf of the Ottoman government who examine the passports of individuals. If it happens that someone does not have a passport, they collect a fee from him and do not molest him. After they inspect the passports, they then open and inspect baggage and personal effects in the customs house. If one knows the language or has a guide or acquaintance, it is possible to make a small payment to the customs agent, and one's baggage and effects are not inspected. In this way, our baggage was not inspected. It is also possible to make a small payment to the oarsmen not to take one to the customs house gate and secretly to drop one off at another spot. They collect customs fees of five per cent from foreign citizens. The customs fee for local citizens does not have a fixed amount; in principle it is ten per cent, but they collect whatever they can, especially for tobacco, cigarette tobacco, opium, and saffron. The duty on these four goods is high.

BROKERS AND BROKERAGE[51]

Many fraudulent brokers of every sort stand at the customs house gate. Most of the wheeling and dealing in this city occurs through the agency of these brokers and brokerage. "The business of this age is conducted through the craft of brokerage." These brokers invite and guide foreigners to find places or lodgings. There

[51] This phrase (*dallâl va delâleh* or *dallâleh*) is ambiguous and could also be translated "male brokers and female brokers."

were several Iranian brokers among [those] at the gate to the customs. One of them served as a guide for [my] companions and me and took us to the khan of Shaykh Dâud, which is one of the lodging places for foreigners and pilgrims. This khan was located in one of the worst quarters of Istanbul, but it had three storeys, its rooms were freshly made, and its rates were cheap.

They charged two qorush per person per night, which is about eleven shâhis. Judging from the large number of pilgrims there, it is more convenient and better for pilgrims' lodging than other places. [117]

All of the travellers who have an acquaintance go to the home or lodging of the acquaintances; everyone who does not have an acquaintance and is not inclined to stint on expenses goes to a hotel. Hotels are plentiful, and the differences between them are endless. [Distinctions between] ritual purity and impurity, Muslim and infidel, are not observed very much in the hotels. The day after arriving, I went to the public bath.

DESCRIPTION OF THE PUBLIC BATHS IN ISTANBUL[52]

[When] one goes to the bath, there is first of all a spacious courtyard parallel to the street. It has a tall, painted roof. The floor of the public bath is usually of marble. There are two tiers of elevated stone platforms along the sides of this cold-bath courtyard. The platforms are covered with mats. Chairs and benches are placed on these platforms, and white towels are pulled over the benches so that they serve as places for undressing. Each bench is reserved for one person. After [the bather] is undressed, he is wrapped in four clean towels. On the mats, he puts on heel-less morocco leather slippers. Whenever [the bather] wishes to move from the mats to the floor of the bath, wooden shoes with leather straps are placed in front of him, which he must wear. Anyone who has not become accustomed to wearing these shoes will have difficulty walking with them on the polished stone [floors].

Next, in order to show the way, one or two masseurs or valets go in front and lead [the bather] to a vestibule which, by comparison, is warmer than the cold-bath. There are some benches and chairs [in it] as well. [The bather] is seated there until he has recovered from his chilly condition. [118] Then they take his towels and cover him with two [fresh] loincloth-like towels and ask what they can do for him. If there is nothing for the masseur to do, [the bather] is guided

[52] Cf. Pirzâdeh, *Safarnâmeh*, 2:117-19.

to the public warm-bath, the floor and socle of which are marble. All around are warm water taps and cold water taps. Below every warm or cold water tap there is a marble basin in which is placed a copper bowl [used for washing and rinsing]. Every [bather] sits at the foot of one of the basins and washes. If he needs massaging, adolescent masseurs, clean and fresh, come at once. The [masseur] selected [by the bather] leads the way to a clean, private, marble place. All around this private place are small rooms for two people; in each room there are two water taps, cold and warm, with a basin and bowl. After entering a room, the masseur insists on hanging a curtain or loin-cloth at the entrance to that room, so that no one sees into it from the outside. Then, standing naked, he massages [the bather] with a rough mitten (*kiseh*) after which he washes him with soap and a soft cloth (*lif.*) By allusion, metaphor, or specific statement, he makes certain "suggestions," but that "depends on the strength of an individual's knee."[53] The rooms and the bath are fully lighted. There is a separate private chamber for depilation. Shaving the head must be done outside the bath; one may not have his head shaven in the warm or cold-bath rooms.

Anyhow, after [the bather] is finished with this business, they bring three towels; they put one towel on his head and two on his body. Then they bring [him] back to the same hallway again and seat [him] on the benches. After a while, when he is sweating less, the first towels are changed and again he is wrapped in four towels. Then he goes to the cold-bath [wearing] the same wooden shoes. When he moves back to the mats, [119] he takes off the wooden shoes and puts on the leather slippers and sits on a bench with clean towels thrown over it. A mirror, coffee, cigarettes, sherbet, or whatever he wishes is brought. The cost for these baths is about two thousand to fifteen thousand Iranian [dinârs?].

It is impossible not to sweat in the bath, but most of the baths of this city are not exclusively for Muslims;[54] every religious group goes [to them.] There are two or three baths to which infidels do not go. Neat people who own houses do not necessarily need to go to a public bath. One small room in their own home is made like a bath and used for washing once a day, in summer or winter.

---

[53] The idioms employed here by Farâhâni have a definitely sexual innuendo.

[54] The sweat of a non-Muslim could make the bath ritually unclean for a Shi'ite; see above, Part Two, p. 74 n. 74.

THE AYÂ SOFYÂ MOSQUE

The Ayâ Sofyâ mosque is one of the ancient mosques. Its [date of] construction and builder are unknown. Originally it was a temple of idolaters. Thus, images of fish and so on, such as I have seen in the temples of idolaters, are on the walls of this mosque. In the time of Justinian I, which was thirty and some [years] before the prophetic mission [of Moḥammad],[55] it became a church and Christian place of worship. It was a church until the time of Solṭân Moḥammad Fâteḥ, who conquered Istanbul and made that place into a mosque. The courtyard of this mosque is a spacious area. The ground is paved with black stone. There are some shade trees in the courtyard. They have constructed a marble and limestone wall one and a half z̲arᶜ high around this area. The mosque is located in the middle of the courtyard. There is a perron all around the mosque. Below this perron there is a cistern with faucets and small stone troughs set up for ritual ablutions. Six steps, each one a chârak high, go up from the courtyard to the perron. From the perron one goes into the mosque. The length of the mosque is about eighty z̲arᶜ. Its width is seventy z̲arᶜ. The height of the dome is about sixty z̲arᶜ. There are thirty-six large lower columns which are of solid marble; twelve large columns of solid porphyry; and thirty-six small marble columns on the upper level. The stone-cutting and fretwork of all of them has been excellently done. [120]

In the gallery of the upper level, they have made a place in which the sultan prays whenever he comes to pray. There is a wide balcony around the mosque situated in such a way that it overlooks the mosque.

There are seventeen small marble columns on this balcony. They have constructed four small marble arches in the interior of the mosque. Fourteen small marble columns are under the four arches. The call to prayer is chanted from atop these four arches. There are two large, round water vases made out of solid marble beside the doors of the mosque. There are two drinking fountains [made] of solid marble with relief work in the interior of the mosque. There are five marble pulpits [*menbar*s] inside the mosque. There are three steps near the mihrab, and each step is elevated one chârak above the other so that the mihrab is three chârak higher than the floor of

---

[55] Aya Sofya (written Ayâ Ṣufi in the text) is the Turkish name for the Byzantine basilica of St. Sophia (Haghia Sofia), dedicated by the Emperor Justinian on Christmas Day, 537. The text reads "three hundred" but this is an apparent mistake for thirty, since Justinian died roughly thirty years before the beginning of Moḥammad's prophetic mission in 610.

the mosque. It is one of the practices of the Sunnis that the prayer-leader's place of prayer must be higher than the place of prayer for the congregation. Shi'ites do not permit this. The main part of the mihrab is oblique because the mosque and this mihrab were not built at the same time.

The floor of this mosque is all made of marble, and the walls of the mosque up to the arch [that supports the dome] are made partly of marble and partly of porphry. Several places have porphyry stone, on which are carved figures of fish and so on, set into the main part of the wall. The roof of the mosque is inlaid and gilded in spots. Old pictures have been effaced. The images of four angels have been drawn under the dome. There are eight [121] plaques on the walls of the mosque on which these names have been written in gold: Allah, Moḥammad, ᶜAli, Fâṭemeh, Ḥasan, Ḥosayn, Abâ Bakr, ᶜOmar, and ᶜOsmân.[56]

There are nine doors to the mosque. These doors are either [made] of inlaid wood or of brass and iron. There are eight marble candlesticks. The diameter of the candle in each exceeds one chârak. Chandeliers, candelabrums, and [glass] balls have been suspended [from the ceiling].

There are three private buildings next to the mosque. In these buildings there are various chambers, each of which is for a particular purpose. Two rooms are for the library and the place for [storing] Korans and lecterns. Its library is very grand; most books can be found [there]. Two rooms are for equipment for lamps and lamp fuel. Several are storerooms for carpets and the curtains for the mosque. Two or three rooms are living quarters for the ferashes and servants.

THE SOLAYMÂNEYYEH MOSQUE

This district and mosque are among the constructions of Solṭân Solaymân Khân I, son of Selim Khân. The city of Solaymâniyyeh is also one of his constructions.

The date of the construction of the mosque is written on top of the gate named the Bâb Khayyâṭâneh in Arabic *solos*[57] script. The

[56] One may note that Farâhâni lists nine names but speaks of only eight plaques. There were (and are) eight plaques in the building with calligraphy by Ebrâhim Effendi (c. 1650); the name of Fâṭemeh is not on them: cf. Farhâd Mirzâ, *Hedâyat*, pp. 55-56; Edwin Grosvenor, *Constantinople* (Boston, 1900), 2:548.

[57] A type of Arabic calligraphy in which the letters are rounded and cursive as in *naskh* style but with longer lines for certain vertical letters. Because of its size and clarity it was often preferred for ornamental inscriptions. See Oktay Aslanapa, *Turkish Art and Architecture* (New York, 1971), pp. 324, 341 and plates 244-45.

gist of its contents is that "the construction of this mosque was begun by order of Solṭân Solaymân Khân in Jomâdâ I 937 [December, 1530/January, 1531] and was completed at the end of the month of Ẕi Ḥejjeh the sacred that same year [July-August, 1531]. Solṭân ᶜAziz Khân repaired [it] in the year 1208 [1793-94]."[58]

Generally, the type of construction of this mosque resembles that of the Ayâ Sofyâ mosque. There are four tall columns of solid marble in this mosque that are noteworthy. This mosque is situated in an elevated quarter which overlooks the straits.[59] The tomb of the founder Solṭân Solaymân Khân is beside the mosque. [122] It has a dome and courtyard and cemetery in which others are buried. Underneath one large dome there are several tombs: one is the grave of Solṭân Solaymân I, whose birth was in 900 [1494-95], his accession in 926 [1520], and his death in 974 [1566]. Another is the tomb of Solṭân Solaymân Khân II, the date of whose death is 1003 of the hegira [1594-95].[60] Another is the grave of Solṭân Aḥmad Khân II.[61] Three other graves are those of their wives. Near this large dome are two other domes which are both tombs of wives of Solṭân Solaymân Khân I. There are custodians, servants, and Koran reciters in these tombs who receive monthly salaries from the wakf endowments of this mosque and cemetery.

THE ELEMENTARY SCHOOL

Beside the mosque there is also an Islamic elementary school which is another one of the constructions of Solṭân Solaymân Khân. It has monthly stipends fixed for the teachers, tutors, ferashes, and the expenses of the pupils.

THE MOSQUE OF SOLṬÂN MOḤAMMAD FÂTEH

The mosque of Solṭân Moḥammad Fâteḥ is next to a madrasah. It is really not a large mosque, but there is a wide open area around it where things for sale are displayed. In the courtyard of the mosque are twenty marble columns. Six of the columns are large; the rest are small. The date of the construction of this mosque commenced in 867 [1462-63]; it was completed in 875 [1470-71]. Before this, no mosques were built in Istanbul.

---

[58] Farâhâni's reading of the inscription was in error (or his memory faulty). In reality, this mosque was begun in 1550 and completed in 1557. See Aslanapa, *Turkish Art*, p. 220. The sultan in 1793-94 was Selim III; if by ᶜAziz Khân he means ᶜAbd ol-ᶜAziz, the latter did not become sultan until 1861.

[59] It is not clear here whether Farâhâni is referring to the Golden Horn or the Bosphorus as the "straits."

[60] The date is in error; Solaymân II died in 1102/1691.

[61] The Ottoman sultan from 1102-6/1691-95.

THE NURI ᶜOS̱MÂN MOSQUE

This mosque is not very large, but it has a very large and high arch [supporting the dome]. There is a school next to it. Solṭân ᶜOs̱mân, son of Solṭân Moṣṭafâ Khân II, built this mosque in the year 1169 [1755-56].[62] [123]

THE MOSQUE OF SOLṬÂN BÂYAZID KHÂN

This mosque is beside the military square and the military guest-house. In its courtyard are twenty columns of solid stone. Inside the mosque there are four stone pillars. Between each pair of pillars there is a large column of solid porphry like the columns of the Ayâ Sofyâ mosque. This mosque is one of the constructions of Solṭân Bâyazid Khân, son of Solṭân Moḥammad Fâteḥ, which was begun in the year 903 [1497-98] and completed in 911 [1505-6].[63]

THE MOSQUE OF SOLṬÂN SELIM KHÂN

In the courtyard of the mosque there are porticos on three sides, with four marble columns on each side. There are also two stout plane trees inside the courtyard. Inside the mosque proper there are six large marble columns, the height and diameter of which are like the columns of Ayâ Sofyâ. On the side of this mosque is the tomb of Abu Ayyub Solṭân,[64] in the courtyard of which there are also three stout plane trees. Like the shrines of holy people in Iran, it has a faience dome and sepulcher. There are silver candlesticks, silver lanterns, and other ornaments inside the dome. In this same place there is a sweet-water well that the people drink and carry away as a cure-all. This mosque and tomb are both among the constructions of the murdered Solṭân Selim Khân III,[65] the son of Solṭân Moṣṭafâ Khân III, and were begun in the year 1208 [1793-94] and completed in the year 1215 [1800-1801]. The date is carved on the sepulcher.

---

[62] The mosque was actually begun by his predecessor Maḥmud I in 1748 but completed by ᶜOs̱man III; see Aslanapa, *Turkish Art*, p. 231.

[63] The inscription at the entrance to the mosque says that construction began in 1501; see Aslanapa, *Turkish Art*, p. 213.

[64] As Farâhâni explains below, Abu Ayyub (known as Eyüp Sultan in Turkey) was a companion of the Prophet Moḥammad who died of dysentery during the first Arab siege of Constantinople (55/674-75). His remains were supposedly rediscovered during the Turkish siege of the city. The mosque complex which Farâhâni is describing is the one built on that site by Solṭân Moḥammad the Conqueror and rebuilt by Selim III in 1800. It is usually called the Eyüp Mosque rather than the mosque of Solṭân Selim. See the discussion with references in Babinger, *Mehmed the Conqueror*, p. 113.

[65] One of the first great reformist Ottoman sultans (1789-1807); see Stanford Shaw, *Between Old and New: The Ottoman Empire under Sultan Selim III* (Cambridge, Mass., 1971).

ABU AYYUB

The proper name of this Abu Ayyub is Khâled, the son of Zayd, the Anṣâri. The dear Prophet [Moḥammad], after entering the city of Medina, when the anṣâr all invited [him] to stay in their own home, ordered, "Wherever my she-camel stops, I will choose that place as my home." When the she-camel knelt down in the place which is [now the site of] the blessed tomb [of the Prophet Moḥammad], Abu Ayyub said, [124] "Since my home is the closest to this place, grant permission that I take [your] clothes and belongings to my house." [The Prophet] granted permission. According to one account, he stayed seven months in the house of Abu Ayyub. His clansmen were brave people, and he was one of the Prophet's cavalry-men at the Battle of Badr and on most of the campaigns. He accompanied the Commander of the Faithful ᶜAli in the battles of the Camel, Siffin, and the [wars against] the Khârijites, and so on, until in the year 53 of the hegira [672-73], when Moᶜâveyyeh (curse him) sent an army under the command of Yazid to fight the Byzantines. Abu Ayyub accompanied that army but fell ill on the way and died just outside Constantinople ["Islambul"]. They buried him near the walls of the city. Assuming that his association towards the end of his life with Moᶜâveyyeh and Yazid did not impair his piety, he was among the greatest of the anṣâr.[66]

THE MOSQUE OF SOLṬÂN AḤMAD KHÂN

This is of the same type and arrangement as the mosque of Ayâ Sofyâ. It has a portico with twenty-six columns of solid marble around the courtyard. Outside the mosque, on three sides, there is a wide open area, resembling an avenue, which belongs to the mosque. There are weekly bazaars there; the markets are held there on Mondays. The great dome of the mosque [rests] on four grooved pillars. The circumference of each pillar is twenty ẕarᶜ.

As for its date, which is above the door, this mosque was begun in the year 1011 [1602-3], during the reign of Solṭân Aḥmad Khân I, and was completed in 1025 [1616], the same year that Solṭân Aḥmad Khân died.[67] They say that Solṭân Aḥmad Khân, after the completion of the mosque, prayed several times in this mosque and [then] died. [125] This [mosque] also has many wakf properties. The

---

[66] The story of Abu Ayyub is found in a number of Muslim sources, notably Moḥammad b. Esḥâq's biography of the prophet: A. Guillaume (tr.), *The Life of Muhammad: A Translation of Ibn Isḥâq's Sîrat Rasûl Allâh* (Oxford, 1955), p. 228. The Umayyad caliphs Moᶜâveyyeh and Yazid are anathema to Shi'ites because of their opposition to ᶜAli and Ḥosayn.

[67] Aḥmad I actually died in 1026/1617.

tomb of Solṭân Aḥmad Khân is also next to this same mosque. The present sultan[68] recently made a thorough restoration of the mosque. Nowadays, the ruler usually prays in this mosque. Inside the mosque, on the upper level, there is a room of stone which is the place for the sultan's prayers. The congregation never sees him at prayer time.

DIKILITASH

On one side of this mosque there is the square of the horse-sellers, which is known as the At-maydân.[69] In the middle of that square, there is a stone which they call Dikilitash.[70] First of all, a square pedestal of stone and limestone has been erected. This pedestal is four ẕarᶜ high. On this stone pedestal an embossed stand of pieces of metal has been made. The monolith, which has four sides, is conical shaped at the top, has a diameter of six ẕarᶜ and a height of twelve ẕarᶜ. It has images of animals and birds drawn on all sides. It is erected on this embossed metal stand. These images also resemble the idols found in pagan temples. Opposite the Dikilitash, a minaret has been constructed out of blocks of stone cemented together with lime.[71] It used to be very high. At present, it has a height of fourteen ẕarᶜ. Both of these are of ancient construction. It might be said that these were built before the people of Constantinople became Christian.

THE JANISSARY MUSEUM

In the middle of this same square which is beside the Solṭân Aḥmad mosque there is a building which is called the Janissary Museum. Everyone is allowed to visit it; indeed, they are encouraged and exhorted to go see it. First, they collect one *qorush-e sâq*,[72] which is about 300 dinars, per person at the door to the building. [126] After entering the building, one goes to the upper storey. There are three wide, long rooms [where] fearsome figures have been made out of wax with clothes and weapons. All are standing up [as if] making ceremonial greetings to the sultan. Some

---

68 ᶜAbd ol-Ḥamid II (1876-1909).

69 This was the hippodrome in Byzantine Constantinople. In Ottoman times it served as a marble quarry as well as a horse market.

70 Text: Tekelitâsh. In Turkish, dikilitaş means stone column or obelisk; here it refers to the obelisk built for the Pharaoh Thutmoses III (1549-1503 B.C.) and later brought to Constantinople by the Emperor Theodosius. See Jelâl Esad, *Eski estânbul* (Istanbul, 1328/1912), pp. 210-14.

71 This "minaret" is the Column of Constantine Porphyrogenitus (912-59); see Asᶜad, *Estânbul*, pp. 217-18.

72 See the discussion of Ottoman coinage which follows below, p. 126.

have turbans, and others large hats. This Janissary faction was at first of Greek Orthodox [origin] and then became Muslim. Gradually, many of them acquired [other] occupations and offices in the Ottoman Empire and possessed power and wealth. Because of this, they obtained dominance in relations with the government and interfered in most state matters. They were rather domineering and oppressive towards the subjects, until in the year 1241 [1826], Solṭân Maḥmud Khân II, son of Solṭân ᶜAbd ol-Ḥamid Khân, annoyed by the behavior of this faction, and having put this secret [matter] to his own private advisors, on a holiday which was [the occasion of] a public audience when the chiefs of the Janissaries were gathered, had those present seized suddenly and put to death. Then they found, seized, and killed everyone from this faction everywhere.[73] Because this great deed was manifested by him, [and] in order that his fame should endure and many of the rebellious be frightened, they have made these figures out of wax with arms and clothes and fearsome manner. To this day, the Ottoman sultans have remembered [this] and think [their] enemies fear these things. Solṭân ᶜAbd ol-Majid Khân built and adorned a very magnificent tomb for this Solṭân Maḥmud Khân, killer of the Janissaries, and established wakf properties [for it], and put some valuable items in it, among which are his aigrette and several silver candlesticks. It is inscribed on his tombstone that this sultan was born in the month of Ramadan 1199 [1784-85], ascended [to power] in the month of Jomâdâ II 1223 [July-August, 1808], [127] and died in Rabiᶜ II 1255 [June-July, 1839].

THE TOWER OF CHEMBERLITASH

Near this tomb of Solṭân Maḥmud Khân there is a tower [*menâreh*], a stone [monument] which they call Chemberlitash.[74] First, a pedestal of small stones has been erected. On top of it, there is a large round tower made of blocks of porphyry put together piece

[73] This crushing of the Janissary order on June 15, 1826 is known in Turkish history as the "Auspicious Event" (*Vak'a-i Hayriye*); it was of critical importance in making possible the Ottoman reform era. See Lewis, *Emergence of Modern Turkey*, pp. 78-80. Farâhâni's observations on the museum commemorating this event are very similar to those of Farhâd Mirzâ, *Safarnâmeh*, p. 59.

[74] Text: *Chenberli tâsh* (the n before b is pronounced "m"; hence the Turkish name Çemberlitaş.) This monument was originally the Column of Constantine, erected to commemorate the foundation of the city on 11 May 330. It was repaired and made more accessible after the great fire of 1865. See Asᶜad, *Estânbul*, pp. 218-19; Zeynep Çelik, *The Remaking of Istanbul: Portrait of an Ottoman City in the Nineteenth Century* (Seattle, 1986), pp. 59-60.

by piece. In certain places where it is broken, they have fixed it with iron bands so it would not fall apart. For this reason they call it "Hooped Stone" [*chenberlitâsh*]. There used to be a capital on top of it which has since been broken. At present its diameter is four z̲arᶜ, and its height is ten z̲arᶜ.

WELL KNOWN DISTRICTS[75]

The Göksu[76] district, from which a little stream flows. The imaret of the sultan's sister and the Sharif ᶜAbd ol-Moṭṭaleb are there.[77]

The Bâb-e ᶜÂli district: the Bâb-e ᶜÂli ["Sublime Porte"] building and the embassy of the state of Iran are in this district.

The Emirg̲ân[78] district: the palace of the Khedive of Egypt is in this district.[79]

The Eslâmbul district: most of the bazaars and shops and mosques are in this district.

The Qalâteh[80] district: a government palace named the Ursi[81] is there. Alongside this district is a narrow strait[82] that is crossed by rowboat.

---

[75] This whole section is marred by repetitions and orthographical errors. Names which are recognizable are given in a form as close as possible to their Ottoman or modern Turkish equivalents; Farâhâni's spelling is given in the footnotes. Ambiguous names are left as spelled in Farâhâni's text (with a guess at the vocalization). A useful description of Istanbul during this period is Moḥammad Râ'ef, *Mer'ât-e estânbul* (Istanbul, 1316/1898), pp. 21 ff.; see also Çelik, *Istanbul*, pp. 34-48.

[76] Text: Kuk-su.

[77] The "sultan's sister" refers to a princess by the name of ᶜAdeleh; ᶜAbd ol-Moṭṭâleb was the former sharif of Mecca who was forced to live in exile in Istanbul after the restoration of Ottoman authority in the Hejaz. See Nâser od-Din Shâh, *Diary*, pp. 378-79.

[78] Text: Amir Kân.

[79] Cf. Nâṣer od-Din Shâh, *Diary*, p. 379; Pirzâdeh, *Safarnâmeh*, 2:80; Mrs. Edmund Hornsby, *In and Around Stamboul* (London, 1858) 1:113-14. The Khedive Esmâᶜil of Egypt (1863-79) invested heavily in building up cordial relations with the sultan ᶜAbd ol-ᶜAziz to secure recognition of his autonomous position in Egypt.

[80] So in the text. This may be a corruption of Ghalaṭeh (Galata), mentioned by Farâhâni with the correct spelling in the following paragraph.

[81] So in the text; it is not clear to what building he is referring. The most important governmental building in Galata was the Sixth District Municipal Palace; see Çelik, *Istanbul*, p. 46. Perhaps "Ursi" is a corruption of a French word (Orsay?) or an orthographical error for the Turkish word *külesi* (meaning the Galata Tower) or *odası* ("room" or "hall"). The latter possibility is appealing because Farâhâni subsequently uses this same term for a royal audience hall (see below, n. 99).

[82] Here Farâhâni almost certainly is referring to the Golden Horn (Halıç in modern Turkish).

The Galata[83] district, Kasımpasha[84] district, Beyoğlu[85] district, Büyükdere[86] district, and Tarabya[87] district: Most of the Europeans and foreign ambassadors are in these five districts.

The Kâvi Kuy[88] district, the Yeni Köy[89] district, the Dolmabahche[90] district, the Tophane[91] district, the Beshiktash[92] district, the Fındıklı[93] district, the Beshkelidâsh [?] district, the Teshvikiye[94] district, the Owlmehbâghchehsi district [*sic*[95]], and the Eski Sarây district. [128]

ROYAL PALACES

The Eski Sarây ["Old Palace"] was built on top of a hill. It is an old building of the Ottoman sultans. At present, no one resides there.

The Beshiktash palace is where the present sultan and the royal family reside. It is one of the constructions of Solṭân ᶜAbd ol-Majid Khân.[96]

The Yâli Cherâghân is one of the grand royal palaces and is one of the constructions of Solṭân Maḥmud Khân.[97]

The Bayglarbayki palace is one of the ornamental royal constructions and where the august Shâhanshâh of Iran lodged.[98]

---

83 Text: Ghalaṭeh. On this district, see Jelâl Esᶜad, *Eski Ghalaṭeh* (Istanbul, 1329/1911).

84 Text: Qâsimpâshâ. On this area, cf. E. De Amicis, *Constantinople* (Philadelphia, 1896), 1:104-6.

85 Text: Baykâwghli.

86 Text: Boyuk-dereh.

87 Text: Ṭarâbyeh.

88 Kadiköy?

89 Text: Yanki Kuy.

90 Text: Dowlmeh-bâghcheh-si.

91 Text: Ṭupkhâneh.

92 Text: Beshekdâsh.

93 Text: Fendeqli.

94 Text: Teshviqeyyeh.

95 Farâhâni is apparently repeating the name of the Dolmabahche district.

96 This passage is somewhat ambiguous. It seems to refer to the Dolmabahche Palace which is near Beşiktaş and was built by ᶜAbd ol-Majid. However, by the time of Farâhâni's visit, the reigning sultan, ᶜAbd ol-Ḥamid II, preferred to reside at the nearby Yildiz Palace. See De Amicis, *Constantinople*, 1:281-303; P. Desjardin, *La Turquie Officielle* (Paris, 1891), pp. 45-65; Hilary Summer-Boyd and John Freely, *Strolling Through Istanbul* (Istanbul, 1973), pp. 470-481; Çelik, *Istanbul*, p. 132.

97 Farâhâni is presumably referring to the Çırağan Palace, which was actually built in 1871 for Solṭân ᶜAbd ol-ᶜAziz. It was destroyed by fire in 1910. See Çelik, *Istanbul*, p. 131.

98 Nâṣer od-Din Shâh visited Istanbul during the period 18-25 August 1873, while returning to Iran from his trip to Europe; he describes his lodgings at this building in the *Diary*, pp. 372-73.

The Göksu palace is a pleasant royal palace. It is one of the constructions of Sultan ᶜAbd ol-Majid Khân. A small stream passes by it.

The Ursi[99] palace is where the royal audiences were formerly held. The royal throne is there.

The Bâb-e ᶜÂli ["Sublime Porte"] is where the officials of the government and the state reside, like the Dâr osh-Shurâ.

The Bâb-e ᶜAskareyyeh, which is like a military barracks, is where the military leaders reside.

The Topkapı[100] palace is famous for this: The blessed mantle of the Prophet is there. Once every year, the sultan goes to make a pilgrimage to the mantle.[101]

If I wished to write a detailed account of every one of these buildings, it would take a long time and cause vexation and inconvenience. I will say this much: Great wealth has been expended on these buildings. They have been built very well, are ornamented, and are attractive. [129] Marble beyond reckoning has been used in every one of them.[102] In general, marble is plentiful in this city and has been utilized everywhere: the baths, the mosques, the houses of the notables, and the royal buildings. They bring some of this marble from an island in the Sea of Marmara which is near Istanbul. Its marble is not of high quality. They bring some from Italy. The marble from there is very white and pure.

THEATERS

Theaters[103] are numerous in this city. I saw some in detail, and I heard descriptions of others, but an account of them is not provided since it could not be understood if one has not actually seen them.

THE SITUATION OF ISTANBUL

Istanbul is situated partly on one side of the Bosphorus and partly on the other. On both sides of the Bosphorus, there are hills,

---

99 This is perhaps a corruption of [ᶜArż] Odası?

100 Text: Tup-qapu.

101 After the conquest of Mamluk Egypt in 1517, the Ottomans took possession of a number of relics of the Prophet Moḥammad (which the Mamluks had received from the Abbasid family), including his mantle, banner, swords, etc. These were preserved in a special room of the Topkapı Palace which the sultans visited on certain ceremonial occasions; they also displayed the relics before going on campaign, etc. See Kemal Çiğ, *Topkapı müzesi mukaddes emanetler resimli rehberi* (Istanbul, n.d.).

102 It should be remembered that Farâhâni, coming from Iran where most buildings were of brick construction, would have been impressed by the seemingly lavish use of marble in Istanbul, where it was common.

103 Text: *tamâshâkhâneh-hâ va bâzigarkhâneh-hâ*. The difference, if any, between these two terms is not clear, since Farâhâni does not describe them further.

valleys, promontories, small mountains with green and pleasant forests, and houses in tiers on the slopes of these hills and promontories. At night the lamps which are lighted are reflected on the water, and the appearance is very attractive. Since the houses are on the slopes of the valleys and promontories, the streets usually go straight up and down. In many of the streets, droshkys and coaches do not go or go with difficulty.

For crossing from this side to that side of the straits, they have constructed a bridge of wood and iron.[104] For every beast of burden or person who crosses it, they collect ten para, which is 285 Iranian krans,[105] as the fee for crossing. A large sum per day is acquired by the government from this bridge. At five hours after nightfall, a seven [130] or eight ẕar[c] [span] of this bridge is taken up and put on top of the next so that no one else crosses from this side to that. Crossing at that time will have to be by rowboat. At night, the oarsmen often throw one or two of the passengers whom they are carrying by rowboat into the sea.[106] Sometimes this is discovered and [the oarsmen] are arrested.

At the foot of this bridge there are three or four small steamers which three times daily at fixed hours transport people on the Bosphorus[107] carrying them to the [various] districts. Each steamer has profits from this of ten or twelve thousand tomans per year. These steamers belong to Austrian and French companies.

There are also some small steamers that travel on the Bosphorus without regularity or fixed hours and which carry people for the sake of recreation. Some also cross or go for recreation by rowboat. To cross the Bosphorus by rowboat requires great discretion because of the coming and going of the steamers, and the crowding and congestion. Repeatedly, by day and night, people get into the rowboats and are drowned.

---

[104] By "straits" Farâhâni is here certainly alluding to the Golden Horn (Halıç) rather than the Bosphorus. He is thus referring to the Galata Bridge, which was finished in 1878. See Çelik, *Istanbul*, p. 88.

[105] In the manuscript, this phrase is written in a shorthand acounting script called *siâq*, which is difficult to read. The amount given is excessive; Farahâni probably meant dinârs rather than krans. For a humorous recollection of the practice of charging a small toll to cross the bridge, see Aziz Nesin, *Böyle gelmiş böyle gitmez*, translated by Joseph Jacobson, *Istanbul Boy* (Austin, 1977), pp. 215-16. See also De Amicis, *Constantinople*, 1:45-57.

[106] The implication is that the rowers rob the passengers and then kill them.

[107] Text: "straits." Some boat lines did run from this bridge up the Golden Horn, but Farâhâni seems to be referring to the larger ships that served the Bosphorus districts.

All the buildings of this city are of two to five storeys. Much wood is used in the buildings, like the buildings of Gilân. Because of this, there are many fires and [other] houses catch on fire from a little fire and wind. Because of the numerous fires, they have made tall towers which overlook all the city. There are several watchmen in these towers who take turns keeping guard by day and night. There are also two cannons raised on top of them. Whenever a place catches on fire, the watchman immediately shoots seven cannon volleys so that they know a fire has broken out. [131] One hundred workers and a superintendent have been taking care of this business and have made equipment such as pumps and so on for putting out the fires. As soon as the superintendent and the employees hear the report of the cannon from the tower, they know there is a fire and immediately come out of the station to put out the fire. There are few days in Istanbul when there is no conflagration.[108]

WATER AND CLIMATE

The weather of this city and its suburbs is very damp and humid. One cannot sleep outdoors. When sleeping, if the doors to the room are open, and one's body is exposed to the wind, it will cause sickness. Because of the humidity, the weather does not get extremely hot or cold. It rains a lot in all four seasons. For this reason the rooftops of the houses are all of red tiles. Its climate strongly resembles the climate of Gilân.

THE STREETS

The streets of this city are mostly wide and clean and paved with cobblestones. Some of the streets are paved with hewn stone blocks. In part of the streets and most of the houses, coffeehouses, theatres, and lodgings, there are shade trees and varieties of potted and garden flowers.

THE CITY'S DRINKING WATER

The water there [comes] from places abounding in springs and streams. They bring some of the water from two or three farsakhs [away]. Two of its water [sources] are famous for purity and wholesome taste. The rest of the water of the city is not pure or wholesome. They have made water storage tanks in the houses and caravanserais so that they do not need water-carriers. However, if someone wants [water] from those two wholesome water [sources], the water-carriers bring it.[109]

---

[108] Cf. Asᶜad, *Estânbul*, pp. 88 ff. (including photograph on p. 91).

[109] Cf. Sayf od-Dowleh, *Safarnâmeh*, p. 94.

THE BAZAARS

There are many bazaars, stores, caravanserais, and guest-houses in this city. [132] Some of the bazaars are covered and some are not. Its covered bazaars are not large, but they are whitewashed and [have] roofs with shallow domes of brick and plaster.

COMMODITIES AND TRADE

There are countless goods here from every province, but demand is low. It has little trade in its own products. The factories in this city are not worth mentioning; there are some woven towel and canvas factories. Textiles here are generally plentiful and cheap. Foodstuffs of every sort are found [but] are expensive.

THE COINAGE

The minted coins of Istanbul are the gold lira, the silver majidi, and the copper para.[110] Its gold and silver money contains 20% alloy. As for the majidi, it is twenty *qorush-e sâq* [*sic*],[111] of which each qorush-e sâq is forty para, so that each qorush equals 285 krans[112] in Iranian money. The value of the majidi in Iranian krans is about 5,500 dinars. There are coins of one qorush, two qorush, and up to ten qorush (which is half a majidi) minted out of silver, but the small coinage is scarce. The majidi is common.

THE GOLD LIRA

As for the gold lira, it is [equal to] 108 qorush-e saq, which is over five silver majidis and eight qorush. [Coins of] half a lira, a quarter of a lira, and five lira are also minted in gold.[113] The value of the lira in Iranian money is from 27,500 dinars to three tomans, according to the time. But merchants, if they want to send a bill of exchange to Iran calculate [it as] three tomans and 1,500 dinars and will send the bill of exchange.

FOREIGN CURRENCY

As for the coinage of foreign countries, such types as the kran, the ashrafi, the manât, the imperial, the guinea, the rupee, the

110 The values of these coins both in relation to each other and to other currencies is complicated by fluctuations in the relative value to silver to gold and consequent debasements of the coinage. See Charles Issawi, *The Economic History of the Middle East* (Chicago, 1966), pp. 521-22; Mehmet Zeki Pakalın, *Osmanlı tarih deyimleri ve terimleri sözlüğü* (Istanbul, 1971), 2:428 (s.v. *mecidiye*), 2:326-28 (*kuruş*), 2:752-53 (*para*); Nuri Pere, *Osmanlı madenî paralar* (Istanbul, 1968); Cüneyt Ölçer, *Sultan Abdülaziz Han devri osmanlı madenî paralar* (Istanbul, 1979).

111 This is a mistake for *qorush-e ṣâgh* (standard qorush), often referred to in English as the gersh or piastre. Theoretically, the qorush was 1/100 of a lira, but, as Farâhâni notes, it was depreciated below this in practice. See Issawi, *Economic History of the Middle East*, pp. 521-22; Pakalın, *Deyimleri*, 3:90-91 (*s. v. sağ akça*).

112 So in the text; the number is written in *siâq* script. This exchange rate is plainly wrong. Farâhâni probably means dinars rather than krans; cf. above, p. 119.

113 The gold lira was worth about $4.40; see Issawi, Economic History, p. 522; Remzi Kocaer, *Osmanlı altınları* (Istanbul, 1967).

Levant dollar,[114] and the currency called the "franc" are all negotiable according to their respective value. At different times, their value will be more or less. [133]

The foreign currency most in circulation in this city is the Levant dollar and the franc. The Levant dollar is usually one or two qorush more than a majidi, and sometimes they are equal. Usually there are twenty-two to twenty-three francs to a lira. The franc is about 1,300 dinars in Iranian money.

WEIGHTS

The weight customarily used in this city is the *ḥoqqeh*.[115] The Istanbuli ḥoqqeh is four hundred drams, which is seventeen and a half sir in Tabriz weights. Most business is transacted with this ḥoqqeh.[116] In the Ottoman Empire, the coins and weights vary and differ in every city.

ETHICS & BEHAVIOR OF THE OTTOMANS IN COMPARISON TO THE RUSSIANS

In general, the people of Istanbul are light complexioned and dark haired. All of them are clean and neat. They are very emphatic about cleanliness. Just as much as the people of Russia are filthy and untidy, the people of this country are clean and neat. As much as a beard in Russia is a matter of worth and esteem, among the people in this country it is without worth or value. As much as the Russians are rude and impolite and rough in speech, the Ottomans are all mild, gentle, and polite.

WOMEN'S RIGHTS

The women of this city are very domineering and venerated.[117] Their dowries are very small, but their expenditures are incalculable. Men in comparison to them are underprivileged. The women do not wear the veil. Men and women are often mixed together sitting in the

---

[114] Text: *riâl-e faranseh* ("French real"). This was the popular name for the Maria Theresa thaler or "dollar" which was a popular medium of exchange throughout the Near East. Burton, *Personal Narrative*, 2:111 n. 1 pointed out that in the Hejaz "the generic term for dollars is 'Riyal Fransah'." Cf. T. F. Keane, *Six Months in the Hejaz* (London, 1887), p. 102. Here and in subsequent occurrences it is translated as "Levant dollar" to avoid confusion with American currency.

[115] Farâhâni has confused (perhaps deliberately; see the following note) the okka (or oke) used in Ottoman Turkey with the ḥoqqeh used in Ottoman Iraq. The okka was equal to 1.283 kg. (the same value as 17.5 sir) while the ḥoqqeh was almost exactly 1 kilogram. See Issawi, *Economic History of the Middle East*, p. 518; Pakalın, *Deyimleri*, 2:723.

[116] Farâhâni seems to be making a pun here since he uses the phrase *ḥoqqeh bâzi*, which can mean "swindle."

[117] Most of the Iranians who wrote about their visit to Istanbul found the women there shockingly "liberated" as compared to their Iranian counterparts: cf. Farhâd Mirzâ, *Hedâyat*, p. 63; Pirzâdeh, *Safarnâmeh*, 2:115-16; Sayf od-Dowleh, *Safarnâmeh*, pp. 96-97.

large coaches for hire and going out for recreation. Most of the wives of the notables are from Circassia. [134]

DESCRIPTION OF THE CIRCASSIANS

The Circassians are a group of Muslims. It is their custom that the menfolk are usually brigands. They entrust their own children from birth to the homes of the peasants. After they reach the age of nine years they are sold if a girl; if a boy, he still does not go back to the home of [his] father until the age of twenty. At that time, he comes to the home of the father and becomes his accomplice. They give a payment for raising their children to the peasants. The notables buy these Circassian girls in childhood, raise them, and take them as wives without a marriage contract or ceremony. Of course, since the Circassians are Muslims, buying and selling them is inconsistent with the enlightened holy law, and possessing them without marriage contract and ceremony is not permissible. One cannot say how these children arrived at such a situation. "I won't bother to explain it to you; if you are a sensitive person, you should tell me."[118]

THE ROYAL WOMEN

Most of the royal women are also Circassians. In the royal household, it is customary that Circassian girls are purchased, brought up, and taught various crafts. After training, some are kept for the royal household. Others are given as presents to the notables along with clothes and necessities.

VARIOUS OBSERVATIONS

People from every clime and country are gathered together in this city.[119]

Muslims and infidels are all mixed together here. There is no avoidance or precaution [as required by religious law], Islam or infidelity. Infidels and Muslims are not differentiated. The men dress like Europeans. Infidels and Muslims cut their hair and wear fezzes. Most of the women's clothes are also of European type. [135]

CRITIQUE OF THE OTTOMAN CHARACTER

The houses are very grand, but the purses are empty and bare. Mosques and places of worship are without equal or peer, but the ones praying [in them] are few and rarely found. "The prayers are entrusted to those whose hearts are closed to prayer."[120] The ulama and the kadis are worldly and lascivious. They are aware of the rules

---

118 This is a poetic expression which is used by Farâhâni quite out of context.

119 Here, Farâhâni quotes a line of poetry to reinforce his point; it is omitted from the translation.

120 This proverb is quoted in Arabic in the text.

and traditions of the religious law, but they are absorbed in the pollution of desire and delusion. They have abolished the rules of Islam [*din-e aḥmadi*] and made imperfect civil law in the manner of the Europeans. "They have been left out of one place and driven away from another."[121] They act with no regard for this world or the next. Of Islam, there is only the name and nothing more. The customs and ceremonies which they have gradually learned completely from the Europeans are the ways of irreligion and indifference about [matters of] doctrine and religious practice. Goshtâsb always used to say, "Those who do not have religion have nothing."[122]

Another of the attributes of their moral imperfection, which has spread greatly among them, is miserliness and stinginess.

Alexander the Great said, "Those endowed with liberality and generosity are always held in honor and esteem even though they be dervishes;[123] those characterized by meanness and miserliness are despised and unworthy even though they be rich." "A beggar is a beggar even if he is given all the world."[124] We do not say that a man should put whatever he has at the disposal of his fellows; rather the point is that the quality of generosity is regarded as the finest virtue. "Do not make your hand to be shackled to your neck, nor stretch it forth to the utmost, lest you should sit down, blamed or stripped."[125] All the individuals of this country, especially the notables, worship the strong and oppress the weak. If they see that a foreign neighbor or a native subject is condescending and submissive, they become bold and behave very harshly. If they perceive a little roughness or toughness, they turn meek.[126] [136]

Their valor and bravery is well concealed. Their speech is all boasting and idle talk. Thus on the subject of Serbia and Bulgaria, they understand perfectly that no side pays any attention to their talk.

---

121 A popular expression; see Ḥayyim, *Proverbs*, p. 20. Farâhâni is, of course, suggesting that the Ottomans have abandoned their own religio-cultural traditions but have not been accepted as Europeans. His assessment is almost identical to that of Farhâd Mirzâ, *Hedâyat*, pp. 63-64. This sense of cultural alienation has provided an important and recurrent theme in modern Persian political and social thought.

122 Goshtâsp was one of the legendary pre-Islamic kings of Iran; see Ferdowsi/Levy, *Epic of the Kings*, pp. 181-219. A line of poetry, which Farâhâni inserts here to emphasize that people who abandon their religion are foolish, is omitted from the translation.

123 That is, indifferent to the materialistic aspects of life.

124 A quotation from Saᶜdi; see Dehkhodâ, *Amsa̱l*, pp. 192-93 and 1268.

125 Koran, 17:29.

126 Farâhâni quotes one line of poetry here; it is omitted from the translation.

In spite of this they consider themselves the masters of the Serbs and Bulgarians. Every month–in writing and talking–they are entering and taking possession [of some place]. In this way they express their opinions. Sometimes, they are dispatching promises and threats to both sides. Sometimes in the consultative assembly they are holding discussions regarding this matter, and talking with foreign ambassadors, and making compromises. Sometimes they are summoning phantom armies for putting those borders into order and sending the phantom armies to the frontier [where] they are waiting to perform their duty. I heard that in order to send an army to Serbia, a command was given to the chief of the arsenal to summon a thousand fit, veteran cannoneers to be sent in that direction. The chief of the arsenal had stated, with a thousand regrets, that whether old or young there were in Istanbul no more than eight hundred cannoneers, and that these eight hundred, first of all, had not received one dinar of their pay, and, secondly, they were needed in ten other places. Nevertheless, they do not listen or take warning and do not see the result of their own actions. They are again continuously arranging the implements of war for themselves. "Don't take all this boasting and bluffing seriously; let there be a limit to bluff and intimidation."[127] Old women who have young and handsome husbands always freshen up their faces with rouge and decorate themselves with clothes and baubles so that their husbands will not know that they are old and will call them young, little knowing that "Young cheeks do not need rouge."[128] [137]

Every month there is a strict prohibition from the Ministry of Information to the offices of the employees of newspapers printed in Istanbul not to write about the irregularities of the government or to enumerate the faults of its officials.[129] Something like that was communicated explicitly in the newspaper Ni'ulu ᶜAvaṣ [*sic*],[130] in which they published, along with some spiteful observations, some stories that were critical of the Ottoman government. They stated, "This type of transgression on the part of the sublime government will not be permitted." Thus, according to the orders of the

---

127 A proverbial saying; see Dehkhodâ, *Amsâl*, p. 350; Ḥayyim, *Proverbs*, p. 49.

128 A verse expressing the same idea is omitted from the translation.

129 Censorship of the press, and all printed materials, was very strict during the reign of ᶜAbd ol-Ḥamid II; see Lewis, *Emergence of Modern Turkey*, p. 188.

130 Unclear in the text. Of the Ottoman newspapers discussed in Selim Nüzhet Gerçek, *Türk gazeteciliği* (Istanbul, 1931), the title which comes closest to matching this is perhaps *Ayenih Vaṭan*.

government, the offices of that newspaper have been closed effective today.

Another example: In order to frighten the Serbians, Bulgarians, and Greeks, they spread rumors and hearsay and instructed the journalists to write: On behalf of the Ottoman Empire, the preparation for war having been perfectly overseen, there are 110,000 Ottoman soldiers on the Thessaly frontier and 60,000 on the Yânieh[131] frontier, along with all their officers and instructors responsible for military training. The reality is that at present the Ottoman Empire does not have 120,000 troops fit for service. And what soldiers they are!

First of all, at this moment, which is four months into the new year, not one dinar of the wages for last year has been received, except only the bare means of livelihood (their payment for living expenses is a ration which is enough for bare subsistence). Secondly, very few of their officers are experienced veterans.[132] [138]

Many of their officers are youths barely past puberty, whose beards have only begun to appear and are very young. All are smooth faced[133] and foppish. "Whichever of them has a spear in hand is like one who has henna on his palm."[134] God forbid that I have told anything wrong. Anyone under those officers will be killed. With eyebrows for bows and eyelashes for arrows, mounds will be made of the slaughtered![135]

Among the things reported is that Zeila[136] and the province of Aden[137] (which are part of Ethiopia and over which the Ottomans have never had and do not now have any form of possession) are considered among their undisputed possessions. The time that Esmâᶜil Pasha, the Khedive of Egypt, had come to Istanbul, the

---

131 Yanina?

132 Two lines of verse quoted here are omitted from the translation.

133 More literally, they have their hair plucked out with a stringed tool the way women do. Farâhâni's point here and in the following proverb is to show his disdain for the Ottoman military by implying that the soldiers are no more threatening than women.

134 This saying is quoted in Arabic in the text.

135 This phrase is often used to describe the way an attractive and flirtatious woman asserts herself among men; Farâhâni is thus continuing to use scornful imagery to suggest the effeminate character of the Ottoman soldiers. A verse to the same effect quoted by Farâhâni is omitted from the translation.

136 Text: Z̲aylaᶜ. Zeila is a port in Somalia near Djibouti. It was seized by Egyptian forces in 1875 and in 1884 became the chief port for British Somaliland; cf. Farhâd Mirzâ, *Hedâyat*, p. 216; Holt, *Fertile Crescent*, p. 208.

137 Text: ᶜAdl.

Ottoman sultan accepted sums as a present from him and presented [Egypt] to him.[138]

AN ANECDOTE

ᶜAlâ' od-Din Marvân Khalji,[139] at a royal audience, divided Iraq and Khorasan, which were not among his possessions, between the attendants. Another time, one of the merchants of that region had lost a great deal of money. A description of the merchant's predicament came to his attention, so he asked, "Where is that man from?" They said, "From Isfahan." He said, "Turn over the government there to him." No one had the courage to say, "Isfahan is not part of your realm." Finally, one of the attendants [in order to help the merchant get some monetary assistance] told him, "That merchant to whom you have given the government of Isfahan needs money to equip his army." This statement touched him, so he gave a large sum for the purpose of equipping the merchant's [fictitious] army. [139] "Therefore, take heed, O you who have eyes."[140]

SITUATION OF THE GOVERNMENT

Despite all the efforts of the functionaries of the Ottoman Empire along these lines for fifty years, Greece and Tunisia slipped out of their grasp all together. Eastern Thrace [*Rumeli*] fell into the possession of the Westerners. All the profits of the state of Sudan were lost.[141] As for the province of Egypt, except for the flag of the moon and the star, no other sign or mark of sovereignty remains. Such of the land of Armenia as they had was given over to the enemy. The inhabitants of the oases and the desert Arabs of the Hejaz never recognize the royal power. The chief of every tribe calls himself sultan. The people of Najd and Jabal [Shammâr] give the empire nothing but deceit and counterfeit, war and controversy. They consider their amirs to be the true rulers. In Arab Iraq, no one has power over life and property because of the incursions and attacks of the tribe of ᶜOnayzeh and so on. These several provinces which now remain in their possession are encumbered with millions in foreign and domestic debts. So from where will the army payments

---

138 Farâhâni is alluding to the way in which Esmâᶜil Pâshâ secured the title of Khedive and recognition of his autonomous and hereditary position as ruler of Egypt. See P. M. Holt, *Egypt and the Fertile Crescent, 1516-1922* (Ithaca, 1966), p. 196. This is followed by a quotation, omitted in the translation, from the poet Jâmi: "What has not partaken of existence can never impart existence to another thing." See Ḥayyim, *Proverbs*, p. 229.

139 Farâhâni is probably referring to the Delhi sultan ᶜAlâ' od-Din Moḥammad Shâh (695-715/1296-1316).

140 Koran, 59:21.

141 To make a pun, Farâhâni uses *sud* for "profits": The Sudan lost its "sud".

and the enormous expenses of government come? I wish that His Highness Moᶜtamad od-Dowleh would write for the Ottoman government the same sort of doleful elegy that he composed for the statue of Napoleon.[142]

At the present day, the condition of the Ottoman Empire resembles a carcass of a dead animal whose corpse has been thrown among many strong dogs. These dogs all around, out of fear of each other, do not have the courage to devour this carcass, unless they suddenly lunge and carry away a piece of it. And if it were not for the fear of these dogs of each other, they would carry away and devour this carcass in a single day.[143] [140]

The amazing thing is that the Ottoman functionaries, in spite of the fact that they have seen and see clearly that England has taken Sudan, Egypt, and Aden out of their grasp, have nevertheless been deceived by the feigned sympathy of this alluring viper and their politics still follows hers. One of the sayings of Darius the Great is "One who mocks you is like an enemy. Like the colocynth, the foliage is verdant [but] the taste is deadly."[144]

A REPUBLICAN OR MONARCHICAL GOVERNMENT?

More curious still is that the status of the Ottoman empire is neither a republic, with the sultan powerless, nor like Russia and Iran in which the monarch is sovereign. If it is a type of republic, why is the monarch involved in [state] affairs? And if it is a form of monarchy, then who are these deputies of the state and what is the alteration [in the status of] the sultan? Although I heard this current sultan[145] is a wise man and has taken all care to make the functionaries of the state and notables of the government independent, for that same reason he observes great caution everywhere lest they machinate and cause injury to him. Since this subject has come up, and republic and monarchy have been

142 While reading a copy of the *London Illustrated News* after the Franco-Prussian War, Farhâd Mirzâ noticed a photograph showing a man destroying a statue of Napoleon. He was so affected by this that he immediately composed an elegaic poem in honor of Napoleon. The poem was apparently translated into French and brought to the attention of Nâṣer od-Din Shâh when he visited Europe in 1873. See Farhâd Mirzâ, *Safarnâmeh* (ed. Ṣafâ), 2:338.

143 One line of poetry quoted here by Farâhâni is omitted from the translation.

144 Quoted in Arabic in the text. The colocynth (*ḥanẓal*), the extremely bitter pulp of which was used for medicinal purposes, served as a poetical metaphor for the harsh experiences of life: see Sami Hamarneh, *Al-Biruni's Book on Pharmacy and Materia Medica* (Karachi, 1973), p. 89.

145 Solṭân ᶜAbd ol-Ḥamid II (1293-1327/1876-1909). He had prorogued the Ottoman Parliament shortly after coming to power and ignored, but did not abolish, the constitution for the rest of his reign.

mentioned, I am compelled to write something [about them], with consideration for the brevity of this chapter.

THE MYSTERY OF UNITY

"There is no refuge and no power except in God."[146] The mystery (*serr*) of unity is a mystery which is flowing in the natures of all extant things. Every existing thing knows innately that all superfluity culminates in a unity. Those superfluities derive benefit entirely from that unity and depend on it. The first oneness which all intelligent people ponder and admire and profess is the oneness of God. "If there were therein gods beside God, then verily both [heaven and earth] had been disordered."[147] [141] The second unity is the unity of the prophets who sprang from the rays of light of the one God. Because light has the attributes of brightness and clarity in the form of the conscience, all were unique in their own epoch, and they brought one religion and one book [i. e., revelation]. In each epoch, one prophet was endowed with [religious] commandments and authority. If there were other prophets [at the same time], they followed that [supreme] prophet and propagated his authority, or else each prophet was sent to one state and one people. Always, from Adam to the seal [of the prophets, Moḥammad], there was only one endowed with the divine law and authority. Also, the Imam of the people was always one and a unity in every epoch; even the imam leading the prayers is one and the faithful, openly or secretly, are able to follow his example. The rational faculty in one person does not obey two [wills]; there is no place in the heart for love for two people. "The requirement of love is one heart and one sweetheart." Obedience will not be realized except in a situation of unity. Unity is the means of joining together; excess is the cause of dissension. "Had you spent all that is in the earth, you could not have united their hearts, but God united them."[148] The mystery of joining together is this same unity that existed in the prophets. Satan instigated opposition and plurality and manifested contrariness to the unity of God. "Verily Satan is an obvious enemy to you. Surely the devil is your enemy so take him for an enemy. If it [the Koran] were from any other than God, they would have found in it many a discrepancy."[149] Everything is witness to this point. The mystery of

146 A well known Arabic saying.

147 Koran, 21:22. Farâhâni is alluding to the concept of *towḥid*, the unity of God, perhaps the most fundamental doctrine of Islam.

148 Koran, 8:63.

149 A conflation of Koran 4:82 and 35:6.

the unity of God is current in everything. As authority and sovereignty are like the heart in the human body, there cannot be two hearts in one body. "God has not put two hearts inside a man."[150] On behalf of the heart, it is the head which is ruler and Grand Vezir in the body; that also is united and one.

SOVEREIGNTY MUST RESIDE IN ONE

It is just so with the authority of the monarchy. Human beings need each other and must congregate in cities so that each one can transact his business with another. [142] After they have congregated together, since they have various intentions, desires, passions, lusts, and different morals, it is inevitable that disputes will occur among them, and murders, pillage, and corruption will become manifest. For this reason, the Lord of the World, out of wisdom, created some of them great and some humble, and some as kings and some as subjects. He has put fear of the king in the hearts of the subjects and made their souls obedient to that ruler [*pâdeshâh*]. Thus millions of people may fear one ruler and accept his commands. It is necessary by all means that this ruler and administrator be one person, and that there be no disputing with him about orders and prohibitions, and that all look with favor on him, so that conflict is alleviated. If there were numerous authorities and rulers in one state, and each one issued orders, of course disputes and quarrels would increase because each group of people would attach themselves to one of them and quarrels and dissension would occur among them accordingly.[151]

For the same reason that there cannot be two prophets for one people at one time, so there cannot be two rulers or authorities in one state. We consider the oneness of the king a proof of the oneness of the Most Merciful [God].

"What is below is like what is above."[152]

EVEN BEES AND BIRDS HAVE [ONLY] ONE RULER

One of the sayings of Kayqobâd[153] is that human beings should not be less than the honeybees and the birds called herons, which consider themselves free to select one [of themselves] for governing and ruling and consider it obligatory to obey that one. [143]

[150] Koran, 33:4.

[151] A line by an unidentified poet is quoted here; it is omitted from the translation.

[152] That is, things on earth reflect the heavenly order. This is a proverbial verse attributed to Mir Abu'l-Qâsem Fendereski; see Dehkhodâ, *Amsâl*, p. 1059.

[153] The first of the semi-legendary Kiânian monarchs of Iran; see Sykes, *History of Persia*, 1:136-37; Huart, *Ancient Persia*, p. 210.

REPUBLICANISM

I do not know the meaning of "republic." If ministers and deputies do not have [sovereign] power, it is not a republic, and if their power is genuine, surely two or three [of their] opinions will not agree with each other and every opinion, position, or plan will clash with the others. Feraydun[154] always used to say, "Two swords cannot be inserted into one scabbard, and one arrow cannot be shot from two bows."

CRITIQUE OF THE MEXICAN AND AMERICAN REPUBLICS

The state of Mexico was in complete disorder at the time it was a republic. After France, in the year 1278 [1861-62], made that republican state into an empire it became tranquil.[155]

Greece, by virtue of republicanism, was disturbed for a while, until, in the year 1279 [1862-63], the European states appointed George, son of the crown-prince of Denmark, as sovereign of Greece.[156] After that, it has been put into order.

America, after it became a republic, had disputes and split into north and south and fought for a while. They have seen no result except ruining the country.

THE FRENCH REPUBLICAN REGIME WILL BE CHANGED

In spite of the fact that France had become the foremost state in terms of income and the prosperity of the country, the notables were nevertheless anxious to have a republic. They lost sight of the grandeur of the monarchy; they did not obey Napoleon [III] as he deserved; and they covertly sought to oppose and weaken him, until as a result the German conquest came to pass. How much they lost and how they fell from grandeur and dignity! In truth, this loss, the ruin of the state, and the capture of the kingdom, all happened because of the demands for this republic. "Whatever happened to me was done to me by my [so-called] friends." It has fallen a hundred years behind, and if they do not have the interests of the state [at heart] any more than this, it will not recover till the Day of Judgment. Wise people see that this great state should become a monarchy again. [144]

---

[154] The legendary king of ancient Iran who dethroned the evil usurper and tyrant Żaḥḥâk; see Ferdowsi/Levy, *Epic of the Kings*, pp. 17-34.

[155] Farâhâni demonstrates here some awareness of the terms of the Treaty of London of 1861 and the subsequent role of Maximillian as Emperor of Mexico (1863-67); he either does not know or at least chooses not to mention the tragic fate of Maximillian, who was overthrown and then executed in 1869.

[156] George I, King of the Hellenes, was appointed to rule Greece by the European powers after a revolt overthrew King Otto in October, 1862. He arrived in Athens on October 30, 1863.

Thus, after the agents of the Ottoman state created a republic, and acted according to their own corrupt opinions, and dauntlessly deposed Solṭân ᶜAbd ol-ᶜAziz Khân and Solṭân Morâd Khân from the sultanate, enemies perceived the plight of the sultans there, pondered the number of the deputies, [and] all at once rushed from the surrounding areas and sealed the fate of the empire.[157] A point about the war with the Russian Empire: First, what a sum and quantity in loss of weapons, money, and troops it caused the Ottoman Empire. Second, they agreed to pay 2,820 *korur*[158] of manâts as compensation for war damages to the Russian government, and they are still burdened with this and have not been able to pay. Third, the government was obliged to separate Bulgaria and the Dobruja from their realm. Fourth, the provinces of Kars, Batum, and Ardahan, which were really the keys to the country, were given up.[159] All these are the inauspicious [results] of a republic. This treatise does not have [enough] room to explain and expand upon this point. God willing, I shall write a special treatise on the futility of a republic, with proofs by reason and example.

More curious than all this is that some ill informed notables and descendants of notables in Iran have taken the deeds and actions of the Ottoman Empire as their own model, and praise them, and call to witness as their own words the sayings of Fakhri Bayk[160] and Khâled Bayk.[161] "So weak are the seeker and the sought, and the witness and the testimony"[162] The panegyric and praise of the former for the latter is like the panegyric and praise that one of the poets of Istanbul has composed in my honor. Several verses from that ode are recorded here.[163] [145]

---

157 Farâhâni is alluding to the tumultuous events which surrounded the promulgation of the Ottoman constitution in 1876, followed by the Russo-Turkish war of 1877-78. See Lewis, *Emergency of Modern Turkey*, pp. 160-69; Joan Haslip, *The Sultan: the Life of Abdul Hamid II* (New York, 1958), pp. 65-80.

158 The *korur* is half a million. It is interesting that Farâhâni should be familiar with such a relatively obscure matter as this war indemnity; see Michael Milgrim, "An Overlooked Problem in Turkish-Russian Relations: The 1878 War Indemnity," *International Journal of Middle East Studies* 4(1978):519-37.

159 According to the terms of the Treaty of San Stefano (1878).

160 Probably the Ottoman ambassador to Iran mentioned by Pirzâdeh, *Safarnâmeh*, 2:126-28; see also the Turkish *Sâlnâmeh-ye devlet-i ᶜâli-ye ᶜos̱mâneyyeh* (Istanbul, 1302/1885), p. 482.

161 Perhaps Khâled Żiâ ᶜOshaqi-zâdeh (1866-1945) the famous poet and founder of the newspaper *Nowruz*. See EI_1, 2:879.

162 A conflation of Koran 22:73 and 85:3.

163 Farâhâni quotes five lines of poetry here. The verses are in Persian, not Turkish; no author is indicated. They are omitted from this translation.

Such panegyric is not appropriate for one as humble as me.[164]

[I] do not understand why we are not warned, do not heed the admonition, and do not display more zeal [because of] what we see and hear.[165]

I suppose that the people who read these words will take them for nonsense and idle talk since the one speaking to them is not a General Ṣâḥeb or Fakhri Bayk or Khâled Bayk. Perhaps, but [still] one must know what a person says and must not be influenced by who is speaking. "Pay attention to what was said, not to who said it."[166] [146]

One of the counsels of Hushang in the *Jâvedân Kherad* [*Eternal Wisdom*][167] is that you must not regard any created thing with contempt because behind every skin there is an intellect, in all balderdash a bit of eloquence, and in every ragged garment a living being. "Pay attention to what is concealed in his tongue, not what is inside his garb."[168] It is proverbial that there is no plant [on earth] for which there is no use.

Anyhow, such matters are none of my business nor of people like me; this is just chatter. "Kings know what is best for their kingdoms."[169]

IMPORTANT OFFICES IN THE OTTOMAN EMPIRE[170]

Grand Vizier; Minister of Justice; Minister of Foreign Affairs; Commander-in-Chief of the Army; Minister of the Navy; Minister of Technology; Minister of Finances; Minister of Public Works; Minister of Commerce; Minister of Customs; Minister of Public Instruction; Tax Inspector; Chief of Staff of the Grand Vizier;[171]

---

164 Farâhâni quotes a couplet by Saᶜdi, omitted in this translation, to make his point. On these proverbial verses see Dehkhodâ, *Amsâl*, p. 1065.

165 Farâhâni quotes another proverbial verse, this time by Ferdowsi, which has been omitted from the translation. On the verse see Dehkhodâ, *Amsâl*, p. 601.

166 An Arabic proverb; see Dehkhodâ, *Amsâl*, p. 304.

167 Hushang was one of the legendary early (Pishdâdiân) kings of Iran credited with discovering fire and having power over demons. The *Jâvedân Kherad* was supposedly a book of wise sayings attributed to this sage. The opening sections of Ebn Meskawayh, *ol-Ḥekmeh ol-khâledeh: jâvedân kherad* (edited by ᶜAbd or-Raḥman Badawi; Cairo, 1952) contain several of these maxims. There were published Persian translations of this work which may have been known to Farâhâni: see Moshâr, *Fehrest*, col. 476.

168 An Arabic proverb in which there is an untranslatable pun on the phrase "what is concealed in his tongue" (*fi ṭayy lisâneh*) and a type of clothing (*ṭaylesân*).

169 A proverb attributed to Saᶜdi; see Dehkhodâ, *Amsâl*, p. 1058; Ḥayyim, *Proverbs*, p. 290.

170 Cf. *Sâlnâmeh*, p. 134 ; Desjardins, *Turquie*, pp. 172-83; Pakalın, *Deyimleri*, 3:81-88 [s. v. *sadrazam*], 3:176-77 [*serasker*], 2:666 [*evkaf nâziri*], 3:644 [*zabtiyye nâziri*].

171 Text: *mostashâr-e ṣadârat*.

Chief of Protocol;[172] Undersecretary of State;[173] Inspector of Wakfs; Secretary to the Sultan;[174] Chief of the Consultative Assembly;[175] Chief of the Police.

RANKS OF ARMY OFFICERS AND THE INSIGNIA OF EACH[176]

The *châvosh* ["sergeant"]: He has [charge of] thirty-two privates. The insignia on his uniform[177] is like this: [Figure A]

The *molâzem-e ṣâni* ["second lieutenant"]: He has [charge of] one hundred privates. His insignia is like this: [Fig. B]

The *molâzem-e avval* ["first lieutenant"]: He has [charge of] one hundred privates. His insignia is like this: [Fig. C]

The *yuzbâshi* ["captain"]: He has charge of 250 privates, and his insignia is like this: [Fig. D] [147]

The *sol qulâqâsi*[178]: He has charge of five hundred privates. His insignia is like this: [Fig. E]

The *ṣâgh qulâqâsi*:[179] He has charge of eight hundred privates. His insignia is like this: [Fig. F]

The *âlây kâteb*: He is the secretary[180] for one thousand soldiers and is a distinguished officer. His insignia is like this: [Fig. G]

The *âlây amin*: He is the secretary for three thousand soldiers and is [the equivalent] to the rank of *lashkar nevis* [in Iran]. His insignia is one [mark] above the âlây kâteb's: [Fig. H]

The *bekbâshi* (which is [pronounced] *binbâshi*[181]): He has [charge of] one thousand privates. His insignia is like this: [Fig. I]

[A] 

[B] 

[C] 

[D] 

[E] 

[F] 

[G] 

[H] 

[I] 

---

172 Text: *âjudân-e ḥożur*.

173 Text: *mostashâr-e vezârat-e khârejeh*.

174 Text: *daftardâr-e solṭân*. Perhaps the "Custos Rotulorum of the Privy Domain" mentioned by Redhouse in his translation of Nâser od-Din Shâh's *Diary*?

175 Text: *re'is-e dâr osh-shurâ*. Farâhâni's terminology is unclear. There was a Dâr osh-Shurâ-yi Bâb-e ᶜÂli in the Ottoman Empire, but it was abolished around 1838; it is possible but unlikely that Farâhâni is using the term Dâr osh-shurâ to refer to the Ottoman Parliament (*Majles-e omumi*), which was in any event prorogued. Perhaps he means the Shurâ-ye Devlet, or council of ministers, established in 1867. See Pakalın, *Deyimleri*, 3:360-61; Findley, *Bureaucratic Reform*, p. 174.

176 Farâhâni's account is a fairly accurate representation of the Ottoman "New Order" (Neẓâm-e Jadid) military following the reorganization of 1826-28. See Mahmud Şevket, *Osmanlı askeri teşkilati ve kiyafeti* (Ankara, 1983), pp. 77-82; Marcel Roubiçek, *Modern Ottoman Troops, 1797-1915* (Jerusalem, 1978), pp. 11 ff.

177 Farâhâni seems to be referring to the decoration on the cuffs of the uniform jackets.

178 Text: *sulghun âqâsi*; an evident mistake for the *sol kolağası*, the military rank between Yüzbashi and Sağ Kolağası. See Pakalın, *Deyimleri*, 3:256-57.

179 Text: *ṣaᶜqul âqâsi*; see the preceding note.

180 That is, he would be responsible for keeping the roster, payroll accounts, etc. See Pakalın, *Deyimleri*, 1:45 [s. v. *Alay Emini*].

181 Text: *minbâshi*. In Ottoman Turkish, the letter for the sound "n" in this word was similar to the letter "k" in Persian.

The *qâ'em-maqâm*: He has [charge of] 3,200 privates. His insignia is like this: [Fig. J]

The *mir âlây*: He also has [charge of] 3,200 privates. His insignia is one [mark] above the qâyem-maqâm. Both are [about equivalent] to the *mir-e panj* [in Iran].

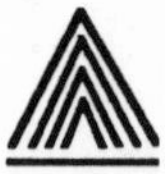

[J]

The *mir-e levâ*:[182] He has [charge of] 8,300 privates and [is equivalent to] the *amir-e tumâni* [in Iran]. His insignia is like this: [Fig. K] [148]

[K]

The *fariq*:[183] He has [charge of] twenty thousand troops (which is equivalent to the rank of *moniᶜ-e sardari* [in Iran]). His insignia is like this: [Fig. L]

[L]

The *moshir-e ᶜâlishân*:[184] He is [equivalent to] the *sepahsâlâr* [in Iran], who commands fifty thousand troops and is commander in chief. His insignia is like this: [Fig. M]

[M]

THE ARSENAL

There are arsenals in two places. One is located between the Fındıklı quarter and the Galata quarter; there are ordinary cannons in it. Also, another arsenal, which has been very grandly and sturdily built, is near the Imperial Palace. There are about six or seven hundred cannon there. Most are breech-loaders. There are also some steel cannons.

BARRACKS

There are also large barracks inside the city and along the straits. Among them is the Selimeyyeh barracks, which is next to the water.

FACTORIES

Further towards Europe,[185] some gunsmith and canvas weaving factories have been built. They also have some good, strong bastions [there].

Punishment [for crimes] in the Ottoman Empire consists of imprisonment; other forms of punishment have been abandoned.[186]

FOREIGN AMBASSADORS

The great ambassador of the exalted Empire of Iran, the Russian ambassador, the English ambassador, the German

---

[182] Under the 1828 reorganization of the military the regiments were renamed *âlây* and the brigade (*levâ*) was established. This officer would thus be roughly equivalent to brigadier general. See Pakalın, *Deyimleri*, 2:545.

[183] See Pakalın, *Deyimleri*, 1:606-7 [s.v. *ferik*].

[184] Cf. Pakalın, *Deyimleri*, 2:636 [s.v. *müşir*].

[185] I.e., in the western districts of the city?

[186] Under the Tanzimat reforms, corporal punishment was abolished and the European system of incarceration adopted.

ambassador, the ambassador of France, the ambassador of Austria,[187] the ambassador of Belgium, the ambassador of South America,[188] the ambassador of the United States,[189] the chargé d'affaires of Spain, the chargé d'affaires of Italy, the chargé d'affaires of Holland, the chargé d'affaires of Greece, the chargé d'affaires of Sweden, the commissioner [*ma'mur*] of Rumania, and the commissioner of Serbia. [149]

Some of these ambassadors have their own yachts which anchor opposite their buildings. Anytime it is necessary, they take their own boats.

MEMBERS OF THE EMBASSY OF IRAN

At the time [of my visit], Ḥâjji Shaykh Moḥsen Khân Moᶜin ol-Molk,[190] the ambassador of the exalted empire of Iran, had gone to Berlin on official business and was not in Istanbul. On his behalf, Ḥâjji Mirzâ Najaf-ᶜali Khân[191] handles legal matters for [Iranian] subjects. The latter is from Tabriz. He is very learned, wise, sedate, sensible, and capable. He is the chief translator for the embassy and the consul-general. He presides over the *qânchâreyyeh*,[192] which is the place court proceedings are held. He has complete command of the Turkish, Arabic, and Persian languages, in speaking and writing, and he has composed many literary works. He is an extremely devout Muslim. He handles most of the business, even when Moᶜin ol-Molk is present.

MIRZÂ JAVÂD KHÂN

One of the important employees of the embassy is Mirzâ Javâd Khân the chargé d'affaires.[193] He is intelligent and *civilisée*.[194] He is

[187] Farâhâni repeats this twice in the text, using the term Aṭrish first and then Nemseh (both mean Austria).

[188] So in the text: *Yanki* [sic] *donyâ[-ye] jonubi.*

[189] This is presumably what Farâhâni means by *Amrikâ[-ye] shomâli.*

[190] Moᶜin ol-Molk (1235-1317/1819-1900) had a long and distinguished career in the Iranian diplomatic service and bureaucracy. He served as ambassador to the Ottoman Empire from 1872-1890. See Bâmdâd, *Rejâl*, 3:204-12; Bakhash, *Iran*, p. 383; Pirzâdeh, *Safarnâmeh*, 2:80-83; Khân Malek-e Sâsâni, *Yâdbudhâ-ye sefârat-e estânbul* (Tehran, 1345/1966-67), pp. 255-64.

[191] Mirzâ Najaf-ᶜali Khân Tabrizi was the founder of the Persian language newspaper *Akhtar* (described by Farâhâni below) published in Istanbul from 1292/1875 to 1313/1895-96. He became secretary of the Iranian embassy in 1300/1882-83. See Bâmdâd, *Rejâl*, 4:330; there is a photograph of him in Sâsâni, *Yâdbudhâ*, p. 258.

[192] A corruption of the term chancery.

[193] Cf. Pirzâdeh, *Safarnâmeh*, 2:83 (there is a photograph of him at the end of that volume).

[194] Although there is other evidence in this text that Farâhâni himself knew at least a little French, he is probably using the term *civilisée* ironically here to emphasize that Javâd Khân is too much of a Francophile.

somewhat excessively Europeanized. He is fluent in speaking and writing the French language. Previously, the sister of Moᶜin ol-Molk was his wife but she died. By her, he has a son named Moḥammad Ṣâdeq Khân,[195] who has studied the French language in an Ottoman state school and some other sciences such as physics, chemistry, and geometry. According to reports, he has become proficient in these sciences.

ḤÂJJI MIRZÂ ḤASAN KHÂN

Another of the important officials of the embassy is Ḥâjji Mirzâ Ḥasan Khân. He has the rank of first secretary general and consul. He is intelligent and eloquent. He writes *shekasteh* and *nastaᶜliq*[196] calligraphy well. He was also at Jedda in the capacity of consul for two years. [150] Also, a house and land have been given to him by the Ottoman sultan.

ḤÂJJI MOḤAMMAD KHÂN

Another of the important officials of the embassy is Ḥâjji Moḥammad Khân, who is the brother-in-law of Moᶜin ol-Molk. He knows the French language. He is also in charge of the consulates [in] Cairo,[197] Alexandria, and Jedda. He is stationed in Cairo[198] in the capacity of consul-general. He has appointed consuls on his own behalf in Jedda and in Alexandria.

There are several other officials whom it is not necessary to mention.

THE IRANIAN EMBASSY

In Istanbul there are two embassy buildings belonging to the government of Iran.[199] One has been there for a long time. They say it was one of the constructions of Moḥammad Khân. Ḥâjji Mirzâ Ḥosayn Khân Moshir od-Dowleh Sepahsâlâr built the other one. The old one has become dilapidated. The tribunal [for Iranian citizens] is there. The one built by the late Moshir od-Dowleh is in excellent [condition] and is currently the residence of the ambassador. It was being repaired this year. Moᶜin ol-Molk has also

[195] On whom see Pirzâdeh, *Safarnâmeh*, 2:82-83.

[196] *Shekasteh* and *nastaᶜliq* are two calligraphic styles for writing the Arabic script; they are both very cursive and rounded, with an emphasis on forming the entire word rather than individual letters. As a result, they were suitable primarily for documents and manuscripts rather than architectural decoration. Both were widely used in Iran but less so in other areas of the Middle East. See Aslanapa, *Turkish Art*, p. 344; Pope, *Survey of Persian Art*, 2:1733-34, 1740-41.

[197] Text: *meṣr*. Although this term usually means Egypt, it can also refer to the city of Cairo; judging from the context, Farâhâni generally seems to use it in the latter sense.

[198] Or Egypt; see preceding note.

[199] Cf. Pirzâdeh, *Safarnâmeh*, 2:80-81; Sâsâni, *Yâdbudhâ*, pp. 8-10, 218.

built a very grand house for himself in Yâli [?].[200] The Ottoman sultan had given the land for it to the aforementioned. Considerable sums were spent on it. This house is situated beside the Bosphorus on the side of an earthen hill.

IRANIAN SUBJECTS

There are about sixteen thousand subjects of Iran in Istanbul and its suburbs, of whom a thousand are merchants and the rest are tradesmen. The chief Iranian place of business is in the Vâledeh khan. The Vâledeh khan is a large inn and place of business. There are only Iranians there. A mosque has been built in that same place. [151] They hold *rowżeh-khvânis* there.[201]

Legal recourse for Iranians is entirely through the embassy. They are never under the jurisdiction of the administration of Istanbul.[202] The procedure of the embassy in court proceedings is this: If both parties are Muslims and Iranian subjects, [the case] is treated according to the laws of the Prophet Moḥammad. If one party is Christian and a foreign subject, [the case] is tried and punishment imposed according to French law.

The Iranians are held in esteem and respect. The embassy is very influential and orderly. There is never any religious dissimulation [*taqeyyeh*].

The embassy provides residence visas every year for the Iranian subjects residing in Istanbul who have trade or work or their own means of livelihood. Half a lira is collected from each person for the cost of the visa. Transit visas are also provided yearly from the embassy to those transiting through Istanbul. Each person is charged half a lira as the cost of the visa, except for notable persons, the poor, and descendants of the prophet [*sâdât*], who are not charged for the cost of the visa. In other words, in Istanbul one must obtain from the Ottoman government a transit visa and pay about four krans for the visa; the embassy endorses the Ottoman visa and charges half a lira as the endorsement fee.

---

200 Yâlı is the Turkish name for the type of mansions built along the Bosphorus; perhaps Farâhâni has confused it with a place name.

201 Cf. Pirzâdeh, *Safarnâmeh*, 2:113-14; Sâsâni, *Yâdbudhâ*, pp. 108-11. On the practice of holding these popular readings or sermons about the suffering of the Shi'ite Imams and other Shi'ite practices in the Ottoman Empire, see Metin And, "The Muḥarram Observances in Anatolian Turkey," in P. Chelkowski (ed.), *Ta'ziyeh: Ritual and Drama in Iran* (New York, 1979), pp. 238-54.

202 On the legal aspects of the system of capitulations in the Ottoman Empire, see N. Sousa, *The Capitulatory Regime of Turkey* (Baltimore, 1933). It is worth noting here that the legal system devised under the capitulatory regime in the Ottoman Empire was used for a Muslim state like Iran as well as the European powers.

MARVELS OF THE CITY

Among the curiosities observed in the city, one was very large ostriches. Another was six-horned sheep with long tails which are as long as the tail of an ox. Another was an Armenian woman half of whose face and body was completely white and [the other] half black. Another was a terrestrial serpent which was three and one quarter z̲arᶜ in length and seven gereh in diameter. [152]

STEAMSHIP COMPANIES

A detailed account of the steamship companies which are in Istanbul, each of which has numerous steamships and goes everywhere, is appended:

The Austrian company, which is reputable in every respect and has a special understanding with the embassy of Iran and has consideration for [Iranian] subjects.

The Arab company, which is run by some people from Cairo, Alexandria, and Suez.

The French company, which is also very excellent and has a close relationship with the embassy of Iran.

The Ottoman company, which is [owned?] by people in Istanbul.

The Russian company, which generally [has service] from Istanbul to Poti and Batum.

There are several steamers [run] by English subjects, but these are not very reputable. They do not belong to a company and are leased.

FROM ISTANBUL TO JEDDA

There are two routes from Istanbul to Jedda. One goes via Port Said to the Suez Canal, and from the canal to Jedda, completely by sea in eleven or twelve days. The steamer goes directly; one does not have to change. Another [route] goes by sea to Alexandria in five days. In the event that one does not wish to remain in Alexandria, one is kept waiting in Alexandria for two days in order to give the ticket for transportation from Istanbul to Jedda which was purchased from the steamship company to the company's agent in Alexandria and to take another ticket [from the agent] to be conveyed both by railroad coach and by the Arab steamers which run between Suez and Jedda (the company in Istanbul being in partnership with the other companies). It takes one day from Alexandria to Suez by railroad coach, and one waits for two more days in Suez. [153] It takes four days to go from Suez to Jedda by steamer, so by this route in this manner, it takes fifteen or sixteen days to go from Istanbul to Jedda. There are good things about going by either of these two routes.

As for the good things about the Alexandria route, [they] are visiting Egypt and its environs, minimizing sea travel, and the comfort of land [travel] and sitting in the railroad [coach].

BENEFITS OF THE ALEXANDRIA ROUTE

As for the good things about the direct route from Istanbul to Jedda, [they] are the economy, the lack of trouble in moving from the steamer to Alexandria and from Alexandria to the railroad, and arriving earlier in Jedda. Every group chooses one of these two routes. "One group prefers this, one that."[203]

BENEFITS OF THE DIRECT ROUTE

As for the matter of the fares from Istanbul to Jedda: First of all, every company has an Iranian broker through whom the fares for Iranian pilgrims are arranged. The broker receives a fixed fee from the company for every person he takes to the steamer. Secondly, the fares vary. Sometimes, the fare per person by third class is six or seven lira, whether by the Alexandria route or the canal route; sometimes the companies are competing with each other and lower the price.

THE FARES

The fare per person to Jedda may be three or four lira. If a group of pilgrims gets together and arranges the fare through the intermediary of the employees of the embassy, it will be even cheaper. Also, the steamship workers behave better and respect the pilgrims. Thus I arranged the fare with the Austrian company through the employees of the embassy. The fare per person in third class by the Alexandria route to Jedda was three and a half lira. The second class fare is twice [that], and the first class fare triple [that]. [154] One hundred and fifty Iranian pilgrims went along with me, and about one hundred other Iranian pilgrims took the English steamer and went by the canal directly to Jedda. Each person paid a fare of four lira.

In the event the steamer fare is arranged through the employees of the embassy, the employees of the embassy collect a fee from the company for transporting the pilgrims, but this is not at the expense of the pilgrim. I will mention one other point concerning economy in the fares, and that is this: On all the steamers, if a person for the sake of comfort wishes to stay in a cabin, it is very expensive in the event he buys a cabin ticket before boarding the steamer. If before boarding the steamer, he buys a third class ticket and then boards the ship, as soon as the ship is a little out to sea, he will be able to make

203 A proverb; see Dehkhodâ, *Amsâl*, p. 1308.

a deal with the cabin stewards, give them a small payment, and openly enter the cabin. This is a profit which goes into the purse of the captain of the steamer. He considers whatever they pay a windfall, and it does not go to the company. As for the first and second captains in regard to this, if it comes to light, they have the opportunity of denial because they never openly interfere in the matter nor do they issue tickets. Inquiries about this matter are left to the cabin stewards. There are also some rooms that are reserved for the steamship workers which are not related to the [regular] cabins. They will rent them for a small fee. They are better and more private than a second class cabin.

DEPARTURE FROM ISTANBUL

The morning of Thursday, the first day of the sacred month of Z̲i Qaᶜdeh [12 August],[204] all the Iranian pilgrims who were in Istanbul gathered together. They took tickets for the Austrian steamer, went to the steamer, and obtained places for themselves. [155]

On the steamship ticket they write that this steamer will stop at so many ports. I sent my companions to the steamship, for I had been invited to have lunch at the residence of Ḥâjji Mirzâ Najaf-ᶜali Khân the consul general. In accordance with the invitation, I went there. Mirzâ Javâd Khân, the chargé d'affaires, and some of the merchants there had prepared a full lunch which was set out on the table. After lunch was eaten, they wrote letters of recommendation to Izmir, Alexandria, and Jedda. Afterwards, we departed, and they all escorted me to the edge of the jetty. I got into a rowboat and went to the steamship. The steamship departed and proceeded very calmly along the Bosphorus for about an hour and a quarter. Summer houses were built on both sides of the Bosphorus, and green and pleasant mountains were visible.

THE PORT OF GALLIPOLI

After leaving the Bosphorus, [the boat] reached Gallipoli in a period of ten hours. The city of Gallipoli is situated on the right-hand side of the Sea of Marmara. It has a population of about 22-23,000.

---

[204] According to the tables in Faik Unat, *Hicrî tarihleri milâdî tarihe çevirme kılavuzu* (Ankara, 1984), the first of Z̲i Qaᶜdeh 1302 fell on Wednesday, 12 August. Since the beginning of a month according to the Islamic lunar calendar is contingent upon an actual sighting of the new moon (and could vary from place to place), such inconsistencies in dating are not uncommon. Because of this discrepancy, the day of the week cited by Farâhâni here is a day in advance of the one given by Unat. For consistency, these dates are converted as given in Unat, ignoring the day of the week as given by Farâhâni. Eventually, Farâhâni's dates are again synchronized with those in Unat (see below, Part Five, p. 206 n. 10.

Most are from European Turkey.[205] From the Bosphorus at Istanbul the distance to Gallipoli is entirely on the Sea of Marmara and is 114 miles. The length of the Sea of Marmara all together is 110 English miles. Its deepest point is not more than 646 fathoms. (Hereafter, whenever a "mile" is mentioned, the Arabic mile is what is meant, which is four thousand qadam or equivalent to two thousand ẕarᶜ-e shâh. The Iranian farsakh is equivalent to six thousand ẕarᶜ, so three miles is one farsakh.)

THE ISLAND OF MARMARA

The island of Marmara is located amidst this same sea. The sea is named for the island. They call this island the island of Marmara because there are marble [*marmar*] quarries there. [156] The island of Marmara was on our port [side].

CHANAKKALE

Passing on twenty-one miles from Gallipoli, we came to Chanakkale. Qumqalᶜeh,[206] which means "Sand Castle", is located between these two ports on the starboard side. Opposite Qumqalᶜeh, to port, or the European side, is the fortress of Sadd ol-Baḥr. Cape Hellas [?],[207] meaning [in Persian] *damâgheh-ye hellas*, is on the port side.

Past Gallipoli is the Mediterranean Sea which [the Turks] call the Ak Deniz.[208] Chanakkale is located on the Mediterranean. The shore of the straits is to the port side of the route. This is a famous port and is part of the province of Balikesir, which is one of the Anatolian provinces and the seat of a mutesarrifat. It has about 2,500 resident households and three hundred shops. Because of the importance of this port, they have built fortresses and strong bastions. They have cannons and arsenals there. There are always a thousand troops and artillerymen garrisoned there.

Excellent pitchers, vases, and dishes just like Chinese [ceramics] are made there. For that reason it has been named Chanakkale.[209] Opposite Chanakkale on the right bank of the straits, on European territory, there is a fortress named Kelid ol-baḥr. There is also a government fortress on the left bank on Asian territory. It has been very stoutly built out of stone, and it has many

[205] Text: *az ṭâyefeh-ye orum*. Farâhâni may mean Greeks.

[206] Modern Turkish Kumkale.

[207] Text: *kayb h-l-s*.

[208] Text: *âq v-ngir*. Strictly speaking, Farâhâni is referring to the Aegean Sea, but he uses the Arabic term for the Mediterranean, *baḥr [ol-]abyaż*, which, like the Turkish Ak Deniz, means "White Sea."

[209] The name means "earthenware castle" in Turkish.

cannons and arsenals. Opposite this, on European territory, there are several other fortresses. From Kelid ol-Baḥr to Chanakkale, a good cannon shot could reach from one [side of the straits] to the other. The steamship stopped at Chanakkale for an hour and a half. Immediately, they brought bread, fruit, vases, and pitchers by rowboat to the steamship for sale. [The boat] loaded and unloaded a little cargo and set out. [157]

THE PORT OF BÂGHCHEH ÂDÂSI

After traversing twenty-five miles from Chanakkale, one reaches a port named Bâghcheh Âdâsi.[210] According to reports, this port has roughly a thousand resident households. It is the residence of a modir and is part of an Anatolian province. The steamship also stopped there for an hour, delivered and picked up the mail, and set out.

THE PORT OF MYTILENE

From Bâghcheh Âdâsi to the port of Mytilene[211] is fifty five miles. As far as Cape Bâbâ[212] (meaning [in Persian] *damâgheh-ye bâbâ* [Cape of the Father]), the steamship stays close to the shore.

The port of Mytilene is situated on the starboard side. It is located on a very nice, green, and pleasant island. On this island, there are forest trees of every type and many olive trees which are even visible from on board the ship. On both sides of this port's straits, low, forested, very attractive mountains come into view. According to reports, there are numerous villages on this island. It has a population of about thirty thousand. It is the seat of a mutesarrifat and has a fortress, bastion, artillery emplacements, and an arsenal. There are always two hundred soldiers garrisoned there. The steamship stopped at this port for about two hours, loaded and unloaded cargo, and set out. From Mytilene to Izmir is a distance of sixty-one miles. Close to Izmir, there is a small island on the right named Uzun Ada, which is also called Smyrna [*sic*],[213] and then the gulf of Izmir.

THE PORT OF IZMIR

On the morning of Sunday, the fourth of the sacred month of Z̲i Qaᶜdeh [15 August], the steamship reached the gulf of Izmir, anchored, and, after receiving permission from the Izmir officials,

---

210 Perhaps Bozcaada?

211 Text: *medelli* (Turkish Midilli); the name of the chief port on the island of Lesbos.

212 Baba Burnu. Farâhâni continues to use the non-Turkish word "kayb" for cape.

213 Text: *s-mirneh*. Smyrna was the Greek name for Izmir, not Uzun Ada.

docked at the Cordon. The Cordon is a place in front of Izmir where they have made a lagoon and jetty. They have put up a platform of large, solid pieces of stone across this lagoon and built several buildings for the companies. [158] The procedure is that the large ships come and dock at this pier. The pier is connected to the city via an avenue, so there is no need to ride in a rowboat. Because of this, they have ordered that each steamship pay two or three lira as a docking fee. In storms, this lagoon protects the ship from damage and sinking. Also, along this seashore there is a very long and wide avenue, the length of which is about three quarters of a farsakh, and the breadth of which a little more than a hundred z̲arᶜ. There is also a railway on this same avenue which goes to the villages and suburban districts. They have built four- or five-storey buildings, shops, and nice coffeehouses along the avenue. They said that this lagoon and avenue, as well as the railway, buildings, and shops along the avenue, used to all be [under] the sea. A French company made an agreement [with the Ottoman government] to fill [the area] in and to build the dock, avenue and railway. All the extra land would be taken [by the company] as construction sites for buildings and shops to sell. The profits from the dock and railway would belong to the company for fifty years and then be given over to the Ottoman government. At present, fifty years have not elapsed, so it has not come into the possession of the government.

HISTORICAL SKETCH OF IZMIR

The best place in Izmir is this very avenue. Izmir used to be an ancient fortress beside the sea, [constructed] of stone and extremely tall and sturdy. Three sides of it adjoined the Mediterranean, and it had a deep trench on the side adjacent to land. A multitude of Christians were gathered there. The Christians used to consider it a holy place and came from other provinces for the purpose of visiting it.

At a distance of one maydân from that large fortress, there was another fortress on top of a tall hill in which the Muslims had settled. They also called that place Izmir. [159] There was always strife between the people of these two fortresses. Solṭân Morâd Khân[214] and Sultan [Y]ilderim Bâyazid Khân[215] the Ottoman repeatedly sent military expeditions there, but they were not successful. Provisions and help for them came by boat from the kings of the Europeans

---

214 The Ottoman sultan Morâd I (1360-89).

215 The Ottoman sultan Bâyazid I "the Thunderbolt" (1389-1402).

["Franks"] and, in fact, it was in the possession of the Europeans, until in the year 840 [*sic*; 1436-37] the Amir Timur Gurakân[216] went to Anatolia, was successful against the large fortress of Izmir, conquered and destroyed [it], killed many of the people, and imposed the poll tax [*jezyeh*] on the rest. The Muslims of the small fortress became powerful and moved to the large fortress. After that, it came into the possession of the Ottoman sultans.

GENERAL DESCRIPTION OF THE PORT OF IZMIR

Izmir is presently one of the flourishing cities of the Ottoman Empire. It is the seat of a governorship [*vâli-neshin*]. It has 50,000 resident households, so that its population is about 200,000 people. There are roughly eight thousand shops and stores there. Its bazaars are mostly covered and have red-tiled roofs. Most of the people of this city are Europeans, Greeks, or Jews. Because the Turks call those outside the religion of Islam "gavur," [the city] is popularly known as "Gavur Izmir." Previously, the inhabitants of the Roman [i.e., Byzantine] Empire had been these same Greeks. Because of this, it used to be called the "Roman Empire." Their religion is Christian, and their doctrines are close to the religion of the Russians. There are large churches there. In any case, the Muslims there number no more than twenty thousand. The Muslims have ten or twelve mosques of various sizes. Some of its public thoroughfares are very clean and paved with large stones. The rest of the streets are paved with cobblestone and are narrow and dirty. The people there, male and female, are very healthy looking and handsome. In no other place have I seen such handsomeness and delicateness. [160] From the healthy appearance of the people, it is obvious that the climate there is very fine and mild.

FRUITS AND PRODUCE

This area is a fine place for [growing] fruits. Most of the fruit for Istanbul comes from here. Its apples, pomegranates, grapes, peaches and figs are highly commendable, especially its figs which are very large, succulent, and lustrous. They are put in very fine boxes and exported to all of Europe. I had never seen figs this good. In Rijâb,[217], which is about four farsakhs from Zohâb, there are very good seedless figs, but they are not this large and succulent.

---

[216] The date 840 is a mistake for 804/1401-2; on the title Gurakân applied to Timur (Tamerlane), see above, Part Two, n. 87.

[217] Dehkhodâ, *Loghatnâmeh*, s.v. Rijâb, says that it is a town in the Shâhâbâd district which is known, among other things, for its figs.

In the gardens of the city, they grow all types of temperate and sub-tropical fruits. The summer retreats and rural districts which surround Izmir are also admiringly described.

In their cemeteries, they have planted and grown very green and beautiful cypresses. There are two abundant springs of wholesome water inside the city, the water being conveyed by pumps to the buildings. This province is a center for merchants. They gather and conduct trade there from Europe, Asia, and America.

Its own goods are maize, barley, raisins, pipe-tobacco, sesame, opium, carpets, figs, and gallnuts.[218]

A gallnut is a wild fruit, the thorn of which they take to export to Europe for tanning. The treasury of the Ottoman Empire collects ten per cent taxes on these ten goods. However, their import duties are still high, especially the duties on tobaccos.[219] [161]

CONSULATE FOR IRANIAN SUBJECTS

There are consulates there for eight countries. On behalf of the government of Iran, there is Âvânes [Hovhannes?] Bayk,[220] who is one of the local Armenians. The subjects of Iran in the city, villages, and suburbs [number] about two hundred, of whom thirty or forty are merchants.

IRANIAN MERCHANTS

The names of the prominent Iranian merchants are: Ḥâjji ᶜAbd ol-Karim Salmâsi; Ḥâjji Mirzâ ᶜAli Salmâsi; Ḥâjji Hâdi Salmâsi; Mirzâ Ḥasan Eṣfahâni; Âqâ Moḥammad Bâqer Eṣfahâni; and Ḥâjji Moḥsen Eṣfahâni.

The Iranian goods which are traded there: shawls, indigo, tobacco of Isfahan and Kashan, gallnuts,[221] silk, carpets of Farahan and Khorasan, and a little opium which is exported to Europe.

The Iranian place of business in this city is mostly in the khan of Ḥosayn Pasha. Inside this khan, Ḥâjji ᶜAbd ol-Karim the merchant has built a mosque. It is also [where] they perform *rowżeh-khᵛâni*.

---

218 Text: *balmut*. This seems to be a corruption of *balluṭ*, an Arabic word (also used in Turkish) for oak or acorn—in this case, specifically the gall oak (*Quercus lusitanicus*). The gallnuts from these trees were exported as a source of tannic acid.

219 *Tutun* (regular dry tobacco for cigarettes) and *tanbaku* (a special moist kind of tobacco for water-pipes); see Dehkhodâ, *Loghatnâmeh*, fascicle 133, p. 982.

220 Cf. Pirzâdeh, *Safarnâmeh*, 2:129-130.

221 Here Farâhâni uses the Persian term *mâzu*, which denotes a particular type of balluṭ or gallnut. See Dehkhodâ, *Loghatnâmeh*, fascicle 133, p. 982. Since Farahâni has just written that these are produced in Izmir itself, it is curious that he should state that they are also imported from Iran.

A TOUR OF THE CITY

After the ship anchored beside Izmir, [my] companions and I went to that khan and visited the residence of Mirzâ Ḥasan Tajer-e Eṣfahâni. Some other of the merchants also gathered there and discussed all sorts of things. Since the embassy had written a letter of commendation from Istanbul to Âvânes Bayk, the consul of the government of Iran, and had sent it by post, he was informed and sent someone to let us know that he would like to come for a visit. Inasmuch as I had a fancy to tour and see the city, I evaded visiting with him, left there, and went about most of the city on foot and by carriage. Two hours before sunset, I went to the steamship. [162] The steamship departed from Izmir one hour before sunset.

THE JOURNEY FROM IZMIR

On the port side, green and pleasant mountains and flourishing villages were visible. Among other things, one farsakh past Izmir, a fortress came into view. They say it is named Qal^{c}eh-ye Now ["New Castle"]. It is a place of cannons, troops, and bastions. There is always a regiment or two garrisoned there.

THE PORT OF CHIOS

From Izmir to the port of Chios[222] is sixty-five miles. The steamship traversed [it] in seven hours and arrived at the port of Chios at dawn. This port is known by the name of the island. On that island a lot of mastic is produced and because of this the port and the island have been given this name. This place is one of the districts of Izmir. There are about two hundred resident households belong to this port. Most are Greeks.[223]

The steamship stopped at this port for an hour and a half, loaded and discharged a little cargo, and departed. There is a sea route from this place that goes to Greece and Europe.

THE JOURNEY FROM CHIOS

Past Chios, the steamship moved between narrow straits. Around the straits, islands came into view. It is said they are the islands of Fourni, Arki, Samos, and Leros.[224]

THE ISLAND OF LEROS

The steamship was also detained at Leros island about an hour to deliver and take on the post. This port and island are districts of

---

222 Text: Ṣaqez. As Farâhâni notes below, the Turkish name Sakız means mastic, one of the main products of the island.

223 Or Greeks?

224 Text: Lârosh. It is interesting that Farâhâni, perhaps getting his information from the captain or a fellow passenger, gives Greek forms for the names of these islands, including "Samus" for Samos instead of the Turkish Sisam.

Izmir and the residence of a modir. In this port, there are about 1,500 inhabitants.

Past there, one leaves the straits. On the port side many islands and populated places were visible. We were told that these are the important ports of Nissiros, Tilos, and Halki. [163]

THE PORT OF RHODES

Passing on from there, [the boat] came to a port named Rhodes, which was located on the right side. From the port of Chios to the port of Rhodes is 166 miles. This island and port are very attractive, green and pleasant. It has countless citrus trees. Its residents are half Muslims and half Greeks and Jews. The Muslims [live] inside the citadel and the non-Muslims outside of the citadel.

The steamship stopped there for an hour and a half, unloaded and loaded a little cargo, and departed.

THE JOURNEY FROM RHODES

Past Rhodes, there is no other island, and the steamship traverses the open sea. The shore was not visible anywhere until, after travelling for thirty hours, the light of a lighthouse, which is burned at night to guide ships, became visible. They said that from Rhodes to this place is three hundred miles, and from this lighthouse to Alexandria is twenty-one miles, so that from Alexandria to Istanbul is 830 miles. Average commercial steamships do not travel at more than eight or nine miles an hour, which makes a trip of ninety-two to ninety-five hours. The remainder [of the time] is taken up by stopping in ports and being detained in the straits. The steamship went from Istanbul to Alexandria in five whole days and a fraction. The captain reported that the depth of the Mediterranean is no more than seven hundred to one thousand fathoms. It also has a route to the Atlantic and Europe going via Gibraltar. [164]

Anyhow, as soon as the steamship came close to Alexandria, because it is shallow near the anchorage and many ships have run aground, it is customary that a guide from the Arabs settled in Alexandria comes in front of the steamship by caique and conducts the steamer to the anchorage.

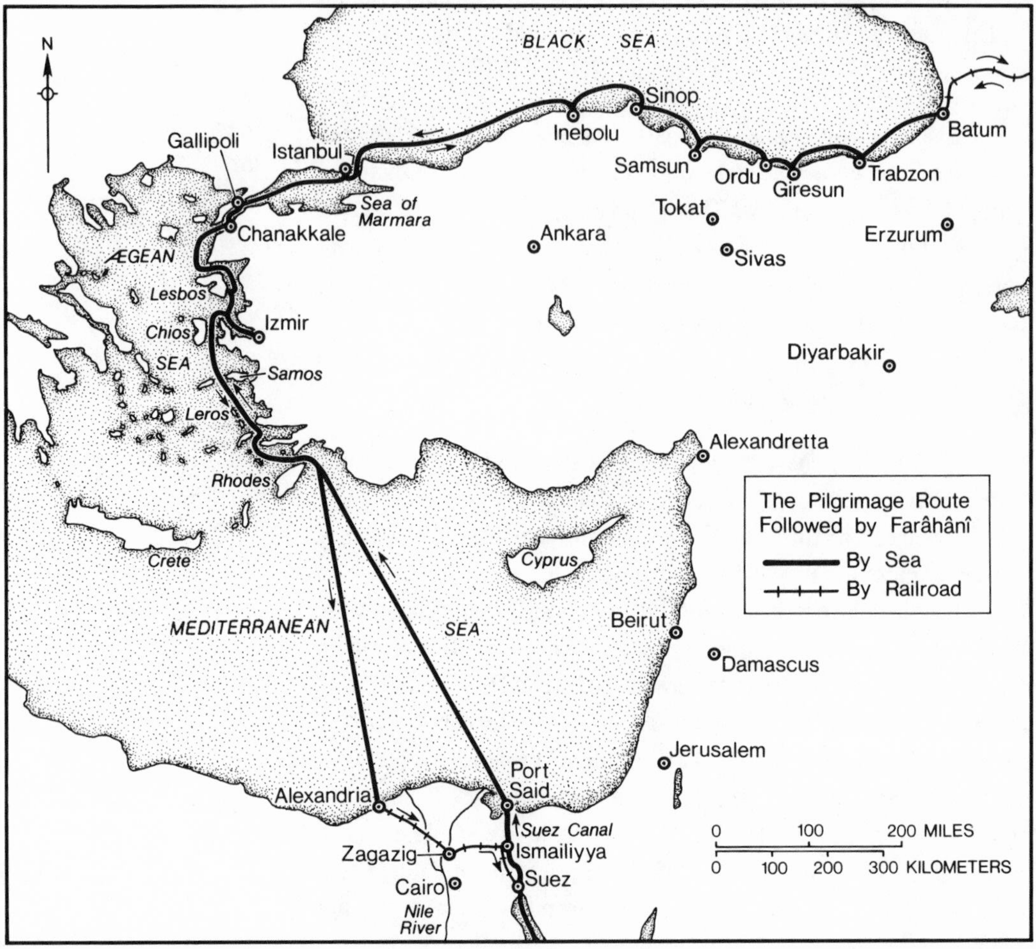

Map 5. The pilgrimage route followed by Farâhâni: Batum to Suez.

PART FOUR
FROM ALEXANDRIA TO JEDDA

THE HARBOR OF ALEXANDRIA

The morning of Tuesday, the sixth of the sacred month of Z̲i Qa^{c}deh [17 August], the steamship entered the harbor of Alexandria, after permission from the Alexandria authorities. Since the English now consider Alexandria their own rightful possession, they have built a fine harbor in Alexandria surrounded by solid stones. The cost of the harbor was about one half million Iranian tomans. As soon as ships enter the harbor, they are protected from wind and storms. Every steamer that enters the harbor must pay something. After the steamship anchored, rowboats came out and people began to disembark. Several Iranian brokers, who reside there, came out to the steamer like alluring vipers, professing camaraderie and making deceptive promises. Each one accompanied several of the pilgrims, who got into rowboats and then got out of the rowboats alongside the pier at an enclosure and building which had no exit and whose doors were closed.

THE CUSTOMS OFFICE

In this enclosure and building at the end of the pier, there are two rooms for those arriving and departing. One has officials who, after examining [the passengers'] passports, give them a small receipt and then take away the passports for endorsement. The passports for each country are collected together and sent that same day to that country's consul. That consul endorses all those passports himself and returns them the next day. [165] The consul or deputy-consul of Iran collects one and a half majidis, which is about eight thousand dinars, per person from the Iranians for processing the passport and then returns the passport.

In this building at the end of the pier, there is also a customs counter where the baggage and belongings of those coming and leaving are carefully inspected, but not with the rigidity of the Russian government. In the event there is nothing dutiable, the employees of the customs house still, in an unfair way, collect a small sum in return for not making trouble. These two counters are something which no one can avoid or elude.

After they take up the passports and inspect the belongings and baggage in the customs house, they then open the door of the enclosure and have the people go out. As soon as we exited from it, coaches and droshkys for hire were waiting there for foreigners to board and be driven to the caravanserais and coffeehouses. We accompanied a broker named Ḥâjji ᶜAbdollah and went to his home. There he provided us with two clean, carpeted rooms. After noon, we came out of the lodgings and rode and walked about most of the city with that broker until three hours after nightfall.

HISTORICAL SKETCH OF THE FOUNDATION OF THE CITY

What has been written in geography books about the circumstances of Alexandria is this:

There is disagreement about its foundation. Some have said that its founder was Alexander the First who had the honorific title of Ẕu'l-Qarnayn ["the Two-Horned"] and whose proper name is Ashk ebn-e Selukus Rumi.[1] Part of his name has been given as ᶜAyyâsh, and some have recorded [it] in this manner: Eskandar [Alexander] ebn-e Yaqṭi[2] ebn-e Yamunân[3] ebn-e S̱ârekh ebn-e Yâfeṣ ebn-e Nuḥ, who went all over the earth, reached the dark regions and the place the sun rises and sets, and imprisoned Yâjuj [Gog] just as God, be He exalted, has announced.[4] And some have said the founder of Alexandria is Eskandar ebn-e Dârâ, [166] the son of the daughter of Filoqus Rumi.[5] They have compared this Alexander with Alexander the First since this Alexander also went to China, the Maghreb, and Iran. And some have said that Alexander

---

1 Muslim traditions concerning the name and history of Alexander are often confused. Some identify him as the son of Philip the Greek, others as the son of the Persian king Darius (Dârâ) by Philip's daughter, and still others (including some of the genealogies cited here by Farâhâni) seem to mistake the Ptolemid Alexanders for Alexander the Great. See for example, Ferdowsi/Levy, *Epic of the Kings* pp. 229-30; Masᶜudi, *Prairies*, 2:248; S̱aᶜâlebi, *Rois des Perses*, p. 400; Southgate, *Iskandarnameh*, appendices; EI_2, 4:127-28. Ashk, incidentally, was the legendary name given to the founder of the Parthian dynasty.

2 This should probably read Labṭ; see Masᶜudi, *Prairies*, 2:248.

3 Probably an error for Yunân; see Masᶜudi, *Prairies*, loc. cit.

4 The story of Ẕu'l-Qarnayn and his prodigious works is found in the Koran, 18:83-98. The identification of this person with Alexander is based entirely on tradition.

5 This genealogy reflects a completely different version of an Alexander romance, based more on Iranian than Koranic tradition. Pre-Islamic Iranian traditions had depicted Alexander as a great villain, but in light of the Koranic traditions, the figure of Alexander was re-interpreted and given heroic proportions as well as an Iranian ancestry (supposedly the son of Darius, as cited here by Farâhâni).

founded [Alexandria] and Alexander the Second renovated it. A few believe that these two Alexanders were one and the same. In any case, in the event that it was one of the foundations of Alexander the Great,[6] it was founded 330-odd years before the birth of Jesus. It has been written that when Alexander set out to build Alexandria, the ruins of an ancient city which Shaddâd ebn-e ᶜÂd[7] had constructed there were in this place. In that city the ruins of buildings and many stone columns were visible. To begin, he offered countless sacrifices. After that he entered one of the Greek temples, made supplications there, and beseeched God to reveal to him whether he would be able to bring this city to completion and what the future of the city would be. In a dream, a mysterious voice told him: "You will finish this city. There will be many inhabited places there, and large numbers of people will come to this city. The venom has been removed from its climate, so the weather will be salubrious and there will not be extreme heat nor cold." After this dream, Alexander summoned architects and engineers and building materials from the surrounding countries and undertook the construction. They say he determined a specific time for the construction [to begin] and ordered that a large bell be rung so that when they rang that bell the builders and laborers everywhere would begin construction all at once. Before that hour which Alexander had determined, a bird landed on that bell; the bell moved; and the builders and laborers began to work. Because that hour was not propitious, that place has repeatedly been destroyed and rebuilt.[8] [167]

It is also written that at the time ᶜAbd ol-ᶜAziz ebn-e Marvân[9] was governor of Egypt, Alexandria was very dilapidated, so he

---

[6] Literally Rumi ("the Greek").

[7] According to the Koran (for example 7:65-72; 89:6), the tribe of ᶜÂd were a people living in the south of Arabia to whom the Prophet Hud was sent. Shaddâd was supposedly one of the kings of these people who built the great city of Eram so as to rival paradise itself. As punishment, he and all his people were struck dead and the great city disappeared. Some traditions held that in addition to building Eram, Shaddâd also built a city on the site later occupied by Alexandria, the ruins of which were uncovered by Alexander.

[8] This story, very similar to one told about the founding of Cairo by the Fatimids, comes from Masᶜudi, *Prairies*, 2:423-25; see K.A.C. Creswell, "The Founding of Cairo," in *Colloque International sur l'Histoire du Caire* (Cairo, 1969), pp. 127-28.

[9] The brother of the Umayyad caliph ᶜAbd ol-Malek; he held the governorship of Egypt for twenty years (65-85/685-705).

brought together the shaykhs there and said, "I am determined to rebuild Alexandria. From you [I want] builders and laborers and hard work. I will provide the funds." The shaykhs requested a grace period of a few days from him to prepare an answer. After they left, they found the skull of a dead person and carried it on an ox and brought it before the governor. They pulled out one of its teeth which [weighed] about twenty *raṭl*s.[10] They said, "The people of the time when Alexandria was built were like this. Now someone like this man must be found in order to rebuild it." ᶜAbd ol-ᶜAziz heeded the lesson, abandoned the rebuilding, and [just] undertook restoration.

THE LIGHTHOUSE OF ALEXANDRIA

One of the wonders of Alexandria was a light house. Its base was square and of hewn stone, with an octagonal lighthouse on top of it, and on top [of that] another round lighthouse. The first storey, which was square, was ninety z̲arᶜ. The second storey, which was octagonal, was also ninety z̲arᶜ. The third storey, which was round, was thirty z̲arᶜ. On top of the third storey, a mirror, which was one of the inventions of the sage Bolinâs,[11] was set up. A person was always delegated to watch that mirror continuously so that if an enemy headed towards Alexandria by sea, the image would appear in the mirror while [they were still] four or five days away. The one appointed would inform the people of Alexandria. That mirror remained until the time of Valid ebn-e ᶜAbd ol-Malek.[12] Several people came from Byzantium [Rum] or [the land of] the Franks to Valid. Some stayed a while, professed Islam, and came to hold positions of trust. One time, while conversing with Valid, they said, "Alexander buried treasures and gold beyond reckoning beneath these stones of the mirror and built this lighthouse on top of that treasure." [168] After hearing this, Valid became very greedy and ordered the lighthouse and mirror to be torn down. Despite his diligence and searching, he found nothing. He summoned those people, and it was learned that they had fled by sea. After that, they rebuilt the lighthouse but they could not set up the mirror in its

---

[10] The *raṭl* was a traditional unit of measure which varied from place to place; in Egypt the conventional measure was equivalent to 449.28 grams. Thus the tooth of this giant wieghted some twenty pounds!

[11] The neo-Pythagorian philosopher Apollonius of Tyana (fl. first century A. D.); see Franz Rosenthal, *The Classical Heritage in Islam* (Berkeley, 1975), p. 267. Cf. Qazvini/Le Strange, *Nuzhat*, pp. 239-40.

[12] An Umayyad caliph (86-96/705-15).

original condition. Some have ascribed these details to the time of the governorship of ᶜAmru [ebn-e] ᶜÂṣ[13] in Alexandria.

Some have written that the mirror could set fire [to things]. Every ship that came to Alexandria was obliged to pass opposite that mirror. Since they passed opposite the mirror, fire could come down from the mirror and burn the ship.

Some say they always oiled that mirror with fat, and it would burn up any ship its rays fell upon.

DESCRIPTION OF THE CITY

Anyhow, the city of Alexandria at present is a nice, prosperous, and attractive city. All of its streets are smooth, clean, wide, and paved with regularly arranged hewn stones joined together with mortar. Its houses generally have four or five storeys and are neat and decorated. Its bazaars are uncovered and are very nicely decorated and full of goods. In many houses they have made flower beds in pots or [on] the ground.

THE FRUITS OF ALEXANDRIA

Tropical and sub-tropical fruits are plentiful, such as dates, bananas, Iranian and European figs, coconuts, chestnuts, olives, citrus fruits, pomegranates and so on. Its pomegranates are sweet; they say it is due to the effects of the climate and the water of the Nile River that the pomegranates do not turn bitter and are sweet. Its lemons are like the lemons of Shiraz but not so fragrant. I do not know why the water and climate have no effect on lemons. Its oranges [169] are very large and full of juice, but their flavor is bitter and flat. Its tangerines are as large as the tangerines from the hill-country in Bandar ᶜAbbâs. Their peel is very thin and moist but flat [tasting]. The tangerine in this country is called "Yusof Afandi." They say it is so called [because] at first the tree did not exist in this country. Someone named Yusof Afandi brought a tree from Malta; cuttings from that tree were planted and grafted, and it multiplied. Thus it became famous under his name. Melons, watermelons, and cucumbers are also plentiful, but they are not very good-tasting or wholesome.

CLIMATE

The climate of Alexandria is not very hot, but because of the humidity one cannot sleep; nevertheless, its humidity is less than that of Istanbul, and its climate is better than there.

---

[13] A prominent personality in early Islamic history, ᶜAmru organized and led the conquest of Egypt in 19/640 and served as its governor on several occasions.

POPULATION

According to reports, it has about sixty thousand resident households, so its population numbers about 250,000. Half the population is Muslim and half is non-Muslim. Both mosques and churches are numerous.

BATHS

The procedure in the baths there is just like that in the baths in Istanbul, except that [they] have a chamber with warm and cold water where everyone goes for religious washing [*ghosl*].

COMMERCE AND ARRANGEMENT OF THE BAZAAR

There are merchants, manufacturers, and craftsmen from foreign countries, especially Europeans, Greeks, and Jews. The bazaars and caravanserais have about twelve thousand shops and stores. Nice theaters and cafés have been built.

THE MOAT AND CITY WALL

The city is [bordered] on two sides by sea and on two sides by land. The two sides by land have a wall all around and two trenches. The width of each trench is nearly twenty z̲arᶜ, and its depth is twelve z̲arᶜ. Its wall has a thickness of about four z̲arᶜ, and its height is twenty z̲arᶜ and a fraction. [170] Its wall is standing between the two trenches. These trenches and the wall are all constructions of Moḥammad ᶜAli Pâshâ.[14] He showed great concern for the inhabited areas there and built great constructions, among them the very strong citadel and bastion built near the harbor in the middle of the city which overlooks the entire city. Large cannons have been placed on top of its towers. In this war of the English with Aᶜrâbi Pâshâ,[15] some of those bastions were destroyed. [Some] of the streets, shops, and houses around the harbor were also destroyed by cannon fire, and Aᶜrâbi Pâshâ burned some [of them]. At the

---

[14] Moḥammad ᶜAli (1769-1849) made himself the commander of the Ottoman expeditionary force sent to reclaim Egypt from the French occupation and used it as a power base to make himself the de facto ruler of Egypt, founding a dynasty which lasted until the Egyptian revolution of 1952. He has been the subject of many scholarly studies, including Afaf Lutfi Sayyid-Marsot, *Egypt in the Reign of Muhammad Ali* (Cambridge, 1984); H. Dodwell, *The Founder of Modern Egypt* (Cambridge, 1931); Shafik Ghorbal, *The Beginnings of the Egyptian Question and the Rise of Mehmet Ali* (London, 1928); and Helen Rivlin, *The Agricultural Policy of Muhammad ᶜAli in Egypt* (Cambridge, Mass., 1961).

[15] Aḥmad Aᶜrâbi or ᶜOrâbi Pâshâ was the leader of a nationalistic military mutiny against the Khedive Tawfiq in 1881 which led to Franco-British intervention to suppress the uprising and, in 1882, the British occupation of Egypt. See Mahmud Zayid, *Egypt's Struggle for Independence* (Beirut, 1965), pp. 21-29; P. M. Holt, *Egypt and the Fertile Crescent 1516-1922* (Ithaca, 1966), pp. 213-16; J. C. B. Richmond, *Egypt 1798-1952* (New York, 1977), pp. 118-31.

present time, many of them have been [re-]built, [but] a few places around the port are still ruined.

DRINKING WATER[16]

One of the improvements [made] by Moḥammad ᶜAlî Pâshâ in Alexandria is the diversion of a branch of the Nile River to there. The river flows everywhere outside the city. In ancient times, water of the Nile River also came to Alexandria, [but] several of its channels went bad. The people dug wells [for] their houses and had cisterns built to collect rain water. For a long time, they were content with this rain and well water, and there are still many of those wells in the houses now. But the well water is not good tasting or wholesome. Moḥammad ᶜAli Pâshâ dug out the channels again and brought in a branch of the Nile River. Because the present city does not obtain [its] water directly from the Nile, a French company has built a factory outside the city. [They] dug pits in an enclosure and large garden and strewed gravel at the bottom of the pits. Water from the river goes into these pits, remains overnight, and is purified. In the morning, they bring up the purified water by [water] wheels and pumps, and it is siphoned into the city. [171] From there it is distributed through iron pipes to the suburbs of the city. In all the houses, on every storey, they put up these iron water pipes and use however many faucets they want on the pipes. Because of the difference in the rate of how much water each person uses in a month, they calculate the charge for the water on this basis and send a bill month by month and collect the fee for the water.

The same system exists in Bombay; however, there is no need for water-wheels and pumps since they have built a dam in the mountains there, and the water is located up high and dominates the entire city.

The French company had agreed that for twenty-five years the revenue would be its own; the period of twenty-five years has expired, so now it belongs to the Khedive of Egypt. Thus, an amount goes to the Khedive yearly.

THE NILE RIVER

The Nile River flows from south to north. Its source is in the Mountains of the Moon, and its mouth is at the Mediterranean Sea [*Baḥr-e Rum*], which is [the same as] the "White Sea" [*Baḥr-e Abyaż*]. Its length is very great; no other river is so long. Its water increases in summer contrary to other rivers and streams. In the

[16] Cf. Sayf od-Dowleh, *Safarnâmeh*, p. 111.

book *Asbâb ol-ᶜajâ'eb* [*Causes of Marvels*] it is written that the reason for the excess of water in summer is that the Mediterranean, which is the mouth of the Nile River, becomes agitated in the summer season. It has waves and becomes like a dam so the Nile water can't pour into it. Because of this, the water backs up and increases.[17] Although the water of the Nile River is muddy, it is still very wholesome.

The author of the *Masâlek ol-mamâlek* [*Roads of the Countries*][18] writes that its source is in the Mountains of the Moon. After passing through some of the African regions [*belad-e zang*] and Ethiopia, it comes to the country of Egypt. There it divides into seven branches. [172] One of its branches goes to Alexandria.

Curious things have been written about the Nile River. For example, in the *Jâmeᶜ ol-ḥekâyât* [*Anthology of Anecdotes*] it is written that "In the age of ignorance [before Islam] the water of the Nile would sometimes stop and not move. They [would] cast beautiful maidens, ornamented and adorned, into it; [then] it would move again and begin to flow. In the time of ᶜOmar ebn ol-Khaṭṭâb, when ᶜAmru [ebn-e] ᶜÂṣ was governor of Egypt, this happened again. ᶜAmru wrote to ᶜOmar [about it, who] answered, 'You act the way they have acted in the past.'"[19] It has been said that hippopotamuses, crocodiles, and skinks are plentiful in this river. As for the crocodile, in ancient times they cast a spell so that it would not come near Egypt. There used to be a gauge for [measuring] the rise and fall of the Nile River. According to the mark, the success or failure of crops that year would be known. If it did not reach the

---

17 This explanation of the flooding of the Nile is an ancient one, supposedly going back to Thales of Miletus; see Herodotus, *History*, 2:19.5; George Sarton, *A History of Science: Volume I: Ancient Science Through the Golden Age of Greece* (Cambridge, Mass., 1952), p. 187. It has not been possible to identify the source cited by Farâhâni; *Asbâb ol-ᶜajâ'eb* may be a variant title of one of several works of this genre of popular explanations of natural phenomena.

18 There are several famous medieval Arabic geographies known by this title, notably the one authored by Eṣṭakhri, which also exists in a Persian translation. However, Farâhâni may have gotten this information secondhand since this and the following paragraph are very similar to Qazvini/Le Strange, *Nuzhat*, pp. 203-4 (which is based on Ebn Khorradâẕbeh). Cf. also above, Part Three, n. 50.

19 Farâhâni is probably referring to ᶜAwf's famous anthology of anecdotes and curious stories, usually known by the title *Javameᶜ ol-ḥekâyât*; in any event, this was a familiar story cited in many sources. Farâhâni's version, however, is entirely different (perhaps because he does not want to say anything nice about ᶜOmar, regarded as an enemy of the Shi'ites): The anecdote usually concludes by pointing out that the caliph ᶜOmar wrote a letter invoking God to make the Nile flood; the letter, instead of a maiden, was thrown into the river and it always flooded thereafter. See Nizámu'd-Din, *Introduction to the Jawámi*, pp. 28, 143.

fourteenth mark, the water was low that year and crops were bad; if it reached the fourteenth or fifteenth mark, the crops were average; if it reached the sixteenth to the eighteenth mark they would be very good and productive that year; but if it passed the eighteenth mark, a flood was indicated and crops would be ruined.

GARDENS

Outside the city along the Nile, there are many gardens that are laid out very meticulously row after row like a kind of flower bed. Varieties of citrus trees, fruit-bearing trees, and potted and garden flowers are carefully arranged and trimmed in numerous rows. They give much care and attention to keeping the gardens neat and clean. Some of the gardens are places for private excursions so that one must go with an acquaintance. Other gardens are places for public excursions; the gardener just collects a fee and allows anyone to enter. [173] Among the gardens that are places for public excursions, there is one park named Nozhat Bâghchehsi ["Garden of Pleasure"] which Esmâᶜil Pâshâ[20] built. It is very attractive and is a wakf property for the recreation of the public. They allow everyone to go there for sightseeing, and they charge no fee except whatever each person gives voluntarily as a gratuity to the gardener. In the afternoon, many city folks, women and men, go to the parks for recreation. Large crowds go especially on Sundays and Fridays.

AGRICULTURE

All sorts of crops and trees are raised on the lands of Alexandria, Cairo, and the suburbs which are very fertile. Because of the great fertility, every piece of land is cultivated two or three times a year and bears crops. Moḥammad ᶜAli Pâshâ established the gardens and encouraged the flower works.

In Mansheyyeh Square[21] in the center of the city, they have set up on a stone pedestal a statue of Moḥammad ᶜAli Pâshâ wearing a turban.

CLOTHING OF THE WOMEN AND MEN

The people of Alexandria, women and men, are generally attractive, but their eyes are often diseased. Their women are very dissolute and pleasure seeking. The dress of the wives of Muslim

[20]The autonomous ruler of Egypt (1863-1879); he assumed the title of Khedive in 1867. On the famous Nozhat gardens, see E. Breccia, *Alexandrea ad Aegypten* (Bergamo, 1922), pp. 21-22; E. M. Forster, *Alexandria: A History and a Guide* (Alexandria, 1938), p. 146.

[21] Text: Monṣeyyeh. On the square and the famous equestrian statue of Moḥammad ᶜAli by Jacquemart, completed in 1873 at a cost of two million francs, see Michael Reimer, "Colonial Bridgehead: Social and Spatial Change in Alexandria," *International Journal of Middle East Studies* 29(1988):536.

dignitaries very much resembles the dress of European women. Most do not wear any covering over the head. Ordinary women wear a black, striped covering on their heads and tie a piece [of cloth] like a veil over the nose so that half the nose, the eyes, the eyebrows, and perhaps the breasts are visible. Most wear a gold ring on the nose.

Muslim men also dress in the European style. They wear the fez as a headdress, except the Bedouin dwelling there who wear Arab dress. These Bedouin [174] are mostly cultivators and are wretched. They have [absolutely] nothing. Often they perform the corvée for the government officials. The government officials dominate them completely and oppress them very much.

Those of the Bedouin of Alexandria, Cairo, and the provinces who go to Mecca or Medina or other places outside Egypt must provide someone from their quarter as guarantor that they will return to their own place again.

THE ENGLISH IN EGYPT

Previously, it used to be the custom in Egypt that they put criminals in boxes and drowned them in the sea or the Nile River. This has been stopped since England penetrated there. Now they either imprison them or banish them to some distant country.

Many Englishmen are employed in Alexandria and Egypt. Most of the employees in the machine factories, the customs officers, the steamship employees, the telegraph officers, the military officers, and the employees of the Ministry of Justice in Egypt and Alexandria are English. About fifteen steamships belong to the Khedive of Egypt. Seven of those steamships are warships. Most are in Alexandria harbor. Eight which are used for commerce or are hired out used to belong to Sa^cid Pâshâ.[22] Their profit goes to the English government on account of the [public] debt.

THE EGYPTIAN ARMY

In the entire kingdom of Egypt, there are altogether about thirty regiments. Two or three regiments of artillerymen and soldiers are always garrisoned in Alexandria. They give every one in these [regiments] about fourteen thousand dinars in Iranian money per month for rations and salary. [175]

THE MONEY OF EGYPT

I did not see the Egyptian gold coinage. However, they have a silver coin named the "qorush" which is different from the qorush of Istanbul. They consider one Ottoman majidi [equal to] twenty-seven

---

[22] Autonomous governor of Egypt (1854-63).

of their own qorush, but because of its low [silver] content, it is not traded at this rate outside Egypt.[23] No country accepts this money, not even in the Hejaz or Anatolia. The coin most used in Egypt is the franc, which is French and is worth about twenty-five shâhis in Iranian money.

THE IRANIAN CONSULATE AND IRANIAN SUBJECTS

There are consuls from most countries in Alexandria. The consul of the government of Iran was Ḥâjji Mirzâ Ḥabibollah Khân Kâshi, who in this year had gone to the consulate in Jedda. In the interim, Ḥâjji Moḥammad Bâqer, a merchant who was highly respected, and Ḥâjji Mirzâ ᶜAli, a Turk [from Iran] who served in the capacity of deputy consul, looked after the affairs of Iranian subjects.

There are about two hundred Iranian subjects in Alexandria. Most are tradesmen, coffeehouse keepers, or inn keepers. There are few merchants there.[24]

MAUSOLEUMS IN THE CITY

In the center of Alexandria, there is at present a crypt over which they have erected a whitewashed mausoleum. This crypt is seven steps lower down than the street level. There are two tombs in the middle of the crypt, one of which they say is the tomb of the Prophet Daniel[25] and the other they think is the tomb of the sage Loqmân.[26] It has a custodian and a lamp and is a place of pilgrimage for the people. However, I have never seen anything in books about the tomb of Daniel or Loqmân being in Alexandria.

Beside this crypt of the tomb of Daniel, there is a large domed building. In this, there are several tombs: [176] One is the tomb of Saᶜid Pâshâ, the governor of Egypt who died in the year 1279 [1862-63]; another is the tomb of Ḥosayn Pâshâ, the governor of the Sudan and son of Saᶜid Pâshâ, who died in the year 1263 [1846-47]. Another is the tomb of Ebrâhim Pâshâ the governor of Egypt.[27]

---

[23] Issawi, *Economic History of the Middle East*, p. 523, notes that Egyptian coinage after 1860 was severely disrupted when the Khedive Esmâᶜil issued large numbers of devalued silver coins; the confusion was ended only in 1885 when Egypt adopted a gold standard.

[24] Cf. Pirzâdeh, *Safarnâmeh*, 2:155-56.

[25] This building is still known as the Mosque of the Prophet Daniel; it is actually the tomb of Shaykh Moḥammad Dânyâl ol-Mowṣoli (d. 810/1407). See Soᶜâd Mâher, *Masâjed meṣr va owliyâhâ oṣ-ṣâleḥin* (Cairo, 1971-83), 1:326-29.

[26] A person mentioned in the Koran (31:12-20). Muslim tradition does not agree whether he should be considered a prophet or simply a wise man. Some Western scholars have attempted to identify him with Aesop.

[27] Moḥammad ᶜAli's immediate successor; he was governor of Egypt for less than a year in 1848. This building was apparently destroyed in 1954 and the tombs removed to Cairo.

The tombs of the admiral Ṭusun Pâshâ, No^caym Pâshâ, and several children of Moḥammad ᶜAli Pâshâ are also there. The tombs in this domed building also have custodians and Koran readers.

THE MAḤMUDEYYEH QUARTER AND ITS COLUMN

Outside the city of Alexandria at the present time there is a place called the Maḥmudeyyeh quarter. The Bedouin dwelling in Alexandria generally stay there. The ancient city used to be near the Maḥmudeyyeh quarter. Ruined traces of the ancient city are still visible there. There is also at present a stone column in the ruins of this same quarter which is of a reddish stone in which are flecks of black.[28] There is at the base a square pedestal four z̲arᶜ [high] of blocks of stone and then a round stone of one piece that is almost twenty z̲arᶜ high.

THE MOṬÂLEBI CLAN

Treasures have repeatedly been found in these ruins. Previously in Cairo and Alexandria there used to be a clan [*ṭâyefeh*] which was always digging up these ruins in search of treasure. They were called the "Moṭâlebi clan." They gave a fifth of whatever they found to the sultan of Egypt. Now there is no one left of this clan, and fewer men engage in this activity.

THE TOMB OF JÂBER

There is a tomb which they call the tomb of Jâber. The popular [story] is that he is one of the companions [of the Prophet Moḥammad], but this is without foundation since, of the well known companions, one is Jâber Anṣâri[29] [177] and another is Jâber Joᶜfi.[30] Both are among the great companions, and both of their tombs are in Medina the Illuminated. [As for] Jâber ebn-e Ḥayyân,[31] who was one of the scholars among craftsmen and alchemists and one of the students of [Imam] Jaᶜfar-e Ṣâdeq and who is well known as a traditionist and a mystic, his tomb also, according to reports, is in Sarakhs. Thus this Jâber [in Alexandria] is not one of the celebrities or the ancients.

---

28 This certainly refers to the so-called Column of Pompey in south-central Alexandria, in an area which used to be outside the old city walls.

29 Perhaps a reference to Jâber b. ᶜAbdollah b. ᶜAmr; on the possible identity of the local saint known as Sidi Jâber see Mâher, *Masâjed meṣr*, 3:96-99.

30 Jâber b. Yazid b. ol-Hâres̲ (d. between 128/745-46 and 132/749-50); see ᶜAsqalâni, *Tahz̲ib*, 2:46-51; EI_2, Supplement, pp. 232-33.

31 Known in the western world as the famous alchemist Geber, who lived in the last half of the eighth century A. D.; see EI_2, 2:357-59 [s.v. "Djâbir b. Ḥayyân"].

THE RAILROAD

One goes from Alexandria to Cairo, which is 130 English miles, by railroad coach in five hours without stopping. (A full English mile is equivalent to 1,019 z̲arᶜ-e shâh plus three and a half gereh, so that six miles and a fraction is equal to one Iranian farsakh, which is one thousand z̲arᶜ.) Thus every hour, the coach goes twenty-six miles, which is about four and a half farsakhs. Sometimes, it takes [only] four hours, so that it travels about five farsakhs per hour. The coach fare from Alexandria to Cairo in third class is about two tomans; in second class about four tomans; and in first class about six tomans. The coach goes from Alexandria to Cairo every day. Although I wanted very much to go to Cairo, [my] travelling companions did not and so dissuaded me from my intention.[32]

THE RAILROAD FROM ALEXANDRIA TO SUEZ

A coach also goes every day from Alexandria to Suez, which is about 260 full English miles or about fifty Iranian farsakhs. Without stopping, it takes ten hours. One train leaves at sunset, but its coaches are open and it is specially adapted for freight. In consequence, its fares are cheaper. Another leaves in the morning and is specially adapted for passengers. [178] Its first class [fare] is about ten tomans, and the second class about seven tomans. Third class is about four tomans, but it is very disorderly and is right behind the engine. The train which leaves at night stops along the way unloading freight until the time the morning train sets out and catches up with it. At that time, they are connected together and leave simultaneously.

Earlier, it was explained that, since pilgrims purchased a through fare from the Austrian steamship company in Istanbul, and the fare for the coach to Suez and the fare for the boat from Suez to Jedda are with the same company, [its] agent in Alexandria collects the pilgrims' tickets and issues the train tickets to Suez and the steamship tickets to Jedda. After the pilgrims gave their own Istanbul tickets to the agent of the company in Alexandria, a few, in order to economize, travelled on the freight train that goes in the evening; others took the early morning train which has the passenger cars.[33]

---

[32] Other Iranian travellers, such as Ḥâjji Pirzâdeh and Amin od-Dowleh, did visit Cairo; one of the most interesting accounts is that of Sayf od-Dowleh, *Safarnâmeh*, pp. 114-21.

[33] This last phrase is a guess at the intent of the Persian phrase *keh az ânjomleh yeki kordun* [?] *ast*, the meaning of which is not clear.

DEPARTURE FROM ALEXANDRIA

Having arrived the morning of Tuesday the sixth of Zi Qaᶜdeh in Alexandria [17 August], [I] took a seat on the train and set out from Alexandria the morning of Thursday the eighth.

From Alexandria to Suez is 260 English miles. In twenty places there are stations, that is, guest-houses and guardhouses, so that every thirteen or fourteen miles there is a station. The employees of the train and its guest-houses are all Egyptians except some Englishmen who operate the locomotive engine. Along the way there are no guards anywhere. In every station, there are variously seven, eight, or ten guards. [179] Also, these stations are not good quality, clean, two storey buildings. Most of the stations are one storey and dirty. All have three or four rooms. In the stations from Baku to Batum all sorts of food and drink for lunch or tea were available. In these stations nothing can be obtained other than water and occasionally a little fruit. In some places, there is neither fruit nor water. On the trains [in Russia], the time for leaving and stopping was specified: They had an alarm bell, and the passengers knew what they were supposed to do. On this train, they never have an alarm bell, and one does not know what one is to do. Sometimes they blow a whistle without any reason. In fact, the whistle was blown once; several people got down from the train, and the train started up and left them. Thus one does not dare get down off the train to go to the guest-house.

On the trains in Russia, the custom was that they would take the luggage in Baku from a traveller who had excess baggage and give him a receipt. In Batum or Tiflis, he would give the receipt and collect his own baggage. Here, they take the baggage but they do not give a receipt or note. After arrival at Suez, within a period of forty hours, everyone who surrendered his baggage collects his own things upon verification. If one has things of value, they are very likely to be lost or taken, and if they are lost or taken, one has no receipt in hand. The custom is that on railway trains and steamships, after they set out, someone comes and looks at the tickets of the passengers and clips off that ticket with scissors and punches a hole [in it] as a sign that the ticket is invalid. On this train, according to custom, someone came [180] and looked at the ticket of one of our companions. He wanted to cut it with the scissors and make a hole, but, however hard he pushed, his scissors would not cut. Finally, he tore the paper of the ticket and got angry with that poor soul and said, "This is all your fault that the scissors will not cut!"

THE CITY OF ZAGAZIG

The Russian trains are clean and without fault or defect. The [Egyptian] trains are usually broken down, their hinges, chains, and equipment have fallen off, and they are held together with ropes. Their furnishings are all old and worn out. As has been recounted, the French company at first operated the trains and the railway and arranged that the profits go to the company for twenty-five years. For those twenty-five years that it was with the company, all was in perfect order. Then the company's term expired, and now the railway has been given over to the Khedive of Egypt. He gives the profits to the English because of the debt.[34]

Anyway, the train reached Zagazig[35] two hours before noon. On both sides along the way from Alexandria to Zagazig there are usually streams, trees, and crops, especially crops of maize, broad-beans, green beans, sugar cane, and millet.

Zagazig is one of the cities of Egypt adjacent to the railway. A nice station has been built there. It is a place with lots of water and trees, but the city does not have a rampart or moat. A branch of the river Nile passes beside there. Most of the houses are located beside the river. It has five or six thousand resident households, which is about twenty thousand people. All are Egyptians. Its streets are mostly narrow and dirty and unpaved. Its houses are of two or three storeys. It has about a thousand shops. There isn't a consul there from any country. There is a [newspaper] correspondent from England there. [181] On behalf of the government of Iran, there is also a man there by the name of ᶜAbdollah Bayk, an Egyptian who is one of the dignitaries and landowners there and who also engages in commerce. There may be twenty-two or -three citizens of Iran in this city, of whom two or three are indigo merchants. The rest are coffeehouse keepers, a surgeon, grocers, and so on.

The train was idle in Zagazig, which is the halfway point on the way, for five hours in order to pick up the Sunni pilgrims who came from Cairo and Zagazig. The freight train, which left at night from Alexandria and had been waiting here, was connected to this train in Zagazig. Also, a train which had come from Cairo to Suez was connected to this train here. Three hours before sunset, [the train] left Zagazig.

[34] According to the Law of Liquidation promulgated in 1880, approximately half of all Egyptian revenues had to be assigned to the *Caisse de la Dette* to pay off Egypt's international debts; see Zayid, *Egypt's Struggle*, pp. 12-16; Holt, *Egypt and the Fertile Crescent*, p. 211; Richmond, *Egypt*, pp. 97-105.

[35] Text: Zaghâz-n-ᶜ.

DEPARTURE FROM ZAGAZIG

From there to the next station, it is again green and cultivated. Then on the left side, there is a desert of fine sand. Hurdles have been erected beside the railway so that the wind doesn't blow sand on the tracks. The right side also has very few habitations or cultivated areas. Five or six miles before Suez, there is a green and pleasant place named Nafiseh.[36]

THE PORT OF SUEZ

The train arrived at Suez at the second hour of the night [before] Friday the ninth of Z̲i Qaᶜdeh the Sacred [19 August]. The Suez station is in the center of the city, and at that time of night it was very crowded. Amid the crowd and throng, several Iranian landlords and coffeeshop keepers appeared and invited the Iranian pilgrims to their own residences. [182] I gathered from the situation that since the coffeemen's homes had not been seen and the rate was not fixed, it might be a cause for dispute, and so I went in person and saw the residences, selected one, and ascertained its rates. They brought the baggage and belongings there. Some of the pilgrims also accompanied me. Other pilgrims had quarrels and disputes and were involved in distraint and consular litigation with the landlords and coffeehouse keepers.

DESCRIPTION OF SUEZ

Suez is a borough which is one of the territories of Egypt and an ancient port. It is to the east of Cairo on the slope of a small mountain which is a continuation of the Moqaṭṭam mountain chain. It is located in a region of fine sand. With a little wind, minute sand is picked up and gets into the eyes. For this reason, the eyes of most of the people of Suez and the environs are blind, injured, or defective. It has about three thousand resident households there, which is approximately twelve thousand people. It has three hundred shops. Its houses are usually three or four storeys. Its bazaars are narrow and dirty and have few goods. Its streets are wide and unpaved. It is located beside the Red Sea, and its climate is bad and humid. Its water is Nile water, as Esmâᶜil Pâshâ dug a canal and brought a branch of the Nile River there. The English, as in the case of Alexandria, have erected mechanical pumps here so that water goes to faucets in the upper storeys of the houses.

---

[36]So in the text. It seems likely that Farâhâni is referring to Nefischa, a suburb of Ismailiyya (not of Suez as indicated by Farâhâni) near the old terminus of the sweet-water canal from the Nile and the junction of the Cairo-Ismailiyya and Alexandria-Suez railway lines; see D. A. Farnie, *East and West of Suez: The Suez Canal in History 1854-1956* (Oxford, 1956), p. 64.

In the environs of Suez, I did not see any greenery or cultivation or trees. In some gardens of the houses in the city, a few shade trees and small palm trees were seen. It seems there are no kinds of crops or fruit in the city. In the villages of the mountain two or three farsakhs away good watermelons are grown, which are large, sweet, abundant, and cheap. [183] They are sent from there to Cairo and Jedda.

I heard that previously Suez used to be more prosperous than this. When the Suez Canal was opened, Port Said, which is adjacent to the Canal, became prosperous and the [main] harbor, so this [city] ceased to flourish.

From Suez to Cairo without stopping is six hours by railroad. Trains come and go every day.

THE CONSULATE AND SUBJECTS OF IRAN

In Suez, there are seven or eight people of Iranian origin. The representative of the exalted government of Iran is a merchant by the name of Aḥmad Afandi, whose father was a well known merchant and a dignitary of Suez, and who is himself a man of property and wealth. He represents the governments of Iran, Austria, and Brazil. He displays the three flags [of these countries] on the rooftop of his house three days a week. [If] citizens of these three countries have any [legal] business, they have recourse to him. He is a man of considerable competence. Here it is again customary that the pilgrims have their passports endorsed. The Ottoman agent signs the passports of the Ottoman pilgrims, and the Iranian deputy and agent signs the passports for the Iranian pilgrims. They charge one and a half majidis per passport, which is about eight thousand dinars.

THE QUARANTINE[37]

Another of the difficulties for the pilgrims at Suez is that the chief physician there on behalf of the Khedive must give health certificates to the pilgrims. As for the fee for writing the certificate, he charges three qorush-e sâq [*sic*] and ten para per person, which is about one Iranian kran. However, it is not necessary that the physician see every pilgrim. [184] That is, the object is to collect the fee. One person goes with the money and gets the health certificates for ten or twenty people.

[37] The establishment of a sanitary regime for maritime traffic in the Red Sea has been studied in some depth by William Roff, "Sanitation and Security: The Imperial Powers and the Nineteenth Century Ḥajj," in *Arabian Studies* 6(1982):143-60. Farâhâni alludes to various aspects of it in more detail later in his account; see below Part Seven, n. 22.

DEPARTURE FROM THE PORT OF SUEZ

We stayed in Suez Friday the ninth, Saturday the tenth, and Sunday the eleventh. The morning of Monday the twelfth of Z̲i Qaᶜdeh [23 August] we took our baggage and belongings and went first to the door of the customs house, which is an enclosure beside the sea. We waited three hours at the door of the customs until all the pilgrims had come and gathered there. After that, the customs inspectors came and looked at the people's baggage. In spite of the fact that all of the pilgrims were being carried by rowboat from one particular place, nevertheless most of the baggage and freight was not inspected and was passed nonchalantly. They did not inspect our baggage. If someone had numerous dutiable goods, it was possible to give money secretly to one of the customs inspectors so that they would not open the baggage. After finishing with the customs, the pilgrims with baggage and goods immediately [left] the customs house enclosure and boarded rowboats. In accordance with Khedival decree, these rowboats which transport people must assemble after a trip of one farsakh over water at a place which the government has built beside the sea. The rowboats with the passengers must line up in an orderly fashion. At this place, there are ten or twelve Arab families who have built houses and have also pitched tents there [to serve] as coffeehouses and groceries. They bring many watermelons and some other food items for sale there on the days pilgrims depart. In this government building, there is an official on behalf of the Khedive. He also has four assistants. The day the pilgrims depart, that official with his assistants comes out of that building near noon. In the event that all of the pilgrims who have come are arranged and waiting in good order on the sea in the rowboats, they then take off the passengers from every rowboat [185] and, person by person, they first inspect one's Ottoman visa which was obtained in Istanbul. Then they inspect the health certificate that was obtained from the physician in Suez. One person also comes on board the rowboat and searches the baggage and freight [to see that] no one without a passport[38] has been hidden under the baggage and freight. They very sternly prevent anyone without a passport from going unless he pays a considerable fee and gets a new passport from this same official.

Anyhow, this official looks at all the people in the rowboats. Meanwhile, he makes an inventory of how many rowboats [there

[38] The meaning of *taz̲kereh* throughout this passage is ambiguous; the sense might be closer to "exit visa." From the context, Farâhâni might also mean "ticket," but he rather consistently uses *belit* rather than *taz̲kereh* for this.

are] and how many people have been transported in each rowboat and the amount of the fares that have been collected. They give two thirds of the fares to the rowboat owners and take one third as the *ḥaqq miri*, that is the government tax. In this matter [the inspector] was very careful that there not be a stowaway or anyone without a passport. Nevertheless, some [people] without passports slipped by.

This day went by with great inconvenience for the pilgrims. Two hours before sunset, they boarded the boat.

BOARDING THE BOAT AND DEPARTURE FOR JEDDA

The steamship did not leave the night [before] Tuesday the thirteenth or on Tuesday until two hours before sunset. It carried many passengers. About one thousand people gathered on this boat, of whom two hundred were Iranians and the rest were Ottomans, Egyptians, and people from Bokhara. The women's place was on a special deck the sides of which had been screened off. The store-rooms and boiler rooms were full of people. It was very crowded. They did not charge extra fare for excess baggage, but they did take [it] below to the hold [where it] could be stained or damaged. [186] They are not as exacting on this ship as is the manner on the European steamships. Everyone cooks things everywhere on the ship. There is no prohibition of water-pipes or samovars.

Two hours before sunset, the steamship departed. Then someone came and took up the steamship tickets that had been given to people. There were about thirty people who were without tickets and had boarded concealed. They stowed away dishonestly and did not pay the boat fare. When they learned about those few persons who had no tickets, they did not interfere with them owing to their poverty and impecuniousness.

This steamship is one of the Khedival steamships and is named the *Maḥalleh*. Aside from the employees of the engine room who are English, the other employees are all Muslims. The steamer was more crowded because of this. Near the time of the pilgrimage, every steamship that goes from Suez to Jedda will be very crowded, especially the steamships which have agreed with the Istanbul companies to carry the passengers of the companies' steamships.

TRAVEL GUIDE FOR IRANIANS VISITING THE HOUSE OF GOD

Thus the best way for someone to travel from Iran is to go by sea from Enzeli [on] the twenty-fifth of Ramadan and travel to Istanbul in ten days, arriving there on the fifth of Shavvâl. One should remain in Istanbul for ten days and then, in the middle of Shavvâl, take a direct boat from Istanbul to Yanbo^{c}, reaching there in twelve days.

There are camel drivers ready in Yanbo^c. Taking a camel and litter [*shoqzof*],[39] one reaches Medina the Agreeable in six days. One waits till the twenty-fifth of Zi Qa^cdeh in Medina the Agreeable and then travels to Mecca the Sublime in the company of the Syrian pilgrims. [187] One would arrive in Mecca on the sixth or seventh of the sacred month of Zi Ḥejjeh. After completing the pilgrimage, the desire to visit Medina the Illuminated is easily fulfilled. One can go any way one wishes without difficulty. This method and arrangement is [best] for anyone whose only aim is to make a pilrimage and be economical and content with expenditures.

As for someone who intends to tour about during the trip and also is not interested in economizing, he [may] go to Istanbul before the month of Ramadan and stay there for the duration of that month. Then he should take a boat from Istanbul to Alexandria and not to Jedda. [Afterwards,] he should go from Alexandria to Cairo and stay there for about a month. [During this time,] he can make some excursions by sea to Beirut, Syria, and other places, and then arrive at Jedda. [Next,] he should go to Ṭâ'ef, and from there he will be able to put on the pilgrim's garb at Qarn ol-Manâzel,which is the *miqât*[40] place for the people of Ṭâ'ef, without any hardship or inconvenience, and finally make his entry into Mecca the Sublime.

THE RED SEA

To sum up: After the steamship left Suez, it entered the Red Sea, which is also called the Qolzom Sea.[41] This sea is a branch of the "Green Sea" which is the Indian Ocean. The eastern side of this sea

---

[39] Eldon Rutter, *Holy Cities of Arabia* (London, 1928), 1:151 offers this description of the shoqzof: "The shugduf, or camel-litter, consists of a pair of stretchers, each of which is over five feet in length and two and a half feet broad. These are constructed similarly to the sirîr, or kursî—of a wooden framework strung with plaited fiber cords. A dome-shaped hood of bent sticks, over which the occupant ties his carpet, acts as a protection from the sun. The two stretchers are fastened together, side by side, with ropes; and they rest one on either side of the camel's saddle. Two little baskets, used for holding water-bottles and food, are sewn with string to the hood of each half of the shugduf." The shoqzof and other vehicles for travelling by camel are also described by Burton, *Personal Narrative*, 1:418 and 2:65; John Lewis Burckhardt, *Travels in Arabia* (London, 1829), p. 295; John Keane, *Six Months in the Hejaz* (London, 1887), pp. 5-6; C. Snouck Hurgronje, *Mekka in the Latter Part of the 19th Century* (translated by J. H. Monahan; Leiden and London, 1931), p. 26; H. Kazem Zadeh, *Relation d'un Pèlerinage à la Mecque* (Paris, 1912), pp. 7-8. "Litter" is not a particularly precise translation for shoqzof, but for convenience it will be used here in lieu of repeating the technical term.

[40] The term for the specific place at which a pilgrim to Mecca must put on the special garments (*eḥrâm*) required for the ritual. Farâhâni discusses this subject more fully later in his account.

[41] An archaic Muslim name for the Red Sea derived from the ancient port of Clysma (near modern Suez).

is part of the land of Arabia and the Yemen. Its western side is Berber[42] and Ethiopia. The northern side is Yasreb and the Tehâmeh.[43] Its south is the Indian Ocean. Pharaoh was drowned in this sea. There are many lodestones in this sea.[44]

All the way, the steamship's movement was towards the south-east. When it had travelled about 120 miles, a mountainous shoreline far away became visible. It is said: There is a prosperous borough behind those mountains named Âdamir,[45] which is one of the dependencies of Egypt. Its people are mostly Zoroastrians and Jews. About 180 miles beyond Suez, the shore of the island of Shadwân[46] is visible to the starboard side. [188] To guide ships from Suez to Shadwân, there are three lighthouses in the midst of the sea. The first and the second are small, [but] the third lighthouse is very large and tall. It has a height of approximately thirty-seven zarᶜ above the sea and a diameter of six zarᶜ. There are always three or four custodians in that place who take turns keeping watch. The steamships bring water and provisions for them. Each of the companies whose steamships traverse this route pays something for the yearly wages and provisions for the custodians and the upkeep of the lighthouse.[47]

Past the island of Shadwân to Jedda, there is no island or other place. The steamship did not stop anywhere else. Numerous steamships which were passing by were seen along the way. In the midst of the sea, there are two high rocks which the Arabs call *Akhavayn*[48] ["Two Brothers"]. Since there are many rocks and mountains in this sea, veteran oarsmen from Jedda, who have repeatedly crossed this sea by rowboat, come to Suez during the [pilgrimage] season. There the captains, in consideration of [their] skill, take them as guides and pay them a fee. Most of the ship's

---

42 That is, the eastern Sudan.

43 The narrow plain along the Red Sea coast of the Arabian peninsula from the Gulf of Aqaba to the Yemen.

44 This passage is very close to the description of the Red Sea in Qazvini/Le Strange, *Nuzhat*, p. 227.

45 It has not been possible to identify the place, which must be somewhere in the vicinity of the Gulf of Suez, to which Farâhâni is alluding. From the spelling, Ibrim or Ed Damer might be possibilities, but both are much too far south to fit the description.

46 Text: Sadvân. Shadwân, also shown on some maps as Shâkir, is the largest of the islands at the exit from the Gulf of Suez into the Red Sea.

47 See also Farhâd Mirzâ, *Hedâyat*, pp. 109-10 (which has a line drawing of some of the lighthouses).

48 So in the text; the actual name is ol-Ekhvân, "the Brothers," shown on most modern maps as El Ikhwân.

movement across the sea is under the direction of that guide. There are three warships from the Ottoman Empire in this Red Sea which are usually anchored in the harbor of Jedda.

THE PORT OF JEDDA

The steamship anchored beside the Jedda pier on Friday the sixteenth of the sacred month of Z̲i Qaᶜdeh [27 August] at one hour past noon. Its entire trip from Suez to Jedda without any delay took sixty-eight hours. Because of the extreme crowding and cramped space on this steamship, three Arabs perished in the hold and several people had become ill. [189]

The steamship was delayed at the Jedda pier for about three hours. No rowboat or launch came near it until the government quarantine doctor with the quarantine employees first boarded the ship, looked and searched around, and ascertained and verified that there was no serious contagious disease on the ship. Then they gave people permission to enter Jedda. Launches and rowboats came and transported people. They charged more than warranted for the rowboat fare. They said this [fare] is divided into three shares: the government takes one, the consul of each state takes one, and the oarsman one. In all places throughout the Ottoman Empire, exorbitant taxes are exacted from the oarsmen, but especially in Jedda.

THE QUARANTINE

First of all, they bring the pilgrims in the launches and rowboats by the quarantine building, which is beside the sea and adjacent to the city. The people disembark, without baggage or belongings, at this guarded enclosure. They give everyone a printed certificate which is the quarantine permit, and they charge each person half a majidi, which is 2,050 shâhis in Iranian money. In this same place, there is another enclosure where they inspect and stamp one's passport.[49] For stamping the passport, they also charge each person half a majidi and several para, which is about three thousand dinars in Iranian money.

THE PASSPORT OFFICE

In this passport office enclosure, there is a consul from every state stationed there who supervises the affairs of the respective

---

[49] According to Roff, "Sanitation and Security," pp. 149-50, the need for passports to enter the Hejaz was a recent innovation, prompted generally by the Ottoman desire to reassert its control over the province and specifically because of the murder in 1880 of the Sharif Ḥosayn of Mecca.

pilgrims so that no injustice is done to them. It is like the story of the baby and the negro slave.[50]

Also in this enclosure, the representatives of the professional pilgrim-guides [*moṭavvefin*] are sitting on chairs from one end to the other, [190] waiting to see under the guidance of which of them the pilgrim will place [himself]. After that, they never let go of one and don't grant one a moment's peace. They become one's guardian and provide one with tutorship. A detailed account of the pilgrim-guides and their activities will be written in the proper place.

CUSTOMS

Anyhow, after one pays the fee for the quarantine permit and the fee for stamping the passport, one then obtains a dismissal ticket, exits from this enclosure, and is free [to go]. As soon as one comes out, one seeks one's baggage and belongings (which had been placed in the rowboat and left [behind] when one had disembarked at the quarantine-house) at the pier among the rowboats beside the open square fronting the gate of the city. In the same square the pilgrims bring their own things and belongings from the rowboats to land. However, there is no way into the city unless one enters by the gate. They search all one's things at the customs house. If one has something dutiable, they collect the customary fee; otherwise, if they do not find any dutiable things, they will charge as much as they can squeeze out of people as "reward" for the customs-officer.

The customs-house closes on Friday one hour before noon. If one disembarks from the steamship then, there is no prohibition against entering the city but the baggage must be left in the square until the next day [when] they inspect the baggage and take it inside the city–except [in the case of] dignitaries who inform the consulates of their own government. The consulate, out of respect, obtains a permit from the customs chief that the belongings not be detained. Thus even on Friday one may enter the city with baggage and belongings. This humble servant sat in the square with other pilgrims in order to guard the baggage and belongings until two men [from] the Iranian consulate came and asked me which one was so

[50] The allusion is to a popular Persian anecdote. A particularly unattractive negro slave [*kâkâ*] was trying repeatedly to get a baby to stop crying; finally, a passerby explained to the slave that the baby was crying because it was frightened at seeing such an ugly person! Here, Farâhâni is probably implying that the pilgrims have as much to fear from the people who are supposed to be protecting them as from those who would exploit them. Farâhâni also quotes a verse from the *Masnavi* of Rumi making a similar point; it is omitted from the translation.

and so. [191] I said, "I don't know him." They asked other pilgrims and learned that I was the one. They came again and said, "We work for the consul of the Iranian government. Since a recommendation has arrived from the embassy in Istanbul that you should be honored, he has sent us [to find out] if you have any problems to report." I then replied, "For the time being, the difficulty that I have is this: the baggage is kept waiting outside the city on account of the customs. They have already inspected the baggage in the customs-houses in Istanbul, Alexandria, and Suez, and now they are checking things again in Jedda. The demands of the customs are out of order. Arrange it so that we can spend the night in the city and not leave our baggage outside." These two deputies of the consul left and returned one hour before nightfall. They brought a letter from the customs chief that no one should hold back our baggage. Then the chief porter of the city, who is appointed by the government and pays a yearly fee to the government for running the porter's business, came. He summoned several porters, arranged the charges, and they carried the baggage. Seven or eight fellow countrymen among the pilgrims attached themselves to us and entered the city evading the customs.

RESTING

We went to an excellent house which the pilgrim-guide's apprentice had indicated. We entered a carpeted room with cushions placed about and sat down tired and hungry until the curtain to a dining room was raised. A very elaborate dining tray had been placed on the floor in which were pilaf and other essentials. It was evident that the servant of the pilgrim-guide had exhorted the owner of the house [to arrange] for provisions and ceremonies. We ate and thanked God. Very delicious foods appeared to gratify the palate, but later, when we paid an exorbitant gratuity to the owner of the house, the flavor of the foods was not so tasty! [192]

THE IRANIAN CONSUL

The next morning, the consul of the government of Iran, Mirzâ Ḥabibollah Khân, who had come to Jedda this year and previously had been the consul at Alexandria, and who is fifty years old and a native of Kashan, came for a visit, along with some of his employees. He was friendly and kind and invited me to his own home. He had written a detailed history about the career of the self-proclaimed Mahdi.[51] He had collected all his sermons and proclamations and

[51] Text: *motamahdi*, i. e. Moḥammad Aḥmad, founder and leader of the Mahdist movement in the Sudan. The Mahdist revolt has been extensively studied;

papers which he had written to the government of the Sudan, the Khedive of Egypt, the Ottoman Sultan, and the English commanders [as well as] the odes of Arab and non-Arab poets which had been composed in praise of him. He had written exhaustively about [the Mahdi's] good qualities and virtues along with details of the career of Aᶜrâbi Pâshâ. It was about twelve thousand lines [long]. I obtained that book from him and extracted and composed this summary from his writings:

CHARACTER SKETCH OF MOḤAMMAD AḤMAD [THE MAHDI OF THE SUDAN]

[He was] black-skinned, of middling stature, corpulent, with eyebrows that touched each other, large eyes, a sparse and short beard, and black hair, a haggard visage, cheerful [disposition], and humble.

HIS APPEARANCE AND CLOTHING

[He] displayed piety and spoke and wrote well. He was severe in meeting out punishment. Some said he liked jokes. Sometimes he practiced the [mystical] invocation and contemplation [of God].[52] He spent two or three hours alone every day, meditating in retreat. No [instances] of personal valor on his part have been recorded, but sometimes he himself made the plans for the campaigns. He was generous and hospitable. He was fond of women and had three legitimate wives. [He wore] a round turban like the turbans of the people of the Hejaz and the short Arab dress.

ACCOUNT OF THE SELF-PROCLAIMED MAHDI

Moḥammad Aḥmad was born in the year 1250 on the fifth of the month of Ṣafar the Victorious [14 June 1834].[53] [193] His father was named ᶜAbdollah. He had four brothers, the first name of all of whom was Moḥammad. His father and brothers were shipwrights. He claimed to be a sayyed and always used to say, "I am one of the descendants of Fâṭemeh and a Ḥosaynid." In his youth he received an elementary education in his own town, which was Dongola. As soon as he came of age, he went to Cairo and was occupied for several years in obtaining a knowledge of Islamic jurisprudence [*feqh*] and so on at the Azhar.[54] After that, he returned to Dongola

---

see F. R. Wingate, *Mahdism and the Egyptian Sudan* (London, 1891); A. B. Theobald, *The Mahdiyya* (London, 1951); P. M. Holt, *The Mahdist State in the Sudan 1881-1898* (Oxford, 1970; second ed.).

52 *Ẕekr va fekr*.

53 The usual date given for his birth is 27 Rajab 1260 (12 August 1844); see Holt, *Mahdist State*, p. 45.

54 There is no indication in other sources that Moḥammad Aḥmad ever went to Egypt either for religious education or any other reason, much less to the Azhar.

and took a wife from among his own relations.[55] For about two years he received training in theology from a traveller from the east (some have said that he was Ḥâjji Moḥammad Jaᶜfar Âqâ-ye Eṣfahâni) who had come on a trip to Dongola.[56]

He and his father were Sunnis of the Mâleki rite. It is said that after studying philosophy [*ḥekmat*] he made rational objections to the four schools of law [recognized by Sunni Islam]. Nonetheless, his deeds and judgments pertaining to religious law were in accordance with the Shâfeᶜi school. After that, he had a liking for commerce. He had a little capital from his wife's property and also was an agent on behalf of a rich man. Mostly he was engaged in buying and selling male and female slaves. In the second year [of this partnership], the rich man perceived that this commerce was causing a loss and urgently terminated the partnership with Moḥammad Aḥmad and demanded back his own funds. Moḥammad Aḥmad requested a grace period of several months before giving back the funds and took over that particular trade himself. By chance, male and female slaves rose in price. Moḥammad Aḥmad made an enormous profit and gave back his partner's money. He obtained considerable capital and engaged in commerce independently until the English government stopped the trade in male and female slaves. He set out for the province of the Hejaz with the intention of trading in jewels and so on. [194] In Medina the Agreeable he joined the Khalvati Shâẕeleyyeh[57] order and received permission to proselytize [for this order] from Shaykh Sajâdeh-ye Sammâneyyeh, who was the head of that order.[58] He returned to the country of the Sudan for the purpose

---

[55] He married one of the daughters of his great uncle; see Holt, *Mahdist State*, p. 46.

[56] This is not confirmed by other sources and seems unlikely; however, it is interesting that there was a strong Shi'ite tendency in the Mahdi's religious ideology which has always been difficult to explain given the Sunni environment in which the movement began.

[57] Text: Shâzleyyeh. This Sufi order was founded by Abu'l-Ḥasan osh-Shâẕeli (1196-1258) and became the most important such movement in North Africa; the Sanusi order was one of its offshoots. See E. Bannerth, "Aspects humaines de la Shâdhiliyya en Egypte," *Mélanges de l'Institut Dominicaines d'Études Orientales du Caire* 11(1972):237-50; Trimingham, *Sufi Orders*, pp. 47-51. It is not clear why Farâhâni calls this a Khalvati order; perhaps he literally means "reclusive."

[58] He was trained and eventually accepted into the Sammâneyyeh order by Shaykh Moḥammad Sharif Nur od-Din od-Dâ'em. The Sammâneyyeh order was founded in Egypt by ᶜAbd ol-Karim as-Sammâni (1718-75) and spread to Sumatra as well as the Sudan. This order was an offshoot of the larger Khalvati group. See Trimingham, *Sufi Orders*, p. 77.

of [offering correct spiritual] guidance. He took up residence on the slopes of a mountain near Kordofan, built a small house, and laid the foundations for [his] missionary work [*da*ᶜ*vat*]. It was not long before he became the [spiritual] authority for the common people and Bedouin [*a*ᶜ*râb*]. The shaykhs and morshids of the [religious] orders which were in Kordofan and its environs were jealous of him. Out of spite they came forward and made out to the government of Kordofan that he was a seditious person and a seeker of power. In that year, because of a drought, people unable to pay the government taxes took refuge with the would-be Mahdi. The latter interceded for the people with the government of Kordofan. Because the government listened to the shaykhs and morshids, it did not listen to Moḥammad Aḥmad. His strength increased because of the refugees going to join him.

There was a short fight between the peasants and the government officials and thus the matter ended in a conflict. The government troops were defeated. The government again sent troops out to capture and to punish Moḥammad Aḥmad and the fugitives [with him], and again they were unsuccessful and were defeated. His fame gradually spread. People from the suburbs and surrounding regions turned to him to avoid paying taxes. The unrest and excitement was evident in some of the provinces of the Sudan. Gradually the flames [of the movement] enveloped the east and the Sudan. The news reached the governor of Egypt. He continuously sent troops to the Sudan to extinguish the conflagration, [but] it was impossible. Meanwhile, the revolt of Aᶜrâbi Pâshâ in Egypt had prospered, and the Khedival authorities were occupied with suppressing it and could not find the opportunity to send help for the Sudanese army. Moḥammad Aḥmad seized the opportunity for getting booty. The Bedouin of the surrounding area gathered around him, and he occupied most of the eastern provinces of the Sudan until the English entered Egypt. [195] At first, the English insisted that the Khedive of Egypt ignore the Sudan for the time being; for a time this was the rumor. The people of the Sudan heard this rumor, became [even] more frightened, and clung more firmly to Moḥammad Aḥmad. The Khedival dignitaries did not accept the English advice and again sent two detachments of troops to the Sudan from Egypt and were defeated. Then they wrote letters [full] of compromises, promises, and threats to him. He gave stern replies. In writings and speeches, he began to claim a kind of divinely inspired leadership[59] so that everyone who went to greet him said, "Peace be upon you O Caliph of God" or "O Proof of God" or "O Deputy of God." He claimed [to have had] a vision while awake of the Prophet Moḥammad. Moreover, in one of his sermons he had written "the spirit is with us [*ol-barrâ maᶜanâ*]." *Barrâ* has been defined as a pure spirit in a pious man which informs him about current and future events.

He fought numerous battles with the Egyptian army. Sometimes he defeated [them], and sometimes he was defeated. Among [these battles], he fought ᶜAbd ol-Qâder Pâshâ the Egyptian[60] several times and was defeated. [At] one point, he was soundly defeated and took refuge on a mountain. Many from his army were killed, and no one from ᶜAbd ol-Qâder's army was killed. Then the English came to the assistance of the Egyptian army. The people of the Sudan, having been [motivated by] religious zealotry and steadfastness, united firmly in support of the would-be Mahdi and persevered. The details of his wars with the English are famous and have been written about in the newspapers. After those wars, his affairs prospered greatly, and the east and west of the Sudan came into his possession. [196] He appointed four "caliphs" on his behalf:[61] Among them is Shaykh ᶜAbd ol-Hâdi[62] [in the eastern Sudan] and Shaykh Sanusi the Maghrebi[63] in the western Sudan and the environs of Tripoli. [Sanusi] is very great and everyone believes in him and accepts what he says. At first he had opposed Moḥammad Aḥmad and then agreed with him and accepted his caliphate, but he did not involve himself in [the Mahdi's] affairs. These two "caliphs" are superiors to the rest of the followers of the would-be Mahdi.

---

[59] The reference is probably to the open declaration or "manifestation" (*ẓohur*) of his claim to be the Mahdi in the year 1881.

[60] ᶜAbd ol-Qâder Pâshâ Ḥelmi was appointed governor of the Sudan in March 1882 and, prior to his recall, was one of the few Egyptian officials to deal effectively with the Mahdi.

[61] Other accounts agree that the Mahdi appointed only three caliphs; see Holt, *Mahdist State*, pp. 119-25.

[62] Perhaps a mistake for Shaykh ᶜAbdollahi?

[63] Here the reference is clearly intended to be to Moḥammad ᶜOs̱mân ol-Merghâni II, the leader of the Sanusi order at the time of the Mahdist revolt. Other sources, such as Wingate, *Mahdism*, pp. 63-72, make clear that while the Mahdi tried to solicit help from the Sanusi, the latter tended to give only lukewarm support to the Mahdists. There is no indication that the Sanusi was named as one of the "caliphs."

ᶜOsmân Dejmeh (or ᶜOsmân Ziqnâ)[64] is his general who repeatedly had many battles with and victories over the Egyptian and English army. The present time is famous for the death of Moḥammad Aḥmad.[65] He was forty-eight years old. According to reports, his followers have still not disbanded. The leader of the west of the Sudan is Shaykh Sanusi the Maghrebi, and authority in the eastern Sudan belongs to Shaykh ᶜAbd ol-Hâdi. What will happen next is up to God.

SAYYED MANṢUR

After I went from the consul's home to my own residence, Sayyed Manṣur, who is one of the Shiʿite pilgrim-guides, and whose servants had informed him that some of the pilgrims had arrived at Jedda, came posthaste by donkey from Mecca the Exalted to visit. He swore such oaths of close friendship that it seemed he was my slave or bondsman or an old friend whom for many years I had the favor of raising.

ACCOUNT OF THE PILGRIM-GUIDES

At this point, I must write a description of the circumstances concerning the professional pilgrim-guides.[66] In Mecca, there are about thirty Shiʿite and Sunni pilgrim guides appointed by the Sharif[67] of Mecca who have permits for leading pilgrimages. Usually they and their fathers have been pilgrim-guides for generations. Each of them has seven or eight assistants and servants. Before the

---

[64] ᶜOsmân b. Abi Bakr Diqnâ; see Holt, *Mahdist State*, pp. 81-87.

[65] The Mahdi died on 9 Ramadan 1302 (22 June 1885), only a few months before Farâhâni's visit. Although Farâhâni's account of the Mahdi, one of the earliest known in Persian, reveals some inaccuracies in the light of modern research, it is nonetheless important as evidence of the intense interest that the Mahdi's movement had created among the ruling elite as well as the ulama of Iran.

[66] Other accounts of these *moṭavvefs* include Snouck Hurgronje, *Mekka*, pp. 24-29; Kazem Zadeh, *Relation*, pp. 9-13; Gaudefroy-Demombynes, *Pèlerinage*, pp. 200-204; F. E. Peters, *Jerusalem and Mecca: The Typology of the Holy City in the Near East* (New York, 1986), pp. 230-31; David Long, *The Hajj Today: A Survey of the Contemporary Makkah Pilgrimage* (Albany, 1979), pp. 27-36.

[67] The term *sharif* (plural *ashrâf*) is used in a general sense to refer to any of the descendants of the Prophet Moḥammad, especially those living in Mecca or a major city; in the technical sense used here, it is a title conferred on certain descendants of the Prophet Moḥammad who served as chief administrators of the city of Mecca. Since the tenth century, this office had been held by members of one family descended from the Prophet's grandson Ḥasan. In modern times, the power of the office increased as the authority of the central Ottoman government over Arabia declined. At the time of Farâhâni's visit the Ottoman sultan was attempting to increase his authority in the Hejaz at the expense of the Sharif. As Farâhâni indicates here, one of the most important (and lucrative) prerogatives of this office was the right to license individuals to transport pilgrims or to serve as pilgrim guides. See Gerald de Gaury, *Rulers of Mecca* (London, 1951), pp. 64-65; Kazem Zadeh, *Relation*, pp. 36-39; Peters, *Jerusalem and Mecca*, p. 46; Long, *Hajj*, pp. 36-37.

pilgrimage season [begins], [197] they go to the cities which are transit points for pilgrims such as Najaf, Karbala, Baghdad, Bombay, Bushehr, Bandar ᶜAbbâs, Rasht, Istanbul, and Odessa. They issue to everyone they locate who wants to go to Mecca the invitation, "You are without information about the practices and activities there; you must have someone knowledgeable and a pilgrim-guide; you will not find [anyone] better than me." Of course, the pilgrims are beseeching God that they might have a knowledgeable man who will work hard on their behalf. Another thing they do is to promise some of the *ᶜakkâm*, *ḥamleh-dâr*s, and *ḥajjeh-forush*es[68] (who are well known and who come to Mecca every year): "I will give you one Levant dollar (which is about six thousand Iranian dinars) for every pilgrim you bring for me." After making these preparations, they return to Mecca near the beginning of the pilgrimage season. For their part, these ᶜakkâm, ḥamleh-dârs, and ḥajjeh-forushes, with a view to making a profit for themselves, assure every pilgrim they see or know of the commendability of that pilgrim-guide: "So and so the pilgrim-guide is a marvelous man, good, very hard working, and not greedy. It's good for you to entrust your pilgrimage to him so that it will be a simple matter in every respect." The pilgrim is deceived and agrees. Another thing they do is to send one of their agents or servants to every port which is a point of entry for pilgrims to the Hejaz, such as Jedda, Yanboᶜ, or Medina the Agreeable, in order to watch out for and to assemble the followers there. As soon as the pilgrim says one word about "my pilgrim-guide is so and so" these agents and servants report to the respective pilgrim-guide that such and such a pilgrim is under your direction; take note [of him]." If the pilgrim is a notable, the pilgrim-guide goes out a day's journey or two to welcome him and also invites him home one night to give him supper. [198] Thus, the pilgrim is totally dependent upon the pilgrim-guide and utterly at his mercy. If, for instance, he has any goods to sell, he is compelled to inform and seek the approval of his

---

[68] The *ᶜakkâm* were servants hired to pack up baggage and handle other routine aspects of managing a caravan. The *ḥamleh-dâr* was the actual organizer of the caravan who drew up contracts to transport pilgrims and then led the caravan to its destination. Islamic law permitted a Muslim who could not make the pilgrimage ritual to Mecca in person to hire someone to make the pilgrimage in his stead; an individual who contracted to make the pilgrimage for someone else in this manner was known as a *ḥajjeh-forush* (literally "pilgrimage seller"). Since these individuals regularly made the pilgrimage (and thus could influence other potential pilgrims who would trust their experience), they could be used by the pilgrimage guides to recruit customers. See Kazem Zadeh, *Relation*, pp. 1-4.

pilgrim-guide, who arranges with the buyer to get half of the money for those goods.

If for instance, the pilgrim wants goods from there for gifts or to buy for commerce, [the guide will] go to the seller [and say] "Let that pilgrim buy at a high price." At least half the profit goes to [the guide].

Or if, for instance, the pilgrim wants to go from Jedda to Sa^cdeyyeh[69] or Mecca, or to hire transport from Mecca to Medina or Yanbo^c, this, of course, must be with the assistance of the pilgrim-guide. Thus this year everyone who went from Jedda to the Sa^cdeyyeh miqât paid eighteen Levant dollars to hire camels. Of these eighteen Levant dollars, seven dollars is the fare for the camel that carries one. For every camel, the pasha, the sharif, the consul, the pilgrim guide, and the *mokharrej*[70] take eleven dollars.

If [the pilgrim] wants to rent a place to stay in Jedda or Mecca, the pilgrim-guide has a role in that and will receive a share. If the pilgrim goes to ^cArafât and Menâ, part of the charge for the beast of burden and the tent goes to the pilgrim-guide.

If the pilgrim or someone in his party dies, a payment to the pilgrim-guide is expected [for] the vows and prayers which are the special duty of the pilgrim-guide. In the end, if the pilgrim is poor and has little money, he must certainly give at least two Levant dollars (which is about twelve thousand Iranian dinars) as remuneration for the pilgrim-guide. If he does not pay or does not have [the money], the matter will result in hostility, disputes, and petitions to the sharif, the governor, and the consuls. It will be collected by force, violence, or the imprisonment of the helpless pilgrim. [199] If the pilgrim is wealthy and a dignitary, the pilgrim-guide will try as hard as [he can] to collect from one to ten lira from him.

The earnings of the pilgrim-guides during the pilgrimage season varies. It may be from two hundred tomans to three thousand tomans for himself, his associates, and his agents.

---

[69] Sa^cdeyyeh is a more modern name for Yalamlam, the place where pilgrims coming from the town of Ṭâ'ef and other areas to the south-east of Mecca, notably the Yemen, put on the ritual pilgrimage garments.

[70] The *mokharrej* or "camel broker," was an official licensed by the Sharif of Mecca to rent out camels and other mounts to pilgrims travelling between Mecca and Jeddah; see Kazem Zadeh, *Relation*, pp. 13-14; Long, *Hajj*, pp. 46-47; Peters, *Jerusalem and Mecca*, pp. 231-32.

ARRIVAL OF NEW PILGRIMS

In the two or three days I was in Jedda, two ships arrived from Bushehr, Basra, and Baghdad. About a thousand Iranian pilgrims were on board them. The ship which came first anchored at the Jedda docks; the other ship followed it and came up beside the first ship with such speed that it struck the anchored ship. The anchored ship was immediately wrecked. The captain, the workers, and the pilgrims were alarmed. They left the cargo and baggage and cast themselves into rowboats. Since the land was near, the ship did not sink, but in the excitement and confusion some of the pilgrims' belongings were lost. Upon investigation and inquiry, it was learned that these two captains had previously had a grudge against each other and had been trying to destroy each other. In the end, they collected indemnities for the wreck from the captain and owner of the ship [that had caused the accident].

ACCOUNT OF THE PILGRIMS

At this point, I must write a brief description of the pilgrims, both Shi'ite and Sunni, Iranian and non-Iranian; and of how many pilgrims came to Mecca from each country, region, or direction; and of how many consuls there are in Jedda.

PILGRIMS FROM JAVA[71]

Every year, from eight to twenty thousand Javanese pilgrims come to Mecca.[72] These Javanese are mostly Dutch subjects, and some are English subjects. [200] All [of them] follow the Shâfeʿi rite. They converted to Islam two hundred years ago [*sic*].

Every year, pilgrim-guides go from Mecca to Java and accompany them. On behalf of the Dutch government, there is always a consul stationed in Jedda.[73] Every pilgrim pays their consul three Dutch reals (which is a qorush and a half more than the Levant

[71] By "Java," Farâhâni is really referring to all the various pilgrims from Indonesia and Malaysia rather than just Java proper. Hurgronje, *Mekka*, pp. 215-92, has a wealth of information about the Indonesian pilgrims and residents in Mecca; see also Kazem Zadeh, *Relation*, pp. 48-49.

[72] Farâhâni's estimate corresponds closely to the records preserved by other authorities. In 1880, for example, W. S. Blunt estimated the number of Malay (mostly Javanese) pilgrims at 12,000; see also the tables in Thomas Patrick Hughes, *A Dictionary of Islam* (London, 1885), p. 159; Roff, "Sanitation and Security," p. 150; Long, *Hajj*, pp. 125-29. Kazem Zadeh, *Relation*, p. 59, on the basis of official statistics, recorded 19,312 Javanese pilgrims in the 1910-11 pilgrimage season—more than any other national group coming from outside Arabia. The relatively large number of Indonesian pilgrims as compared to those from Iran, Egypt, North Africa or the Ottoman Empire, may, ironically, be attributed in large part to the efforts of Western, especially Dutch and British, shipping companies.

[73] The Dutch were among the first of the European powers to open a consulate in Jedda (1872); the various arrangements they made to facilitate (and to control) the pilgrimage by Indonesians are discussed in Roff, "Sanitation and Security,"

dollar, so three reals is equivalent to eighteen thousand dinars) for the visa. It is their custom, before initiating the pilgrimage, to notify the administration of their city of residence that "we are making the pilgrimage this year; and we will supply you with an amount of funds, so that you may inform the Dutch Consulate in Jedda that you have received such in our names, and that throughout the Hejaz region, upon requesting the funds, we shall receive them in exchange for your draft." Upon arrival in the Hejaz, they present the draft, which they have in hand, to the Dutch Consulate, whereupon they are enabled to make successive withdrawals, as needed, up to the amount for which they have contracted For this service, the pilgrims also pay a fee to the government and the consulate. Often, their stay in Mecca and Medina is as long as two years. The shape of their faces is usually like that of Chinese people. Their skin is copper-colored, and they have little hair. This year, about twelve thousand Javanese came to Mecca. They entered the Hejaz via Jedda and Yanboʿ.

PILGRIMS FROM INDIA

Every year from five thousand to twenty-five thousand Indian pilgrims come to Mecca the Exalted. They are mostly paupers and come by begging on sailing ships.[74] They beg in the streets and alleys. At night, they usually sleep in the alleys of Mecca and Jedda. They pass their time in utter misery. Many perish because of [their] poverty. Most are Ḥanafis, but there are also a few Shiʿites. [201]

Apart from these, pilgrims from Sind, Musqat, and Bahrain were also present. The Bahrainis are Shiʿites, and the Musqatis are Khârejis. All are subjects of the English government. There is

p. 149. See also Hurgronje, *Mekka*, p. 218; idem, "Der Hadji-politiek der Indischen Regerung," in *Verspreide Geschriften* (Bonn & Leiden, 1924), pp. 173-98; Carl Rathjens, *Die Pilgerfahrt nach Mekka: Von der Weihrauchstrasse zur Ölwirtschaft* (Hamburg, 1948), pp.103 ff. It is interesting to contrast Farâhâni's observations here about the relative financial security afforded the Javanese pilgrims with the poverty of the Indian and Malay Muslims under British rule, who were often regarded as the most impecunious of pilgrims; cf. John Lewis Burckhardt, *Travels in Arabia* (London, 1829), pp. 259 ff. The assessment of Rutter, *Holy Cities*, 1:88, was that "although the Malays never go on pilgrimage unless they have sufficient money for the purpose, they often suffer great hardship by reason of their inability to cope with the deceit and greed of the Arabs." For the views of southeast Asian pilgrims about the pilgrimage, see V. Matheson and A. C. Milner (eds.), *Perceptions of the Haj: Five Malay Texts* (Brookfield, 1986).

74 Cf. Burckhardt, *Travels*, p. 256-59. Keane, *Six Months in the Hejaz*, pp. 292 ff., noted the appalling conditions on the British ships bringing pilgrims from India and rightly observed the contrast between the energy the British placed into suppressing the maritime slave trade and their reluctance to do anything to improve the lot of Indian pilgrims (such as regulating shipping standards or supporting medical quarantines).

always a consul on behalf of the English government stationed in Jedda. Because most are paupers, there is little visa money and profit from them for their consul. He receives only a salary from his government. However, if someone deposits funds at the consulate, [the consul] charges a tenth of the deposit [as a fee]. If a person of property dies while in the Hejaz, the consulate takes charge [of his estate] and sends it home to his heirs. In this event, [the consul] will also receive some benefits.

Many wealthy inhabitants of India now reside in Jedda, Mecca, and Medina and thus have become neighbors of the holy places [*mojâver*]. This year no more than five thousand people had come to Mecca the Exalted from India, Sind, Musqat, and Bahrain owing to the disease in those regions. All entered the Hejaz via Jedda.

NORTH AFRICAN PILGRIMS

From two to ten thousand North African pilgrims come to Mecca every year. These are French subjects from Tunis and Algeria. They are of the Mâleki rite. They are generally corpulent, swarthy, have little hair, and are seditious, bellicose, and fanatical about their own religious rite. All come armed. There is always a deputy consul in Jedda on behalf of the French government. For the visa fee, each person pays five francs (each franc equals one Iranian riâl) to his consul. [202]

This year a few more than four thousand had come. They entered the Hejaz via Jedda and Yanbo[c].

PILGRIMS FROM HERZEGOVINA AND BOSNIA

Every year, from one hundred to four hundred pilgrims from Herzegovina and Bosnia come to Mecca the Exalted. These are usually blonde and fair, resembling the people of Europe. They are Austrian subjects. Most of them are of the Ḥanafi rite. There is always an Austrian consular deputy in Jedda to look out for them and to supervise the ships of the Austrian company. Each of these pilgrims pays his consul about one and a half Levant dollars for the visa. This year about two hundred people had come. All entered the Hejaz via Jedda.

GREEK PILGRIMS

Every year from one hundred to five hundred Greek pilgrims came to Mecca the Exalted. They used to be Ottoman subjects, but because of the Treaty of Berlin they became subjects of Greece. Their rite is Ḥanafi, but they are never fanatical about it. On behalf of the Greek government, there is an "agent-consul," that is a consular delegate, stationed in Jedda. Each of them also pays about one Levant dollar (which is about six thousand Iranian dinars) to their agent-consul for the travel document. About one hundred and fifty Greeks who are Christians live in Jedda. Each pays half a lira to their agent-consul for a residence permit. This year, about three hundred Greek pilgrims had come.

PILGRIMS FROM AFGHANISTAN

Every year, from two hundred to six hundred Afghan pilgrims come to Mecca the Exalted. They are subjects of the Amir of Afghanistan. They have no consulate. The English consul is in charge of their affairs. They do not pay anything for a visa. [203] They are of the Ḥanafi, Ḥanbali, and Shâfeᶜi rites. Also, a few are Shiʿites. They are armed and fanatical about their religious rite. This year about three hundred people had come. Most came by way of India and entered [the Hejaz] via Jedda.

PILGRIMS FROM BOKHARA AND TURKISTAN

Every year from two hundred to one thousand pilgrims from Bokhara and Turkistan come [to Mecca].[75] Some of them are Russian subjects, and some of them are of indeterminate nationality. There is also no representative of Russia in the Hejaz. They are mostly of the Ḥanafi and Shâfeᶜi rite. A few, too, are Shiʿites. This type is very corpulent, large-headed, pale, with little hair, hot-tempered, ill-fed, and dirty. Many become ill and die. In this area, they are known as "Tatars." Since some are Russian subjects, the Ottoman government does not collect the toll [*khâveh*] from them. This year about seven hundred had come. Most came by way of Istanbul and entered [the Hejaz] via Jedda.

PILGRIMS FROM THE CAUCASUS

Every year from three hundred to six hundred pilgrims from the Caucasus come to Mecca the Exalted. Some are inhabitants of Daghestan and [belong to the ethnic] groups of the Chechen and Lezg. This type is robust, tall in stature, with long beards; their dress resembles that of the Turkomans. Their origin goes back to the Mongols. They are Shâfeᶜis. All of them always come armed. Some others are from Ganjeh, Shemakha, Baku, Tiflis, and Shirvân and are considered to be Georgians. They are mostly Shiʿites. They also have a few Sunnis. They bring lots of money and sumptuous things. [204] All are Russian subjects, but they also do not pay the toll. This year, there were five hundred [of them]. All had come by way of Istanbul and arrived via Jedda and Yanboᶜ.

[75] Cf. Kazem Zadeh, *Relation*, pp. 51-55.

IRANIAN PILGRIMS

Every year from one thousand to eight thousand Iranian pilgrims come to Mecca the Exalted. All of them are subjects of the lofty government of Iran. They are of the Shi'ite sect except for a few who come from Kurdistan and some of the ports of Fârs who are Sunnis. There is a consul on behalf of the Iranian government in Jedda. Sometimes he is permanently stationed in Jedda, such as previously [was the case with] Aḥmad Bayk, who was for years the consul stationed in Jedda. Other times, he is [there] on a temporary basis; that is to say, he comes to Jedda three months before the pilgrimage season and leaves two months after the end of the pilgrimage. Thus for several years now, Ḥâjji Mirzâ Ḥasan Khân, Moḥammad Khân, or Rażi Khân, who are all employees of the Istanbul embassy, have at times been consuls [there]. This year, Ḥâjji Mirzâ Ḥabibollah Khân Kâshi was the consul. A privilege that the consul of Iran has–beyond that of the consuls of other countries–is that since he is a Muslim he can enter Mecca, Medina, ᶜArafât, etc., and accompany the [Iranian] subjects everywhere. The Sharif and the Pâshâ also have high regard for him. Each of the Iranian pilgrims who enter the Hejaz via Jedda pay the consul in Jedda one and a quarter Levant dollars (which is about 7,500 dinars in Iranian money) for the visa. If the consul learns that a pilgrim who is an Iranian subject dies in the Hejaz he takes a part of his estate. A tenth of whatever is involved in litigation also goes to the consul. For each camel the Iranian pilgrims hire to either Saᶜdeyyeh or Mecca, a fee goes to the consul, the pilgrim-guide, and the camel broker. For every camel that is hired from Mecca to Medina and Yanboᶜ another sum will also go to the consulate. [205] The ḥamleh-dârs who go along the Syrian and Mountain[76] routes are supposed to pay one imperial or one lira as the transport tax for each of the Iranian pilgrims (other than the ḥajjeh-forush) they transport. However, the ḥamleh-dârs cheat and do not tell how many pilgrims they have transported. Often they have transported fifty people and only report thirty.

IRANIAN SUBJECTS

At the most, there are no more than twenty-five Iranian subjects who reside in Jedda and Mecca. Of these, several, as follows, are

[76] Text: *jabal*. By Jabal ("Mountain"), Farâhâni is referring to the Jabal Shammâr region of north central Arabia. The caravan route, which going from the Hejaz to southern Iraq via Hâil, which Farâhâni discusses more fully later in his account, passed through this area. Hereafter, this will be referred to as the "Mountain Route" or "Mountain Caravan."

Iranian merchants: Ḥâjji Moḥammad Kâzeruni, a Shi'ite; Ḥâjji Mollâ Ḥosayn Lâri, a Shi'ite; Ḥâjji Moḥammad Bâqer Lâri, a Shi'ite; Ḥâjji ᶜAbdollah Kâẓem, of Bandar Lengeh, a Sunnite; Zayn[77] ᶜAli Rezâ, of Bandar Lengeh, a Sunnite; Zayn Abo'l-Qâsem ᶜEvażi, a native of Bandar ᶜAbbâs and a Sunnite.[78] The rest of those twenty-five people are laborers.

Each of these Iranian subjects also pays half a lira to the consul of Iran for the residence visa.

ACCOUNT OF THE PILGRIMS FROM IRAN THIS YEAR

This year, a few more than three thousand [pilgrims] had come from Iran to Mecca the Exalted. That is to say, eight hundred came by the Syrian route, of whom fifty had died from [the effects of] thirst and the simoom. About one hundred people came via the Mountain Route by clandestine means or in disguise. Twelve hundred people came by way of Bushehr, Bandar ᶜAbbâs, and Baghdad and entered via Jedda. Also, more than a thousand came by way of Istanbul and entered via Jedda and Yanboᶜ. About seven hundred of these pilgrims were ḥajjeh-forushes, ᶜakkâm, dervishes, and paupers, so no one got any profit from them. There were a few more than two thousand [actual] pilgrims. The Iranian pilgrims, compared to other pilgrims, were better [provisioned] and organized, in respect of expenses, housekeeping necessities, tents, and so on. [206] This year there were no prominent Iranian ulama or dignitaries in Mecca. The individuals among the group who were somewhat well known included:

Ḥâjji Mollâ Reżâ-ye Astarâbâdi, who looks like a eunuch[79] and is one of the ulama of Astarâbâd.

Ḥâjji Mir Moḥammad ᶜAli Mojtahed Ṭehrâni, son of the late Âqâ Sayyed Mortażâ Ṭehrâni, who usually resides in the ᶜAtabât.[80]

---

[77] Here and in the following name, the text reads Zinal rather than Zayn.

[78] Several of these individuals were still active in 1910 when Kazem Zadeh wrote his account. He noted that Ḥosayn Lâri was a very well known merchant who had been established in Jedda for forty years; Moḥammad ᶜAli Lâri, a merchant and sometime member of the Iranian consular staff, was his son; Zaynal ᶜAli Reżâ and his brother ᶜAbdollah were directors of the Nâṣeri navigation company, an Iranian enterprise founded by merchants in southern Iran in the time of Nâṣer od-Din Shâh to provide transportation from Bushehr to Jedda. See Kazem Zadeh, *Relation*, pp. 3-5, 8.

[79] Presumably Farâhâni means no disrespect by this remark but is merely noting that this man, unlike most members of the ulama, is beardless. However, it may be recalled that Farâhâni's comments on Mollâ Reżâ's actions during the storm on the Black Sea (Part Three, p. 98) were also tinged with a degree of sarcasm.

[80] The ᶜAtabât are the Shi'ite holy cities in Iraq such as Karbala (site of Imam Ḥosayn's martyrdom) and Najaf (burial place of Imam ᶜAli).

Abu'l-Ḥasan Mirzâ Shaykh or-Ra'is,[81] a resident of the Holy Land, who had fled from Âṣaf od-Dowleh.[82]

Ḥâjji Mirzâ Fażlollah, who is one of the mojtaheds of Shiraz.

Mirzâ Reżâ, the secretary to the late ᶜAla' od-Dowleh, who now is a *lashkar-nevis*.[83]

Mirzâ Musâ, son of Mirzâ ᶜAli Reżâ, the *mostowfi* [state accountant] of Khorasan, who was also a refugee from Âṣaf od-Dowleh.

Ḥâjji Mirzâ Aḥmad Khorâsâni, the mostowfi of [the shrine of] Ḥażrat-e Emâm Reżâ, [and] the son of Moᶜtamad ot-Towleyyeh.

The wife of the Navvâb Nayer od-Dowleh Parviz Mirzâ.

The wife of ᶜAlâ' ol-Molk.[84]

Ḥâjji Amir Khân the Sarhang, son of Amin-e Divân Gilâni.

OTTOMAN TURKISH PILGRIMS

There are from five thousand to twelve thousand pilgrims from Istanbul, Anatolia, Rumelia, and Trabzon every year. Although they belong to the four [Sunnite] rites, most are like dervishes and are Sunni mystics [*sonni-ye ṣufi*]. A few Shi'ites can also be found among them. [207]

They are never fanatical about religious rites. They are usually very peaceable. All are Ottoman subjects. Each person pays one and a quarter majidis (about seven thousand dinars in Iranian money) for the visa to the agent of the Ottoman government in

---

[81] Shaykh or-Ra'is (1264-1336/1847-1918) was the only prince of the Qâjâr royal family to become a member of the ulama. See M. Farhâd-Moᶜtamad, "Nâṣer od-Din Shâh va Shaykh or-Ra'is," *Yaghmâ* 3(1329/1950-51):343-344; ᶜAli Javâher-kalâm, "Shâhzâdeh Abu'l-Ḥasan Mirzâ Shaykh or-Ra'is Qâjâr," *Armaghân* 40(1350/1971-72):165-70; ᶜAli-naqi Behruzi, "Shaykh or-Ra'is Qâjâr va moṭâyebât-e u," *Armaghân* 40(1350/1971-72):352-54; Bâmdâd, *Rejâl*, 1:42-43.

[82] The reference is to ᶜAbd ol-Vahhâb Khân Shirâzi, the extremely stern governor of Khorasan (1301-3/1883-86); see Benjamin, *Persia and the Persians*, pp. 235-236; Bamdâd, *Rejâl*, 2:301-17; ᶜAbbâs Eqbâl, "Mirzâ ᶜAbd ol-Vahhâb Khân Âṣaf od-Dowleh," *Yâdgâr* 5/vi(1327-28/1948-49):27-37. Farhâd-Moᶜtamad, "Nâṣer od-Din," and Bâmdâd, *Rejâl*, 1:42-43, confirm that he attempted to arrest Shaykh or-Ra'is, but the latter was forewarned and managed to flee via Ashkabad, eventually taking asylum in the Ottoman Empire. This was probably because Shaykh or-Ra'is was the son of Âṣaf od-Dowleh's rival, Moḥammad Taqi Mirzâ Rokn od-Dowleh, whom Âṣaf od-Dowleh replaced as governor of Khorâsân. In exile, Shaykh or-Ra'is became a supporter of the pan-Islamism of Jamâl od-Din Afghâni and the Ottoman Sultan ᶜAbd ol-Ḥamid II. Even after his death he had powerful enemies in Khorâsân who prevented his burial in Mashhad.

[83] An officer responsible for keeping records of the army roll call and salary assignments; on the origin and duties of this office in earlier times see V. Minorsky, *Tadhkirat al-Mulûk: A Manual of Safavid Administration* (London, 1943), pp. 75; 141-42; Dehkhodâ, *Loghatnâmeh*, 39:199.

[84] According to Eᶜtemâd os-Salṭaneh, *Ma'âs̱er*, p. 237, this title was held (in 1306/1889) by a certain Ḥâjj Mirzâ ᶜAbdollah Khân.

Jedda. This year about seven thousand people had come. Most entered the Hejaz via Jedda and Yanbo[c].

PILGRIMS FROM EGYPT AND ITS DEPENDENCIES[85]

Every year from two thousand to seven thousand pilgrims from Egypt and its dependencies come. They are subjects of the Khedive of Egypt. Most are Shâfe[c]is or Ḥanafis. There might also be Esmâ[c]ilis, Zaydis, and Twelver Shi'ites[86] among them. There are many women and children with them. Each person pays the administration of Jedda one and a quarter majidis for the visa. Also, for every camel that carries Egyptian pilgrims, one-quarter majidi goes to the administration. Two Levant dollars, which is about twelve thousand dinars in Iranian money, goes to the governor of the Hejaz and the Sharif of Mecca for each of the camels which goes from Egypt and its dependencies towards Medina and transports pilgrims as a tax for grazing rights. According to what some of them said, about six thousand had come this year in order to make the "Greater Pilgrimage."[87] They accompanied the [ma]ḥmal of [c]Âyesheh,[88] which is conveyed with veneration and respect through all areas of the Hejaz by soldiers and the *amin-e ṣorreh*.[89] They

---

[85] The Egyptian pilgrimage has been described in great detail by the leader of the caravan for many years, Ebrâhim Ref[c]at Pâshâ, *Mer'ât ol-ḥaramayn* (Cairo, 1344/1925).

[86] These are the three major Shi'ite sects still in existence.

[87] A pilgrimage year in which the day of [c]Arafât falls on a Friday; see Burton, *Personal Narrative*, 2:218; Keane, *Six Months in the Hejaz*, p. 106.

[88] The *maḥmel* (colloquial *maḥmal*) was a framework box, covered with a richly embroidered cloth and other ornaments, carried on camelback to Mecca. One, popularly known as the Maḥmal of [c]Âyesheh, came with the Egyptian caravan; another, the Maḥmal of the Prophet, came with the Syrian caravan. This practice was probably an innovation dating from the thirteenth century, when it was introduced by some of the Mamluk rulers of Egypt to convey the presents bestowed on the shrines and inhabitants of Mecca and Medina. By Farâhâni's time, as Rutter, *Holy Cities*, p. 169, puts it, "the Mahmal serves no purpose save that of a banner or emblem of state." The continuation of this practice became a matter of contention after the Sa[c]udi takeover of the Hejaz and was eventually abandoned. See E. W. Lane, *Manners and Customs of the Modern Egyptians* (London, 1860), pp. 444-46; Kazem Zadeh, *Relation*, pp. 45-48; Gaudefroy-Demombynes, *Pèlerinage*, pp. 157-66; Ref[c]at, *Mer'ât*, 1:5-12 etc.; Long, *Hajj*, pp. 108-109; A. Robinson, "The Mahmal," *JRAS* 18(1931):117-27; J. Jomier, *Le Mahmal et la caravan égyptienne des pèlerins de la Mekke, xiii[e]-xx[e] siècles* (Cairo, 1953).

[89] Known in Turkish as the Sürre Emini, a dignitary entrusted with delivery of the gifts sent annually by the ruler to Mecca; see Pakalın, *Deyimleri*, 3:283. The *ṣorreh* or "purse" was especially intended to provide the funds to pay the Bedouin tribesmen to allow the pilgrims to pass safely through their territory. On the financial aspects of the pilgrimage in Ottoman times, see R. Tresse, *Le pèlerinage syrien aux villes saints de l'Islam* (Paris, 1937), pp.71-74; Peters, *Jerusalem and Mecca*, pp. 48-49, 185-86, 199-206; W. Ochsenwald, "Ottoman Subsidies to the Hejaz, 1877-1886," *International Journal of Middle East Studies* 6(1975):300-307.

accompany the *kesveh*[90] every year. The Khedival government spends exorbitant sums yearly on the expenses for the [ma]ḥmal and the kesveh. They come overland to Mecca and Medina.

PILGRIMS FROM JABAL [SHAMMÂR] AND ARAB IRAQ

Every year from two hundred to six hundred pilgrims from Jabal [Shammâr] and Arab Iraq come to Mecca the Exalted. They are Ottoman subjects. They pay nothing for visas. They come by land. Some of them are Shi'ites, and some [208] are Sunnis. This year three hundred people had come.

PILGRIMS FROM SYRIA

Every year from five hundred to fifteen hundred Syrian pilgrims come. They are Ottoman subjects. Most are of the Shâfeᶜi rite. They also have [some] Khârejis and Yazidis. They come overland with the [ma]ḥmal of the Prophet. For years, Saᶜid Pâshâ has brought the [ma]ḥmal to Mecca in perfect order and regularity, [accompanied by] the amin-e ṣorreh, soldiers, and cannons. Enormous sums are given by the Ottoman government for this purpose. Since the Syrians are accompanying the [ma]ḥmal, they pay nothing for visas, tolls, etc. This year, due to it being the "Greater Pilgrimage," about 1,600 people had come.

PILGRIMS FROM THE ARABIAN PENINSULA

The pilgrims of the Yemen, Medina, Mecca, Ṭâ'ef, Jedda, Yanboᶜ, Râbegh, and the Bedouin, who are all subjects of the province of the Hejaz, are all Sunnis of the four [Sunni] rites. A few Twelver and Zaydi Shi'ites are also found among them. Every year, from forty thousand to fifty thousand attend the pilgrimage. They pay nothing to the government or the Sharif, except for the camel drivers and ḥamleh-dârs who will pay various fees to the sharif and the pâshâ for each camel they hire to a pilgrim, according to whether from Jedda to Mecca, Jedda to Saᶜdeyyeh, Mecca to ᶜArafât, or Mecca to Medina and Yanboᶜ. This year about fifty thousand people of the Hejaz performed the pilgrimage.

FARES FOR PILGRIMS IN THE PROVINCE OF THE HEJAZ

In order for the pilgrims to hire riding animals throughout the Hejaz–from Jedda to Saᶜdeyyeh and Mecca or from Mecca to ᶜArafât or from Mecca to Medina and Yanboᶜ–a camel broker [*mokharrej*] is designated by the Sharif for each [national] group of pilgrims.[91] That is, six people have been designated as camel

[90] A special cloth covering for the Kaaba, traditionally donated by the ruler of Egypt. See Lane, *Manners and Customs*, p. 486 and below Part Five, n. 51.

[91] Cf. Long, *Hajj*, pp. 46-47.

brokers: one is the [209] camel broker for the Iranian pilgrims; another is the camel broker for the Ottoman pilgrims; another is the camel broker for the people of Java; another is the camel broker for the Indian pilgrims; another is the camel broker for the North African pilgrims; and another is the camel broker for the Egyptian pilgrims. Their work is that they sit down together and take counsel and fix the hiring rates every year according to the situation. The hiring of riding animals by the pilgrims in every part of the Hejaz is with their knowledge, assignment, and assistance. For example, the camel brokers fix whatever rate they desire for the fare from Mecca to Medina, or from Medina to Yanboᶜ or Jedda. Whatever the amount of the fare they determine is put into practice, and no one will disagree. For each camel, a fee is expected for the Sharif, the consul, the pilgrim-guide, and themselves and is added to the fare. The camel broker for the Iranians is an individual named Moḥammad Kâboli, whom the late Ḥosâm os-Salṭaneh[92] had bastinadoed. Every Iranian must hire riding animals with his advice and approval. All of these camel brokers have gotten very wealthy.

THE PLACE FOR PUTTING ON THE EḤRÂM

One of the subjects [I] must write about at this point [concerns] the place at which the pilgrims who have travelled from afar must put on the *eḥrâm*.[93]

[92] Prince Solṭân Morâd Mirzâ Ḥosâm os-Salṭaneh (1233-1300/1818-83), the brother of Moḥammad Shâh (and uncle of Nâṣer od-Din Shâh), was a distinguished member of the Qâjâr royal family, who served as governor of Khorasan, helped arrange Nâṣer od-Din's visit to the Ottoman empire, and accompanied the shâh on his trip to Europe. See Eᶜtemâd os-Salṭaneh, *Târikh-e montaẓam*, 3:381; idem, *Ruznâmeh*, p. 143; Dehkhodâ, *Loghatnâmeh*, 16:536; Bakhash, *Iran*, p. 380; Bâmdâd, *Rejâl*, 2:104-10. The narrative of his visit to Mecca in 1297/1880, entitled *Dalil ol-anâm fi sabil ziârat baytollah ol-ḥaram*, is extant but unedited: see Storey, *Persian Literature*, p. 1157.

[93] An area surrounding Mecca for several miles in all directions constitutes the sacred territory (*ḥarâm*). Upon entering this territory, usually at certain specified places on the perimeter of the harâm, would-be pilgrims must declare their intention to perform a pilgrimage and put on the ritual eḥrâm garments. For men, this consists of two pieces of cloth measuring about six feet by three and a half feet each; they may be of any material (except silk) or color (but white is much preferred) but must be seamless. One is worn wrapped around the waist; the other is draped over the back, leaving the right arm and shoulder exposed. The head and the instep of the foot must be left uncovered. Having done this, the pilgrim becomes *moḥrem*; that is, he is obligated to follow a number of special regulations (discussed below) to maintain his ritual purity. On this ritual, see M. Gaudefroy-Demombynes, *Le Pèlerinage à la Mekke* (Paris, 1923), pp. 168-91; Rutter, *Holy Cities*, 1:96; Refᶜat, *Mer'ât*, 1:100-107; Querry, *Droit Musulman*, 1:240-48. According to Muslim tradition, Moḥammad designated five specific spots as the stations, or *miqât*, at which this ritual should be performed: Ẕu'l-Ḥolayfah for pilgrims coming from Medina; Joḥfeh for those coming from Syria; Qarn ol-Manâzel for those coming from Najd (central Arabia);

As for the pilgrims who enter the province of the Hejaz via the port of Yanbo^c^, there are only two options: whether to go from Yanbo^c^ to Medina the Agreeable or not to go [that way]. If they go to Medina and want to go from Medina towards Mecca, the Shi'ites must put on the eḥrâm at the Masjed-e Shajareh ["Mosque of the Tree"], popularly known as Be'r ^c^Ali.[94] It is the miqât place of Z̲u'l-Ḥolayfeh.[95] It is one and a half farsakhs from Medina. The Sunnis do not put on the eḥrâm at the Masjed-e Shajareh. [210] They go to the village of Râbegh and put on the eḥrâm there.

If the transit of the pilgrims who come via the Syrian route should be by Medina the Illuminated, the Shi'ites put on the eḥrâm at the Mosque of the Tree and the Sunnis in the village of Râbegh which is nearly opposite the miqât place of Joḥfeh. Joḥfeh used to be a village beside the sea three farsakhs from Râbegh.[96] Now it has fallen into ruins. Traces of its ruins are extant.

Since the pilgrims who come by the Mountain route do not transit via Medina, the Shi'ites put on the eḥrâm in the Wadi ^c^Aqiq, which is three days journey from Mecca in the desert. The Sunnites enter the state of eḥrâm two days journey from Mecca at the place they call [Z̲at-e] ^c^Erq, which is a village.[97]

As for the Sunni pilgrims who come via the Suez route to Jedda, they are usually not fastidious about these matters. They are common people. As soon as the steamer is twelve hours out of Suez, they put on the eḥrâm group by group [while] on board the steamer. Their elite people and holy men put on the eḥrâm twelve hours before [reaching] Jedda, which they say is parallel to Joḥfeh. The

---

Yalamlam for those coming from the Yemen; and Z̲ât-e ^c^Erq for those coming from Iraq. See, for example, Moḥammad ol-Azraqi, *AkhbârMakkeh* (ed. Roshdi Molḥas; Madrid, n.d.), 2:130-31 and 2:310 (appendix 2); Aḥmad b. Moḥammad ol-Ḥadrâvi, *Ketâb ol-^c^eqd os̲-s̲amin fi fażâ'el ol-balad ol-amin* (Mecca, 1314/1896), pp. 10-11; Kazem Zadeh, *Relation*, pp. 55-57; Rutter, *Holy Cities*, 1:98; Gaudefroy-Demombynes, *Pèlerinage*, 16-25. As Farâhâni's account implies, the problem of when pilgrims arriving by sea should perform eḥrâm was not anticipated in the traditions: Farâhâni discusses two of the possible solutions to this problem—putting on the eḥrâm when parallel to one of the canonical miqât or making a second trip to one of those spots and performing the eḥrâm a second time. See also Gaudefroy-Demombynes, *Pèlerinage*, pp. 21-22.

94 Explicitly vocalized Bor ^c^Ali in the text. It is a place about about ten miles southwest of Medina. See Azraqi, *Akhbâr*, 2:310; Gaudefroy-Demombynes, *Pèlerinage*, p. 20. On the mosque, see below, Part Six, p. 256.

95 Text: Z̲u'l-Khalifeh. Cf. Farhâd Mirzâ, *Hedâyat*, pp. 172-73.

96 See Abdollah Wohaibi, *The Northern Hijaz in the Writings of the Arab Geographers* (Beirut, 1973), pp. 102-12.

97 See ^c^Atiq b. Ghays̲ Belâdi, *Mo^c^jam ma^c^âlem ol-ḥejâz* (Ṭâ'ef, 1978-), 6:77-78.

captain, ulama, and knowledgeable people announce that [the boat] is at the parallel of Joḥfeh. The Shi'ites consider wearing the eḥrâm cloth when opposite [the correct place] to be correct, and they put on the eḥrâm when the captain, ulama, knowledgeable people, and other good Muslims say they have determined that [they] are parallel [to the correct place], likewise twelve hours before [reaching] Jedda.[98] They enter Jedda and Mecca in the same eḥrâm clothes. Some others, in order to be sure of being correct, go in this same eḥrâm dress to Saᶜdeyyeh, which is the miqât place of Yalamlam.[99] There, they put on the eḥrâm again and enter Mecca with the second eḥrâm clothes. [211] A few do not consider putting on the eḥrâm when parallel [to the usual place] to be correct at all. They say nothing has come down in the traditions that putting on the eḥrâm when parallel [to the usual place] is proper. Thus, they do not put on the eḥrâm at sea; they enter Jedda in their ordinary dress, then go from Jedda to Saᶜdeyyeh, and in Saᶜdeyyeh, which is the canonical [*sharᶜi*] miqât place, put on the eḥrâm and enter Mecca.

It is a three day journey from Jedda to Saᶜdeyyeh by camel and litter. That is, one reaches the well of Saᶜdeyyeh on the third day. One stops there for a day, and from there to Mecca is a two day trip, so one reaches Mecca the morning of the sixth day. However, the Saᶜdeyyeh route is rather waterless, desolate and hot.

The fare for [the camel for] a litter from Jedda to Saᶜdeyyeh and Mecca is fifteen Levant dollars.[100] The litter itself is rented for three Levant dollars. Thus the fare for camel and litter is eighteen Levant dollars.

A few of the Shi'ites also put on the eḥrâm [while] on board ship opposite Joḥfeh and entered Jedda and Mecca wearing that same eḥrâm. They circumambulated the House of God and [then] took off the eḥrâm. Then, for the sake of correctness, they went from Mecca to Qarn ol-Manâzel and put on the eḥrâm again there. They entered Mecca and again performed the lesser circumambulation of the Kaaba in compliance with the *ᶜomreh-ye tamattoᶜ*.[101]

---

[98] Sayf od-Dowleh, *Safarnâmeh*, p. 124, says the Sunnis put on the eḥrâm at the parallel of Râbegh but the Shi'ites do so at the parallel of Joḥfeh.

[99] This miqât was the one visited in 1925 by Rutter, who approached Mecca from the south; see Rutter, *Holy Cities*, pp. 94-95.

[100] As noted above, Part Three, n. 114, Farâhâni is referring to Levant dollars (Maria Theresa thalers), the preferred currency in the Hejaz. For another very detailed account of the transport fares, see Refᶜat, *Mer'ât*, 1:65-71.

[101] This term refers to one of several different ways of performing the ritual visit to Mecca. It is discussed more fully below.

[QARN OL-]MANÂZEL AND THE MIQÂT PLACE

From Mecca to Qarn ol-Manâzel is ten farsakhs, or five [farsakhs] from the miqât place. It is the miqât place for the people of Yemen and has been mentioned in the resplendent divine law. It is situated on the outskirts of Ṭâ'ef. It has very good water and climate. In this area there are running streams and varieties of fruit, especially pomegranates, grapes, and figs. [212]

THE BOROUGH OF ṬÂ'EF

The borough of Ṭâ'ef is half a parasang from Qarn ol-Manâzel. The tomb of ᶜAbdollah ebn-e ᶜAbbâs,[102] cousin of the prophet, is in this town. It is a shrine with a lofty white-washed tomb. This ᶜAbdollah was one of the pupils and disciples of Ḥażrat-e Amir ol-Mo'minin ᶜAli ebn-e Abi Ṭâleb. He had disputes with ᶜÂyesheh and some of the Companions [of the prophet.] He was among the retinue with [ᶜAli] at the Battle of Ṣiffin. After the death of [ᶜAli], he was not subservient to [the Umayyad caliph] Moᶜâveyyeh and consistently vilified him. To the end of [his] life, he stayed at home and gave lessons on the science of jurisprudence [*feqh*]. He was born three years before the hegira and died in the year 68 [687-88] in Ṭâ'ef. The length of his blessed life has been recorded as seventy-one or seventy-two years.

ᶜARAFÂT

ᶜArafât[103] is on the Qarn ol-Manâzel route. All along the Qarn ol-Manâzel route there are coffeehouses and good water [sources]. Usually one traverses that route by ambling-paced horses, donkeys, or mules. For cautious [or] indolent people, going by the Qarn ol-Manâzel route is very good. They might spend several days in these villages which are in the suburbs of Ṭâ'ef and enjoy themselves.

The situation for Shi'ite pilgrims who come via Basra and Bushehr to Jedda is just like that of the pilgrims who come from the direction of Suez to Jedda. There is not much difference.

---

[102] ᶜAbdollah, son of the Prophet Moḥammad's uncle ᶜAbbâs, was one of the most famous ancestors of the later Abbasid dynasty of caliphs. He was highly regarded for his knowledge of hadith and a supporter of ᶜAli in his struggle against the Umayyads. He was expelled to Ṭâ'ef during the revolt of Ebn Zobayr in Mecca (65-73/684-93). On the ruined condition of this shrine following the bloody Wahhâbi conquest of Ṭâ'ef, see Rutter, *Holy Cities*, 2:29. On Ṭâ'ef in general see Refᶜat, *Mer'ât*, 1:344-53.

[103] ᶜArafât (or ᶜArafeh) is the name of a hill and adjacent plain located several miles east of Mecca; it serves as the site of one of the major ceremonies of the pilgrimage. Cf. Refᶜat, *Mer'ât*, 1:335-41; Burton, *Personal Narrative*, 2:186-89.

THE CITY OF JEDDA

As for the city of Jedda,[104] it is next to the sea. Its water [source] is rainwater. All around it is a wall, three zar^c high, of stone and mud. Jedda has two gates. One is to the east, which is the direction of Mecca (and thus the kiblah in Jedda is towards the east). One gate is on the west side, towards the sea. [213]

Outside the eastern gate is a mosque in which they say [the Prophet Moḥammad] took shelter and performed the ritual prayers. Outside the gate beside the sea they have built some houses and coffeehouses. There are about 16,000 families residing in Jedda, which is 45,000 people. It has about 1,300 shops. Its bazaars are spacious and made of platforms with awnings. Its streets are also wide. However the bazaars and streets are dirty and unpaved. Many of its buildings are of three or four storeys. It has numerous coffee houses.

CLIMATE

Its air and ground are both very damp, but the air is more humid than the ground. One can never sleep outdoors. Because of this humidity, its heat is not very severe.[105] The rain water is collected in pools and cisterns. Water-carriers bring [it] to the houses and sell [it]. Due to the humidity, the water is warm and does not get cold. It is also a little salty.

TRADE AND PRODUCTS

This city is a commercial center. There are Iranian, Indian, Dutch, and Greek merchants. The products of this city which are exported to [other] areas are white and black coral [*yosr*], [other varieties of] coral [*merjân*], and pearls. The various coral items that are exported to the bordering countries are made in Jedda itself. They have several coral-working shops.

AGRICULTURE AND FRUITS

There are no cultivated areas, date-groves, or trees here. All the food and drink is imported. They bring pomegranates, grapes, and green vegetables from Ṭâ'ef. Some fruit also comes from Mt. Sinai. They import good watermelons from Suez. [214]

---

104 For other accounts of Jedda, see Burckhardt, *Travels*, pp. 1-52; Kazem Zadeh, *Relation*, pp. 19-33; Wohaibi, *Northern Hijaz*, pp. 91-101; Ref^cat, *Mer'ât*, 1:19-24 (with many contemporary photographs).

105 So in the text. One would think that the humidity would make the weather seem even more oppressive, especially to someone like Farâhâni coming from the arid climate of Iran.

ADMINISTRATION

Jedda is the seat of a qâ'em-maqâm. Its qâ'em-maqâm is appointed by Istanbul, but he is under the authority of the governor of the Hejaz who is in Mecca. The qâ'em-maqâm administers the city of Jedda. The Sharif of Mecca does not interfere in any way with it.[106] The city is not disorderly, but outside the city, [things] are extremely chaotic. The Bedouin of the desert are lying in wait for a chance to steal [something]. Three or four people, even ten or twelve, are not bold enough to go from Jedda to Mecca. [The Bedouin] are constantly robbing people. There are two hundred foot soldiers and a hundred dromedary-mounted [troops] here on behalf of the Ottoman government. The soldiers come every year from Istanbul; the dromedary-mounted [troops] are from the province of the Hejaz itself. They also have about twenty cannons in Jedda.

THE CEMETERY

To the northeast, outside the citadel of Jedda, there is a cemetery, popularly known as the Jedda Cemetery, which has a two zar^c high wall around it. Just as one enters the door of that enclosed cemetery, there is another structure, shaped like a tomb, which is about 150 zar^c long and forty zar^c wide. They say this is the tomb of the grandmother of the human race, i. e. Eve.[107] At the door of the cemetery, there is a small mausoleum which they say is the place [where] Eve's head is [located].

In the middle of this double-walled tomb-like building, there is a dome under which there is a cenotaph[108] and a stone set up. They say this is the site of Eve's navel. The end of the grave is in another place which they say is the site of Eve's foot.

The grave of ^cOsmân Pâshâ, [former] governor of Jedda, is also in the same area as Eve's grave. I heard that one of the main requests

---

106 One of the results of the opening of the Suez Canal was that the Ottoman government after 1870 was in a better position to attempt to assert its control over the Hejaz at the expense of the Sharifate. One of the first steps in this process was the reinforcement of its position in Jedda: see Gaury, *Rulers of Mecca*, pp. 253 ff.

107 See Burton, *Personal Narrative*, 2:273-75; Kazem Zadeh, *Relation*, pp. 25-27; Angelo Pesce, *Jiddah. Portrait of an Arabian City* (Cambridge, 1974), pp. 126-30 (which includes a detailed sketch of the structure). This shrine was destroyed by the Wahhâbis in 1928.

108 Text: *żariḥ*. There is no precise English equivalent for this term which can refer to a variety of structures, usually of stone, wood, or precious metals, built over a burial site. There are drawings of this supposed tomb of Eve in Burton, *Personal Narrative*, p. 274, and Pesce, *Jiddah*, pp. 128-29, which will help in visualizing the structure Farâhâni is trying somewhat awkwardly to describe.

of his eminence Navvâb Mo^c^tamad od-Dowleh to the Ottoman government is the disinterment of this ^c^O̱smân Pâshâ.[109] [215]

The tomb of Eve is a shrine for Shi'ites and Sunnites. It has an ignorant, stupid custodian who insists that the pilgrims kiss the place which [represents] the navel of the grandmother [Eve]. For this same reason, the city of Jedda has been named "Grandmother" [*jaddeh*].[110]

According to reports, Solṭân Solaymân the Ottoman extended the present wall around the city.

GENERAL LOCATION OF JEDDA AND ITS BOUNDARIES

This Jedda [marks] the beginning of the province of the Hejaz, which is one of the Arab lands. The lands of the Arabs and Yemen, as Nâṣer-e Khosrow has defined them in his *Safarnâmeh* [*Travel Book*],[111] are: The land of Yemen [which] is located to the south of the Hejaz (so the Hejaz and Yemen are adjacent). The [people of] Yemen are called Himyarites, and [those of] the Hejaz Arabs. The eastern border of both lands is the Sea of Oman, and the western [border] the Qolzom Sea, which is also called the Red Sea. Their southern [border] is the ocean. The length of this peninsula, which [consists] of Yemen and the Arab lands, from Kufa to Aden is 500 parasangs from north to south. Its breadth, which [goes] from the city of Oman to Jâr,[112] is 400 parasangs from west to east. The Arab land is from Kufa to Mecca, and the Himyarite land is from Mecca to Aden. In the Arab lands, there are few inhabited places. The people are mostly Bedouin. In the Himyarite lands, there are three

---

109 See Farhâd Mirzâ, *Hedâyat*, p. 204. He says that this ^c^O̱smân Pâshâ died in 1261/1845. Keane, *Six Months in the Hejaz*, p. 285, mentions an ^c^O̱smân Pâshâ responsible for repairing the tomb of Eve. He may have been the father of the ^c^O̱smân Pâshâ who was the governor at the time of Farâhâni's visit and is famous for his rivalry with Sharif ^c^Awn.

110 The proximity of the supposed tomb of Eve to Jedda seems to be the inspiration for this popular etymology. However, it is a fanciful explanation since the proper vocalization of the name of the city is *joddeh*, an altogether different word in Arabic from *jaddeh.*

111 The rest of this paragraph closely follows Nâṣer-e Khosrow's account; cf. Schefer, *Sefer Nameh*, pp. 190-92 (Thackston, p. 43). Other descriptions of the boundaries of the Hejaz may be found in Wohaibi, *Northern Hijaz*, pp. 17-31; Ref^c^at, *Mer'ât*, 1:143-49.

112 Text: "to B-khâr" (*tâ b-khâr.*) Schefer, *Sefer Nameh*, p. 191 (p. 69 in the Persian text), reads "à Djar" (*tâ be-jâr*); in medieval times, Jâr was the main port on the Arabian coast of the Red Sea, at which passengers sailing from Qolzom to Medina disembarked. It has been identified with the village of Ra'is south of Yanbo^c^. See Jâser, *Shemâl gharb el-jazireh*, pp. 207-14 and map p. 193; Wohaibi, *Northern Hijaz*, pp. 84-90.

parts. One part of it is called the Tehâma, which is on the shore of the Qolzom [Red] Sea and on the west side [of the peninsula]. Another part of the Himyarite [lands] is mountainous and is called Najd. There is little habitation there, and it is very stony and cold. Another part is towards the east, which is inhabited. Many of the cities and cultivated districts of the Yemen are there. It is about 200 parasangs by 150 parasangs. [216]

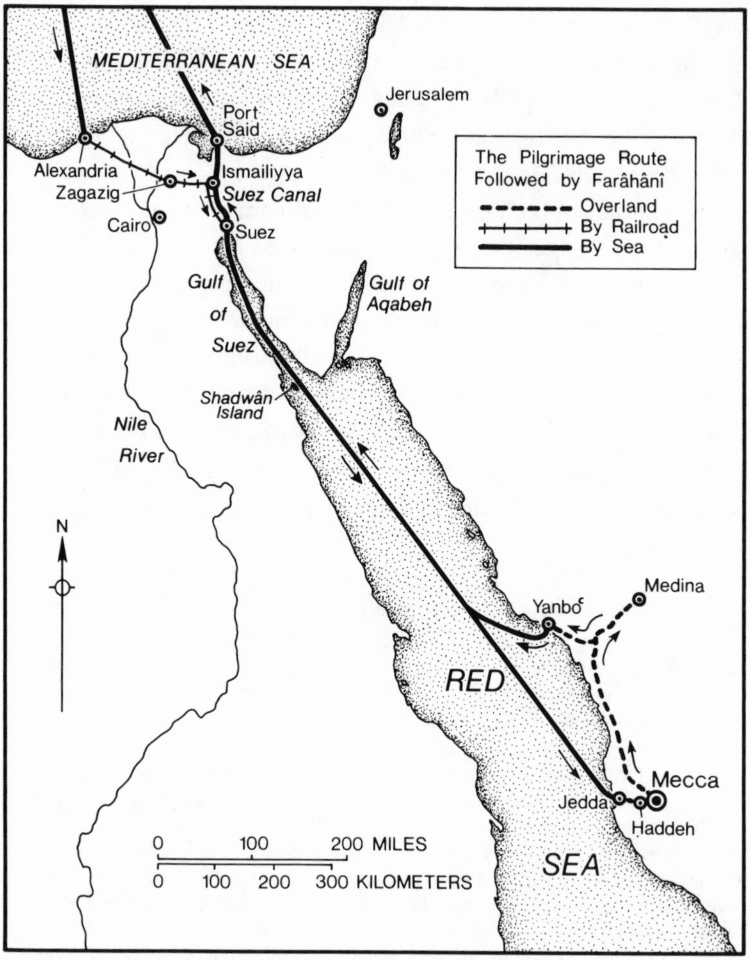

Map 6. The pilgrimage route followed by Farâhâni: Alexandria to Mecca and Return.

PART FIVE
THE PILGRIMAGE TO MECCA

DEPARTURE FROM JEDDA FOR MECCA

Anyway, [I] had arrived at the city of Jedda on Friday, the sixteenth of the sacred month of Zi Qa^cdeh [27 August] and was there Saturday the seventeenth, Sunday the eighteenth, Monday the nineteenth, and Tuesday the twentieth [28-31 August]. Then, wearing the eḥrâm garments and seated on an uncovered litter and camel, [I] set out. Some of the pilgrims sent their baggage by camel and set out individually on hired, easy-paced packhorses or donkeys and arrived in Mecca at first light. The rate for a passenger camel from Jedda to Mecca is three and a half Levant dollars. The rate for a donkey or packhorse is four [Levant] dollars. The rate for a camel with litter is seven [Levant] dollars.

Going by donkey or packhorse is very much better than by camel and litter, especially for Shi'ites. Sunnis consider it permissible to be shaded while travelling in a state of eḥrâm, but the Shi'ite position about this is that it is not permissible to be shaded while travelling in a state of eḥrâm. Thus they ride in litters and covered camel-panniers and see no harm [in being in the shade] if it is sunny. Since the Shi'ite litters do not have coverings, it is a cause of hardship if they travel by day. At this point, it is necessary to recount briefly the things which are forbidden to the *moḥrem* [while] in the state of eḥrâm:

EḤRÂM AND ITS PROHIBITIONS

The essential aspect of eḥrâm is taking off [one's ordinary] dress, putting on two pure white robes, and reciting the *talbeyyeh*.[1] Some of the Shi'ite ulama have said that there are twenty-four things

[1]The *talbeyyeh* is a ritual formula to be recited immediately after putting on the eḥrâm, on approaching Mecca, and during the pilgrimage. The text is translated by Hughes, *Dictionary*, p. 626, as "I stand up for Thy service, O God! I stand up! I stand up! There is no partner with Thee! I stand up for thy service! Verily Thine is the praise, the beneficence, and the kingdom! There is no partner with thee!" Cf. Burton, *Personal Narrative*, 2:139-40; Rutter, *Holy Cities*, 1:97; Gaudefroy-Demombynes, *Pèlerinage*, pp. 179-84; M. Jawâd Mughniyyah, "The Hajj According to Five Schools of Islamic Fiqh," *Al-Tawhîd* 3/i(1406/1985-86):70-71.

which are forbidden to a person in a state of eḥrâm; some reckon twenty-two; and a few sixteen.[2] In detail, they are thought [to be]:

First, hunting any type of land or sea animal or bird.[3] [217]

Second, coition with or taking pleasure from women.

Third, intentional emission of sperm.

Fourth, using or smelling perfume.

Fifth, rubbing oneself with ointment.

Sixth, telling lies, using foul language, or swearing.

Seventh, looking in a mirror.

Eighth, wearing knotted, sewn, or seamed garments; wearing boots and stockings; putting on rings for ornamentation.

Ninth, covering the head or ears.

Tenth, deliberately drawing one's own blood.

Eleventh, seeking shade; that is, going under a covering while travelling. For example, one must not sit in the litter or covered camel-pannier and one must not use a parasol.

Twelfth, cutting or plucking the hair and nails.

Thirteenth, killing lice or removing them from the body and removing ticks from camels or sheep.

Fourteenth, killing any living thing except mice and scorpions.

Fifteenth, cutting or pulling up the grass and trees of the sanctuary.

Sixteenth, wrestling and fighting.

The moḥrem must abstain from all these things that have been indicated [in the case of] intention and free will, not in the case of error or constraint. In the event any one [of them] is violated, intentionally or inadvertently, the eḥrâm is not invalidated. For each offense there is a specific expiation which must be complied with. [218]

---

[2] The precise formulation of the restrictions imposed on the *moḥrem* vary considerably, both in number and detail, among and within the various schools and sects of Islam. The view according to the Shâfeᶜi school is summarized in Burton, *Personal Narrative*, 2:281 ff.; see also Mughniyyah, "Hajj," *Al-Tawhîd* 3/i:72-78; Rutter, *Holy Cities*, 1:98-99; Gaudefroy-Demombynes, *Pèlerinage*, pp. 185-91; Refᶜat, *Mer'ât*, 1:115-25. The teachings of the Ḥanbali school may be found in Ebn Qodâmeh, *ol-ᶜOmdeh*, translated by H. Laoust, *Le Précis de droit d'Ibn Qudâma*, (Beirut, 1950), pp. 77-78. For other Shi'ite accounts see Querry, *Droit Musulman*, 1:250-55 (where Ḥelli lists 20 prohibitions); Kazem Zadeh, *Relation*, p. 58. A modern Shi'ite account, from the perspective of a layman, is Ali Shariati, *Hajj*, translated by Ali Behzadnia and Najla Denny (Houston, 1980), pp. 17-18.

[3] The details and significance of the restrictions on killing animals and uprooting plants are discussed at considerable length by Gaudefroy-Demombynes, *Pèlerinage*, pp. 6-16.

STAGES FROM JEDDA TO MECCA[4]

It is twelve farsakhs from Jedda to Mecca. [The rate per] farsakh, in so far as I determined it through experience with a watch, is this: One who travels mounted on horseback goes one farsakh per hour. Mules or pack-horses [guided by a] sumpter go one farsakh over level ground in an hour and a half. A file of camels, loaded, travels one farsakh in an hour and forty five minutes. Thus one reaches Mecca from Jedda in twelve hours if one goes mounted on ambling-paced pack horses or donkeys.[5] It takes from sixteen to eighteen hours if one goes by pack-mule and litter. If one goes by litter and camel-train, it is a twenty-one hour trip without stopping. Since I took the litter and camel-train, I travelled for twenty-one hours.

COFFEEHOUSES ALONG THE WAY TO BAḤREH

Going out from Jedda there are coffeehouses, which the Arabs call simply *qahveh*, at intervals of one farsakh or more along the way in this order: First, the coffeehouse of Râs Qâ'em.

Second, the coffeehouse of Roghâmeh, up to which is open plain.[6]

Third, the coffeehouse of ᶜAbd on-Naṣif. From here the road is situated below two mountain chains. The mountains are about half a farsakh and one maydân away from the road.

Fourth, the coffeehouse of Jarâdeh.[7]

Fifth, the ᶜArab coffeehouse.[8] From here, the road is level and there are no more mountains.

Sixth, Baḥreh.[9]

THE VILLAGE OF BAḤREH

[I] arrived at Baḥreh one hour before sunset and lodged there. It is sparsely populated. They have erected some houses which are

---

4 A meticulous geographical study of this route is provided by J. J. Hess, *Die geographische Lage Mekkas und die Strasse von Gidda nach Mekka* (Freiburg, 1900); see also Farhâd Mirzâ, *Hedâyat*, pp. 202-3; Refᶜat, *Mer'ât*, 1:24-30; D. G. Hogarth, *Hejaz Before World War I* (revised edition; London, 1978), pp. 108-9.

5 Cf. Burckhardt, *Travels*, p. 58: "I travelled several times afterwards between Mekka and Djidda, in both directions. The caravan's rate of march is here very slow, scarcely exceeding two miles an hour. I have ridden from Mekka to Djidda upon an ass in thirteen hours. The distance may, perhaps, be fairly estimated at sixteen or seventeen hours' walk, or about fifty-five miles; the direction a trifle to the northward of east."

6 Cf. Burckhardt, *Travels*, p. 53; Farhâd Mirzâ, *Hedâyat*, p. 202 (vocalizes the name as Roghâmeh); Refᶜat, *Mer'ât*, 1:25; Hess, *Strasse*, p. 18; Belâdi, *Ḥejâz*, 4:61.

7 See Hess, *Strasse*, p. 19; Refᶜat, *Mer'ât*, 1:25-26.

8 The reading ᶜArab may be a mistake for ᶜAbd; a Qahvat ol-ᶜAbd in this locale is discussed in detail by Hess, *Strasse*, p. 20.

9 Cf. Burckhardt, *Travels*, p. 54; Hess, *Strasse*, p. 21; Belâdi, *Ḥejâz*, 1:183-84; Refᶜat, *Mer'ât*, 1:26.

[more] like huts in which the Bedouin stay. In their imagination, this [seems like] a village. [219] There are also three large, dirty coffeehouses there, so it is a place for pilgrims and those passing through to stop. Scorpions are abundant in these houses and coffeehouses. In spring, fall, and summer, one cannot enter or spend the night in the coffeehouses unless it is a bright day and the scorpions go into their holes.

Baḥreh is very hot. Other than one tree, there is nothing green there. No food can be obtained. Its water [supply] is rainwater. It is brought from ditches beside the road.

DEPARTURE FROM BAḤREH

[I] was in Baḥreh Wednesday the twenty-second of Z̲i Qaᶜdeh [2 September[10]] and left there two and a half hours before sunset. At an interval of one hour after setting out from Baḥreh one reaches the Qandahur[11] coffeehouse. That place is the half-way point. Travelling another hour beyond the Qandahur coffeehouse one reaches the village of Ḥaddeh.

THE VILLAGE OF ḤADDEH[12]

The village of Ḥaddeh has a flowing stream that comes from the Wadi Fâṭemeh. The water of the Wadi Fâṭemeh is very sweet and wholesome, but since it comes through some salty land, it becomes a little salty. But there is also a sweet-water well. [The village] has twenty-two resident households and a mosque. Date-groves and fresh gardens have been created and planted [there] which belong to one of the relatives of the Sharif of Mecca. Traces of a [ruined] canal [*qanât*] are visible there. Most of the halting places between Jedda and Mecca are like Ḥaddeh. There are always ten foot-soldiers and ten dromedary-mounted troops garrisoned in Ḥaddeh.

COFFEEHOUSES BETWEEN JEDDA AND MECCA

Going on from Ḥaddeh to Mecca there are, in order, these several other coffeehouses:

First, the Shemeysâ[13] coffeehouse. [220]

Second, the ᶜAlamayn coffee-house,[14] at which they have built two small pillars to mark the boundaries of the *ḥarâm* [sacred territory]. This is the frontier of the ḥarâm.

---

10 Farâhâni's dating, which has consistently been a day off, now corresponds to the correct day of the week.

11 Cf. Farhâd Mirzâ, *Hedâyat*, p. 203.

12 Cf. Burckhardt, *Travels*, p. 55; Hess, *Strasse*, p. 22; Burton, *Personal Narrative*, 2:262; Refᶜat, *Mer'ât*, 1:27.

13 Farhâd Mirzâ, *Hedâyat*, p. 202, vocalizes the name as Shomaysâ; cf. Burckhardt, *Travels*, p. 56; Refᶜat, *Mer'ât*, 1:28; Hess, *Strasse*, p. 22.

14 Cf. Burton, *Personal Narrative*, 2:262; Hess, *Strasse*, p. 23.

Third, the Sâlem coffeehouse.[15]

Fourth, the Maktaleh[16] coffeehouse.

Fifth, the Omm od-Dâud[17] coffeehouse.

Sixth, the Bostân coffeehouse.[18]

From Ḥaddeh to here, the road is usually smooth, level, and sandy. Nearby and at a distance, low mountains are visible alongside the road.

Seventh, the city of Mecca.[19] This city is situated in the midst of mountains so that, from whatever direction one approaches the city, no trace of it is visible until one reaches the city [itself].

THE CITY OF MECCA

[When] I arrived in Mecca the morning of Thursday the twenty-third of the sacred month of Z̲i Qaᶜdeh [3 September], I had a fever. Because of the fever, I did not go to the Masjed ol-Ḥarâm[20] that day, even though I had on the eḥrâm garments. This fever is due to the influence of the hot weather and lasts for three or four days. Humectives are the cure for it.[21]

This fever is common in Mecca the Exalted and is called "Abu Rokkâb." Most of the pilgrims are afflicted by this fever, but it is not serious and they get over it. Almost no one has died of this illness.

The residence which the guide had arranged for me was undistinguished and hot. I stayed at another residence which was cool and private and which had a bath. [221]

HOUSES FOR RENT

The houses of this city have from one to five storeys. They rent out most of them to pilgrims.[22]

Some houses are like caravanserais. That is to say, about fifty or sixty people are gathered together in one house. Several people stay

---

15 Burckhardt, *Travels*, p. 56; Hess, *Strasse*, p. 23.

16 Farhâd Mirzâ, *Hedâyat*, p. 202, gives this vocalization and spelling. Other sources suggest Maqtaleh: see Moḥammad Ṣâdeq Pâshâ, *Dalil ol-ḥajj* (Bolâq, 1313/1897), p. 45; Hess, *Strasse*, p.23; Refᶜat, *Mer'ât*, 1:28.

17 Hess, *Strasse*, p. 23 has "Umm e-Dûd 'Mutter der Würmer,'" as does Hogarth, *Hejaz*, p. 109; cf. Refᶜat, *Mer'ât*, 1:29.

18 Cf. Refᶜat, *Mer'ât*, 1:29.

19 [Marginal note]: "That exalted town has been called Mecca and also called the Mother of Cities [*Omm ol-qorrâ*] and Mother of the Lands [*Omm ol-arżin*]. They also say Mecca is the Home of the Kaaba as is indicated in verses from the Koran."

20 The Masjed ol-Ḥarâm is the sanctuary in Mecca surrounding the Kaaba. The pilgrim should visit it immediately upon his arrival in Mecca; Farâhâni is thus careful to point out the reasons for his departure from the normal custom.

21 On this illness, from which many visitors to Mecca suffered, cf. Keane, *Six Months in the Hejaz*, p. 17. It may be noted that Farâhâni suggests a remedy based on traditional Galenic medical theory.

22 Cf. Hurgronje, *Mekka*, pp. 31-38.

on one floor room by room. The rent for this type of house is cheaper.

They rent some others in entirety to particular individuals. This type of house is, by comparison, more expensive.

The houses are not customarily rented by the month or day but rather for however many days during the pilgrimage season one must spend in Mecca in these lodgings.

The rent for the houses [ranges] from two hundred Levant dollars (which is about 120 tomans) to twenty Levant dollars. That is for good houses with room furnishings, table, chairs, sofa, and cushions.

All the houses have flat roofs suitable as a place to sleep.

In some houses, the landlord is also responsible for paying for the water-carriers and water.

THE FEVER BREAKS

Friday the twenty-fourth of Z̲i Qaᶜdeh [4 September], feeling better and my fever having come down a little, [I] performed the ritual ablutions again and went outside the lodgings in a state of eḥrâm to perform the ᶜomreh-ye tamattoᶜ with my pilgrim guide.

OBLIGATORY RITUALS OF THE PILGRIMAGE

Here, in order that discerning [readers] may be informed about the rituals of the pilgrimage, I will recount a brief summary of the obligatory rituals of the pilgrimage.[23]

Briefly, there are twenty duties. Five of them are related to the ᶜomreh-ye tamattoᶜ, [222] and fifteen are related to the *ḥajj-e tamattoᶜ*.[24]

---

[23] See Querry, *Droit Musulman*, 1:244-90. Refᶜat, *Mer'ât*, 1:29-31, gives a useful chart outlining the requirements according to the four Sunni schools of law.

[24] The ᶜomreh, or "lesser pilgrimage," is nothing more than a meritorious ritual visit to Mecca requiring circumambulation of the Kaaba and running between the hills of Ṣafâ and Marveh. The ḥajj, or pilgrimage proper, is the obligatory ritual pilgrimage which is performed during the month of Z̲i Ḥejjeh and involves many additional ritual requirements beyond those of the ᶜomreh. Most pilgrims, who will probably visit Mecca only once, take the opportunity to perform both the ᶜomreh and the ḥajj. Thus Islamic law recognizes three varieties of the ḥajj: the *ḥajj-e efrâd* (performing the ḥajj but not the ᶜomreh); the *ḥajj-e qerân* (performing both ḥajj and ᶜomreh in the month of Z̲i Ḥejjeh, remaining in a state of eḥrâm until the completion of the ḥajj); and the form which many pilgrims (such as Farâhâni) opt to perform, the *ḥajj-e tamattoᶜ* (both ᶜomreh and ḥajj are performed, but the state of eḥrâm is ended after completion of the ᶜomreh and need not be resumed until the first day of the ḥajj ceremonies on the eighth of Z̲i Ḥejjeh). The attractiveness of the latter option is that it frees the pilgrim from the many uncomfortable restrictions of eḥrâm for at least part of his stay in Mecca waiting for the ḥajj to begin. See Querry, *Droit Musulman*, 1:233-40; Kazem Zadeh, *Relation*, pp. 55-57; Burton, *Personal Narrative*, 2:281; Ali, *Religion of Islam*, pp. 577-78; Gaudefroy-Demombynes, *Pèlerinage*, pp.

The ᶜomreh-ye tamattoᶜ is what must be done at the time of entering Mecca the Exalted. The ḥajj-e tamattoᶜ is what must be done at ᶜArafât[25] and [on] the Day of Sacrifice [*ᶜId-e Qorbân*].[26]

As for the five duties connected with the ᶜomreh-ye tamattoᶜ, [they are]:

First, putting on two pure white robes at one of the five places that are the eḥrâm stations, saying the talbeyyeh, and avoiding those things that are forbidden at the time of eḥrâm.

Second, performing the seven circumambulations [*ṭavâf*] of the Kaaba, beginning at the Black Stone [*Ḥajar ol-Asvad*]. The Black Stone should be located on the left side [as one goes round].[27]

Third, after completing the seven circuits [*showṭ*] of the circumambulation, performing the two cycles [*rakᶜat*][28] of prayer of the *ṭavâf-e ᶜomreh-ye tamattoᶜ*.[29]

Fourth, performing the *saᶜy* ["going back and forth"] seven times between the marketplaces of Ṣafâ and Marveh, beginning at Ṣafâ and finishing at Marveh.[30]

Fifth, after going back and forth between Ṣafâ and Marveh, trimming one's nails or mustache.[31]

192-200, 307-9; Anis Matthews, *A Guide For Hajj and 'Umra* (Lahore, 1979), pp. 51-55.

25 At ᶜArafât and in its environs, the pilgrims perform a number of rituals, including the one known as the "standing" (*voquf*) on the ninth of Z̲i Ḥejjeh from noon until sunset. On ᶜArafât, see above, Part Four, p. 198 n. 103; on the rituals, see also Querry, *Droit Musulman*, 1:256-59; Gaudefroy-Demombynes, *Pèlerinage*, pp. 235-55.

26 This is the concluding ceremony of the pilgrimage on the tenth of Z̲i Ḥejjeh in which the pilgrims offer an animal sacrifice, commemorating Abraham's sacrifice of a sheep in place of his son. It is a major Muslim holiday, celebrated all over the Muslim world as well as at Mecca. See Hughes, *Dictionary*, pp. 192-94; Kazem Zadeh, *Relation*, p. 76; Gaudefroy-Demombynes, *Pèlerinage*, pp. 277-91.

27 Cf. Kazem Zadeh, *Relation*, pp. 60-64; Rutter *Holy Cities*, 1:108-10; Gaudefroy-Demombynes, *Pèlerinage*, pp. 205-24; Refᶜat, *Mer'ât*, 1:107-9; Mughniyyah, "Hajj," *Al-Tawhîd*, 3/ii:57-65; EI_1, 4:702-3 [s.v. "Ṭawâf"].

28 In the Muslim prayer ritual, each cycle of standing, genuflecting, and prostration constitutes one *rakᶜat*. Various numbers of rakᶜat are performed in each of the five daily prayers (for example, two in the morning prayer and four in the noon prayer). See EI_1, 4:99 [s.v. "Ṣalât"].

29 Rutter, *Holy Cities*, 1:110 calls this "sunnat et towâf (the 'rule for towâf')."

30 Cf. Querry, *Droit Musulman*, 1:282-85; Kazem Zadeh, *Relation*, pp. 67-69; Rutter, *Holy Cities*, 1:111-12; Gaudefroy-Demombynes, *Pèlerinage*, pp. 225-34; Refᶜât, *Mer'ât*, 1:109-10; Mughniyyah, "Hajj," *Al-Tawhîd*, 3/iii:63-66; and below n. 77.

31 When the ᶜomreh is performed as tamattoᶜ (in conjunction with the ḥajj) only a token clipping of the nails and hair (*taqṣir*) is necessary. A full shaving of the head is thus delayed until the end of the ḥajj. Cf. Querry, *Droit Musulman*, 1:272-73; Rutter, *Holy Cities*, 1:112-13; Gaudefroy-Demombynes, *Pèlerinage*, pp. 231-32; Mughniyyah, "Hajj," *Al-Tawhîd*, 3/iii:66-68.

As for the fifteen duties of the ḥajj-e tamatto^{c}, [they] are:

First, wearing the eḥrâm garments in the precincts of Mecca.

Second, staying at ^{c}Arafât from noon of the ninth day to sunset.[32]

Third, spending the night [before] the tenth until sunrise at Mash^{c}ar.[33]

Fourth, coming to Menâ the day of the Feast of Sacrifice and throwing seven stones at the Jamreh-ye ^{c}Aqabeh.[34] [223]

Fifth, making a sacrifice on the day of the Feast in Menâ.[35]

Sixth, after making a sacrifice, and on the same day, shaving the head or paring the nails.

Seventh, coming to the Masjed ol-Ḥarâm and going seven times around the House [of God, the Kaaba], beginning at the Black Stone and keeping the House on the left side [as one goes round].

Eighth, performing the two cycles of the prayer of the ḥajj-e tamatto^{c}.

Ninth, performing the sa^{c}y seven times between Ṣafâ and Marveh.

Tenth, performing seven circumambulations [of the Kaaba] as the *ṭavâf-e nesâ'*.[36]

Eleventh, performing the two cycle prayer of the ṭavâf-e nesâ'.

---

[32] Pilgrims must be on the plain at ^{c}Arafât on the ninth of Z̲i Ḥejjeh for the "standing" (*voquf*) from afternoon until sunset; this constitutes the first ritual of the ḥajj or pilgrimage proper. It is described at length by Rutter, *Holy Cities*, 1:151-63; see also Gaudefroy-Demombynes, *Pèlerinage*, pp. 248-53; Ref^{c}at, *Mer'ât*, 1:111-12; Mughniyyah, "Hajj," *Al-Tawhîd*, 3/iii:68-72; EI$_1$, 4:1141 [s.v. "Wuḳûf"].

[33] Also called Mozdalefeh; see below, n. 151.

[34] The Jamreh-ye ^{c}Aqabeh, often called the "Great Satan," is a stone marker at the western end of the town of Menâ. The pilgrims are obliged to make a ritual lapidation (*rami*) of it just prior to the ritual sacrifice. See Burton, *Personal Narrative*, 2:203-4; Kazem Zadeh, *Relation*, p. 76; Rutter, *Holy Cities*, 1:154, 170-71, 183-85; Gaudefroy-Demombynes, *Pèlerinage*, pp. 256-76 (especially p. 268); Querry, *Droit Musulman*, 1:263-65; Ref^{c}at, *Mer'ât*, 1:113-15; EI$_2$, 2:438 [s. v. "Djamra"].

[35] This offering of a sacrificial animal is the culminating ritual of the ḥajj, celebrated not only by the pilgrims in Menâ but by Muslims everywhere on the tenth of Z̲i Ḥejjeh. For Shi'ite law pertaining to the sacrifice, see Querry, *Droit Musulman*, 1:265-72.

[36] Most authorities recognize three types of circumambulation: the *ṭavâf-e qodum* ("circumambulation of arrival," performed upon arrival in Mecca); the *ṭavâf-e ziyâreh* ("circumambulation of visitation") or *ṭavâf ol-efâżeh* ("circumambulation of completion") performed between the tenth and twelfth of Z̲i Ḥejjeh; and the *ṭavâf-e vadâ^{c}* ("circumambulation of farewell," made just before leaving Mecca). The *ṭavâf ol-efâżeh* marks the end of the pilgrimage ritual proper; after completing it the various restrictions placed on the pilgrim are ended. To this, however, the Shiites add the circumambulation known as the *ṭavâf-e nesâ'* ("circumambulation of women") since the prohibition against having intercourse with women is not lifted until it is performed; it is not recognized by the Sunnis. Cf. Querry, *Droit Musulman*, 1:273; Kazem Zadeh, *Relation*, p. 77; Mughniyya, "Hajj," *Al-Tawhîd* 3/ii:59.

Twelfth, remaining the night [before] the eleventh in Menâ.

Thirteenth, throwing seven stones at the first Jamreh, seven stones at the middle Jamreh, and seven stones at the last Jamreh on the eleventh day.[37]

Fourteenth, being in Menâ on the night [before] the twelfth.

Fifteenth, on the day of the twelfth, throwing seven stones at the first Jamreh, seven stones at the middle Jamreh, and seven stones at the last Jamreh. Then one is through and [obtains] peace of mind.

PERFORMANCE OF THE ᶜOMREH-YE TAMATTOᶜ

Anyhow, [I] entered the new Masjed ol-Ḥarâm by the Dâr os-Salâm Gate [*sic*] and went into the Masjed-e ᶜAtiq by the Bani Shaybeh Gate.[38] First of all, I kissed the Black Stone, rubbed my head, body, and eyes, and invoked God. Then I carried out the obligatory seven circuits of the circumambulation of the ᶜomreh-ye tamattoᶜ, performed the two-prostration prayer of circumambulation at the Station of Abraham [*Maqâm Ebrâhim*],[39] and drank a little water from the [well of] Zamzam[40] and poured [some] on my head and body. Leaving by the Ṣafâ Gate, I performed the saᶜy [between] Ṣafâ and Marveh seven times. Since I was not well and had a fever, I sat down and drank [some] water between [each] saᶜy. [224]

After finishing, I returned home. Along the way, these verses came to mind due to the joy and enthusiasm I felt, and I wrote them down.[41]

THE NEW MASJED OL-ḤARÂM

As for the details about the Masjed ol-Ḥarâm and its gates, buildings, corners [*rokn*], and stations [*maqâm*], they are [as described] in the following presentation:

---

[37] The Jamreh-ye ᶜAqabeh and the two other markers are stoned by the pilgrims over a three day period known as the days of *tashriq*. See above, n. 34.

[38] The Masjed ol-Ḥarâm is the entire mosque-sanctuary in Mecca; the Masjed-e ᶜAtiq refers to the ancient monuments surrounding the Kaaba in the center of the mosque. The Bani Shaybeh Gate (also known as the Gate of Peace or Bâb os-Salâm) stands northeast of the Kaaba, just behind the building known as the Station of Abraham, at the entrance to the inner circuit of the Kaaba. Members of the clan of Bani Shaybeh have been custodians of the Kaaba from ancient times to the present. Perhaps the most thorough discussion of these areas of the sacred precincts is that of Gaudefroy-Demombynes, *Pèlerinage*, pp. 26-154; see also Refᶜat, *Mer'ât*, 1:227-62; Kazem Zadeh, *Relation*, pp. 59-67; Burckhardt, *Travels*, pp. 134-70; Burton, *Personal Narrative*, 2:159-77, 294-326; Rutter, *Holy Cities*, 1:248-69.

[39] A stone and building near the Kaaba; it is discussed more fully below.

[40] The name of the well near the Kaaba; it is discussed more fully below.

[41] The seven verses, which contain Farâhâni's pen-name (Golbon), are omitted from the translation. Perhaps owing to his excitement and inspiration, they are among the best he has composed.

GATES OF THE NEW MASJED OL-ḤARÂM

The gates of the present Masjed ol-Ḥarâm: Some [consist of] three doors side by side, some are two doors, and some are one door. They are all detailed in the following appendix:

Bâb os-Salâm, three doors; Bâb od-Doraybeh, one door; Bâb ol-Maḥkameh, one door; Bâb oz-Zeyâdeh,[42] three doors; Bâb ol-Qoṭbi, one door; Bâb ol-ᶜAtiq, one door [225]; Bâb ol-Bâseteyyeh, one door; Bâb ol-ᶜOmreh, one door; Bâb Ebrâhim, one door; Bâb ol-Vedâᶜ, two doors; Bâb on-Noᶜush, two doors; Bâb Omm Hâni, two doors; Bâb Jiâd, two doors; Bâb osh-Sharif Manṣur, two doors; Bâb oṣ-Ṣafâ, five doors; Bâb ol-Khalifatayn, two doors; Bâb ᶜAli, three doors; Bâb ol-ᶜAbbâs, three doors; Bâb on-Nabi, two doors; Bâb Qâyt Bayk, one door; Bâb os-Salâmeyyeh, one door; Bâb Elmâs, two doors; Bâb oz-Zamâmeyyeh, one door.[43]

MINARETS OF THE NEW MASJED OL-ḤARÂM

Beside some of these doors which have been built, they have also erected minarets, according to the description which follows:

The minaret of the Bâb os-Salâm; the minaret of the Bâb oz-Zeyâdeh;[44] the minaret of the Bâb ol-Maḥkameh; the minaret of the Bâb ol-ᶜOmreh; the minaret of the Bâb ol-Vedâᶜ; the minaret of the Bâb ᶜAli, and the minaret of the Bâb Qâyt Bayk.[45]

CONSTRUCTIONS INSIDE THE NEW MASJED OL-ḤARÂM

After entering the Masjed ol-Ḥarâm, there is first of all an arcade which has been covered over, plastered, and painted all around the perimeter of the Masjed ol-Ḥarâm. The width of this

[42] Text: Ziâreh.

[43] On the gates of the sacred mosque, see Refᶜat, *Mer'ât*, 1:230-34; Gaudefroy-Demombynes, *Pèlerinage*, pp. 131-53; Rutter, *Holy Cities*, 1:253-56; Burckhardt, *Travels*, pp. 152-53; Burton, *Personal Narrative*, pp. 294-317; Ṣâdeq Pâshâ, *Dalil*, pp. 52-53; *Nozhat ol-nâẓerin* (MS. Leiden Or. 14.026), f. 5b. This passage presents a number of difficulties in that Farâhâni's list of the names of the gates does not correspond completely to the list of any other authority. The six names which differ from those given by Rutter are those of the ᶜAtiq, Sharif Manṣur, Noᶜush, Khalifatayn, Salameyyeh, and Elmâs gates. Refᶜat, *Mer'ât*, 1:234, points out that the ᶜAtiq is another name for the gate of ᶜAmr b. ᶜÂṣ (the latter individual is anathema to Shi'ites and Farâhâni would naturally be reluctant to use this name for the gate.) The same source, 1:232, gives what appears to be Khalifatayn as an alternate name for the Ejyâd gate (called the Raḥmeh gate in most other sources). Ṣâdeq Pâshâ, *Dalil*, p. 53, has the name Noᶜush as an alternative for the Baghleh gate of other sources. What Farâhâni calls the Bâb osh-Sharif Manṣur may be a mistake for the Bâb osh-Sharif ᶜAjlân. Since Farâhâni describes the Salâmeyyeh Gate has having only one door, it could match either the Da'udeyyeh or Madrasah Gates in Rutter's list. The remaining Salâmeyyeh and Elmâs gates cannot be identified from other sources, although they probably correspond to the Madraseh and Bâzân gates. For a map and summary of the problems in identifying these gates, refer to the Appendix, Figure 2 (below, p. 328).

[44] Text: Ziâreh.

[45] Cf. Rutter, *Holy Cities*, 1:258; Refᶜat, *Mer'ât*, 1:234-35.

arcade is, in all places, nineteen *qadam*.[46] Below the arcade some areas have rooms and chambers throughout that are places for servants, rugs, brooms, offices, libraries, lamps, and so on.

By whichever door of all the aforementioned doors one enters, the first [place] one reaches will be this arcade.

All around the arcade there are columns. The interval between each column and the next is four qadam. At spaces of every three columns there is one large column. The small columns are of black stone,[47] and the large columns are of plaster and brick. So in twenty-five qadam there are three small stone columns and one large brick column. [226]

There are thirty-six columns on each of the two sides for the length of the Masjed ol-Ḥarâm. There are twenty-four columns on each of the two sides of the width of the Masjed ol-Ḥarâm, in the arrangement which has been described. All of these columns are located at the front of the arcade all [the way] around.

In the middle of this arcade there is another row of columns of plaster and brick in the same pattern. The floor of the arcade is paved with black stone.

The [parts] of the floor of the courtyard of the new Masjed ol-Ḥarâm that [serve as] walkways are all paved with black stone. The spaces [between] the walkways are somewhat lower than the level of the walkway and have been covered with tiny pebbles in the manner of a little garden.

THE ANCIENT MASJED OL-ḤARÂM

As for the ancient Masjed ol-Ḥarâm, it is much smaller than this and surrounds the House [of God, the Kaaba]. In order to mark its boundaries stone columns have been set up and painted. The tops of the columns are connected together with iron [bars]. There is a brass knob at the top of each column, and lanterns and lamps are suspended [from them]. There are thirty-four columns all around this Masjed-e ᶜAtiq. Thirty-two of them are of stone, and two of them of brick and plaster. A brick and plaster arch has been constructed over these two plaster columns. It is known as the Bâb Bani Shaybeh.

---

[46] A unit of measurement equal to approximately 15 inches.

[47] Text: *sang-e siâh*. This term is used for a variety of stones such as sandstone and basalt, but Farâhâni is probably using it here to refer to the common dark-grey stones found near Mecca. According to Burton, *Personal Narrative*, 2: 295, the columns were built of various stones including white marble, granite, and a kind of yellow sandstone; cf. Rutter, *Holy Cities*, pp. 252-53.

The circumference of this old Masjed ol-Ḥarâm is 250 qadam. The building of the Kaaba, the *Ḥejr* of Ishmael,[48] the Station of Abraham, the well of Zamzam, and the pulpit [*menbar*] of the Messenger of God [Moḥammad] are all located inside this ancient Masjed ol-Ḥarâm.

The floor of the Masjed-e ᶜAtiq is completely paved with marble. Each of the two sides [that make up] the width of the Kaaba building is eleven qadam [long]. The two sides [that make up] the length [of the Kaaba] are eighteen qadam [each], including the *shâdorvân*, that is, the stones which are set up around the base of the House [of God, the Kaaba]. [227] The perimeter of the Kaaba, excluding the Ḥejr of Ishmael is sixty-six qadam and including the Ḥejr of Ishmael is ninety-three qadam. One side of the Ḥejr is adjacent to the House; the three other sides are twenty-seven qadam [long]. There is a wall of marble raised up around the Ḥejr of Ishmael, the height of which is one and a half z̲arᶜ. The Mizâb-e Raḥmat ["Spout of Mercy"], which is called the "Golden Gutter", is next to the Ḥejr, and rainwater from it flows onto the Ḥejr.[49] The Ḥejr is flush with the Kaaba. One must enter the Ḥejr [when performing] the circumambulation. The height of the House is about twenty-seven z̲arᶜ. The walls of the House are made of black stone and plaster. Its thickness is six *vajab*.[50] It is completely covered with a black cloth of silk. It is a very thick cloth which is brought every year from Egypt.[51] "There is no God but God" and "Moḥammad is the Messenger of God" and the names of the rulers of the Ottoman [Empire] and Egypt are embroidered on it.

---

[48] The Ḥejr is a semi-circular area opposite the north-west face of the Kaaba, bounded by a low stone wall known as the Ḥaṭim. The Koran attributes the construction of the Kaaba and sanctuary at Mecca to Abraham and Ishmael (2:127) and, according to Muslim tradition, the Ḥejr contains the tombs of Ishmael and his mother Hagar. See Refᶜat, *Mer'ât*, 1:305-307; Gaudefroy-Demombynes, *Pèlerinage*, pp. 35-37; Hawting, "Origins of the Muslim Sanctuary," pp. 33-34.

[49] The grave of Ishmael was supposed to be underneath the spot marked by this waterspout: See, for example, Ebn Baṭṭuṭeh, *Reḥleh,* translated by H.A.R. Gibb; *The Travels of Ibn Battuta*, (Cambridge, 1958), p. 196; Kazem Zadeh, *Relation*, p. 67.

[50] The *vajab* or span would equal about nine inches.

[51] [Marginal note:] "According to the narrative of Abu'l-Fatḥ, author of the *Ketâb-e maᶜâref*, and Moḥammad ebn-e Jarir Ṭabari, the younger Tobbaᶜ Ḥesân, son of the elder Tobbaᶜ, was the first person who covered the Kaaba with cloth. It is written in some books by the biographers that Tobbaᶜ the Ḥimyarite was the first person who covered the Kaaba with cloth. In any case, one of the rulers of Yemen known as Tobbaᶜ, about a thousand years before the Prophet appeared, used to cover the Kaaba with cloth." [Ṭabari was a famous Muslim historian (d. 923). The identify of Abu'l-Fatḥ is uncertain; the best known *Ketâb ol-maᶜâref* is by Ebn Qotaybeh (Abu ᶜAbdollah). Tobbaᶜ was the title of various South Arabian kings; cf.

THE CORNERSTONES OF THE KAABA

There are four cornerstones [*rokn*] for this House of the Kaaba:[52]

The Rokn-e Yamâni is to the southwest. The *Mostajâb*[53] is affixed to it. The Mostajâb is a green-colored stone which is outside the covering [cloth] of the Kaaba. [People] rub [their] hands and bellies on it and kiss it.

The Rokn-e Shâmi is to the northwest, adjacent to the Ḥejr of Ishmael.

The Rokn-e ᶜErâqi is to the northeast, so it is also adjacent to the Ḥejr of Ishmael. [228] Some believe that this corner between east and north is the Rokn-e Ḥejâzi or Ḥabashi and [that] the Rokn-e ᶜErâqi is the one in which the Black Stone is embedded. Most books have written [about it] this way.

The Rokn-e Ḥajar ol-Asvad is to the southeast. The Black Stone is embedded in it. [The Black Stone consists] of seventeen broken fragments of stone which have been stuck together and surrounded with silver. Its color is black tending to reddish. It is outside the cloth. [Pilgrims] kiss it. The Black Stone is set into the corner in such a way that whenever a man of middling stature stands his forehead is parallel to the stone.

The Bâb Baytollah [door to the Kaaba] is between the Rokn-e Ḥabashi and the Black Stone. It is very near the Black Stone. Over the door to the House, this blessed verse has been inscribed: "Surely the first house appointed for mankind is the one at Bakka..." to the end of the verse "...a blessed place, a guidance to the people."[54] This door to the House of God is of one leaf and is gilded. Its height is one and a half z̲arᶜ. It is one and a half z̲arᶜ higher than ground level. Whenever they want to go inside the House they put up a wooden or iron ladder and go. They do not allow everyone to go inside the House. The dignitaries of the sanctuary take various amounts of money from people for admission to it and allow them [to enter].[55]

Qazvini/Le Strange, *Nuzhat*, p. 7. There is a very detailed account of the cloth used to cover the Kaaba (the *kesveh*) and its history in Refᶜat, *Mer'ât*, 1:281-98.]

[52] On these "corners" and the traditions and significance attached to them, see Ḥadrâvi, *ᶜEqd*, pp. 26 ff.; Gaudefroy-Demombynes, *Pèlerinage*, pp. 211-12; Hawting, "Origins of the Muslim Sanctuary," pp. 38-40; Refᶜat, *Mer'ât*, 1:264.

[53] Text: *mostajâr*. See Burton, *Personal Narrative*, 2:303.

[54] Koran, 3:95.

[55] The term translated here as "dignitaries" is *âghâvât* in the text, which usually refers specifically to the black eunuchs who served as custodians of the mosque. However, other officials usually attended the opening of the Kaaba as well in order to collect gratutities; thus the more general word "dignitaries" is used in this case. Burton, *Personal Narrative*, 2:210, says he paid eight dollars for the privilege of

CONSTRUCTIONS INSIDE THE OLD MASJED OL-ḤARÂM

After a person enters, it is very awesome. The inside walls of the House are also of black stone and plaster. Its floor is marble. There is also one large, reddish colored slab of stone among the stones covering the floor on which they say the Messenger [Moḥammad] has prayed. [229]

Inside the House there are three columns and a marble staircase [going up] to the flat-roof of the House in the direction of the Ḥejr of Ishmael. There are several inscribed stones set up on the walls. Each of the rulers [who] made repairs inscribed his name and the date of the repairs on a stone and set it up. One is in the name of Malek ol-Ashraf Barsbây,[56] who repaired the House in the year 826 [1422-23] and [who] was one of the rulers of Egypt. Another is [in] the name of Moḥammad Khân the Ottoman; the date of his repair work is not known. Another is the name of Qâyt Bây,[57] who made repairs in 884 [1479-80] and [who] was one of the rulers of Egypt.

The Station of Abraham is located at a space of fifteen qadam from the House, opposite the House to the northeast, which is in the direction of the Rokn-e ᶜErâqi. It resembles a small chamber.

THE STATION OF ABRAHAM

The width of the Station of Abraham[58] is four qadam. There is a small portico in front of it, the floor of which is marble. It has two small columns, also of marble. The length of the Station, including its portico, is eight qadam. The top of both the Station and the portico are covered. Although the door to the Station itself is closed, it has an iron [grated] window so that the inside of the Station can be seen. A chest has been placed inside the Station, and the top of the chest is [covered with] a black woolen broadcloth with filigree embroidery of gold braid. Various Koranic verses dealing with Abraham have been formed out of the gold braid. Inside it is a stone which they say has the footprints of Abraham, who stood on it while building the House. They pour water on this stone and give it to

---

admission into the Kaaba, and his companion thought he escaped cheaply at the price; cf. Rutter, *Holy Cities*, 1:210-11; Refᶜat, *Mer'ât*, 1:41.

56 A Mamluk sultan of Egypt (1422-37).

57 Mamluk sultan of Egypt (1468-96).

58 This is a small covered building to the east of the Kaaba, containing a stone on which the Prophet Abraham is supposed to have stood. Thus the Koran (2:125) states, "Take as your place of worship the place where Abraham stood [*maqâm Ebrâhim*]." See Gaudefroy-Demombynes, *Pèlerinage*, pp. 102-9; G. R. Hawting, "The Origins of the Muslim Sanctuary at Mecca," in G. H. A. Juynboll, *Studies on the First Century of Islamic Society* (Carbondale, 1982), pp. 30-33; M. J. Kister, "Maqâm Ibrâhîm, a stone with an inscription," *Museon* 84(1971):477-91; Sayf od-Dowleh, *Safarnâmeh*, p. 131; Refᶜat, *Mer'ât*, 1:242-46.

people as a remedy. On the foundation-stone of the Station of Abraham is the name of Malek ol-Ashraf Inâl Nâṣeri[59] who repaired [it] in the year 858 [1454]. [230]

The name of Qânsuh Ghuri,[60] who made repairs in the year 915 [1509-10], is also on two sides of the foundation-stone of the Station of Abraham. Both [Inal and Qânsuh] were Circassian rulers of Egypt.

The pilgrims pray after the circumambulation on the portico and in front of the portico of the Station of Abraham. This is the place of prayer for the Shâfeᶜi rite. Their leader stands on this portico and they perform the prayers.

THE PROPHET'S PULPIT

At a space of eight qadam in the same direction as the Station of Abraham, opposite the Rokn-e Ḥabashi, there is a pulpit of ten steps [made] of marble. They say this is the pulpit of the Messenger of God,[61] and the Imam of the Age–may God hasten the interval [until his return]–will ascend this pulpit upon [his] advent.[62]

THE WELL OF ZAMZAM

[The Well of Zamzam][63] is located to the east of the House, near the Station of Abraham. It faces the Black Stone. An arch has been constructed over it, and they have made [it] like a chamber and put a door [on it]. The base of the well is in the middle of that chamber. Its sides are made out of marble and are raised up more than one zarᶜ above the floor. They have set up a winch and draw water with a pulley and jug. The water is a little salty, but it does not taste bad.

The mouth of the well is three zarᶜ [wide]. The rope which goes down to water level in the well is thirteen zarᶜ [long]. A terrace has been fashioned over the chamber of the well, and a wooden arch has been raised over it. The Shâfeᶜi muezzin gives the call to prayer from it.

[59] The reference is presumably to ol-Ashraf Sayf od-Din Inal, Mamluk sultan of Egypt (1453-61).

[60] The next to the last Mamluk sultan of Egypt (1501-17).

[61] Other sources make no mention of this pulpit being associated with the Prophet Moḥammad. Cf. Refᶜat, *Mer'ât*, 1:252-55.

[62] In "Twelver" Shi'ism (the form practiced in Iran), the last recognized Imam, Moḥammad ol-Mahdi, went into "occultation" in the year 260/873-74; it is believed that he is still alive and will return to usher in the Shi'ite equivalent of the millenium. Shi'ites frequently pray or utter such pious formulas as the one used by Farâhâni for his reappearance; see A. Sachedina, *Islamic Messianism* (Albany, 1981), pp. 150-79.

[63] According to Muslim tradition, Zamzam was the name given to the well which appeared to save Hagar and Ishmael when they were abandoned in the desert near Mecca and which was later re-opened by the Prophet Moḥammad's grandfather; see Gaudefroy-Demombynes, *Pèlerinage*, pp. 71-96; Refᶜat, *Mer'ât*, 1:255-59.

In back of the chamber of the Well of Zamzam, in the direction of the Station of Abraham, they have placed a [movable] iron stairway which is [shaped] like a pulpit. On holy days they place it at the door to the House of the Kaaba and can enter the House [by means of it]. [231]

On three sides, the west, east, and south of the House, next to the old Masjed ol-Ḥarâm, three square, covered porticos have been built. The sides are open. They are prayer places for the Ḥanafi, Ḥanbali, and Mâleki imams [prayer-leaders]. The length and breadth of each portico is eight qadam. All four Sunni rites pray in the Masjed ol-Ḥarâm.[64]

The prayer-place for the Shâfeᶜi imam is the Station of Abraham which is north of the House of the Kaaba.

The Ḥanafi imam prays in the portico to the west of the House, beside the Ḥejr of Ishmael.

The Mâleki imam performs prayer in the portico to the south of the House.

The Ḥanbali imam prays in the portico to the east of the House.

The method of ablution and prayer for all four sects is this:

THE SUNNI METHOD OF ABLUTIONS

None of the four [Sunni] rites considers washing the face upwards or downwards to be correct or incorrect [performance] of ablutions. All four rites wash from the fingers [up] to the elbow, not from the elbow [down] to the fingers. Shâfeᶜis, Ḥanafis, and Ḥanbalis do not practice rubbing [*masḥ*] the head and feet, they wash [them]. The Mâlekis do not wash [them]; in the Shi'ite manner they practice rubbing.[65]

---

[64] On the arrangements for prayers in the mosque, cf. Rutter, *Holy Cities*, 1:262-63; Refᶜat, *Mer'ât*, 1:248-52.

[65] The performance of a "lesser ablution" (*vożuᶜ*) is an obligatory preparation for the daily ritual prayers in Islam. As Farâhâni indicates, the way in which these ablutions are practiced differs in some details among the four Sunni rites (or "schools" of law) and between the Sunni and Shi'ite sects. The major difference in this regard pertains to the practice of *masḥ* (rubbing or wiping rather than actually washing the feet and head.) The practice seems to be authorized by the Koran (5:6) which states, "O ye who believe! When ye rise up for prayer, wash your faces, and your hands up to the elbows, and rub your heads and your feet up to the ankles." On this basis, Shi'ites and the Mâleki school allow rubbing of both the head and the feet. The other Sunni schools, however, argue that the verb "wash" in the verse applies to the feet as well; they thus allow rubbing the head but require washing the feet. This issue should not be confused with the more serious one of whether it is permissible to purify one's shoes by wiping them (*ol-masḥ ᶜalâ'l-khoffayn*) which the Shi'ites vehemently reject: See R. Strothmann, *Kultus der Zaiditen* (Strassburg, 1912), 2:21-26; A. Wensinck, *The Muslim Creed* (Cambridge, 1932), pp. 158-60; Ignaz

SUNNI PRAYER RITUALS [66]

In the prayers, none of these four rites says, "I testify that ᶜAli, Commander of the Faithful, is the Deputy of God" nor "Come to the best of works."[67] The [Sunnis] do not recite the *qonut*.[68] They consider it valid [to perform] the prostration on anything pure, whether of stone, wood, cotton, etc. The Ḥanbalis consider a prostration on ritually impure things to be valid.[69] The Ḥanbalis and Ḥanafis either do not say "In the name of God" or they say it in a low voice. They say the praise God [*ḥamd*][70] loudly. The Shâfeᶜis and Mâlekis say, "In the name of God" loudly like the Shi'ites. After reciting the ḥamd, all four groups either read a long chapter [of the Koran] or recite several verses from one of the chapters of the Koran. In the witnessing part of the prayer service [*tashahhod*], the four groups do not utter prayers of blessing for Moḥammad and the family of Moḥammad. [232] In accordance with the preferred custom [*esteḥbâb*], they usually say something approximately like this after the tashahhod: "Salutations to the Prophet and to his companions and his descendants."[71] In the concluding salutation [*salâm*], they say "Peace be upon you, and the mercy of God and his

---

Goldziher, *Introduction to Islamic Theology and Law* (translated by Andras and Ruth Hamori; Princeton, 1981), p. 207 n. 110; EI_1,4:1140 [s.v. "Wuḍû'"].

66 A good summary, with illustrations, of the prayer rituals may be found in Hughes, *Dictionary*, pp.465-69; see also EI_1, 4:96-105 [s.v. "Ṣalât"].

67 These pious expressions are regularly included by the Shi'ites (but never the Sunnis) in the call to prayer (*aẕân*) performed by the muezzin and in the *eqâmeh* (a kind of announcement in the mosque that the prayer service should begin). See Khomayni, *Clarification of Questions*, pp. 126-27.

68 The term *qonut* has several meanings, but generally speaking it is a prayer of supplication. Sunnis typically include it in *veṭr* prayers (a special cycle of ritual prayer usually appended to the last of the five daily prayers at night). Shi'ites include such prayers of supplication in the regular prayer rituals. See Querry, *Droit Musulman*, 1:81; Maulana Muhammad Ali, *The Religion of Islam* (Cairo, n.d.), pp. 425-27; EI_2, 5:395.

69 During the prostration (*sejdah*) part of the prayer, the worshipper's palms, knees, toes, and forehead must touch the ground. Shi'ite law holds that the surface on which the prostration is performed must be made either of earth, or certain stones, or non-edible plants. To insure this, Shi'ites often place a prayer stone (which is known to be ritually pure and often made of earth taken from the precincts of the tomb of an Imam) on the ground or floor and press the forehead to it.

70 One of the first parts of the prayer service, during which the worshippers recite the opening chapter of the Koran, which begins "Praise be to God, Lord of the Worlds." The correct way of beginning the prayer is a matter of some controversy; see J. Chelhod, "Les attitudes et les gestes de la prière rituelle dans l'Islam," *Revue de l'Histoire des Religions* 156(1959):172 n. 2; Querry, *Droit Musulman*, 1:71.

71 The Shi'ites add several expressions of salutation and blessings for the Prophet and his descendants during this part of the prayer. It is not clear whether the point Farâhâni is trying to make is that the Sunnis offer the blessing after rather than during the tashahhod or that they also include blessings on his companions instead of just his family.

blessings" only two times. They glance one time towards the left, so that the face turns away from the kiblah, and they glance one time to the right.[72]

The Shâfeᶜis, Ḥanbalis, and Ḥanafis pray with hands folded. The Mâlekis pray with hands open like the Shi'ites.[73] [233]

[Map of the Masjed ol-Ḥarâm[74]]

SERVITORS OF THE MASJED OL-ḤARÂM

[234] The servitors of the Masjed ol-Ḥarâm are specifically as follows: the black eunuchs of the sanctuary, six persons; sweepers of the streets and the sanctuary, twenty-one persons; ferashes of the sanctuary, twelve persons; muezzins for the sanctuary, twenty-two persons; *moshdiât* (that is, heralds) for the sanctuary, twelve persons.[75]

There are many pigeons in the sanctuary which the pilgrims treat charitably. They take seeds and throw them in front of [the pigeons]. [The pigeons] also get a fixed ration from the wakf endowments of the sanctuary. They do not fear or take flight from people.

ṢAFÂ AND MARVEH

The markets of Ṣafâ and Marveh are behind the Masjed ol-Ḥarâm. Formerly, Ṣafâ and Marveh were two hills. Mount Ṣafâ is to the east of the Masjed ol-Ḥarâm on the lower slopes of Mount Abu Qobays. Mount Marveh is to the north-east of the Masjed ol-Ḥarâm. Shops and houses have been built between these two hills on both sides. Houses have also been built on top of these two hills. Now the way to the houses which are located on top of Mount Ṣafâ goes up very high. In particular, the house of the Sharif ᶜAbd ol-Moṭṭaleb[76] is on top of Mount Ṣafâ, who had it leveled and built [there].

---

[72] During the *salâm* ("salutation") Shi'ites prefer to sit still and recite such formulas as "Salutations to you O Prophet and the mercy of God and His blessing;" "Salutations to you all and God's mercy and blessing;" or "Salutations to us and to God's pious servants." See Querry, *Droit Musulman*, 1:115 ff.; Khomayni, *Clarification of Questions*, pp. 149-50; Chelhod, "Attitudes," p. 174.

[73] In the part of the prayer cycle during which the worshipper is standing (the *qeyâm*), Sunnis from the three schools mentioned by Farâhâni place the right hand over the left holding them just below the navel or on the chest; Shi'ites keep their hands over their thighs: See Hughes, *Dictionary*, p. 466; Khomayni, *Clarification of Questions*, p. 134; Ali, *Religion of Islam*, p. 414; Chelhod, "Attitudes," p. 172.

[74] Farâhâni's sketch map is reproduced in the Appendix, Figure 1 (p. 327).

[75] Cf. *Ḥejâz velâyati sâlnâmehsi* (Mecca, 1303/1886), p. 82; Burckhardt, *Travels*, pp. 157-59; Rutter, *Holy Cities*, 1:264-66; Peters, *Jerusalem and Mecca*, pp. 160-65.

[76] The allusion is to ᶜAbd ol-Moṭṭaleb b. Ghâleb, who held the office of Sharif of Mecca from 1851-56 and was reappointed 1880-82; see De Gaury, *Rulers of Mecca*, pp. 240-56; Refᶜat, *Mer'ât*, 1:354-66; EI_1, 3:446-47 [s.v. "Mecca"].

The pilgrims perform saʿy (that is, they walk along) down the middle of this wide street, on the two sides of which are houses and shops.[77] Two pillars have been built in the middle of this street towards the side on which the Masjed ol-Ḥarâm is situated. The place for *harvaleh*[78] is between these two pillars. [As] guideposts, which at the present time indicate [the site of] Ṣafâ and Marveh, they have constructed open porticos on both Ṣafâ and Marveh and have built three arches, like doors, of brick and plaster [on them]. These two porticos are raised four steps above the street level. Pious people say that when performing the saʿy one must go [up] and come [down] the steps of those two porticos in such a way that the foot is extended but does not leave the ground. [235]

It is five hundred qadam from the base of the Ṣafâ stairway to the base of the Marveh stairway. That is, from Mount Ṣafâ to the first pillar is one hundred qadam; from the first pillar to the second pillar is one hundred and thirty qadam (and these one hundred and thirty qadam between the two pillars is the place for harvaleh, that is, one must go fast enough to agitate one's limbs). From the second pillar to the base of Marveh is two hundred and seventy qadam. So all together it is a space of five hundred qadam from Ṣafâ to Marveh. In addition to the pilgrims on this street, there are also wayfarers with all sorts of camels, donkeys, and dogs passing by. It is not prohibited.

This is a current description of the Masjed ol-Ḥarâm and the Kaaba.

BUILDING OF THE KAABA

There are many disagreements about the construction of the Kaaba and its inhabitation. Everyone has something to say about it.[79]

---

[77] The performance of *saʿy*, racing seven times between the two hills, is one of the obligatory rituals of the pilgrimage. It is generally understood to commemorate Hagar's frantic search for water for her son Ishmael; the well Zamzam appeared miraculously to save them. A less common tradition is that Adam was standing on Mt. Ṣafâ when he saw Eve for the first time on Marveh, and the two then ran towards each other. See Burton, *Personal Narrative*, 2:288-89; Ali, *Religion of Islam*, p. 538; Gaudefroy-Demombynes, *Pèlerinage*, pp. 225-34; Refʿat, *Mer'ât*, 1:320-21; Querry, *Droit Musulman*, 1:282-83; EI_1,4:199-200.

[78] The term for the distinctive brisk pace used by the pilgrims performing the saʿy between Ṣafâ and Marveh.

[79] The best known account of the history of the Kaaba was that given by the early Arab historian Azraqi supplemented by various later writers; they have been collected and edited by F. Wüstenfeld, *Die Chroniken der Stadt Mekka* (Leipzig, 1857-61). A summary of these accounts may be found in Burckhardt, *Travels*, pp. 162-70 and Esin, *Mecca*, pp. 15-27; see also Rutter, *Holy Cities*, 1:117-23; Gaudefroy-Demombynes, *Pèlerinage*, pp. 26-70; Refʿat, *Mer'ât*, 1:235-42, 262-308; Peters, *Jerusalem and Mecca*, pp. 104-17; *Ḥejâz sâlnâmehsi*, pp. 119-42.

According to the best known [story], Abraham Khalil [the "Friend" of God] wanted to send Hagar and Ishmael away from Sarah. At God's command, he brought them to this land of Mecca, where there was no water or habitation. By the miracle of this prophet, the well of Zamzam appeared. The tribe of Bani Jorham,[80] since they saw that water had appeared, gathered there. Ishmael was brought up among them. It was thus for a while, until Abraham the Friend and Ishmael, by God's command, built a house of stone from Mount Qoᶜayqeᶜân[81] there and dedicated that house to God. The Black Stone was sent from Paradise, and they placed it in a corner of the House so that it might be a place of pilgrimage. At first that stone was white. Impure people touched it with impure hands and gradually it became black. Thus a tradition of the prophet [Moḥammad] has been handed down: "The Black Stone from Paradise was whiter than milk, but the sins of humanity made it black."[82] After it became a place of pilgrimage [236], crowds [of people] gathered [there] from the surrounding areas and it became populous. That House was revered and because of the reverence for that House, rulers were concerned with the well-being of the people. The notables of Mecca were respected very much. The custodians of the House were descendants of Abraham and Ishmael from generation to generation until ᶜAbd ol-Moṭṭaleb, grandfather of the Messenger of God found golden gazelles and weapons there. [The tribe of] Qoraysh was covetous [of them] and the affair led to contention.[83] In the end, it was decided that whatever had been obtained be spent on repairing that House. Repairs were carried out, and the door to the House was gilded with those golden gazelles. A courtyard was laid out. The prosperity of the House and the Masjed ol-Ḥarâm increased. The Black Stone was inside the House, [but] the Messenger [of God, Moḥammad] brought the black stone outside the house and placed it in the present Rokn-e ᶜErâqi. After the [death of the] Messenger [Moḥammad], the Umayyads sacked the Masjed ol-Ḥarâm, wrecked the walls of the House, and carried off its decorations. ᶜAbdollah [ebn-e] Zobayr repaired [it] again and took the Black Stone inside the House and fastened it up on the

---

[80] See Burton, *Personal Narrative*, 2:322; Masᶜudi, *Prairies*, 3:99 ff.; Esin, *Mecca*, pp. 27-35.

[81] A mountain northwest of Mecca located between Mt. Hindi and Mt. Laᶜlaᶜ.

[82] Cf. Ali, *Religion of Islam*, p. 536; Burton, *Personal Narrative*, 2:300 n. 3.

[83] Cf. Qazvini/Le Strange, *Nuzhat*, p. 4; Esin, *Mecca*, p. 74.

wall.[84] Ḥajjâj ebn-e Yusof S̱aqafi[85] enlarged the mosque, altered the form of ᶜAbdollah's building, brought the Black Stone outside the House, and replaced it in the present Rokn-e ᶜErâqi.[86] Valid ebn-e ᶜAbd ol-Malek[87] built grand buildings in that mosque. [Abu] Jaᶜfar [Manṣur] the "Penny-pincher" [*Davâneqi*][88] and his son Mahdi[89] enlarged the Masjed ol-Ḥarâm and improved its condition. At the time of Moqtader the Abbasid,[90] in the year 317 [929-30], the Qarâmeṭeh[91] poured into Mecca and killed the pilgrims and people to [such] an extent that the well of Zamzam was full of the slaughtered.[92] They tore up the covering of the Kaaba and carried off the Black Stone. [237] In the year 339 [950-51], they sold [it] for a paltry sum to agents of the Caliph Motiᶜ. The caliph sent it to the Kaaba, and it was again placed in the present Rokn-e ᶜErâqi. Thereafter, it remained in this manner. The rulers of Egypt and the Ottomans made some repairs.

THE CITY OF MECCA

The city is situated in the middle of a valley, the eastern border of which is Mount Abu Qobays and Mount Qoᶜayqeᶜân and the

---

[84] Ebn-e Zobayr had revolted in Mecca against the Umayyad caliph Yazid in 61/680. Umayyad forces besieged the city of Mecca in 64/683; during the siege, the bombardment of the city destroyed the Kaaba. When Yazid died, the Umayyad general lifted the siege and Ebn-e Zobayr was able to rebuild the Kaaba. The revolt was not finally crushed, and Ebn-e Zobayr killed, until 72/691. See Burton, *Personal Narrative*, 2:323-24; William Muir, *The Caliphate* (reprint, Beirut, 1963), pp. 329-31; 344-46; A. Dixon, *The Umayyad Caliphate* (London, 1971), passim.

[85] Ḥajjâj (d. 95/714) was a governor of Arabia and Iraq during the Umayyad period; he was notorious for the ruthless efficiency of his government. See S. R. Chowdhry, *Al-Hajjaj Ibn Yûsuf* (Delhi, 1972).

[86] Cf. Burton, *Personal Narrative*, 2:234.

[87] The Umayyad caliph Walid I (86-96/705-15.)

[88] The Abbasid caliph Abu Jaᶜfar Manṣur (136-158/754-75); see above, Part One, n. 101.

[89] Abbasid caliph (158-69/775-85).

[90] Another Abbasid caliph (ruled 295-320/908-32).

[91] The Qarâmaṭeh, or Carmathians as they are often called in English, were followers of an Esmâᶜili Shiᶜite sect founded by one Ḥamdan Qarmaṭ in the late ninth century A. D. They were responsible for inciting several revolts against Abbasid rule and in 899 established their own state in the Aḥsâ' region of eastern Arabia. From there, they launched numerous raids into the Arabian peninsula and Iraq, the most famous of which was the capture and sack of Mecca in 930. See M. J. de Goeje, *Memoire sur les Carmathes de Bahrain* (Leiden, 1886); P. K. Hitti, *History of the Arabs* (tenth edition; New York, 1970), pp. 444-46; M. A. Shaban, *Islamic History A. D. 750-1055* (Cambridge, 1976), pp.128-35.

[92] [Marginal note:] "The belief of the Qarâmeṭeh was that the Black Stone was a magnetic rock which pulled people from wherever they were towards it. Thus people came to Mecca because of the attraction of that stone. After they carried away the Black Stone from Mecca and this effect did not materialize, they sold it for a paltry sum." Cf. Qazvini/Le Strange, *Nuzhat*, p. 9.

western border of which is Mount Sâmâ and Mount Shirvân [*sic*]. Mount Shirvân overlooks Menâ and Mash^{c}ar.[93] They say Ishmael came down from that mountain [after] the sacrifice. Its houses are from one to four or five storeys [high]. Most are made of stone and lime. The streets which are its thoroughfares are wide. The other streets are very narrow. The surface of the streets is dirt. There are no paving-stones.

[The city] has about twenty thousand resident households, so its population is 120,000. Most of its bazaars are covered. The roofs of some of them are like scaffolding. It has about 1,600 shops. All sorts of goods can be found, especially at pilgrimage time, when [people] come from the surrounding areas and regions specifically with the intention of trading and bring along all sorts of goods and fabrics. However, food, drink, and merchandise are usually expensive, especially during the season the pilgrims come.

As for animals, sheep and camels are plentiful there. The mutton is very tender and delicate. What they say about its sheep eating senna for fodder so that the meat of the sheep causes diarrhea has no foundation.[94]

First of all, senna is scarce in the wilderness of Mecca. [238]

Second, there are always people who, if they find senna, immediately cut it and bring [it] to Mecca to sell, for there is a market for this product there.

Third, sheep do not eat senna for fodder. In a warm climate [whenever] one eats a lot of any meat and drinks copious amounts of warm water, it inevitably causes diarrhea.

There are many fish there and countless domestic fowl. A few francolins are also found. There are also gazelles in the desert there, but no one hunts [them]. In the mountains of Ṭâ'ef there are also wild goats and sheep.

---

93 This passage is either corrupt or confused. Mt. Qo^{c}ayqe^{c}ân is opposite Mt. Abu Qobays, on the western (not eastern) side of the valley. There is neither a Mt. Sâmâ nor a Mt. Shirvân near Mecca. Since Farâhâni says that "Mount Shirvân" overlooks Menâ, it would seem that he is referring to the whole valley leading from Mecca to Menâ, not just the valley of the city itself. The name of the mountain at Menâ is S̱abir. On these mountains, see Aḥmad b. Moḥammad ol-Ḥadrâvi, *Ketâb ol-^{c}eqd ol-s̱amin fi fażâ'el ol-balad ol-amin* (Mecca, 1314/1896), pp. 12-15; Belâdi, *Ḥejâz*, 7:89, 146-47; Ref^{c}at, *Mer'ât*, 1:178.

94 This appears to have been a popular belief which Farâhâni feels obliged to discredit. The notion that sheep in the environs of Mecca grazed on senna and that consequently eating this mutton would cause diarrhea may have been based on the fact that one variety of senna, which was widely used as a laxative, was known as *sennâ makki*: see Biruni, *Ṣaydaneh*, p. 57.

AGRICULTURE AND FRUITS OF MECCA

Crops of plants and trees do not grow in its soil except for some wild plants and trees, lote trees,[95] and small palms. Some European flowers are also occasionally grown there in pots.

Its grain, green-vegetables and fruit are all brought from Ṭâ'ef. It is ten farsakhs to Ṭâ'ef.

There are these fruits there: melons, watermelons, cucumbers, bananas, Frankish figs [?], sweet and bitter pomegranates, black and white grapes, sweet and bitter lemons, and oranges. Its sweet pomegranates and white grapes are noteworthy. Its sweet pomegranates are better than the pomegranates of Kan.[96]

CLIMATE OF MECCA

The soil of the city of Mecca is dry and has no moisture. Its climate is also dry, warm, and healthy. There is usually a breeze. They [can] sleep in the open air and on the flat roofs. That breeze there cools the water very much. Its water is very wholesome, sweet, light, and aids digestion. [239]

Its water [supply] is canal water which water-carriers take in water-skins and sell at the houses. During non-pilgrimage seasons, a water-skin costs about one shâhi and one hundred dinârs [in] Iranian [money.] In the season pilgrims come, it costs about five shâhis and two ᶜabbâsis [in] Iranian [money].[97]

They take animals to where water is flowing and water them [there].

The source of this water is from the mountainous region of Ṭâ'ef. They have dug a canal which comes to ᶜAfarât, from the wadi of ᶜArafat to Menâ, and from Menâ to the city. It has a wide water-channel [made] of stone and plaster. It is one and a half z̲arᶜ deep and one z̲arᶜ wide. In many places, it has been stopped from flowing by the amount of water they take out or by someone getting [in it].

It is well known and written that Zobaydeh, the wife of Hârun or-Rashid, had a dream [that] she was stark naked and people passing by were having sexual intercourse with her and taking their pleasure from her. She awoke in a fright and out of shame would not divulge it to anyone until finally she told her personal slave girl: "Go

---

[95] Text: *derakht-e konâr va sedr*. The konâr or sedr refers to the *Zizyphus jujuba*, a fruit-bearing tree (also known as the *nabaq*) common to Arabia and the Mediterranean region. Strictly speaking, *sedr* refers to the fruit rather than the tree. See Biruni, *Ṣaydaneh*, p. 180; Burton, *Personal Narrative*, 1:404-5.

[96] Text: *kand*. This is a colloquial name for Kan, a village near Tehran which is famous for its pomegranates.

[97] On the Meccan water-supply, see Refᶜat, *Mer'ât*, 1:207-24.

to Ḥażrat-e Musâ ebn-e Jaᶜfar and tell him, as if speaking about yourself, 'I had such a dream' and see how he interprets it." The slave girl went and told about it. The Ḥażrat smiled and said, "This is the dream of your mistress. She shall perform some charitable work so that people and passersby will derive pleasure from her." Therefore Zobaydeh came out to this place and had the water brought [in] at considerable expense.[98]

In the reign of Moqtader the Abbasid[99] this canal fell into ruin and [he] repaired it. In the reign of ol-Qâ'em-bellah[100] and the Caliph Nâṣer[101] it also fell into ruin and they repaired it too. [240] After the fall of the Abbasid caliphate it was in ruins for a while until, in the reign of the Mongol Amir Chupân[102] it was repaired and improved. Afterwards, it sometimes became ruined, and the Circassian rulers of Egypt and the Ottoman Sultans repaired it. It is still in existence now.

MALE AND FEMALE SLAVES

The people are generally dark colored, but many whites are also found. Most of their servants and workers are slave men and women. Many people, such as the notables and so on, take possession of the slave girls and accept them in marriage. Their children are often by slave girls.[103]

Slave girls and male slaves are plentiful here and relatively inexpensive. There are three enclosed areas in the middle of the bazaar specifically for selling male slaves and slave girls. They put wooden benches arranged in three tiers [there]. Those on the first tier are well dressed [with] clean, fresh clothes, are very beautiful, with pretty eyes, and full of charm, banter, and coquetry. [Those on] the second tier are of a little lower quality than these. [On] the third tier are the very black, thick-lipped, and dirty slave girls, most of whom are brought to Iran where people like us are willing to own

---

[98] The pilgrimage of Zobaydeh to Mecca and her many charitable works are celebrated by many of the Muslim historians; the water source at ᶜArafât is still known as ᶜAyn Zobeydeh. See Ṭabari, *Târikh*, 3:81, 486; Masᶜudi, *Prairies*, 8:295-99; Nabia Abbott, *Two Queens of Baghdad* (Chicago, 1946), pp. 246-47; Refᶜat, *Mer'ât*, 1:209; Peters, *Jerusalem and Mecca*, p. 48; S. al-Rashid, *Darb Zobaydeh* (Riyadh, 1986), pp. 31-35.

[99] Abbasid caliph (285-320/908-32).

[100] Abbasid caliph (422-67/1031-75).

[101] Abbasid caliph (575-622/1180-1225).

[102] Chupân was a powerful general in the army of the Ilkhânid ruler of Iran, Abu Saᶜid (717-35/1317-35). He incurred the wrath of the ruler and was executed in 1327.

[103] Cf. Hurgronje, *Mekka*, pp. 106-8.

them. Their price is from thirty or forty tomans to two hundred tomans. Male slaves are cheap. Good eunuchs, young and old, can be obtained there.[104] Thus the wife of ᶜAlâ' ol-Molk who, I heard, had come to Mecca this year bought a young eunuch for two hundred tomans and took [him] back.

The people of Egypt, Arab Iraq, and the Syrians buy many slave girls and male slaves. Transporting them by sea is a source of trouble and dispute.[105] They must be carried by way of Syria and the Jabal [Shammâr]. It costs twenty or thirty tomans each to get [them] to Tehran. [241]

PRACTICES AND CUSTOMS

One of the customs and practices of the people of Mecca is that they cut marks on the cheeks and the space behind the ears of their children [during] childhood.[106] When they grow up, the scar is visible on the cheeks and behind the ears of the women and men. They have settled on this as a means of distinguishing between those of Meccan and non-Meccan identity. If their faces are white, this method of cutting the face increases their beauty.

RELIGIOUS RITES

The people are mostly of the Shâfeᶜi and Ḥanafi rites.[107] There are also Mâlekis and Ḥanbalis. [The city] has about sixty Shi'ites who are often pilgrim-guides who associate with the Iranians[108] and [who] may be descendants of Ḥosayn. These Shi'ites do not practice dissimulation [*taqeyyeh*] very much at the present time. They clearly and openly practice Shi'ism. Some of these Shi'ites hold rowzeh-khᵛânis during the days of ᶜÂshurâ. Among them is Sayyed Abu'l-Fażl, who is one of the pilgrim-guides and the son-in-law of Musâ Baghdâdi. (Musâ Baghdâdi is also a Shi'ite, who is a respected merchant and who often conducts business with the Sharif of Mecca and the notables.)

---

[104] Cf. the contemporary account of the Mecca slave market in Hurgronje, *Mekka*, pp. 10-20; also note Rutter, *Holy Cities*, 1:133-36.

[105] This "trouble" was of course due to British efforts to suppress the slave trade by blocking the transport of slaves by sea routes; see J. B. Kelly, *Britain and the Persian Gulf 1795-1880* (Oxford, 1968), pp. 411-51 and 576-37. There had long been no slave market as such in Iran, andthe import of slaves into Iran by sea had been outlawed since 1852, but ownership of slaves, assuming they could be acquired through other means, was not yet prohibited. Such slaves were used strictly for domestic purposesand often became in effect members of the household.

[106] These scars (*masâli*) were made to protect the children against the evil eye; see Hurgronje, *Mekka*, p. 97.

[107] Cf. Hurgronje, *Mekka*, pp. 182-84.

[108] Text: *ᶜajam*, which can be used generally for any non-Arab but usually refers specifically to Iranians.

PRACTICES OF ᶜÂSHURÂ

Previously, the people of Mecca, on the pretext that Noah's ark came to rest on Mount Judi on [the day of] ᶜÂshurâ, and the Muslims had [thus] been saved from the abyss of destruction by Noah, held festivals on ᶜÂshurâ and brought out instruments of play and sport.[109] After the reign of Sharif ᶜAbd ol-Moṭṭaleb, since Sharif ᶜAbdollah[110] and the present sharif, Sharif ᶜAwn, were not hostile towards Shi'ism, this practice was abolished and stopped out of respect for the death of the Prince of Martyrs [Ḥosayn].[111]

EMÂM JAᶜFAR-E ṢÂDEQ'S BOOK OF TAFSIR

I heard from many [people] that Sayyed Abu'l-Fażl the pilgrim guide had a book of *tafsir*[112] by Ḥażrat-e Jaᶜfar-e Ṣâdeq in which he had provided exegesis of many verses about the virtues of his forefathers and descendants. Many had seen that tafsir. [242] Since this subject was something new, and since at this time nothing was known about a tafsir by Ḥażrat-e Jaᶜfar-e Ṣâdeq, I made inquires and looked specifically for Abu'l-Fażl. He said, "It is true. This year, I took that tafsir with me to India. One of the Rajas of India, thanks to [offers of] money and persistence, took the book to be copied and printed and published there. He will return the original tafsir to me."

ATTITUDE OF THE PEOPLE TOWARD SHI'ITE PILGRIMS

Previously, in Mecca the populace greatly persecuted the Iranian pilgrims who were Shi'ites, so they had to practice complete

---

109 According to the Koran (11:44) Noah's ark came to rest on Mt. Judi. Various Muslim commentators held that this was a mountain near the city of Mosul in Iraq and that the date Noah left the ark was the tenth of Moḥarram, which is also ᶜÂshurâ, a holy day of mourning for Shi'ites. Farâhâni is implying that the Sunni Arabs used this as an excuse for merrymaking on the day of Imam Ḥosayn's martyrdom in order to annoy the Shi'ites.

110 On ᶜAbd ol-Moṭṭaleb, see above n. 76. ᶜAbdollah was Sharif from 1858-77. See EI_1, 3:446-47 [s.v. "Mecca"].

111 In this regard, it is interesting to note that the Sharifs of Mecca were originally Zaydi Shi'ites in rite but changed to the Shâfeᶜi rite in order to conform with the majority of the population; see Hurgronje, *Mekka*, p. 183; Richard T. Mortel, "Zaydi Shiᶜism and the Ḥasanid Sharifs of Mecca," *International Journal of Middle East Studies* 19(1987):455-72; *idem*, "The Genealogy of the Ḥasanid Sharifs of Mecca," *Journal of the College of Arts, King Saud University* 12(1985):221-50. Farâhâni's comments reflect one of several ways in which the Sharifs were consciously cultivating the favor of Muslim visitors to Mecca in order to get support for their position in resisting the extension of Ottoman political power in the Hejaz. See Butrus Abu-Manneh, "Sultan Abdülhamid and the Sharifs of Mecca," *Asian and African Studies* 9(1973):4-5.

112 *Tafsir* is exegesis of the Koran. One of the cardinal beliefs of Shi'ism is that the Imams were entrusted with full understanding of the inner meaning (*bâṭen*) of the holy scriptures. There is a *Tafsir ol-qur'ân* attributed to the Imam Jaᶜfar-e Ṣâdeq: See Fuat Sezgin, *Geschichte des arabischen Schriftums* (Leiden, 1967), 1:529. Sezgin makes no mention of a published version of the text, but does indicate that some of the manuscripts are in India (none are listed in Meccan libraries).

dissimulation. These days, because of the weakness of the Ottoman government and the European style civil law which is practiced there, and the strength of the Iranian government, this practice is completely abandoned. There is no harm done to the Iranians. No one would molest them, even if they did not practice dissimulation. They treat the Iranians very respectfully, especially the ones who do not show meanness in expenditures and appearance.[113]

APROPOS THE MANNER OF DRESS AND NOT PRACTICING DISSIMULATION

In Mecca, Medina, and along the way, I wore Iranian garb everywhere. I put an Iranian hat on my head, and I never practiced dissimulation, Yet, not only did no one ever bother me physically or verbally, I was afforded complete respect. My opinion is that in this day and age, dissimulation is unlawful, and one must not curse the caliphs.[114] Changing dress and concealing the Jaᶜfari [Shi'ite religious] rite results in nothing but hardship and hypocrisy. All the Sunni people know that the Iranians are of the Jaᶜfari rite and that their rite differs from the Sunnites in methodology and substance [*oṣul* and *foru*ᶜ]. They consider the dissimulation of the Iranians an instrument of hypocrisy. For this reason, they call the Iranians hypocrites. [I] have discussed this with their ulama more often than there is room to relate in this short account. How is it that Shi'ites [worship] differently in public on the Day of ᶜArafeh or at the miqât, and no one remonstrates with them and nothing happens to them, [243] and yet when it comes to the stations of prayer and the ablutions, they [feel] obliged to pray with hands folded to perform the *qonut,* even though the Mâlekis also pray with hands open and perform the wiping of the head and feet [in lieu of ablutions]?[115]

BELIEF OF THE IMMACULATE IMAMS ABOUT THE PROPRIETY OF DISSIMULATION

The fact that the immaculate Imams have commended dissimulation [in religious matters] can be explained by the weakness of faith which they had observed in people. This blessed verse [of the Koran] implies that one should avoid the practice of

---

113 Farâhâni's remarks may be contrasted with those of the rather sour-dispositioned Sayf od-Dowleh in his *Safarnâmeh,* where he has only bad things to say about the people of both Mecca and Medina.

114 The Shi'ite practice of ritually cursing various early Muslim leaders, especially the caliph ᶜOmar, would be particularly offensive to Sunni Muslims.

115 The Persian text, particularly for this last sentence, is confusing, but Farâhâni's feeling that Iranian Shi'ites no longer need to practice dissimulation is clear enough. As his discussion of *taqeyyeh* suggests, the concept of dissimulation was an important one in Shi'ism. It was based in large part on traditions from the Imams; however it was also derived by Shi'ites (and others) from the Koran (3:20): "Whether ye hide that which is in your breasts or reveal it, Allah knoweth it." On

dissimulation: "How should I fear that which you have associated [with God], when you fear not to associate with God that for which He has revealed to you no authority? Which of the two factions has more right to safety, if you know? Those who believe and do not obscure their belief by wrongdoing, theirs is safety, and they are rightly guided."[116]

CAPITAL OF THE HEJAZ

The capital of the province of the Hejaz is Mecca. The governor resides there, and Ṭâ'ef, Jedda, Medina, Yanboᶜ, and Râbegh are under his authority. In some of these places, there is a qâ'em-maqâm, and in some a modir. The governor has jurisdiction over them.

THE SHARIF

The sharif really acts like the chief custodian [*motavalli-bâshi*] of the House [of God, the Kaaba]. The work of the sharif at the present time is [dealing with] matters [concerning] the Masjed ol-Ḥarâm. He is also in charge of many of the affairs of the pilgrims. The Bedouin of the desert, since for years they have known and listened to the sharifs, do not obey anyone else and refer their own affairs to him. The governor also automatically has recourse to the sharif for dealing with the Bedouin. Otherwise, matters of city administration, the army, Ṭâ'ef, etc. are all under the governor; by no means does the sharif get involved. Previously, the sharifs were very powerful in the Hejaz. They never submitted to nor obeyed the

the concept itself, see Ignaz Goldziher, "Das Prinzip der Taḳijja im Islam," *Zeitschrift der Deutschen Morgenländischen Gesellschaft* 60(1906):213-226; E. Kohlberg, "Some Imami Shii Views on Taqiyya," *Journal of the American Oriental Society* 95(1975):395-402; Seyyed Hossein Nasr et al. (eds.), *Shi'ism: Doctrines, Thought, and Spirituality* (Albany, 19880, pp. 203-12; EI_1, 4:628-29; Momen, *Shi'i Islam*, p. 183. In earlier times, particularly when the Ottoman Empire and Safavid Iran were at war with each other, the open practice of Shi'ism, especially during the pilgrimage, could result in persecution or death. J. L. Burckhardt, *Travels in Arabia*, p. 251, records, for example, that some Iranian Shi'ites were executed for not renouncing their beliefs in 1625 and that Shi'ites were actually forbidden to enter Mecca in 1634. As late as 1877-78, Keane, *Six Months in the Hejaz*, p. 80, noted that Iranian pilgrims were "under a cloud" and felt obliged to "keep very much to themselves and pray together in parties." By the time of Farâhâni's visit, this situation had changed considerable for a number of reasons: improving Ottoman-Iranian relations, the visit of Nâṣer od-Din Shâh to the holy cities of Iraq, mutual Ottoman-Iranian interest in curbing the Wahhabi movement in Arabia, the Ottoman sultan ᶜAbd ol-Ḥamid's efforts to revive the title of caliph and consequent concern for his image in the larger Muslim world, and the interest of the Sharifs of Mecca in buttressing their autonomy by cultivating the favor of non-Ottoman Muslims (their descent from the Prophet Moḥammad would naturally be an asset in dealing with Iranian Shi'ites). Against this more tolerant background, the use of dissimulation would no longer seem necessary to protect Shi'ites from persecution.

[116] Koran, 6:81-82.

governor of the Hejaz and the Ottoman sultan. But these days, the governor is powerful, and the sharif does not have such power.[117] I heard [that] Sharif ᶜAwn, the present sharif, is at heart very annoyed with this situation and this governor.[118] [244]

SHARIF ᶜAWN

Sharif ᶜAwn[119] is well disposed to Shiᶜism. He is modest, scholarly, well-bred, knowledgeable about history, and eloquent. He knows a little Persian and Turkish. He seeks and is eager to meet any of the Iranian notables and well-bred people who come to Mecca.

INTERVIEW WITH SHARIF ᶜAWN

In order to obtain an interview with him, I went in Iranian dress with an interpreter from the consulate. His house is five storeys [high]. A squad of Ottoman soldiers were stationed as sentinels at the door of the house, and two people with silver maces stood in three places–at the head of the stairs and the doorways. I went first to his chancery. Five clerks and secretaries were seated [there]: One was the Arab secretary [*monshi*]; two were Arab accountants; one was also a secretary and the Arabic-Turkish translator; and one was the registrar and secretary of documents. [I] waited there three or four minutes [while] they informed the sharif. I was admitted to the presence of the sharif. Two Ottoman military officers were present with the sharif. The room was covered with Persian carpets. Two linen covered sofas and six chairs were arranged irregularly; there was no table or desk. The sharif [wore] a turban and Arab dress. He had a trimmed salt-and-pepper beard. He was about forty-three or -four years old. [He] was seated with the two Ottoman military officers on the chairs in a circle. The custom is that whoever enters the presence of pashas and sharifs pays homage and greetings in the Ottoman manner and kisses the hand of the sharif. I saluted only in

[117] On the complicated relationship between the Ottoman government and the Sharifs, see *Ḥejâz sâlnâmehsi,* pp. 143-53; Kazem Zadeh, *Relation*, pp. 36-39; Hogarth, *Hejaz*, pp. 47-48; Hurgronje, *Mekka*, 1:138-89; Ṣâleh ol-Amr, *The Hejaz Under Ottoman Rule 1869-1914* (Riyadh, 1978); Tresse, *Pèlerinage syrien*, pp. 50-66; Abu-Manneh, "Sharifs," pp. 1-21; W. Ochsenwald, *Religion, Society, and the State in Arabia: The Hijaz under Ottoman Control 1840-1908* (Colombus, 1984)

[118] So much so, in fact, that he, his relatives, and many of his supporters finally left Mecca in the fall of 1886 and refused to return until the Sultan removed the offensive governor: See De Gaury, *Rulers of Mecca*, pp. 259-60; Abu-Manneh, "Sharifs," pp. 12-15.

[119] ᶜAwn or-Rafiq, the Sharif of Mecca from 1882-85; see Hogarth, *Hejaz*, p. 48; De Gaury, *Rulers of Mecca*, pp. 257-61; Hurgronje, *Mekka*, 1:176-79 (and photograph, plate VII); *Mokhtaṣar târikh omarâ makkeh ol-mokarrameh* (MS. Leiden Or. 14.025), f. 11b.

the Iranian manner. He got up and seated me on a chair facing him. He made polite conversation in Arabic and inquired about the health of Moᶜin ol-Molk. Then he said, "Today I was involved with some [people of] Ghaznin." The translator from the consulate said, "What did Qazvinis have to request that we had not been informed [about]?" He said, "I am talking about the Ghaznin which is the homeland of Seboktegin."[120] [245] He asked me about Qazvin and Ghaznin. I talked nearly half an hour about Ghaznin and Sultan Maḥmud. Meanwhile they brought coffee in cups studded with jewels on a gold tray. A filigreed dish cover was placed over the tray. The coffee had a lot of cardamom and spices. After coffee, he took one of his own cigarettes and gave a cigarette to me. This is a sign of close friendship. When I begged permission to leave, he expressed gratefulness [for the interview] and hoped to have another meeting and escorted [me] for four steps [to the door].

MUSICAL TROUPE

In the evenings, one hour before sunset, a troupe of musicians play with great accomplishment in the middle of the street on which the sharif's house fronts, and crowds of people gather. Three hours after nightfall, these same musicians play for a whole hour at the gate of the Pâshâ's house.[121]

TREATMENT OF NON-MUSLIMS

Non-Muslims never enter Mecca, Menâ, Mashᶜar, ᶜArafât, and the frontiers of Mecca. Sometimes travellers of religions other than Islam come in disguise to tour about. If someone finds out and they catch them, they are imprisoned and will be punished.

MONEY

All sorts of currency are [used] in Mecca. For example, the lira, the majidi, the Levant dollar, the rupee, the English guinea, the imperial, and the Dutch real are in circulation–especially the Levant dollar which is most often used.[122]

In Mecca, they accept the Ottoman lira at 150 qorush. The Ottoman silver majidi in Mecca is 27 qorush. The Levant dollar [246] is 28 qorush. The imperial is 135 qorush. The English guinea is 163 qorush. The English rupee is 13 qorush. The Dutch real is 30

---

120 Seboktigin (366-87/977-97) was the founder of the Ghaznavid dynasty which ruled in Afghanistan and India from its capital at the city of Ghazneh (also called Ghaznin). Farâhâni's point is that the interpreter misunderstood the term the Sharif used for "people of Ghazneh" as "people from Qazvin."

121 Cf. Kazem Zadeh, *Relation*, p. 44.

122 A few years later, Kazem Zadeh, *Relation*, p. 23, reported that the Indian rupee had become the most common currency in the area.

qorush. In Mecca, each qorush is 60 para, but in Istanbul the qorush is 40 para, and each lira is 108 qorush and each majidi is 20 qorush.

HOLY PLACES IN MECCA REMAINING FROM THE TIME OF THE PROPHET

Near the house of the sharif, there is a place which they say is the quarter of Abi Ṭâleb[123] and the birthplace of [the Prophet Moḥammad].[124] One first goes ten steps down from the level of the street [to where there] is a round stone house. In the middle of it there is another round stone, in the middle of which there is also a black stone. They say the blessed birth was in the house on this rock. It is a place of pious visitation.[125]

This house has two custodians and a modest wakf endowment. On the door of the house it has been written that it is the place of birth of the Seal [of the Prophets, Moḥammad].

BIRTHPLACE OF FÂṬEMEH

Near the bazaars of Ṣafâ and Marveh there is another building [where], after going down seven steps, there is a whitewashed stone house. They have built a cenotaph [there]. They say this place is the place of birth of Ḥażrat-e Fâṭemeh.[126] This is also a place of pious visitation and has a custodian and a wakf endowment.

THE STONE WHICH GREETED THE PROPHET

Near this same street there is a stone fixed on the wall. They say this stone spoke a salutation to the Prophet [Moḥammad]. On the stone, these two verses are inscribed:

> I am the stone [which] always greeted the best of all
> men, so the tidings of joy are mine. [247]
> A merit was bestowed by his excellency, by it I am
> distinguished above [all other] stones.[127]

THE ḤAJUN CEMETERY

On the left [side] as one goes towards ᶜArafât and Menâ, at the end of the houses of Mecca, there are two very extensive enclosed

[123] Abu Ṭâleb was the uncle of the Prophet Moḥammad and his protector after the death of his father as well as the father of the caliph and Shi'ite Imam ᶜAli.

[124] Cf. ᶜAli b. Abi Bakr ol-Harawi, *Guide des Lieux de Pèlerinage* (trans. Janine Sourdel-Thomine; Damascus, 1957), p. 199; Burckhardt, *Travels*, p. 171; Burton, *Personal Narrative*, 2:254. Rutter, *Holy Cities*, 1:270, notes that this shrine was badly damaged after the Wahhâbi occupation of Mecca.

[125] Text: *ziârat*. This term could be translated as "pilgrimage" but the more awkward "pious visitation" will be used here in order to avoid confusion with the *ḥajj* or pilgrimage proper.

[126] Cf. Harawi, *Guide*, p. 199; Burckhardt, *Travels*, pp. 171-72; Burton, *Personal Narrative*, 2:251; Rutter, *Holy Cities*, 1:273; Refᶜat, *Mer'ât*, 1:189.

[127] The building was supposedly the shop of Abu Bakr; one day when Moḥammad knocked at the door, the stone greeted him and informed him that Abu Bakr was not at home. See Ḥadrâvi, *ᶜEqd*, p. 24; Burckhardt, *Travels*, p. 172; Burton, *Personal Narrative*, 2:253-54; *Ḥejâz sâlnâmehsi*, 2:149.

areas at the foot of and on the slopes of the mountain. A wall two z̲arᶜ [high] of stone has been built all the way around them. This place is known as the Ḥajun cemetery.[128] Shi'ites and Sunnis are often buried there.

MAUSOLEUM OF KHADIJEH

In the last enclosure, there is first of all a mausoleum which is whitewashed inside and out. Ḥażrat-e Khadijeh-ye Kobrâ[129] is buried in this mausoleum. It has a cenotaph [made] of wood and covered with a cloth of gold-braided velvet. It has a custodian, servant, a *ziâret-nâmeh* reader, and a *ziârat-nâmeh*.[130]

MAUSOLEUM OF ÂMANEH

Near this mausoleum of Khadijeh, there is another mausoleum which is also whitewashed and has a sepulcher, custodian, and servant. They say it is the tomb of Ḥażrat-e Âmaneh, the mother of the Messenger of God.[131] One of the sharifs is also buried in this mausoleum, beside the tomb of Ḥażrat-e Âmaneh.

THREE OTHER MAUSOLEUMS

Going a little further up the side of the mountain from there, there is also a small enclosed area. Two houses are built there and are inhabited. There are two mausoleums in this enclosure. Ḥażrat-e ᶜAbd ol-Moṭṭaleb[132] and Ḥażrat-e ᶜAbd ol-Manâf[133] are

---

128 Strictly speaking, Ḥajun ("Twisting") is the name of the valley between Mt. Kadâ and Mt. Laᶜlaᶜ where the cemetery, which is named the Maᶜlâ ("Heights"), is located. It is not uncommon, however, for either name to be applied to the cemetery or even to distinguish two cemeteries, one known as Maᶜlâ and the other as Ḥajun. See Belâdi, *Ḥejâz*, 2:236-40; Burton, *Personal Narrative*, 2:248-50; references to medieval sources in Harawi, *Guide*, p. 203 n. 15. These accounts should be contrasted with that of Rutter, *Holy Cities*, 1:274, who visited this holy site after the occupation of the Hejaz by the Saᶜudi/Wahhâbis, who objected violently to the practice of building and visiting elaborate tombs: "The tombs of these personages were formerly crowned by small but handsome domes, but these, without exception, have now been demolished, together with most of the tombstones. The guardians of each tomb, who formerly derived considerable incomes from the hâjjis, now no longer dare to spread their handkerchiefs on the ground to receive the pilgrims' alms. The cemetery is silent and deserted, save when a funeral party quickly bears in one more departed Muslim to join the millions whose dust lies there."

129 The first (and during her lifetime the only) wife of the Prophet Moḥammad; on the tomb see Burckhardt, *Travels*, pp. 172-73; Burton, *Personal Narrative*, p. 249; Refᶜat, *Mer'ât*, 1:31 (photograph #28).

130 A book of prayers to be read while performing a pious visitation [*ziârat*] to a shrine; see Donaldson, *Shi'ite Religion*, pp. 89, 185, 346.

131 Burton, *Personal Narrative*, 2:249-50, reports that this tomb had been destroyed during the first Wahhâbi occupation of Mecca but recently rebuilt. See also Burckhardt, *Travels*, p. 173; photograph in Refᶜat, *Mer'ât*, #29.

132 The Prophet Moḥammad's grandfather.

133 The great-great-grandfather of the Prophet Moḥammad and the progenitor of both the Umayyad and Hashimite clans of the tribe of Qoraysh in Mecca.

buried in one, and Ḥażrat-e Abi Ṭâleb is buried in the other mausoleum. They are also places of pious visitation. [The tomb of] Ḥażrat-e Abi Ṭâleb is a frequent place of pious visitation for Shi'ites and Iranians.

MOUNT [A]BU QOBAYS

Mount [A]bu Qobays[134] is located to the east of the Masjed ol-Ḥarâm and is inside the city. There are two sanctuaries on top of it. One is an unroofed stone building. The splitting of the moon took place there.[135] It is a place of pious visitation. Another is a building of stone with a roof. [Moḥammad], they say, prayed there, and Belâl gave the call to prayers. [248]

THE JABAL ON-NUR OR MOUNT ḤERÂ

Another [site] is the Jabal on-Nur ["Mountain of Light"], which used to be called Mount Ḥerâ.[136] When the Messenger of God circumambulated that mountain, it began to shake violently. He commanded, "Be still, O Ḥerâ!"

It is one farsakh from the city of Mecca to the Jabal on-Nur. Along the way there is a place from which flood waters used to come towards Mecca and caused destruction. A very strong dam has been built there. [It] is about seven hundred qadam [long]. They say the Ottoman Solṭân Solaymân built this dam.

This Jabal on-Nur is a tall rocky mountain. The road has been built [in such] a way that one can go, with difficulty, mounted on a donkey. Before reaching the summit of the mountain, a large cistern has been built which is filled with rain-water. After that, one comes to a domed structure. There is a large stone under the middle of the dome. That stone has been split down the middle. It is well known that the cleaving open of the chest of the prophet took place on top

---

134 This mountain is very close to the eastern corner of the sacred mosque in Mecca. In Muslim tradition, it is famous as the first mountain created by God, the site of Adam's tomb, the place where the Black Stone was found, and a spot where the Prophet Moḥammad used to pray. It has thus always been a popular site for pious visitation. See, for example, Ḥadrâvi, *ʿEqd*, p. 12; Ebn Baṭṭuṭeh, *Travels*, p. 210; Harawi, *Guide*, p. 201; Burckhardt, *Travels*, pp. 174-75; Burton, *Personal Narrative*, p. 160 n. 2; Rutter, *Holy Cities*, 1:276.

135 In popular tradition, Moḥammad, when urged by the tribe of Qoraysh to perform a miracle, showed the moon split in half (based on a loose interpretation of the Koran, 54:1-2: "The hour drew nigh and the moon was rent in twain. And if they behold a portent they turn away and say: Prolonged illusion!").

136 This famous mountain is located about five miles north-east of Mecca overlooking the town of Menâ. See Ebn Baṭṭuṭeh, *Travels*, p. 211; Qazvini/Le Strange, *Nuzhat*, p. 8; Burckhardt, *Travels*, pp. 175-76; Rutter, *Holy Cities*, 1:280-82; Gaudefroy-Demombynes, *Pèlerinage*, p. 237; Keane, *Six Months in the Hejaz*, p. 65; Refʿat, *Mer'ât*, 1:56-60.

of this stone, and the chapter [from the Koran beginning] "Did we not expand ..." was revealed.[137] The custodian there lets people lie down on the middle of this rock in order to obtain some money to supply himself with provisions. There is a cave at the foot of this same mountain. The door to the cave is [made] of two very large stones. There is just enough [room] between these two stones for a man to enter the cave with difficulty. It is a small cave, rounded out of the stone, which [used to be] a place of worship for [Moḥammad.][138] This is also a place of pious visitation.

MOUNT S̱OWR

Another [site] is the Jabal os̱-S̱owr. [Moḥammad] took refuge in [one of] its caves. It is a place of pious visitation. [249]

Jabal os̱-S̱owr is one and a half farsakhs from Mecca, to the south of the city. However, [I] did not go and see [it] because the way [to] it is terrible and precipitous. I will not write anything about it in this section.[139]

DISPOSITION OF THE PILGRIMS DURING THE PILGRIMAGE

Beginning on the second and third days of the month of Ẕi Hejjeh a squad of soldiers goes to Menâ, and a squad of soldiers to ᶜArafât. There are about a hundred shops on the road to Menâ. The shopkeepers also take goods to those shops [beginning] on the fourth and fifth of the month. Tents, tent-supplies, and kitchen equipment are continuously being carried to Menâ and ᶜArafât over

---

137 Koran, 94:1, "Have we not caused thy bosom to dilate." This is interpreted literally in some early Muslim tradition. In A. Guillaume, *The Life of Muhammad: A Translation of Ibn Isḥaq's Sirat Rasul Allah* (Oxford, 1955), p. 72, it is related thus: "Thaur b. Yazîd from a learned person who I think was Khâlid b. Maᶜdân al-Kalâ'i told me that some of the apostle's companions asked him to tell them about himself. He said, 'I am what Abraham my father prayed for and the good news of Jesus. When my mother was carrying me she saw a light proceeding from her which showed her the castles of Syria. I was suckled among the B. Saᶜd b. Bakr, and while I was with a brother of mine behind our tents shepherding the lambs, two men in white raiment came to me with a gold basin full of snow. Then they seized me and opened up my belly, extracted my heart and split it; then they extracted a black drop from it and threw it away; then they washed my heart and my belly with that snow until they had thoroughly cleaned them."

138 Many Muslims believe that Moḥammad received the first of the revelations that make up the Koran while meditating in this cave on Mt. Ḥerâ.

139 It is a well known story in Muslim tradition that when Moḥammad fled Mecca to make the hegira to Medina, he hid in this cave in order to elude those pursuing him; a spider miraculously wove a web across the entrance to the cave to mislead the guide tracking him. See Harawi, *Guide*, p. 202; Ebn Baṭṭuṭeh, *Travels*, p. 212; Burckhardt, *Travels*, p. 176; Belâdi, *Ḥejâz*, 2:96-99; Refᶜat, *Mer'ât*, 1:60-63. As Rutter, *Holy Cities*, 1:283, confirms, "very few of the Mekkans have climbed Jebel Thowr, on account of the difficulty of the ascent, and because, prior to the Wahhâbi occupation, the surrounding country was always infested with dangerous Bedouins."

these several days. If a person has his own tent, so much the better. If one will be travelling with the Syrian ḥamleh-dârs via the Syrian route, those ḥamleh-dârs have numerous tents for the pilgrims under their guidance. They carry the tents to Menâ and ᶜArafât and set [them] up and do not collect a rental fee for the tents from them. If not, many pilgrims rent tents in the city and send them to Mena and ᶜArafât.

The fare for pack-animals from Mecca to ᶜArafât and Menâ is three and a half Levant dollars per camel. The charge for camel-pannier and litter is seven dollars. The charge for the tent in ᶜArafât and Menâ is not a fixed sum; it depends on the size and quality of the tent.

THE DAY OF TARVEYYEH

From the morning of the eighth of the sacred month of Z̲i Ḥejjeh, which is the day of Tarveyyeh,[140] until three hours after nightfall, some [people] first perform the major ablution at home or [their] lodgings and put on the eḥrâm clothes. [Others] take their eḥrâm clothes, go to the Masjed ol-Ḥarâm, perform the eḥrâm ablutions beside the Well of Zamzam, put on the eḥrâm clothes at the Station of Abraham or the Ḥejr of Ishmael, and recite the talbeyyeh. They set out towards Menâ on camel and litter or by horse or donkey or on foot. [250] On this day, owing to the multitudes of people, [going] by camel and litter and camel-pannier is a cause of trouble and perdition. Going by horse or donkey is better. The sharif and the pasha also accompany the pilgrims to Menâ and ᶜArafât along with crowds, parade horses, and very splendid soldiers. They had put on the eḥrâm clothes, except that their eḥrâm clothes were [made of] two pieces of cashmere shawl. The consul of the government of Iran also has eḥrâm clothes of two pieces of cashmere shawl out of consideration for the dignity of the state.[141]

---

140 It is not known why the eighth day of the month of pilgrimage, when the pilgrims begin the trek to the plain of ᶜArafât, is called the day of Tarveyyeh. One common explanation is that the term means "satisfying thirst" and was used because the pilgrims watered their camels on that day (or perhaps because it was a vestige of a more ancient rain ritual); another is that it means "noticing" and refers to Abraham's "taking notice" of his divine orders; still another that it refers to the ceremonial washing of the Kaaba: See Hughes, *Dictionary*, p. 628; Burton, *Personal Narrative*, p. 289 n. 1; Gaudefroy-Demombynes, *Pèlerinage*, p. 236.

141 Cf. Kazem Zadeh, *Relation*, pp. 14-15, 69-75.

MENÂ

At the outskirts of Menâ, there are about two hundred houses and shops which are rented out to pilgrims and shopkeepers during this season.

Menâ is located to the east of the city of Mecca between two low mountains.

THE KHAYF MOSQUE

When one goes to the outskirts of Menâ, the Khayf mosque[142] is on the right side on the slopes of the mountain. It has been raised up four steps above ground level and has had a wall of stone and lime and plaster erected [around it]. On top of its door the foundation of the mosque has been written–that it was built in the year 894 [1488-89]. This sentence is also written: "The sultan of the lands and the seas, the servant of the noble holy places, Solṭân Aḥmad Khân, son of Solṭân Moḥammad Khân,[143] may God perpetuate his caliphate to the end of time, ordered the repair of the Khayf Mosque and the Place of the Scales of the Prophet, dated in the year 1025 [1616]."

After entering the mosque there is first of all a very expansive courtyard, the periphery of which is whitewashed and [has] false archways. The length of the courtyard is 140 qadam, and the width of the courtyard is 120 qadam. In the middle of the courtyard there is a domed [structure] which has a mihrab and four stone benches. All four of its sides are open. The mosque proper has four columns [along] its width (which is about 16 qadam), and [along] its length (which is 90 qadam) [it has] twenty-one columns. [251] The name of Qâyt Bây, the founder of the mosque, is written in Kufic script above the mihrab.

It is a two hour trip from Mecca to Menâ by camel and litter. The initial boundary of Mena is at ᶜAqabeh-ye Ulâ, which is adjacent to Mecca, and its end is Wadi Moḥasser.[144]

THE WADI MOḤASSER

The Wadi Moḥasser is on the way to Mashᶜar the sacred. It is a place which is elevated a little above the [surrounding] terrain. One can climb up a little ways. There it is recommended conduct [*mostaḥabb*] to move oneself about a little, mounted or on foot, as in the harvaleh.

---

142 Khayf or "declivity" is another name for the plain where Menâ is located. The mosque there was opened only during the pilgrimage season; see Rutter, *Holy Cities*, 1:178-79; Refᶜat, *Mer'ât*, 1:322-25. Gaudefroy-Demombynes, *Pèlerinage*, p. 239, reports a tradition that the body of Adam was buried under this mosque.

143 I.e., the Ottoman sultan Aḥmad I (1603-17).

144 These are two ravines to the west and east of Menâ respectively.

SPENDING ONE NIGHT IN MENÂ

In any case, one must spend the night [before] the ninth in Menâ in accordance with recommended religious conduct. Each group of pilgrims has a specified place in Menâ so that no one goes to another place. The next day, that is the ninth, the pilgrims leave at the crack of dawn and go to ᶜArafât.

ᶜARAFÂT

It is a trip of four hours from Menâ to ᶜArafât by camel and litter.[145] To denote the boundaries of ᶜArafât, they have built two milestones, three z̲arᶜ [high], of brick and plaster, [one] on this side and [one on] that side of the road. The Iranians say that the late Ḥâjji Sayyed Moḥammad Bâqer Eṣfahâni,[146] on a trip to the House of God, delimited ᶜArafât and, as a sign of the boundaries, built these two milestones.

THE MOSQUE OF ABRAHAM

After arriving at the valley of ᶜArafât, there is a small mosque on the left named the Mosque of Abraham.[147] They say it is one of the constructions of Ḥaẓrat-e Khalil [Abraham] which has subsequently been repaired. Each [ethnic group] of pilgrims also has a special place at ᶜArafât and must pitch their tents there. For example, the place for the Iranians is on the right of the wadi near the cistern which is next to the Zobaydeh aquaduct [*nahr*] and is filled with the canal water. [252]

The Zobaydeh aquaduct runs beside the valley from the mountain side.

ᶜArafât is a very wide valley which is located at the base of a mountain named the Jabal or-Raḥmat ["Mount of Mercy"]. It is located east of Mecca and [runs] towards the south. This plain of ᶜArafât is about two farsakhs [wide] and is situated between small mountains, the largest of which is the Jabal or-Raḥmat. Ruins of buildings and constructions are visible on top of the Jabal or-Raḥmat, which they say were built by Shâd-del [?], the Amir of the Yemen. The climate of ᶜArafât is very pleasant, owing to its being open to the north and because of the elevation of the terrain and the proximity to Ṭâ'ef. It is not at all like the climate of the city of Mecca or Menâ.

---

145 On this route, see Refᶜat, *Mer'ât*, 1:335-41.

146 Moḥammad Bâqer Eṣfahâni was one of the prominent members of the ulama; he died in 1301/1883. See Eᶜtemâd os-Salṭaneh, *Ma'as̲er*, p. 142; Momen, *Shi'i Islam*, p. 141, and the genealogical chart on p. 133.

147 This is apparently the mosque called the Masjed Nemreh in other sources; see Refᶜat, *Mer'ât*, 1:336; Burton, *Personal Narrative*, 2:182 n. 3.

ARRIVAL OF THE MAḤMALS OF THE PROPHET AND ᶜÂYESHEH

The evening of the ninth day, the Maḥmal of the Prophet and the Maḥmal of ᶜÂyesheh, which accompany the Syrian and Egyptian pilgrims, are both brought out to the foot of the Mount of Mercy. The pilgrims congregate around them, and the preacher [*khaṭib*] stands on top of a big camel and reads a sermon. However it is not known what he says because of the multitudes of people. After the sermon, handkerchiefs are scattered and dispersed about, and the maḥmals are carried to their [proper] place.

A DIFFERENCE BETWEEN THE SHIʿITES AND SUNNIS

If there is no disagreement between Shiʿites and Sunnis about ᶜArafât, the masses of Shiʿites and the Sunnis will wait until sunset the day of the ninth to leave. Otherwise, there will be a different [procedure between them]. Thus in this year the Sunnis observed ᶜArafât on Friday and, so they said, performed the Greater Pilgrimage. The Shiʿites observed ᶜArafât on Saturday.[148]

REASONS FOR SCHEDULING ᶜARAFÂT ON FRIDAY

One reason that the Sunnis want ᶜArafât to fall on a Friday is to obtain a Greater Pilgrimage.[149] Another is because if ᶜArafât falls on a Friday the kadis will get a bonus from the government because there are more vows and prayers [involved in] the Greater Pilgrimage. [253] In every [period of] seventy years, ᶜArafât must fall on a Friday ten times. But for the considerations [cited], they move ᶜArafât to Friday every three years. This year, too, they moved ᶜArafât to Friday. They left ᶜArafât at sunset on Friday. The sharif and the pâshâ had also submitted to this and left. The Shiʿites, who numbered about six thousand and were mostly subjects of Iran, spent Saturday at ᶜArafât since no one had seen the moon.[150]

SPENDING ONE NIGHT AT ᶜARAFÂT

They observed the Standing [*voquf*] at ᶜArafât the night [before] Saturday. The Iranian consul requested soldiers and sentinels from the sharif and the pasha in order to protect the pilgrims. They kept guard that night over the pilgrims until morning for fear of harm by thieves. All of a sudden, several Bedouin swarmed over a tent and carried off a very few goods. Two camels belonging to the guides were also carried off. To remunerate the soldiers and the guards for

---

[148] Cf. Kazem Zadeh, *Relation*, p. 73.

[149] Cf. Burckhardt, *Travels*, p. 285; Burton, *Personal Narrative*, 2:281; Gaudefroy-Demombynes, *Pèlerinage*, p. 252 n. 5.

[150] The visual confirmation of a new moon marks the beginning of the new month in the Muslim lunar calendar.

their trouble that night, the consul collected from his countrymen among the pilgrims about four hundred Levant dollars (which is about 230 tomans in Iranian money).

MASHᶜAR

Anyhow, the pilgrims left ᶜArafât after sunset the day of ᶜArafât and arrived at Mashᶜar three hours after nightfall.

Mashᶜar is also a valley which is located at the foot of a mountain. It has no water or inhabited areas. This Mashᶜar is also called Mozdalefeh.[151]

Three hours past nightfall [before] the holiday, they arrive at Mashᶜar and go on the slopes and sides of this nearby mountain in order to gather stones for the lapidation of the Jamreh.[152] The stones for the lapidation of the Jamreh must be stones from the valley of Mashᶜar. After returning from collecting the stones, they usually sleep with [their] baggage and belongings and do not pitch tents again since it is night and the weather is pleasant. [254] It is obligatory that one be at Mashᶜar until sunrise the day of the holiday.

RETURN TO MENÂ

They leave Mashᶜar after sunrise and go to Menâ. In Menâ, tents are pitched near the Khayf Mosque. After arriving at the tents and refreshing [themselves], the pilgrims go on foot or mounted to stone the Jamreh-ye ᶜAqabeh. In the market of Menâ they have built three markers, two z̲arᶜ high, out of plaster and brick at intervals of one thousand z̲arᶜ from each other. They call one the First Jamreh; another the Second; and another the Third. On the day of the holiday all the pilgrims must each cast seven of the stones they have collected at Mashᶜar at the last Jamreh, which is on the side adjacent to Mecca in such a way that the stones [actually] strike that Jamreh.

THE SACRIFICE

After returning from stoning the Jamreh, they perform the sacrifice at that time, each whatever sacrifice he can.

The sheep there are of the fat-tailed variety[153] and are generally similar to those in Iran. They are brought in from the surrounding areas in such quantity that one flock runs into another. Their price varies from fifteen Iranian krans to six thousand [dinârs?].

---

151 See Refᶜat, *Mer'ât*, 1:331-34; Belâdi, *Ḥejâz*, 8:169; Rutter, *Holy Cities*, 1:165-67. Mashᶜar is the Koranic form of the name.

152 On the ritual of *rami* (lapidation), see above n. 34 and n. 37.

153 Text: *bozumish* ("goat-like" sheep?).

On this holiday, about 200,000 sacrificial animals were slaughtered at Menâ. They had prepared large pits as a place for performing the sacrifice.[154] Nevertheless, they threw many of the sheep's heads and trotters, the guts, flesh, and bones of the sacrificial animals amid the tents and along the road. It was made filthy everywhere as far as the Khayf Mosque. Even though two hundred black slaves, who are the street cleaners, work under the careful scrutiny of their supervisors and clean all the filth from the roads, and [although] they immediately pour a mixture of lime over the pits where the sheep are killed and cover them up [255], still the air is infected by the odor of carcasses to the extent that smelling it causes disease. For this reason, illness and the plague first appear in Menâ.

The government physicians keep a watch on Menâ. Every day of these three days [at] Menâ, they get a list from the undertakers and ascertain that each day a certain number [of people] died, and what illness was the cause. If the disease is contagious, they inform Istanbul and the frontier posts.

In Istanbul, they determine at a meeting of the public health [officials] how many days there should be a quarantine and in what place. After it is determined that there is disease in Menâ, they raise a yellow flag on top of the mountain as a sign of there being disease, so that the pilgrims will know what precautions to take. This raising of the yellow flag causes terror, and many die out of fear. If the disease is not contagious, still, out of precaution, they determine [in] Istanbul that the pilgrims should be quarantined for two or three days. Whichever way they go, they will have a quarantine, unless via the route to Bombay or Bushehr.

The particulars about the quarantine will be recounted in detail in the proper place.[155]

CIRCUMAMBULATION OF THE KAABA

After slaughtering the sacrificial animals on the holiday, the pilgrims then perform *taqṣir*, that is they shave the head or trim the nails and mustaches. After that, in order to perform the circumambulation of the Kaaba, they go on foot or by hired donkeys

---

[154] Cf. Kazem Zadeh, *Relation*, p. 78.

[155] These measures were all part of the health regime instituted to prevent the spread of cholera during the pilgrimage season following a wave of cholera epidemics which swept the Middle East and Europe during the early nineteenth century. On the international sanitary conferences that producèd these and other reforms, see Long, *Hajj*, pp. 69-75; Roff, "Sanitation and Security;" cf. below, Part Seven, n. 22.

to the city of Mecca to perform ablutions at the Masjed ol-Ḥarâm and to perform the seven circuits of the circumambulation of the ḥajj-e tamattoᶜ. [256] Then they pray the two-prostration prayer of the circumambulation at the Station of Abraham. Then they perform sayᶜ seven times between Ṣafâ and Marveh.

After performing the circumambulation of the ḥajj-e tamattoᶜ and the sayᶜ [between] Ṣafâ and Marveh, the Shiʿites perform the seven circuits of the ṭavâf-e nesâ, go to their residence, take off the eḥrâm clothes, and put on [ordinary] clothes. All those things which were forbidden to them become lawful. Returning to Menâ, they spend the nights [before] the eleventh and twelfth in Menâ. On each of the two days they stone the First Jamreh seven times, the Second Jamreh seven times, and the last Jamreh seven times with the stones from Mashᶜar.

CELEBRATION AND HAPPINESS OF THE PILGRIMS

The night [before] the eleventh, there is rejoicing among the pilgrims for having completed the rituals. The Syrians and Egyptians who accompanied the [ma]ḥmal have elaborate fireworks displays. The sharif also gives a fireworks display. The soldiers stationed in the Hejaz also fire various elaborate volleys.[156]

I heard that for several years before the last two, Ḥâjji Mirzâ Ḥasan Khân, who was the consul in Jedda and Mecca, also gave very elaborate fireworks displays the night [before] the eleventh.

After noon of the twelfth, most [people] were returning to Mecca. Some spent the night [before] the thirteenth in Menâ also, stoned the pillars before noon on the thirteenth, and went to Mecca after noon on the thirteenth. Although one is finished with the obligatory duties, it is recommended conduct to perform circumambulation of the Kaaba as often as possible if one stays in Mecca for another day or two.

THE ᶜOMREH-YE MOFRADEH

At this time, some of the pilgrims also spend [a few] days in Mecca [257] in order to perform the *ᶜomreh-ye mofradeh* at Tanᶜim (which is the name of a place one farsakh beyond Mecca on the way to Medina on the left side).[157] They perform the ablutions there, put

156 Cf. Kazem Zadeh, *Relation*, pp. 39-45.

157 People residing in Mecca need not go all the way to one of the miqât to put on the eḥrâm when they wish to perform ᶜomreh; they simply go to one of the suburbs of the city, of which Tanᶜim is the most convenient for this purpose. See Rutter, *Holy Cities*, 1:284-85; Gaudefroy-Demombynes, *Pèlerinage*, p. 190.

on the eḥrâm, say "Labbayka,"[158] go to the Masjed ol-Ḥarâm, perform the seven circuits of the circumambulation, and pray the prayer of two cycles. They call this the ᶜ*omreh-ye mofradeh*.

ORGANIZING A MARKET

After returning from Menâ and ᶜArafât, the pilgrims start thinking about leaving and making preparations for the journey. Beside the sharif's house, in the middle of the street, a market may be held where there are all sorts of goods for travelling and provisions such as litters, camel-panniers, tents from Istanbul and Isfahan, leather goods, etc. Everyone buys whatever he wants in that market.

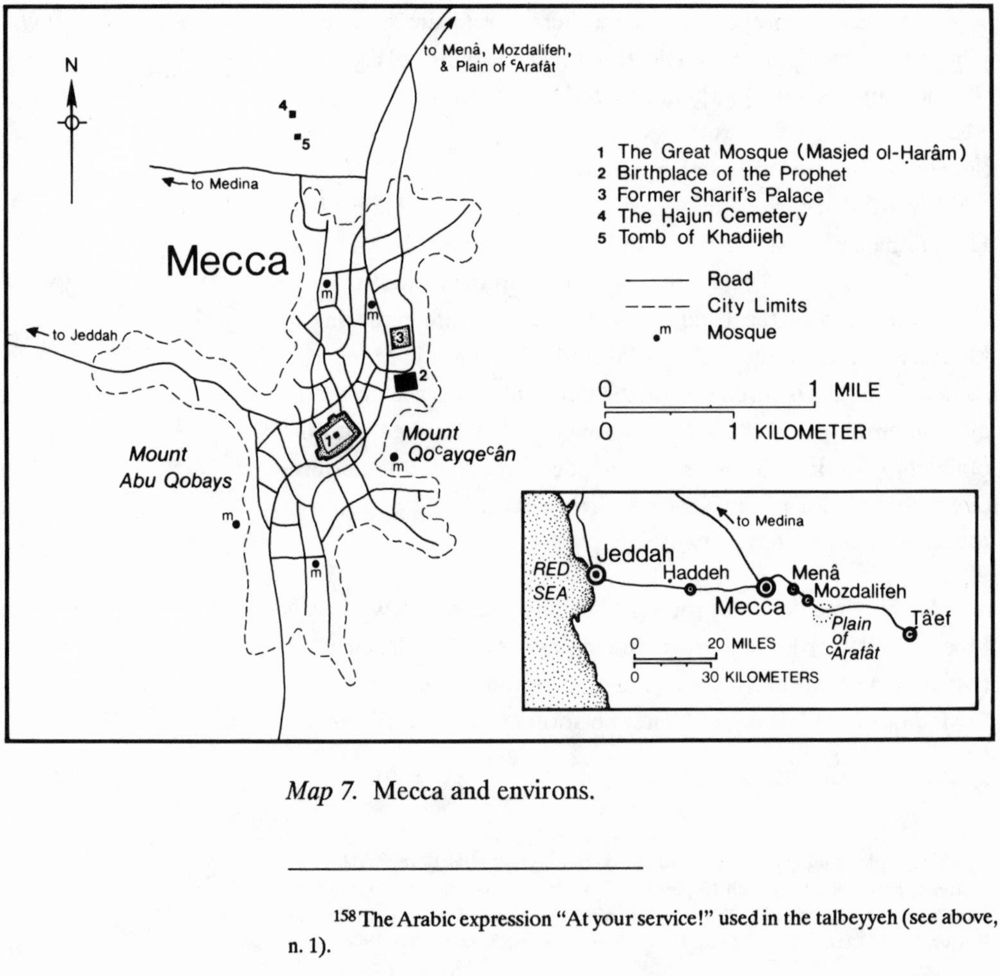

Map 7. Mecca and environs.

[158] The Arabic expression "At your service!" used in the talbeyyeh (see above, n. 1).

PART SIX
THE VISIT TO MEDINA

DEPARTURE OF THE PILGRIMS

The pilgrims leave Mecca the Exalted in various ways.[1] It is easier for those who came via Yanboᶜ or the Syrian route and have already visited Medina the Illuminated. They leave Mecca on the eighteenth or nineteenth of Z̲i Ḥejjeh and go to Jedda. If there is no disease, they go from there wherever they wish. If there is a contagious disease, they go to Bombay or Bushehr to avoid being delayed in the quarantine.

MURDER OF A NUMBER OF PILGRIMS

The news this year concerning what had happened to the Jedda caravan was that the Bedouin waylaid a group of pilgrims from Greece, Herzogovina, Albania[2] etc., who were travelling along the way from Mecca to Jedda by night. They killed ten or twelve people among them and stole about ten thousand tomans [worth] of property from them. Their consuls received news [of this] and informed the governor of the Hejaz and Istanbul. In the end, the matter was handled weakly, and this irregularity was considered to be due to the incompetence of the qâ'em-maqâm of Jedda. They deposed him. [258]

ROUTES TO MEDINA

As for those who have not gone to Medina the Agreeable and must go [there], they will go with one of these three caravans:

THE SYRIAN CARAVAN

One is the Syrian caravan which is [accompanied] by the pasha, the *amin-e ṣorreh*, soldiers, and artillery, and is orderly and regular. Everyone who goes with it is in complete security. However these

---

[1] The various pilgrimage routes are discussed in Adolphe D'Avril, *L'Arabie contemporaine avec la description du pèlerinage de la Mecque* (Paris, 1868); pp. 167-84; Jomier, *Mahmal*, pp. 181-204; Kazem Zadeh, *Relation*, p. 15; Tresse, *Pèlerinage syrien*, pp. 67-192; S. Tamari, "Darb ol-Hajj in Sinai. An Historical-Archaeological Study," *Accademia Nazionale dei Lincei: Memorie* 25(1982):431-525; Burton, *Personal Narrative*, 2:58; Wohaibi, *Northern Hijaz*, pp. 315-95; Refᶜat, *Mer'ât*, 1:369-82; Hogarth, *Hejaz*, pp. 94-149; *Ḥejâz sâlnâmehsi*, pp. 193-94.

[2] Text: Lebantâ.

days few Iranians go via this route because of the long trip, the great trouble, and the untold expense.[3]

The Syrian caravan sets out from Mecca from the twenty-fifth of the month of Ẕi Ḥejjeh to the end of the month.

THE "MOUNTAIN CARAVAN"

Another is the "Mountain [*Jabal*] Caravan."[4] Every year, the ḥamleh-dârs of Arab Iraq conduct some Iranian and Ottoman pilgrims with the party of the Amir-e Jabal ("Amir of the Mountain")[5] and convey his standard to Mecca in good order and regularity. This caravan leaves very early. Since it has a guard, the way is secure. Less of the pilgrims' money is lost. The expenses for it are by comparison less than by the Syrian route. However, it has some faults–faults which Najm ol-Molk knows full well.[6] This year,

---

[3] Previously, this had been the more or less officially sanctioned route for pilgrims from Iran, who joined the Syrian caravan in Damascus. Under the terms of a treaty dating back to Nâder Shâh, they theoretically had the right to travel with the Syrian caravan under the leadership of their own *amir ol-ḥajj*. Farâhâni's own journey is a classic example of how even this overland route was declining rapidly, at least until the opening of the Hejaz Railway, in favor of easier and safer sea transportation provided by various European and Muslim entrepreneurs. See D'Avril, *Arabie contemporaine*, p. 168; Jacob Landau, "A New Manuscript on the Muslim Pilgrimage," *Ve Congrès International d'Arabisants et d'Islamisants: Actes* (1970), 307-16; idem, *The Hejaz Railway and the Muslim Pilgrimage* (Detroit, 1971); Robert W. Olson, *The Siege of Mosul and Ottoman-Persian Relations 1718-1743* (Bloomington, 1975), pp. 100-106. Tresse, *Pèlerinage syrien*, p. 229 has a map showing the placement of the Iranians in the encampments of the Syrian caravan.

[4] In earlier times, the main alternative to the Syrian route was this "mountain route" through the Jabal Shammâr country of north central Arabia. The itinerary of this route from Baghdad to Mecca (ca. 1214/1800) was described by Mirzâ Khayrât-ᶜali in his *Manâzel ol-ḥajj;* see Storey, *Persian Literature* 2/i:148-49. In the 1860s, it was the preferred route for Iranian pilgrims; D'Avril, *Arabie contemporaine*, pp. 173-175 noted the preference of the Iranians to travel by this route, and the willingness of the amir of the region to protect them for a price, but pointed out that the Iranians were still mistreated and abused while travelling through Najd. See also Rashid, *Darb Zobaydah*, p. 66; Kazem Zadeh, *Relation*, pp. 15-16; C. Guarmani, *Northern Najd* (tr. Lady Capel-Cure; London, 1938).

[5] The region of Jabal Shammâr was dominated in the nineteenth century by shaykhs from the dynasty of Ebn Rashid, whose capital was at Ḥâil: See Charles Doughty, *Travels in Arabia Deserta* (London, 1936; third edition of the work first published in 1888), 1:503-4 etc. Kazem Zadeh, *Relation*, p. 16, notes that this was a title given to the chief of the Arabs in this part of Arabia. According to Kazem Zadeh, he was, at that time (ca. 1910), an individual named Nâṣer Kheshmân.

[6] Najm ol-Molk was the title (awarded in 1290/1873) of Ḥâjj Mirzâ ᶜAbd ol-Ghaffâr Khân; see Eᶜtemâd os-Salṭaneh, *Ma'âṣer*, pp. 219, 230; Bâmdâd, *Rejâl*, 2:273-74. He may have performed the pilgrimage in 1299/1881-82 (see Eᶜtemâd os-Salṭaneh, *Ruznâmeh*, p. 212), but it is not clear to what exact event or events Farâhâni is referring. However, Iranian pilgrims travelling across Arabia by this route in the mid-nineteenth century were subject to frequent harassment, particularly by Mohannâ, the Amir of Boraydeh, who annihilated virtually the entire Iranian pilgrimage caravan in 1856 (see D'Avril, *Arabie contemporaine*, pp. 174-75).

no more than fifty or sixty Iranian subjects had come via this route owing to an [Iranian] governmental prohibition, and those [went] secretly and in Bedouin dress.[7] Nevertheless, the guides with ʿAbd or-Raḥman, the deputy of the Amir-e Jabal, who is the leader of the Jabal route pilgrims, came again to Mecca and invited the Iranian pilgrims to be conveyed via the Jabal route. Since most of the revenue of the Amir-e Jabal [comes] from the Iranian pilgrims, and the Iranian pilgrims have not come by this route for two years due to the government prohibition, it is [a matter of] great regret and remorse for the Amir-e Jabal. [259] He behaved extremely well in every respect to the few Iranian pilgrims who had accompanied them. He wrote an explanation to the Iranian consul who was in Mecca through the intermediary of his agent ʿAbd or-Raḥman, requesting the removal of the ban on pilgrims travelling via the Jabal route. He made many promises [such as] "I will look after the pilgrims in every way, and no sort of injustice or disrespect will befall them."

The Jabal guides were willing to give nearly seven hundred liras (which is 2,100 Iranian tomans) for allowing the pilgrims [to go] via the Jabal route. Nevertheless, because there was a prohibition, permission for the pilgrims to go by the Jabal route was not given. Furthermore, those Iranians who went by stealth with the Jabal ḥamleh-dârs were caught on the way, in a most humiliating manner, brought back to Mecca, fined, and imprisoned. The amounts which accrued from this matter became the perquisite of the Iranian consul.

Since the profit of the Amir-e Jabal has been greatly reduced, owing to this two year prohibition, it is now possible that this will effect benefits for the pilgrims [who go] via this route. All sorts of guarantees about the tranquility of the pilgrims will be made, and then, because of that, it will be the best route.

This Mountain Caravan will also set out from Mecca around the twenty-fourth to the twenty-eighth.

W. G. Palgrave, *Personal Narrative of a Year's Journey Through Central and Eastern Arabia* (seventh edition; London, 1875), pp. 160 ff. gives a detailed description of how Mohannâ, in order to extort as much money as possible, held hostage another Iranian caravan in 1866-67 which was carrying Tâj Jehân, wife of Âṣaf od-Dowleh.

[7] Doughty, *Travels*, 2:64 ff. comments on the arrival of this much reduced pilgrimage caravan in Ḥâil, central Arabia.

[8] Cf. Burton, *Personal Narrative*, 2:50; Hogarth, *Hejaz*, pp. 112-14.

THE "FLYING CARAVAN"

Yet another [caravan] is the "Flying Caravan."[8] The Flying Caravan is that by which one or two of the chiefs of the tribes of the Hejaz convey the pilgrims with the assistance of Bedouin camel drivers. They go by Medina the Agreeable, and from there to Yanbo[c] or to Jedda. [260] These Bedouin chiefs offer guarantees for the safe arrival of the pilgrims with the knowledge of the consul in the presence of the Sharif of Mecca. They give two people [as] pledge and hostages. If the pilgrims do arrive safely, the Sharif releases these hostages. If not, he imprisons and punishes [them]. Thus most pilgrims of all nationalities go with this caravan.

There is no method in the departure of this caravan. It sets out from Mecca going to Medina group by group from the twentieth of the month of Z̲i Ḥejjeh to the end of the month. There is no order or regularity in anything about this caravan. There is much thievery both from within and without [the caravan]. Most of the camel drivers are thieves and robbers. Along the way, if something is lost, it is the responsibility of the camel driver. Because of this, few belongings of people are lost along the way. After an individual arrives at the lodgings, if he is a little careless, they steal his belongings at once. If 100,000 tomans [worth] of the pilgrims' belongings are carried off one night, or fifty pilgrims are killed, or if [some] of the thieves are killed, there is no redress or calling to account. Usually, the pilgrims stay awake from nightfall to morning, with weapons in hand, saying "Keep away, keep away!"

Thieves from Egypt, Syria, and Arab Iraq come to Mecca especially for the pilgrimage season. They accompany these caravans until the pilgrims reach Jedda or Yanbo[c]. A great amount of personal property is lost.

THE TOLL (KHÂVEH)

One of the problems with this caravan is the matter of the toll which the chiefs of the tribe of Ḥarb[9] collect in their territory (which is a place of passage for the caravan) as a toll from those passing through. This tax for passage is named the *khâveh*.[10] The Ottoman

---

[9] This Arab tribe had come in modern times to dominate the region between Mecca and Medina. It was far easier for the Ottoman government to pay the Ḥarb tribesmen to allow the pilgrims to pass safely through their territory than to try to control them by force; moreover, the Ḥarb served as a shield against the more dangerous prospect of Wahhâbi tribesmen from the interior of Arabia threatening the pilgrimage routes. See Burckhardt, *Travels*, pp. 307-308; Burton, *Personal Narrative*, 2:119-21; Hogarth, *Hejaz*, pp. 38-39.

[10] See Kazem Zadeh, *Relation*, pp. 16-18. There is a little irony in the name for this tax, which is derived from the word for "fraternity."

government [261] contracts to pay the Bedouin a yearly amount on behalf of its citizens and the citizens of foreign countries. No one interferes with them. However, citizens of Iran must themselves pay the toll individually. The toll is added to the fare and is paid to the chief of the caravan who provided the hostages. If that chief does not covet the toll and gives it rightly to the tribal chiefs, the caravan will arrive safely and they will not be hindered by anyone. If not, the chiefs of Ḥarb prevent the pilgrims from going in order to exact the toll. It will cause delays. Thus in earlier years, the pilgrims were delayed for a month or two months in Râbegh and elsewhere for this reason, and the chiefs of the caravan who had collected the toll from the pilgrims fled. They charge ten Levant dollars per pilgrim for the toll, which is about six tomans in Iranian money.

Another difficulty with this caravan is that the pilgrims are charged an excessive fare. That is, for each camel that transports a pilgrim, something must go to the sharif; something must go to the pasha; something for the chief of that caravan; something for the pilgrim-guide of that pilgrim; something for the camel-broker; something for the consul; and something for the caravan followers.[11] All this is added to the fare, and the fare becomes very exorbitant. They charge seventy-one Levant dollars for the fare from Mecca the Exalted to Medina the Illuminated and from Medina to Yanboᶜ, including the toll and one litter capable of transporting two pilgrims. A cook and pack-camel are assigned for each litter. They charge twenty-two Levant dollars for the cook and [also] for the pack-camel. In reality, the toll is not charged for the pack-camel and cook. They charge the pilgrim passenger forty-six Levant dollars for the camel, including the toll. [262] For every seven pilgrim passengers, one does not pay the toll. Anyone who wants to go from Mecca to Medina, and from Medina to Jedda, is charged on the same basis. At most, they will collect two or three Levant dollars [extra] per camel.

Despite all these problems regarding this caravan, it is still the best of the caravans since one is more quickly delivered from the hands of the Bedouin. Most people these days go via this "Flying Caravan." I left Mecca the Exalted along with three hundred Iranian pilgrims on the last day of the month of Z̲i Ḥejjeh [9 October] and set out with this caravan.

---

[11] Text: *fožul-hâ*, which might be translated as "busybodies." This probably refers to the many poor youths who would follow along with the caravan in hope of receiving some small gratuity for performing odd errands for the pilgrims.

THE WADI FÂṬEMEH

The first stage is the Wadi Fâṭemeh.[12] It is four farsakhs from Mecca to the Wadi Fâṭemeh but by camel train it takes seven hours. A little way past Mecca, there is a cemetery on the left side of the road. They say the martyrs of Fakhkh[13] are buried there. Near this same cemetery, on the slopes of the mountain, they have constructed a large government building; whichever pasha accompanies the Syrian caravan stays in it. All the way to Wadi Fâṭemeh, the road is smooth and level ground. However, the Wadi Fâṭemeh has running water alongside the road. There are thirty-four canals and springs in this wadi. There are mostly villages [there], and they grow maize, millet, barley, wheat, peas, and beans. It has many date groves.

That particular canal which bears the name of the wadi (the entirety being known by the name of the part) [comes from] a spring. It has about one sang of water. Alongside this spring, there is a small date grove and cultivated area. Its water is very wholesome. Near [263] this spring next to the road there is an enclosed area. In that enclosure there are twenty shops [constructed] of stone and mud and date-palm [branches]. The Bedouin bring all sorts of foodstuffs to sell there during the season the pilgrims come. In the village of this Wadi Fâṭemeh, there are many Twelver Shi'ites and Zaydis. There were all types of pilgrims in the valley. We left the valley and set out for Be'r ᶜOsfân[14] the first day of Moḥarram the Sacred [10 October].

BE'R ᶜOSFÂN OR BE'R EṢFAHÂN

From the wadi to Be'r ᶜOsfân is a trip of eight farsakhs. By pack-mule it takes twelve hours. By camel train it takes fourteen hours. Just a little beyond the valley, the road goes through a narrow pass for about two hours. It was a stony area, with forbidding mountains around it. After that, there were mountain chains, near and far, all along the right side of the road until near the stopping point.

This Be'r ᶜOsfân is popularly known among the Iranians as Be'r Eṣfahân.[15] It is located amid a desert which is near mountains in two directions. It has three wells near each other. The mouth of each one

---

[12] This is the valley north of Mecca which runs west towards Jedda; see Burckhardt, *Travels*, p. 292-93; Farhâd Mirzâ, *Hedâyat*, p. 153; Sayf od-Dowleh, *Safarnâmeh*, pp. 135-36.

[13] The "martyrs of Fakhkh" are those killed in the wadi of Fakhkh during the revolt of Ḥosayn b. ᶜAli b. Ḥasan b. Ḥasan b. Ḥasan b. ᶜAli against the Abbasids in 169/786. See C. van Arendonk, *Les Débuts de l'imamat Zaidite au Yemen* (translated by J. Ryckmans; Leiden, 1960), pp. 61-65; Farouq Omar, *The Abbasid Caliphate* (Baghdad, 1976), pp. 252-57.

[14] See Burckhardt, *Travels*, p. 297.

[15] Cf. Farhâd Mirzâ, *Hedâyat*, p. 175; Wohaibi, *Northern Hijaz*, pp. 284-89.

is fifteen z̲arᶜ, and each is thirty z̲arᶜ deep. The sides of the wells were raised up with stone and brick about one z̲arᶜ [high]. Their water is sweet. A little maize is grown around these wells which is irrigated manually with water from the wells.

Twenty shops out of stone and mud have also been built beside these wells. In pilgrimage season, foodstuffs are brought and sold. At this stage, about ten or twelve thousand Egyptian, Javanese, Indian, Iranian, and Turkestani pilgrims had gathered together. The Bedouin collecting the toll were preventing them from leaving. [264]

The reason for this was that the previous year some of the regular stipend which the Ottoman government had agreed to pay every year for the toll to the Bedouin shaykhs for its subjects and foreigners had not arrived. The shaykhs demanded [it] and were preventing the pilgrims from going. Because of this, the pilgrims camped for three days at this stage.

The pilgrims were engaged from night till dawn and fighting and skirmishing with the thieving bandits[16] and robbers. One of the Egyptians and one of the robbers were killed. It was not known who he was or to which tribe he belonged. Finally, the news reached the Sharif and the governor of the Hejaz. They pacified the shaykhs through flattery and obsequiousness, and the pilgrims set out.

DEPARTURE FROM BE'R ᶜOSFÂN

We left Be'r ᶜOsfân the fifth day of Moḥarram the Sacred [14 October] and set out for the Qożaymeh stopping point.[17] It is nine farsakhs from Be'r ᶜOsfân to Qożaymeh. It takes sixteen hours by camel train. The terrain is mostly fine sand. Some wild trees were seen. Most were lotus trees and tamarisk trees.

One farsakh beyond ᶜOsfân, a pass is reached to the right and left of which are rocky mountains. Previously a dam had been constructed in the middle of the pass for the purpose of collecting rain water. Some of its remains were visible. So earlier there used to be a respectable settlement in this place. Past there, [the route is] again over fine sand desert. There are wild trees in the environs. Until we arrived at Qożaymeh there were two mountain chains on both the right and left, one and a half farsakhs from the road.

---

[16] Text: *khersis*; this is certainly a mistake for the Turkish word *hırsız* (thief or burglar). The same term (although again slightly misspelled) is used by Farhâd Mirzâ, *Hedâyat*, p. 171.

[17] Sometimes the caravans stopped at the larger village of Kholays (see Burckhardt, *Travels*, pp. 297-99); others pressed on to Qożaymeh (Rutter, *Holy Cities*, 2:168).

QOŻAYMEH

Qożaymeh[18] [consists of] two water-wells in the middle of the desert, which are eleven z̲arᶜ deep and each with a mouth five z̲arᶜ [wide]. The water is a little salty and bad tasting. [265] Three shops have been built out of stone. In the pilgrimage season they bring fodder, dates, and meat to sell. Otherwise there is no habitation. Three nights previously the pilgrims had come and struggled with robbers at this stage. Two pilgrims had been killed.

DEPARTURE FROM QOŻAYMEH

We set out for Râbegh from Qożaymeh on the sixth [15 October]. It is about nine farsakhs from Qożaymeh to Râbegh, which takes fifteen hours by camel. [The way] is open, level desert. There are saltpans in some places and fine sand in others. The Red Sea was often visible on the left-hand side until we arrived at Râbegh.

THE VILLAGE OF RÂBEGH

Râbegh is a settled area with many date groves.[19] It has a population of about one thousand people. There are ten or twelve villages surrounding it. It has about fifty or sixty shops which are set up during the season the pilgrims come. Varieties of fish, sheep, bread, other foodstuffs, cucumbers, watermelons, sour oranges, and limes can be obtained.

A fort has also been built there by the Ottoman government. There are fifty foot soldiers, twenty dromedary mounted troops, and three artillery pieces there. But what soldiers they are–naked and bare, no rifles, no bullets, no gunpowder! Their means of livelihood is selling water and stealing. They have run up an Ottoman flag in that fort, but even the flag is worn and tattered.

In Râbegh, there are several shaykhs of the Ḥarb [tribe] who are held in some esteem. Among them is Ḥovayfeż, who in some years becomes the chief of one of the "Flying Caravans." [266]

There are numerous water wells in Râbegh. They are seven or eight z̲arᶜ deep. However, their water is often salty and bad tasting.

In the place beside Râbegh where the flood [waters] flow like a river, water comes out [if] one digs down one or two z̲arᶜ. In this flood channel, many wells have been dug. Their water is by comparison better than the [other] well water, but again it is a little salty and bad tasting. It is one farsakh from Râbegh to the seashore.

---

[18] Or Qażimeh; see Belâdi, *Ḥejâz*, 7:141. Sayf od-Dowleh, *Safarnâmeh*, p. 137, has Każimeh.

[19] Cf. Burckhardt, *Travels*, p. 301; Rutter, *Holy Cities*, 2:170-71; Wohaibi, *Northern Hijaz*, pp. 223-25; Belâdi, *Ḥejâz*, 4:5-8; Farhâd Mirzâ, *Hedâyat*, pp. 169-70; Sayf od-Dowleh, *Safarnâmeh*. pp. 137-38.

Râbegh is part of the Tehâmeh. It is the miqât place for the Sunnis. It is approximately at the parallel of Johfeh. Johfeh is three farsakhs from Râbegh. [Johfeh] used to be beside the sea, but now it is in ruins.

Anyhow, the pilgrims all encamped in Râbegh on the seventh [16 October]. The night [before] the eighth of ᶜÂshurâ, the Iranian pilgrims gathered together and held a lengthy rowżeh-khᵛâni without [any need for] dissimulation. Many people from Râbegh also attended.

DEPARTURE FROM RÂBEGH

We left Râbegh the eighth of Moḥarram [17 October]. [From] there the pilgrims went by different ways. Some went by the eastern route, which is the "Sultan's Highway"[20] and the way of transit for the Syrian pilgrims. Some [others], since they had hired pack animals from camel drivers from Forᶜ,[21] went by the Forᶜ road. The people of Forᶜ are mostly Twelver Shiʿites. The Forᶜ route is more populous, but it is three or four farsakhs longer.

It is six farsakhs from Râbegh to Be'r Mastureh. A camel travels [it] in ten hours. For five hours of that [time], the sea is usually visible one farsakh away. The terrain is fine sand. [267]

MASTUREH

Mastureh is a well, the water of which is very bad tasting and salty.[22] Usually pilgrims bring drinking water along [with them] from Râbegh. There is also one stone shop in Mastureh where they bring fodder and dates to sell.

DEPARTURE FROM MASTUREH

We left Be'r Mastureh on the ninth [18 October]; the stopping place that day was Be'r Raḥṣân or Raṣṣân. It is twelve farsakhs to this stopping place, but by camel train it takes seventeen hours. The way was all fine sand so that the camels moved with great difficulty until we arrived at Raḥṣân.

---

[20] Text: *Râh-e Solṭâni.* This highway, better known in Arabic as the *Darb os-Solṭâni*, was one of the securest and consequently the most frequently travelled route for the pilgrimage traffic; see Burton, *Personal Narrative*, 2:58; Rutter, *Holy Cities*, 2:171.

[21] A village located at approximately the same latitude as Mastureh but several miles further east: See Ḥamad ol-Jâser, *Fi shamâl gharb el-jazireh* (Riyadh, 1401/1981), p. 193 (map); Wohaibi, *Northern Hijaz*, pp. 69-71; the route is mentioned by Rutter, *Holy Cities*, 2:171; Hogarth, *Hejaz*, pp. 120-21.

[22] Cf. Burckhardt, *Travels*, p. 304; Rutter, *Holy Cities*, 2:176; Sayf od-Dowleh, *Safarnâmeh*, p. 138; Belâdi, *Ḥejâz*, 8:139-41.

BE'R RAḤṢÂN OR RAṢṢÂN

Be'r Raḥṣân is located at the foot of a tall mountain. There is one well that is about twenty zarᶜ deep and seven zarᶜ wide. It is revetted with stone, and its water is sweet. Near this well an enclosure has been built. In that enclosure, the Bedouin from the environs bring and sell fodder and dates during the season the pilgrims come. That night, which was the eve of ᶜÂshurâ, the pilgrims held a lengthy rowżeh-khᵛâni and a taᶜzeyyeh.

DEPARTURE FROM BE'R RAḤṢÂN

We set out for Be'r ᶜAbbâs from Be'r Raḥṣân on the day of ᶜÂshurâ [10 Moḥarram/19 October]. It is seven farsakhs from there to Be'r ᶜAbbâs, but by camel it takes twelve or thirteen hours to traverse. Alongside the road were two mountain chains until [they came together to] form a pass and defile. This pass was rocky, difficult, narrow, and acclivitous. We went steadily uphill through this pass for about four hours; then we reached an open expanse, bordered by mountains. The terrain was level [for an area of] half a farsakh by half a farsakh. At the top of this high plateau which we had reached, the temperature dropped ten degrees. It was plainly evident that one area was a warm region, and the other area a cold region. Thus, it has been repeatedly observed that any place which has a difference in climate is separated [from the other] by a pass—that side of the pass which is lower is warmer [268], and that side which is higher is colder. For example this is the case with the pass of Ṭâq-e Gerreh.[23] As soon as one comes down from the pass and arrives at the foot of the Ṭâq it is quite perceptible that in the pass and on the side of the pass which is higher it is cold, and at the bottom of the pass, which is lower, it is warm. Similarly, [as] one goes from Shiraz towards Bushehr there is a difficult pass which one descends very sharply. There, the difference in temperature is also perceptible. The heights of the pass are by comparison cold, and at the foot it is very warm. Also, there is a pass from Kerman to Khabiṣ[24] where the drop in temperature between one side and the other side of the pass is perceptible. The Kharzân pass is the same way. [Going] through the pass and descending to Pâchenâr, which is at the end of the descent, one notices the difference in temperature. At the beginning and [in] the middle of the pass there is a cold region, and [at] the end of the descent is a warm region.

---

[23] Text: Ṭâq-e Gerrâ. Ṭâq-e Gerreh is on the road from Qaṣr-e Shirin to Kermânshâh (between Sar-e Pol-e Zohâb and Karand).

[24] Now known as Shâhdâd.

Medina and its environs are a cold region in comparison with Mecca and its environs. There is a considerable difference in climate. The variation in the climate between the two places is perceptible. Anyhow, there were mountains near and far all the way until we arrived at Be'r ᶜAbbâs. ᶜAbbâs is the grandfather of Naṣṣâr; Naṣṣâr is one of the shaykhs of Ḥarb. He is still alive and has houses in Ḥamrâ' and Ṣafrâ'.

BE'R ᶜABBÂS

Be'r ᶜAbbâs[25] is a well, the water of which is sweet and wholesome. It is twenty-three z̲arᶜ deep, and its diameter is nine z̲arᶜ. The well is completely [lined] with hewn stone extending up [above ground level], and it has steps made out stone that enable one to go [down] to the bottom of the well. There is a ruined fort beside it [made of] stone and plaster. Formerly it used to be a place for government soldiers. There are several stone steps where fodder and dates are sold.

DEPARTURE FROM BE'R ᶜABBÂS

We left Be'r ᶜAbbâs on the twelfth of the month of Moḥarram the Sacred [21 October] for Sharyuf. [269] From Be'r ᶜAbbâs to Be'r Sharyuf is nine farsakhs, which takes sixteen hours by camel train. Three hours past Be'r ᶜAbbâs, we passed between two rocky mountain chains. After an interval of four more hours, we reached a water well which was named Be'r Rowḥâ'.[26] The mouth of that well was eight z̲arᶜ, and it was twenty-seven z̲arᶜ deep. It had sweet and wholesome water. Travelling five more hours past Be'r Rowḥâ', we arrived at a well which is popularly known as the Be'r Shohadâ' ["Well of the Martyrs"].[27] They say several martyrs from among the companions of [Moḥammad] are buried very close to this well.

Past there, one reaches Be'r Sharyuf after several hours.

BE'R SHARYUF

This well is also in the middle of the desert, and there is no settlement around it. The well is revetted with stone. Its mouth is nine z̲arᶜ [wide], and it is twenty-two z̲arᶜ deep. The water is good and sweet. They bring fodder, dates, and bread to sell.

DEPARTURE FROM BE'R SHARYUF

We left Be'r Sharyuf on Thursday the thirteenth of Moḥarram the Sacred [22 October] and set out for Medina the Agreeable.

[25] Cf. Rutter, *Holy Cities*, 2:183; Sayf od-Dowleh, *Safarnâmeh*, p. 139; Belâdi, *Ḥejâz*, 1:163.

[26] Cf. Ebn Baṭṭuṭeh, *Travels*, p. 184; Belâdi, *Ḥejâz*, 4:85-88; Wohaibi, *Northern Hijaz*, pp. 226-30; Farhâd Mirzâ, *Hedâyat*, p. 124.

[27] Cf. Burton, *Personal Narrative*, 1:274; Farhâd Mirzâ, *Hedâyat*, p. 124.

From there to Medina is eleven hours by camel. From Mt. Manqur (or Manjur),[28] which is two farsakhs away from Medina, the city of Medina is visible. The road is smooth and level all the way.

BE'R ᶜALI (MASJED-E SHAJAREH)

One and a half farsakhs before Medina, beside the road, there is the Masjed-e Shajareh ["Mosque of the Tree"],[29] which is the miqât place for Shi'ites in the event they are travelling [to Mecca] via Medina the Illuminated.

The Masjed-e Shajareh is known among the people of Medina these days as Be'r ᶜAli.[30] Several wells have been dug there, where the pilgrims perform the major ablution and put on the eḥrâm. Some date groves have also been planted there. It has become a pleasant place. [270]

The Masjed-e Shajareh is a little mosque with an arcade on one side. A tradition has been inscribed on the middle of it about the virtue of the mosque and [Moḥammad's] having prayed there. A little past the Masjed-e Shajareh, on the right hand [side], at an interval of one maydân, a large ruined fort is visible. They say it is the fort of Ḥosun ol-ᶜAqiq[31] in which the Jews used to dwell before the mission of the Prophet [Moḥammad]. After the hegira, that fort was conquered and was inhabited for years, [but] it gradually fell into ruins. Near Medina there is an elevated area or tell which has been revetted with stone. [From] the top of that eminence, all of Medina is revealed.[32]

From the day we left Mecca the Exalted, the kiblah was very nearly due east. Day by day, it departed a little from east. The kiblah in Medina is also still very much in the direction of the east but not so much as at the stages along the way.

---

[28] Cf. Farhâd Mirzâ, *Hedâyat*, p. 124; Belâdi, *Ḥejâz*, 8:280-81. Farâhâni was probably uncertain about the spelling of this name because "j" is often pronounced in the local dialect as "g."

[29] This is more commonly known as the Mosque of Ẕu'l-Ḥolayfeh; see Ebn Baṭṭuṭeh, *Travels*, p. 184 and n. 106; ᶜAbd ol-Qoddus Anṣâri, *Asâr ol-madinat ol-monavvareh* (Medina, 1353/1935), p. 87; Belâdi, *Ḥejâz*, 8:147; Burton, *Personal Narrative*, 1:279 n. 2. Burton explains that it is called the Mosque of the Tree because the Prophet sat under a fruit tree there.

[30] Shown as Abyâr ᶜAli on modern maps; see above. Cf. Burckhardt, *Travels*, p. 316. H. A. R. Gibb in Ebn Baṭṭuṭeh, *Travels*, p. 185 n. 112, identifies Be'r ᶜAli with a well near Rowḥâ, but that does not seem plausible because of the much greater distance from Medina.

[31] "Castles of ᶜAqiq," i. e., in the Wadi ᶜAqiq southwest of Medina: see Ebn Baṭṭuṭeh, *Travels*, p. 185 n. 10, (with reference to Ebn Taymeyyeh); cf. Farhâd Mirzâ, *Hedâyat*, p. 136; Anṣâri, *Asâr*, pp. 141-49.

[32] Cf. Burton, *Personal Narrative*, 1:279.

MEDINA

Thursday, the thirteenth of the month of Moḥarram the Sacred [22 October], the Syrian and Jabal [route] pilgrims and the "Flying Caravan" that went to Jedda and Yanboᶜ all arrived safely at Medina the Agreeable by whichever route they had taken. It is about eighty farsakhs from Mecca the Exalted to Medina the Illuminated. This city is located on the slopes of Mt. Oḥod. Its suburbs are also in the mountains but are not near Mt. Oḥod. Oḥod is located to the north of Medina. It is one farsakh to Medina. There are many gardens and date groves on this mountainside. This is a detailed list of the villages in the suburbs near Medina:

Bâb ol-Jomᶜeh; ᶜAvâli;[33] Qorbân; Qobbeh; ᶜOyun; Berkeh; Qobâ; and two villages that they say are in the territories of Fadak. [271]

POPULATION AND THE SHI'ITE GROUPS

There are 15,000 households residing in the city and the villages around it, which is about 80,000 people. [Of] this population, 70,000 are Sunnis, who are mostly of the Ḥanafi and Shâfeᶜi rites. About 10,000 are Shi'ites. The Shi'ites there are of these groups:

The Nakhâveleh;[34] whose homes are in part of the city and outside the city wall near the Baqiᶜ cemetery. [The members of] this group are usually poor. They cultivate and irrigate the fields and gardens around the city. The Shi'ite pilgrims often stay in the houses of the Nakhâveleh.

The Bani ᶜAli, Howb [?], and Firuh [?]:[35] Some of these three groups are Bedouin, and the rest are in the villages surrounding Medina. Some are people of Arab Iraq whose fathers and grandfathers came to Medina and stayed. They have homes within the city wall of Medina and outside.

---

[33] Text: Avâli. Farâhâni must have collected his topographical information from oral rather than written sources since here, and in several other places, he has trouble determining the correct spelling of an Arabic name and simply writes it the way it sounds to him.

[34] Burton, *Personal Narrative*, 2:1-3, explains this name as the plural form of *nakhvali* (date farmer) and reports some of the esoteric Shi'ite beliefs these people were supposed to hold; cf. Burckhardt, *Travels*, p. 354; Rutter, *Holy Cities*, 2:245-46; M. S. Makki, *Medina, Saudi Arabia* (Avesbury, 1982), pp. 118-20.

[35] Burton, *Personal Narrative*, 2:3 n. 3, and Makki, *Medina*, p. 118, mention the Banu ᶜAli, a division of the tribe of Ḥarb, but not the other two groups or tribes. Howb may be an error for Vohub; see the anonymous *Vasf ol-madineh ol-monavvareh* in Ḥ. ol-Jâser, *Rasâ'el fi târikh ol-madineh* (Riyadh, 1972), p. 31. Golzâri (p. 220) has Firuzeh instead of Firuh.

There are some Ḥasani Ashrâf[36] who also live in the city and are some of the distinguished landowners in the city.

About four thousand of the Shi'ites there [reside] in the city, and six thousand are in the villages around the city.

THE MARKET

There are about six hundred shops inside the city walls of Medina and outside the wall. There will be more shops than this during the season the pilgrims come. Its markets are usually not covered.[37]

THE HOUSES IN MEDINA

The houses in Medina are mostly of one, two, or three storeys.

The streets inside the city wall are very narrow. The streets outside the city wall are wide. [272] None of the streets are paved.

THE CITY WALL OF MEDINA

ᶜAżod od-Dowleh the Daylamite[38] began construction of the city wall of Medina in the year 365 [975-76]. After that wall fell into ruin, Jamâl od-Din Moḥammad ebn-e ᶜAli, known as ol-Javâd ol-Eṣfahâni,[39] constructed a small inclined wall in place of the earlier wall. After Solṭân Solaymân the Ottoman[40] repaired Jamâl od-Din's wall, the other Ottoman sultans did not allow [it] to fall into ruin; they made minor repairs yearly. This wall is made of stone and lime and plaster. Its thickness is three ẕarᶜ, and its height is seventeen ẕarᶜ. At present, most of the settled area and houses are outside this wall. Outside the wall at the outskirts of the city towards the north, which is the way pilgrims come and go, they have constructed a gateway and a wide street by which one arrives at Wadi Boṭḥân and the ancient Trench [*khandaq*].[41]

THE TRENCH

The Prophet [Moḥammad] ordered the digging of the trench at the Battle of the Clans on the advice of Salmân.[42] ᶜAmru ebn-e ᶜAbd

[36] Distinguished descendants of Emâm Ḥasan. Burton, *Personal Narrative*, 2:3-4, noted that they subsisted on income from landed property to which they had title deeds supposedly going back to the time of the Prophet.

[37] On the markets in Medina, see Makki, *Medina*, pp. 148-53.

[38] One of the most brilliant of the Buyid rulers (338-72/949-83).

[39] This refers to Jamâl od-din Abu Jaᶜfar Moḥammad b. ᶜAli b. Abi Manṣur ol-Eṣfahâni (d. 559/1163-64), the minister of the Zangid ruler of Mosul, Qoṭb od-Din Mawdud (1149-69). He was known as Javâd because of his generosity. See Ebn ol-Aṯir, *Kâmel*, 11:306.

[40] Solaymân the Magnificent (1520-1566).

[41] On the wall and the related topography of the city, see Anṣâri, *Aṯâr*, pp. 101, 105, 109; Makki, *Medina*, pp. 34-39; Burckhardt, *Travels*, p. 323; Burton, *Personal Narrative*, 1:391-395; Rutter, *Holy Cities*, 2:208-209; Jâser, *Rasâ'el*, pp. 3-81.

[42] The Meccan opponents of Moḥammad laid siege to Medina in the fifth year of the hegira (March 627) with an army numbering as many as 10,000 men. Rather

Vodd[43] was killed at this same battle. Now the trench is filled in, [but] many vestiges of it remain. The length of the trench used [to extend] from the beginning of Wadi Boṭḥân. The Wadi Boṭḥân runs from north to south. Now there are many settled areas and buildings in it.

To the west [of the trench] there is a lava field [*ḥarreh*],[44] which comes to an end at two small mountains. To its east is Mt. Salᶜ.[45] The slopes of Mt. Salᶜ are near the old wall of the city, so Mt. Salᶜ is situated to the west of the [present] wall. Near the aforementioned mountain, they have built an arsenal, the site of which used to be a small hill. It is still elevated six steps above ground level. [273]

THE SQUARE

There is a spacious square near this arsenal which is beside the city wall. One side of that square is [adjacent to] the city wall of Medina, and the other three sides [front] the houses outside the wall. In the season the pilgrims come, they set up a market in this square and bring all sorts of foodstuffs and grains there. The Syrian pilgrims camp in this square. Various pilgrims stay in the houses and gardens outside [of the wall].

GATES

The city wall of Medina has four gates. One, the western gate, is next to the square and is very wide. It is named the Bâb ol-Jabal ["Gate of the Mountain"]. Another is the eastern gate, which is adjacent to the Baqiᶜ cemetery. The coming and going of the pilgrims is via these two gates.[46]

CLIMATE

The climate of this city is very nice. It is ten degrees cooler than the climate of Mecca. It is very pleasant and bright. Earlier, I had read in [some] books that the fragrance of attar was pronounced in Medina. Insofar as I could determine, this point has [some] truth. It is caused by the great purity of the air there. The ground is never damp, nor the weather overcast. The people [can] sleep outdoors on the roofs for five months [of the year].

The waters of Medina are plentiful. Even most houses have wells. There is also canal water and spring water. One stream, which

---

than engage this force in open combat, Moḥammad, relying on the advice of Salmân, a Persian convert to Islam, had a trench dug to protect the city from assault.

43 One of the Meccan cavalrymen; he was killed in single combat with ᶜAli: See Guillaume, *Life of Muhammad*, pp. 454-56.

44 See Makki, *Medina*, pp. 19-21.

45 See Farhâd Mirzâ, *Hedâyat*, p. 132; Anṣâri, *Aṣ̱âr*, p. 131.

46 Farâhâni is referring to the four gates of the inner city wall. Burton, *Personal Narrative*, 1:391, gives Bâb ol-Jomᶜeh ["Friday Gate"] as the name of the eastern gate and Bâb ol-Maṣri ["Egyptian Gate"] for the western gate.

is in the city, [comes] from the Wadi Boṭḥân. Another stream comes from the Wadi Rânunâ.[47]

In Medina and its suburbs citrus fruits, varieties of dates, pomegranates, figs, and green vegetables are grown and are plentiful. [274]

THE MOSQUE OF THE PROPHET

The Mosque of the Prophet of God is inside the city walls.[48] When the prophet made the hegira to Medina, this place was vacant, so he bought it and built a house and small mosque out of sun-dried bricks and palm wood. The blessed burial place [of the Prophet Moḥammad] was in this same house which was next to the mosque. Now the cenotaph is located at the site of the house. After [Moḥammad's] death, ᶜOmar made some minor repairs to that mosque and incorporated part of the house into the mosque.[49] ᶜOs̱mân added something to the sides of the mosque and covered its roof with teak wood.[50] Valid ebn-e ᶜAbd ol-Malek built a grand building to serve as the mosque. He brought architects from the Byzantine Empire [Rum] and constructed the foundation of the mosque out of lime and stone. He erected marble columns into the middle of which he poured melted iron and covered [them] with a high roof. He spent exorbitant amounts [on this].[51] Ol-Mahdi-bellah the Abbasid and Ma'mun [son of the caliph Hârun] or-Rashid also repaired it.[52] After that, the Circassian sultans of Egypt[53] and the

---

47 See Farhâd Mirzâ, *Hedâyat*, p. 132; Anṣâri, *As̱âr*, pp. 150-52; Belâdi, *Ḥejâz*, 1:233.

48 On this extremely important sanctuary, see Ebn Baṭṭuṭeh, *Travels*, 164-75; Burckhardt, *Travels*, pp. 329-52; Burton, *Personal Narrative*, 1:304-75; Rutter, *Holy Cities*, 2:189-205, 230-40; Anṣâri, *As̱âr*, pp. 54-59; Farhâd Mirzâ, *Hedâyat*, pp. 339 ff.; Refᶜat, *Mer'ât*, 1:448-82; Jâser, *Rasâ'el*, pp. 85-92; G. Bisheh, "The Mosque of the Prophet at Madinah Throughout the First Century A.H." (Thesis; Michigan, 1979). It should be noted that religious scholars encouraged the pious visitation of this mosque and other shrines and tombs in Medina, but this is not a requirement ḥajj or pilgrimage proper: See Querry, *Droit Musulman*, 1:290-91, where Shi'ites are advised to visit the tombs of the Prophet, Fâṭemeh, the imams, Ḥamzeh, etc.

49 The caliph ᶜOmar enlarged the mosque in 17/638; see the passage from Samhudi's account translated in Burckhardt, *Travels*, p. 350; Refᶜat, *Mer'ât*, 1:426.

50 ᶜOs̱mân is supposed to have torn down the old walls, despite the opposition of the populace, and expanded the size of the mosque, as well as adding the teak roof, in 29-30/649-51; see Burckhardt, *Travels*, p. 350; Refᶜat, *Mer'ât*, 1:426.

51 This major renovation of the mosque took place in 87/706. The Byzantine emperor is said to have made contributions of gold and materials for the project. See Jean Sauvaget, *La Mosquée omeyyade de Médine* (Paris, 1947); Refᶜat, *Mer'ât*, 1:427; Esin, *Mecca*, pp. 130-34.

52 Mahdi's renovation of the mosque took place in 191/806-7; Ma'mun's expansion of the mosque was in 202/817-18. See Burckhardt, *Travels*, p. 351.

53 The Borji Mamluk sultans (784-922/1382-1517).

Ottoman sultans added to the building of Valid ebn-e ᶜAbd ol-Malek and made repairs, especially Qâyt Bây the Egyptian,[54] and Solṭân Solaymân and Solṭân ᶜAbd ol-Majid Khân the Ottomans.[55] These three have done the most in regard to renovations.

GATES OF THE MOSQUE OF THE PROPHET

The present mosque has five gates. Four of the gates are in the small ancient mosque that the Messenger of God had built.[56]

The Bâb Jebre'il ["Gate of Gabriel"]–by whom the revelation was sent down–is on the eastern side.

The Bâb os-Salâm ["Gate of Peace"] is on the west side of the mosque. Whenever someone comes from outside Medina, he must enter by this door.[57]

The Bâb or-Raḥman ["Gate of the Merciful"] or the Bâb or-Raḥmeh ["Gate of Pity"] is also on the western side of the mosque. Whenever [Moḥammad] returned from his campaigns, he entered by this door. [275]

The Bâb on-Nesâ' ["Gate of the Women"] is also on the eastern side of the mosque. The wives [of the Prophet] and women entered the mosque by this gate.

The Bâb ol-Majidi, which is also called the Bâb ot-Tavassol ["Gate of Refuge"], is on the north side and is one of the new constructions which formerly did not exist. Solṭân ᶜAbd ol-Majid Khân the Ottoman, who repaired and enlarged the mosque, built this gate and it was named for him.

CONSTRUCTIONS INSIDE THE MOSQUE

The length of the courtyard of the present mosque, which is uncovered, is one hundred qadam. The width of the courtyard is fifty-seven qadam. In the middle of this uncovered courtyard there is a well and a small garden. The well is known as Fâṭemeh's Well.[58] Its water has a slightly salty taste. It uses a rope five z̲arᶜ [long.] Its mouth is about two z̲arᶜ[wide]. It seems that the well of Be'r Boẕâᶜeh

---

54 The Mamluk Sultan Sayf od-Din Qâytbây (872-901/1468-96). He had the mosque repaired on several occasions, most notably in 888/1483-84, after it had been damaged by lightning. See Burckhardt, *Travels*, p. 352; Esin, *Mecca*, p. 160.

55 This last renovation of the mosque took place in 1853-54, about the time of Burton's visit to Medina; see also Refᶜat, *Mer'ât*, 1:465; Esin, *Mecca*, pp. 183-84.

56 Cf. Refᶜat, *Mer'ât*, 1:476-79. For the location of these gates and other features of the mosque mentioned by Farâhâni, refer to the map in the Appendix, Figure 4 (p. 330).

57 It is customary for visitors to the mosque in Medina to enter by this gate, located at the southern end of the western wall of the mosque. On this and the other gates, see Burckhardt, *Travels*, pp. 341-42; Rutter, *Holy Cities*, 2:235.

58 According to Burton, *Personal Narrative*, 1:337-38, the garden is known as Fâṭemeh's Garden or Orchard, and the well as the Prophet's Well.

is this same well.[59] [The Prophet Moḥammad] performed ablutions at this well. Owing to the blessedness of his auspicious ablutions, the water has become a cure for illnesses. Its garden has four small palm trees and one *ili* [?] tree and one *bih* [?] tree,[60] which are both wild fruit-bearing [trees]. They grow a few green shrubs in the garden. They pull up water from this well by a wheel and irrigate the garden.

Each of the four sides of this open courtyard [has] a portico which is covered, and columns have been erected inside. One side, on the west of the mosque, which is covered over, is 107 qadam in length and has three rows of stone columns. Each row has twelve columns, and each column is separated from the next by 8 qadam. The width of this same area is 26 qadam. [276] Another side of the courtyard, the eastern, which is roofed over, is 107 qadam in length and 17 qadam wide. It has two lines of columns. The interval between each column and the next is 8 qadam. That is the women's area, and the Bâb on-Nesâ' is on that same side.

One side on the north of the courtyard, the top of which is covered, is 57 qadam in length and 18 qadam wide. It has two rows of columns. Each column is at an interval of 8 qadam from the next.

One side on the south of the courtyard, which is covered over and used to be the old mosque, and which is where the tomb [of Moḥammad] is located (in the eastern corner), is 80 qadam long. That is to say, from parallel with the Bâb os-Salâm to the boundary of the blessed tomb [of Moḥammad] is 50 qadam, and from the boundary of the blessed tomb to the Bâb Jebre'il is 30 qadam. It has 54 columns. The width of this side is 68 qadam. It is nine columns across.

---

[59] Actually, the Be'r Bożâᶜeh, which was famous for the healing properties of its water, was located in the date groves outside Medina: see Burton, *Personal Narrative*, 1:414 n. 2; Anṣâri, *Asâr*, p. 167.

[60] It is very difficult to be certain of the translation of this sentence, particularly since other descriptions of Fâṭemeh's Garden do not correspond to Farâhâni's. Both Burton, *Personal Narrative*, 1:337, and Refᶜat, *Mer'ât*, 1:449, mention only the palm trees and a *nabaq* or lotus tree. Although in other places Farâhâni uses the terms *sedr* or *konâr* for the lotus, it is possible that the term given as *bih* in the text also refers to this type of tree: A Persian recension of Biruni's botanical text by Abu Bakr b. ᶜAli Kâsâni, known as the *Ṣaydaneh* (edited by M. Sotudeh and I. Afshâr; Tehran, 1358/1979-80), 1:367, notes that the lotus tree (*sedr* or *konâr*) is known in India as the *bir* tree—a word that could easily be misread as *bih*. (The same text, 2:688, says that the fruit of the *nabaq* is known as *b-b-r*, another word that could be misread as *bih*.) It may be recalled that Farâhâni did live for a while in India and could have been familiar with this word. Kâsâni, *Ṣaydaneh*, 2:768, also mentions a plant called *il* which might be the *ili* mentioned by Farâhâni, but it cannot be identified.

The width of the old mosque [encompasses] two square pedestals and four columns. In detail, they have been inscribed [with the names]: (1) Pillar of the Cot;[61] (2) Pillar of the Guardian;[62] (3) Pillar of the Delegations;[63] (4) nothing has been inscribed on it.

The length of the old mosque [contains] one square pedestal and six columns in two lines. These sorts of things are written on the columns:

(1) Abi Lobâbeh's Pillar;[64] (2) ᶜÂyesheh's Pillar;[65] (3) nothing is written [on this column]; (4) the Perfumed[66] Pillar.

The mihrab of [the Prophet Moḥammad] is between the third and fourth pillars. [277]

The plinth of the mihrab is of marble, and the rest is stucco. It is painted and gilded. Nothing has been written on the fifth and sixth columns either. The blessed pulpit, which is of marble and has been gilded and has seven steps, is between the fifth and sixth columns. This is not the pulpit of [the Prophet Moḥammad], but since [the Prophet's] pulpit used to be placed in this particular spot, they set up the pulpit in the same place. In the second row of columns, at the pillar opposite the pulpit, they have inscribed "the Pillar of Compassion."[67]

There are 260 columns in the entire blessed mosque and the periphery of the courtyard. The columns of the old mosque are of fluted and gilded marble. There are 23 columns, each of which has the mark: 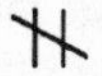. The columns of the new mosque are of ordinary stone which has been painted over, and a number has been inscribed on each one. On some of the columns the names of the companions [of the prophet] have also been inscribed. The roof [over] all the

---

61 *Sarir.* Moḥammad had a cot beside it and slept there while engaged in *eᶜtekaf* (spending the last ten days of Ramadan in a mosque). On these columns, see Burton, *Personal Narrative*, 1:335-336; Farhad Mirzâ, *Hedâyat*, pp. 339-342.

62 *Ḥaras.* It is also called the Pillar of ᶜAli since ᶜAli used to pray and stand guard beside it.

63 *Vofud.* So named because Moḥammad used to receive delegations coming to learn about Islam in front of this pillar.

64 Abu Lubâbah felt that he had betrayed the Prophet Moḥammad by warning the Jews of the tribe of Qorayzeh that Moḥammad intended to kill them. To repent, he tied himself to one of the pillars in the mosque and would not leave until Moḥammad forgave him: See Guillaume, *Life of Muhammad*, p. 462.

65 Farhad Mirzâ, *Hedâyat*, p. 339 gives a different location for this pillar.

66 Text: *moḥalleqeh*; read *mokhalleq*; see Burton, *Personal Narrative*, 1:335.

67 *Ḥanâneh.* Burton, *Personal Narrative*, 1:335 calls this the "Weeping Pillar." Prior to the introduction of the minbar, the Prophet gave the Friday sermon while standing next to this pillar; it was subsequently moved to an uncertain location.

columns [forms] an arcade. It has been whitewashed, gilded, and painted. The diameter of the columns varies.

The marble columns are three chârak [in diameter]. Some of the other columns are three ẕarᶜ, and some are two ẕarᶜ or a little less. Some are one and a half ẕarᶜ.

There are three mihrabs on this side of the mosque. One is known as the mihrab of the Messenger. It is in the old mosque. Another mihrab is one of the constructions of ᶜOs̱mân, which is in the new mosque and is situated in such a way that anyone who stands at the mihrab must turn his back to the tomb of the prophet. Another one is the mihrab of Solṭân Solaymân, which is a stone set up behind the other mihrab. This passage [in Arabic] is inscribed [on it]: [278] "The victorious King, Solṭân Solaymân Shâh, son of Solṭân Selim Khân, son of Bâyazid Khân, may God make glorious his victories on behalf of Moḥammad and his family, erected this noble mihrab; dated in the month of Jomâdâ I, the year nine hundred and eight of the hegira of the Prophet [November-December 1502]."

They have also built two benches of marble for the call to prayer and the *mokabber*.[68]

THE PROPHET'S CENOTAPH

As for the blessed cenotaph [of the Prophet Moḥammad], of which the tomb of the immaculate saintly lady [his daughter Faṭemeh] is also a part, it is at most sixty qadam all [the way] around.[69] Lengthwise, there are six chambers and false arches; breadthwise, there are three chambers and false arches. One of its eastern chambers, next to the Gate of Gabriel, is the tomb of her saintly eminence [Faṭemeh] and, also, another of its eastern chambers is the place of revelation where they say the visitation by Gabriel [took place].

The [walls of the] blessed cenotaph incorporate four large pedestals, each of which is two and a half ẕarᶜ in breadth. The domed roof is also supported on these pedestals. There are three small pillars, two of which are in the direction of the holy sepulcher of the immaculate saintly lady [Faṭemeh]. There is also another pillar above it [which is] the minaret of Belâl, who used to give the call to

[68] A ritual announcement of the beginning of the prayer service, usually delivered from a raised platform; see Burton, *Personal Narrative*, 1:311n.

[69] Moḥammad was buried in the house he shared with his wife ᶜÂyesheh, which was adjacent to the Mosque of the Prophet on one side and Fâṭemeh's house on another. As the mosque was expanded, these other buildings were enclosed within it; they were separated from the mosque by the walls of the sepulcher and a curtain. See Burckhardt, *Travels*, pp. 331-35.

prayer. There are fifteen columns and four doors on the sides and inside of the blessed sepulcher.

DOORS TO THE PROPHET'S CENOTAPH

There is one door on the east side, by which one enters the tomb of [Faṭemeh]. From the chamber of [Faṭemeh], one enters the blessed cenotaph [of Moḥammad].

There is one door to the west which is between the Pillar of the Delegations and the Pillar of the Guardian.

There is a door to the south, near which is the holy sepulcher of the prophet.

One door [is] to the north. Above the door, the name of Malek ol-Ashraf Qâyt Bây, [279] who was one of the Circassian sultans of Egypt and the builder of this cenotaph and dome, has been inscribed. It was built in the year 888 [1483-84]. There are steel windows colored green [on] three sides of this cenotaph, and there is a bronze window on one side of it. The names of [Moḥammad] the best of mankind, Fâṭemeh Zahrâ, the twelve Imams, Abâ Bakr, ᶜOmar, ᶜOs̱mân, Ḥamzeh, ᶜAbbâs, Ṭalḥeh, Zobayr, Saᶜd, Saᶜid, Abu ᶜObaydeh, Tamim, Osâmeh, Noᶜmân, ᶜAbd or-Raḥman ebn-e ᶜAwf, etc.[70] have been written above the pillars on the south behind the cenotaph. They say the courtyard of the new mosque and its pillars are among the constructions of Solṭân ᶜAbd ol-Majid Khân the Ottoman.

DIGNITARIES AND SERVITORS

There are about thirty dignitaries and thirty miscellaneous servitors for the blessed Garden [*Rowżeh*] of the Prophet.[71] The dignitaries and servitors are mostly wealthy people and respected landowners in Medina. The *shaykh ol-ḥarâm* and the *nâyeb ol-ḥarâm* supervise them. The shaykh ol-ḥarâm is the qâ'em-maqâm of Medina, who is under the jurisdiction of the governor of the Hejaz. The nâyeb ol-ḥarâm is one of these dignitaries.[72] When it is time [to light] the lamps, these two people put on white, clean garments, enter the holy sepulcher of the prophet by the door of the tomb of [Fâṭemeh], and light the lamps with their own hands.

70 These are all names of relatives of the Prophet, caliphs, generals, and other more or less famous companions of the Prophet.

71 The area around the tomb in the Prophet's Mosque is often referred to as the Garden on the basis of one of his reported sayings, "Between my house and my place of prayers is a Garden of the Gardens of Paradise."

72 Burton, *Personal Narrative*, 2:371, reports that the *shaykh ol-ḥarâm*, or chief official of the sanctuary, was appointed from Istanbul; his deputy, the *nâyeb*, was the chief of the black eunuchs. Cf. Burckhardt, *Travels*, pp. 343-45; Rutter, *Holy Cities*, 2:238-40.

ORNAMENTS

There are candlesticks, chandeliers, and numerous candelabra in this mosque. There are two large jewel-studded candlesticks inside the cenotaph above the blessed tomb, which are lit at the time the pilgrims come. Three lamps which burn olive oil have also been suspended in each niche. [280]

Among the decorations in the blessed Garden are nineteen trays of aloe and sandalwood incense, over which embroidered coverings have been placed. Every year, on the nineteenth of the month of Z̲i Qaᶜdeh, whatever is left over of the old incense is divided among the servitors and fresh incense is put out. The reason for choosing nineteen trays and the nineteenth of Z̲i Qaᶜdeh is unknown.

Two prayer leaders perform prayers in this mosque. One is a Ḥanafi master, and one is a Shâfeᶜi master.

BRINGING THE MAHMAL

They bring both the Maḥmal of the Prophet and the Maḥmal of ᶜÂyesheh to the blessed mosque.[73] Both are there until the day the Syrian and Egyptian pilgrims leave Medina. These two maḥmals are like those false [models of] fountains which processions escort around the streets during the days of ᶜÂshurâ in Iran. Each one has several gold and silver bosses, and an embroidered covering is over them.

The invention of these maḥmals [dates] from the time of the Circassian sultans of Egypt. At the time either of these two maḥmals enter or exit Mecca the Exalted and Medina the Agreeable, the ruler, soldiers, servants of the sanctuary and others go to welcome [it] and escort [it] and respectfully take [it] in or out.

EXTORTION IN THE PROPHET'S SANCTUARY

I heard that previously [people] used to annoy and pick quarrels with Iranian and Shi'ite pilgrims in the sanctuary of the prophet in order to extort money. The late [Grand Vizier] Mirzâ Ḥosayn Khân Moshir od-Dowleh Sepahsâlâr, during his trip to Mecca, ordered Sayyed Moṣṭafâ to be bastinadoed. He then decreed that every Iranian pilgrim pay to the Iranian pilgrim-guide one Levant dollar (which is about six thousand Iranian dinars) for the servitors of the [sanctuary of the] Prophet and the pilgrim-guides at that threshold. [281] That pilgrim-guide divides [it] among the servitors. Other than that, the servitors are not to molest the Iranian pilgrims in any way. Now this is the customary practice. One pays one Levant dollar to

---

73 See Refᶜat, *Mer'ât*, 1:384-85.

Sayyed Ḥasan,[74] the Iranian pilgrim-guide, who is the son of SayyedMoṣṭafâ, and he divides it between himself and the servitors. No one ever bothers the Iranian pilgrims, and they are at complete liberty. Even if someone does not wish to practice dissimulation in the prayers and ablutions, no one will argue with him. If, however, someone does not want to pay the one Levant dollar, they will certainly collect [it] from him. As I heard, several Iranian pilgrims wanted to slip away by night [so as] not to pay a Levant dollar. Sayyed Ḥasan was informed and took one of the dignitaries of the sanctuary, two of the soldiers under the governor of Medina, and three of his own men. They fell on the lodgings of the pilgrims in the middle of the night. They collected the one Levant dollar that very night and left. They do not charge anything from paupers and the ḥajjeh-forushes. By custom, dignitaries pay more than one Levant dollar.

The door to the sanctuary of the prophet is open during the time the pilgrims are in Medina till three hours after nightfall. The pilgrims go to visit it group by group. There is never any hindrance or inconvenience for the Shiʿites.

HOLY PLACES

A detailed account may be appended [here] about the holy Baqiᶜ cemetery and all the blessed places in Medina that are places of pious visitation.

THE BAQIᶜ CEMETERY

The Baqiᶜ cemetery is a spacious cemetery located to the east of the city wall of Medina adjacent to the city wall gate.[75] They have put up a wall three ẕarᶜ [high?] of stone and lime all around it. It has four gates. Two of its gates are on the western side on the street behind the city wall. One gate is on the south side. Another of its gates is on the east beside the Ḥashsh Kawkab on the street [by] the gardens outside the city. [282] So many [people] have been buried on top of each other in this cemetery that most of the cemetery is elevated more than one ẕarᶜ above ground level.

At the time the pilgrims come to Medina, the gates to this cemetery are open everyday until sunset. Anyone who wishes [may] go. At times other than the pilgrimage, it is opened Thursday noon until about sunset on Friday. Then it is closed unless someone dies and is buried there.

---

[74] Also mentioned by Farhâd Mirzâ, *Hedâyat*, p. 125.

[75] This famous cemetery is described by Burckhardt, *Travels*, pp. 362-64; Burton, *Personal Narrative*, 2:24-38; Refᶜat, *Mer'ât*, 1:425-27. The tombs there described by Farâhâni were destroyed following the Wahhâbi/Saᶜudi seizure of the Hejaz; see Rutter, *Holy Cities*, 2:245, 256-57.

FAMOUS PEOPLE BURIED IN THE BAQI^c CEMETERY

First, three or four of the twelve Imams are to be found in a large mausoleum built like an octagon.[76] Its interior and dome are whitewashed. The builder of this mausoleum or when it was built is unknown. However, Moḥammad ᶜAli Pâshâ the Egyptian repaired it in the year 1234 [1818-19] at the command of Solṭân Maḥmud Khân the Ottoman. Now, each year, on behalf of the Ottoman sultans, this blessed mausoleum and the rest of the mausolea located in the Baqiᶜ are repaired. Inside the blessed mausoleum there is a large coffer [made] of very fine forest wood.

Inside this large coffer there are two other wooden coffers. Five persons are buried under these two coffers. One is Emâm Momtaḥen Ḥażrat-e Ḥasan.[77] One is Ḥażrat-e Sayyed Sajjâd.[78] One is Emâm Moḥammad Bâqer.[79] One is Ḥażrat-e Jaᶜfar-e Ṣâdeq.[80] And one is ᶜAbbâs, the uncle of the prophet, from whom the Abbasid [caliphs] were descended.

Inside this same blessed mausoleum, there is a tomb by the western false arch. They have built an iron cenotaph by the wall on one side of it. [283] They say it is the tomb of Fâṭemeh Zahrâ.

VARIOUS NARRATIVES CONCERNING THE LOCATION OF [FÂṬEMEH'S] CENOTAPH

After the death of [Fâṭemeh],[81] the Commander of the Faithful [ᶜAli], out of broken-heartedness at the behavior of the hypocrites, and in accordance with [Fâṭemeh's] testament, buried her blessed body by night and concealed [the location] of the blessed sepulcher. Several places are known as the tomb of [Fâṭemeh]: One is inside the mosque of the prophet beside the blessed tomb [in] what used to be Fâṭemeh's own home.[82] Now a tomb has been built [there], and the Sunnis generally believe in it. Another is inside the mosque beside the tomb of the Messenger. Its pulpit is very grand. The noble tradition "Between my pulpit and my tomb is a garden of the gardens of paradise" referred to this very [site]. There is no obvious tomb in

---

76 Burton, *Personal Narrative*, 2:39-41, describes this building and records the prayer of supplication recited by Iranian pilgrims there.

77 The oldest son of ᶜAli and the second Shi'ite Imam (d. 50/670).

78 The fourth Imam, ᶜAli b. Ḥosayn (d. 95/712), known as Sajjâd ("the Prostrator") because he spent most of his life engaged in worship.

79 The fifth Imam (57-114/675-732).

80 The sixth Imam (83-140/702-57).

81 For conciseness, the various pious formulas and circumlocutions used by Farâhâni when referring to the Prophet's daughter are replaced here with the name in brackets.

82 Known as the *ḥojreh* ("chamber"); this house of the Prophet's daughter was adjacent to that of the Prophet and his wife ᶜÂyesheh (which contains the tomb of the Prophet and the first two caliphs).

that place, but they say [it is there]. Another is in the Baqiᶜ, in a chamber they call the Bayt ol-Aḥzân ["House of Sorrows"]. In view of this, most [pious people] also recite the visitation [prayer for Fâṭemeh] at the Bayt ol-Aḥzân. Another [proposed site] is this blessed mausoleum in the Baqiᶜ where they have built the tomb.[83] Sunnites and Shi'ites recite the visitation [prayer] there. At the front of this tomb, an old embroidered curtain has been hung up. The gold-braiding [reads]: "Solṭân Aḥmad, son of Solṭân Moḥammad, son of Solṭân Ebrâhim, son of Solṭân Aḥmad, son of Solṭân ᶜOs̱mân, the thirty-first year after the year one thousand, 1131 [1718-19]."[84] Some believe that this is the burial place of Ḥażrat-e Fâṭemeh, the daughter of Ḥażrat-e Emâm Ḥasan Mojtabâ ["the Chosen"], who was the mother of Emâm Moḥammad Bâqer.

ORNAMENTS OF THE MAUSOLEUM

There is no other decoration in this blessed mausoleum, except for two small chandeliers and some bronze candlesticks. The floor of the mausoleum is covered with a mat. [284]

CUSTODIANS AND SERVANTS

It has four or five custodians and servants who [hold the posts] from generation to generation. They do not apply themselves to the job; their aim is [just] to get money from pilgrims.

EXTORTION OF MONEY FROM THE SHI'ITE PILGRIMS

Sunni pilgrims rarely make a visitation to this blessed tomb. There is no hindrance to them in [making] a visitation, and no money is collected from them. However, none of the Shi'ite pilgrims are allowed to enter the mausoleum without paying the tax, unless they give the servants approximately one kran to five shâhis every time they want to make the pilgrimage and enter the mausoleum. Of the money that the servants collect from the pilgrims in this manner, a share must go to the nâyeb ol-ḥarâm and a share to Sayyed Ḥasan, son of Sayyed Moṣṭafâ, who is the pilgrim guide for the Iranians. After paying the money, there is no need for dissimulation in the pilgrimage and prayer. One is free to recite any visitation [prayer] one wishes, secretly or openly. No harm by word or deed ever befalls the Shi'ite pilgrims.[85]

---

[83] Burton, *Personal Narrative*, p. 41 n. 2, comments on the confusion surrounding the burial place of the Prophet's daughter.

[84] The reference is thus to the Ottoman Sultan Aḥmad III (1703-30).

[85] This again reflects an improvement in the treatment of Iranians in the Hejaz; earlier, travellers such as D'Avril, *Arabie contemporaine*, pp. 171-72, had observed that "les gamins de Médine exercant leur malice contre les Persans."

THE TOMB OF SHAYKH AḤMAD AḤSÂ'I

The holy dome of the tomb of Shaykh Aḥmad Aḥsâ'i,[86] to whom the Shaykhis are devoted, is behind the blessed mausoleum in the Baqi^c^, below the gutter-spout. It has an iron cenotaph. The tomb is of plaster and brick, raised up one zar^c^, and whitewashed. There is a large marble stone on top of it. These [Arabic] phrases are inscribed on it in *nasta^c^liq* script:

"The holy tomb of the great Shaykh, the paragon, the luminous, the proof, the believer of the age, the crown of glory, the most erudite of the epoch, the authoritative source for the ulama of Islam, the renewer [*mojadded*] of the thirteenth century, our master and the master of the Muslims, Aḥmad son of Zayn od-Din ol-Aḥsâ'i, may God hallow his heart and perfume his grave. He passed away, may God make his station lofty, in the year one thousand two hundred and forty-three [1827-28]. This is the subject of his date, may God exalt his rank.[87]" [285]

Another marble stone is affixed to the side of this same tomb. A two-verse chronogram is inscribed [on it].[88]

[The tomb] is known as the grave of the "Chief of the Heretics" among the Sunnis.[89] Nevertheless, [both] Sunnis and Shi'ites recite the opening chapter of the Koran over it. In Medina, one of [the shaykh's] miracles is famous: Several years ago, when this stone had recently been erected over the tomb, two Bedouin who were employed as tombstone makers saw that the stone was of marble and decided together to come over the wall into the Baqi^c^ cemetery by

---

[86] Shaykh Aḥmad Aḥsâ'i (1754-1826) was the founder of the movement within Twelver Shi'ism known as Shaykhism, the most novel idea of which was that there must always be a religious leader in the world capable of explaining the will of the hidden Imam. This idea may have helped lay the foundations for the subsequent Babi/Bahai movement. He died while on pilgrimage from Iran to Mecca. See Tonakâboni, *Qeṣaṣ*, pp. 47-55; Bâmdâd, *Rejâl*, 1:76-77; Morteżâ Modarresi-Chehârdehi, "Shaykh Aḥmad Aḥsâ'i," *Yâdgâr* 1/iv(1323-24/1944-46):30-47; Momen, *Introduction to Shi'i Islam*, pp. 225-31; A. Nicolas, *Essai sur le Sheikisme* (Paris, 1910); H. Corbin, *L'École Shaykhie en théologie shi'ite* (Tehran, 1957); Mangol Bayat, *Mysticism and Dissent* (Syracuse, 1982), pp. 37-58; Denis MacEoin, "From Shaykhism to Babism: a study in charismatic renewal in Shii Islam," (dissertation; Cambridge, 1979); EI_1, 4:279-80.

[87] This last phrase may be intended as a chronogram. Modarresi, "Aḥsâ'i," and most other authorities give the date of his death as 1241/1826; Bâmdâd, *Rejâl*, 1:77 says 1242/1826-27. It is not clear here if the tombstone or Farâhâni's reading of it is faulty.

[88] The two verses giving the date are quoted in the text but have been omitted in this translation.

[89] He denied the literal truth of the resurrection of the body and was accused of many additional heresies which he apparently never actually believed; see EI_2, 1:326.

night, take the stone from there, carry [it] to their home, erase the writing from it, inscribe the name of someone else over it, and sell it for an exorbitant price. [That] night, they went over the wall into the Baqiᶜ cemetery. As soon as one of them struck the tomb with a pick, a voice issued from the tomb three times [saying], "Leave the stone!" They thought that this voice was from outside the cemetery [and] that someone had seen [them] and had spoken these words. Finally, the hands, legs, and tongue of the one who was using the pick became incapacitated, and it was as if he were paralyzed and speechless. His distraught companion carried him on [his] back over the wall of the cemetery, getting down with difficulty. [By coincidence] that night, three or four holy men of Medina who were on their way to a meeting arrived there. They seized the Bedouin [and asked], "What were you going to do in the middle of the night?" After [being] imprisoned for two days, [the man's] companion who had been paralyzed died. He himself told the details and was set free. The responsibility for this story rests with the one who told it [to me]! [286]

TOMB OF THE SHAYKH OL-ESLÂM OF SHIRAZ

Beside the tomb of the late Shaykh Aḥmad is the tomb of Shaykh Abu'l-Qâsem, the Shaykh ol-Eslâm of Shiraz. It is without a cenotaph and has a small [tomb]stone. He died in the year 1286 [1869-70].

THE BAYT OL-AḤZÂN

Behind the dome of the Imams [in] the Baqiᶜ, in the same direction as the tomb of the late Shaykh Aḥmad, there is a small mausoleum which is the Bayt ol-Aḥzân of Ḥażrat-e Fâṭemeh Zahrâ.[90] There is one small cenotaph made of iron in this mausoleum. They say inside the cenotaph there is a place where a palm tree grew owing to one of [Fâṭemeh's] miracles.

TOMBS OF THE DAUGHTERS OF THE PROPHET

To the south of the mausoleum of the Imams [in] the Baqiᶜ, there is a mausoleum which is whitewashed and has a bronze cenotaph and is the tomb of Zaynab, Roqayyeh, and Omm Kolṡum, daughters of the Messenger of God [Moḥammad], of whom two were wives of ᶜOṡmân.[91] [287]

---

90 On this third possible resting place of the Prophet's daughter, see Burton, *Personal Narrative*, 2:42n.

91 Marginal note: "In the *Qorb ol-esnâd*, under the *Mosnad* of Ḥażrat-e [Jaᶜfar-e] Ṣâdeq, it is recorded that Khadijeh bore the Prophet [his sons] Qâsem and Ṭâher (whose proper name was ᶜAbdollah) and [his daughters] Fâṭemeh, Omm Kolṡum, Zaynab and Roqayyeh. He gave Fâṭemeh in marriage to the Commander of the Faithful [ᶜAli]; Zaynab to Abu'l-ᶜÂṣ b. Rabiᶜ, who was a member of the

MOSQUE OF EBN ABI KAᶜB

To the west of this mausoleum of the daughters of the Messenger, there is a mosque, roofed over like a small room, on the door of which is written, "This is the mosque of Ebn Abi Kaᶜb,[92] and the Messenger prayed in this mosque."

TOMBS OF THE PROPHET'S WIVES

To the south of this mausoleum of the daughters of the prophet, there is a whitewashed mausoleum. It has a cenotaph that [contains] the tomb of eight of the prophet's wives. The name and ancestry of each is written on a plaque suspended over the cenotaph. In order to make a pious visitation [to the tomb of] ᶜÂyesheh, many Sunnis visit [this mausoleum].[93]

TOMB OF ᶜAQIL

Near this mausoleum, there is another whitewashed mausoleum which has a bronze cenotaph. It is the tomb of ᶜAqil ebn-e Abi Ṭâleb.[94]

TOMB OF ᶜABDOLLAH JAᶜFAR

Near this mausoleum, there is another whitewashed mausoleum that is the tomb of ᶜAbdollah [ebn-e?] Jaᶜfar.[95]

THREE OTHER TOMBS

Near this mausoleum, there is another mausoleum that is the tomb of Nâfiᶜ, who was one of the seven reciters[96] of the Koran

---

Umayyad family; Omm Kols̱um to ᶜOs̱mân b. ᶜAffân; and Roqayyeh to ᶜOtbeh b. Abi Lahab. Before Omm Kols̱um went to ᶜOs̱mân's house, she died. ᶜOtbeh divorced Roqayyeh before consummating the marriage. Then Roqayyeh was married to ᶜOs̱mân. She also died in Medina during the lifetime of the Prophet. These four daughters were all buried in Medina. Qâsem and ᶜAbdollah both died in Mecca the Exalted and were buried there. In Medina, Mary [text: Mâreyyeh] the Copt bore Ebrâhim; he died in Medina and was buried in the Baqiᶜ cemetery. Mary the Copt was presented to the Prophet by the ruler of Alexandria." [The *Mosnad* of Jaᶜfar-e Ṣâdeq is contained in the *Qorb ol-esnâd* by ol-Ḥemyari ol-Qommi: see Sezgin, *Geschichte*, 1:165.]

92 So in the text; the name should probably read Obayy ebn-e Kaᶜb. Obayy (died ca. 20/640-41) was a close friend and scribe of the Prophet; Moḥammad used to visit his home and pray there. See Khalil b. Aybek oṣ-Ṣafadi, *Ketâb ol-vâfi be'l-vafayât*, (ed. Sven Dedering et al.; Wiesbaden, 1962-in progress), 6:190-91.

93 Although Farâhâni is loath to say so directly, the implication is that ᶜÂyesheh is one of the prophet's wives buried here; Shi'ites would not care to visit her tomb since she was a notorious enemy of their first Imam, ᶜAli.

94 Although a relative of the Prophet Moḥammad, ᶜAqil was a late convert to Islam; at the battle of Ṣiffin, he deserted his own brother ᶜAli and fought for Moᶜâveyyeh. He died in 60/679-80. See EI_1, 1:239.

95 This probably refers to ᶜAbdollah b. Jaᶜfar b. Abi Ṭâleb (d. ca. 80/699-700), a traditionist and relative of ᶜAli who lived in Medina. See ᶜAsqalâni, *Tahẕib*, 5:180-81; EI_1,1:23.

96 Muslims recognized seven acceptable readings of the Koran, with that of Nâfiᶜ (a slave owned by the caliph ᶜUmar who died ca. 117/735) representing the reading used in Medina: See W. Montgomery Watt, *Bell's Introduction to the Qur'ân* (Edinburgh, 1970), p. 49.

[*qorrâ'*]. Near this mausoleum is the mausoleum of Mâlek,[97] who [was] the founder of the Mâleki rite. Near these is a whitewashed mausoleum [which] has a bronze cenotaph. This is the tomb of the sons of the Messenger.[98]

TOMB OF ḤALIMEH-YE SAᶜDEYYEH

In the corner of the Baqiᶜ cemetery, to the northeast, there is a small, white mausoleum which has a wooden cenotaph. It is the tomb of Ḥalimeh-ye Saᶜdeyyeh,[99] [Moḥammad's] wet-nurse.

TOMB OF ᶜO͟SMÂN EBN-E ᶜAFFÂN

Beside the Baqiᶜ cemetery, to the east, there is a large whitewashed and painted dome which they say is the tomb of ᶜO͟smân ebn-e ᶜAffân. What is known is this. This place first had the name Ḥashsh Kawkab and was not part of the Baqiᶜ cemetery. [288] According to what the traditionists have written, ᶜO͟smân's grave was in a plot between the Baqiᶜ cemetery and the Jewish cemetery. Moᶜâveyyeh ebn-e Abi Sofyân, out of consideration of [their] kinship, made that place part of the Baqiᶜ enclosure.[100] Others believe that this is the tomb of ᶜO͟smân ebn-e Maẓᶜun.[101] Since no one knew where the grave of ᶜO͟smân ebn-e ᶜAffân [was], this was imagined to be his tomb. The mausoleum was built and enclosed in the Baqiᶜ cemetery. This supposition is unwarranted.

TOMB OF FÂṬEMEH

Behind the Baqiᶜ cemetery, in the same direction as the mausoleum of the Lady Ḥalimeh, there is a small whitewashed mausoleum. There are two tombs in it that are adjacent to each

97 Mâlek b. Anas (94-179/716-95) lived his entire life in Medina; in addition to founding the "school" of law named for him, he compiled one of the most important collections of traditions of the Prophet.

98 On these tombs, see Burton, *Personal Narrative*, 2:37-38. Although the text reads "sons," this contradicts the earlier marginal note (n. 91 above) in which Farâhâni correctly states that only Ebrâhim, the child of Mary the Copt, is buried in Medina; the graves of the other two sons are in Mecca.

99 It was the custom in Arabia to entrust children to a wet-nurse who would serve as a foster mother until the child was about six years old. As Burton, *Personal Narrative*, p. 37 n. 1, notes, the term Saᶜdeyyeh is a pun: it literally means "auspicious" and is also the name of the tribe to which Ḥalimeh belonged.

100 The caliph ᶜO͟smân was murdered in 35/656; the mob responsible for his death prevented his burial for three days. Because of his unpopularity, it was thus impossible to inter him in the Prophet's mosque with his predecessors; he was finally buried on the plot of land known as the Ḥashsh Kawkab, which his kinsman Moᶜâveyyeh annexed to the Baqiᶜ upon becoming caliph.

101 Text: Maṭᶜun. This ᶜO͟smân was one of the emigrants from Mecca; he died in Shaᶜbân 3 A.H. (Jan.-Feb. 624) and was buried on the plot of land which became the Baqiᶜ cemetery at the command of the Prophet. See Burton, *Personal Narrative*, p. 32.

other and are raised up to the extent of one z̲arᶜ above ground level with plaster and brick. As you enter the door, the tomb of Ḥażrat-e Fâṭemeh, daughter of Asad, who is the mother of Ḥażrat-e Amir ol-Mo'menin [ᶜAli], is on the right.

TOMBS OF THE PROPHET'S PATERNAL AUNTS

Behind the Baqiᶜ cemetery, at a distance of a street's width or ten z̲arᶜ, near the city gate, there is a whitewashed mausoleum where the paternal aunts of the Messenger are buried.

There are some small mausoleums in the Baqiᶜ cemetery where the leaders of Sunnism are buried. They are not worth describing or elaborating on.

TOMB OF ESMÂᶜIL EBN-E JAᶜFAR OṢ-ṢÂDEQ

Just as you enter the city via this city gate which is beside the Baqiᶜ cemetery, there is the high frame of a dome on the street behind [it]. It has an open space in front, a courtyard, and a bronze cenotaph. It is the tomb of Ḥażrat-e Esmâᶜil ebn-e Jaᶜfar oṣ-Ṣâdeq, who is the founder of the Esmâᶜileyyeh sect.[102] It has a custodian and servants. It is often a place of pilgrimage for the Boḥreh and Khowjehs. [289]

The Boḥreh and the Khowjehs are two sects of the Esmâᶜilis.[103] They dwell for the most part in India, Sind, Egypt, and [their] environs. There was a disagreement between these two sects a hundred and fifty years ago. The Khowjehs are disciples of Âqâ

---

[102] This is one of the three major divisions of Shi'ite Islam (the other two being the "Twelvers" and the Zaydis). Esmâᶜil (died between 133/750 and 145/762) was the oldest son of the sixth Imam Jaᶜfar oṣ-Ṣâdeq. Jaᶜfar supposedly recognized Esmâᶜil as his successor but later withdrew this recognition, or, according to other accounts, Esmâᶜil died before his father. In any event, this branch of Shi'ism split into two groups, the Twelvers (who traced a line of twelve Imams through Jaᶜfar's second son Musâ) and the Esmâᶜilis or "Seveners" (who variously held that the imamate ended with Esmâᶜil or alternatively recognized a series of Imams descended from him). See Marshall Hodgson, *The Order of Assassins* (Gravenhage, 1955); Bernard Lewis, *The Origin of Ismai'ilism* (Cambridge, 1940); W. Ivanow, *The Rise of the Fatimids* (Calcutta, 1942) and *A Guide to Ismaili Literature* (London, 1933); John Hollister, *The Shi'a of India* (Delhi, 1979; second edition), pp.195-220.

[103] Following the death of the Fatimid Caliph Mostanṣer in 487/1094, there was a schism within the Esmâᶜili movement when his oldest son Nezâr was replaced in the succession by a younger son Mostaᶜli. Those activists who supported the right of Nezâr to rule formed the Nezâri branch of Esmâᶜilism (more popularly known as the "Assassins"). The Boḥrehs in India (Bohorâs, "traders" or "merchants") were among those who supported the succession of Mostaᶜli; the Khowjehs were part of the Nezâri Esmâᶜili sect. On these groups see T. Lokhandwalla, "The Bohoras, a Muslim Community of Gujarat," *Studia Islamica* 5(1955):117-35; Asgharali Engineer, *The Bohras* (Sahibabad, 1980); S. Mujtaba Ali, *The Origins of the Khodjas* (Bonn, 1936).

Khân Maḥallâti[104] and his descendants. The Boḥrehs do not accept this. They believe in Mollâji Boḥreh and his descendants. Both sects consider Ḥażrat-e Esmâᶜil the legitimate Imam.[105] They consider the eldest son and the son of the eldest son [to be] the [legitimate] successor, no matter what. Thus, Âqâ Khân was the eldest son of Shâh Khalilollah and became his successor. The eldest son of Âqâ Khân, ᶜAli Shâh, was [his] successor. After the death of ᶜAli Shâh, although two older sons of Âqâ Khân were qualified, nonetheless Ḥosayn Shâh, son of ᶜAli Shâh, was the successor.

TOMB OF ᶜABDOLLAH, THE PROPHET'S FATHER

In one of the streets of Medina inside the city walls, near the Mosque of the Prophet, is the tomb of Ḥażrat-e ᶜAbdollah, father of the Prophet [Moḥammad], who died four months before the birth of the Prophet.[106] It is a large whitewashed mausoleum and has a bronze cenotaph and a lofty dome. In there, too, the servants and custodians collect whatever money they can from the visitors. [290]

THE MASJED OL-FATḤ

The Masjed ol-Fatḥ ["Mosque of Victory "] is one of the holy sites [in] Medina which is a place of pilgrimage. There are five small mosques on the western slope of Mount Salᶜ, all of which are called the Masjed ol-Fatḥ.[107] It is known that the Messenger of God prayed in all [of them]. The tomb of Nafs-e Zakeyyeh Moḥammad ebn-e ᶜAbdollah, who [was] one of the sons of Ḥasan ebn-e ᶜAli, is near Mount Salᶜ.

---

104 Ḥasan ᶜAli Shâh (1804-81), popularly known as Âqâ Khân Maḥallâti, became leader of this sect after the murder of his father, Shâh Khalilollah, in 1817. He had married a daughter of Fatḥ-ᶜali Shâh and was appointed governor of the city of Qomm. In 1840, however, he led a revolt in southeastern Iran; after his defeat, he and his followers, with British assistance, settled in Bombay. See Sykes, *History of Persia*, 2:336-37; EI_2, 5:1221-22; H. Algar, "The Revolt of Agha Khan Mahallati and the Transference of the Isma'ili Imamate to India," *Studia Islamica* 29(1969):55-81.

105 The technical term used in the text is *moftareż oṭ-ṭâᶜeh* ["the one to whom obedience is obligatory"].

106 [Marginal note:] "There is disagreement about the time of the death of Ḥażrat-e ᶜAbdollah. Some have written that it was two years after the birth of the Prophet, and others seven months after he was born. Still others believe that he died before the birth of the Prophet. In any event, he died in a house in Medina called the Dâr ot-Tâbeᶜeh ['Home of the Female Servant'] and was buried there. He was twenty-five years old."

107 The "Mosque of Victory" is supposed to be on the spot where Moḥammad prayed for victory over the Meccans during the Battle of the Trench (and is also occasionally held to be the place where the forty-eighth chapter of the Koran was revealed). The mosque most often accepted as the authentic one is also called the Masjed ol-Aḥzâb [Mosque of the Troops]. See Burton, *Personal Narrative*, 2:47-48; Burckhardt, *Travels*, p. 327; Anṣâri, *Aṣ̱âr*, pp. 76-78; Refᶜat, *Mer'ât*, 1:416-17.

THE MOṢALLÂ OR MASJED OL-GHAMÂMEH

To the southwest of Medina, outside the city wall, there is a small mosque which they call the Moṣallâ [or] the Masjed ol-Ghamâmeh[108] ["Mosque of the Clouds"]. The excellence of the Masjed ol-Ghamâmeh or Moṣallâ is great.

TOMBS OF THE MARTYRS OF ḤARREH

Another of the holy sites that is a place of pilgrimage is the tomb of the martyrs of Ḥarreh[109] who were killed fighting Yazid ebn-e Moᶜâveyyeh in the year 63 after the hegira [682-3].[110] It is located to the southwest of the city of Medina. This Ḥarreh is adjacent to the Wadi Boṭḥân and is near the city wall of Medina.

TOMB OF ḤAMZEH

Another of the holy sites of Medina which is a place of pilgrimage is the tomb of Ḥażrat-e Ḥamzeh, Prince of the Martyrs, which is located near Mt. Oḥod.[111]

Just as one goes out the gate in the direction of Mt. Oḥod, there is an unroofed mosque which they call the Mosque of Abi Z̲arr Gheffâri.[112] The Prophet [Moḥammad] prayed there. For going to Oḥod, there are easy-paced donkeys, pack-horses, and small ox- or mule-carts at the gate, which are present at the season the pilgrims arrive in Medina. Every day, the pilgrims go in groups, on foot or mounted, to visit [it]. From Medina to the tomb of Ḥażrat-e Ḥamzeh is three quarters of a farsakh. It is one farsakh to Mt. Oḥod.

---

[108] Text: Qamâmeh. A *moṣallâ* (literally "place of prayer") is usually a mosque on the outskirts of a town where prayer services are held on the major Islamic holy days. Moḥammad is supposed to have delivered the holiday prayers at this spot upon his arrival in Medina. It may also have been called the Mosque of the Clouds because prayers for rain were offered there. On the building, see Burton, *Personal Narrative*, 1:395; Qazvini/Le Strange, *Nuzhat*, p. 15; Refᶜat, *Mer'ât*, 1:420-32.

[109] As noted above, this term designates a lava flow; here it is also being used as the name of a particular lava field near Medina, site of the famous battle.

[110] A delegation of prominent citizens of Medina to the Umayyad Caliph Yazid was reportedly so shocked by his impious behavior that they incited a revolt against him; it was brutally suppressed a few months before the caliph's death. See J. Wellhausen, *The Arab Kingdom and Its Fall* (translated by Margaret Weir; Calcutta, 1927), pp. 152-65; M. Kister, "The Battle of Ḥarra: Some Socio-Economic Aspects," in M. Rosen-Ayalon (ed.), *Studies in Memory of Gaston Wiet* (Jerusalem, 1977), pp. 33-50; EI_2 3:326-27 [s.v. "al-Ḥarra."]

[111] Ḥamzeh, one of the Prophet's paternal uncles, was a celebrated warrior, "the Lion of God and His Prophet." The story of his treacherous ambush and murder at the battle of Oḥod, and the subsequent mutilation of his corpse by Hind (mother of Moᶜâveyyeh) is one of the most famous in early Islamic history. On Ḥamzeh and this mosque, see Burton, *Personal Narrative*, 1:426-33; Burckhardt, *Travels*, pp. 364-65; Rutter, *Holy Cities*, 2:242-48; Refᶜat, *Mer'ât*, 1:390-94.

[112] Abu Z̲arr Jondob b. Jonâdeh or-Rabaz̲i (d. 32 or 33/652-53) was a celebrated companion of the Prophet, known for his asceticism and piety and, later, his outspoken criticism of Umayyad rule.

The terrain is level. This desert is a very attractive desert. [291] There are date groves along the road.

Mt. Oḥod is a red mountain located to the north of Medina. The blessed tomb of Ḥamzeh is near this mountain. The original tomb of Ḥamzeh is a building located on top of a hill. It is elevated five or six steps above the ground. One enters a clean enclosure made of plaster and brick via a door and hallway. The floor of the enclosure is strewn with gravel. There are two wide, tall parlors on the two sides of this enclosure. One is the mosque, and two tombs are in the other one. The one inside the parlor which has a large wooden sarcophagus is the blessed tomb of Ḥażrat-e Ḥamzeh. The other one is a small tomb which is the tomb of ᶜAbdollah ebn-e Jaḥsh. (ᶜAbdollah is the brother of Zaynab, the wife of the prophet and the niece of Ḥażrat-e Ḥamzeh. He is one of the martyrs of Oḥod.)[113] There are visitation-prayer benches and various works of calligraphy in this mausoleum.

They say [other] martyrs of Oḥod are also buried in this mausoleum and enclosure, but the [location of their] tombs are not certain.

This blessed mausoleum is one of the constructions of Solṭân ᶜAbd ol-Majid Khân the Ottoman. The exterior of the dome is of dark blue tiles. There is a large hill opposite this building on top of which some houses have been built. Some are ruined, and a few are still inhabited.

The servants of [the shrine of] Ḥażrat-e Ḥamzeh stand at the door of this hallway during the pilgrimage season and collect money from the pilgrims. If they do not collect [money], they do not allow one to enter. At this building, there is a coffeehouse and a water fountain.

Twenty qadam towards the mountain from Ḥamzeh's mausoleum, [292] there is a small enclosure, unroofed, where they also say there are tombs of some of the martyrs of Oḥod. Just before this enclosure, one climbs up seven steps to where the enclosure stands. It has a large pool. Very warm running water flows into that pool. It [has a flow of] about two sang. This is a place where the pilgrims may wash. It is like a [public] bath. Going up towards the mountain again 130 qadam from there, there is a small mosque which has an enclosure and a portico. They say the blessed tooth of

[113] See Guillaume, *Life of Muhammad*, pp. 286-89; 388.

the prophet was broken there.[114] Past there, going a little further up near the mountain at the end of the valley, there is a small mosque. They say the day of the battle of Oḥod the archers of the division commanded by ᶜAbdollah ebn-e Jobayr had advanced in eagerness to get spoils.[115] The opposing army swarmed out of the valley, and the Messenger [of God, Moḥammad] was wounded. He prayed in this place.

One is not able to come to this place other than when the pilgrims are passing through. At this season, too, four foot soldiers and four cavalrymen are stationed there every day in order to protect the pilgrims from bandits. Nonetheless, if one is a little careless, the Bedouin bandits kill pilgrims and carry off their property.

THE QOBÂ MOSQUE

Another of the holy places that is in Medina the Illuminated and is a place of pilgrimage is the Qobâ Mosque, concerning which the blessed verse "A mosque which was founded upon fear of God..."[116] was revealed. It is located half a farsakh from Medina to the south of the city. Most of the way from Medina to there, there are gardens and palm groves. There is a guardhouse in the middle of the road. Two artillery [pieces] and twenty soldiers are there. This Qobâ Mosque is a small mosque. It does not have a roof. Three sides of it are ruined, and one side is in good shape. [293] There is a well in the palm grove of the Qobâ Mosque which they call the Well of Aris.[117] The signet ring of the prophet, which ᶜO̱smân was wearing, fell into that well. No matter how much they searched, it could not be found.

---

[114] During the Battle of Oḥod, when the Muslim forces were routed, the Prophet was struck in the face and had a tooth knocked out by a rock hurled by one of his enemies.

[115] The Prophet had ordered ᶜAbdollah to protect his flank against attack by the Meccan cavalry. His disobedience as a result of his desire to seize booty from the Meccan camp gave the Meccans an opportunity to turn the tide of battle and rout the Muslims.

[116] Koran, 9:108. Upon his arrival in Medina, the Prophet rested for a few days in the suburb of Qobâ, about three miles south of the city. The Koranic reference contrasts the "Mosque of Piety" which was built there at that time with the "Mosque of Mischief" which some of those opposed to Islam later constructed in the same area. On this mosque, see Burckhardt, *Travels*, pp. 367-69; Burton, *Personal Narrative*, 1:398-411; Rutter, *Holy Cities*, 2:254-55; Esin, *Mecca*, pp. 92-93; Sayf od-Dowleh, *Safarnâmeh*, p. 144; Refᶜat, *Mer'ât*, 1:394-99 (with many photographs); Anṣâri, *A̱sâr*, pp. 55-59.

[117] Text: Aresh. Cf. Qazvini/Le Strange, *Nuzhat*, p. 15; Ebn Baṭṭuṭeh, *Travels*, p. 180; Burton, *Personal Narrative*, 1:413-14; Rutter, *Holy Cities*, 2:255-56; Anṣâri, *A̱sâr*, p. 164. The caliph's loss of the ring was regarded as symbolic of the inauspiciousness of his reign.

THE MOSQUE OF FAŻIKH

Near the Qobâ Mosque, to the south of Medina, there is a mosque without a roof. It is twenty-seven qadam long and four qadam wide. It also has a courtyard around which most of the wall is still extant. They call this place the Mosque of Fażikh.[118] Beside this mosque also there is a pleasant palm grove and a garden which are the property of one of the notables of the Ḥasanids and the Shi'ites. There are very good sweet pomegranates and all sorts of green vegetables in this garden. They are irrigated [with] water drawn up from the well by camel. They said the Garden of Omm Ebrâhim[119] is near this mosque. However, this humble servant did not see [it] and will not write details about it.

SECURITY IN THE CITY

There are disturbances and disorders in Medina and its environs. All sorts of robbery and murder occur. One cannot travel at night alone and unarmed. Even the citizens of Medina itself do not go anywhere alone and unarmed at night. By day also, going alone to the villages in the environs is not [possible], especially for the pilgrims.

CITIES UNDER OTTOMAN JURISDICTION

In all the province of the Hejaz, except for the cities of Jedda, Mecca, Medina, and Yanbo^{c}, the Ottoman government never commands any authority and obedience. It has no mastery over the people of the villages, the Bedouin of the desert, and the tribes. The roads and highways of the Hejaz are utterly insecure. Some of the tribes and Bedouin of the desert at least obey the Sharif of Mecca. Since Jedda and Mecca are closer to the Sharif, they are more orderly. However, Medina and Yanbo^{c} do not have any security. [294]

MONEY

In Medina, all types of money such as the Levant dollar, the Ottoman lira and majidi, the English guinea and rupee, the Russian imperial, and the Dutch real are in circulation. The lira is accepted at 163 qorush. The majidi is 31 qorush; the rupee is 15 qorush; and the Levant dollar is 33 qorush. Each qorush is 70 para. Most transactions are in Levant dollars. The imperial has less value than any [of the others].

---

118 Throughout, the text has Fażiḥ. Some companions of the Prophet were said to be drinking date liquor (*fażikh*) at this mosque when they heard that alcoholic beverages had been forbidden and immediately emptied their cups. See Burton, *Personal Narrative*, 2:45-46; Farhâd Mirzâ, *Hedâyat*, p. 134; Anṣâri, *Asâr*, p. 88; Ref^{c}at, *Mer'ât*, 1:418.

119 That is, Mary the Copt. See Burton, *Personal Narrative*, 2:46-47.

CONSULATE AND IRANIAN SUBJECTS

There are no Iranian citizens in Medina. It also does not have a consul on behalf of the Iranian government. At the season the pilgrims come, if the Iranian pilgrims have any problem, it is referred to the same Ḥasan, son of Sayyed Moṣṭafâ, who is the pilgrim-guide for the Iranians. In some years, a man also comes temporarily to Medina on behalf of the consul [in] Jedda and is there until the pilgrims leave. This year, [a man] named Mirzâ ʿAli Khân, an Azerbayjani Turk, had come to Medina on behalf of the consul [in] Jedda.

This year, the pilgrims in Medina were at complete liberty. Every night, [they] gathered in the Nakhâveleh quarter and held rowżeh-khᵛânis and taʿzeyyehs [in commemoration of] the Lord of Martyrs [Ḥosayn]. Sometimes, the Sunnis also came to the rowżeh. In particular, a prayer for the endurance of the government of the Shâhanshâh of Iran was recited after the completion of the rowżeh.

The Syrian, Egyptian, and Jabal [Shammâr] pilgrims, who come via the land routes, did not stay more than five days in Medina. However, the Iranians who had come by the "Flying Caravan" stayed nine days in Medina.

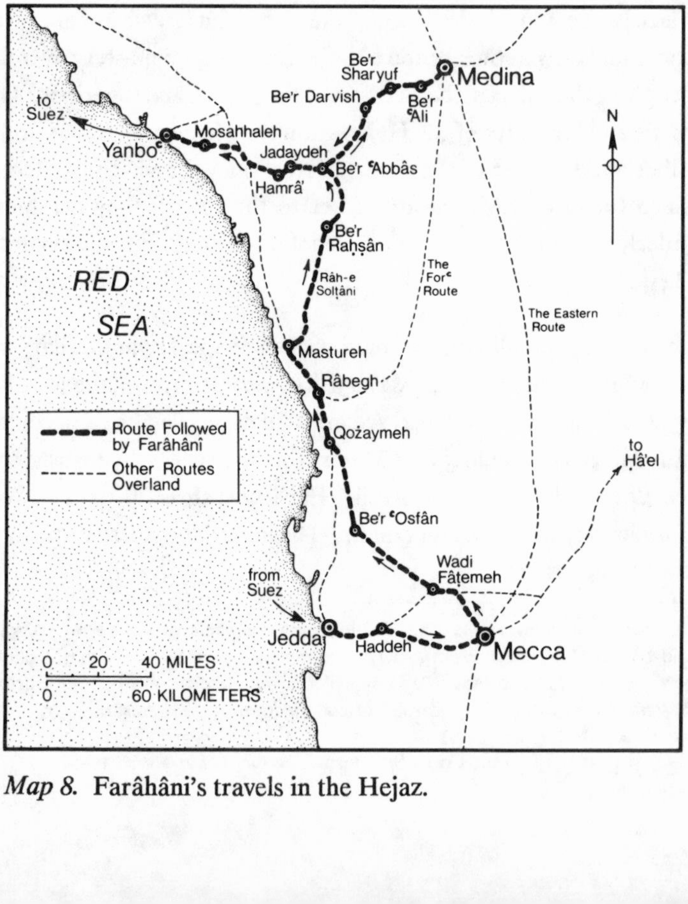

Map 8. Farâhâni's travels in the Hejaz.

PART SEVEN
THE RETURN TO IRAN

DEPARTURE FROM MEDINA

Having entered Medina the Agreeable the morning of Thursday the thirteenth of the sacred month of Moḥarram [22 October], we left Medina Friday the twenty-first of Moḥarram [30 October]. [295] This caravan at that time was limited to four hundred Iranians, whose leaders and guides were named Ḥovayfeż of Râbegh and Nâṣer and Shâker, sons of Naṣṣâr, who were all leaders of the tribe of Ḥarb.[1] In Mecca, the transport of the Iranian pilgrims was confirmed, and hostages were given [to guarantee safe arrival].

One and a half farsakhs outside Medina, one arrives at the Masjed-e Shajareh and Be'r ᶜAli. The Masjed-e Shajareh is beside the road. A description of it was written [in the account of my] arrival in Medina, and there is no need [to repeat it].

BE'R DARVISH

The stopping place for the day [was] Be'r Darvish.[2] It takes sixteen hours from Medina to Be'r Darvish by camel train. The road is smooth and level. There are no mountains near the road. Acacia trees[3] are seldom found. Be'r Darvish is a new well which a dervish [or someone named Darvish?] has been digging for several years. He has spent exorbitant sums, and it is still unfinished. Its depth is twenty-two z̲arᶜ. Its mouth is nine z̲arᶜ. Its water is sweet and wholesome. There is also one wattle hut at the well where they bring and sell fodder and dates from the environs.

BE'R ᶜABBÂS

We left Be'r Darvish and set out for Be'r ᶜAbbâs on Saturday the twenty-second of the sacred month of Moḥarram [31 October]. It takes fifteen hours by camel train from Be'r Darvish to Be'r ᶜAbbâs.

---

[1] Some of these same guides are mentioned by Amin od-Dowleh, *Safarnâmeh*, p. 251; on the tribe of Ḥarb, see Belâdi, *Qabâ'el*, pp. 99-100. Farâhâni's route may be contrasted with that taken overland to Syria by Sayf od-Dowleh, *Safarnâmeh*, pp. 146 ff.

[2] Cf. Rutter, *Holy Cities*, 2:183; Belâdi, *Ḥejâz*, 1:161.

[3] Text: *moghilân*. The tree (*Acacia arabica*) is more correctly known as the *omm ghaylân*; see Biruni, *Ṣaydaneh*, pp. 43-44; Massé, "Le Voyage de Farhâd Mirzâ," p. 353.

[There are] acacia trees along the way. One must pass between two chains of rocky mountains. Be'r ᶜAbbâs is a large well around which a stone fence has been built. It has sweet water. I also stopped at this well at the time [I was] on the way to Medina, and I have already written a description of it.

DEPARTURE FROM BE'R ᶜABBÂS

We left Be'r ᶜAbbâs on Sunday the twenty-third of the sacred month of Moḥarram [1 November]. The caravan of Iranian pilgrims divided there into two [groups]: [296] One went towards Jedda (their guide was Ḥovayfeż), and the other towards Yanboᶜ (their guides were Shâker and Nâṣer). The stopping place for the day for people going to Yanboᶜ is Ḥamrâ'.

THE ḤAMRÂ' ROUTE

From Be'r ᶜAbbâs to Ḥamrâ' is more than five farsakhs. It takes nine hours by camel train. Along the way, there are numerous acacia trees.

THE WADI JADAYDEH

One arrives first at the Wadi Jadaydeh.[4] Many gardens, palm groves, and citrus fruits of all kinds can be found in the Wadi Jadaydeh. There are three villages which are named Khaddâmi, Omm Zayyân, and Khayf ol-Kesâ'. They call these three villages Jadaydeh. There are about three thousand people in these three villages.

THE WADIS OF ḤAMRÂ' AND ṢAFRÂ'

The wadis of Ḥamrâ' and Ṣafrâ' are one farsakh past Jadaydeh. Ḥamrâ' and Ṣafrâ' are two wadis which intersect each other.[5] There are three springs of running water and gardens in Ṣafrâ' and the two villages which are part of it. There are about four thousand people in these three villages.

Ḥamrâ' is a very prosperous village.[6] It is located at the foot of a mountain. It has a spring where about three sang of flowing water comes out of the base of the mountain. Its water is very warm and sweet. It has countless gardens, which are mostly palm groves and citrus fruits. Grape vines can also be found. The village of Ḥazmâ' is also beside Ḥamrâ'. Ḥamrâ' and Ḥazmâ' have a population of four thousand people. The inhabitants of these two wadis are mostly

---

[4] Cf. Burckhardt, *Travels*, p. 404; Burton, *Personal Narrative*, 1:262. Rutter, *Holy Cities*, 2:270, vocalizes the name as Jodayyedeh; Belâdi, *Ḥejâz*, 2:135, gives Jadideh.

[5] Cf. Farhâd Mirzâ, *Hedâyat*, p. 120; Wohaibi, *Northern Hijaz*, pp. 236-42; Belâdi, *Ḥejâz*, 5:148-52.

[6] Cf. Burton, *Personal Narrative*, 1:253-61; Belâdi, *Ḥejâz*, 3:57-58.

of the tribe of Ḥarb and are Ḥanafis and Shâfeᶜis. There are also Malekis and Zaydis. It also has a few Shi'ites. The names of the important shaykhs who live in these wadis of Jadaydeh, Ḥamrâ', and Ṣafrâ' are listed below: [297]

Naṣṣâr, Ebrâhim ebn-e Salâmeh, Ebrâhim ebn-e Saᶜid, Jovaybar, ᶜAbd or-Raḥman, and ᶜAbdollah ebn-e ᶜAbd or-Raḥman.

WADI RABAZEH

The Wadi Rabaẕeh adjoins the Ḥamrâ' and Ṣafrâ' wadis. Formerly, Rabaẕeh was a very prosperous village, [but] now it is ruined. The remains of it are visible. The tomb of Ḥażrat-e Abi Ẕarr is near the ruins of Rabaẕeh.[7] It does not have a dome or cenotaph.

It takes three hours by camel train to go or come from Ḥamrâ' to that place. It is along a frightful road. There must be seven or eight people able to travel [together]. Few of the inhabitants there know about Rabaẕeh or the tomb of Abi Ẕarr, except the shaykhs and old people of Ḥamrâ'. Anyhow, we arrived at Ḥamrâ' on Sunday the twenty-third of Moḥarram [1 November] and encamped there on Monday the twenty-fourth also. Some of the pilgrims visited the tomb of Abi Ẕarr. Since Nâṣer and Shâker, the sons of Naṣṣâr, the guides of this Shi'ite caravan, have their homes and dwellings in this same village of Ḥamrâ', they brought most of the fellow traveller pilgrims a sheep as an act of courtesy.[8] Each of the pilgrims also gave from one lira to three lira to them in recompense for the sheep. There is a ruined fortress in the village of Ḥamrâ' which formerly used to be an Ottoman military site. Now it is ruined, and there are no soldiers in it.

DEPARTURE FROM ḤAMRÂ'

We left Ḥamrâ' on Tuesday the twenty-fifth of the sacred month of Moḥarram [3 November]. After travelling for one farsakh, there was a cemetery in which there were several old, roofed-over tombs. One of these roofed-over tombs had inscribed on it: "Abu ᶜObeydeh ol-Ḥâreṣ, cousin of the Messenger of God, may God bless him and his family." The Bedouin who inhabit the wadi consider this place to be sacred land. They bury most of their dead in this place. [298]

---

[7] The famous ascetic Abu Ẕarr did withdraw to a town known as Rabaẕeh, but it was located on the Darb Zobaydeh leading from Mecca to Iraq rather than on this route; Farâhâni's comments are probably based on some popularized version of this event. See Sa'ad al-Rashid, *al-Rabadhah* (Riyadh, 1986), pp. 8-9; maps and discussion in Saᶜd b. ᶜAbdollah b. Jonaydel, *ol-Moᶜjam ol-joghrâfi le'l-belâd ol-ᶜarabeyyeh os-saᶜudeyyeh* (Riyadh, 1978), 2:571 ff.; Belâdi, *Ḥejâz*, 4:20-27. On Abu Ẕarr, see above, Part Six, n. 112.

[8] Cf. Farhâd Mirzâ, *Hedâyat*, p. 120.

They recounted that these are the graves of the martyrs of [the battles of] Badr and Ḥonayn.[9] One farsakh past there, there was a water well. Its mouth was three zarᶜ, and its depth was [?] zarᶜ. However much I inquired, no one knew its name. Its water was sweet. This well is in the Wadi Zaferân. One farsakh past this well, one arrives at a difficult mountainous area. We travelled about one and a half farsakhs in this towering, rocky highland. Once again, the climate changed. This warm depression and its climate were similar to that of Yanboᶜ. It was like a tropical country. After that, the road was level again, and acacia trees were visible everywhere along the road. After travelling for sixteen hours from Ḥamrâ', we halted at the foot of the Nesᶜ mountains at a place where there was no water, well, or habitation. Some of the pilgrims had brought water. Some gave money to the camel drivers, [who] brought water for them from a farsakh away from the road. In this place, it was rather hard on the pilgrims due to the lack of water.

YANBOᶜ

We left this waterless and desolate stopping place on Wednesday the twenty-sixth of the sacred month of Moḥarram [4 November] and set out for the borough of Yanboᶜ.[10] We travelled for fifteen hours. The road was usually smooth and level, and there were acacia trees. Five hours before Yanboᶜ, there is an enclosure with a water well named Mosahhaleh.[11] It is a post for dromedary-mounted troops. Sometimes, passersby also stay there. They said Mount Rażvâ is twelve miles from Yanboᶜ, one and a half farsakhs from the road. In the belief of the Kaysâneyyeh [sect], Moḥammad ebn ol-Ḥanafeyyeh went into occultation on that mountain and will reappear [there]. They consider him to be the [living] Imam of the Age [*Emâm-e Zamân*].[12]

[9] The Battle of Badr, a raid on a Meccan caravan, took place in the second year after the hegira (624 A.D.) and was Moḥammad's first great military victory. The Battle of Ḥonayn (8/630) was a hard-fought victory by Moḥammad over an anti-Islamic tribal alliance and was the prelude to the capture of the city of Ṭâ'if. It is mentioned in the Koran (9:25). On this region, see Burckhardt, *Travels*, pp. 405-8; Sayf od-Dowleh, *Safarnâmeh*, p. 138.

[10] There is an interesting historical and geographical account of this region by Ḥamad ol-Jâser, *Belâd Yanboᶜ* (Riyadh, n. d.); see also Burckhardt, *Travels*, pp. 410-25; Wohaibi, *Northern Hijaz*, pp. 304-12.

[11] Burton, *Personal Narrative*, 1:245, gives the name as Mosahhal; Farhâd Mirzâ, *Hedâyat*, p. 117, as Mosahheli.

[12] The Kaysâneyyeh, a heretical Shi'ite sect, held that the imamate was inherited by certain descendants of ᶜAli not through his wife, the Prophet's daughter Fâṭemeh, but through another wife of the tribe of Ḥanifeh; thus their first Imam,

After that, we arrived at Yanbo[c]. It is forty farsakhs from Medina to Yanbo[c], [299] which by camel train takes fifty-seven or fifty-eight hours.

Yanbo[c] is a large town located beside the sea. It is the site of a qâ'em-maqâmate. It has some villages and Bedouin in the environs. In the town itself, there are about 2,500 households, which is about 8,000 and some people. It has two hundred shops. The inhabitants are all Bedouin. Their religious rite is usually Ḥanafi, Zaydi, or Kaysâni. There are no consuls or foreign subjects resident there. On behalf of the Ottoman government, 160 infantry troops, five artillery pieces, and one hundred dromedary-mounted troops are always stationed there. They have also built a special fort for the troops and artillery of the Ottoman Empire.

CLIMATE

The climate of Yanbo[c] is very warm and oppressive. Its soil and air are very damp. In most places, one hits water by digging down one chârak and half a zar[c]. Sometimes it is foggy. One can never sleep outdoors. Because of the closeness of the climate, there are so many flies that one cannot open one's mouth. Its lands are brackish, and no crops or trees are grown. There aren't even any wild trees. Everything is brought in from elsewhere. Fish are one of the foodstuffs produced locally, so excellent varieties of fish can be found. One type of very large fish there, which is about twenty zar[c] long or more, is named by the Arab nomads the *tabbân*[13] fish.

The water of Yanbo[c] is very bad. Rainwater is collected in cisterns. Owing to the nearness of the brackish land, it is bad tasting, salty and warm. [300] Because of the badness and warmth of the water and climate, many of the pilgrims were afflicted with diarrhoea.

FROM YANBO[c] TO JEDDA

There is no steamboat from Yanbo[c] to Jedda. There are rowboats, launches,[14] and sailboats which do not have a schedule for their departure or how often they go. Occasionally a steamship

---

Moḥammad, was known as "the son of the Ḥanafi woman" (Ebn ol-Ḥanafeyyeh). For a translation of a traditional account of the beliefs of the sect and related subsects, see Moḥammad b. [c]Abd ol-Karim Shahrâstâni, *Ketâb ol-melal va'n-neḥal*, translated by A. K. Kazi and J. G. Flynn, *Muslim Sects and Divisions* (London, 1984), pp. 126-32. See also Farhâd Mirzâ, *Hedâyat*, pp. 117-18; Jâser, *Belâd Yanbo[c]*, pp. 186-88.

[13] The vocalization is given explicitly by Farhâd Mirzâ, *Hedâyat*, p. 112.

[14] Text: *mâshveyyeh-hâ*; Farâhâni is apparently using a colloquial Arabic term for boat.

passes by this port. From Yanbo^c to Jedda is 180 miles. It takes from seventeen to twenty hours by commercial steamship. For their third class [fare], they usually charge a fare of four majidis, except during the season the pilgrims return from Mecca and Medina. The companies know the schedule for the arrival of the pilgrims in Yanbo^c, and at that time there are steamships for whoever comes to Yanbo^c, and there is no delay. For whoever comes later than that schedule, the ships that come to transport pilgrims [will] have loaded and left. There will [then] be cause for delay. In this year, when we arrived in Yanbo^c, about ten or twelve thousand pilgrims from various places had assembled in Yanbo^c and wanted to leave. Six steamships were also anchored there and were waiting for the pilgrims. Three passenger ships were going to Istanbul, two via Beirut, and two via Basra. At first, the deck-class fare to Istanbul or Basra was fixed at seven lira and the fare to Beirut at five lira. Then the pilgrims haggled with the ship companies about the fare, and in the end the fare to Basra was four lira, to Istanbul five lira, and three lira to Beirut. Cabin class to Istanbul was fourteen lira.

THE BEIRUT ROUTE

As for the pilgrims who went to Beirut, most were residents of Syria. A few were residents of Arab Iraq. About twenty of the Iranians went by that route. It was said they were [members] of the Bâbi sect who were going to Beirut and would go from Beirut to Acre to visit in Acre Mirzâ Ḥosayn ^cAli, the chief of the Bâbis, who is there.[15] [301] Acre is near Beirut. From Yanbo^c to Beirut, without stopping, takes six days to seven days by steamship, and one arrives on the seventh day. However, nowadays it will take more than six days because the passengers to Beirut must stop for two days for quarantine at the wadi of Mount Sinai. From Beirut to Damascus by train takes twelve hours. For people who want to go from Beirut to Baghdad, it is two days at sea by steamship from Beirut to Alexandretta,[16] and from the port of Alexandretta to Aleppo

[15] In 1844, a certain Mirzâ ^cAli Moḥammad of Shiraz proclaimed himself the Bâb ["Gate"] leading to the hidden Imam, the messianic figure in Twelver Shi'ism, whose advent was longed for by the Shi'ites; he subsequently introduced a new scriptural revelation, the *Bayân*, to supplant the Koran. Bâbism rapidly became the most significant sectarian and insurrectionary movement in nineteenth century Iran, culminating in the execution of the Bâb in 1850. After his death, the great majority of his followers accepted the leadership of Mirzâ Ḥosayn ^cAli, who became known as Behâ'ollah, the real founder of Bahaism. He resided in Acre until his death in May 1892. Cf. Browne, *Year Amongst the Persians*, p. 67; Bâmdâd, *Rejâl*, 1:434-38; 2:469-82.

[16] Now the port of Iskenderun in Turkey.

overland by mule or pack horse is five days. From Aleppo to the river bank[17] is a trip of three days, and from the river bank to Baghdad by small steamer is a trip of five days. However, boats are not always present there. Sometimes it happens that an individual waits ten or twelve days for a boat to appear.

THE BUSHEHR ROUTE

As for the pilgrims who go via the ports of Bushehr, Basra, and Baghdad, they go from Yanboᶜ in one day to Jedda; from there by steamship to the port of Ḥodaydeh[18] in three days; and from there to Aden in thirty hours. From Aden one reaches Musqat in five days; and from Musqat to Bandar ᶜAbbâs is three [more] days. From there to Bushehr is a trip of forty-five hours. One goes from Bushehr to Basra and Moḥammareh in one day. From Basra, one takes a small steamer, enters the Shaṭṭ [ol-ᶜArab] and reaches Baghdad in five days. Along the way one sees the towns of Emâreh and Madâ'en.[19] So all together, it is a trip of twenty-two days at sea by steamship, without stopping, from Yanboᶜ to Baghdad. [302] I myself have heard about [but] have not travelled by [the route] from Yanboᶜ to Musqat. However, I have travelled at length from Musqat to Baghdad during the journey when I returned from India. If I wanted to write an account of it, it would have to be separate from this travel account, as much needs to be said about it.

DEPARTURE FROM YANBOᶜ

Anyhow, having arrived at Yanboᶜ on Wednesday the twenty-sixth of the sacred month of Moḥarram [4 November], and having been in Yanboᶜ Thursday the twenty-seventh, Friday the twenty-eighth, Saturday the twenty-ninth, and Sunday the last day of Moḥarram the Sacred [5-8 November], we took a boat from Yanboᶜ and set out on the evening of Monday, the first day of the month of Ṣafar the Victorious [9 November]. We took the Arab steamship named the *Maḥalleh*, which belonged to Saᶜid Pâshâ, the former Khedive of Egypt, and set out. This steamship usually operates in the Red Sea. On our way to Mecca, we had taken this same steamship from Suez to Jedda. Although it is old, its furnishings are worn out, and it is not clean or orderly, still it is swift and large. If the wind is

17 Although the text has *labb-e daryâ*, which usually means seashore, Farâhâni must be referring to the Euphrates.

18 Text: Jadaydeh.

19 Madâ'en ("the Cities") is the Arabic name for the site of ancient Ctesiphon, capital of the Sassanid Empire. By "Emâreh," it is not clear whether Farâhâni means ᶜAmâreh or Kut ol-Emâreh, either of which could be reached by the Basra-Baghdad steamer. On this route, see Issawi, *Economic History of the Middle East*, pp. 146-53.

not unfavorable, and there is no storm, it can go ten miles an hour. Since its captain and crew are Arabs and Muslims, and they are not harsh to the pilgrims, there were many pilgrims on this steamship. There were about eight hundred pilgrims. Most were inhabitants of Istanbul and Anatolia. There were two hundred Tatars and people from Turkestan and seventy Iranians. Amazingly, there was an epidemic of diarrhea among the pilgrims, and about sixty or seventy persons on board the ship died. None of the Shi'ites or Iranians died. The depth of this Red Sea, according to the captain, is no more than 1,060 fathoms. This sea is also called the Baḥr-e Qolzom and the Baḥr-e Nubeh ["Sea of Nubia"]. Qolzom is the name of a city which used to be on the shores of this same sea.[20] It was a distance of thirty parasangs from Cairo. Previously, one used to travel from or to Mecca [via it]. After arriving at the city of Qolzom, there were two routes, one by sea and one by land. [303] Via the land route, one reached Mecca in fifteen days. After water covered the place and it was ruined, Suez flourished.

Nubia of Ethiopia is also on the shores of this same sea. This sea adjoins the Indian Ocean (which is the "Green Sea" [*Baḥr-e Akhżar*]) From there, one goes to the Sea of Oman. In most places of this sea, there are black and white corals [*yosr*], pearls, and many other corals [*marjân*]. It is a very bountiful sea.

MOUNT RADVEH

Twenty seven miles past Yanbo[c], the shore was nearby on the eastern side. A mountain was visible which is named Mount Radveh,[21] but it is not a stopping place for boats and is uninhabited.

MOUNT SINAI

We were en route Tuesday the second of the month of Ṣafar [10 November]. Wednesday the third [11 November] at nine o'clock, the steamship anchored at the wadi of Mount Sinai, which was the quarantine site this year. When the captain first informed the quarantine officials, ten or twelve government rowboats came below the steamship and transported the pilgrims without charging a fare. Although the oarsmen took one and a half qorush from the pilgrims as a gratuity, this was not in addition to a fare. On land, they went

[20] Clysma; see above, Part Four, n. 41.

[21] This is actually identical to the Mt. Rażvâ mentioned earlier. Burton, *Personal Narrative*, 1:222 n. 2, mentions the confusion caused by the variant spellings of the name. In addition to its importance to the Kaysâneyyeh sect, Rażvâ was also one of the "mountains of paradise" that were fragments of the original Mt. Sinai. See Qazvini/Le Strange, *Nuzhat*, p. 181; Belâdi, *Ḥejâz*, 4:54-56; Farhâd Mirzâ, *Hedâyat*, p. 112.

on foot. A government building had been constructed at the edge of the landing. Most of its rooms were like very spacious storage rooms or halls.

THE QUARANTINE [STATION][22]

The employees of the quarantine are as follows: chief doctor, one person; doctors, two persons; inspector, one person; assistant inspector, one person; accountant, one person; official in charge of security, called the *moḥâfeẓ*, one person; foot soldiers, two hundred persons. [304]

These troops do not allow the pilgrims to wander around. As soon as all the people of a steamer have assembled in the open area in front of the building, they announce that the pilgrims must obtain tickets and enter the quarantine. The inspector, assistant inspector, and accountant are seated in one of the rooms. All the pilgrims must pay them one and a quarter Levant dollars per person and take tickets. They charged some of them who were not knowledgeable about the operation of the quarantine from one and a half to two Levant dollars for the tickets. They cheated in some other ways, too. For example, they took imperials, liras, and other gold money for less [than they were worth]. They gave printed tickets to each person, couple, ten people, or whatever. As soon as they had collected the money from all the pilgrims and given out the tickets, then the accountant stood at the door to the building with two soldiers and inspected the people's tickets. They entered the building group by group. In some of the rooms of this building, there is fumigating equipment present like a *bokhur kebrit*,[23] etc. If people

[22] Farâhâni has frequently alluded to various sanitary measures affecting the pilgrimage traffic, but the Sinai quarantine is perhaps the most important of them. Largely because of the influx of poor pilgrims from British India, the Hejaz had been swept by cholera epidemics, some of which, like the great epidemic of 1817, spread to Europe. Since there was little sound medical information about cholera, the main response aimed at preventing the spread of the epidemics was an effort to control the physical movement of the pilgrims. This led to the establishment of an Egyptian Quarantine Board in 1831, the Conseil Supérieur de Santé de Constantinople in 1839, and the Paris Sanitary Conferences of 1851 and 1859. These were largely ineffective, however, due to the opposition of some maritime countries (notably Britain) to any restraints on the pilgrimage transport industry. After a severe cholera epidemic in 1865, however, a Third International Sanitary Convention met in Istanbul in 1866 at which the Ottomans agreed to construct quarantine stations at several key spots along the maritime pilgrimage routes, including the site at Sinai. Thorough discussion of the sanitary regime may be found in Daniel Panzac, *La Peste dans l'empire Ottoman* (Louvain, 1985) and *Quarantaines et Lazarets* (Aix-en-Provence, 1986); see also Long, *Hajj*, pp. 69-75; Roff, "Sanitation and Security;" F. Duguet, *Le Pélerinage de la Mecque* (Paris, 1932.)

[23] Apparently a device used for burning sulphur to fumigate or purify a room.

do not have a disease known to be contagious, they do not have to be fumigated.

THE FIELD TENTS

At another door to the building by which the people exit, there is a vast plain. On that plain, four groups of military field tents[24] had been pitched, so that each group was at an interval of about one maydân from the next. Each group had three rows of white tents, and each row had twenty-five tents. So all together, there were three hundred tents. In front of each group of tents, there were also six tents where shopkeepers stayed. There were two coffeehouses and four grocer's tents. They also have fruit and sell everything at exorbitant prices. Those six shopkeepers are Arabs. There is also a tent in each group for two Jewish money changers and two Armenian butchers. [305] Live sheep can also be obtained but they are extremely expensive. Beside each group of tents there are also two iron water tanks. Each one has two or three spigots. They draw water from those spigots. The water is brought in continuously by government camels and poured into the tanks. They give water, however much is desired, to the pilgrims for free. These four groups of tents are the collective property of the four steamers. Each steamer that comes to the quarantine must lodge all its passengers in one of these groups of tents. Variously, every five, seven, eight, or ten people will have one tent. There are thirty soldiers to take care of each group of tents. They watch out for the pilgrims' belongings at night, and by day they also insure that the people of one ship and group of tents do not mix with the group or people of another ship. Thus, after our arrival at the quarantine, two other ships came which were visible from afar, but we did not see the people of that ship nor did they see us.

At one spot in the desert, near the government building, there are some trees, date palms, and a little greenery where ten or twenty tents have been pitched. It is the residence of the soldiers and the employees of the quarantine. The only inhabited place in this desert is a village named Ḥammâm Musâ, located half a farsakh from the tents. It has twenty Arab households resident there. It has fresh water and date palms. Eggplants and fresh green vegetables are grown there and sold at the quarantine. They bring the drinking water consumed at the quarantine from there.

---

[24] Text: *châdorhâ-ye qalandari sarbâzi*. Refᶜat, *Mer'ât*, has photographs of the encampment at Sinai showing the type of tents Farâhâni is attempting to describe.

From this aforementioned wadi to Mount Sinai, [306] according to what they said, is an overland trip of forty hours by camel. Mount Sinai is located in the middle of a mountainous area. Its environs have many gardens, streams, and trees. Its climate is extremely cold. They brought fruits from there to here to sell. There were quinces, large sweet apples, and oranges in abundance. Carobs (which is a fruit with a flavor resembling wild plums) had been brought from the villages in the suburbs of Cairo. However, all these are very expensive.

THE QUARANTINE

To sum up, it was noted earlier in the description of ᶜArafât and Menâ that this quarantine was set up by the Ottoman government's bureau of health in Istanbul. If there is no contagious disease, the period the pilgrims stay in the quarantine is forty-eight hours. If during the forty-eight hours, someone dies [while] on land, the period will be renewed. However, its employees are [employed] by the Khedive of Egypt. The Sinai wadi is also part of the kingdom of Egypt. It seems that the service and fealty and obedience which the Khedive of Egypt renders to the Ottoman Empire is no more than using the moon and star flag and this matter [of the quarantine.] This quarantine in no way causes any loss or expense for the Ottoman Empire. Whatever they expend on it, they get back double from the pilgrims. Exorbitant sums go to the employees of the quarantine. When officials are posted to the quarantine, it is as if [they had been appointed] officials in charge of fleecing and plundering the pilgrims. One of the circumstances that makes this clear is that the authorities of the quarantine, especially the chief doctor, take something from the captains of the steamers so they won't cause any trouble: If someone dies during the two days stopped at the quarantine, they don't renew the period and do not delay the steamer.[25] [307]

Anyhow, since it was the first of Qows[26] and the spell of hot weather was broken and the land at this place was less humid and had

[25] Farâhâni's observations are remarkably consonant with those of Hurgronje, *Mekka*, p. 218, that "the whole quarantine arrangement has no other genuine purpose than exploitation" and that the "health authorities in Constantinople succeed in convincing the highest medical authorities in Europe (to whom the real conditions of the Orient are unknown, and remain unknown despite fleeting visits) as to the wholesome working of their system of extorting money."

[26] Qows is the name for the zodiacal constellation Sagittarius, and is the old name for the ninth month of the Iranian solar calendar (*Âzar*); it thus corresponds to November-December.

wholesome water, it was not too hard on the pilgrims at the quarantine. Having arrived at the quarantine on Wednesday the third of the month of Ṣafar the Victorious [11 November], and having been released from the quarantine on Friday the fifth of Ṣafar [13 November] and having gone to the landing, government rowboats carried the pilgrims to the steamer for free. The steamer left one hour before sunset.

THE PORT OF SUEZ

Saturday the sixth [14 November] at seven o'clock in the morning, [the ship] arrived at the Suez landing and anchored. It stopped opposite Suez the day of Saturday the sixth and the night [before] Sunday the seventh and took on water and coal. The ship was refurbished, and all sorts of food and drink were brought to sell on board the ship. However, no one was permitted to leave and go freely except those who were stopping in the area of Egypt and had residence permits. They entered after being inspected by the quarantine doctor in Suez.

THE SUEZ CANAL

The morning of Sunday the seventh of the month of Ṣafar the Victorious [15 November], [the ship] went from Suez towards the canal. Everyone who wants to transit through the canal must first inform the canal commission. After the employees of the commission have collected the toll and given permission, the ship proceeds to the canal. Every ship that wants to pass through the canal pays the customary toll in proportion to its tonnage. The canal makes enormous income yearly. This canal was dug at great trouble and incalculable expense by a French company. [308] It was completed in the year 1286 on the twelfth of Shaʿbân [November 17, 1869].[27] It connects the Mediterranean and the Red seas. The work lasted for ten years. About 40,200,800 tomans[28] were expended on the canal. The engineer for this work was the French engineer Ferdinand de Lesseps. A statue of him has been made out of gun-metal and set up on a stone at the harbor of Suez (which is at the mouth of the canal). Because a number of people had shared in the expenses of the canal, and it has enormous income, [ownership of it] has been divided into 400,000 shares [of stock]. The Khedive of Egypt received 176,000 shares as compensation for the land, the permits, and assistance [in building it.] The rest of the shares went to the numerous individuals of the French company. In order to

[27] This is the date of the ceremony marking the official opening of the canal.
[28] Literally, "80 *korur* and 200,800 tomans."

commemorate the share[holders?], they divided each mile [of the canal] into ten parts, and at each part they set up signboards with [the names in?] French written [on them].[29] After several years, the Khedive of Egypt sold the shares he had in the canal for nearly ten million ["twenty *korur*"] Iranian tomans and gave that for his debts.[30]

DESCRIPTION OF THE CANAL

The description of the canal is as follows:

The length of the canal from Suez to Port Said is eighty-five English miles,[31] which is about sixteen farsakhs. Its width varies from forty French meters to one hundred meters.[32] [309] Its depth varies from nine Iranian z̲arᶜ to ten z̲arᶜ. At three places per mile, a sentinel is posted for protection. They have also constructed guardhouses every three miles. Some places, there is nothing but the guardhouse. In other places, there are inhabited areas, trees, and several resident households of those employed by the road- and ship-building industries, in addition to the guardhouse. They have also constructed guest-houses and stations. They have brought water from the Nile River to those places. All together, there are inhabited areas and stations in eleven places. Most are located on the left [bank of the canal]. A telegraph line has been run the whole way. From the harbor of Suez to the mouth of the canal (that is, the sea), they have put up buoys so that the steamers pass between them and do not run aground. After entering the canal, they have made stone revetments alongside the canal in some places, and in other places they are engaged in repairing the revetment, until one arrives at the Karin[33] station. From the Karin station to near Ismailiyya the

[29] The meaning of the Persian sentence here is extremely unclear, and this is simiply a guess at what Farâhâni was attempting to explain.

[30] Farâhâni's information is fairly accurate. The Khedive Saᶜid had received 177,642 shares in the canal company; Disraeli purchased these shares for the British government from Saᶜid's successor Esmâᶜil in 1875 for £E 3,975,580. See Zayid, *Egypt's Struggle*, pp. 8-12; Holt, *Egypt*, pp. 200-208. On de Lesseps and the *Compagnie financière de Suez*, see Farnie, *East and West of Suez*; John Pudney, *Suez; De Lesseps' Canal*, (New York, 1969); Sir Arnold Talbot Wilson, *The Suez Canal: iIs Past, Present, and Future*, (London, 1939); and Patrick Balfour Kinross, *Between Two Seas: The Creation of the Suez Canal* (London, 1968); Richmond, *Egypt*, pp. 91-97.

[31] [Marginal note:] "A full English mile equals 1090 zarᶜ-e shâh, with three and a half gereh left over. The geographical English mile, which is also called a nautical mile, equals 1043 z̲arᶜ and three gereh-ye shâh. The Iranian farsakh is taken to be equivalent to 6000 zarᶜ-e shâh. This is the meaning of the English geographical or nautical mile."

[32] [Marginal note:] "The French meter is equivalent to fifteen and a half gereh (half a gereh is less than one Iraqi z̲arᶜ)."

[33] So in the text. From the detailed map in G. Blake *et al.*, *Cambridge Atlas of the Middle East & North Africa* (Cambridge, 1987), pp. 102-3 this should probably read Kabret; otherwise, it might be a mistake for Kubri.

waterway goes through the desert. They have made a small lake which is about eight or nine miles in length. For these nine miles they have erected signs on two sides. The steamers go between those signs so they do not run aground. Twenty-five miles from Suez, they have built a tower in the middle of the canal. There is a large lighthouse on top of it. At night, they put a lamp in it. After that, there is another lighthouse in the middle of the canal which is smaller. In some places along the canal near this small lighthouse, there are [areas of] reed-beds. As soon as you pass out of that large lagoon, the waterway again passes for a span of four miles through the desert. [310] Another small lake and lagoon has been made. They have erected signs on two sides. The ships pass between them. Since in most places the depth and width of the canal is small, and steamers are continuously passing through, and they did not make the mouth of the canal large enough for steamers going and coming to pass each other, the steamers therefore travel very slowly and deliberately and are constantly stopping. For this same reason, no steamer traverses the canal by night even if it is moonlit. At sunset, they must stop wherever they may be. [Our] steamer arrived at Ismailiyya at about sunset and anchored.

ISMAILIYYA

Ismailiyya is located on the left bank of the canal and, according to accounts, it is a green and pleasant port. It has many palm groves and coconut palms. It is one of the constructions of Esmâᶜil Pâshâ, the Khedive of Egypt, who also erected nice buildings there and brought in water from the Nile River. There are about two thousand households resident there, so it has [a population of] eight thousand. Because of the quarantine, they did not allow anyone to go into Ismailiyya. However, they brought foodstuffs and fruit by rowboats to the steamer to sell, in particular oranges which were very large and inexpensive.

DEPARTURE FROM ISMAILIYYA

The morning of Monday the eighth of the month of Ṣafar the Victorious [16 November], the steamer left from opposite Ismailiyya. It travelled very slowly; whenever another ship came along, it moved to the side and stopped until [the other ship] passed by. Because it was frequently delayed, it was not possible to exit the canal, and so [the ship] stopped for another night along the canal. That day, the terrain alongside the canal was mostly a region of fine sand. Thus in most places the sides [of the canal] were revetted with stone so that the sand and earth would not run into the canal. [311]

Nevertheless, with a little wind, the sand ran into the canal, and they continually [have to] clean it out. They have built some strange equipment for cleaning it out that defies description.

The morning of Tuesday the ninth [17 November], the steamer set out again. After travelling a mile along the canal, the waterway was again situated in the desert and was shaped like a lagoon. In this lagoon, there were many birds such as the *changar*[34] and so on.

PORT SAID

The steamer arrived at Port Said at nine o'clock in the morning on Tuesday the ninth [17 November]. It anchored and took on coal and water. Because of the quarantine, they did not allow anyone to enter Port Said. However, they brought all sorts of foodstuffs and fruit to sell aboard the ship.

Port Said is one of the ports of Egypt. It is located beside the Mediterranean Sea at the end of the canal. After the construction of this canal, it became very prosperous and it will continue to be. Consuls of the European countries stay there. The ship companies have constructed large warehouses for coal and provisions. They have built nice houses. Its water is also from the Nile River. They have planted citrus trees. According to reports, it currently has about three thousand resident households, so its population is twelve thousand. It has 850 shops. There, they brought many parrots of all colors to sell on the ship. Most of the pilgrims purchased [them]. I likewise bought two parrots. None of the pilgrims, not even the people from Istanbul, reached home [with them], but praise be to God, [my] two parrots arrived home safely. [312]

DEPARTURE FROM PORT SAID

The steamer left Port Said two hours before sunset on Tuesday and set out on the Mediterranean Sea. The night and day of Wednesday the tenth [18 November], Thursday the eleventh, and the night [before] Friday the twelfth, it travelled continuously without stopping at any port until it arrived at Izmir at noon on Friday the twelfth [20 November]. It intended to anchor, but navy sailors came by rowboat and forbade [that]. They said: "If you want to stop here and have the passengers enter Izmir, you must go to the quarantine post for Izmir (which is a two hour trip by steamer from Izmir) and get a health certificate from the quarantine doctor. Then you may enter Izmir." Since the steamer had many passengers from

---

[34] This is the name, in Gilaki dialect, for a certain type of sea duck (*Fulica atra*); see Sotudeh, *Farhang-e gilaki* (Tehran, p. 79.

Izmir, it had to turn back. After travelling for two hours, it arrived at a place at the foot of a green and attractive mountain beside the sea where a large building for the quarantine had been constructed. Tents were pitched alongside it. The steamer anchored there. The second captain got in the steamer's launch and went to the coast to the doctor of the quarantine. He saw him, returned to the steamer, and informed the sick people that they should get up and not sleep until the doctor came and left. Then the chief doctor of the quarantine and several of his employees came to the steamer and looked at the passengers and left. Even though a group of people on the steamer were afflicted with dysentery, the chief doctor nevertheless looked the other way and ignored the fact. Out of friendship and previous acquaintance with the second captain, he issued a health certificate and left. They said the chief doctor took a bribe from the captain as the price for [his] silence. Then the steamer left and arrived at the Izmir landing near sunset. Since it was night, and it did not have permission to enter, it anchored at that same place. The morning of Saturday the thirteenth of the month of Ṣafar the Victorious [21 November], after the captain went into town and showed the health certificate from the chief doctor of the Izmir quarantine to the security officer [*moḥâfeẓ*] of Izmir, they gave permission for the pilgrims to enter the city of Izmir. [313] We also entered [the city] and went to the khan of the Iranians, the residence of Mirzâ Ḥasan Tâjer-e Eṣfahâni–the same place we had gone the time before.[35]

DEPARTURE FROM IZMIR

[The ship] left Izmir the afternoon of Saturday the thirteenth of Ṣafar [21 November], one hour before sunset. Two hours after nightfall, the weather got stormy, it rained hard, and there was a tempest. The storm lasted until one hour before sunset on Sunday the fourteenth [22 November] when [the ship] reached Chanakkale. Many people had swooned and were insensible. [The ship] stopped two hours in Chanakkale in order to take refuge from the storm. Several of the passengers got off. The storm gradually died down. One hour after nightfall [the evening before] Monday the fifteenth, the steamer set out from Chanakkale. The description of this route and the ports along the way was written when I was on my way [to Mecca]; there is no need to repeat it.

---

[35] Farâhâni quotes a line of poetry here which is omitted from the translation.

THE STRAITS AT ISTANBUL

The morning of Monday the fifteenth of the month of Ṣafar the Victorious [23 November], the ship arrived at the Istanbul straits at nine o'clock in the morning. After informing the maritime authorities and obtaining permission, it passed into the Bosphorus and travelled very slowly through the straits for one hour. A small steamer came out to serve as guide until [the] boat anchored near the customs house. The second captain took the health certificates that had been obtained from the quarantine doctors to the director of the Ministry of Health and obtained permission for the disembarkation of the passengers. Because there were many pilgrims from Istanbul on this steamer, women and men came out to welcome [them] on small steamers and rowboats. Also, various women spectators, well-groomed and wearing sumptuous clothes, had each taken a bouquet of flowers and fruits in hand, gotten into rowboats, and had come to see the pilgrims for the sake of [doing] a good deed or for amusement. [314] It was a strange scene: some were crying, some were laughing; they were waving handkerchiefs, scattering flowers and sweet basil, and casting fruit and dried nuts onto the ship. The passengers were disembarking from the steamer until one hour past noon. We also got into rowboats and got off at the door to the customs house. In the customs house, a little of the baggage was opened for customs purposes. They took a small gratuity [in exchange for] not searching [baggage]. From there we went to the Fenjân-chi Inn and lodged there. This inn is two-storeyed. Because it is antiquated, it is not commendable. It is a lodging place for Iranians.

INVITATION OF MOᶜIN OL-MOLK TO HIS MANSION

The day after [our] arrival in Istanbul, Mirzâ Javâd Khân the chargé d'affaires, Ḥâjji Mirzâ Najaf-ᶜali Khân the consul-general and head translator, and Ḥâjji Mirzâ Ḥasan Khân came to visit. Via them, Moᶜin ol-Molk asked after our health, expressed his concern, and invited us to his mansion [*yâli*].[36] The fourth day [after our] arrival, we went to the mansion in accordance with the invitation. It was a very attractive tall building. One side of the building adjoined the Bosphorus, and one side of the building was located next to a small earthen hill. The courtyard of the building was paved with

[36]This is a Turkish term (derived from the Greek) for the waterside residences which were often built overlooking the Bosphorus near Istanbul. There are some photographs of the Iranian consular buildings in Khân Malek-e Sâsâni, *Yâdbudhâ-ye sefârat-e estânbul*, p. 10 etc.

small, colored pebbles, from which something like a picture of flowers and bushes had been fashioned. The spaces between the pebbles had been pointed with plaster. Inside and outside, attractive flowerbeds and a garden had been constructed, and varieties of flowers were grown. It had large, nice, decorated rooms and salons in which there was excellent furniture of Iranian, European, and Ottoman types.

MOᶜIN OL-MOLK

Moᶜin ol-Molk[37] seemed to be a very sociable, good-natured person, an eloquent conversationalist and good company. [315] I observed his affairs to be in order and understood his actions and deeds to be reasonable. I had the opportunity to visit with [him] at numerous meetings; for example, in the Mosque of the Vâledeh khan (which is especially for Iranians). The merchants were holding a rowżeh-khᵛâni there. Abu'l-Ḥasan Mirzâ, known as Shaykh or-Ra'is-e Khorâsâni,[38] was in the pulpit. Moᶜin ol-Molk had come to the mosque in order to propagate the Shi'ite religion and to honor Shaykh or-Ra'is. One must pardon [me] for not being able to write bits of praise or reproach of people according to their merits. It is not possible to write or talk about everyone and everything one knows. "You know how many notes the lyre and the lute produce." "The kernel is [part of] the ear [of grain]."

During these days [we were] staying in Istanbul, Ḥâjji Mirzâ Najaf-ᶜali Khân and some of the important merchants extended invitations [to me and my] companions. We also went to several theatres and playhouses. All together, fifteen days were spent in Istanbul during our return stop.

OFFICES OF THE NEWSPAPER "AKHTAR"

Among the places we visited during these several days, one was the bureau of the newspaper *Akhtar*,[39] which is in the Vâledeh khan. It has five or six employees such as writer, translator, etc. The head

---

[37] See above, Part Three, n. 190.

[38] See above, Part Four, n. 81. According to Moshâr, *Ketâbhâ-ye châpi*, col. 961, there is a printed edition of a *Safarnâmeh-ye estânbul* by Shaykh or-Re'is; it has not been possible to find a copy of this text, which might shed some light on the matters Farâhâni discusses here. In any case, it is known that Shaykh or-Ra'is became an apologist for Sultan ᶜAbd ol-Ḥamid's version of Pan-Islamism; see Hamid Enayat, *Modern Islamic Political Thought* (Austin, 1982), p. 122.

[39] The *Akhtar* ("Star") was a weekly newspaper published in Persian in Istanbul from 1875-96; its political tone was generally more subdued than that of some of the other Persian newspapers published abroad. However, it would reach its greatest fame a few years after Farâhâni's visit when it published articles sharply criticizing the concession of a tobacco monopoly in Iran to a British entrepreneur (1890-91).

of the bureau is Mirzâ Ṭâher. He is a native of Tabriz and an Iranian national. He is well bred, learned, quiet, experienced, temperate, and straightforward. He had come to Istanbul years ago and stayed. Previously, he had a business; at present, also, he has a little capital which is his main means of subsistence. As he is religious, he has good ideas and considers the welfare of the government of Iran to be one of the articles of his religion and faith. [316] If once in a while he writes something in his newspaper [critical of] the government of Iran, he has no motive other than public-spiritedness. He means this as a kind of sincere faith and patriotism.

THE IRANIAN ELEMENTARY SCHOOL

Another [place visited] was the Iranian elementary school which has been established for several years.[40] To begin the establishment of the school, Moʿin ol-Molk gave an elaborate banquet and extended official invitations to the notables and emissaries. At the meeting, he mentioned that such an idea was being considered. Each of the guests, as is customary, made charitable contributions of whatever amount they could. The funds were collected, and they deposited those funds with one of the Iranian merchants. After a planning council met and after consulting the Iranians, they established the school. The Iranian merchants decided, out of civility and patriotism, that each would make charitable contributions according to his ability, a fixed amount paid per month, whether he had a child in the school or not. Then they selected the pupils and decided on a special uniform for them, rented a building, purchased things for the place such as tables, chairs, mirrors, books, etc. out of the funds that had been collected, and hired Arabic, Persian, and French teachers, a tutor, servant, shoe-keeper, and ferash. They appointed a man named Ḥâjji Mirzâ Mahdi as the principal; the aforementioned is eloquent, perceptive, religious, efficient, and learned. There are more than sixty children. They have numerous classes, and their lessons vary according to their different levels of comprehension. They come in the morning and leave in the afternoon. They eat lunch at school. That is, they have brought their own cook to the school compound. That cook prepares various dishes every day. [317] He sets the price for each.

See E. G. Browne, *The Press and Poetry of Modern Persia* (Cambridge, 1914), pp. 36-37; idem, *Persian Revolution*, pp. 46-49; H. Rabino, "La Presse persane depuis ses origines jusqu'à nos jours," *Revue du monde musulman* 22(1913):287-315: Bakhash, *Iran*, pp. 241, 318; Khân Malek-e Sâsâni, *Yâdbudhâ-ye sefârat-e estânbul*, pp. 205-7.

[40] Cf. Khân Malek-e Sâsâni, *Yâdbudhâ-ye sefârat-e estânbul*, pp. 103-5.

Each of the students and workers of the school tells what he wants and the cook brings [it]. If the student has the financial means, he either pays cash or charges it and pays at the end of the month. If a child has no relatives, or is an orphan, or is poor, his expenses for what he eats are paid by the school. Also, if he has no place [to spend] the night, he sleeps at the school itself. The expenses for this [school] are of several types: One is the rental of the building, which is about two hundred tomans. Another is the monthly salaries of the principal, teachers, and workers, each of whom has a different fixed monthly salary. Another [expense] is the repair of old equipment and the purchase of new equipment for the classes. Another is the expense for the food and clothes of the impecunious and orphan children, which the school must pay. The monthly fees that the merchants pay are now not enough for those expenses. Whatever deficit or loss there may be is taken from the funds which had been collected earlier at the banquet meeting. They keep a record of the monthly fees that the merchants pay along with the specific expenses of the school in a ledger so that all those who make charitable donations know there is no wrongdoing or irregularity in this regard. When I went to the school, they were examining the students. They knew Arabic, Persian, geometry, arithmetic, and geography very well. One can say that in this short time they have made great progress. "This child travels a journey of a hundred years overnight."[41] If it continues this way, they will make considerable progress in a short time, and it will be a source of pride for Iranians abroad. [318]

THE SITUATION FOR IRANIAN PILGRIMS

Anyhow, Iranian pilgrims who pass through Russia must again have their passports endorsed in Istanbul at the Iranian embassy. Each person pays half a lira to the officials as the fee for endorsement. They also send the passport for the endorsement of the Russian embassy. They pay one manât as the fee for its endorsement. If someone does not have his passport endorsed by the Russian embassy, they will not permit him to enter at Batum. He will be compelled to go back unless, upon arriving in Trabzon, he sends his passport for the endorsement of the Russian consul who is in Trabzon. Thus, the passport belonging to one of the fellow travellers which had been obtained in Istanbul was lost at sea. As

[41] A popular Persian proverb usually applied to a person (child or adult) who seems to have a promising future; see Y. Jamshidi-pur, *Farhang-e amsâl-e fârsi* (Tehran, n.d.), p. 42.

soon as he reached Trabzon, he obtained a passport from the Iranian consulate in Trabzon and sent it for the endorsement of the Russian consul stationed in Trabzon.

STEAMSHIP FARES

On the advice of the officials of the embassy, we booked passage on a steamer of the Austrian company. The steamer fare to Batum, third class, was one and a half liras, which is about four and a half Iranian tomans. Second class was three lira, thirty-five qorush (which is about ten tomans in Iranian money). The fare for a first class cabin was four and a half lira (which is about thirteen tomans and a fraction in Iranian money).

DEPARTURE FROM ISTANBUL

Monday, the last day of the month of Ṣafar the Victorious [7 December], we boarded the steamer along with a group of pilgrims one hour before sunset, and the steamer departed. It reached Inebolu on Tuesday the first day of the month of Rabiᶜ ol-Avval [8 December] five hours before sunset. It discharged and took on cargo and passengers. Two hours after nightfall [before] Wednesday, it left from there. Wednesday the second [9 December], it arrived at Samsun one hour before noon. [319] It also anchored there and discharged and took on cargo and passengers. After stopping for two hours, it set out one hour past noon. It did not stop in any [other] port.

TRABZON

Thursday the third [10 December], it arrived at Trabzon one hour after sunrise. Since it had a lot of cargo for Trabzon, the passengers were informed that the steamer would stop there until sunset. Anyone who wished could enter the city. Most of the passengers went into the city. Some of my travel companions and I also entered the city and went to the home of Ḥâjji Sayyed ᶜAli Âqâ-ye Tâjer due to acquaintance [with him].

HOSPITALITY OF ḤÂJJI MIRZÂ ḤOSAYN KHÂN

They gave news [of our arrival] to Ḥâjji Mirzâ Ḥosayn Khân, the consul-general of Iran in Trabzon. He insisted that we visit his home. They had prepared an elaborate feast and had fixed a lunch with varieties of Ottoman foods arranged on a table. He was very friendly and kind. He is self-possessed, reasonable, and temperate. He has a good command of Arabic and Persian learning. In my estimation, he is a scholarly, refined person.[42]

[42] Farâhâni quotes here a proverbial verse from a poem by Shabestari which implies that he was delighted to have been in Trabzon; see Dehkhodâ, *Amsâl*, p. 597.

DEPARTURE FROM TRABZON

We conversed about all sorts of things. We went to the steamer one hour before sunset. The sons of Mirzâ Ḥosayn Khân, who were courteous and knew the language, along with several of the merchants, accompanied us to the steamer. Three hours after nightfall [before] Friday, the steamer left Trabzon. It arrived opposite Batum the morning of Friday the fourth of the month of Rabi^c ol-Avval [11 November] one hour past daybreak. [320] So from Trabzon by commercial steamship is a trip of eight to nine hours. From Istanbul to Batum takes five nights, three days, and a little more.

HARBOR OF BATUM

Before the entrance of the steamer into the harbor, the captain requested permission for the entrance of the passengers. First, the Russian doctor of the quarantine at Batum came, looked at the health certificate that was obtained from the doctor at the Russian embassy in Istanbul, ascertained the health of the people on the boat, and then gave permission for the entrance of the passengers. If the people on the boat are not well, or if the steamer does not have the health certificate from the doctor of the Russian embassy in Istanbul, the passengers will be compelled to stay in quarantine for five days on the ship.

After [receiving] permission from the doctor of the quarantine in Batum, the passport authorities came on board the ship and took up passports from the people. Whoever did not have a passport was turned back. Whoever had a passport in hand, they gave him, after taking his passport, a entry permit in place of the passport. They took all the passports from the people, and [the next] day the passport owners went to the passport bureau. They returned their entry permits and received their endorsed passports. They charged each pilgrim one manât as the fee for the passport.

STAY IN BATUM

We arrived in the city of Batum the fourth of the month of Rabi^c ol-Avval [11 December] in the morning and stayed in Batum Saturday the fifth [12 December]. Sunday the sixth [13 December] we took a railway coach at the station and set out. The Batum customs house is in this same railway coach station, [321] and a description of it is as follows.

THE CUSTOMS AT BATUM

In Russia, they usually collect exorbitant customs duties for any goods that are brought in at the point of entry and do not collect customs duties on goods that are taken out. [But] since they are striving very hard [to make] Batum prosper, they want many goods to be brought into but not taken out of it. Thus they do not charge customs duties on whatever goods are brought into Batum. However, if one wishes to carry out of Batum those goods which were brought into Batum from abroad, then they will, with great diligence and rigor, charge extraordinary duties [on them] at Batum. For example, they will collect on one mann-e tabriz of dates, the value of which is one kran, the equivalent of one kran in customs duties. For five zarᶜ of broadcloth, they demand its value in customs duties. It can be said that they collect duties equal in value to all goods. Even if someone has two mann of oranges or two mann of *sokhâri* bread[43] to take along for his food, the equivalent of its value will be collected in customs duties. Sometimes it happens that someone who had figs, dates, onions, etc. in the way of food or drink has discarded [them] out of fear of the customs duties, since he knew that he could not take [them with him] and no one would buy [them] from him. Thus we ourselves had brought along several boxes of Izmir figs and seven or eight mann of dates from Medina and gave them gratis to the Iranian brokers out of fear of the high customs duties.

They even charge duties on clothing apparel that is not well used and old. If, for example, one has a new unworn pair of socks, they will demand customs duties. They charge customs duties on all things without exception, even for a chicken coop! [322]

For each person, they do not charge customs duties on dutiable goods up to the value of one manât. For dutiable goods above one manât, there is no allowance even for this one manât, and customs duties are collected from one on everything in entirety.

They search inside all baggage, packages, bundles, boxes, bags, and containers. They even undo back cushions, quilts, and pillows and inspect them. They search peoples' pockets and breast-pockets. If for example someone has a couple of knives or a couple of prayer-beads in his pocket or breast-pocket, they will collect customs duties from him.

Inside the customs building, there is an iron railing. The reason for this is lest people smuggle anything past customs. The owners of the property stand on one side, and they put their belongings, without the owner, on the other side, so that the customs employees

---

43 A kind of dried bread resembling Melba toast which, not being very perishable, was often carried by travellers.

can search and inspect the goods meticulously without the owners being present.

Their customs workers and the soldiers who are the sentinels and guards there are usually thieves and swindlers. With utter dexterity and agility they pilfer whatever possible from the baggage, especially during all that crowding and confusion and noise. Thus one Iranian there took a manât out of his own purse and a soldier noticed and quickly stole the purse. The point is this: Many belongings of the travellers are lost or disappear, and whatever is left will be damaged. Since the train is ready to go, and the individual wants to leave, he must tolerate the loss of property. If one does not overlook it, and waits, and makes a fuss, it will produce no results, and no one will listen to his case. [323]

Owing to the wickedness of this kind of customs house in Batum, travellers pass through there in great hardship. This city is the worst place for pilgrims, especially on the way back. After the travellers understood the situation at this customs house, they were upset. Some of the men who had acquaintances or friends in Trabzon, sent their things, even clothes that had been worn, back to Trabzon again in order for the merchants to send their things by that route. Some concealed a few things that they had, such as knives, fezzes, prayer-beads, etc., inside back-cushions, pillows, turbans, hats, pockets, or their breast-pockets. A few were caught and had to pay an additional customs fine, and most of their effects were also confiscated.

BEHAVIOR OF RETURNING PILGRIMS

Today, not only did everyone wear his new and clean clothes, some, out of fear lest they be charged customs duties, wore two [garments] on top of each other. A pilgrim who the day before was wearing an old peasant's felt hat and a ragged caftan, today had wrapped two Egyptian shawls on his head and wore cloak, tunic, and a vest of broadcloth, put a watch in his vest pocket, and wore glasses and carried amber prayer beads.

IRANIAN CHARLATANS

In this city, a hardship which is worse than the customs business for Iranian pilgrims is this. Several Iranian brokers stay there who have been rascals and rogues since way back. They are divided into two factions. Each faction has several followers, and they are occupied with robbing and vexing the pilgrims. The names of their leaders are as follows:

Tekrân the Armenian, who is an Iranian by origin and sometimes has consular authority in Batum.

Ḥâjji Gholâm who is an Iranian and has become one of the soldiers and employees of the customs house; [324] Karbalâ'i Moḥammad ʿAli; Mashhadi Reżâ; and Mashhadi ʿAli Yazdi.

First of all, they insist that travellers and pilgrims are responsible for passport fees which are not customarily paid there, so that each person pays about two tomans passport fee. Secondly, [they get money for] every lodging rented by a traveller in Batum. If, for example, that lodging costs 5000 [dinars or half a toman], they, by force or cajolery or sharp talk, hold a person responsible for paying [them] two tomans. Third, everything that one wants to buy there costs double its value since they have an understanding with the merchants and tradesmen. If a traveller wants to sell anything, they belittle his goods so much that he sells for half the value or no one will buy it at all. Fourth, if the broker for this helpless traveller belongs, for example, to Tekrân's faction, the faction of Ḥâjji Gholâm tries to harm him or to steal his property. Or if he smuggles something past customs, this faction will reveal his delinquency and thus entangle him with imprisonment and fines. The helpless Iranian traveller is confused: What should he do? Where should he go? To which gang should he entrust himself? How can he renounce his baggage, clothes, food and drink? How can he bear this amount of customs duties? How can he take refuge from these Russian thieves and Iranian swindlers? On whom can he rely? How can he flee?

Really, it is a strange situation. "These days a father doesn't know his own son." "It is like doomsday." "It is a day when a man flees from his brother."[44] It is in this place that all the travellers are utterly distraught and upset. Since I did not have anything dutiable, I was at ease and merely observing [what was going on].

ANECDOTE

They tell the story about Shaykh Shebli[45] that on one of his trips, he was with a caravan. [325] Bandits fell on the caravan, and the people were distraught out of grief and sorrow over the loss of property. They were weeping and lamenting. They saw the shaykh seated in a corner laughing. They said, "What reason is there for laughter?" He said, "The bandits stole whatever all these [people]

[44] These are all proverbs, some in Arabic and some in Persian, to drive home the point that the pilgrims have a very difficult time in Batum. See Jamshidi-pur, *Farhang*, p. 143.

[45] Abu Bakr Dolaf osh-Shebli (247-334/861-945) was a celebrated Sufi from Baghdad. He is mentioned frequently in Ḥojviri/Nicholson, *Kashf al-Maḥjub*, which gives a biographical notice (pp. 155-56.)

had, and thus they are upset and weeping. I didn't have anything for the thieves to steal. Therefore I am at ease and laughing!" "The lightly burdened shall be saved."[46]

DEPARTURE FROM BATUM

Anyhow, the morning of Friday the fourth of Rabi^c ol-Avval [11 December], which was the second of Jady,[47] I had arrived at Batum. The morning of Sunday the sixth, after a thousand delays and difficulties, I was seated on the train and set out from Batum. Batum never gets any snow, and the weather was not cold. As soon as we were six stations from Batum snow was visible on some mountains far and near, but the weather was not very cold. The coach arrived at the Tiflis station six hours after nightfall, so the travel time from Batum to arrival in Tiflis, including delays along the way at the stations, took thirteen hours. It stopped for one hour in Tiflis, took on passengers, and set out. Past Tiflis, the weather was very cold, but the cold was not noticeable in the cabins on the train since they had been equipped with steam heaters. The coach set out en route [the night before] Monday the seventh [14 December]. Normally it reaches Baku near sunset (that is, it does not take more than seventeen hours from Tiflis to Baku). Owing to the cold weather, the disrepair of the track, and meeting other trains along the way, it arrived at the Baku station after nightfall [the day before] the eighth [15 December]. [326] So the travel time from Tiflis to arrival in Baku, including delays along the way, took twenty-one hours.

THE BAKU STATION

Beside the Baku station, which is three quarters of a farsakh distant from the city, there were many one and two horse-drawn coaches for hire to transport the passengers. This humble servant and [my] companions also took coaches and lodged at the caravanserai of Mashhadi Ḥâjji Âqâ, which is the lodging place for Iranians. [We] stayed three nights at the caravanserai. Then Âqâ ᶜAziz, son of Ḥâjji Ghaffâr of Baku, who was one of [our] acquaintances, came and invited [us] to his house. We stayed five nights at his house. Thus on the return [journey], there were eight days spent at Baku. During these eight days, the weather was very

---

[46] Text: *bakhâ ol-mokhaffafun*; read *najâ ol-mokhaffufun*. See above, Part One, n. 9. Farâhâni also quotes a verse here; it is omitted from the translation.

[47] Literally, Capricorn; the old name for Dey, the tenth month in the Iranian solar calendar (December-January).

cold, the wind and snow were continuous, and the storm was very severe.

DEPARTURE FROM BAKU

The good steamers on this sea are the post steamers which are always going back and forth between Baku and Enzeli. These post steamers make return trips once or twice a week to Enzeli in spring, summer, and fall. In winter, they make a round trip once a fortnight. During these several days spent in Baku, the wind and rain and snow calmed down, but the post steamer did not come. Out of fear lest the weather become disturbed again, and the trip delayed, [I] made haste and, the morning of the fifteenth of Rabi^{c} ol-Avval [22 December], took the steamer of Ḥâjji Yunes of Baku which was going to Enzeli. This steamer was very small, old, worn out, broken down, and was really like a caricature of a steamship. The name of its captain was Karbalâ'i Solṭân Qoli, whom they called Karbalâ'i Qapitân ["Captain"]. He wore a large *marghazi* hat[48] on his head, an old Khorâsâni pelisse[49] on his back, and slippers. He wrapped a Bokhârâ shawl[50] ten ẕar^{c} long [around himself] from chest to navel. Several [327] things were fastened on top of this shawl. One side of it had a tobacco pouch and a long stemmed pipe with bronze chain, and one side an iron pen-case with a patched chintz pouch for papers. A beaten up telescope of bronze and iron, which strongly resembled a *sornâ*,[51] was also girded on. He wore eyeglasses, on one side of which the stem was broken and was tied [together] with string. His compass was [a small] portable [one]; his desk a chicken-coop. Instead of an alarm bell, he had fashioned something out of a goat's horn like a dervish's bugle which he played every moment. Instead of an iron ladder such as the steamers have for boarding passengers onto the steamer from the launches, this [boat] had a rope ladder. Whenever he wanted someone to board the steamer, he tossed down that ladder. Even though there was no wind or storm, nevertheless [the boat] was constantly bobbing up and down fiercely. There was room in its cabin for no more than four persons. It had also been

[48] *Marghazi* is a term used to denote something or someone from the environs of the city of Marv; here it is applied to a distinctive type of sheepskin hat worn in that region.

[49] Text: *pustin*, a coat usually made from a sheepskin worn with the hide on the outside and the wool next to the body.

[50] Text: *shâl-e bokhur*. This is probably an orthographical error. Bokhârâ seems a plausible reading since that city was famous for its shawls, and Farâhâni has indicated that the captain's hat and coat were of fashions common in that same region.

[51] A musical instrument similar to an oboe.

freshly painted, and it had a putrid smell. If one was inside the cabin, the stench of the paint and the odor of the coal would give one a headache and make one nauseous. If one went outside the cabin, the cold weather would paralyze one's hands and feet. Every two hours, he would lose the way and go off to one side to look for land with that telescope. In short, we were in a curious situation that words can't describe. "The Muslim does not hear; the unbeliever does not see."

THE PORT OF ENZELI

After countless troubles, fears, frights, prayers, invocations [of God], vows and oaths, [the boat] arrived off Enzeli and anchored on the morning of the seventeenth of the month of Rabiᶜ ol-Avval [24 December], which was the festival of the birthday of the Prophet [Moḥammad].[52] [328] The trip, which should have taken twenty-three hours, lasted for fifty-five hours. Deliverance from this boat was by the grace of God alone.

RECEPTION BY AMIN-E DIVÂN

Since the time [I] left Gilân, Ḥâjji Amir Khân the Sarhang, son of Amin-e Divân, had been [my] travelling companion. By [mutual] agreement, he was [with me] everywhere. In truth, he behaved with complete nobility, affection, and fidelity. Since young men have not become hardened in their ways, generosity and fidelity are established in their nature to an extent which old[er] men do not share.[53]

Upon returning to Baku, the aforementioned informed his father Amin-e Divân of our arrival. Amin-e Divân, out of regard for his son and affection for this humble servant, had come as soon as he was informed with some of his men to meet [us] in Enzeli and was waiting for us to arrive. [When] the steamer reached Enzeli, and we came ashore by launch, Amin-e Divân and his men were informed, came to the seaside, escorted us to his home, and performed the customary ceremonies and formalities.

ENZELI AT THE BEGINNING OF WINTER

At this time, which was the middle of Jady, Enzeli was having unusually pleasant weather about which one cannot write [only] briefly. All the streets and walls were green and pleasant; fresh violets were sprouting up, and the citrus trees, like adorned brides,

---

[52] [Marginal note:] "When we left Mecca the Exalted, the direction of prayer was in an easterly direction. As we got further from Mecca, it gradually deviated from east until in Istanbul it was between west and east [i. e., southerly]. After leaving Istanbul, it gradually changed to a westerly direction."

[53] Here Farâhâni quotes one line of poetry; it is omitted from the translation.

were peeking over all the houses showing off the yellow and red unripe fruit among the leaves. [329] Sometimes it rained, and sometimes it was sunny. The cold of winter was not at all evident. Very good and cheap citrus fruits ("And fruits that they prefer")[54] and varieties of fish and land and water fowls such as pheasant, *changar*,[55] etc. ("And the flesh of fowls such as they desire")[56] were abundant. None of the ports [we] saw along the way to the House of God were as pleasant and had as easy living and as good weather as this one.[57]

DEPARTURE FROM ENZELI

[I] spent that day, the seventeenth [24 December], and the night [before] the eighteenth in Enzeli and set out from Enzeli for the city of Rasht around noon. We disembarked from the launch at Pir Bâzâr. Although the road from Pir Bâzâr to Rasht has been revetted with stone in some places, it was built a long time ago. Most of it is muddy and in bad shape, and it was very difficult to traverse. Most of the notables and merchants of Gilân came to welcome [us] out of regard for Amin-e Divân. They brought parade horses and heralds. The heralds were reciting these verses:

> "We are coming from the House of God
> We are separated from the things we love."

With benedictions, salutations, and greetings, we entered the city of Rasht and went to the residence of Amin-e Divân. After stopping four days in Rasht, I decided to go to Lâhijân since I had heard so much about the pleasantness and good weather of Lâhijân.[58]

THE ROUTE FROM RASHT TO LÂHIJÂN

There are two routes from Rasht to Lâhijân. One is by way of the village of Kucheṣfahân. This route is comparatively shorter. It is six farsakhs to Lâhijân. That is, from Rasht to the Safid Rud River is four farsakhs, and from the Safid Rud to Lâhijân is two farsakhs. [330] In fall and winter, the road for those four farsakhs is in bad shape and full of mud so that it is very difficult to traverse. There are pits of slime and mud along the way as deep as pools and wells. If

---

54 Koran, 56:20.

55 See above, n. 34.

56 Koran, 56:21.

57 Farâhâni quotes a proverbial verse, the point of which is that "there's no place like home."

58 Lâhijân is famous for having the best climate of any area in Gilân.

someone didn't know the way and was careless, he would wind up in the next world![59]

The muleteers of Lâhijân and Rasht have strong, sturdy pack horses that are familiar with the road. They traverse the road by means of them. It is not possible to traverse this road with one's own horse.

Another route goes by way of the village of Naṣrollahâbâd and Bâzâr-e Sangar. This route is longer. It is eight farsakhs; that is, from Rasht to the banks of the Safid Rud is six farsakhs by this route, and from the banks of the Safid Rud to Lâhijân is two farsakhs. These six farsakhs are also full of mud and are in bad shape. However, the mud and dilapidation is much less than by that [other] route. Both these roads are in need of repair and [re]building. Every two or three years, they are repaired all at once by unpaid laborers,[60] but a year later they are just like before.

These two roads were first built and paved by Shâh ᶜAbbâs I. The stone paving is still extant in some places. By either of the routes one is obliged to cross the Safid Rud. A large ferry has been built. Beasts of burden and people go on it and cross over. They collect a small toll for this for each beast of burden and person.

This Safid Rud River is very large. It is very beneficial and profitable. Most of the crops of Gilân are irrigated from this river. In springtime, it floods a great deal, to such an extent that villages located on its banks may be damaged. [331] Among the places that have been damaged because of the quantity and flooding of the water of the Safid Rud is the shrine of Ashrafeyyeh, where Sayyed Jalâl od-Din Ashraf is buried.[61] According to the author of the *Baḥr ol-Ansâb*,[62] he is one of the direct descendants of Ḥażrat-e Musâ ebn-e Jaᶜfar.[63] This mausoleum was situated next to the Safid Rud,

---

[59] Farâhâni quotes a line of poetry here; it is omitted from the translation.

[60] Text: *iljâr*. These workers were unpaid volunteers; they were not forced to work on such projects as part of a corvée.

[61] See Mirzâ Ebrâhim, *Safarnâmeh*, p. 163; Sotudeh, *Âstârâ*, 2:179-83.

[62] See above, Part One, n. 99.

[63] [Marginal note:] "Sayyed Jalâl od-Din Ashraf, the brother of Ḥażrat-e ᶜAli ebn-e Musâ (or Reżâ), ruled in Lâhijân for nineteen years. He had many followers and partisans. In the end, someone whose ancestry went back to Shemr ebn-e Z̲i'l-Jowshan and who was staying in Gilân rebelled against him. There was a battle between him and Sayyed Jalâl od-Din in the environs of Lâhijân. During that battle, Sayyed Jalâl od-Din received an arrow wound and was martyred. Sayyed Kiâ ᶜAli buried him." [Shemr was the man who killed Imam Ḥosayn at Karbelâ. Since ᶜAli Kiâ came to power in 769/1368, it is hardly plausible that Jalâl od-Din could have been the brother of ᶜAli b. Musâ (d. 203/818.) A much more likely candidate might be the Ashraf b. Zayd ol-Ḥasani who proclaimed his imamate in Lâhijân in 544/

and there was a marketplace in front of the mausoleum where visitors and the inhabitants of the village bought and sold [things]. Because of the multitude of visitors, the inhabitants of that village derived considerable profit from the market. Then, in the year 1285 [1868-69], the waters of the Safid Rud flooded an extraordinary [amount]. The market in front of the mausoleum was completely demolished, and some of of the houses of peasants in that village were also damaged. The courtyard and portico of the mausoleum were ruined, and the lofty dome of the mausoleum was also damaged. [The flood] created a natural dike that prevented water from getting into the tomb; thus the cenotaph and tomb remained safe. In [recent] years, the peasants have wanted to divert the water another way and [re]build the mausoleum, but it has not been possible. That is, because of the considerable expense, it is not within their financial ability. Thus it has remained this way.

In short, by either of these two routes, it is two farsakhs from the Safid Rud to Lâhijân. [332] The road for these two farsakhs is not so bad. Sometimes Amin-e Divân repairs it at his own [expense] and sometimes the governor of Lâhijân, on orders from the governor-general of Gilân, has unpaid laborers work on the road on the orders of the governor of Gilân. Thus in this year, Mirzâ Ḥasan Khân, the governor of Lâhijân had the unpaid laborers engaged in repairing and [re]building these two farsakhs on the orders of Moshir os-Salṭaneh. Since it is [done] by unpaid laborers, it will be ruined again in a year's time.

LÂHIJÂN

Lâhijân is one of the ancient cities of Gilân.[64] The popular [story] among the Gilânis is that it is one of the constructions of Lâhij, son of the Prophet Noah.[65] However, I have not seen in the chronicles that anyone named Lâhij was a son of Noah. Perhaps someone named Lâhij who was not the son of Noah was the founder of this city. Previously, this city was very prosperous, its people were beyond counting, and it was usually the capital of Gilân. Several

1149; see W. Madelung, *Arabic Texts Concerning the History of the Zaydi Imams of Ṭabaristân, Daylamân and Gîlân* (Wiesbaden, 1987), pp. 158, 168. On the problematic history of this shrine, see Sotudeh, "Baḥr-e naṣâb," pp. 298-303; Gilâni, *Târikh-e ʿolamâ*, p. 24; on the Kâr Kiâ'i sayyeds, see below, n. 79.]

[64] Cf. Mirzâ Ebrâhim, *Safarnâmeh*, pp. 162-64; Sotudeh, *Âstârâ*, 2:69-214; Jackson, *Constantinople*, pp. 88-89; Rabino, *Provinces*, pp. 291-334.

[65] Actually, the local tradition is that Lâhijân was founded by a Lâhij, *son of Sâm*, son of Noah: see Kharegat, *Tourist Guide*, p. 83; Sotudeh, *Âstârâ*, 2:70; Rabino, *Provinces*, pp. 291-92.

severe natural disasters caused its destruction. For example, in the year 703 [1303-4], a calamitous plague raged in Lâhijân. Many of its people died and the rest dispersed. Most of its houses and buildings fell into ruin. This calamity was during the lifetime of Shaykh Zâhed Gilâni.[66] The followers of Shaykh Zâhed took care of enshrouding and burying people. After the alleviation of this calamity, a few [people] who had fled to the hinterland gathered together. The population increased again with the passing of time, and [the town] [re]gained some of its prosperity. In the year 850 and something [after 1446-47], a severe fire occurred which completely ruined and destroyed Lâhijân. The people were totally dispersed. Once again, the populace gradually regathered and built clean, good quality buildings. Then in the year 1230 [1814-15] there was a tremendous earthquake, and much destruction occurred. In the year 1246 [1830-31], another calamitous plague befell Lâhijân.[67] [333] The plague this time was more severe than the first plague was. There was widespread death. It reached the point where it was not possible to wash and to bury the corpses. Many of the corpses remained unburied and were eaten by vermin. For instance, in one house where there were twenty people, no more than three survived. The people died, and the houses became utterly desolate and ruined. After the alleviation of this act of God, the few who had fled to the hinterland returned. A group of merchants [from] Qazvin, Kashan, Yazd, Isfahan, etc. congregated [there] out of greed to conduct business. Since the people were few, and the profits from silkworms was great, the inhabitants became wealthy and affluent. Then in the year 1273 of the hegira [1856-57], a great plague befell the silkworms of Gilân. The silkworms of this locality were also lost. The dirth of silkworms lasted for several consecutive years and caused the inhabitants to become impoverished, distraught, and dispersed. The merchants who had come out of greed for silkworms and profits scattered. The caravanserais and markets remained without

---

[66] Shaykh Zâhed, whose proper name was Tâj od-Din Ibrâhim b. Rowshan, was the leader of a Sufi order in Gilân in the seventh/thirteenth century. He became the spiritual guide (*pir*) of the ancestor of the Safavid dynasty in Iran, Ṣafi od-Din (647-735/1249-1334). Ṣafi od-Din married the daughter of Shaykh Zâhed and became the head of the order, which soon became the Ṣafaveyyeh order, after Zâhed's death (700/1301). See Saᶜid Nafisi, *Shaykh Zâhed-e Gilâni* (Rasht, 1307/1928-29); Trimingham, *Sufi Orders*, pp. 99-101; Michel Mazzaoui, *The Origins of the Ṣafavids* (Wiesbaden, 1972), p. 53; Roger Savory, *Iran under the Safavids* (Cambridge, 1980), pp. 3-9. Shaykh Zâhed is discussed more fully by Farâhâni below.

[67] Cf. Rabino, *Provinces*, p. 293, on the great plague, which he dates to 1832.

residents. The businessmen and artisans all remained without work [because] of the poverty. Thus formerly there used to be several weaving workshops in this town. They wove all sorts of silk fabrics and exported them to the environs. The inhabitants of one of the quarters of Lâhijân, which is named the Shaᶜrbâfân ["Silk-Weavers"] quarter,[68] were mostly weavers and owners of workshops. They used to be wealthy and affluent: Now weaving has been completely abandoned. After all these destructions, there was a fire several years ago. Its dating goes like this:[69] [334]

In this fire one area of Lâhijân, where most of the houses of the notables were, was completely burned down and ruined and destroyed and was no longer inhabited. About 300,000 tomans [worth] of dwellings, chattels, and furniture belonging to Amin-e Divân burned; you can imagine what happened to others.

THE QUARTERS

The currently inhabited areas of this city are as follows:[70]

It consists of seven quarters. The names of the quarters and the number of people in them are as detailed in this appendix:

The Khamir Kalâyeh quarter:[71] It consists of 184 households, so its population is 1,350 people.

The Gâboneh quarter:[72] It consists of 175 households, so its population is 1,280.

The Maydân quarter: It consists of 240 households, and its population is 1,700.

The Shaᶜrbâfân quarter: It consists of 180 households, and its population is 1,100.

The Ordu Bâzâr quarter: It consists of 190 households, and it has a population of 1,300. [335]

The Pordesar quarter:[73] It consists of 130 households. Its population is 750.

---

68 See Sotudeh, *Âstârâ*, 2:79.

69 The verse chronogram cited by Farâhâni is omitted from the translation. Kharegat, *Tourist Guide*, p. 84, states that this destructive fire occurred in 1880; Rabino, *Provinces*, p. 293, gives the exact date as 21 Safar 1297 (4 February 1880).

70 Cf. G. Melgunof, *Das südliche ufer des Kaspischen Meeres* (Leipzig, 1868), pp. 231-32; Mirzâ Ebrâhim, *Safarnâmeh*, pp. 162-63; Rabino, *Provinces*, pp. 293-98; Sotudeh, *Âstârâ*, 2:77-78; Kharegat, *Tourist Guide*, pp. 83-85. Since Farâhâni's population figures may be compared with those given later by Rabino, this passage is of some interest for studying the demography of this region.

71 The vocalization is given by Mirzâ Ebrâhim, *Safarnâmeh*, p. 163, and Melgunof, *Kaspischen Meeres*, p. 232.

72 Mirzâ Ebrâhim, *Safarnâmeh*, p. 162, has Gâvboneh, as does Melgunof, *Kaspischen Meeres*, p. 231.

73 Text: Pordehsar; cf. Sotudeh, *Âstârâ*, 2:78.

The Kâravânsarâbar quarter: It consists of 75 households, so its population is 500.

There are about three hundred thatch-roofed houses[74] on the outskirts of the quarters. Their population is a thousand and something. So all together, the population [of the town] is 10,000-odd. It has about five hundred shops, and three small commercial caravanserais.

THE SABZEH MAYDÂN

On the eastern side of the city there is a field. It is a level, four-sided, open area which is named Sabzeh Maydân. This field is like a meadow and is green and pleasant in [all] four seasons. It really is a "Green Field" [*sabz maydân*]. This field is rectangular; its length is 800 qadam, and its breadth is 450 qadam.

THE LAKE OF LÂHIJÂN

At the eastern end of this field there is a lake which is 1000 qadam long and 450 qadam wide. This lake is full of water in spring and winter. In fall and summer, its water is taken for agricultural usage to the surrounding cultivated areas. The lakebed, if there is no water, is perfectly verdant and pleasant. The areas around this lake have been planted by hand with trees at regular [intervals].

There is a tall mountain to the east of this lake. The lake is adjacent to the mountain. The surface of this mountain is [covered with] flowers and tulips and greenery. It has [some] isolated forest trees. The range of this mountain extends to the province of Ṭabarestân. There are few places to be seen as attractive as this field, lake, and mountain. The source for the water of this lake is rainwater from the mountain. [336] There is a stream of this runoff [rainwater] passing alongside the city, which overlooks the lake. This Sabzeh Maydân and the lake are among [the properties] reclaimed from Khân Aḥmad Khân, who was one of the rulers of Gilân with his capital at Lâhijân and who was the son-in-law of Shâh Esmâᶜil Ṣafavi. In the time of Shâh ᶜAbbâs I he was deposed; rendered homeless, he took refuge with the Ottoman sultans.[75] In the middle

[74] Text: *kâli-push*; read *gâli-push*. See Sotudeh, *Farhang*, p. 209.

[75] Khân Aḥmad Khân became governor of the area around Lâhijân ca. 943/1536. He reportedly intrigued with the Ottomans and revolted against Shâh ᶜAbbâs in 1000/1592 but was defeated and forced into exile. Before becoming shâh, Esmâᶜil had spent almost five years in hiding in Lâhijân (1494-95), where he was protected by the local ruler Kâr Kiâ Mirzâ ᶜAli. Khân Aḥmad was a later member of this same family, but since Esmâᶜil died in 930/1524 it is hard to see how Khân Aḥmad could have been Esmâᶜil's son-in-law. Some of his letters are edited in an appendix to Rabino's edition of Mir Ẓahir od-Din Marᶜashi's *Târikh-e gilân va daylamestân* (Rasht, 1330/1911-12); see also ᶜAli b. Shams od-Din Lâhiji, *Târikh-e khâni* (edited

of the lake, there is a green and pleasant hill which is called Miân Poshteh. The author of the ᶜ*Âlam Ârâ* [*World Adorner*] writes that "Shâh ᶜAbbâs I, after putting Khân Aḥmad to flight, constructed a building in the middle of the lake. Whenever he stopped in Lâhijân, he lived in luxury and pleasure there. Frequently it was illuminated so that the lights were reflected on the water."[76] Now the ruins of the foundations of this palace are visible.

There are ruins of a building on the summit of the mountain overlooking the lake which they have named Shâh-neshin. They say this building is one of the constructions of Khân Aḥmad Khân.

THE MOṢALLÂ

On the southern side of the lake there is a perfectly pleasant plateau which is named the Moṣallâ. The aforementioned lake is located in front of the plateau. From the side of the Moṣallâ there is a road which goes beside the mountain and ends at a garden and a building which Mirzâ Kâẓem Khan, brother of Amin-e Divân, constructed on the mountain overlooking the lake. It is named Manẓareyyeh and is a very attractive and pleasant [place]. In this same direction, beside this field, there are also some houses which have a view of the lake and field.

THE MAUSOLEUM OF ÂQÂ MIR SHAHID

Beside the Sabz[eh] Maydân field, on the north side, there is a mausoleum named for Âqâ Mir Shahid.[77] The mausoleum is situated on the heights. The field is located in front of the mausoleum, and the mausoleum overlooks it. [337]

MAUSOLEUMS

Among the mausoleums which are in the city, one is this same mausoleum which is known as the Âqâ Mir Shahid and is named for Sayyed Aḥmad Kiâ, [who] was one of the descendants of Musâ ebn-e Jaᶜfar.

CHEHÂR PÂDESHÂH MAUSOLEUM

Another mausoleum is known as the Chehâr Pâdeshâh[78] ["Four Kings"] which is located in the Maydân quarter. Four of the rulers of Gilân are buried in this mausoleum. Their names are as follows:

---

by M. Sotudeh; Tehran, 1352/1973); Eskandar Beg Monshi, *History of Shah 'Abbas the Great*, pp. 182-88; 621-25; Sotudeh, *Âstârâ*, 2:71; Rabino, *Provinces*, p. 226.

[76] The ᶜ*Âlam Ârâ* is the *History of Shah 'Abbas the Great* by Eskandar Monshi cited in the preceding note; it mentions (p. 624) the Shâh's stay in Lâhijân after the defeat of Khân Aḥmad, but not the construction of this building.

[77] Cf. Kharegat, *Tourist Guide*, p. 84; Sotudeh, *Âstârâ*, vol. 2, plates 53-57.

[78] Cf. Kharegat, *Tourist Guide*, p. 84; Sotudeh, *Âstârâ*, 2:98-115 and plates 73-85.

Sayyed Khorram Kiâ; Sayyed Rażi Kiâ; Sayyed ᶜAli Kiâ; Sayyed Moḥammad Kiâ.[79]

The date of the construction of this mausoleum is the year 770 of the hegira [1368-69].

THE MAUSOLEUM OF MIR SHAMS OD-DIN

Another [of the mausoleums] is the mausoleum of Mir Shams od-Din,[80] which is located in the Ordu Bâzâr quarter. The date of its construction is unknown.[81] However, in the year 1267 [1850-51], someone named Ḥâjji Mirzâ ᶜAbbâs made extensive repairs of the mausoleum.

THE MAUSOLEUM OF PIR ᶜALI

Another is the mausoleum of Pir ᶜAli, which is located in the Gâboneh[82] quarter. The date of its construction and the identity of the occupant of the mausoleum are both unknown.

THE MAUSOLEUM OF MIR EBRÂHIM

Another is the mausoleum of Mir Ebrâhim.[83] It is located in the Gâboneh quarter. They say [it is the tomb] of one of the descendants of Ḥażrat-e Musâ ebn-e Jaᶜfar. The date of the mausoleum's construction is not indicated.

THE MAUSOLEUM OF ÂQÂ SAYYED MOḤAMMAD

Another is the mausoleum of Âqâ Sayyed Moḥammad known as the Yamani, which is located in the Shaᶜrbâfân quarter.[84] The [date of] the construction of the mausoleum and the identity of the occupant of the mausoleum are both unknown.

---

[79] All of these were members of the Kâr Kiâ'i family, which traced its ancestry (and its claim to be sayyeds) back to the Aḥmad Kiâ mentioned above (n. 63) as one of the descendants of the Imam Musâ b. Jaᶜfar. Khorram (or Khor) Kiâ, the founder of the dynasty, was killed in 647/1249-50. ᶜAli Kiâ came to power around 769/1368 and was killed in 791/1389. He was succeeded by his nephew Moḥammad Kiâ. Rażi Kiâ died in 829/1426. See Marᶜashi, *Târikh-e gilân* , p. 41; H. L. Rabino, "Rulers of Lahijan and Fuman," *Journal of the Royal Asiatic Society* (1918), pp. 85-92; idem., "Dynasties locales du Gilân et de Daylam," *Journal Asiatique* 237(1949):323-37; idem., *Provinces*, pp. 397-409; Madelung, *Texts*, passim. Melgunof, *Kaspischen Meeres*, p. 231, gives a different list of names for the tombs in this mausoleum.

[80] More properly, the Âqâ Mir Shams od-Din mausoleum; see Sotudeh, *Âstârâ*, 2:82 (and plates 58-63).

[81] Kharegat, *Tourist Guide*, p. 85, says that it is the tomb of Shams od-Din Musavi and that it was constructed in 1017/1608-9. Sotudeh, *Âstârâ*, 2:82 also gives the date of construction as 1017.

[82] Text: Kâboneh. On this mausoleum, see Sotudeh, *Âstârâ*, 2:94-96.

[83] Or Âqâ Mir Ebrâhim; see Sotudeh, *Âstârâ*, 2:94.

[84] See Sotudeh, *Âstârâ*, 2:91-92.

THE MAUSOLEUM OF SAYYED JAMÂL OD-DIN

Another is the mausoleum of Sayyed Jamâl od-Din which is located in the Pordehsar quarter.[85] His ancestry is unknown, and the date of its construction is not indicated. [338]

MOSQUES

There are about fifteen mosques of various sizes in this city. An account may be appended of the large and well known mosques as follows:

THE MASJED-E JÂMEᶜ

One is the Masjed-e Jâmeᶜ which is of very old and stout construction. It is very bright and cheerful. It contains three herculean pillars and eight vaults. The date of construction and its builder are unknown. On the wall at the threshold[86] of the mosque, a decree by Shâh Solṭân Ḥosayn Ṣafavi is inscribed on four slabs of marble that have been fastened together.[87] [339/340/341]

THE AKBAREYYEH MOSQUE

Another mosque is the Akbareyyeh,[88] which is located in the Gâboneh quarter. It is one of the constructions of Ḥâjji ᶜAli Akbar, grandfather of Amin-e Divân. For years it was in good condition; then its façade was damaged. Amin-e Divân proposed to repair the mosque. On the same site as the first building, he raised up a very spacious and lofty building. He spent great sums on that place. The construction had reached [the point of being] vaulted, [but] meanwhile there occurred the ruin and extinction of the silkworms so it could not be completed. The mosque remained in this incomplete condition. Thus it is still uncompleted.[89] Despite the incompleteness, it is quite noteworthy; however, if it remains in this condition for another year it will certainly be damaged by the shocks of snow and rain.

---

[85] Kharegat, *Tourist Guide*, p. 85, locates this in the Kâravânsarâbar quarter; cf. Sotudeh, *Âstârâ*, 2:78.

[86] Text: *kafsh-kan*; literally the place where worshippers deposit their shoes before going into the mosque.

[87] This long and florid inscription, dated Shavvâl 1106 [May-June 1694], has been omitted from the translation. It is quoted or described by Sotudeh, *Âstârâ*, 2:115-19 (and plate 87) and Kharegat, *Tourist Guide*, p. 84. Shâh Solṭân Ḥosayn (1105-35/1694-1722) was a weak ruler who was often influenced by powerful Shiʿite religious leaders such as Moḥammad Bâqer Majlesi. The inscription, which prohibits such vices as prostitution, gambling, and cock-fighting, is typical of his policies. See Momen, *Introduction to Shiʿi Islam*, p. 115.

[88] See Sotudeh, *Âstârâ*, 2:96-97 and plates 70-72.

[89] Kharegat, *Tourist Guide*, p. 85, states that this mosque was built in 1239/1823-24 by Ḥâjji Akbar, the governor of Lâhijân. According to Kharegat, the reason the mosque was left unfinished was that enemies of the governor persuaded the Shâh that he was building a fortress (implying that he was considering a revolt).

THE SOLAYMÂNEYYEH MOSQUE

Another mosque is the Solaymâneyyeh, which is next to the mosque of Sayyed Solaymân.[90] This mosque has the same name as the shrine. They say that the builder of the mosque is this same sayyed. According to [his] will, they buried him beside the mosque. A date for the construction of the mosque and mausoleum was not seen.

THE SHAᶜRBÂFÂN MOSQUE

Another mosque is the Shaᶜrbâfân, which is in the Shaᶜrbâfân quarter.[91] The people of this quarter built [it] in an earlier time. Then it became ruined. The late Mirzâ Ḥosayn ᶜAli the Mojtahed made extensive renovations [of it] in the year 1276 [1859-60].

THE KÂRAVÂNSARÂBAR MOSQUE

Another mosque is the Kâravânsarâbar. It is also one of the large mosques. The late Mirzâ Ḥosayn ᶜAli the Mojtahed renovated it. The renovations remain unfinished.

MADRASAHS

There are four madrasahs for the inhabitants of Lâhijân, which are:

The Jâmeᶜ madrasah, which is next to the Masjed-e Jâmeᶜ.

The Solaymâneyyeh madrasah, which is next to the Solaymaneyyeh mosque.

The Shaᶜrbâfân madrasah, which is next to the Shaᶜrbâfân mosque [342].

The madrasah known as the Ṣâdeqeyyeh.

These schools each have a small wakf endowment. There are ten or fifteen students at each.

BATHS

There are seven public baths in all of Lâhijân. Its baths are not below ground owing to the dampness of the soil but are at street level. However, most of the baths are quite good, solidly built, and furnished with much marble and exquisite tiles.

ICE-HOUSES

The ice-houses of Lâhijân are pits without lime or brick that have been dug into the slopes of the mountain and dry elevated lands. In winter they fill [them] with snow and ice and cover them with [a kind of] herbage. They call that herbage *karaf*.[92] It is naturally cold, like camel's thorn.[93] This fodder protects the ice and snow from

[90] According to Sotudeh, *Âstârâ*, 2:77, this is located in the Kalâyeh quarter.

[91] See Sotudeh, *Âstârâ*, 2:92-93, plate 69.

[92] Cf. above, Part One, n. 164.

[93] Text: *khâr-e shotor*. This shrub, which was used for insulation, is known by various names such as *ḥaj*, *oshtorkhâr*, *showk ol-jamal*, or *ᶜaqul* (hedysarum, alhagi,

warmth. There is more snow and ice in Lâhijân than in Rasht and the surrounding areas of Gilân. Usually snow and ice are brought from Lâhijân to Rasht. One reason for this is that the climate of Lâhijân is colder. In comparison to Rasht, it is summer-estate country. Another reason is that in former times many wells and pits were dug on the mountains, so that snow or ice might be retained for two years. If, for example, one year the weather is not cold and it does not snow, snow and ice may still be found in them.

CLIMATE

The climate of this city is moderate in all four seasons. Neither the cold nor the heat is very severe there. Since the city is located on high ground on the slopes of the mountain and has [land] like summer-estates, its humidity is consequently less by comparison than other [places in] Gilân. Its weather is better than all other areas of Gilân. Its fields and hills are quite verdant and pleasant in every season. [343] Various types of fragrant flowers such as violets, hyacinths, narcissus, and iris are very numerous on its fields and mountains. Hyacinth, narcissus, iris, and violets grow even on the walls of the houses in the city.

The water and drinking water of the city of Lâhijân comes mostly from wells that have been dug in the houses. One reaches water having dug down two or three zar^{c}. There is a river from the west beside the city. In summer, it has fifty or sixty sang of water. Its water is more agreeable to the taste than the well-water. However, since the river is down low and the city is located on high ground, it cannot be diverted into the city quarters. According to reports, a long time ago there used to be a dam so it was brought into the city. Traces of that dam remain. The source of this river is in the mountainous area of Lâhijân. Passing beside the city, it irrigates the surrounding villages. The river opens into the sea. According to reports, it would be a source of prosperity and welfare for the people of Lâhijân in the event this river should be harnessed. It would be perfectly easy for a boat to come up this river and bring foreign merchants into the region. [Then the people] could buy and sell whatever goods they need to buy or sell without the hardship, delay and loss of hiring [transport]. Just as in Rudsar, owing to the

---

etc.). See Biruni, *Ṣaydaneh*, p. 119; Hamarneh, *Materia Medica*, p. 87; Schefer, *Sefer Nameh*, p. 270; Dehkhodâ, *Loghatnâmeh*, fascicle 55, p. 32. Much of this passage repeats Farâhâni's earlier mention of the ice-pits in his discussion of Gilân's climate (above, Part One, p. 37).

harnessing of the river, a thousand kinds of prosperity befell the province. Because of the trade with Baku and the area of Shirvân, many people there derived and are deriving benefit. But in Lâhijân foreign merchants never pass through. Whatever goods [the people] want to sell must be transported either to Rasht or to Langarud, paying exorbitant fares and being delayed. In the end, [the goods] will be sold with trouble and loss. [344]

Thus its commodities, goods, and crops which are suitable for the market in [Persian] ʿErâq must first have taxes[94] paid in Lâhijân and be transported to Rasht; then a second tax is paid in Rasht, and they are conveyed to Qazvin. There is a road from Lâhijân to Qazvin which is six farsakhs shorter than the route via Rasht. However, owing to the disrepair of that road, no one traverses it. In the event this road should be [re]built, the people of Lâhijân would not need to take their goods to Rasht. It would become a place caravans could pass through, and [this] would be a source of prosperity for this city.

It is about four farsakhs from Lâhijân to the [Caspian] sea. It is said that in olden times the sea used to be near Lâhijân, but with the passing of time it receded and became distant. A very big river one farsakh south of there is named the Shimrud, which rises in the mountainous country of Daylamân and flows into the Safid Rud.

DISTRICTS

The districts of Lâhijân at present are as follows:[95]

Lashteneshâ, the north of which borders the sea. Some of the villages of this district are crown property, and the rest are privately owned. Its crown lands are outside Gilân and Lahijan proper and are under the jurisdiction of Amin os-Solṭân's foremen.

The Pashmechâh[96] district, one side of which is adjacent to the sea. It has no crown lands.

The Gukeh[97] district, which ends at the territory of Daylamân.

The Kuh Pâyeh district: This district is very small and is no more than a few villages.

There are some villages around the city which are conventionally called the "suburban district" [Ḥowmeh]. [345]

---

94 Literally customs duties (*gomrok*), but Farâhâni must be using this term to refer to some sort of local transportation tax

95 Cf. Sotudeh, *Âstârâ*, 2:79; Adamec, *Gazetteer*, 1:410-11; Rabino, *Provinces*, pp. 306-7.

96 Cf. above, Part One, p. 38 n. 170.

97 Text: Kukeh. See Rabino, *Provinces*, p. 306; Sotudeh, *Âstârâ*, 2:79. *Farhang*, 2:262 has Gokeh.

CROPS

Silk and rice are the [chief] crops of the province of Lâhijân. The production of silk in olden times used to be great, and silk also used to be very expensive. For the last twenty years, however, there is much less silk, and its price has become very cheap. Good silk is produced in some of the villages of Lâhijân, such as Sareshkeh,[98] Kisom,[99] and Lafmajân.

The silk of these villages is the best silk in Gilân. The difference in price is also considerable. The commercial measure of rice in Lâhijân is the quti. A quti is four kayl; a kayl is more than one and a quarter mann-e shâh. Thus a quti is nine mann-e tabriz in the new kayl measurements.[100]

ULAMA

The ulama of Lâhijân are as follows:

Ḥâjji Mirzâ Fatḥ-ᶜali Shams ol-ᶜOlamâ'; Âqâ Mirzâ Ḥasan the Emâm Jomᶜeh; Âqâ Shaykh Mahdi, chief of the Shaykheyyeh sect[101] of Rasht and Lâhijân; Ḥâjji Mirzâ Ḥasan, known as the Mojtahed; Mirzâ Maḥmud, known as Shariᶜatmadâr; Âqâ Sayyed Ḥosayn-e Qâżi; Âqâ Sayyed Mahdi, son of the Emâm Jomᶜeh; Shaykh Aḥmad; Ḥâjji Mollâ Ḥosayn-e Emâm; Âqâ Sayyed Reżâ-ye Emâm; Mirzâ Ebrâhim the Ṣadr ol-ᶜOlamâ'.

NOTABLES

The notables of Lâhijân: Mirzâ Moḥammad ᶜAli Khân Amin-e Divân[102] and his sons, brothers, cousins, and clan.

ANCESTORS OF AMIN-E DIVÂN

The ancestors of Amin-e Divân are as follows: Mirzâ Moḥammad ᶜAli Khân is the son of Mirzâ Kâẓem-e Ḥâkem. Mirzâ Kâẓem is the son of Ḥâjji Abu'l-Qâsem-e Ḥâkem and the nephew of Ḥâjji ᶜAli Akbar-e Ḥâkem. Ḥâjji ᶜAli Akbar had no descendants. [Ḥâjji ᶜAli Akbar] was one of the servants and adherents of the pious Shâh Âqâ Moḥammad Shâh. [346] Since Hedâyat Khân-e Rashti

---

98 On the vocalization, see Rabino, *Provinces*, pp. 328-30 (on the villages of Râh-e Shâhbâlâ). *Farhang*, 2:248 suggests Sereshkeh.

99 See Adamec, *Gazetteer*, 1:376; Mirzâ Ebrâhim, *Safarnâmeh*, pp. 165-66.

100 Cf. above, Part One, notes 168 and 169.

101 On the Shaykhis, see above, Part Six, n. 86.

102 Amin-e Divân, with whom Farâhâni stayed in Rasht and whose son accompanied him to Mecca, has been mentioned repeatedly throughout Farâhâni's account. Although he resided in Rasht, he is given prominence here as a notable of Lâhijân because he and his family were the major landowners and richest silk producers in that region, possessing some 366 villages and serving as virtually hereditary governors of the district. See Nâyeb oṣ-Ṣadr Shirâzi, *Ṭarâ'eq ol-ḥaqâ'eq* (edited by M. Maḥjub; Tehran, 1345/1967), 3:616; Mirzâ Ebrâhim, *Safarnâmeh*, p. 162; Amin od-Dowleh, *Safarnâmeh*, pp. 23, 47; Rabino, *Provinces*, p. 300; Benjamin, *Persia and the Persians*, p. 421.

had revolted [against the Shâh], he wanted [Ḥâjji ᶜAli Akbar] to be obedient and submissive to him. [Ḥâjji ᶜAli] refused, so Hedâyat Khân bastinadoed him severely, to such an extent that for a long time he couldn't move or speak. For this reason, he came to be childless. Ḥâjji ᶜAli Akbar and Ḥâjji Abu'l-Qâsem are both sons of Ḥâjji Ṣâdeq-e Ḥâkem. Ḥâjji Ṣâdeq was the son of Ḥâjji Mahdi Ḥâkem. From the time of Ḥâjji Mahdi to the present, [the family of Amin-e Divân] has had the position of governorship and authority in Lâhijân.

SONS OF AMIN-E DIVÂN

The sons of Amin-e Divân are as follows:

His oldest son, Mirzâ Ḥosayn Khân, is very intelligent, of good disposition, polite, honest, and meek. He is wealthier than the other sons. He has insignia for the rank of brigadier general [*sartip*] from the state.

Mirzâ Ḥasan Khân, the second son, is very self-possessed and capable. He is quite proficient in knowledge of diplomacy and government. He deserves important posts and employment in the government. He is now in charge of the government of Lâhijân and treats the people very well and [with] administrative [ability]. He has staff officer's insignia from the government for the rank of adjutant general.

Mirzâ Hâdi Khân does not have a rank in the government service. He is very suitable for his post as headman of the village of ᶜAli Shohuz.[103]

Mirzâ Jaᶜfar Khân is very self-possessed, upright, pious, polite in speech and correct in behavior. He is one of the accountants [*mostowfi*] for the King's Council [*Divân-e Aᶜlâ*] and is usually stationed in Tehran.

Ḥâjji Amir Khân is the youngest son of Amin-e Divân. He is very clever and smart. He is intelligent and has mastered accounting. He has complete knowledge of the ways of [government] service and skill. [347] He has the post and staff officer's insignia for the rank of colonel [*sarhang*].

THE GARDEN OF DIVSHAL

While I was staying in Lâhijân, since they highly commended and praised the garden of Divshal, which is part of Langarud and is about two farsakhs from Lâhijân, I set out for that place.

---

103 This probably refers to the village of ᶜAli Shahvâz (or ᶜAlishâh-ᶜevaż) located 30 km. from Tehran on the road to Qazvin; see Sayf od-Dowleh, *Safarnâmeh*, p. 327.

THE MAUSOLEUM OF SHAYKH ZÂHED GILÂNI

The mausoleum of Shaykh Zâhed Gilâni is along the way one farsakh from Lâhijân.[104] Amin-e Divân constructed the one farsakh of road from Lâhijân to the mausoleum very well. There is no mud or slime. The mausoleum is located on top of a mountain that overlooks the area of Lâhijân. A huge mountain overlooks that mountain and the mausoleum also. The top of the mountain on which the Shaykh's mausoleum [is located] is smooth and level for the area of a maydân. The mausoleum is in the middle of this field. The terrain of the field is meadow-like. There are huge citrus fruit trees here and there around this field. There is a village beside this mausoleum named Shaykhâneh-bar.[105] About one sang of water flows from the top of the mountain there and goes down below, where the people of the village raise crops. The area in which this mausoleum is located is a most pleasant and delightful place. Its climate is healthy and invigorating. Formerly, this mausoleum used to be very prosperous. Pools, brooks, and water-fountains were fashioned alongside the stream that comes from the mountain. Traces of [them] are found at the present time. They say [348] Shâh ᶜAbbâs I had either repaired or built this place. Fifteen years ago this mausoleum was damaged and ruined. Amin-e Divân made extensive, good reparations and spent exorbitant sums [on it]. He built rooms around it as places for visitors to stay. Several years after its renovation, a hot wind blew up, such as is natural in Gilân. Usually the hot wind comes at the beginning of winter and is the precursor of snow. The village located beside the mausoleum caught fire in this wind, and it couldn't be extinguished. It was transmitted to the mausoleum. The mausoleum building burned, but the dome that was on top of the mausoleum of the saint's shrine survived intact and is still standing. After that, there was not a complete renovation of the mausoleum; only two rooms and a small mosque were built next to it.

---

104 [Marginal note:] "There is a mausoleum adjacent to the tomb of Shaykh Zâhed which has a white dome of tiles. There is an emâmzâdeh in it by the name of Moḥammad, who is one of the descendants of Ḥażrat-e Sayyed Sajjâd [the fourth Shi'ite Imam]. It has a wooden cenotaph. There is also a grave in it which they say is the grave of one of the daughters of Tamerlane." [On Shaykh Zâhed, see above, n. 62. On the mausoleum, see Matheson, *Persia*, p. 71; Sotudeh, *Âstârâ*, 2:148-57.]

105 Or Shaykhân-bar; see Aḥmad Kasravi, *Chehel maqâleh* (Tehran, 1953), pp. 9-11; Rabino, *Provinces*, p. 309.

SHAYKH ZÂHED

According to what has been written, Shaykh Zâhed [was] the disciple of Sayyed Jamâl od-Din Tabrizi, who was the disciple of Shaykh Shehâb od-Din Ahiri.[106] Shaykh Zâhed was the spiritual guide and mentor of Shaykh Ṣafi od-Din of Ardabil, who was the ancestor of the Safavids. On the journey that the shaykh had made to the environs of Shirvân, he became ill. He sent his disciple named Moḥammad Jalilâ to the Golkhᵛârân [district] of Ardabil to seek Shaykh Ṣafi od-Din. Shaykh Ṣafi od-Din went to him in person. He died at the end of the year 700 of the hegira [1300-1301]. Shaykh Ṣafi od-Din, in accordance with his will, carried the corpse of Shaykh Zâhed to Gilân. They buried him there in the place that had been his place of worship and spiritual exercise.[107] From this mausoleum to Divshal is about one farsakh; this one farsakh of road is very difficult and in bad shape.

THE VILLAGE OF DIVSHAL

Divshal is a village which is located on the slopes of the mountain. It has about sixty resident households and two sang of flowing water. It was the property of the late Mirzâ Mahdi Khân Monajjem-bâshi.[108] [349] He built a garden there comprised of five lanes and five plots. One plot of it is entirely red roses. It also has a few fruit trees. Four other plots are all citrus fruit [trees] that have been planted in an orderly and regular fashion. In the middle of each plot of citrus [trees], many hyacinths, narcissus, tuberoses, and lilies have been planted at regular [intervals]. There is a brook of running water in the middle of the lanes, all alongside of which there are also narcissus and violets. It has two buildings. One is at the beginning of the garden which has upper and lower rooms constructed of wood. Another is in the middle of the garden, which is a grand, lofty building with upper and lower [storeys] of lime and brick. A complete kitchen was also constructed near this same building. In the lifetime of Mirzâ Mahdi Khân this garden used to be very pleasant and attractive, but nowadays, when it is in the possession of Mirzâ Musâ Khân Monajjem-bâshi, it has become very dilapidated.

---

[106] This represents the *selseleh*, or sequence of spiritual guides through whom instruction in Sufi mysticism was passed on to Shaykh Zâhed.

[107] Cf. Eskander Monshi, *History*, pp. 22-24.

[108] The title Monajjem-bâshi (which literally means Chief Astrologer) was first held by Mirzâ Ṣâdeq, a follower of Âqâ Moḥammad Khân Qâjâr. Mirzâ Ṣâdeq was the great-grandfather of Ḥâjji Âqâ Bozorg; Farâhâni cites a genealogy of the family from Ḥâjji Âqâ Bozorg to Mirzâ Mahdi Khan and his son Mirzâ Musâ Khan above, Part One, p. 41. See also Rabino, *Provinces*, p. 345; Sotudeh, *Âstârâ*, 2:157-58, 249-58; Bamdâd, *Rejâl*, 4:165-68.

If it remains in this condition much longer, it will be in very bad shape. This Monajjem-bâshi is the son of Amin-e Divân's daughter. He is very remiss, pleasure-seeking, and incompetent. His governorship of Langarud is hereditary, similar to that of ᶜAbd ol-Ḥosayn Khan in Fuman. This was the season for narcissus flowers in this garden, and it was very pleasant. I spent the night there and returned to Lâhijân in the morning.

DEPARTURE FROM LÂHIJÂN

Anyhow, [I] had set out for Lâhijân on the night [before] the twenty-third [evening of 29 December] from Rasht via the Kuchesfahân route that is utterly ruined, and arrived in Lâhijân the afternoon of the twenty-third [30 December]. After staying there fifteen nights, [I] left Lâhijân on the eighth of Rabiᶜ II [14 January 1886] via the Naṣrollahâbâd and [Bâzâr-e] Sangar route. [I] entered Rasht on the ninth [15 January]. [I] remained there three days and set out for Tehran on the twelfth of Rabiᶜ II [18 January] at about noon [350] by the postal service riding animals. Even though it was the tenth and even the twelfth of Jady, there was no cold weather or snow anywhere. The weather was extremely fresh, especially in Rudbâr Zeytun, where the trees and [the ground] under the trees were all green and verdant. I have rarely seen weather as fine as the very good weather observed [here]. The weather was like this until [we] reached the middle of the Kharzân pass. On the side of the pass that was part of Gilân, it was raining and the weather was not cold. As soon as [we] were near the top of the pass and in the territory of Qazvin, the weather became very cold. It sleeted fiercely, and there was much snow on the ground, especially on both sides of the village of Kharzân. Across from the village of Esmâᶜilâbâd, it snowed so hard that the postal service riding animals travelled with great difficulty. A little past Esmâᶜilâbâd, the road improved, and there was less snow [when we arrived] at Qazvin.

ARRIVAL IN TEHRAN

The morning of the fourteenth of the month of Rabiᶜ II [20 January], [we] arrived in Qazvin and stayed there that day till one hour before sunset. From Qazvin, [I] took a coach and entered the capital city of Tehran safely on the morning of the fifteenth of the month of Rabiᶜ II [21 January].

Blessings on Our Prophet Moḥammad and His Immaculate Family
In the Year 1303 [1886]

APPENDIX

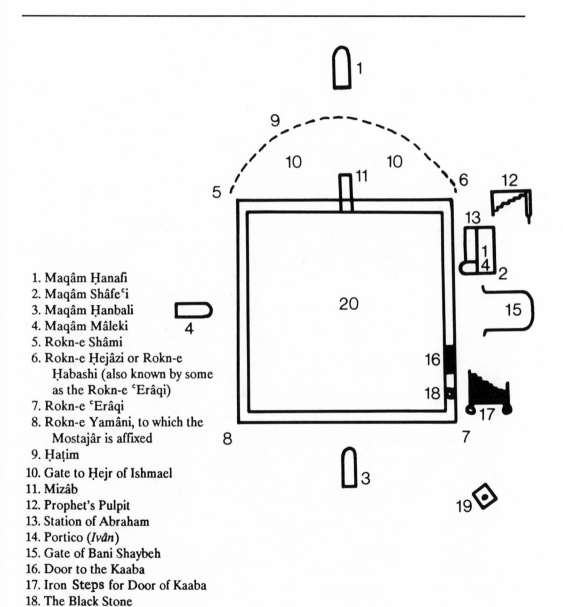

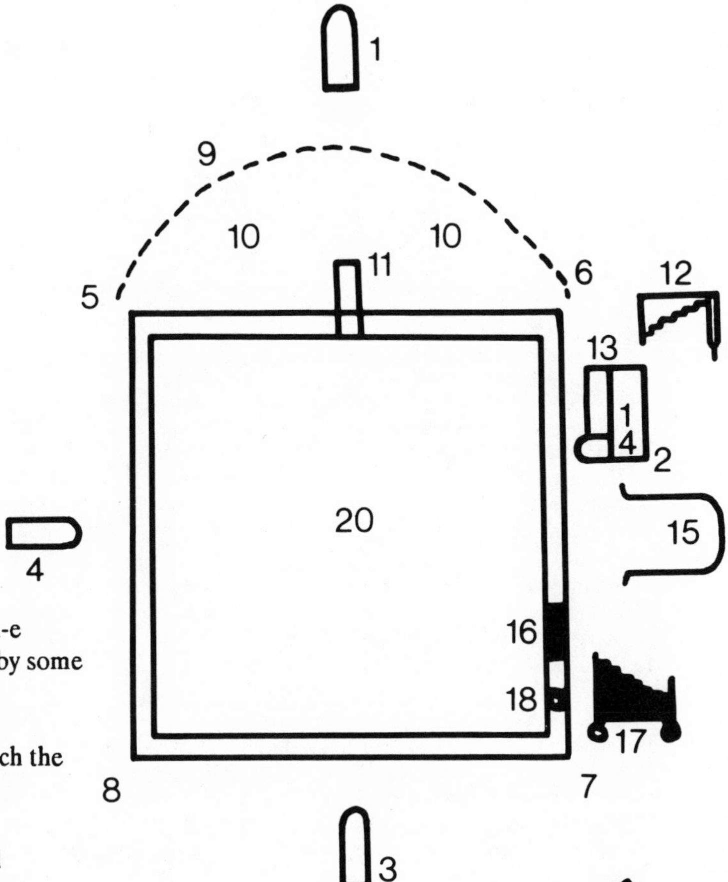

1. Maqâm Ḥanafi
2. Maqâm Shâfeᶜi
3. Maqâm Ḥanbali
4. Maqâm Mâleki
5. Rokn-e Shâmi
6. Rokn-e Ḥejâzi or Rokn-e Ḥabashi (also known by some as the Rokn-e ᶜErâqi)
7. Rokn-e ᶜErâqi
8. Rokn-e Yamâni, to which the Mostajâr is affixed
9. Ḥaṭim
10. Gate to Ḥejr of Ishmael
11. Mizâb
12. Prophet's Pulpit
13. Station of Abraham
14. Portico (*Ivân*)
15. Gate of Bani Shaybeh
16. Door to the Kaaba
17. Iron Steps for Door of Kaaba
18. The Black Stone
19. Well of Zamzam
20. Interior of the Kaaba

Farâhâni's map of the Masjed ol-Ḥarâm.

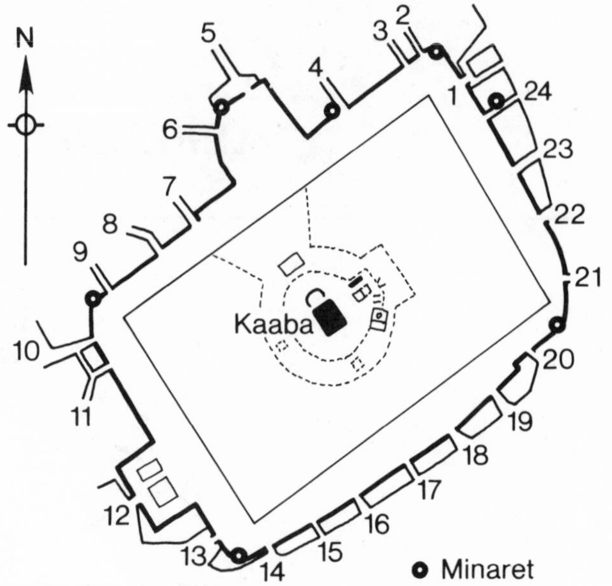

Farâhâni	*Burton/Ali Bey*	*Ṣâdeq Pâshâ*	*Ref^c at Pâshâ*	*Rutter*
1. Salâm	Salam	Salâm	Salâm	Salâm
2. Doraybeh	Duraybah	Doraybeh	Doraybeh	Durayba
3. (Salâmeyyeh?)	-----	Madraseh	[Madraseh]	Madressa
4. Maḥkameh	-----	Maḥkameh	[Maḥkameh]	Mahkama
5. Ziâreh [Zeyâdeh]	Ziyadah or Nadwah	Ziâdeh	Ziâdeh (Sovayqeh)	Ziyâda
6. Qoṭbi	Kutubi	Qoṭbi	Qoṭbi	Qutbi
7. Bâseṭeyyeh	Ajlah or Basitiyah	Bâseṭeyyeh	^cAjleh (Bâseṭeyyeh)	Bâsita
8. Zamâmeyyeh	-----	Zamâmeyyeh	Zamâmeyyeh	Zamâmiyah
9. ^cAtiq	Atik	^cAmr	^cAtiq (^cAmr b. ^cÂṣ)	Amr ibn el Aas
10. ^cOmreh	Bani Saham or Omrah	^cOmreh	^cOmreh	Omra
11. Dâudeyyeh	-----	-----	[Dâudeyyeh]	Dâûdîya
12. Ebrâhim	Ibrahim or Khayyatin	Ebrâhim	Ebrâhim ol-Khayyâṭ	Ibrâhim
13. Vedâ^c	Widaa	Vedâ^c	Vedâ^c or Hazvareh	Widâ
14. Omm Hâni	Umm Hani	Omm Hâni	Omm Hâni	Umm Hâni
15. Sharif Manṣur	Ujlan or Sharif	Takyeh	Bani Tayyem (Madraseh Sharif ^cAjlân or Takyeh)	Ajlân
16. Jeyyâd	Jiyad	Jeyyâd	Raḥmeh (Mojâhedeyyeh)	Jiyâd
17. (Khalifatayn?)	Rahmah	Manṣuri	Ejyâd (Khalafin?)	Rahma
18. Ṣafâ	Safa	Ṣafâ	Ṣafâ	Safa
19. (No^cush?)	Baghlah	No^cush	Baghleh	Baghla
20. (Elmâs?)	Zayt, Asharah, Yunus or Bazan	Baghleh	Bâzân	Bâzân
21. ^cAli	Ali or Bani Hashem	^cAli	^cAli (Bani Hâshem)	Ali
22. ^cAbbâs	Abbas	^cAbbâs	^cAbbâs	Abbâs
23. Nabi	Nabi	Nabi	Nabi (Janâ'ez)	Nabi
24. Qâyt Bâyk	-----	-----	[Qâytbây]	Câit Bey

Gates of the Masjed ol-Ḥarâm according to various authorities.

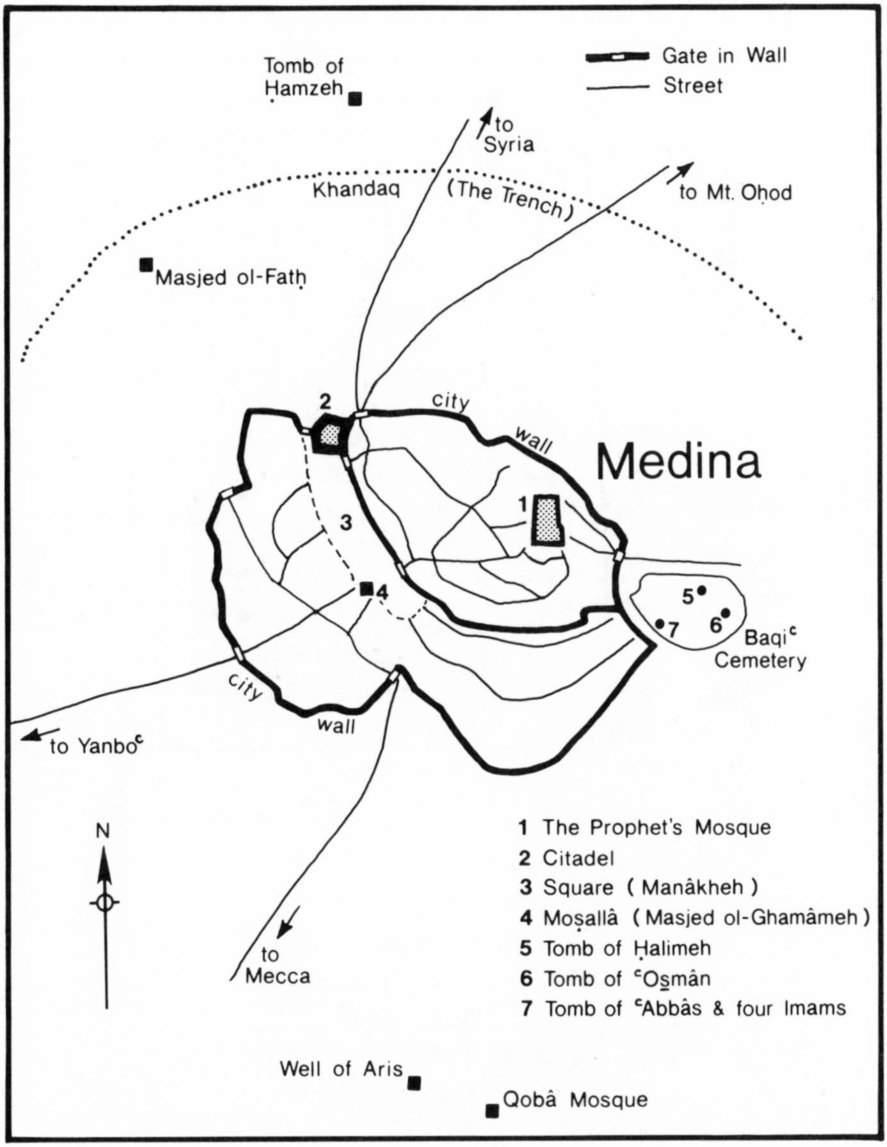

Plan of Medina.

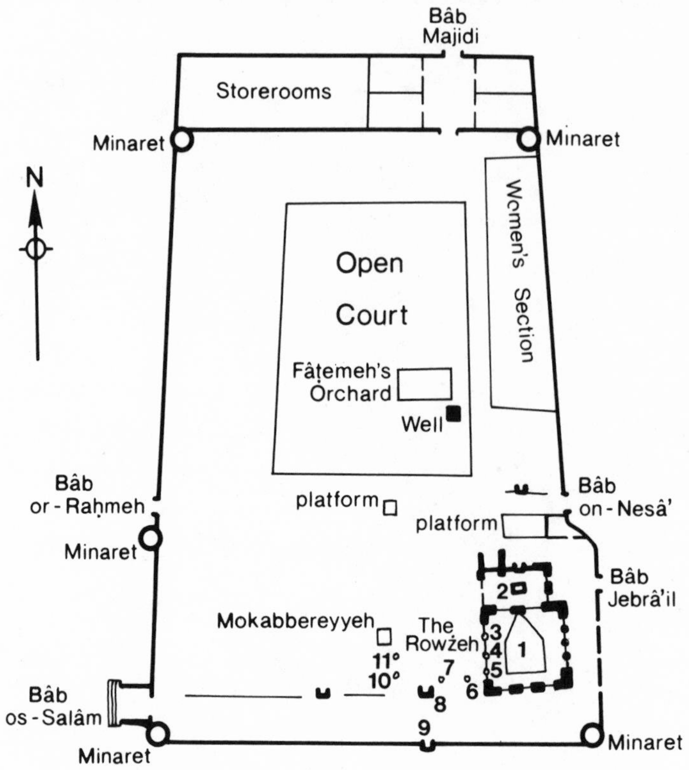

1. The Prophet's Cenotaph.
2. Tomb of Fâṭemeh.
3. Pillar of the Delegations.
4. Pillar of the Guardian.
5. Pillar of the Cot.
6. Pillar of Abu Lobâbeh.
7. Pillar of ʿÂyesheh.
8. The Prophet's Mihrab.
9. ʿOsmân's Mihrab.
10. The "Perfumed" Pillar (Mokhalleq).
11. Pillar of Compassion.

Plan of the Prophet's Mosque in Medina.

GLOSSARY

The following glossary lists various terms used in this translation which might prove confusing to readers who are not specialists in Islamic or Middle Eastern studies. It includes (1) technical terms which are defined in the notes and used frequently throughout the text, (2) some general terms which are not explained in the text or notes, and (3) a few common English equivalents, with transliterations, of technical terms that need further explanation. References to the more detailed notes in the translation are given in brackets. Terms which are used only once or twice and whose meaning is clear in the context are generally not included in this glossary.

ᶜakkam	servants employed to handle baggage and other duties on a caravan [Part Four, n. 68]
amin-e ṣorreh	dignitary entrusted with delivery of gifts from the Ottoman government to Mecca and thus responsible for safe arrival of the official pilgrimage caravan [Part Four, n. 89]
anṣâr	"helpers," i. e., people of Medina who accepted Islam and supported the Prophet Moḥammad after his move to that city [Part One, n. 91]
arg	citadel
b.	an abbrevation for ebn[-e], q.v.
bâb	door or gate, especially as a monumental entrance
bayk	title of respect, usually after a personal name, denoting "gentleman" or "sir" (from the Turkish *bey*)
chârak	"one fourth" of a z̲arᶜ or about ten inches [Part Two, n. 48]
dâng	unit for measuring real estate, equal to one sixth of the total property [Part One, n. 82]
dissimulation	see *taqeyyeh*
Divân-e Aᶜlâ	advisory council to the Shah, combining aspects of a chancery and a treasury [Part One, n. 22]

ebn-e "son of" (Persianized Arabic expression) [Part One, n. 4]

eḥrâm process of sacralization for the pilgrimage [Part Four, n. 93]

emâm among "Twelver Shiʿites," a title given to ʿAli, the Prophet Moḥammad's cousin and son-in-law, and eleven of his descendants, all regarded as sinless and infallible religious authorities; Sunni Muslims also use the term for the leader of the ritual prayers (given in English as Imam and imam respectively)

emâmzâdeh a term meaning "offspring of an Imam," also applied to the shrine where such a dignitary is entombed; there are hundreds of such shrines in existence in Iran [Part One, n. 36]

ʿErâq[-e ʿajam] a district in Iran comprising the area between Qazvin and Hamadan, known today as Arâk; not to be confused with the country of Iraq [Part One, n. 148]

farsakh unit of distance, usually about four miles (six km.) [Part One, n. 15]

farsang (or parasang); a synonym for farsakh

gereh a measurement of length; equal to about two and a half inches [Part Two, n. 61]

gaz a measurement of length; approximately equal to the English ell (45 inches) [Part Three, n. 43]

ḥajjeh-forush a professional who contracts to perform the pilgrimage on behalf of someone unable (or unwilling) to perform the pilgrimage in person [Part Four, n. 68]

ḥajj-e tamattoʿ a form of the pilgrimage combining ḥajj and ʿomreh [Part Five, n. 24]

ḥâjji respectful title bestowed on a person who has made the pilgrimage to Mecca

ḥâkem in Persian usage, title of an administrative official serving as governor or magistrate of a district

ḥamleh-dâr organizer and leader of a caravan [Part Four, n. 68]

Ḥanafi a Sunni maẕhab, i. e. one of the four mutually recognized "rites" or comprehensive "schools of law" of Sunni Islam; named for Abu Ḥanifeh [d. 150/767]

Ḥanbali another of the Sunni maẕhabs or "schools of law"; named for Aḥmad b. Ḥanbal [d. 241/855] *harvaleh* a distinctive, quick-paced amble supposed to be used while performing pilgrimage rituals such as the saᶜy [Part Five, n. 78]

Ḥażrat a term of respect often used in addressing or mentioning the names of religious or political dignitaries [Part One, n. 34]

Ḥejr area near the Kaaba reputed to enclose the graves of Hagar and Ishmael [Part Five, n. 48]

Imam see emâm

Jady "Capricorn," a name for the tenth month in the Persian solar calendar (December-January) [Part Seven, n. 46]

jamreh a market indicating one of the spots at which pebbles must be hurled during the pilgrimage ritual of lapidation [Part Five, n. 34 and n. 37]

jarib a measurement of land, equal to about a quarter of an acre [Part One, n. 27]

Jomâdâ I *Jomâdâ ol-Ulâ*; fifth month of the Islamic lunar calendar

Jomâdâ II *Jomâdâ ol-Okhrâ;* sixth month of the Islamic lunar calendar

kayl a measure of volume and weight; it varied from region to region but in Gilân was equivalent to approximately 7.25 kg. [Part One, n. 169]

khan an inn or caravanserai (English form of Turkish *han/khân*)

Khân originally a Turko-Mongol title for a prince or noble; later a title added to the personal name of any powerful individual, especially tribal chieftains

khâneh-nozul obligation to provide accomodations for visiting government officials [Part One, n. 87]

khâqân Turko-Mongol title for a king or emperor [Part One, n. 5]

Khâreji[te] generic name applied to several Muslim religio-political groups active primarily in early Islamic history; in Farâhâni's usage, it appears to refer only to the contemporary Ebâżeyyeh sect of Islam

khâveh a toll or transit tax on travellers to Arabia collected by the Ottoman government and paid to chiefs of Bedouin tribes to guarantee safe conduct for caravans [Part Six, p. 248 n. 10]

khowrdeh-mâlek a jointly owned piece of real estate; the term usually refers to rural areas where pieces of property were jointly owned by peasants without the presence of a landlord [Part One, n. 124] kiblah [*qebleh*] direction of the compass pointing to Mecca, towards which the Muslim faces for the prayer ritual; also, a niche in the wall of the mosque oriented towards Mecca

korr a unit of volume for measuring water; the exact quantity is a matter of dispute in Islamic law [Part Two, n. 65]

kran [*qerân*] a silver coin; one tenth of a toman [Part One, n. 16]

lashkar-nevis officer responsible for keeping the army muster and salary records [Part Four, n. 83]

lira an Ottoman gold coin [Part Three, n. 110]

madrasah an institution of education and instruction in the Islamic legal disciplines, usually supported by charitable endowments (wakf)

maḥmal [properly *maḥmel*]; symbolic emblems conveyed to Mecca with the Syrian and Egyptian caravans [Part Four, n. 88]

majidi an Ottoman silver coin [Part Three, n. 110]

Mâleki a Sunni maẕhab, i. e. one of the four mutually recognized "rites" or comprehensive "schools of law" in Sunni Islam; named for Mâlek b. Anas (d. 179/795-96)

mann also *mann-e shâh, mann-e tabriz;* units of weight varying from approximately three to six kg. [Part One, n. 168]

maqâm "station," used as a technical term to denote the places assumed by various prayer leaders in the mosque in Mecca

Mashhadi term added before a personal name, indicating that one has made a ritual visit to the shrine of Imam Reżâ in Mashhad

masjed mosque

*masjed-e jâme*ᶜ the principle mosque of a city, suitable for use for the Friday noon congregational prayer service and sermon [Part One, n. 56]

Masjed ol-Ḥarâm the mosque surrounding the Kaaba in Mecca [Part Five, n. 20, n. 38]

maydân "square," also a unit of measurement [see *maydân-e asb*]

maydân-e asb a vague term of measurement equal to about one forth of a farsakh

menbar	the "pulpit" or dais, usually in the form of a platform at the head of a staircase, used by the person giving the sermon at the Friday noon prayer service
mihrab [*mehrâb*]	a niche in the wall of a mosque indicating the direction to Mecca, towards which worshippers orient themselves during the prayer ritual
miqât	locality specified in Islamic religious law for beginning the sacralization (eḥrâm) for the pilgrimage [Part Four, n. 40]
mirzâ	a title of respect; if it precedes the personal name, it indicates that the person belongs to the learned class; if it comes after the name, it indicates a prince or person of royal birth (e.g. ᶜAbbâs Mirzâ)
miskal [*meṣqâl*]	a unit of weight usually equivalent to 4.6 grams [Part Two, n. 52]
modir	"director"; in the Ottoman empire, an official in charge of an administrative subdistrict [Part Three, n. 5]
mohâjer	plural *mohâjerin*; term applied to the "emigrants" who left their homes in Mecca to follow Moḥammad to Medina [Part One, n. 91]
Moḥarram	the first month of the Islamic lunar calendar; the first ten days of the month (ᶜÂshurâ) are important to Shi'ites as commemorating the martyrdom of the Prophet Moḥammad's grandson Ḥosayn
moḥrem	pilgrim who has entered the state of sacralization known as eḥrâm (q.v.) [Part Five, n. 2]
mojtahed	a scholar of Islamic law qualified to practice ejtehâd, "independent legal reasoning" [Part One, n. 81]
mokharrej	an official licensed to hire out camels, etc. to pilgrims [Part Four, n. 70]
mollâ	title for a person who has completed training in Islamic law, often used as part of a personal name; generally speaking, it denotes the lowest position in the clerical hierarchy of the Iranian Shi'ite ulama (sometimes spelled mullah in English usage)
manât	a Persian term, derived from the Russian, to refer to Russian currency, especially the rouble [Part Two, n. 2]
mostowfi	title of a government accountant
moṭavvef	professional guides who helped pilgrims with accomodations, travel and correct performance of the pilgrimage rituals [Part Four, n. 66]

mutesarrifat	English form of the Turkish *mutasarrıflık*; in the Ottoman Empire, a subdivision of a province [Part Three, n. 5]
nasta^c^liq	a cursive style of Arabic script, very popular in Iran for books and decoration [Part Three, n. 196]
nâyeb	"headman" of a village; more generally, anyone to whom some power has been delegated (for example, an official acting on behalf of an absent governor)
nâyeb ol-ḥarâm	title of the official appointed as chief superintendent of the Prophet's Mosque in Medina
^c^omreh	the "lesser pilgrimage" or ritual visit to Mecca, often combined with the hajj or pilgrimage proper (*^c^omreh-ye tamatto^c^*) [Part Four, n. 101; Part Five, n. 24]
pâdeshâh	a king or ruler
para [*pâreh*]	a generic term for a very small denomination of currency; specifically, the smallest unit of Ottoman coinage, nominally valued at one fortieth of a qorush [Part Three, n. 110]
pâshâ	a Turkish title bestowed on the highest ranks of military and civilian officials
qadam	the "pace," a unit of measurement equivalent to about 15 inches [Part Five, n. 46]
qâ'em-maqâm	in the Ottoman empire, the chief official (a kind of lieutenant governor) of a district [Part Three, n. 5]
qal^c^eh	castle, fortress, citadel; also a large residence owned by the landlord of a village [Part One, n. 28]
qanât	an underground canal [Part One, n. 29]
qonut	a special prayer of supplication [Part Five, n. 68]
qorush[-e ṣâgh]	a small coin used in the Ottoman Empire and Egypt; often referred to as the "piastre" in English [Part Three, n. 111; Part Four, n. 23]
quti	unit of weight and volume used especially for measuring rice in Gilân; equivalent to approximately 30 kg. [Part One, p. 38]
Rabi^c^ I	*Rabi^c^ ol-Avval;* the third month of the Islamic lunar calendar
Rabi^c^ II	*Rabi^c^ ol-Akhar* (or *os-S̲âni*); the fourth month of the Islamic lunar calendar

Rajab seventh month of the Islamic lunar calendar

rakᶜat "cycle" of standing, genuflecting and prostration during the Muslim prayer ritual [Part Five, n. 28]

Ramażân Ramadan, the tenth month of the Islamic lunar calendar, during which the ritual fast is observed

raṭl an archaic unit of weight; equivalent to almost half a kilogram [Part Four, n. 10]

rokn cornerstone or pillar; specifically one of the corners of the Kaaba [Part Five, n. 52]

rowżeh-khᵛâni a public reading from popular collections of stories about the martyrdom of Shi'ite religious figures, especially to commemorate the martyrdom of Ḥosayn at Karbala [Part Three, n. 201]

Ṣafar the second month of the Islamic lunar calendar

sang a unit for measuring the flow of water [Part One, n. 30]

sarhang a military rank similar to that of a colonel [Part One, n. 203]

saᶜy ritual running between the hills Marveh and Ṣafâ in Mecca during the pilgrimage [Part Five, n. 30 and n. 77]

sayyed term of respect for someone descended from the Prophet Moḥammad [Part One, n. 38]

Shaᶜbân eighth month of the Islamic lunar calendar

Shâfeᶜi a Sunni maẕhab, i. e. one of the four mutually recognized "rites" or comprehensive "schools of law" of Sunni Islam; named for Abu ᶜAbdollah Moḥammad b. Edris osh-Shâfeᶜi (d. 204/820)

shâhi a copper coin equal to one twentieth of a kran [Part One, n. 16]

sharif "dignitary," especially certain descendants of the Prophet Moḥammad; used most often to denote the chief administrator of Mecca [Part Four, n. 67]

Shavvâl the ninth month of the Islamic lunar calendar

showṭ one counter-clockwise circuit around the Kaaba during the performance of ṭavâf *shaykh ol-eslâm* title used for a religious official usually serving as the chief judge for a town or district [Part One, n. 88]

shekasteh a calligraphic style for writing Persian, especially suitable for documents [Part Three, n. 196]

shoqẕof a special litter used for riding a camel [Part Four, n. 39]

siâq a kind of shorthand script for writing numbers and accounting records [Part Three, n. 105]

sir[-e tabriz] a weight equivalent to about 74 grams [Part Two, n. 52]

ṯolos̱ a special calligraphic style for writing the Arabic script [Part Three, n. 57]

solṭân transliterated form of the title sultan; often used as part of a personal name

tâjer "merchant"

takyeh in Iran, a special hall used for the performance of plays about the martyrdom of Imam Ḥosayn (taᶜzeyyeh); also a retreat or domicile for members of Sufi mystical orders [Part One, n. 159]

talbeyyeh ritual formula recited throughout the pilgrimage ceremonies [Part Five, n. 1]

taqeyyeh as used by Farâhâni, the Shi'ite concept that one's true religious beliefs and actual ritual practices can, or even should, be concealed in the presence of non-Shi'ites; normally this concealment should only be used when drawing attention to one's sectarian identity might lead to persecution, but in practice Shi'ites often used it routinely when among non-Shi'ites whether such a danger actually existed or not [Part Two, n. 73; Part Five, n. 115]

taqṣir trimming the hair and clipping the nails after performing certain rituals of the pilgrimage, part of the process of desacralization [Part Five, n. 31]

ṭavâf ritual circumambulation of the Kaaba [Part Five, n. 27]

ṭavâf-e nesâ' in Shi'ite Islam, a final circumambulation of the Kaaba which removes the prohibition against intercourse imposed by the sacralization (eḥrâm) [Part Five, n. 36]

taᶜzeyyeh an expression of mourning for the Shi'ite Imam Ḥosayn and his family, particularly a performance of a "passion play" reenacting his martyrdom at the Battle of Karbalâ; in Qâjâr Iran, this religious ritual was very popular and was used to commemorate the death of many saints and martyrs

tojjâr	plural of tâjer
toman [*towmân*]	a coin, usually silver, worth about eighty cents [Part One, n. 14]
ulama [ᶜ*olamâ*]	"scholars," i. e. that group of Muslims regarded as having a sound and extensive knowledge of the Islamic religious sciences, especially those having been trained in the principles and substance of Islamic law
vajab	the "span," a measurement equivalent to about nine inches
vâli	governor of a major province
vaqf	see wakf
voquf	the "standing" or waiting on the plain of ᶜArafât from noon to sunset on the ninth of Z̲i Ḥejjeh [Part Five, n. 32]
wadi [*vâdi*]	a valley or other water channel that is dry except after a rainfall
wakf [*vaqf*]	tax-exempt and theoretically inalienable donation of real property, the income from which is used to support specific charitable institutions [Part One, n. 49]
Yazidi	a highly eclectic but nominally Islamic sect popular among some Kurdish peoples in the environs of Mosul
yuzbâshi	military rank roughly equal to captain [Part One, n. 58]
*z̲ar*ᶜ	a measurement of length, equal to 41 inches [Part One, n. 27]
Zaydi	a branch of Shi'ite Islam especially widespread in the Yemen; the name is derived from the sect's recognition of Zayd rather than Moḥammad Bâqer as the fifth imam
ziârat	ritual visitation of a sacred site, especially a tomb [Part Five, n. 125]
Z̲i Ḥejjeh	the name of the twelfth month of the Islamic lunar calendar, during which the ḥajj takes place; this spelling is the one typically given by Farâhâni; it is also written more correctly as Z̲i'l-Ḥejjeh
*Z̲i Qa*ᶜ*deh*	the name of the eleventh month of the Islamic lunar calendar; also written Z̲i'l-Qaᶜdeh.

SELECT BIBLIOGRAPHY

Works in Persian, Arabic and Turkish

ᶜAbd ol-Bâqi, M. F. *ol-Moᶜjam ol-mofahras le-alfâẓ ol-qor'ân ol-karim*. Cairo, 1364/1945.

ᶜAbd ol-Karim. *Bayân-e vâqeᶜ*. MS. London: British Library, Add. 8909.

Adib ol-Molk, ᶜAbd ol-ᶜAli Khân. *Safarnâmeh-ye Adib ol-Molk beh ᶜatabât*. Edited by Masᶜud Golzâri. Tehran, 1362/1985.

Afshâr, Iraj. *Fehrest-e maqâlât-e fârsi*. Tehran, 1340/1961-77. [Also known as *Index Iranicus*.]

—. "Negâhi be-safarnâmeh-nevisi-ye Nâṣer od-Din Shâh." *Âyandeh* 9(1362/1983):757-769.

—. "Negâhi degar be-safarnâmeh-nevisi-ye Nâṣer od-Din Shâh." *Âyandeh* 11(1364/1985):39-48.

—. "Nokteh-i dar bâb Eᶜtemâd os-Salṭaneh." *Râhnamâ-ye Ketâb* 11(1347/1968-69):190-191.

Âghâ Bozorg-e Ṭehrâni, Moḥammad Moḥsen. *Ṭabaqât aᶜlâm osh-shiᶜeh*. Tehran, 1954-58.

—. *oz̲-Z̲ariᶜeh elâ taṣânif osh-shiᶜeh*. Tehran, 1936-78.

ᶜAlam ol-Hodâ, S. Morteżâ [?]. *Ketâb kanz ol-ansâb maᶜruf be-baḥr ol-ansâb*. Bombay, 1898.

ᶜÂmeli, Moḥsen. *Manâsek ol-ḥajj*. Sidon, 1340/1922.

Amin od-Dowleh, Mirzâ ᶜAli Khân. *Safarnâmeh-ye Amin od-Dowleh*. Edited by ᶜAli Amini. Tehran, 1354/1975.

—. *Khâṭerât-e siyâsi-ye Mirzâ ᶜAli Khân-e Amin od-Dowleh*. Edited by Ḥâfeẓ Farmânfarmâ'iân. Tehran, 1977. [Second edition.]

Anṣâri, ᶜAbd ol-Qoddus. *Âs̲âr ol-madineh ol-monavvareh*. Medina, 1353/1935.

—. *Mowsuᶜeh târikh madineh joddeh*. Cairo, 1402/1982.

Arabic Texts Concerning the History of the Zaydi Imams of Ṭabaristân, Daylamân and Gîlân. Edited by W. Madelung. Wiesbaden, 1987.

Arseven, Jelâl Esᶜad. *Eski estânbul âbedât ve mebânisi*. Istanbul, 1328/1912.

Asᶜad, Jelâl. *Eski estânbul*. Istanbul, 1328/1912.

—. *Eski ghalaṭeh*. Istanbul, 1329/1913.

Ashraf, A. "Alqâb-e divâni dar ᶜahd-e qâjâreyyeh." *Âyandeh* 9/i(1362/1983):29-33.

ᶜAsqalâni, Aḥmad b. ᶜAli (Ebn Ḥajar). *Tahz̲ib ot-tahz̲ib*. Haydarabad, 1325-27/1907-9.

ᶜAṭṭâr, Aḥmad. *Qâmus ol-ḥajj va'l-ᶜomreh*. Beirut, 1399/1979.

ᶜAyyâshi, Ebrâhim. *Madineh bayn ol-mażi va'l-ḥâżer*. Medina, 1392/1972.

Azraqi, Moḥammad b. ᶜAbdollah. *Akhbâr makkeh va mâ jâ'a fihâ men ol-as̲âr*. Madrid, n. d.

Bâbâzâdeh, Shahlâ. *Fehrest-e towṣifi safarnâmeh-hâ-ye âlmâni mowjud dar ketâbkhâneh-ye melli-ye irân*. Tehran, 1978. [Also entitled *Katalog der deutschprächigen Reisebeschreibungen in der iranischen Staatsbibliothek*.]

Bahmânyâr, Aḥmad. *Ṣâḥeb ebn-e ᶜAbbâd: sharḥ-e aḥval va âs̱âr*. Edited by M. Bâstâni-Pârizi. Tehran, 1965.

Bakr, ᶜAbd ol-Majid. *Ashhar ol-masâjed fi'l-eslâm. Ol-Beqâᶜ ol-moqadaseyyeh*. Jedda, 1400/1979-80.

Balâẕori, Aḥmad b. Yaḥyâ. *Ketâb fotuḥ ol-boldân*. Edited by M. J. de Goeje. Leiden: 1866.

Bâmdâd, Mahdi. *Târikh-e rejâl-e irân*. Tehran, 1966-74. [Also known as *Sharḥ ḥâl-e rejâl-e irân* and *Dictionary of National Biography of Iran 1700-1960*.]

Barimâni, Aḥmad. *Daryâ-ye khazar*. Tehran, 1326/1947-48.

Bâsalâmeh, Ḥosayn. *Târikh ᶜemârat ol-masjed ol-ḥarâm*. Jedda, 1400/1980.

al-Baṭanuni, Moḥammad Labib. *or-Reḥleh ol-ḥejâziyyeh*. Cairo, 1329/1911.

Bayhaqi, Abu'l-Fażl. *Târikh-e Bayhaqi*. Edited by ᶜAli Akbar Fayyâż. Mashhad, 1971.

Bayrak, M. Orhan. *Istanbulun tarihi yerler kılavuzu*. Istanbul, 1966.

Behruzi, ᶜAli Naqi. "Shaykh or-Re'is-e Qâjâr va moṭâyebât-e u." *Armaghân* 40(1350/1971-72):352-354.

Belâdi, ᶜAtiq b. Ghays̱. *Maᶜâlem makkeh ot-târikheyyeh va'l-as̱areyyeh*. Mecca, 1980.

—. *Moᶜjam maᶜâlem ol-ḥejâz*. Ta'ef, 1978-[in progress].

—. *Moᶜjam qabâ'el ol-ḥejâz*. Mecca, 1979.

Bu-Rowaybeh, Rashid. "Masjed ol-madineh fi ḥadâ'eq ol-kotob os̱-s̱amineh." In ᶜA. Anṣâri, (ed.), *Sources for the History of Arabia*. Riyadh, 1979. Volume 1, pp. 183-197.

Daḥlân, Aḥmad. *Omarâ' ol-balad ol-ḥarâm*. Beirut, 1978.

Dehkhodâ, ᶜAli Akbar. *Ams̱âl va ḥekâm*. Tehran, 1352/1973-74. (Fourth edition.)

—. *Loghatnâmeh*. Tehran, 1946-83.

Ebn Dohaysh, ᶜAbd ol-Laṭif. "Derâseh mowjezeh le-baᶜż mo'allafât Keristeyân Snuk Hurgrunye ᶜan ol-jazireh ol-ᶜarabeyyeh." In ᶜA. Anṣâri (ed.) *Sources for the History of Arabia*. Riyadh, 1979. Volume 2, pp. 91-94.

Ebn Khallekân, Shams od-Din. *Ketâb vafayât ol-aᶜyân va anbâ' oz-zamân*. Edited by F. Wüstenfeld. Göttingen, 1835-50.

Ebn Meskavayh, Abu ᶜAli Aḥmad b. Moḥammad. *ol-Ḥekmeh ol-khâledeh: jâvidân kherad*. Edited by ᶜAbd or-Raḥman Badavi. Cairo, 1952.

Eqbâl, ᶜAbbâs. "Mirzâ ᶜAbd ol-Vahhâb Khân Âṣaf od-Dowleh." *Yâdgâr* 5vi(1327-28/1948-49):27-37.

Eṣbahâni, Abu'l-Faraj. *Maqâtel oṭ-ṭâlebeyin*. Edited by Aḥmad Ṣaqr. Cairo, 1368/1949.

Eṣṭakhri, Abu Esḥâq Ebrâhim. *ol-Masâlek va'l-mamâlek*. Edited by M. de Goeje. *Bibliotheca Geographorum Arabicorum*. Volume I. Leiden, 1870.

—. *Masâlek va mamâlek*. Anonymous Persian translation. Edited by Iraj Afshâr. Tehran, 1347/1969.

Eᶜtemâd os-Salṭaneh (Ṣaniᶜ od-Dowleh), Moḥammad Ḥasan Khân. *Safarnâmeh-ye Ṣaniᶜ od-Dowleh az teflis beh ṭehrân*. Edited by Moḥammad Golbon. Tehran, 2536/1977.

—. *ol-Ma'âs̱er va'l-âs̱âr*. Tehran, 1306/1889. [Also edited by Iraj Afshâr. *Chehel sâl-e târikh-e irân dar dowreh-ye pâdeshâhi-ye Nâṣer od-Din Shâh*. Vol. I. Tehran, 1362/1983.]

—. *Maṭla*ᶜ *osh-shams*. Tehran, 1301-1303/1884-86.

—. *Mer'ât ol-boldân*. Tehran, 1293-96/1877-79.

—. *Ruznâmeh-ye khâṭerât*. Edited by Iraj Afshâr. Tehran, 1345/1966-67.

—. *Ṣadr ot-tavârikh*. Tehran, 1349/1970.

—. *ot-Tadvin fi aḥvâl jebâl shirvân*. Tehran, 1311/1894-95.

—. *Taṭbiq-e loghat-e joghrâfiyâi-ye qadim va jadid-e irân*. Edited by M. Moḥaddeṯ. Tehran, 1363/1984.

—. *Târikh-e montaẓam-e nâṣeri*. Tehran, 1298-1300/1881-83.

Farâhâni [Golbon], Mirzâ Moḥammad Ḥosayn. *Ḥâlat [va] âdâb os-sorur*. Tehran, 1311/1924.

—. *Safarnâmeh*. Edited by Ḥâfeẓ Farmân-Farmâ'yân. Tehran, 1342/1964.

—. *Safarnâmeh*. Edited by Masᶜud Golzâri. Tehran, 1362/1983.

Farhâd Mirzâ, Moᶜtamad od-Dowleh. *Ketâb hedâyat os-sabil va kefâyat od-dalil [yâ] ruznâmeh-ye safar-e madinat os-salâm va baytollah ol-ḥarâm*. Shiraz, 1294/1877.

Farhâd-moᶜtamad, Maḥmud. "Ḥâjji Mirzâ Ḥosayn Khân Moshir od-Dowleh va Ḥosâm os-Salṭaneh." *Yâdgâr* 2/vii(1324-25/1945-47):50-54.

—. "Nâṣer od-Din Shâh va Shaykh or-Ra'is." *Yaghmâ* 3(1329/1950-51):343-344.

—. "Tasleyatnâmeh-ye Nâṣer od-Din Shâh dar marg-e shâhzâdeh Farhâd Mirzâ." *Yagmâ* 2(1328/1949-50):159-160.

Farhang-e gil va daylam. Tehran, 1987.

Farhang-e joghrâfiyâi-ye irân. [See under Iran. Artesh.]

Farhi, Yusef. "Râjeᶜ beh marḥum Farhâd Mirzâ." *Yâdgâr* 2/vi(1324-25/1945-47):117-124.

Farmân-farmâ'iân, Ḥâfeẓ. "Eshâreh-i bar sharḥ-e zendegi va âṯâr-e Mirzâ Moḥammad Ḥosayn Farâhâni." *Yaghmâ* 17(1343/1964-65):18-24.

Fâsi, Moḥammad b. Aḥmad Taqi od-Din. *Shefâ ol-ghoram be-akhbâr ol-balad ol-ḥaram*. Edited by F. Wüstenfeld. *Chroniken der Stadt Mekka*, vol. 2. Leipzig, 1857.

Firuzâbâdi, Moḥammad b. Yaᶜqub. *ol-Maghânem ol-moṭabeh*. Riyadh, 1969.

Fumani, ᶜAbd ol-Fattâḥ. *Târikh-e gilân*. Edited by B. Dorn. *Muhammedanische Quellen zur Geschichte der südlichen Küstenländer des Kaspischen Meeres*. Vol. III. *ᶜAbdu'l-Fattâh Fûmeny's Geschichte von Gîlân*. St. Petersburg, 1858.

Gilâni, Shaykh Ḥasan Shams. *Târikh-e ᶜolamâ va shoᶜarâ-ye gilân*. Tehran, 1327/1948.

Golchin-e Maᶜâni, Aḥmad. "Ḥâj Mirzâ Âqâsi va solṭân-e qâjâr." *Yaghmâ* 20(1346/1967-68):547-549.

Hadrâvi, Aḥmad. *Ketâb ol-ᶜeqd oṯ-ṯamin fi fażâ'el ol-balad ol-amin*. Mecca, 1314/1896.

Ḥâfeẓ, ᶜAbd os-Sallam. *ol-Madineh ol-monavvareh fi't-târikh*. Cairo, 1381/1972.

Ḥaykal, Moḥammad Ḥosayn. *Fi manzel ol-waḥy*. Cairo, 1356/1937.

Hedâyat, Reżâ-Qoli Khân. *Rowżat oṣ-ṣafâ-ye nâṣeri*. Tehran, 1270-74/1853-57. [Reprint; Tehran, 1339/1960-61.]

Ḥejâz velâyati sâlnâmehsi. Mecca, 1302-5/1885-88.

Ḥelli, Jaᶜfar b. Ḥasan. *Sharâ'eᶜ ol-eslâm fi masâ'el ol-ḥalâl va'l-ḥarâm*. Edited by ᶜAbd ol-Ḥosayn ᶜAli. Najaf, 1389/1969. [See also below, s. v. Querry.]

Ḥosâm os-Salṭaneh, Abu'n-Naṣr Mirzâ. *Safarnâmeh-ye tavâlesh*. Edited by Esmâᶜil Ṣafâ'i. Tehran, 1346/1967.

Ḥosâm os-Salṭaneh, Solṭân Morâd Mirzâ. *Dalil ol-anâm fi sabil ziârat baytollah ol-ḥarâm*. MS. Tehran: Majles, #693.

Ḥosayni, Jamâl od-Din. *Rowżat ol-aḥbâb fi siar on-nabi va'l-âl va'l-aṣḥâb*. Lucknow, 1297/1880.

Iran. Artesh. Setâd-e Artesh. Dâyereh-ye joghrâfiyâi. *Farhang-e joghrâfiyâi-ye irân*. Tehran, 2535/1976. [Reprint.]

Jaktaji, M. *Fehrest-e towṣifi-ye safarnâmeh-hâ-ye farânsavi mowjud dar ketâbkhâneh-ye melli-ye irân*. Tehran, 2535/1977. [Also entitled *Catalogue descriptif des récits de voyages en langue française conservés à la Bibliothèque Nationale d'Iran*.]

—. *Fehrest-e towṣifi-ye safarnâmeh-hâ-ye engelisi mowjud dar ketâbkhâneh-ye milli-ye irân*. Tehran, 2535/1976. [Also entitled *Descriptive Catalogue of the English Itineraries in the National Library of Iran*.]

Jamâlzâdeh, M. ᶜAli. "Ḥajji Mirzâ Âqâsi." *Yaghmâ* 17(1343/1964-65):123-125.

Jamshidi-pur, Yûsof. *Farhang-e amṯâl-e fârsi*. Tehran, n. d.

ol-Jâser, Ḥamad. *Belâd Yanboᶜ*. Riyadh, n. d.

—. *Fi shamâl gharb ol-jazireh*. Riyadh, 1401/1981.

—. "Kotob ol-manâzel min ravâfed od-derâsât ᶜan joghrâfeyyeh jazireh ol-ᶜarab. " In ᶜA. Anṣâri, (ed.) *Sources for the History of Arabia*. Riyadh, 1979. Volume 1, pp. 229-241.

—. *Rasâ'el fi târikh ol-madineh*. Riyadh, 1972.

Javâher-kalâm, ᶜAli. "Shâhzâdeh Abu'l-Ḥasan Mirzâ Shaykh or-Re'is Qâjâr." *Armaghân* 40(1350/1961-62):165-70.

Jonaydel, Saᶜd b. ᶜAbdollah. *al-Moᶜjam ol-joghrâfi le'l-belâd ol-ᶜarabeyyeh os-saᶜudeyyeh*. Riyadh, 1978.

Kaḥḥâleh, ᶜOmar. *Moᶜjam qabâ'el ol-ᶜarab*. Damascus, 1949.

Kâsâni, Abu Bakr b. ᶜAli. *Ṣaydaneh*. Edited by M. Sotudeh and I. Afshâr. Tehran, 1358/1979-80.

Kasravi, Aḥmad. "Baku." *Armaghân* 10(1311/1932-33):81-87.

—. *Chehel maqâleh*. Tehran, 1335/1955.

—. *Nâmhâ-ye shahrhâ va dehhâ-ye irân*. Tehran, 1335/1956.

Keshâvarz, Karim. *Gilân*. Tehran, 1347/1968.

Khân Malek-e Sâsâni, Aḥmad. *Siâsatgarân-e dowreh-ye qâjâreyyeh*. Tehran, 1338-45/1960-67.

—. *Yâdbudhâ-ye sefârat-e estânbul*. Tehran, 1345/1966-67.

Kharbuṭli, ᶜAli. *Târikh ol-kaᶜbeh*. Beirut, 1396/1976.

Khayrat ᶜAli. *Manâzel ol-ḥajj*. MS. London: British Library, Add. 16741.

Khomayni, Âyatollah Ruḥollah. *Manâsek-e ḥajj*. Tehran, 1361/1982-83.

Kindi. *Ketâb ol-omarâ' va ketâb ol-qodât*. Edited by R. Guest. *Governors and Judges of Egypt*. London, 1912.

Kocaer, Remzi. *Osmanlı altınları*. Istanbul, 1967.

Koran [*Qor'ân*]. Edited Cairo, 1347/1928.

Kushâ, Jaᶜfar. "Shilât." *Nâmeh-ye farhang* 1(1330-31/1952-53):230-231.

Lâhiji, ᶜAli b. Shams od-Din. *Târikh-e khâni*. Edited by M. Sotudeh. Tehran, 1352/1973.

Mâher, Soᶜâd. *Masâjed meṣr va owleyyâhâ oṣ-ṣâleḥin*. Cairo, 1971-83.

Makâteb-e Khân Aḥmad Khân Edited by H. Rabino. In *Mîr Zahîr-ed-Din's History of Gîlân and Deilemistân*. Rasht, 1330/1911-12.

Marᶜashi, Mir Ẓahir od-Din. *Târikh-e gilân va daylamestân*. Edited by H. Rabino. *Mîr Zahîr-ed-Din's History of Gîlân and Deilemistân*. Rasht, 1330/1911-12.

Masᶜud, Ḥajji Mirzâ. *Safarnâmeh-ye Khosrow Mirzâ be peṭerzburgh*. Edited by M. Golban. Tehran, 1349/1970-71.

Maṭar, Ḥosayn. *Târikh ᶜemârat ol-ḥaram ol-makki osh-sharif*. Jedda, 1402/1982.

Mehr, Farhang. "Nâṣer od-Din Shâh dar teflis." *Anjomân-e Târikh* 1(1359/1980):15-17.

Tadẕkerat ol-molûk. Facsimile in V. Minorsky. *Tadhkirat al-Mulûk: A Manual of Ṣafavid Administration*. London, 1943.

Mirzâ Ebrâhim. *Safarnâmeh-ye astarâbâd va mâzanderân va gilân*. Edited by Masᶜud Golzâri. Tehran, 2535/1976.

Moᶜayyer ol-Mamâlek, Dust ᶜAli Khân. *Rejâl-e ᶜaṣr-e nâṣeri*. Tehran, 1361/1983.

—. *Yâddâsht-hâ-i az zendegâni-ye khoṣuṣi-ye Nâṣer od-Din Shâh*. Tehran, 1361/1982.

Mobarak, ᶜAli Pâshâ. *ol-Kheṭaṭ ot-towfiqeyyeh ol-jadideh*. Bulâq, 1887-1889.

Modarresi-Chehârdehi, Morteẓâ. "Shaykh Aḥmad Aḥsâ'i." *Yâdgâr* 1/iv(1323-24/1944-46):30-47.

—. "Shaykh Morteżâ Anṣâri." *Armaghân* 28(1338/1959-60):117-124.

Modarresi-Ṭabâṭabâ'i, Ḥosayn. *Bargi az târikh-e qazvin, târikhcheh-ye az âstâneh-ye Shâhzâdeh Ḥosayn*. Qomm, 1361/1982-83.

Mofakhkham-Pâyân, Loṭfollah. *Farhang-e âbâdi-hâ-ye irân*. Tehran, 1976.

Mokhtaṣar târikh omarâ makkeh ol-mokarremeh. MS. Leiden: University Library, Or. 14.025.

Moᶜin, Moḥammad. *Farhang-e fârsi*. Tehran, 1362-4/1983-85.

Moshâr, Khânbâbâ. *Fehrest-e ketâb-hâ-ye châpi-ye fârsi*. Tehran, 1337-42/1958-63.

Moᶜtażed, Khosrow. *Ḥâjj Amin ož-Ẓarb: târikh-e tejârat va sarmâyeh gozâri sanᶜati dar irân*. Tehran, 1987.

Nafisi, Saᶜid. *Shaykh Zâhed-e Gilâni*. Rasht, 1307.

Nâṣer-e Khosrow. *Safarnâmeh*. Edited and translated by Charles Schefer. *Sefer Nameh; relation du voyage de Nassiri Khosrau*. Paris, 1881.

Nâṣer od-Din Shâh. *Ketâb-e ruznâmeh-ye safar-e homâyun bi mâzandarân*. Tehran, 1294/1877. [Reprint. *Ruznâmeh-ye safar-e mâzandarân*. Tehran, 2536/1977.]

—. *Safarnâmeh-ye ᶜatabât*. Edited by Iraj Afshâr. Tehran, 1363/1984-85.

Nâyeb oṣ-Ṣadr Shirâzi, Moḥammad Maᶜṣum-ᶜalishâh. *Toḥfat ol-ḥaramayn*. Bombay, 1306/1889.

—. *Safarnâmeh-ye Nâyeb oṣ-Ṣadr Shirâzi dar ziârat-e makkeh*. Tehran, 1362/1983-84.

—. *Ṭarâ'eq ol-ḥaqâ'eq*. Tehran, 1316-19/1898-1901. [Edited by Moḥammad Maḥjub. Tehran, 1345/1966.]

Nozhat ol-nâẓerin fi târikh beladollah ol-amin. MS. Leiden: University Library, Or. 14.026.

Nuri, Ḥosayn Sa^c^âdat. "Ḥâjj Mirzâ Âqâsi." *Yaghmâ* 20(1346/1967-68):17-25.

—. "Mosâferat-e Nâṣer od-Din Shâh beh khorâsân." *Yaghmâ* 11(1326-27/1947-48):61-67.

—. "Mo^c^tamad od-Dowleh-hâ." *Yaghmâ* 10(1336/1957-58):30-32.

—. *Rejâl-e dowreh-ye qâjâr*. Tehran, 1364/1985.

—. "Rokn od-Dowleh-hâ." *Vaḥid* 4(1345/1967-68):585-593.

—. *Ẓell os-Solṭân*. Tehran, 1347/1968.

—. *Zendegi-ye Ḥâjj Mirzâ Âqâsi*. Tehran, 1356/1977.

Nüzhet [Gerçek], Selim. *Türk gazeteciliği*. Istanbul, 1931.

Ölçer, Cüneyt. *Sultan Abdülmecid devri osmanlı madenî paraları*. Istanbul, 1978.

Pakalın, Mehmet Zeki. *Osmanlı tarih deyimleri ve terimleri sözlügü*. Istanbul, 1971.

Pere, Nuri. *Osmanlılarda madenî paralar*. Istanbul, 1968.

Pirzâdeh, Ḥâjji Moḥammad ^c^Ali. *Safarnâmeh*. Edited by Ḥâfeẓ Farmân-farmâ'iân. Tehran, 1342-43/1963-65.

Qâ'em-maqâmi, Jehângir. "Rejâl-e dowreh-ye qâjâreyyeh: Malek ol-Kottâb ^c^eshrat-e Farâhâni." *Yâdgâr* 4/viii(1326/1947-48):22-34.

Qâsem, Jemâl. "od-Davâfe^c^ os-siyâseyyeh le-reḥlât ol-urobeyin ilâ najd va'l-ḥejâz khelâl ol-qarn ot-tâse^c^ ^c^ashr va avâ'el ol-qarn ol-^c^ashrin." In ^c^A. Anṣâri (ed.), *Sources for the History of Arabia*. Riyadh, 1979. Volume 2, pp. 9-28.

Qazvini, Ḥamdollah. *Târikh-e gozideh*. Edited by ^c^Abd ol-Ḥosayn Navâ'i. Tehran, 1339/1961.

Qazvini, Moḥammad. "Vafiyât-e mo^c^âṣerin." In *Yâdgâr* 3(1325/1946-47)/iii:27-39, iv:7-21, v:38-39, vi/vii:50-59, x:12-25; 5(1327-28/1948-49)/i:89-110, iii:51-72, iv/v:79-91, vi/vii:122-135, viii/ix:66-72.

Râ'ef, Moḥammad. *Mer'ât-e estânbul*. Istanbul, 1316/1898.

Rafi^c^, Moḥammad. *Makkeh fi'l-qarn ol-râbe^c^-^c^ashar ol-hejri*. Mecca, 1401/1981.

Râ'in, Esmâ^c^il. *Farâmushkhâneh va frâmâsunri dar irân*. Tehran, 1348/1969.

Razmârâ, General ^c^Ali. *Joghfrâfiyâ-ye neẓâmi-ye irân*. Vol. III. *Gilân va mâzanderân*. Tehran, 1320/1941-42.

Ref^c^at, Aḥmad [Yağlıkçızde]. *Loghât-e târikheyyeh va joghrafeyyeh*. Istanbul, 1299-1300/1882-83.

Ref^c^at Pâshâ, Ebrâhim. *Mer'ât ol-ḥaramayn*. Cairo, 1344/1925.

S̲a^c^âlebi, Abu Manṣur. *Ghorar os-siar*. Edited and translated by H. Zotenberg. *Histoire des rois des perses*. Paris, 1900.

Ṣabri Pâshâ, Eyyub. *Mer'ât ol-ḥaramayn*. Istanbul, 1304/1886. [Two volumes.]

Ṣâdeq Pâshâ, Moḥammad. *Dalil ol-ḥajj*. Bulaq, 1313/1897.

Ṣafâ, Esmâ^c^il Navvâb. *Sharḥ ḥâl-e Farhâd Mirzâ Mo^c^tamad od-Dowleh*. Tehran, 1987.

Ṣafadi, Khalil b. Aybak. *Ketâb ol-vâfi be'l-vafayât*. Edited by Sven Dedering, et al. *Das Biographische Lexikon des Ṣalâḥaddin H̲alil ibn Aibak aṣ-Ṣafadi*. Wiesbaden, 1962-[in progress].

Sâlnâmeh-ye devlet-e âli-ye ^c^os̲mâneyyeh. Istanbul, 1302-3/1885-86.

Sanusi, Moḥammad. *or-Rehleh ol-ḥejâzeyyeh*. Edited by ^c^Ali Shenufi. Cairo, 1976.

Sayf od-Dowleh, Solṭân Moḥammad. *Safarnâmeh-ye makkeh*. Edited by ᶜAli Akbar Khodâparast. Tehran, 1364/1985.

Sebâᶜi, Aḥmad. *Târikh makkeh*. Mecca, 1372/1952-53.

Şevket, Mahmud. *Osmanlı askeri teşkilâti ve kiyâfeti*. Ankara, 1983.

Shafiᶜzâdeh, Moḥsen. "Maᶜni-ye shilât." *Yâdgâr* 2/iv(1324/1945):33.

Sharqâvi, Maḥmud. *Makkeh ol-mokarremeh*. Cairo, 1972.

Shaykh or-Ra'is, Abu'l-Ḥasan Mirzâ. *Badâyeᶜ os-samr va vaqâyeᶜ os-safr*. Edited by S. Vahidneyâ. Tehran, 1352/1973.

—. *Montakhab-e nafis*. Tehran, 1950.

Shirâzi, Mirzâ Ṣâleḥ. *Safarnâmeh*. Edited by Esmâᶜil Râ'in. Tehran, 1347/1968.

Sotudeh, Manuchehr. *Az Âstârâ tâ astarâbâd*. Tehran, 1349-53/1970-74.

—. "Baḥr-e naṣâb." *Râhnamâ-ye Ketâb* 11(1347/1968):298-303.

—. *Farhang-e gilaki*. Tehran, 1332/1953.

—. "Târikhcheh-ye shahr-e qazvin." *Bar-rasihâ-ye Târikhi* 4(1348/1969-70):95-132, 165-210.

Ṭabari, Abu Jaᶜfar Moḥammad b. Jarir. *Târikh or-rosol va'l-moluk*. Edited by M. J. de Goeje. Leiden, 1879-1903.

Ṭâheri, Abu'l-Qâsem. *Joghrâfiyâ-ye târikhi-ye gilân, mâzandarân va âzarbâyjân az naẓar-e jahân-gardân*. Tehran, 1347/1968-69.

Ṭâleqâni, Abu'l-Ḥasan. *Beh suy-e khodâ miravim: bâ ham beh ḥajj beravim*. Tehran, 1332/1953.

Ṭarabzun velâyateneh makhṣuṣ sâlnameh. Trabzon, 1316/1898.

Taymuri, Ebrâhim. *ᶜAṣr-e bi-khabari yâ târikh-e emteyâzât dar irân*. Tehran, 1332/1953-54.

Tonakâboni, M. Solaymân. *Qeṣaṣ ol-ᶜolamâ*. Tehran, n. d. [Published with edition of Murtażâ b. Dâᶜi, *Tabṣirat ol-ᶜavâmm*.]

Unat, Faik. *Hicrî tarihleri milâdî tarihe çevirme kılavuzu*. Ankara, 1984.

Yâqut, Shehâb od-Din Yaᶜqub b. ᶜAbdollah. *Moᶜjam ol-boldân*. Cairo, 1323-25/1906-7.

Works in European Languages (Including Translations)

Abbasi, Muhammad Y. "Arabia in the Accounts of the South Asian Travellers." *Islamic Studies* 18(1979):49-63.

Abbott, Keith. "Notes on Ghilan." *Proceedings of the Royal Geographical Society* 3(1858-59):30-95.

Abbott, Nabia. *Two Queens of Baghdad*. Chicago, 1946.

ᶜAbd ol-Karim. *Bayân-e vâqeᶜ*. Translated by Frances Gladwin. *Memoirs of Khojeh Abdulkarrem*. Calcutta, 1788.

Abdel-Hamid, M. S. "Literature of Eastern Travel and the Romantic Movement." *Bulletin of the Faculty of Arts* (University of Cairo) 19(1957):25-32.

Abu-Manneh, Butrus. "Sultan Abdülhamid II and the Sharifs of Mecca (1880-1900)." *Asian and African Studies* 9(1973):1-21.

Abu Ṭâleb Khân. *Travels in Asia, Africa and Europe*. Translated by Charles Stewart. London, 1810.

Adamec, Ludwig (ed.). *Historical Gazetteer of Iran*. Vol. I, *Tehran and Northwestern Iran*. Graz, 1976.

Akhtar, Waḥid. "Al-Sayyid al-Murtażâ: Life and Works." *Tawhid* 4/i(1407/1986):125-152.

—. "Shaykh al-Ṭâ'ifah al-Ṭusi: His Life and Works." *Tawhid* 4/ii(1407/1986):126-167.

Akiner, Shirin. *Islamic Peoples of the Soviet Union*. London, 1986. [Revised edition.]

al-Alem, Mustafa. "A Guide to Hajj Rituals." *Muslim World League Monthly Magazine* 3/x (1385/1966):52-58.

Alexander, Grant. "The Story of the Ka'ba." *Muslim World* 28(1938):43-53.

Algar, Hamid. "An Introduction to the History of Freemasonry in Iran." *Middle Eastern Studies* 6(1970):276-296.

—. *Religion and State in Iran 1785-1906: The Role of the Ulama*. Berkeley, 1969.

—. "The Revolt of Agha Khan Mahallati and the Transference of the Isma'ili Imamate to India." *Studia Islamica* 29(1969):55-81.

Ali, Maulana Muhammad. *The Religion of Islam*. Cairo, n.d.

Ali Bey Al Abbassi (Domingo Badia Y Leiblich.) *Voyages en Afrique et en Asie pendant les années 1803 à 1807*. Paris, 1814.

Ali Khan, Hadji Gazanfar, and Sparroy, Wilfred. *With the Pilgrims to Mecca: The Great Pilgrimage of A.H. 1319, A.D. 1902*. London, 1905.

Allen, W.E.D. and Muratoff, Paul. *Caucasian Battlefields*. Cambridge, 1953.

Amin, Hassan. *Islamic Shi'ite Encyclopaedia*. Beirut, n. d.

al-Amr, Ṣâleḥ. *The Hejaz Under Ottoman Rule 1869-1914*. Riyadh, 1978.

And, Metin. "The Muḥarram Observances in Anatolian Turkey." In P. Chelkowski (ed.), *Taᶜziyeh: Ritual and Drama in Iran*. New York, 1979. Pp. 238-254.

Anet, Claude. *Through Persia in a Motor Car*. New York, 1908.

Ankawi, Abdullah. "The Pilgrimage to Mecca in Mamluk Times." *Arabian Studies* 1(1974):146-170.

Anṣâri, ᶜAbd or-Raḥman (ed.). *Sources for the History of Arabia*. Riyadh, 1979.

Arendonk, C. van. *Les Débuts de l'imamat Zaidite au Yemen*. Translated by J. Ryckmans. Leiden, 1960.

Arjomand, Said Amir (ed.) *Authority and Political Culture in Shi'ism*. Albany, 1988.

Arnold, A. *Through Persia by Caravan*. London, 1877.

Asgharali Engineer. *The Bohras*. Sahibabad, 1980.

Aslanapa, Oktay. *Turkish Art and Architecture*. New York, 1971.

ᶜAṭṭâr, Farid od-Din. *Manṭeq oṭ-ṭayr.* Translated by Afkham Darbandi and Dick Davis. *The Conference of the Birds*. New York, 1984.

Augustinovic, A. *"El-Khader" e il Profeta Elia*. Jerusalem, 1971. [English translation. *El Khader and the Prophet Elijah*. Jerusalem, 1972.]

Ayoub, Mahmoud. "Dhimmah in Qur'an and Hadith." *Arab Studies Quarterly* 5(1983):172-182.

—. *Redemptive Suffering in Islam: A Study of the Devotional Aspects of Ashura in Twelver Shi'ism*. The Hague, 1978.

Babinger, Franz. *Mehmed der Eroberer und seine Zeit*. Translated by Ralph Manheim. *Mehmed the Conqueror and His Time*. Princeton, 1978.

Baker, V. *Clouds in the East*. London, 1873.

Bakhash, Shaul. *Iran: Monarchy, Bureaucracy & Reform under the Qajars*. London, 1978.

Baktash, Mayel. "Ta'ziyeh and Its Philosophy." In P. Chelkowski (ed.), *Ta'ziyeh: Ritual and Drama in Iran*. New York, 1979. Pp. 95-120.

Balâẕori, Aḥmad b. Yaḥyâ. *Ketâb fotuḥ ol-boldân*. Translated by P. K. Hitti and F. C. Murgotten, *The Origins of the Islamic State*. New York, 1916-24.

Bannerth, E. "Aspects humaines de la Shâdhiliyya en Egypte." *Mélanges de l'Institut Dominicaines d'Etudes Orientales du Cairo* 11(1972):237-250.

Barbir, Karl. *Ottoman Rule in Damascus*. Princeton, 1980.

Barois, Jean. *Le Mecque, ville interdite*. Paris, 1938.

Barthold, W. *An Historical Geography of Iran*. Translated by Svat Soucek. Princeton, 1984.

Bayat, Mangol. *Mysticism and Dissent*. Syracuse, 1982.

Baye, Baron de. *Tiflis, souvenirs d'une mission*. Paris, 1900.

Bazin, Marcel. *Le Tâlesh: Une région ethnique au nord de l'Iran*. Paris, 1980.

— and Bromberger, C. *Gilân et Âzarbâyjân orientales: cartes et documents ethnographiques*. Paris, 1982.

Beeman, William O. *Language, Status and Power in Iran*. Bloomington, 1986.

Bell, R. "The Origin of the Id al-Adha." *Muslim World* 23(1933):117-120.

—. "Muhammad's Pilgrimage Proclamation." *Journal of the Royal Central Asian Society* 24(1937):223-244.

Benda, H. J. "Christian Snouck Hurgronje and the Foundations of Dutch Islamic Policy in Indonesia." *Journal of Modern History* 30(1958):338-347.

Benjamin, S. G. W. *Persia and the Persians*. London, 1887.

Bernard, E. *Le Conseil Sanitaire et Quarantinaire d'Egypte*. Alexandria, 1897.

Bidwell, Robin. *Travellers in Arabia*. London, 1976.

Bilge, Mustafa. "Arabia in the Works of Awliya Chalaby." In ᶜA. Anṣâri (ed). *Sources for the History of Arabia*. Riyadh, 1979. Vol. 2, pp. 213-227.

Biruni, Abu Rayḥân. *Ketâb oṣ-ṣaydaneh fi'ṭ-ṭebb*. Translated by H. M. Said. Karachi, 1973.

Bisheh, Ghazi Izzedin. *The Mosque of the Prophet at Madinah throughout the First Century A.H.* Thesis, University of Michigan, 1979.

Blackwood, P. "The Pilgrimage in 1934." *Muslim World* 25(1935):287-292.

Blake, G., Dawbney, J., and Mitchell, J. *The Cambridge Atlas of the Middle East & North Africa*. Cambridge, 1987.

Blake, G. and King, R. "The Hejaz Railway and the Pilgrimage to Mecca." *Asian Affairs* 3(1972):317-325.

Blake, G. and Swearingen, W. *The Suez Canal: A Commemorative Bibliography*. Durham, 1975.

Blunt, Anne. *A Pilgrimage to Najd*. London, 1888. [Reprint; London, 1968.]

Boital, Fabius. *Nasser-ed-Din Schah et la Perse*. Paris, 1878.

Bondoqji, Ḥosayn Ḥamzeh. *Maps of Hajj to the Holyland–Mecca, Medina*. Cairo, 1397/1977.

Bosworth, C. E. *The Ghaznavids*. Beirut, 1973. [Second edition.]

—. *The Islamic Dynasties*. Edinburgh, 1967.

— and Hillenbrand, C. (eds.). *Qajar Iran: Political, Social and Cultural Change 1800-1925*. Edinburgh, 1983.

Boulangier, Edgar. *Voyage à Merv: Les Russes dans l'Asie Centrale et le Chemin de Fer Transcaspien*. Paris, 1888.

Bousquet, G. H. *Kitâb et-Tanbîh ou le Livre de l'Admonition touchant la Loi Musulmane selon le rite de l'Imâm Ech-Châfé^c^i par le Cheikh et Imâm Abou Ish'aq Ibrahîm ben ^c^Alî Ech-Chirâzî el-Fîrouzabâdhî*. Algiers, 1949.

—. *Les grandes pratiques rituelles de l'Islam*. Paris, 1949.

— and Schacht, J. (eds.). *Selected Works of C. Snouck Hurgronje*. Leiden, 1957.

Bradley-Birt, F. B. *Through Persia, from the Gulf to the Caspian*. London, 1909.

Brandenburg, D. *Die Madrasa--Ursprung, Entwicklung, Ausbreitung und künstlerische Gestaltung der islamischen Moschee-Hochschule*. Graz, 1978.

Breccia, Evarish. *Alexandrea ad Aegyptum*. Bergamo, 1922.

Brent, Peter. *Far Arabia*. London, 1977.

Bretannitsky, L. "Baku's Historic Inner City." *Crossroads* 1(1977):37-40.

Brockelmann, Carl. *Geschichte der arabischen Literatur*. Leiden, 1934-39.

Brosset, M. "Rapport de M. Brosset sur les voyages exécutés sous les auspices du Prince Vorontsov, lieutenant du Caucase, par M. Dimitri Méghwineth-Khoutsésov." *Mélanges Asiatiques* 2(1852-56):69-89.

Browne, Edward. *A Literary History of Persia*. Cambridge, 1930. [Reprint.]

—. "The Persian Press and Persian Journalism." London, 1913. [Lecture.]

—. *The Persian Revolution of 1905-1909*. Cambridge, 1910.

—. *The Press and Poetry of Modern Persia*. Cambridge, 1914.

—. *A Year Amongst the Persians*. London, 1926. [Second edition.]

Brownson, M. J. "Mecca: The Socio-Economic Dynamics of the Sacred City." In Z. Sardar and M. A. Badawi (eds.). *Hajj Studies*. 1(1978):117-136.

Brugsch, Heinrich. *Im Lande der Sonne*. Berlin, 1886.

Bulliet, Richard. "The Shaikh al-Islâm and the Evolution of Islamic Society." *Studia Islamica* 35(1972):53-67.

Burckhardt, John Lewis. *Travels in Arabia*. London, 1829.

Burton, Sir R. F. *Personal Narrative of a Pilgrimage to al-Madineh and Meccah*. London, 1893. ("Memorial Edition.")

Bushnak, A. "The Hajj Transportation System." In Z. Sardar and M. A. Badawi (eds.), *Hajj Studies* 1(1978):87-116.

Busse, Heribert. *Chalif und Grosskönig*. Beirut, 1969.

Calmard, J. "Le mécénat des representations de ta'ziye. I. Les Précurseurs de Nâseroddin Châh." *Le Monde Iranien et l'Islam* 2(1974):73-126.

—. "Le mécénat des representations de ta'ziye. II. Les débuts de règne de Nâseroddin Châh." *Le Monde Iranien et l'Islam* 4(1976-77):133-162.

—. "Muharram Ceremonies and Diplomacy (a preliminary study)." In C. E. Bosworth and C. Hillenbrand (eds.), *Qajar Iran: political, social and cultural change 1800-1925*. Edinburgh, 1983. Pp. 213-228.

Çelik, Zeynep. *The Remaking of Istanbul: Portrait of an Ottoman City in the Nineteenth Century*. Seattle, 1986.

Chelhod, J. "Les attitudes et les gestes de la prière rituelle dans l'Islam." *Revue de l'Histoire des Religions* 156(1959):161-188.

Chelkowski, Peter (ed.). *Ta'ziyeh: ritual and drama in Iran*. New York, 1979.

Cherif, Ahmed. *Le Pèlerinage de la Mecque. Essai d'histoire, de psychologie et d'hygiène sur le voyage sacré de l'Islam*. Beirut, 1930.

Chodzko, Aleksander. *Le Gîlân; ou, les Marais Caspiens: description historique et géographique du pays qui borde au sud de la Mer Caspienne*. Paris, 1850.

Chowdhry, R. *Al-Hajjaj Ibn Yûsuf*. Delhi, 1972.

Ḥâfeẓ. *The Dîvân-i Ḥâfeẓ*. Translated by H. Wilberforce Clarke. Calcutta, 1891.

Clemens, C. "Der ursprungliche Sinn des *hagg*." *Der Islam* 10(1920):161-177.

Clemow, F. G. "The Constantinople Board of Health." *Lancet* 1(1923):1074-1080.

Cole, Juan. "Imami Jurisprudence and the Role of the Ulama." In N. Keddie (ed.), *Religion and Politics in Iran*. New Haven, 1983. Pp. 33-46.

Corbin, H. *L'École Shaykhie en théologie shi'ite*. Tehran, 1957.

Cordier, G. "Un Voyage à la Mecque." *Revue du monde musulman* 14(1911):510-513.

Courtellemont, G. *Mon Voyage à la Mecque*. Paris, 1896.

Cragg, Kenneth. "Pilgrimage Prayers." *Muslim World* 45(1955):269-280.

Creswell, K. A. C. *Early Muslim Architecture*. Oxford, 1932-40.

Cunynghame, Arthur. *Travels in the Eastern Caucasus*. London, 1872.

Curzon, George. *Persia and the Persian Question*. London, 1892. [Reprint; London, 1966.]

Damiani, Anita. *Enlightened Observers: British travellers to the Near East 1715-1850*. Beirut, 1975.

D'Avril, Adolphe. *L'Arabie contemporaine, avec la description du pèlerinage à la Mecque*. Paris, 1868.

DeAmicis, Edmondo. *Constantinople*. Philadelphia, 1896.

Desjardins, P. A. *La Turquie Officielle*. Paris, 1891.

Dethier, P. A. *Le Bosphore et Constantinople*. Vienna, 1875.

De Windt, Harry. *A Ride to India Across Persia and Baluchistan*. London, 1891.

Dixon, A. *The Umayyad Caliphate*. London, 1971.

Dodwell, H. *The Founder of Modern Egypt*. Cambridge, 1931.

Donaldson, Dwight. *The Shi'ite Religion*. London, 1933.

Dorn, B. *Bemerkungen auf Anlass einer Wissenschaftlichen Reise in dem Kaukasus und den Südlichen Küstenländern des Kaspichen Meeres in den Jahren 1860-61. Reise nach Masanderan im Jahre 1860*. St. Petersburg, 1895.

—. "Bericht über eine wissenschaftliche Reise in dem Kaukasus und den Küstenländern des Kaspischen Meeres." *Mélanges Asiatiques* 4(1860-63):429-500.

—. *Beiträge zur Geschichte der kaukasischen Länder und Völker*. Leipzig, 1967. [Reprint.]

—. "Geschichte Schirwans unter den Statthaltern und Chanen von 1538-1820." *Mémoires de l'Académie Impériale des Sciences de St.-Pétersbourg, VIme Série, Sciences Politiques, Histoire et Philologie* 5(1842):317-434.

—. *Muhammedanische Quellen zur Geschichte der südlichen Küstenländer des Kaspischen Meeres*. St. Petersburg, 1850-58.

—. *Reise nach Masanderan im Jahre 1860*. St. Petersburg, 1895.

—. "Versuch einer Geschichte der Schirwanschahe." *Mémoires de l'Académie Impériale des Sciences de St.-Pétersbourg, VIme Série, Sciences Politiques, Histoire et Philologie* 4(1841):523-602.

Doughty, C. M. *Arabia Deserta*. Cambridge, 1888.

Douglas, E. H. "Al-Shâdhilî, a North African Sufi." *Muslim World* 38(1948):257-279.

Drouville, G. *Voyage en Perse pendant les années 1812 et 1813*. St. Petersburg, 1820.

Druzhinin, V. *Molokane*. Leningrad, 1930.

Duguet, F. *Le Pèlerinage de la Mecque au point de vue religieux, social et sanitaire*. Paris, 1932.

Dunlop, D. M. *The History of the Jewish Khazars*. Princeton, 1954.

Eastwick, Edward. *Journal of A Diplomate's Three Years' Residence in Persia*. London, 1864.

Ebn Baṭṭuṭeh, Moḥammad b. ᶜAbdollah. *Reḥleh*. Translated by H. A. R. Gibb. *The Travels of Ibn Baṭṭuṭa A. D. 1325-1354*. Cambridge, 1958. [Volume I.]

Ebn Esḥâq, Moḥammad. *Sirat rasul ollah*. Translated by A. Guillaume. *The Life of Muhammad: A translation of Ibn Ishaq's Sirat Rasul Allah*. Oxford, 1955.

Ebn Khallekân, Shams od-Din. *Ketâb vafayât ol-aᶜyân*. Translated by Bⁿ Mac Guckin de Slane. *Ibn Khallikan's Biographical Dictionary*. Paris, 1842-43.

Ebn Qodâmeh, Movaffaq od-Din. *Ketâb ol-ᶜomdeh fi'l-feqh*. Translated by Henri Laoust. *Le Précis de droit d'Ibn Qudâma*. Beirut, 1950.

L'Écluse, Charles de. *Monnaies de tous les pays du monde*. Paris, 1887.

Edib, Mehmet. *Manâsek ol-ḥajj*. Translated by M. Bianchi. *Itineraire de Constantinople à la Mecque*. Paris, 1825.

EI_1. [See *Encyclopaedia of Islam*.]

EI_2. [See *Encyclopaedia of Islam: New Edition*.]

Eichwald, E. *Periplus des Caspischen Meeres*. Stuttgart, 1834.

—. *Reise auf dem Caspischen Meere und in den Caucasus, unternommen in den Jahren 1825-1826*. Stuttgart & Tubingen, 1834-38.

Encyclopaedia of Islam: A Dictionary of the Geography, Ethnography and Biography of the Muhammadan Peoples. Edited by M. Th. Houtsma *et al*. Leiden, 1913-38.

Encyclopaedia of Islam: New Edition. Edited by H. A. R. Gibb *et al.* Leiden, 1954-[in progress].
English, Paul W. "The Origin and Spread of Kanats in the Old World." *Proceedings of the American Philosophical Society* 112(1968):170-181.
Esin, Emel. "Episodes of the Last Restoration of the Kaᶜbah (1039-40/1629-30)." *Islam Today* 1(1983):21-25.
—. *Mecca the Blessed, Madinah the Radiant*. London, 1963.
Eskandar Beg Monshi. *Târikh-e ᶜâlam ârâ-ye ᶜabbâsi.* Translated by R. Savory. *History of Shah 'Abbas the Great*. Boulder, 1978.
Ettinghausen, Richard. "Die bildliche Darstellung der Ka'ba im Islamischen Kultur Kreis." *Zeitschrift der deutschen Morgenländischer Gesellschaft* 87(1933):111-137.
Eusebius. *The History of the Church*. Translated by G. A. Williamson. New York, 1965.
Euting, Julius. *Tagbuch einer Reise in Inner-Arabien.* Leiden, 1896-1914.
Fabri, Felix. *The Wanderings of Felix Fabri*. Translated by A. Stewart. London, 1893.
Fahd, T. "Le Pèlerinage à la Mecque." In F. Raphael *et al. Les Pèlerinages: De l'antiquité biblique et classique à l'occident médiéval*. Paris, 1973. Pp. 65-94.
Farmayan, Hafez F. "The Forces of Modernization in Nineteenth Century Iran: A Historical Survey." In William Polk & Richard Chambers (eds.), *Beginnings of Modernization in the Middle East*. Chicago, 1968. Pp. 119-151.
—. "Amin od-Dowleh: Portrait of a Nineteenth Century Iranian Statesman." *International Journal of Middle East Studies* 15(1983):337-351.
—. *Iran's Fateful Years 1870-1907: Khâtirât-i Sîyâsîy-i Mirzâ 'Alî Khân-i Amînu'd-Dowla, The Political Memoirs of Mîrzâ 'Alî Khân Amînu'd-Dowla*. Tehran, 1977.
Farsi, Zaki M. *City Map and Hajj Guide of Makkah al-Mukarramah.* Jedda, 1983.
Ferdowsi, Abu'l-Qâsem. *Shâhnâmeh*. Abridged translation by R. Levy. *The Epic of the Kings*. London, 1967.
Ferrand, Gabriel. "Notes de Voyage au Guilân." *Bulletin de la Société de Géographie d'Alger* 7(1902):281-320.
Fesch, Paul. *Constantinople aux derniers jours d'Abdul-Hamid*. Paris, 1907.
Feuvrier, Jean-Baptiste. *Trois ans à la cour de Perse*. Paris, 1889.
Findley, Carter. *Bureaucratic Reform in the Ottoman Empire*. Princeton, 1980.
Flandin, Eugène and Coste, Pascal. *Voyage en Perse*. Paris, 1851-54.
Floor, W. M. "The Merchants (*tujjâr*) in Qajar Iran." *Zeitschrift der Deutschen Morgenländischen Gesellschaft* 126(1976):101-135.
Flügel, G. *Concordantiae Corani Arabicae*. Leipzig, 1842.
Forster, E. M. *Alexandria: A History and a Guide*. Alexandria, 1938.
Fraser, James Baillie. *Travels and Adventures into the Persian Provinces on the Southern Banks of the Caspian Sea*. London, 1826.
Freeth, Zahra and Winstone, H. V. F. *Explorers of Arabia*. New York, 1978.
Freygang, Frederika. *Lettres sur le Caucase et la Géorgie suivies d'un relation d'un voyage en Perse en 1812*. Hamburg, 1816.

Freygang, W. *Briefe über den Kaukasus und Georgien*. Hamburg, 1817.

Gabriel, Alfons. *Die Erforschung Persiens*. Vienna, 1952.

Gaudefroy-Demombynes, M. *Le Pèlerinage à la Mekke. Étude d'histoire religieuse*. Paris, 1923.

Gaury, Gerald de. *Rulers of Mecca*. London, 1951.

General Instructions for Pilgrims to the Hedjaz and a Manual for the Guidance of Officers and Others Concerned in the Red Sea Pilgrim Traffic. Calcutta, 1922.

Gervais-Courtellement, Jules. *Mon voyage à la Mecque*. Paris, 1896.

Ghorbal, Shafik. *The Beginnings of the Egyptian Question and the Rise of Mehmet Ali*. London, 1928.

Gmelin, Samuel. *Reise durch Russland zur Untersuchung der Drey Natur-Reiche. 3er Theil: Reise durch das nördliche Persien in dem Jahren 1770, 1771 bis in April 1772*. St. Petersburg, 1774.

Goblot, H. *Les Qanats: une technique d'acquisition de l'eau*. Paris, 1979.

Goeje, M. J. de. *Bibliotheca Geographorum Arabicorum*. Leiden, 1870-77.

—. *Memoire sur les Carmathes de Bahrain*. Leiden, 1886.

Goldziher, Ignaz. "Das Prinzip der Taḳijja im Islam." *Zeitschrift der Deutschen Morgenländischen Gesellschaft* 60(1906):213-226.

—. *Introduction to Islamic Theology and Law*. Translated by Andras and Ruth Hamori. Princeton, 1981.

Gouilly, Alphonse. "Le Pèlerinage à la Mecque." *Revue juridique et politique* 18(1964):99-106.

Graham, Stephen. *A Vagabond in the Caucasus*. London, 1911.

Grosvenor, Edwin. *Constantinople*. Boston, 1900.

Grunebaum, G. E. von. *Muhammadan Festivals*. London, 1951; reprint, London, 1976.

Guarmani, Carlo. *Il Neged Settentrionale*. Jerusalem, 1866. Translated by Lady Capel-Cure. *Northern Najd*. London, 1938.

Guillini, E. "Essai sur le Ghilan." *Bulletin de la Société de Géographie de Paris* (1866). Section V/ii:81-104.

Haidari, I. *Zur Soziologie des Schiitischen Chiliasmus: Ein Beitrag zur Erforschung das irakischen Passionsspiels*. Freiburg, 1975.

Hakimian, Hassan. "Wage Labor and Migration: Persian Workers in Southern Russia, 1880-1914." *International Journal of Middle East Studies* 17(1985):443-462.

Hamarneh, Sami. *Al-Biruni's Book on Pharmacy and Materia Medica*. Karachi, 1973.

Hamidullah, M. *Le pèlerinage à la Mecque*. Paris, 1960.

Hanway, Jonas. *An Historical Account of the British Trade Over the Caspian Sea*. London, 1753.

Harawi, ᶜAli b. Abi Bakr. *Ketâb ol-eshârât elâ maᶜrefat oz-ziârât*. Translated by Janine Sourdel-Thomine. *Guide des Lieux de Pèlerinage*. Damascus, 1957.

Ḥasan-e Fasâ'i. *Fârsnâmeh-ye Nâṣeri*. Translated by H. Busse. *History of Persia under Qâjâr Rule*. New York, 1972.

Haslip, Joan. *The Sultan: the Life of Abdul Hamid II*. New York, 1958.

Hawting, G. R. "The Origins of the Muslim Sanctuary at Mecca." In G. H. A. Juynboll. *Studies on the First Century of Islamic Society*. Carbondale, 1982. Pp. 30-33.

—. "'We were not ordered with entering it but only with circumambulating it.' Ḥadith and fiqh on entering the Ka^cba." *Bulletin of the School of Oriental and African Studies* (London) 47(1984):228-242.

Ḥayyim, Solaymân. *Persian-English Proverbs*. Tehran, 1956.

Henry, J. D. *Baku: An Eventful History*. London, 1905.

Herodotus. *History*. Edited by A. D. Godley. *Herodotus*. Cambridge, Mass., 1922-38.

Hess, J. J. *Die geographische Lage Mekkas und die Strasse von Gidda nach Mekka*. Freiburg, 1900.

Hinz, Walther. *Islamische Masse und Gewichte umgerechnet ins metrische System*. Leiden, 1955.

Hitti, P. K. *History of the Arabs*. Tenth edition; New York, 1970.

Hodgson, Marshall. *The Order of Assassins*. Gravenhage, 1955.

Ḥodûd ol-ᶜâlam. Translated and annoted by V. Minorsky. *Ḥudûd al-ᶜÂlam: The Regions of the World, a Persian Geography 372 A.H.-982 A.D.* London, 1970. [Second edition, edited by C. E. Bosworth.]

Hogarth, D. G. *Hejaz Before World War I*. London, 1917. [Revised edition; London, 1978.]

Hollister, John. *The Shi'a of India*. Second edition; Delhi, 1979.

Holmes, William R. *Sketches of the Shores of the Caspian*. London, 1845.

Holt, P. M. *Egypt and the Fertile Crescent*. Cornell, 1966.

—. *The Mahdist State in the Sudan 1881-1898*. Oxford, 1970. [Second edition.]

Hommaire de Hell, Xavier. *Voyage en Turquie et en Perse*. Paris, 1854.

Hone, J. M. and Dickinson, Page. *Persia in Revolution with Notes of Travel in the Caucasus*. London, 1910.

Horak, Stephan. *Guide to the Study of the Soviet Nationalities*. Littleton, 1982.

Hornsby, Mrs. Edmund. *In and Around Stamboul*. London, 1858.

Howard, I. K. A. "Great Works of Shii Islam: *Tahdhib al-Ahkam* and *al-Istibsar* by al-Shaikh al-Tusi." *Al-Serat* 2(1976):22-26.

Huber, Charles. *Journal d'un voyage en Arabie (1883-84)*. Paris, 1891.

Hujviri, ᶜAli b. ᶜOs̱mân. *Kashf ol-maḥjub*. Translated by R. Nicholson. *The Kashf al-Mahjub of Al-Hujwiri*. London, 1911.

Hughes, Thomas. *Dictionary of Islam*. London, 1895.

Hurgronje, Christian Snouck. "Der Hadji-politiek der Indischen Regerung." In *Verspreide Geschriften*. Bonn & Leiden, 1924. Pp. 173-198.

—. *Het Mekkaansche Feest*. Leiden, 1880.

—. *Mekka*. The Hague, 1888-89.

—. *Mekka in the Latter Part of the Nineteenth Century*. Translated by J. H. Monohan. London, 1931.

—. "Some of My Experiences with the Muftis of Mecca (1885)." *Asian Affairs* 64(1977):25-37.

Ibrahimoff. "Les noms ethniques actuels des divers peuples du Caucase." *Revue du monde musulman* 11(1910):97-99.

—. "Les Tourkmens: leur steppes et leur coutumerie." *Revue du monde musulman* 9(1909):124-143.

Issawi, Charles. *The Economic History of Iran 1800-1914*. Chicago, 1971.

—. *The Economic History of the Middle East, 1800-1914*. Chicago, 1966.

—. "The Tabriz-Trabzon Trade, 1830-1900: rise and decline of a route." *International Journal of Middle East Studies* 1(1970):18-27.

Ivanow, W. *The Rise of the Fatimids*. Calcutta, 1942.

—. *A Guide to Ismaili Literature*. London, 1933.

Izzedine, Cassim. *Le Choléra et l'Hygiène à la Mecque*. Paris, 1909.

Jackson, A. V. Williams. *Constantinople to the Home of Omar Khayyam*. New York, 1911.

—. *Persia, Past and Present*. New York, 1906.

Jomier, J. "La Figure d'Abraham et le pèlerinage musulman de la Mekke." *Mélanges Eugène Tisserant*. Paris, 1964. Pp. 229-244.

—. *Le Mahmal et la caravane égyptienne des pèlerins de la Mekke, xiiie-xxe siècles*. Cairo, 1953.

Jondet, Gaston. *Atlas historique de la ville et des ports d'Alexandrie*. Cairo, 1921.

Juynboll, T. W. *Handbuch des islamischen Rechtes*. Leiden, 1910.

Kabir, Mafizullah. *The Buwayhid Dynasty of Baghdad*. Calcutta, 1964.

Kamal, Ahmad. *The Sacred Journey: Being Pilgrimage to Makkah*. New York, 1961.

Karny, Azriel. "The Premierships of Mirzâ Ḥossein Khan and His Reforms in Iran." *Asian and African Studies* 10(1974-75):127-156.

Katz, Zev *et al.* (eds.). *Handbook of Major Soviet Nationalities*. New York, 1975.

Kazemzadeh, Firuz. *Russia and Britain in Persia, 1864-1914*. New Haven, 1968.

Kazem Zadeh, H. *Relation d'un Pèlerinage à la Mecque en 1910-1911*. Paris, 1912.

Keane, T. F. *My Journey to Medinah*. London, 1881.

—. *Six Months in Mecca*. London, 1881.

—. *Six Months in the Hejaz*. London, 1887.

Kelly, J. B. *Britain and the Persian Gulf 1795-1880*. Oxford, 1968.

Kelly, Laurence (ed.). *Istanbul: A Traveller's Companion*. New York, 1987.

Khanikof, Nicholas de. "Voyage scientifique de M. Dorn dans le Mâzandérân, le Caucase et le Dâghestân." *Journal Asiatique* (1862), pp. 214-225.

Kharegat, Rustam. *A Tourist Guide to Iran*. Bombay, 1935.

Kholaif, Ali Ibrahim. "The Hejaz Vilayat, 1869-1908: The Sharifate, the Hajj, and the Bedouins of the Hijaz." Ph.D. Thesis. Madison, 1986.

Khomayni, Âyatollah Ruḥollah. *Resâleh towżiḥ ol-masâ'el*. Translated by J. Borujerdi. *A Clarification of Questions*. Boulder, 1984.

Kiernan, R. H. *The Unveiling of Arabia*. Harrap, 1937.

King, Geoffrey. "Some European Travellers in Najd in the 19th and Early 20th Centuries." In ᶜA. Anṣâri (ed.), *Sources for the History of Arabia*. Riyadh, 1979. Volume 2, pp. 255-265.

Kinross, Patrick Balfour. *Between Two Seas: the creation of the Suez Canal*. London, 1968.

Kister, M. J. "The Battle of the Ḥarra. Some Socio-economic Aspects." In M. Rosen-Ayalon (ed.), *Studies in Memory of Gaston Wiet*. Jerusalem, 1977. Pp. 33-50.

—. "Maqâm Ibrâhîm, a stone with an inscription." *Museon* 84(1971):477-491.

—. "Some Reports Concerning Mecca from Jahiliyya to Islam." *Journal of the Economic and Social History of the Orient* 15(1972):61-93.

Klibanov, A. I. *History of Religious Sectarianism in Russia*. London, 1982.

Kohlberg, E. "Some Imami Shii Views on Taqiyya." *Journal of the American Oriental Society* 95(1975):395-402.

Koran. Translated by Marmaduke Pickthall. *The Meaning of the Glorious Qur'an*. London, 1930.

Kortepeter, C. M. "A Source for the History of Ottoman-Hijaz Relations: The *Seyahatname* of Awliya Chalaby and the Rebellion of Sharif Sa[c]d b. Zayd in the Years 1671-1672/1081-1082." In A. Anṣari (ed.), *Sources for the History of Arabia*. Riyadh, 1979. Volume 1, pp. 229-246.

Krimly, H. "The Oldest Tour in the World: Mecca Pilgrimage." *World Health* 20(1967):10-13.

Kudsi-Zadeh, A. A. "Iranian Politics in the late Qajar Period." *Middle Eastern Studies* 5(1969):251-257.

Lambton, Ann. *Landlord and Peasant in Persia*. Oxford, 1953.

—. *Qâjâr Persia*. Austin, 1988.

Lammens, Henri. *La Mecque à la vielle de l'Hégire*. Beirut, 1924.

"Le Pèlerinage de la Mecque en 1902: Journal d'un pelerin Egyptien." *Bulletin des missions Belges* (Brussels), 1904.

Landau, Jacob M. "A New Manuscript on the Muslim Pilgrimage." Ve Congrès International d'Arabisants et d'Islamisants. *Actes* (1970):307-316.

—. *The Hejaz Railway and the Muslim Pilgrimage: A Case of Ottoman Political Propaganda*. Detroit, 1971.

Lane, E. W. *Manners and Customs of the Modern Egyptians*. London, 1860.

"Le Feu Perpétuel de Baku." *Journal Asiatique* (second series) 11(1833):358-384.

LeStrange, Guy. *Lands of the Eastern Caliphate*. Third impression; London, 1966.

Lewis, Bernard. *The Emergence of Modern Turkey*. Oxford, 1968.

—. *The Origin of Ismai'ilism*. Cambridge, 1940.

Lockhart, L. *Nâdir Shâh*. London, 1938.

Lokhandwalla, T. "The Bohoras, a Muslim Community of Gujarat." *Studia Islamica* 5(1955):117-135.

Long, David Edwin. *The Hajj Today: A Survey of the Contemporary Makkah Pilgrimage*. Albany, N.Y., 1979.

Loutfi, Z. E. *La Politique sanitaire internationale*. Paris, 1906.

MacEoin, Denis. "From Shaykhism to Babism: a study in charismatic renewal in Shii Islam." Dissertation; Cambridge, 1979.

MacGregor, C. *Journey Through Khorasan*. London, 1878.

Maclean, Fitzroy. *To Caucasus, the End of all the Earth*. London, 1976.

Madelung, W. "A Tradition of the Sharif al-Murtażâ on the Legality of Working for the Government." *Bulletin of the School of Oriental and African Studies* 30(1980):18-31.

—. *Arabic Texts Concerning the History of the Zaydi Imams of Ṭabaristân, Daylamân and Gîlân*. Wiesbaden, 1987.

Makki, M. S. *Medina, Saudi Arabia*. Avesbury (Amersham), 1982.

Makky, G. A. *Mecca: The Pilgrimage City. A Study of Pilgrimage Accomodation*. London, 1978.

Maltzan, H. von. *Meine Wallfahrt nach Mekka*. Leipzig, 1865.

Marsot, Afaf Lutfi Sayyid. *Egypt in the Reign of Muhammad Ali*. Cambridge, 1984.

Martellaro, J. A. "The Acquisition and Leasing of the Baku Oilfields by the Russian Crown." *Middle Eastern Studies* 21(1985):80-88.

Marvin, Charles. *The Region of the Eternal Fire*. London, 1891.

Massé, H. "Le Voyage de Farhâd Mirzâ." In *Mélanges de géographie et d'orientalism offerts à E. F. Gautier*. Paris, 1937. Pp. 348-356.

Masᶜudi, Abu'l-Ḥasan ᶜAli. *Moruj oẕ-ẕahab*. Edited and translated by C. Barbier de Meynard and Pavet de Courteille. *Les Prairies d'or*. Paris, 1861-77.

Matheson, Sylvia. *Persia: an Archaeological Guide*. London, 1972.

Matheson, V. and Milner, A. C. (eds.). *Perceptions of the Haj: Five Malay Texts*. Brookfield, 1986.

Matthews, Anis Daud. *A Guide for Hajj and 'Umra*. Lahore, 1979.

Mazzaoui, Michel. *The Origins of the Ṣafawids*. Wiesbaden, 1972.

McKay, J. P. "Entrepreneurship and the Emergence of the Russian Petroleum Industry, 1813-1883." *Research in Economic History* 8(1982):47-91.

Medlicott, W. N. *The Congress of Berlin and After*. London, 1938.

Melgunof, G. *Die Südliche Ufer des Kaspichen Meeres ofer die Nordprovinzen Persia*. Leipzig, 1868.

—. "Essai sur les dialectes de Mâzandérân et du Ghîlân." *Zeitschrift der Deutschen Morgenländische Gesellschaft* 17(1868):195-224.

Meulen, D. "The Mecca Pilgrimage and its Importance to the Netherlands East Indies." *Muslim World* 31(1941):48-60.

Mey, Jean de. *Repertoire de la numismatique française contemporaine*. Brussels, 1969.

Mikhailovich, Georgii. *Monnaies de l'empire de Russie, 1725-1894*. Paris, 1916.

Minorsky, V. *A History of Sharvân and Darband*. Cambridge, 1958.

—. *Ḥudûd al-ᶜÂlam: The Regions of the World, a Persian Geography 372 A.H.-982 A.D.* London, 1970. [Second edition, edited by C. E. Bosworth.]

—. *Tadhkirat al-Mulûk: A Manual of Ṣafavid Administration*. London, 1943.

Mofakhkham-Pâyân, Loṭfollah. *Étude géographique de la mer Caspienne*. Mashhad, 1969.

—. *Les principales rivières de la région de Guilan*. Mashhad, 1347/1969. [Second edition.]

Momen, Moojan. *An Introduction to Shi'i Islam*. New Haven, 1985.

Monteith, W. "Journal of a Tour through Azerbaijan and the Shores of the Caspian." *Journal of the Royal Geographical Society* 3(1833):1-58.

Moosa, Matti. *Extremist Shiites: The Ghulat Sects*. Syracuse, 1988.
Morgan, David. *Medieval Persia, 1040-1797*. London, 1988.
Mounsey, Augustus. *A Journey Through the Caucasus and the Interior of Persia*. London, 1872.
Mughniyyah, M. Jawâd. "The Hajj According to Five Schools of Islamic Fiqh." *Al-Tawhîd* 2/iv(1405/1984-85):54-70; 3/i:(1406/1985-86):66-79; 3/ii(1406/1985-86):57-65; 3/iii (1406/1985-86):63-93.
Muir, William. *The Caliphate*. Reprint; Beirut, 1963.
Mujtaba Ali, S. *The Origins of the Khodjas*. Bonn, 1936.
Musil, A. *Northern Neğd*. New York, 1928.
Nasr, Seyyed Hossein et al. (eds.) *Shi'ism: Doctrines, Thought, and Spirituality*. Albany, 1988.
Nâṣer-e Khosrow. *Safarnâmeh*. Edited and translated by Charles Schefer. *Sefer Nameh; relation du voyage de Nassiri Khosrau*. Paris, 1881.
—. *Safarnâmeh*. Translated by Wheeler Thackston, Jr. *Nâser-e Khosraw's Book of Travels (Safarnâma)*. Albany, N. Y., 1986.
Nâṣer od-Din Shâh. *Ruznâmeh*. Translated by J. W. Redhouse. *The Diary of H. M. the Shah of Persia during his Tour through Europe in A.D. 1873*. London, 1874.
—. *Ruznâmeh*. Translated by Albert Houtum Schindler and Baron Louis de Norman. *A Diary Kept by His Majesty the Shah of Persia During His Journey to Europe in 1878*. London, 1879.
Nashat, Guity. *The Origins of Modern Reform in Iran 1870-80*. Urbana, 1982.
Nesin, Aziz. *Böyle Gelmiş, Böyle Gitmez*. Translated by Joseph Jacobson. *Istanbul Boy*. Austin, 1977.
Neẓâm ol-Molk. *Siâsatnâmeh*. Translated by Hubert Darke. *The Book of Government or Rules for Kings*. New Haven, 1960.
Nickjoo, Mahvash. "A Persian Statesman (Malcom Khân) on the Eastern Question." *Journal of Asian History* 13(1979):1-14.
Nicolas, A. *Essai sur le Sheikisme*. Paris, 1910.
Niebuhr, Karsten. *Voyage en Arabie et en d'autres pays circonvoisins*. Translated by F. L. Mourier. Amsterdam, 1770-80.
—. *Travels Through Arabia*. Edinburgh, 1792.
Nizámu'd-Din, Muḥammad. *Introduction to the Jawámiʿu'l-Ḥikáyát*. London, 1929.
Ochsenwald, W. "Ottoman Subsidies to the Hejaz, 1877-1886." *International Journal of Middle East Studies* 6(1975):300-307.
—. "The Financial Basis of Ottoman Rule in the Hijaz 1840-1877." In W. Haddad, *Nationalism in a Non-national State*. New York, 1977. Pp. 129-149.
—. *The Hijaz Railroad*. Charlottesville, 1980.
—. "The Jidda Massacre of 1858." *Middle Eastern Studies* 13(1977):314-326.
—. *Religion, Society, and the State in Arabia: The Hijaz under Ottoman Control, 1840-1908*. Columbus, 1984.
O'Donovan, E. *The Merv Oasis*. London, 1880.
Omar, Farouq. *The Abbasid Caliphate*. Baghdad, 1976.

Orsolle, E. *Le Caucase et la Perse*. Paris, 1885.
Palgrave, W. G. *Personal Narrative of a Year's Journey Through Central and Eastern Arabia 1866-67*. Seventh Edition. London, 1875.
Panzac, Daniel. *Quarantaines et Lazarets: L'Europe et la peste d'Orient*. Aix-en-Provence, 1986.
—. *La Peste dans l'empire Ottoman*. Louvain, 1985.
Partin, Harry. "The Muslim Pilgrimage: Journey to the Center." Ph. D. thesis; Chicago, 1967.
Peres, Henri. "Voyageurs musulmans en Europe aux XIXe et XXe Siècles." *Mélanges Maspéro. III. Mémoires...de l'Institut français d'archéologie orientale du Caire* 68(1935):185-195.
Perry, John. *Karim Khan Zand: a History of Iran, 1747-1779*. Chicago, 1979.
Pesce, Angelo. *Jiddah. Portrait of an Arabian City*. Cambridge, 1974.
—. *Mecca a Hundred Years Ago, or C. Snouck Hurgronje's Remarkable Album*. London, 1986.
Peters, F. E. *Jerusalem and Mecca: The Typology of the Holy City in the Near East*. New York, 1986.
Peterson, Samuel. "The Ta'ziyeh and Related Arts." In P. Chelkowski (ed.), *Ta'ziyeh: Ritual and Drama in Iran*. New York, 1979. Pp. 64-87.
Petrov, V. I. *Catalogue des monnaies russes*. Graz, 1964.
Philby, H. St. John B. *Arabia of the Wahhabis*. London, 1928.
—. "Mecca and Madina." *Journal of the Royal Central Asian Society* 20(1933):504-518.
Pirenne, Jacqueline. *A la découverte de l'Arabie*. Paris, 1957.
Pope, Arthur Upham (ed.). *A Survey of Persian Art*. Tehran, 1977. [Third edition.]
Prokhorov, A. M. (ed.). *Great Soviet Encyclopaedia*. New York, 1973-83.
Pudney, John. *Suez; De Lesseps' Canal*. New York, 1969.
Qazvini, Ḥamdollah. *Nozhat ol-qolub*. Translated by G. Le Strange. *The Geographical Part of the Nuzhat al-Qulub*. London, 1919.
Querry, A. *Droit musulman: Recueil de lois concernant les musulmans schyites*. Paris 1871-72. [Translation of Ḥelli, *Sharâ'e^c^ ol-eslâm*.]
Rabino (di Borgomale), H. L. *Coins, Medals & Seals of the Shahs of Iran (1500-1941)*. Hertford, 1945.
—. "Dynasties locales du Gilân et de Daylam." *Journal Asiatique* 237(1949):323-337.
—. *Mâzandarân and Astarâbâd*. London, 1928.
—. "La Presse persane depuis ses origines jusqu'à nos jours." *Revue du monde musulman* 22(1913):287-315.
—. *Les Provinces Caspiennes de la Perse: Le Guîlân*. Paris, 1917. [*Revue du monde musulman* 32(1916-17); there is also a separate volume of illustrations.]
—. "Rulers of Gilan." *Journal of the Royal Asiatic Society* (1920), pp. 287-315.
—. "Rulers of Lahijan and Fuman." *Journal of the Royal Asiatic Society* (1918), pp. 85-92.
— and Lafont, D. F. *L'Industrie séricole au Perse*. Montpelier, 1910.
Radde, Gustav. *Reisen an der Persisch- Russischen Grenze. Talysch und seine Bewohner*. Leipzig, 1886.
—. *Die Sammlungen des Kaukasischen Museums*. Tiflis, 1901-12.

Rahman, F. "The Pre-Foundations of the Muslim Community in Mecca." *Studia Islamica* 43(1976):5-24.

Railli, A. *Christians at Mecca*. London, 1909.

Ramazani, Rouhallah. *The Foreign Policy of Iran*. Charlottesville, 1966.

al-Rashid, Saad. *Darb Zubaydah: the Pilgrimage Road from Kufa to Mecca*. Riyadh, 1980.

—. *al-Rabadhah*. Riyadh, 1986.

Rastorgeva, V. S., *et al*. *Gilanskij jazyk*. Moscow, 1971.

Rathjens, Carl. *Die Pilgerfahrt nach Mekka: Von der Weihrauchstrasse zur Ölwirtschaft*. Hamburg, 1948.

Reggio, Milla (ed.). *Taziyeh: Ritual and Popular Belief in Iran*. Hartford, 1988.

Reid, John. *The Telegraph in America*. New York, 1879.

Reimer, Michael. "Colonial Bridgehead: Social and Spatial Change in Alexandria, 1850-1882." *International Journal of Middle East Studies* 29(1988):531-553.

Rhinelander, L. H. "Russia's Imperial Policy: The administration of the Caucasus in the first half of the nineteenth century." *Canadian Slavonic Papers* 17(1975):218-235.

—. "Viceroy Vorontsov's Administration of the Caucasus." In R. G. Suny, (ed.), *Transcaucasia*. Ann Arbor, 1983.

Richmond, J. C. B. *Egypt 1798-1952*. New York, 1977.

Rivlin, Helen. *The Agricultural Policy of Muḥammad ᶜAli in Egypt*. Cambridge, Mass., 1961.

Robinson, Arthur. "The Mahmal of the Moslem Pilgrimage." *Journal of the Royal Asiatic Society* 18(1931):117-127.

Roff, William R. "Pilgrimage and the History of Religions: theoretical approaches to the Hajj." In R. C. Martin (ed.), *Approaches to Islam in Religious Studies*. Tucson, 1985. Pp. 78-86.

—. "Sanitation and Security: The Imperial Powers and the Nineteenth Century Ḥajj." *Arabian Studies* 6(1982):143-160.

Roman, Jean. *Le Pèlerinage aux lieux saints de l'Islam*. Algiers, 1954.

Rosen, Fritz. *Persian Grammar*. Reprinted; New Delhi, 1979.

Rosenthal, Franz. *The Classical Heritage in Islam*. Berkeley, 1975.

Roubiçek, Marcel. *Modern Ottoman Troops, 1797-1915*. Jerusalem, 1978.

Rutter, Eldon. *The Holy Cities of Arabia*. London, 1928.

—. "The Muslim Pilgrimage." *Geographical Journal* 74(1929):271-273.

Rutter, Owen. *Triumphant Pilgrimage: An English Muslim's Journey from Sarawak to Mecca*. Philadelphia, 1937.

Rypka, Jan (ed.). *History of Iranian Literature*. Dordrecht, 1968.

S̱aᶜâlebi, Abu Manṣur. *Ghorar os-seyar*. Edited and translated by H. Zotenberg. *Histoire des rois des perses*. Paris, 1900.

Sabini, John. *Armies in the Sand: The Struggle for Mecca and Medina*. London, 1981.

Sachedina, Abdulaziz. *Islamic Messianism*. Albany, 1981.

Sadlier, George F. *Diary of a Journey across Arabia*. Bombay, 1866.

Salmis, M. *Fatima-Body of the Light, Daughter of the Holy Prophet Muhammad*. Bombay, 1939.

Sarton, George. *A History of Science, Volume I: Ancient Science Through the Golden Age of Greece*. Cambridge, Mass., 1952.

Sauvaget, Jean. *La Mosquée omeyyade de Médine*. Paris, 1947.

Savory, R. M. *Iran under the Safavids*. Cambridge, 1980.

Schindler, A. H. "Notes on the Length of the Farsakh." *Proceedings of the Royal Geographical Society*, second series, 10(1888):584-588.

—. "Reisen in nördlichen Persien." *Zeitschrift der Gesellschaft für Erdkunde zu Berlin* 14(1879):112-124.

Schoenberg, P. E. "The Evolution of Transport in Turkey (Eastern Thrace and Asia Minor) under Ottoman Rule, 1856-1918." *Middle Eastern Studies* 13(1977):359-372.

Schwarz, Paul. *Iran im Mittelalter, nach den arabischen Geographen*. Leipzig, 1896-1926.

Serjeant, R. B. "Haram and Hawtah, the Sacred Enclosures in Arabia." In A. Badawi, (ed.), *Mélanges Taha Husain*. Cairo, 1962. Pp. 41-58.

Seyf, A. "Silk Production and Trade in Iran in the 19th Century." *Iranian Studies* 16(1985):51-71.

Sezgin, Fuat. *Geschichte des arabischen Schriftums*. Leiden, 1967-75.

Shaban, M. A. *Islamic History A. D. 750-1055*. Cambridge, 1976.

Shahrâstâni, Moḥammad b. ᶜAbd ol-Karim. *Ketâb ol-melal va'n-neḥal*. Translated by A. K. Kazi and J. G. Flynn. *Muslim Sects and Divisions*. London, 1984.

Shariati, Ali. *Hajj*. Translated by Ali Behzadnia and Najla Denny. Houston, 1980.

Shaw, Stanford. *Between Old and New: The Ottoman Empire under Sultan Selim III*. Cambridge, Mass., 1971.

Shaykh-e Mofid, Abu ᶜAbdollah Moḥammad ol-Baghdâdi. *Ketâb ol-ershâd*. Translated by I. Howard. *Kitâb al-Irshâd: The Book of Guidance*. London, 1981.

Siraj ad-Din, A. B. "Pilgrimage to Mecca." *Studies in Comparative Religion* 1(1967):171-180.

Smith, W. Robertson. *The Religion of the Semites*. New York, 1956.

Somogyi, J. "Ibn al-Jauzi's Handbook on the Makkan Pilgrimage." *Journal of the Royal Asiatic Society* 25(1938):541-546.

Soubhy, Saleh. *Pèlerinage à la Mecque et à la Médine*. Cairo, 1894.

Sourdel, Dominique. "L'Imamisme vu par le Cheikh al-Mufid." *Revue des Études Islamiques* 40(1972):217-296.

Sousa, N. *The Capitulatory Regime of Turkey*. Baltimore, 1933.

Southgate, Minoo. *Iskandarnamah: A Persian Medieval Alexander-Romance*. New York, 1978.

Spiro Beg, S. *The Moslem Pilgrimage*. Alexandria, 1932.

Stahl, Alexander F. *Reisen in Nord- und Zentral-Persien*. Gotha, 1895.

Stanton, H. U. W., and Pickens, Claude Leon. "The Muslim Pilgrimage." *Muslim World* 24(1934):229-235.

Steingass, Francis J. *A Comprehensive Persian-English Dictionary*. London, 1963. [Reprint.]

Storey, C. A. *Persian Literature, A Bio-Bibliographical Survey*. London, 1953.

Strothmann, R. *Kultus der Zaiditen*. Strassburg, 1912.

Suard, Abbé. *Alexandrie, ancienne et nouvelle*. Alexandria, 1899.

Sumner-Boyd, Hilary and Freely, John. *Strolling Through Istanbul*. Istanbul, 1973.

Sykes, Percy. *A History of Persia*. Third edition; London, 1951.

Tabatabai, H. M. *An Introduction to Shii Law: A Bibliographical Study*. London, 1984.

Tamari, S. "Darb al-Hajj in Sinai. An Historical-Archaeological Study." *Accademia Nazionale dei Lincei: Memorie* 25(1982):431-525.

Tamisier, M. O. *Voyage en Arabie. Séjour dans le Hejaz. Campagne d'Asir*. Paris, 1840.

Theobald, A. B. *The Mahdiyya*. London, 1951.

Thielman, Max von. *Journey in the Caucasus, Persia and Turkey in Asia*. London, 1875.

Thornton, L. *Images de Perse. Le Voyage de Colonel F. Colombari à la cour du Chah de Perse de 1833 à 1848*. Edited by J. Soustiel. Paris, 1981.

Tresse, R. *Le pèlerinage syrien aux villes saints de l'Islam*. Paris, 1937.

Trimingham, J. Spencer. *The Sufi Orders in Islam*. London, 1971.

Turkey. Dairei Umuru Sihhiye. *Le Lazaret de Camaran et la quarantaine des pèlerins pendent cinq années d'exercise. Rapport du docteur Duca, directeur du Service, au Conseil supérieur de santé, publié par l'Administration sanitaire ottomane*. Constantinople, 1887.

—. *Mouvement générale du pèlerinage du Hedjaz par les ports de la mer Rouge, A.H. 1318 (1900-1901)*. Constantinople, 1906-7.

—. *Rapport de la commission des lazarets*. Constantinople, 1894.

Turki, H. and Souami, H. *Récits de Pèlerinage à la Mekke*. Paris, 1979.

United States. Office of Geography. *Iran; Official Standard Names Approved by the U. S. Board on Geographic Names*. Washington, 1956.

Useinov, M., Bretanitskii, L., and Salamzade, A. *Istoriia Arkhitektury Azerbaidzhana*. Moscow, 1963.

Vaughan, H. B. *A Journey Through Persia*. London, 1893.

Vaujany, H. de. *Alexandrie et la basse-Égypte*. Paris, 1885.

Vredenbregt, J. "The Haddj: Some of its features and functions in Indonesia." *Bijdragen tot de Taal- Land- en Volkenkunde von Nederlandsch-Indie* (1962):pp. 91-154.

Wagner, Moritz. *Travels in Persia, Georgia and Koordistan with Sketches of the Cossacks and the Caucasus*. London, 1856.

Waldman, Marilyn. *Toward a Theory of Historical Narrative*. Columbus, 1980.

Wallin, George A. "Narrative of a Journey from Cairo to Medina and Mecca." *Journal of the Royal Geographical Society* 24(1854):115-207.

—. "Notes Taken During a Journey through Part of Northern Arabia in 1848." *Journal of the Royal Geographical Society* 20(1851):293-344.

Watson, Robert Grant. *A History of Persia from the Beginning of the Nineteenth Century to the Year 1858*. London, 1866.

Wavell, A. J. B. *A Modern Pilgrim in Mecca*. London, 1912.

Weber, Shirley. *Voyages and Travels in the Near East During the XIX Century*. Princeton, 1952.

Weeks, Edwin. *From the Black Sea Through Persia to India*. New York, 1896.

Wellhausen, Julius. *Das Arabische Reich und sein Sturz.* Translated by Margaret Weir. *The Arab Kingdom and Its Fall.* Calcutta, 1927.

—. *Reste arabischen Heidentums*. Berlin, 1897.

Wensinck, A. J. *A Handbook of Early Muhammadan Tradition*. Leiden, 1927.

—. "The Ideas of the Western Semites concerning the Navel of the Earth." *Verhandelingen der Koninklijke Acad. van Wetenschappen*. 1916.

—. *The Muslim Creed*. Cambridge, 1932.

Wills, Charles. *In the Land of the Lion and Sun*. London, 1883.

Wilson, Sir Arnold Talbot. *The Suez Canal; Its Past, Present, and Future*. London, 1939.

Winder, R. Bayly. *Saudi Arabia in the Nineteenth Century*. New York, 1965.

Wingate, F. R. *Mahdism and the Egyptian Sudan*. London, 1891.

Wixman, Ronald. *The Peoples of the USSR: An Ethnographic Handbook*. Armonk, 1984.

Wohaibi, Abdullah. *The Northern Hijaz in the Writings of the Arab Geographers*. Beirut, 1973.

Wolf, E. "The Social Organization of Mecca and the Origins of Islam." *Southwestern Journal of Anthropology* (1951), pp. 330-377.

Wollaston, A. N. *The Pilgrimage to Mecca*. Leiden, 1880.

Wüstenfeld, H. F. *Die Chroniken der Stadt Mekka*. Leipzig, 1857-61.

— and Mahler, E. *Vergleichungs-Tabellen zur muslimischen und iranischen Zeitrechnung*. Revised by J. Mayr and B. Spuler. Wiesbaden, 1961.

Xenophon. *Anabasis*. Edited and translated by C. L. Brownson. In *Xenophon in Seven Volumes*. Cambridge, Mass., 1968-80. [Revised edition; Volume 3.]

Yâqut, Shehâb od-Din Ya^c^qub b. ^c^Abdollah. *Mo^c^jam ol-boldân.* Excerpts translated by C. Barbier de Meynard. *Dictionnaire géographique, historique et littéraire de la Perse et des contrées adjacentes, extrait du Mo'djem el-bouldan de Yaqout*. Paris, 1861.

Zambaur, Eduard von. *Manuel de généalogie et de chronologie pour l'histoire de l'Islam*. Hanover, 1927.

Zwemer, S. M. "Al Haramain: Mecca and Medina." *Muslim World* 37(1947):7-15.

—. "The Palladium of Islam." *Muslim World* 23(1933):109-116.

—. "Snouck Hurgronje's 'Mecca.'" *Muslim World* 22(1932):219-226.

TABLE OF SUBJECT HEADINGS

PART THREE: THE OTTOMAN EMPIRE

PART FOUR: FROM ALEXANDRIA TO JEDDA

PART FIVE: THE PILGRIMAGE TO MECCA

PART SIX: THE VISIT TO MEDINA

PART SEVEN: THE RETURN TO IRAN

INDEX

3493

WITHDRAWN

JUL 0 3 2024

DAVID O. McKAY LIBRARY
BYU-IDAHO